THE SOUTH CAROLINA
RICE PLANTATION
as Revealed in the Papers of
Robert F. W. Allston

SOUTHERN CLASSICS SERIES

John G. Sproat and Mark M. Smith, Series Editors

THE SOUTH CAROLINA RICE PLANTATION

as Revealed in the Papers of Robert F. W. Allston

Edited by

J. H. EASTERBY

New Introduction by
Daniel C. Littlefield

UNIVERSITY OF SOUTH CAROLINA PRESS

Published in cooperation with the Institute for
Southern Studies of the University of South Carolina

Original text © 1945 The University of Chicago
New introduction © 2004 University of South Carolina

First cloth edition published by the University of Chicago Press, 1945

This paperback edition published in Columbia, South Carolina, by the
University of South Carolina Press, 2004

Manufactured in the United States of America

08 07 06 05 04   5 4 3 2 1

Library of Congress Cataloging-in-Publication Data

Allston, Robert F. W. (Robert Francis Withers), 1801–1864.
  The South Carolina rice plantation as revealed in the papers of Robert F. W.
Allston / edited by J. H. Easterby ; new introduction by Daniel C. Littlefield.
     p. cm. — (Southern classics series)
  Originally published: Chicago : University of Chicago Press, [1945].
  "Published in cooperation with the Institute for Southern Studies of the Univer-
sity of South Carolina."
  Includes bibliographical references and index.
  ISBN 1-57003-569-5 (pbk. : alk. paper)
  1. Plantation life–South Carolina–History–19th century. 2. Slaves–South
Carolina–Social conditions–19th century. 3. Slavery–South Carolina–History–
19th century. 4. Rice–Planting–South Carolina–History–19th century. 5. South
Carolina–History–1775–1865. 6. Allston, Robert F. W. (Robert Francis Withers),
1801–1864–Manuscripts. 7. Alston family. I. Easterby, J. H. (James Harold),
1898–1960. II. Institute for Southern Studies. III. South Caroliniana Society. IV.
Title. V. Series.
  F273.A6E23 2004
  975.7'03'092—dc22   2004016465

Publication of the Southern Classics series is made possible in part by the generous
support of the Watson-Brown Foundation.

CONTENTS

SERIES EDITORS' PREFACE

IN 1860, only fourteen southern planters owned more than five hundred slaves. Robert F. W. Allston was among them. Edited originally by J. H. Easterby and published as *The South Carolina Rice Plantation,* Allston's papers offer careful readers extraordinary access to the political, economic, and cultural world of one of the Old South's most prominent planters. In an elegant new introduction to this enduring work, Daniel C. Littlefield places Allston in context, explains what the papers reveal about plantation slavery and southern life, and offers judicious and enlightening commentary on both Allston the planter and Easterby the historian.

Southern Classics returns to general circulation books of importance dealing with the history and culture of the American South. Sponsored by the Institute for Southern Studies and the South Caroliniana Society of the University of South Carolina, the series is advised by a board of distinguished scholars who suggest titles and editors of individual volumes to the series editors and help establish priorities in publication.

Chronological age alone does not determine a title's designation as a Southern Classic. The criteria also include significance in contributing to a broad understanding of the region, timeliness in relation to events and moments of peculiar interest to the American South, usefulness in the classroom, and suitability for inclusion in personal and institutional collections on the region.

Mark M. Smith
John G. Sproat
SERIES EDITORS

NEW INTRODUCTION

WHO WAS Robert F. W. Allston, and why should we care? And why should we be interested in his papers? The answers to these questions are various, depending on one's perspective and interests. He was governor of South Carolina just before the outbreak of the Civil War and a firm proponent of southern rights. In that, he was a sound representative of his class and his region. He was also one of the wealthiest planters in the richest rice-producing region in the United States—the lowcountry of South Carolina. His region produced one-third of the nation's rice crop in 1860 and nearly equaled the combined output of the rest of the state. He owned four plantations along the Pee Dee River in 1860 and another at the northern end of the Waccamaw River on Sandy Island. He managed two other Waccamaw plantations for his nephews until 1857, one of which enjoyed the highest yield per acre in All Saints Parish. Allston belonged to a select group. As historian Charles Joyner reports, the census of 1860 counted only eighty-eight planters in the whole country who owned more than 300 slaves; twenty-nine of these were rice planters. Only fourteen planters owned more than 500 slaves, and nine of these were rice planters. Robert Allston owned 630 slaves in 1860. He and neighboring planters dominated their region politically and set the tenor of its social environment.[1] The details of his dynastic succession (as it may be called) and the minutia of his genealogical connections are disclosed by the editor of these papers and will not bear repeating. Nor will I recall the names and locations of all his plantations. What follows are reflections on a planter's life and thought and on what his papers, particularly those collected here by J. Harold Easterby, mean for the study of slavery and the Old South.

Born in Georgetown District in April 1801, Robert Allston assumed responsibility for his father's Matanzas plantation (later renamed Chicora Wood by his wife) on the Pee Dee River after his mother's death in 1824. His father had died when he was young, and he was raised largely by his mother. Between 1817 and 1821 he attended West Point, an institution he credited with providing him the scientific background fundamental to his success as a planter. His mother, left a widow with children, was strong-willed but not, the editor of these papers writes, "one to bear her burdens with gentle submission" (13). Allston called her "judicious" and lauded the training he received under her tutelage but perhaps benefited more than usual from the masculine environment of the military academy. There, he thought, he acquired or improved "the discipline of mind and body, the justness of thinking, the decision and promptness to execution," which were responsible for his success

---

[1] See Charles Joyner, *Down by the Riverside: A South Carolina Slave Community* (Urbana: University of Illinois Press, 1984), 12–37; see also George C. Rogers Jr., *The History of Georgetown County, South Carolina* (Columbia: University of South Carolina Press, 1970), 224–341, which informs much of what follows.

in life.[2] Beginning in 1827 he gave serious attention to planting and, at the same time, became interested in politics. He developed views consonant with those of the planters around him, nearly all of whom favored limited government. He was a Jeffersonian republican in an age of Jacksonian democracy, and although he supported Jackson's war on the monied interests of the time, interests he thought had a regional bias, he objected to Jackson's nationalism. Indeed, he came to political prominence in South Carolina during the Nullification Controversy and remained among those less willing to compromise on the issue of states' rights. He may not have been as rabid a southern nationalist as Robert Barnwell Rhett, who gave up a seat in the United States Senate because his state was not more aggressive in its opposition to the growing powers of the federal government, but was evidently more consistent than James Henry Hammond, who first condemned John C. Calhoun as too moderate but later assumed much of his stance.[3] Although ambitious, Allston was not unreservedly so and, these papers reveal, resisted his wife's urging that he run for Congress. He was elected to the state senate in 1832, where he remained until he assumed the governorship in 1856. He was a strong supporter of John C. Calhoun and, like Calhoun, believed that state unity was vital for South Carolina, that the state would have greater influence in national politics if it acted with unanimity rather than dividing along the fissures of national politics. He wrote his wife after the Nullification Convention of 1832 that "there ought now to be but one party in the State, & that comprising *the whole state*—I would give all that I am worth . . . [to] consummate this event."[4] Like Calhoun and most of the planters of his district, he objected to the Compromise of 1850, believing that the South surrendered too much. In his eulogy of Calhoun, addressed to citizens of Georgetown District in April 1850, he doubtless expressed his own philosophy as he summarized that of the man he honored. Calhoun had died, he said, "in the midst of a contest for 'Equality or Independence,'" opposing "the grasping cupidity and unjust aggressions of a Northern majority." The Constitution was "the result of a compact between the States as States, instituted and agreed to by the people thereof." He was convinced that Calhoun had "demonstrated, irresistibly, to minds unprejudiced and candid, that, by this Constitution, the States, each sovereign and independent before its adoption, have parted with no more of their sovereignty than is embraced in the powers expressly granted" in that document. A mere act of Congress, though passed by a majority, had no validity if it were inconsistent with the powers allowed by the Constitution, and he obviously considered a protective tariff to be among those powers not specifically provided. He explained Calhoun's support for the Tariff of 1816 as necessitated by the exigencies of the late war with Great Britain and "actuated by public-spirited, and generous motives, which the

---

[2] See the sketch of Allston published in *DeBow's Review*, copy evidently corrected in Allston's hand, in RFW Allston Papers, 1164.02.01 (12/4/8), South Carolina Historical Society, Charleston. The society (hereafter SCHS) has recently added to its collection of Allston papers.

[3] For Rhett, see Walter Edgar, *South Carolina: A History* (Columbia: University of South Carolina Press, 1998), 306; for Hammond, see Drew Gilpin Faust, *James Henry Hammond and the Old South: A Design for Mastery* (Baton Rouge: Louisiana State University Press, 1982), 296–303.

[4] Rogers, *Georgetown County*, 251.

mere politician is incapable of appreciating." But the intention had never been "to establish permanently the policy of Protection," which operated unfavorably "upon the Southern planting interest" and was in conflict with the "spirit of the Constitution." He went on to argue that "an unchecked majority is a despotism. It is the purpose of a Constitution to impose limitations and checks upon the majority."[5]

Essential to Allston's opposition to the Compromise of 1850 was his position as a slaveholder. In keeping with his desire that the state be politically united in defense of slavery—in association with other southern states if possible, alone if necessary—he objected to sending Carolina delegates to the Democratic national convention in 1848 and denounced a delegate who attended anyway. He let it be known that he supported neither party's candidate that year. The vote of his district split, with larger planters, nominally Democrats, choosing the slaveholding Whig Zachary Taylor as safer than Democrat Lewis Cass of Michigan. He would have taken little comfort in the fact that small farmers voted for Cass. The next year Allston chaired a public meeting in Georgetown that resolved that passage of the Wilmot Proviso, forbidding slavery in the Mexican Cession, would mean destruction of the Union. Elected as a secessionist to a state convention that met in 1852, he voted in the minority for a motion authorizing the state legislature to leave the Union. The convention majority merely declared that the state had a right to do so.

The papers included here shed light on many of these issues and refer to many others. They reveal, for example, that Allston approved of Franklin Pierce and advised his son to seek an introduction. They indicate that Allston's wife considered Henry Clay a traitor to his region and predicted, correctly, that his compromise measure would not pass. (It was subsequently broken apart and passed piecemeal under the stewardship of Stephen Douglas.) She, like many others, favored extension of the Missouri Compromise line to the Pacific. The papers detail Allston's meeting with soon-to-be-president James Buchanan in Lancaster, Pennsylvania, and suggest Buchanan's proslavery views. In a preview of the Supreme Court's thinking in the Dred Scott decision, Allston heard one of the justices debate the issue of slavery in Kansas "as fearlessly & fairly as it could be done in Carolina," though, he was careful to add, "more calmly however." They document Allston's heavy involvement in southern activities to secure Kansas for slavery and indicate he was quite willing to put his money where his mouth was. As he declared in his eulogy of Calhoun:

> [The northern states] allege that their object is, by means of the General Government to prevent the extension of our domestic system. We contend for non-intervention; that the General Government has no power to legislate thus partially, invidiously, oppressively; and insist upon the right of property; the individual right to emigrate with our social institutions, and upon our rights as States, under the Constitution of the Union. They, arrogating to themselves superior purity and patriotism, are for usurping the powers of the

[5] Robert F. W. Allston, *Eulogy on John C. Calhoun, Pronounced at the Request of the Citizens of Georgetown District, on Tuesday, 23d April, 1850* (Charleston, S.C.: Miller & Browne, 1850), 8, 10–12, 17, respectively.

Union from out the Constitution, and consolidating them, in the keeping of the tender consciences of a ruling majority of Congress—that majority being made up of their own representatives. We, on the other hand, avow, and will maintain for the Southern States, their "Equality or Independence."[6]

In an era when the South's "peculiar institution" was very much under attack, he had reason to be defensive. He responded enthusiastically to James Henry Hammond's *Two Letters on Slavery in the United States*, writing Hammond: "As a planter, also, representing others who like himself, have half their Capital invested in slaves, my warm and grateful acknowledgements [*sic*] for inditing & publishing the said letters," which would, he thought, "be found hereafter among the papers elucidating the history of the State, the character of her people, and the spirit of her institutions" (95). In that he was correct, though not in the manner he supposed. While he believed firmly in the justice of slavery and thought Hammond's letters vindicated the institution, they are read now as the relics of a not-quite-vanished past.[7] Slavery is gone, but its residue remains and, in some places, its mentality.

These papers reveal also that while Allston spent much of his time in Columbia, and could be convivial, he remained aloof from some of the salacious gossip making the rounds. He apparently was not close to the family or the circle of Wade Hampton II and had not heard of the scandal involving Hammond and Hampton's daughters (Hammond's nieces), whom Hammond molested. He therefore played no part in Hampton's vengeful efforts to derail Hammond's political career, voting in the affirmative to send Hammond to the United States Senate in 1846 "not having been enlighten'd as to his conduct 'till the day after" (97). But this knowledge lent unintended irony to his comments to Hammond a few months before the vote, when he thanked him for scientific and political publications:

I beg leave to congratulate you on the taste for which you have given your preference i e, the life and pursuits of a Planter which if view'd aright, regulated by the principles of Religion, that highest Philosophy, enlighten'd and aid'd by Science, affords both the means & opportunity to do as much good, and contributes to the true dignity of man, the elevation and just influence of his character, quite as much as any other avocation whatever. (95)

He did not realize at the time that Hammond's retirement to private life and seclusion at Silver Bluff had not been entirely voluntary. Hampton had moved anticipating the storm of criticism resulting from his moral lapses and personal misdeeds.[8]

Allston also tried his hand at justifying slavery, though he did not publish so detailed an exposition as Hammond did. In notes for a lecture on the institution, he took as his point of departure a speech before a Boston audience in 1847 by Charles Sumner of Massachusetts. Sumner had lectured on white slavery in the Barbary States and noted that before its conquest by the French, Algiers was called

---

[6] Ibid., 16.
[7] See J. H. Hammond, *Two Letters on Slavery in the United States: Addressed to Thomas Clarkson, Esq.* (Columbia, S.C.: Allen, McCarter, 1845).

the "Wall of the Barbary World." He applied that analogy to the Missouri Compromise line, 36° 30' west of the Mississippi River, which he termed the "Wall of Christian Slavery" in the United States. He styled Virginia, Carolina, Mississippi, and Texas, lying, in his estimation, on approximately the same parallel as the Missouri Compromise line, as "the American complements to Morocco, Algiers, Tripoli, & Tunis," and he designated the southern slaveholding states as the "Barbary States of America." Allston took umbrage at Sumner's satire and set out to show that slavery was of great antiquity, beginning in the time of Abraham. He noted that these white slaves were captives in war. He seemed to suggest a transition from white to black slavery in his discussion of the sixteenth-century Spanish *asiento* authorizing the importation of Africans into the West Indies, and moved rapidly to their coming to seventeenth-century English North America. In a common rationalization, he placed the blame for slavery in South Carolina not on its planters but squarely upon the English: it was merchants in Bristol and Liverpool who prospered from the trade. When "in 1760 the province of S° Carolina pass'd an Act prohibiting the further importation of Negroes—it was rejected by the Government at home, on the ground that the trade was beneficial to the Mother Country. . . . When the Colonists of S°Ca petition'd the Lord Proprietors for a larger supply of cattle, as the natural pastures were good, they were answer'd that they were intended to be *Planters* not Graziers—accordingly they were supplied after with slaves."[9] So much for British critics of southern institutions!

The issues of race and religion were inescapably involved in the problem, and he introduced them without elaboration but with clear implications. Replying to an apparent statement of Sumner that after the conquest of Algiers by France, "The Barbary States seem less Barbarous," he interjected:

> No Wonder this. The Christian Slaves were intelligent, ingenious, useful. They were Mechanics & Artisans who were highly estimated, and treated accordingly. They exercised no little influence in directing the attention of the barbarians to the beauties & excellencies of the Christian Religion,—to the beauty and Utility of Civilization. Oppressive & odious as it was in the estimation of all Nations, yet in the order of a wise Providence, it (Slavery in Barbary) has been the means of conveying a knowledge of the Redeemer, and of his Religion into portions of Africa where the Bible was never heard of before and where perhaps but for this it would not have been known at all.[10]

In a defense of white slavery in Barbary, he implied a vindication of black slavery in South Carolina. Not only was slavery part of God's plan for bringing the gospel to those without knowledge of it, but Africans in South Carolina had nowhere near the skill and intelligence of Europeans enslaved in Barbary. Or if they had, they owed it all to the whites. He blamed the failure of planters to use an advanced

[8] For the scandal involving Hammond and his nieces see Faust, *Hammond*, 241–58, and Hammond, *Secret and Sacred: The Diaries of James Henry Hammond, a Southern Slaveholder,* ed. Carol Bleser (New York: Oxford University Press, 1988), 165–78.

[9] "Alston Lecture," RFW Allston Papers, 1164.02.01 (12/4/10), SCHS.

[10] Ibid.

plow in rice fields, for example, apparently on the incapacity of the slaves: the so-called drill plough requiring "more minute attention and judgement than could be calculated on, among the field-laborers of that day." He intended to introduce it again, however, so he was not without hope they could master the craft, being taught, perhaps, by a Scottish "laborer who is familiar with its use."[11] He made clear his opinion of Africans and their prospects of manumission in a letter to his son: "The computations of intricate calculation has proved the impracticability of emancipation by deportation, and the other alternative cannot be contemplated, namely, the giving up of our beautiful country to the ravages of the black race & amalgamation with the savages" (132). So while he praised the bey of Tunis for abolishing slavery within his dominions and listed the progress of emancipation in other areas of the world, he could not envision it in his own region.

His alternative to emancipation was to emphasize the human face of slavery and highlight its efficacy. He advised his son to read William Grayson's *The Hireling and the Slave* and sent him a copy of it. Grayson's work is an extended poem contrasting the mistreatment of hired labor to the benign treatment of bondsmen. Grayson makes clear in his preface that race is a prime element of his conceptualization: "Slavery is the negro system of labour. He is lazy and improvident. Slavery makes all work and it ensures homes, food and clothing to all. It permits no idleness, and it provides for sickness, infancy and old age. It allows no tramping or skulking, and it knows no pauperism." He conceded that cruelty might exist but it "is an abuse; does not belong to the institution; is punished and may be prevented and removed." He was convinced that conditions for slaves had improved over the years as they had for British soldiers and sailors.[12] In other words, slaves were not the only people who had suffered or been mistreated, and everywhere circumstances were changing for the better. Slaves were merely "apprentice[s] for life" and were owed support for life. Benjamin Allston would have read verses such as these:

> How small the choice, from cradle to the grave,
> Between the lot of Hireling and of Slave!
> To each alike applies the stern decree,
> That man shall labour; whether bond or free,
> For all that toil, the recompense we claim—
> Food, fire, a home and clothing—is the same. (19)
> . . . .
> In squalid hut—a kennel for the poor,
> Or noisome cellar, stretched upon the floor,
> His clothing rags, of filthy straw his bed,
> With offal from the gutter daily fed,
> Thrust out from Nature's board, the Hireling lies—
> No place for him that common board supplies. . . . (21)

[11] R. F. W. Allston, *Memoir of the Introduction and Planting of Rice in South Carolina: A Description of the Grass, and Some Account of the Exports, with an Appendix Prepared for the Agricultural Survey of the State* (Charleston, S.C.: Printed by Miller & Browne, 1843), 15–16.

[12] William Grayson, *The Hireling and the Slave* (Charleston, S.C.: J. Russell, 1854), vii–viii.

This unhappy picture contrasts with that of the slave. It is true he suffers ill fortune in the method of his acquisition, but Africans themselves participate in the process and, anyway, it is all for a greater good:

> Companions of his toil, the axe to wield,
> To guide the plough, to reap the teeming field,
> A sable multitude unceasing pour
> From Niger's banks and Congo's deadly shore;
> No willing travellers they that widely roam,
> Allured by hope, to seek a happier home,
> But victims to the trader's thirst for gold,
> Kidnaped by brothers, and by fathers sold. (30–31)
>
> . . . .
>
> But Providence, by his o'eruling will,
> Transmutes to lasting good the transient ill,
> Makes crime itself the means of mercy prove,
> And avarice minister to works of love;
> In this new home, whate'er the negro's fate
> More blest his life than in his native State! (31)

The poem goes on to paint a canvas of linear fields of snowy cotton and golden grains wrought from fetid swamps and steamy morasses. "And, borne by commerce to each distant shore, / Supplies the world with one enjoyment more" (33). Slavery brought benefits to civilization and civilization to the slave.[13] It was not a poetry of great art, but it was in earnest and provided all the arguments for the archaic institution in succinct formulation.

The reality of slavery was somewhat different from its idealization, and the value of these papers is to reveal the face behind the mask. Allston considered himself a patriarch, in his dealings with his family and in his dealings with his slaves. His daughter Elizabeth Allston Pringle, who achieved fame as an author, illustrates this patriarchal role in both spheres. In one instance, she discusses her father's relationship with her mother at the beginning of their marriage. Allston wanted his wife to accompany him to the quarters to see a sick slave. His wife did not want to go: "'I know nothing about sickness, and there is no earthly use for me to go with you. I have been having the soup made and sending it to him regularly, but I cannot go to see him for I can do him no good.' He answered with a grave, hurt look: 'you are mistaken; you can do him good. At any rate, it is my wish that you go.'"[14] The wife yielded unwillingly to her husband's authority, eventually saw the wisdom of his judgment and the goodness in his intentions, and was happy to have obeyed. Insofar as these papers display, Allston did not speak of slaves as part of his extended family, the way eighteenth-century planters were wont to do, but he adopted an attitude that said much the same thing. In one of her stories, Elizabeth

[13] Ibid., 19–36.

[14] Elizabeth Waties Allston Pringle, *Chronicles of Chicora Wood* (New York: Charles Scribner's Sons, 1922), 63.

Pringle remembered the distribution of clothing to the bondsmen at Christmas. This story was composed in the early twentieth century, years after slavery had died, when she had discovered a "fierce Huguenot conscience" that would have made her unhappy under the burden of owning slaves—a conscience nowhere in evidence among her family in these published documents—so the story has a romantic edge and yet is instructive. The distribution, she writes,

> was an interesting thing to watch: a name was read out by mamma, papa, or my sister from the book, and up the step came the little girl, dropped a courtesy to each of us and then to Maum Mary, and stood before her to be measured. Maum Mary was sometimes inclined to be very impatient and cross, but she dared not give way to the inclination openly, with us all watching her. She would just jerk the timid one around a little; but if papa was there he would say quite sternly: "Gently, Mary, gently." The little girl, as she went out loaded with her things and the things of her little brothers and sisters, would drop another courtesy of thanks.[15]

In such a formal setting the patriarch was enabled ceremoniously to reenforce his authority, celebrate his generosity, demonstrate his ability to arbitrate, and emphasize his fairness and firmness. He was the source of benevolence and also of righteous anger and the power to punish.

Allston sought to minimize the ill-treatment of his slaves and to shield his children from evidence of cruelty to slaves. On more than one occasion he protested brutal behavior toward bondsmen. Yet he demanded the obeisance due a patriarch, obeisance rendered cheerfully and speedily. Like many slaveholders, he expected his self-image to be reflected in his slaves, and he did not react kindly when it was not. His correspondence indicates that he had no trouble selling or otherwise disciplining errant or recalcitrant servitors. In most cases, this was done through intermediaries and substantiates the comment of one historian that many masters and slaves had fond memories of each other because the overseer effected the unpleasantness. But sometimes the master was forced to act himself. Allston records how on a fine spring day in 1859, with the scent of jasmine in the air, he rode in pleasure down a shady lane reveling in the pastoral setting, when, suddenly, he came face-to-face with an ox "which had been abused by John and turn'd out of the cart. This quite upset me because of the poor animal, and because of the penalty which I had to impose" (153). He does not say what the penalty was: it could have ranged from a whipping or a few licks to a demotion or a withdrawal of privileges. Listen to his daughter describe her punishments in *Chronicles of Chicora Wood*. Allston punished her just twice, once when she told a lie and once when she threw a childish tantrum. In the first instance her father calmly lectured her on the evils of lying, expressed his distress that she had done so, and sent her to a shed-room to await his attention:

> I sat in the rocking-chair and rocked, trying to make believe to myself that I did not care and was not frightened. After a while my father came and gave

[15] Ibid., 8, 154.

me a severe switching. When he had finished he kissed me, put me on the bed, and threw a light linen coverlet over me, and I went to sleep. I slept a long time, for when I woke up it was nearly dark, and I felt like an angel in heaven—so happy and peaceful and, above all, filled with a kind of adoration for my father. It is strange what a realization of right and wrong that gave me, baby though I was. I have never ceased to feel grateful to papa for the severity of that punishment. It *had* to be remembered, and it meant the holding aloft of honesty and truth, and the trampling in the dust of dishonesty and falsehood. No child is too young to have these basic principles taught them.[16]

The next chastisement, which she describes as a "severe whipping," followed a similar pattern. He never had to lay hands on her again.

The point is not that the patriarch treated members of his immediate family in precisely the same way as he treated that part of an extended family comprising his slaves, but that the punishment differed in quality not in kind (and even, in some cases, differed in quantity and not in quality) and had the same purpose: to instill his own sense of proper order and good behavior.[17] The role he played was the same in both spheres. In a social environment that included corporal punishment as an omnipresent possibility, where one assumed that correct deportment and suitable demeanor required reenforcement with stripes and lashes, compartmentalizing that world and drawing impermeable lines between house and field was not easily done. It is a situation that punctuates Frank Tannenbaum's dictum that in a slave society "nothing escaped, nothing, and no one."[18] Moreover, the disruption of Allston's revelry on a spring day in March uncovered the troublesome dynamics of slaveholding and suggests why it could seldom, if ever, approach the ideal so frequently drawn. The slave he encountered, obviously unhappy, may have been transferring to the animal his onus against the master or the overseer or both. Or maybe he was just expressing a general dissatisfaction by imitating the insensitivity he saw all around him. Allston recognized the threat to his authority as well as his sympathy for the animal in the incident and realized that all was not right in his world. Owning slaves obliged more than the daily reading of "the evening psalm and the morning chapter *en Francais*" (153).

Patriarchal control worked best when there were no competing sources of authority, when the planter operated in a closed system with himself as deus ex

---

[16] Ibid., 110–11.

[17] See, for example, Landon Carter's assumption of his patriarchal role when his grandson ignored a command to come to breakfast: Carter "reached for his whip and 'gave' the child 'one cut over the left arm,' and 'the other over the banister by him.' The outraged mother 'then rose like a bedlamite,' and 'up came her Knight Errant'; there were 'some heavy God damnings,' but the son, the old man took pains to note, 'prudently did not touch me. Otherwise my whip handle should have settled him if I could'" (cited in Gerald W. Mullin, *Flight and Rebellion: Slave Resistance in Eighteenth-Century Virginia* [New York: Oxford University Press, 1972], 68). Also see Jack P. Greene's introduction in *The Diary of Colonel Landon Carter of Sabine Hall, 1752–1778*, ed. Jack P. Greene (Charlottesville: University Press of Virginia, 1965) and Daniel C. Littlefield, "John Jay, the Revolutionary Generation, and Slavery," *New York History* 81, no. 1 (January 2000): 126–28.

[18] Frank Tannenbaum, *Slave and Citizen* (1946; repr., Boston: Beacon Press, 1992), 117.

machina. Consequently, Allston disapproved of laboring situations that provided the bondsman with too much leeway, personal autonomy, or inadequate supervision. He distrusted the lumber industry, whether cutting wood or collecting turpentine, as unconducive to the "steady habits of the negro." He objected to railroad work for the same reason.[19] The success of his management system depended upon a regular organization. Whether in working the fields or at the artisan's station, he desired order. Both his son and daughter elaborate the structure on his plantations, where he commonly trained enslaved men for jobs preserving or marketing a crop or for service on his estates as carpenters, coopers, blacksmiths, and so forth, and women for domestic pursuits such as sewing, washing, and cooking. Although his ideological writings seem sometimes to argue otherwise, son and daughter both thought he had several slaves of unusual intelligence and ability. Elizabeth Pringle even thought that two of her family's favorites had royal blood "for they were so superior to the ordinary Africans brought out"—which is a way of acknowledging efficiency and affection without vanquishing a stereotype.[20] (That is to say, Pringle could recognize the humanity, nobility, and intellectual capacity of those she admired and still maintain a racial bias.)

As part of his plantation management, Allston was quite willing to recognize and reward talent. For example, he paid his coopers 25 cents for every barrel over their task of three barrels a day. If the staves were prepared beforehand, he said, a slave could make five barrels a day, and his policy obviously encouraged them to do just that. Of course, both slave and master benefited from the extra work, and he left the choice to the slave's initiative. His daughter claimed, and there is some evidence in these documents to support her claim, that he had a system of rewards for every job on the plantation: "pretty bright-colored calico frocks to the women, and forks and spoons; and to the men fine knives, and other things that they liked—so that there was a great pride in being the prize ploughman, or prize sower, or harvest hand, for the year."[21] Nor did being out of the master's sight mean being beyond his control, for many of the tasks for which he trained his men—as salt-makers and boatmen among other tasks—he let them accomplish without the supervision of any white man. Minimizing the leeway of slaves did not mean allowing no leeway at all. The threat of being reduced to fieldwork was sufficient to compel obedience. For what the exceptional cases obscure and Allston's papers make clear is that most work on the plantation was mere drudgery, repeated day in and day out with little variance in routine. There was every reason for slaves, the skilled ones at least, to be the efficient models of production adduced in the cliometric calculations of historians Robert Fogel and Stanley Engerman.[22] It might well have been, as Allston wrote in his *Essay on Sea Coast Crops*, that "in fine April weather

[19] R. F. W. Allston, *Essay on Sea Coast Crops; Read before the Agricultural Association of the Planting States on the Occasion of the Annual Meeting, Held at Columbia, December 3d, 1853* (Charleston, S.C.: A. E. Miller, 1854), 10, 18a.

[20] Pringle, *Chronicles*, 53.

[21] Ibid., 15, and Allston, *Sea Coast Crops*, 37.

[22] Robert W. Fogel and Stanley L. Engerman, *Time on the Cross: The Economics of American Negro Slavery* (Boston: Little, Brown and Company, 1974).

it is pleasing to behold the steady, graceful progress of a good sower," but it must have been mind-numbing to be the sower.[23] No wonder a slave on a fine day in March might take in mind to mistreat an ox.

There is little reason to doubt that Allston seriously believed in the religious justification of slavery; that God, for reasons of his own, permitted the institution to exist, and that men who served God, as he believed he did, had a Christian duty to their bondsmen. He ended his lecture on sea coast crops with the plea that "the young negroes . . . [be] taught specially; and to all, the way of salvation" ought to be preached. "But it is not enough . . . that the preaching of the Gospel is provided for our negroes," he intoned; "they must be induced to seek an interest in it—they must be won to obedience to the divine law—to love the truth." He advised that "the strongest inducement is example on our part; next, a just, consistent, systematic administration of domestic government."[24] He thereby imparted his recipe for success. And he practiced what he preached in religion as well as in plantation regime. The planters in his district countenanced a mission to the slaves, and he complimented his wife in a letter herein on her decision "to have the Chapel open'd. . . . It is good for the people to assemble themselves together, if it is only to hear the word of God read, and preparations should be made there for the visit of the Bishop" (92–93). Religion, not properly regulated, could be dangerous of course, and he noted in another letter that some denominations encouraged abolitionist thinking. But rightly conceived and directed (that is to say from his viewpoint), it united master and slave in a hierarchical community and gave religious approbation to his patriarchal position. So when the bishop confirmed Allston's driver Daniel in an "impressive" ceremony "doubtless new" to the people, he added mystery and spiritual sanction to the master's secular authority. Time and again Allston ruminated on the duties and burdens of slaveownership and clearly imparted that message to his children. It is one of the themes of Elizabeth Pringle's somewhat romantic and defensive depiction of slavery and race relations in *Chronicles of Chicora Wood*. When her mother talked with a favorite servant about the tragedy of the woman's capture and removal from Africa, Maum Maria rose to her full height and, with clasped hands and a fervent expression, declared her complete satisfaction at having been brought to the light of Christ.[25] It was something they could all believe without reflecting on the deeper meaning of the relationship.

Self-delusion is an interesting phenomenon. Or perhaps it is better to say that the inability to put oneself in another person's shoes, to discover a "fierce Huguenot conscience" before a different reality intrudes itself, is a common human attribute. In a Fourth of July oration during the 1850s, Allston exhorted his fellow citizens: "Venerate the plough, the hoe & all the impliments [*sic*] of Agriculture. Honor the men who, with their own hands maintain their families, and raise up their Children inured to toil, & capable of defending their country. Reckon the necessity of labour not among the curses but among the blessings of life." He contrasted

[23] Allston, *Sea Coast Crops*, 32.
[24] Ibid., 41; Pringle, *Chronicles*, 36.
[25] Pringle, *Chronicles*, 54.

the virtues of rural existence with the evils inherent in urban living and factory
work. He was pleased to consider that "a great majority of your country must &
will be yeomanry, who have no other dependence than on Almighty god, for his
usual blessing on their daily labour. From the great excess of the number of such
independent farmers in these states, over & above all other classes of inhabitants,
the long continuance of your liberties may be reasonably presumed."[26] While Allston undoubtedly considered himself among those who venerated the plough and
the hoe, he was not a yeoman and did not labor with his own hands. Of course,
he probably considered the work he did in supervising his bondsmen, in "wring-
ing his bread from the sweat of other men's brows," to use Lincoln's phraseology,
as exemplary labor. He once advised his son Benjamin to ride his horse rather than
walk through tall corn because it could be "hotter than a cane-break." Supervising
could be hard work indeed! Obviously Allston did not labor with his "own hands"
as an "independent farmer" the way "yeomen" did, and he would not have wanted
to do so. Even less would he have wanted to work as a slave did, for then he would
not be free. His oration reified a lifestyle not his own and for which he had only
an idealized regard. Certainly he engaged in a form of work, and clearly he had
a high regard for liberty, but in both instances of a restricted kind. He personified
the paradox and myopia of a Jeffersonian republicanism based on hierarchy and
anchored in racial vassalage.

The masks behind which both groups, masters and slaves, operated began to
slip during the war, though they did not fall completely away until its conclusion.
Allston's hope of receiving a commission in the Confederate army was disappointed, and he had to content himself with raising crops and making salt for the
cause. Perhaps his looming presence exercised a restraining influence because the
Allstons had many suspicions of but little trouble with their slaves until after Allston's death. Even then relatively few absconded. Perhaps they thought it best to
bide their time. Certainly if they received any news of the Yankees' posture toward
blacks in the regions where they trod (and there is no overt evidence in these papers
that they did), it would have reenforced their natural caution. There is a story, perhaps apocryphal, about two slaves discussing the war and what their attitude toward
it ought to be. One concluded that it was like two dogs fighting over a bone: "You
never saw the bone get up and fight, did you?" In fact, many claimed their freedom and did fight, and others contributed to the fight in smaller and no less important ways. But the story referenced a suspicion that Union soldiers did not always
assuage. When the Allston slaves did finally begin to desert, it was not en masse
but in a trickle. In response, Adele Allston assumed the avenging spirit of the Old
Testament and sought to assess collective punishment. She would hold the old people responsible for the behavior of the young, and she singled out one women in
particular. When three children and a brother of Mary ran off, Mrs. Allston wrote:
"It is too many instances in her family for me to suppose she is ignorant of their
plans and designs. She has been always a highly favoured servant, and all her family have been placed in positions of confidence and trust. I think this last case

[26] See RFW Allston Papers, 1164.02.01 (12/4/9), SCHS.

should be visited in some degree on her" (200). Adele Allston was probably correct that it was unlikely Mary had no idea what her relatives intended. Allston's sense of betrayal was undoubtedly more painful because the offending servants were trusted ones, pointing to the apparent anomaly that the best treated were sometimes the first to turn and vitiating the hypothesis that those closest to the master were most likely to remain faithful. It was, of course, unreasonable to expect a mother to betray her children, and it was right of Mrs. Allston to be suspicious in this case, but it was another matter to attempt to establish the general principle of guilt she did.

While the Allston family seemed to suffer few deprivations during the conflict, there is evidence the slaves did. They lacked shoes in particular, sometimes having to work barefoot, and they probably did not get enough to eat. On one hand, these conditions would argue in favor of running away, but on the other hand, the slaves might have thought it better to face the devil they knew. Nonetheless, when Yankee soldiers arrived at Chicora Wood, the freedpeople vented their dissatisfaction by ransacking the house. Surprised and disappointed, Mrs. Allston began occasionally to refer to her former charges, previously described in more personal terms, as "nigs." Students of nineteenth-century American society however will not be astonished to learn that the first unabashed and extended use of the term "nigger" in these papers is by a northern correspondent, who writes Benjamin Allston that "*people* at the North are not more desireous [*sic*] of being *ruled* by the nigger than you are in the South" (234), thereby illustrating how widespread such racial attitudes were among whites and helping to show why Reconstruction was a failure. It is significant, too, that the correspondent was a champion of white labor, rural rather than urban in this case (the "independent farmers" that R. F. W. Allston idealized), and an Irishman to boot, the Irish being traditional adversaries of African Americans at this period.[27] Mrs. Allston prepared herself to accept the new circumstances and wrote Benjamin that "Negroes will soon be placed upon an exact equality with ourselves, and it is in vain for us to strive against it" (226). Benjamin seemed disposed to give the experiment a try. But with no encouragement from the White House and evidence of the substance of northern opinion, this predisposition gave way. Elizabeth Pringle indicates in *Chronicles of Chicora Wood* that her brother was glad his father did not live to see a prostrate South ruled by carpetbaggers and Negroes.[28]

In a final example of the revelations these papers contain, it is interesting to reflect upon the meaning of two small comments Allston makes about Jews in these letters. In the midst of political controversy in 1850 he wrote his wife, "The

[27] The writer was Oliver H. Kelley who founded the Patrons of Husbandry. See Thomas A. Woods, *Knights of the Plow: Oliver H. Kelley and the Origins of the Grange in Republican Ideology* (Ames: Iowa State University Press, 1991). Also see O. H. Kelley, *Origin and Progress of the Order of the Patrons of Husbandry in the United States; A History from 1866 to 1873* (Philadelphia: J. A. Wagenseller, 1875), 14, where Kelley talks about his trip to South Carolina and mentions his visit with Benjamin Allston. For black-Irish antagonism, see, inter alia, Leon Litwack, *North of Slavery: The Negro in the Free States, 1790–1860* (Chicago: University of Chicago Press, 1961).

[28] Pringle, *Chronicles*, 36.

opposition . . . is strong and the excitement considerable; and to make it doubly mortifying to me, they have set up 'the jew Moses' against me" (105–6). In the other instance he opines "old Brown (the jew) charged him $8, for the oil" (194). South Carolina had a reputation for unusual toleration of its Jewish community and evidence supports that assessment. When James Henry Hammond, as governor, offended the community with his Thanksgiving Day proclamation of 1844, he had not initially intended to pick a fight, though he refused to back away from this one. The Jewish reaction indicated they would not be intimidated as they proceeded to make the dispute a public issue.[29] But people obviously were not without prejudice. Allston put his first reference in quotation marks, suggesting that perhaps people commonly talked about Moses in that fashion—though maybe not to his face—leaving Allston "doubly mortified" to have to run against him. In the second reference, Brown may not even have been Jewish but simply fit a stereotype about Jews grasping for money. So much and more is illuminated by these documents.

But what of the editor of these papers, J. Harold Easterby? How are we to know that he did not load the dice, that his selection of papers did not predetermined how we view Allston? In some ways we cannot know without looking at all the papers from which he chose.

Born in Charleston, South Carolina, in 1898, James Harold Easterby received most of his early education there before going away to Harvard for a master's degree and, later, to Chicago for his doctorate. Easterby worked under Avery Craven at the University of Chicago, where he completed a dissertation in the 1940s. He studied at a time when social attitudes and historiographical trends were different than now. Yet the first rumblings of change were in the air, and he may indeed have been always of a more liberal disposition than most of his contemporaries. In a valuable forty-nine-page introduction, Easterby explains the circumstances of his editing of the Allston papers, his organizational procedures, and part of his rationale for the choice of what to include and what to leave out. He refers to all the important primary sources that related to rice cultivation, some of which were eighteenth-century reports, such as James Glen's *A Description of South Carolina* (1761) and John Drayton's *A View of South Carolina as Respects Her Natural and Civil Concerns* (1802). Other citations are to personal memoirs, such as Elizabeth Pringle's *Chronicles of Chicora Wood* (1922). He consulted the current work on the Gullah, including stories in dialect, which, at the time he wrote, excluded the pioneering research of Lorenzo D. Turner into the sources of the Gullah language. The authoritative work on slavery was that of Ulrich B. Phillips; on agriculture, Lewis C. Gray's *History of Agriculture in the Southern United States*; and on South Carolina, David Duncan Wallace's four-volume *History of South Carolina*. This literature suggests the academic climate in which he worked and which could have influenced his choice of documents. Gray's work is a classic, but Wallace's, while packed with information, is embarrassing to present-day readers with its repeated

[29] Faust, *Hammond*, 249.

reference to slaves as "heathen barbarians," its calling African American soldiers "barbarians, intoxicated with equalitarian ideas," its quoting—with apparent approval—William Harper's suggestion that "the nobility of Southern manhood and the purity of Southern womanhood" is accounted for partly "by the welcome which slave women offered to their master's intimacy" (an attempt to dignify the shameless exploitation of defenseless slave women), and its praise for the Ku Klux Klan. Wallace's abridged 1951 version, which Easterby helped to prepare for publication after Wallace's death, is slightly more moderate in tone but only, perhaps, because it is shorter.[30] Phillips's work has also been surpassed and somewhat discredited but still has value. As Eugene D. Genovese has pointed out, Phillips, despite racial blinders, asked more and better questions than many historians since. He had a scientific outlook evidenced in an intense and abiding concern for a rigorous and methodical use of primary documents, except where they interfered with his avowed intention of upholding the tenets of white supremacy.[31] Phillips's interest in the economics of the plantation is reflected in Easterly's division of the documents, especially in the sections titled "Production and Marketing" and "Plantation Finance."

Craven may have asserted some influence on his intellectual perspective, but Easterby already had a solid professional foundation. As fellow southerners, they may even have shared a racial outlook common to the time, but, surprisingly in view of the academic environment already described, Easterby appears to have been racially moderate, even more so than his putative mentor. Craven received his higher education and spent his academic career at northern universities, but his southern background was reflected in his profound interest in southern topics. His southern birth was not determinative, however; he came to an interest in the South at Harvard, where Frederick Jackson Turner suggested he expand an agricultural paper on New England to include Maryland and Virginia. Historian Kenneth

[30] See Lorenzo Dow Turner, *Africanisms in the Gullah Dialect* (Chicago: University of Chicago Press, 1949) for Turner's most influential work; it was recently republished by the University of South Carolina Press (2002). The most memorable works of Ulrich Bonnell Phillips are *American Negro Slavery: A Survey of the Supply, Employment and Control of Negro Labor as Determined by the Plantation Regime* (New York: D. Appleton, 1918), and *Life and Labor in the Old South* (Boston: Little, Brown, and Company, 1929). Phillips was an avid document collector; see, for example, his early ten-volume *A Documentary History of American Industrial Society* (Cleveland: A. H. Clark Company, 1910–11). Lewis Cecil Gray, *History of Agriculture in the Southern United States to 1860,* 2 vols. (Washington, D.C.: Carnegie Institute of Washington, 1933); David Duncan Wallace, *The History of South Carolina,* 4 vols. (New York: American Historical Society, 1934); quotations appear respectively in 1:371; 3:226; 2:494; and 3:275. Also see Wallace, *South Carolina: A Short History, 1520–1948* (1951; Columbia: University of South Carolina Press, 1984), passim. The preface (p. viii) explains Easterby's involvement.

[31] For Phillips, see, inter alia, Merton L. Dillon, *Ulrich Bonnell Phillips: Historian of the Old South* (Baton Rouge: Louisiana State University Press, 1985); and John David Smith and John C. Inscoe, eds., *Ulrich Bonnell Phillips: A Southern Historian and His Critics* (New York: Greenwood Press, 1990), which contains an assessment by Eugene D. Genovese (113–30). Also see Peter Novick, *That Noble Dream: The "Objectivity Question" and the American Historical Profession* (Cambridge: Cambridge University Press, 1988), passim.

Stampp even considered him a "doughface"— a northern man with southern principles. He was part of a "revisionist" school of Civil War history that rejected the idea of the conflict between North and South as a moral crusade against slavery, as an "irrepressible conflict" between divergent civilizations (though he thought they did diverge), or as a war of democracy against aristocracy. He considered it, rather, a misguided effort impelled "by politicians and pious cranks!" The disagreement was "the product of purely local conditions," not transcendent ideals.[32] He had written a sympathetic biography of Edmund Ruffin, one that Frank Owsley, a member of the so-called Southern Agrarians and whose *I'll Take My Stand* was a strident defense of the region, believed ought to be read by all southerners who subscribed to the Agrarians' credo.[33] Craven agreed with Phillips, with whom he was friendly, in his attitudes toward blacks and slavery. "Slavery rendered ignorant Africans economically profitable and solved the race problem that the presence of a dangerous foreign element created," he wrote in *Edmund Ruffin, Southerner.* "It was apparently a happy solution of a pressing situation."[34] Easterby, however, seemed to avoid such gratuitous insults. Widely published, not all he wrote would have provided an outlet for expressing racial animosity, but he did have occasion for such expressions, had he been so inclined. In his introduction to *Wadboo Barony, Its Fate as Told in Colleton Family Papers, 1773–1793*, which he edited in 1952, he writes, "In recruiting their laborers they had resorted to an institution far older than feudalism with the result that their tenants were Negro slaves instead of the white leaseholders and villeins that the original plan had contemplated. In the primitive system of plantation justice there was no place for courts baron and leet and views of frank-pledge."[35] He could easily have written that "primitive savages" required a "primitive system," as Phillips suggested in *Life and Labor in the Old*

---

[32] For Craven, see Novick, *That Noble Dream,* passim, and 349 for Stampp's characterization of Craven as a "doughface"; John Higham, *History: Professional Scholarship in America* (Baltimore: Johns Hopkins University Press, 1985), 198–232, and Joe Gray Taylor, "The White South from Secession to Redemption," in *Interpreting Southern History: Historiographical Essays in Honor of Sanford W. Higginbotham,* ed. John B. Boles and Evelyn Thomas Nolen, 162–98 (Baton Rouge: Louisiana State University Press, 1987). Later in life, Craven retreated from his earlier position that the war was a needless one brought on by a blundering generation. He now argued in "Why the Southern States Seceded," in his *An Historian and the Civil War* (Chicago: University of Chicago Press, 1964), that "blundering southern leadership had . . . placed their section squarely across what northern men had begun to think of as progress" (208); and that northern politicians "had lifted the issue [of slavery] to the abstract level of right versus wrong and had thereby created a situation with which the democratic process of toleration and compromise could not deal" (204). For the quotation that expressed his earlier position, see page 29. Craven wrote about his introduction to southern history in "Some Historians I Have Known," *Maryland Historian* 1 (Spring 1970): 1–11. Even as a young man he had no trouble addressing the Association for the Study of Negro Life and History and publishing in the Association's journal: see Craven, "Poor Whites and Negroes in the Antebellum South," *Journal of Negro History* 15 (January 1930): 14–25.

[33] Novick, *That Noble Dream,* 227.

[34] Avery Craven, *Edmund Ruffin, Southerner; a Study in Secession* (New York: D. Appleton and Company, 1932), 120–21.

[35] J. H. Easterby, *Wadboo Barony, Its Fate as Told in Colleton Family Papers, 1773–1793* (Columbia: University of South Carolina Press, 1952), x. His other publications include "The Charleston

South.[36] As written, the implied criticism is more of those who ran the system than those who worked under it.

Perhaps the clearest example of his more liberal attitude in race relations is to be found in his lectures before students at the College of Charleston. In this relatively more private setting, away from the commitment to measured statements destined for public dissemination in print, he might be expected to relax his guard and express sentiments close to his innermost feelings. Not that one would regard the lectern as a confessional. His notes reveal that he was very much a traditional southerner in his belief that Reconstruction had been a disaster in its attempt to achieve racial equality and that the Congressional regime had been a "carnival of corruption." In this he was merely reflecting the historiographical consensus of the time. W. E. B. DuBois's *Black Reconstruction,* advancing a different view of the era, had appeared, but it was largely ignored by the historical profession and Easterby did not mention it. (He did, however, mention DuBois in relation to the slave trade, naming him a "rather brilliant negro who is so outstanding in negro affairs today." He noted that DuBois was editor of the *Crisis* magazine, a "negro magazine," he termed it, rather than the organ of the NAACP. But his mention suggests that he was familiar with it and may even have ventured to read it at some point.) "Through the great door of the State House in Columbia under the sculptured portraits of George McDuffie and Robert Y. Hayne[,] the black man passed to occupy the seat of his former master," Easterby's lecture continued. Although the tone was demurring, even here he refers to the "black man," not employing an insulting epithet. An appeal to base passions was clearly not his style. His was more the "patrician's quietude" than the demagogue's frenzy if he subscribed to Phillips's cardinal test of a southerner. In his discussion of the Denmark Vesey conspiracy, he calls Vesey a "boy" more from custom, perhaps, than malice, and in jocular fashion relates that after Vesey won his freedom, "He immediately became as a free negro one of the colored dandies of the town and he quickly acquired a very bad reputation as a heart smasher. He seems to have won the hearts of many negro women and was responsible for breaking up many homes. In fact it was said that, ugly as the charge may be, one of Vesey's reason[s] for his plot was his resentment that a number of his illegitimate children were held in slavery." Much of this was

---

Commercial Convention of 1854," *South Atlantic Quarterly* 2 (April 1926): 181–97; entries on the Hamptons in Allen Johnson and Dumas Malone, eds., *Dictionary of American Biography* (New York: Charles Scribner's Sons, 1931–32), 4:212–15; *A History of the College of Charleston, Founded 1770* (Charleston, S.C.: College of Charleston, 1935); "The South Carolina Rice Factor as Revealed in the Papers of Robert F. W. Allston," *Journal of Southern History* 7 (May 1941): 160–72; *The Study of South Carolina History* (Columbia: Historical Commission of South Carolina, 1951); ed., *Transportation in the Ante-bellum Period* (Columbia: Historical Commission of South Carolina, 1951); *One Small Candle May Light a Thousand: An Address* (Charleston, S.C.: College of Charleston, 1956); and with W. Edwin Hemphill, *The South Carolina Archives Building; Its Attainment, Purpose, and Design* (Columbia: South Carolina Archives Department, 1960). This listing is not meant to be exhaustive and largely excludes his archival and historical guides and editing work, perhaps the most important of which is his multivolume *The Journal of the Commons House of Assembly.*

[36] Phillips, *Life and Labor in the Old South,* 194.

for dramatic effect for he goes on to say, "He lived not far from here, around at 20 Bull Street and there he had his meetings where he planned over a space of some four years." Easterby must have been an engaging lecturer, and one can image students sitting in rapt attention as he wove a riveting tale of crisis in their city. For our current purpose, however, the most interesting feature of this lecture, aside from the fact that he considers the topic at all and in some detail, is the way he introduces Vesey: "Denmark offers amazing opportunities for someone who would have the courage to touch a subject with a good deal of dynamite. He would make a wonderful character for another play like EMPEROR JONES. There are some Charlestonians who have him in mind for a play, but do not think it wise at this time to do so."[37] This does not sound like the typical white southern male in 1940s Charleston, and one wonders whence came his more flexible caste of mind. Evidence suggests that Easterby was far from typical and, moreover, the stereotype of the southern white male, like many stereotypes, can be misleading.

Neither Craven nor Phillips seemed to presume any innate antipathy between black people and white people, evidence of the complexity in southern thought that northerners often found difficult to comprehend. "The negro . . . prospered under the Southern sun," Craven wrote, "and white men and women learned to love him." (He meant, of course, so long as the Negro remained in his place.) Although he had an image of slavery that was essentially benign, he viewed the institution with a sharper eye and was more willing to report the misfortune if not the injustice of it than Phillips was. He noted that Ruffin, "contrary to the usual custom" divided families when he set out to settle a new plantation. He also reported the high death rate among slave children on Ruffin's plantation.[38] Perhaps Craven

---

[37] See William Edward Burghardt DuBois, *Black Reconstruction; An Essay toward a History of the Part Which Black Folk Played in the Attempt to Reconstruct Democracy in America, 1860–1880* (New York: Harcourt, Brace and Company, 1935). The reference to Phillips is to his "The Central Theme of Southern History," where he says of the South that "it is a land with a unity despite its diversity, with a people having common joys and common sorrows, and, above all, as to the white folk a people with a common resolve indomitably maintained—that is shall be and remain a white man's country. The consciousness of a function in these premises, whether expressed with the frenzy of a demagogue or maintained with a patrician's quietude, is the cardinal test of a Southerner and the central theme of Southern history" (*American Historical Review* 34 [October 1928]: 31). For Easterby's comments on Reconstruction, see his lecture on Reconstruction in folder XI, labeled "History of South Carolina"; for his comments on Denmark Vesey see folder XXII, labeled "Depression and States Rights. Nullification Controversy," "lecon de 12 April 1943"; for his comments on W. E. B. DuBois see folder XIX, labeled "Introduction of Cotton and Subsistence of Sectionalism," "Lecon de 17 March 1943" in the Easterby Papers, P900172, South Carolina Department of Archives and History. I am indebted to Charles H. Lesser, accessions archivist in the department, for bringing these papers and other information to my attention and for taking time from a busy schedule to read and comment on one version of this introduction. He is not responsible for any of its faults or opinions.

One should note that there is renewed historical controversy over whether Vesey actually plotted insurrection. See the forum "The Making of a Slave Conspiracy, pts. 1 and 2," *William and Mary Quarterly* 58 (October 2001): 913–76 and 59 (January 2002): 135–202.

[38] Craven, *Edmund Ruffin, Southerner*, 120 and 18–20, respectively.

imparted this sharper eye to Easterby. More likely, Easterby needed no such instruction. In any case, Easterby features in his introduction and includes in the documents examples to indicate such unfortunate facts as the number of slave deaths
on the Allston plantations (which "does not support the general belief that Negroes
enjoyed almost complete immunity from the diseases of the Rice Coast" [30]), the
fragility of slave family life and the number of broken homes in the records (two),
and the size of slave families ("not excessively large" [29] and, besides, "childbearing was the order of the day in the planter's family as well as among the slaves"
[30]). Allston's wife bore ten children, he points out, only five of whom lived to
maturity. Of course, there is much here that will interest genealogists, and while
his vision of the slaves is largely from the viewpoint of the master class, he provides information that lends itself to other views. He includes almost as many pages
of documents in his section on the slaves as in the section on the Allston family
and more than in the section on the overseers. This may be somewhat misleading
because there are other sections on the Allstons and they clearly overshadow all.
In fact, the divisions, as Easterby admits, were arbitrary and slaves appear in all the
sections, as does the Allston family, and subjects are cross-referenced.

Scholars of various disciplines have found this collection of Allston documents
useful, and any student of plantation culture can find here documents that he or
she will recognize as having been quoted elsewhere. Easterby transcribed more
documents than he could print, and one sometimes wonders whether the impression of Allston might change if different documents had been included. For example, in 1858 Allston describes a fight that broke out among slaves at a religious
congregation, and the trial and punishment of the participants. He relates that one
slave was sentenced to receive one hundred lashes, two others fifty, and several
others twenty-five each. But the accomplishment "was cruelly severe. The consta-
ble employed was not the regular one, but he was gotten from an adjoining District, for the occasion, as I heard alleged, on account of his known severity in his
treatment of negroes. The public indignation was aroused by the unmerciful manner in which the negroes were whipped, and I have been informed that it rose to
such a height that a forcible interposition might have been made to prevent the
second infliction of fifty lashes on Jim, if it had been attempted by the same con-
stable." Allston had already indicated that one of his slaves was implicated in the
affair although he doubted his guilt. Yet, he was "unwilling to interpose to arrest
the punishment which my neighbours thought should be inflicted on him."[39] Whatever considerations caused Easterby to omit this document in favor of another one,
it could not have been because slaves were whipped, he includes evidence of this;
nor because of individual cruelty, he includes evidence of that as well. Indeed, the
story suggests public opposition to undue harshness. If one were to be distressed
at Allston's failure to intervene on behalf of one of his own slaves he believed to

[39] See the letter dated "Orangeburg, Dec. 24, 1858" in Allston, Robert F. W., Miscellaneous
Papers, 1775–1895, South Caroliniana Library, University of South Carolina, Columbia. Easterby
deposited the transcriptions of the documents he used with the South Caroliniana Library, including those of documents excluded from publication.

be innocent, it is well to reflect that Allston was governor at the time and may not have wanted to appear to be exercising undue influence for his own advantage. In other words, there is nothing here to suggest that Easterby's editorial hand tipped the scales toward excessive sentimentality in either the protagonist or his region when he decided what to include or exclude.

As first director of the newly renamed South Carolina Archives Department, Easterby contributed much to the collection and conservation of the state's historical legacy and was instrumental in the acquisition of a new archives building. He was described as "a historian first, an archivist second," but he found the two careers to be interrelated. "As a historian, he demonstrated the instincts of an archivist," a eulogist wrote, "and when he became an archivist, he remained a historian."[40] Patently, he was a historian of more rigorous standard and more generous spirit than many of his generation. His historian's vision guided his capacious understanding of what to consider a plantation record, "believing," as he said in his preface to this collection, "that neither the materials which throw light upon the planter's role in politics nor those which reflect his views on religion and his interests in the arts and sciences could properly be excluded from this category" (xxix). In that way he provided entry into a nineteenth-century world that engages the general reader curious about the Old South as much as the student seeking to dissect and reconstruct it. If, to some extent, one might view South Carolina's modern archival system as partly his monument, this engrossing collection is an equally signal accomplishment, as readers past and future will doubtless testify.

Daniel C. Littlefield

[40] W. Edwin Hemphill, "James Harold Easterby, 1898–1960," *American Archivist* 24 (April 1961): 159. Also see the sketch on Easterby in Wallace, *History of South Carolina,* 4:5.

PREFACE TO THE FIRST EDITION

Several years ago the editor of the present volume, in quest of materials for an article on the life of Robert Francis Withers Allston, applied to the late Mrs. Charles Albert Hill, of Charleston, Allston's youngest and then only surviving child. The result was one of the rich strikes which occasionally reward the efforts of those who spend their time, as Professor Ulrich B. Phillips used to say, in "panning the sands of the stream of southern life." Numerous trunks, great and small, poured forth a treasure of family papers, all of which Mrs. Hill agreed, without reservation of any kind, should be used for historical purposes.

Time did not permit any extensive use of the Allston manuscripts for the article in hand,[1] but with some idea of preparing a longer biography the writer assembled those documents which could be made in any way to serve such a purpose. Further examination revealed, however, that the Allston papers were valuable chiefly as records of the South Carolina rice plantation. In view of the fact that relatively little contemporary material concerning this phase of southern agriculture is now available, it was decided that the publication of a selected group of documents illustrating Allston's career primarily as a rice-planter might well precede any attempt at a more general biographical treatment. This plan was approved by the committee of the American Historical Association representing the Albert J. Beveridge Memorial Fund, and with their assistance it now reaches completion.

It has been neither an easy nor a simple task to decide what documents of the several thousand which comprise the Allston Collection should be included in this volume. A statement of the principles which guided selection will be found in that part of the Introduction devoted to a description of the manuscripts, but it may be well to say here that the editor has adopted a broad interpretation of the term "plantation records," believing that neither the materials which throw light upon the planter's role in politics nor those which reflect his views on religion and his interests in the arts and sciences could properly be excluded from this category. A number of the documents omitted in the text have been summarized in the Introduction, which has been made somewhat longer than is customary, partly for this reason and partly with the object of reducing the need of numerous and lengthy explanatory notes to the documents themselves. Even so, it is hardly to be expected that the selection will satisfy every interest. To those who may wish to range more widely in the papers the editor finds some satisfaction in being able to say that a calendar, prepared in the course of this study, has been deposited with the originals in the South Carolina Historical Society.

The arrangement of the documents here presented has been made with the idea of facilitating their reading and study. In general, letters treat too great a variety of

---

[1] "Robert Francis Withers Allston," in *Dictionary of American Biography*, ed. Allen Johnson and Dumas Malone (New York, 1928–37), I, 223–24.

subjects to permit any better classification than that which draws those written by a given person into one group and places all those written to that person in another class. More was to be lost than gained, it was felt, by following such a method in the present collection. Accordingly, the majority of the letters written and received by Allston, as well as those of other members of his family, have been arranged in simple chronological order in one section. But many of the letters (in certain instances more properly described as reports) in the Allston Collection were written by persons who were engaged in performing some special service for their correspondents and have a unity which invites classification on a basis of their contents. Such are the letters of the overseers and the factors, and these have been arranged in separate sections. The documents relating directly to the slaves have also been given a classification by themselves; and, finally, other papers which fitted into none of these classes have been gathered together in a section labeled "Miscellany." Whatever disadvantages there may be in this departure from a general chronological arrangement the editor has endeavored to offset by a liberal use of cross-references and by listing the documents of all classes in one calendar. No effort has been made to identify every person mentioned in the records. Where it seemed that identifications, in addition to those given in the Introduction, would contribute to a better understanding of the context, the information has been inserted, in the usual form of a footnote, at that point where it would be of most service to the reader. The names of all persons, however, have been listed in an index which has been designed to serve also as a complete guide to other subjects.

It is perhaps unnecessary to add that the greatest care has been exercised in preparing accurate copies of the materials selected for printing. No alterations have been made except to reduce superior letters to the line and to make eccentricities of punctuation conform to what seemed to be standard contemporary usage. The editor has felt compelled, however, in the interest of economy to delete such parts of individual documents as the addresses and formal closings of letters (except in a few instances in which this information has special significance) and passages of trivial content wherever found. With the same object he has given the place and date of the writing of a letter in a single line instead of the usual two and has placed the salutation at the beginning of the first line of the text, though it may have been set apart by itself in the original. For the letters the name of the writer followed by that of the recipient has been made to serve as a title; for other documents a title descriptive of the content has been supplied. It will be understood that, with the exception of two letters written by Allston to James H. Hammond and indicated as copies obtained from the Library of Congress, all the documents in this volume have been selected from the Allston Collection in the South Carolina Historical Society.

The editor wishes to acknowledge his indebtedness to the late Mrs. Hill and other members of the Allston family, especially to Miss Susan Lowndes Allston, for information concerning the authors of the documents; to Miss Ellen M. Fitz-Simons for cordial assistance at every step in the preparation of this book; to Messrs. Duncan C. Waddell, Archer M. Huntington, and William Ancrum, present owners of former Allston, or neighboring, plantations, for pleasant and profitable hours spent at their places; to Mrs. Faith Cornish Murray and the Reverend H. D. Bull for expert guidance through the Georgetown region; to Mr. William F. Allston for permission to reproduce the portrait of Robert F. W. Allston; to Mr. E. Milby Burton and Mr. John R. Lofton for photographs of plantation scenes which, though of necessity omitted from this volume, have been of great value to the editor; to the officials of Darlington, Marion, Marlboro, and Georgetown counties, particularly to Mr. Benjamin P. Fraser of the last, for expediting the use of records in their custody; to the officers of the University of North Carolina Library and the Library of Congress for the use of Allston manuscripts in their possession; to the late Professor Ulrich B. Phillips, chairman of the Beveridge Committee, and his successors, Professors Roy F. Nichols and Richard H. Shryock, for patient direction in the preparation of copy for the printer; to Professor A. L. Geisenheimer for aid in the interpretation of the documents relating to marketing; to Professor Paul R. Weidner for criticism of the Introduction from the standpoint of style; to Professor Robert L. Meriwether for kindnesses too numerous to mention; to the staff of the University of Chicago Press, especially Miss Mary D. Alexander, for interest in designing and producing this book; and, above all others, to Miss Virginia A. Rugheimer for the care which she exercised, while acting as the editor's secretary, in preparing type scripts of most of the Allston papers selected for publication.

While this volume was still in the early stages of preparation, the editor was appointed to a Julius E. Rosenwald Fellowship for graduate study at the University of Chicago. There, under the supervision of Professor Avery O. Craven, the work was completed, and, in the form in which it now appears, it was accepted as a dissertation in partial fulfilment of the requirements for the degree of Doctor of Philosophy. To Professor Craven the writer desires to express appreciation not only of his expert counsel but of many kindnesses which quickly led to friendship.

J. H. Easterby

COLLEGE OF CHARLESTON

CALENDAR

UNDATED

The South Carolina Rice Plantation
as Revealed in the Papers of
Robert F. W. Allston

To
W. A. E.

INTRODUCTION

I. THE ALLSTON PAPERS*

O F THE making of many books concerning the South Carolina rice plantation it would seem that there is to be no end. From the date of the introduction of rice into the region about Charles Town to the day, some two centuries later, when its culture was seen to be rapidly disappearing, the subject was a favorite theme of contemporary writers. In recent years a renewed interest has assumed the proportions of a revival.[1]

The rice industry quickly found a place in the official records of the province; in these and, after 1732, in the newspapers certain phases of its progress may be traced. As early as 1731 Captain Fayrer Hall in a pamphlet entitled *The Importance of the British Plantations in America* called attention to the "prodigious Advantage" of the production of rice in Carolina, and few, whether casual travelers or professional commentators, who essayed descriptions of this region prior to 1900 failed to touch at some length upon the topic.[2] Meanwhile, beginning with Alexander Hewat in 1779, the historians had taken up the theme with the usual show of erudition if not always with the strictest attention to accuracy.

But it was the planters themselves who did most to swell the volume of rice-plantation literature. During the nineteenth century, while the industry was still active, they filled scores of pages in the publications of their agricultural societies and in such journals as the *Southern Agriculturist* and *DeBow's Review* with discussions of the methods of cultivation. One planter's son, while a student in Germany, was inspired to write a thesis on the subject;[3] and the daughter of another, when a sentimental aura was beginning to gather about

---

* Unless otherwise indicated all statements made in this introduction are based on the Allston papers.

[1] For a list of many of the writings on the subject see A. S. Salley, "Bibliography of the Rice Industry in South Carolina," in David Doar, *Rice and Rice Planting in the South Carolina Low Country* ("Contributions from the Charleston Museum," Vol. VIII [Charleston, 1936]).

[2] E.g., [James Glen], *A Description of South Carolina* (London, 1761); J. F. D. Smyth, *A Tour in the United States of America* (London, 1784); John Drayton, *A View of South Carolina as Respects Her Natural and Civil Concerns* (Charleston, 1802); Robert Mills, *Statistics of South Carolina, Including a View of Its Natural, Civil, and Military History, General and Particular* (Charleston, 1826); [Solon Robinson], "Description of Rice Planting on Jehosse Island, S.C.," in *DeBow's Review* (New Orleans), IX (1850), 201–3; Frederick Law Olmstead, *A Journey in the Seaboard Slave States* (New York, 1856); [Harry Hammond], *South Carolina, Resources and Population, Institutions and Industries* (Charleston, 1883).

[3] Philip Tidyman, *Commentatio inauguralis de Oryza Sativa* (Gottingae, 1800).

1

the fading industry, contributed for several years to a New York newspaper an almost daily account of planting routine.[4] Finally, after rice-planting had been abandoned on the South Carolina coast, former planters were encouraged to record their reminiscences in such works as Elizabeth W. Allston Pringle's *Chronicles of Chicora Wood*,[5] David Doar's *Rice and Rice Planting in the South Carolina Low Country*,[6] and Duncan Clinch Heyward's *Seed from Madagascar*,[7] all excellent within their respective limits.

In the meantime, as interest in the whole plantation regime was reviving among historians, the rice plantation was not being neglected. Early in the present century Henry A. M. Smith began to contribute to the *South Carolina Historical and Genealogical Magazine* a notable series of cartographic studies,[8] and more recently works of a similar nature have appeared in Louisa Cheves Stoney's *Day on Cooper River*[9] and John R. Todd and F. M. Hutson's *Prince William's Parish and Plantations*.[10] While Alexander S. Salley was seeking to determine at precisely what date and under what circumstances rice culture was introduced into South Carolina[11] and George R. Taylor was tracing the rise and fall of rice prices in the Charleston market,[12] others were at work on studies of a more general character. In 1918 Ulrich B. Phillips traced the history of the North Carolina and the Georgia as well as of the South Carolina sector of the Rice Coast in his *American Negro Slavery;*[13] this was later supplemented at several points by chapters in Lewis C. Gray's *History of Agriculture in the Southern United States to 1860;*[14] and eight years ago Herbert Ravenel Sass ventured the first popular historical account of rice-planting in *A Carolina Rice Plantation of the Fifties*.[15]

But the present-day interest in the old Rice Coast is not restricted to historians. Alice R. Huger Smith, supplementing memory with an intimate knowledge of physical remains, has recorded the plantation scene in her deli-

[4] These articles were written for the *New York Sun* between 1904 and 1907 by one of Robert F. W. Allston's daughters, Mrs. Elizabeth W. Allston Pringle. They were later collected and published under the title, *A Woman Rice Planter* (New York, 1913).

[5] New York, 1922.

[6] See n. 1 above.

[7] Chapel Hill, 1937.

[8] Some of these were later reprinted under the title, *The Baronies of South Carolina* (Charleston, 1931).

[9] John B. Irving, *A Day on Cooper River*, enlarged and edited by Louisa Cheves Stoney (Columbia, 1932).

[10] Richmond, 1935.

[11] *The Introduction of Rice Culture into South Carolina* ("Bulletin of the Historical Commission of South Carolina," No. 6 [Columbia, 1919]).

[12] "Wholesale Commodity Prices at Charleston, South Carolina," *Journal of Economic and Business History*, IV (February, 1932), 356–77; *ibid.*, August, 1932, pp. 848–68.

[13] New York, 1918.

[14] Washington, 1933.   [15] New York, 1936.

cate water colors.[16] By means of the photograph, the measured drawing, and much searching in family muniments, Samuel G. Stoney has rescued the architectural details of many a ruinous plantation house,[17] and less tangible survivals are not being overlooked. A society formed for the purpose of preserving the spirituals that were once sung by plantation slaves has published a stout volume describing the conditions out of which they arose and giving the words and music of the favorite ones.[18] John Bennett and Reed Smith have written serious studies of the Gullah patois of the region,[19] while Ambrose E. Gonzales and, more recently, Samuel G. Stoney have employed it effectively in telling the humorous folk tales of the plantation Negroes.[20] Descendants of these same Negroes are now to be found bearing such names as Black April and Scarlet Sister Mary in the novels of Julia Peterkin,[21] and their culture patterns have recently been outlined by Mason Crum.[22]

Members of the family whose papers have been drawn upon to fill the present volume were not lacking in contributions to the literature of the rice plantation. Mrs. Pringle, one of the younger generation, described her own experiences as a planter in *A Woman Rice Planter* and later in the *Chronicles of Chicora Wood* wrote of plantation life in her father's day.[23] The father himself, many years before, had written the *Memoir of the Introduction and Planting of of Rice in South Carolina*, which is still considered the best scientific treatise on the subject. Later he prepared an *Essay on Sea Coast Crops* dealing with all the agricultural interests of the region.[24]

[16] These have been reproduced in color in *A Carolina Rice Plantation of the Fifties*, which also contains the recollections of Miss Smith's father, D. E. Huger Smith, concerning rice-planting.

[17] Albert Simons and Samuel Lapham (eds.), *Plantations of the Carolina Low Country* (Charleston, 1938). Also of interest in this connection is Samuel Lapham, Jr., "Architectural Significance of the Rice Mills of Charleston, S.C.," *Architectural Record*, LVI (August, 1924), 178–84.

[18] Augustine T. Smythe *et al.*, *The Carolina Low-Country* (New York, 1931).

[19] John Bennett, "Gullah: A Negro Patois," *South Atlantic Quarterly*, October, 1908, and January, 1909; Reed Smith, *Gullah* ("Bulletin of the University of South Carolina," No. 190 [Columbia, 1926]).

[20] Best known among the former's writings is *The Black Border: Gullah Stories of the Carolina Coast* (Columbia, 1922); the latter's written work in this connection will be found in S. G. Stoney and G. M. Shelby, *Black Genesis* (New York, 1930).

[21] A series of novels and stories published between 1924 and 1933.

[22] *Gullah: Negro Life in the Carolina Sea Islands* (Durham, 1940).

[23] See nn. 4 and 5 above.

[24] The first was originally prepared for Edmund Ruffin, *Report of the Commencement and Progress of the Agricultural Survey of South Carolina for 1843* (Columbia, 1843). It appeared in separate form the same year; in 1846 it was printed in *DeBow's Review*, I (April, 1846), 320–57, and in 1847 in the *Supplement to the Proceedings of the State Agricultural Society, of South Carolina* (Columbia, 1847). The *Essay on Sea Coast Crops* was read before the Agricultural Association of the Planting States in 1853 and published the next year by this society. It

Justification for the addition of another book to this already crowded field, even though the people and the plantations with which it deals have been treated by Mrs. Pringle in the *Chronicles of Chicora Wood*, might be found in the interest which the subject has aroused and still arouses, but the editor believes that a better defense may be offered. One is a little surprised after reading all that has been written about the South Carolina rice plantation to discover that so few records of the type that are contained in the Allston papers have been used. With the exception of a few documents published by Professor Phillips,[25] virtually nothing of this kind is to be had in print, and even manuscripts have been slow in finding their way into libraries.[26] This is not to say that what has been written is without documentary foundation— a word in the Gullah dialect, a spiritual sung by descendants of the original chanters, or even a moldering pile of brick is a document in its way, but these documents tell much less than the whole story. They give little direct information concerning such matters as the organization, supervision, and performance of labor, the methods of cultivation, the marketing of the crops, and the financial returns. Here the planters' published writings are of help, but the most truthful of men do not always practice in private what they advise in print; and it is always necessary to remember that while slavery was under attack the authors of these writings were strongly tempted to claim for the plantation system every possible merit. Much better for this purpose are the records of daily operations which the planters made in great numbers but without any idea of their some day reaching the public eye. Perhaps it is not too much to say that, until a solid basis of this kind of documentary evidence is provided, the rice-plantation tradition will be in danger of suffocation at the hands of sentimentalists.

Planters might be expected to preserve their muniments, account books, and possibly their business letters, but all did not have the Allstons' zeal in preserving their personal correspondence. The habit of saving letters appears to have been strong in Robert Allston from an early age, for at twenty he was writing to one of his correspondents: "It affords me great pleasure to read over, at some leisure hour, all my old letters." These he carefully arranged in chronological order, tying them up in tight little bundles each of which was labeled by means of a bit of shingle. Less care was exercised in retaining

---

was reprinted in *DeBow's Review*, XVI (June, 1854), 589–615. For a listing of Allston's contributions to *DeBow's Review* the writer is indebted to Professor Otis C. Skipper.

[25] Ulrich B. Phillips, *Plantation and Frontier Documents: 1649–1863* (Cleveland, 1909).

[26] Since the present work was commenced, however, the Grimball Family Diaries have been deposited in the Charleston Library Society; the Cheves Papers have been presented to the South Carolina Historical Society; and the Frost Records have been given to the Library of Congress. For other important holdings of rice-plantation materials see *A Guide to the Manuscripts in the Southern Historical Collection of the University of North Carolina* (Chapel Hill, 1941).

copies of his own letters, only an occasional rough draft being preserved; but during his frequent absences from home Allston wrote almost daily letters to his wife, giving directions concerning the work on the plantations, and in later life he sent long missives to his children. His wife and children having adopted the practice of saving their letters—those from other correspondents as well as those from members of the family—the result, there is reason to believe, was a truly vast collection.

Unfortunately, these papers have not been preserved intact. With his usual care, Allston appears to have taken some precautions for their protection during the Confederate War;[27] but after his death they were, according to his son, Benjamin, "ruthlessly torn, destroyed, & given to the winds of heaven by the negroes, his own, during their insanity." Those that remained were returned to Chicora Wood, where they were carefully preserved until the place was sold in 1926. They were then moved to Charleston and a short time later placed in the custody of the writer. There is evidence of their having been examined by Mrs. Pringle, but she used them only in a general way, if at all, in the preparation of the *Chronicles of Chicora Wood*.[28]

Benjamin Allston did not think that enough of his father's papers had survived to enable him to prepare the biography that he had contemplated, but Benjamin's requirements for this purpose probably differed greatly from those of the professional historian. The collection now includes approximately eight thousand items, besides twenty account books, a volume of overseers' receipts, fragments of diaries kept by three different individuals, and a miscellaneous assortment of memorandum books. Excepting a few scattered rec-

[27] A memorandum in one of his notebooks seems to indicate that at least a part of the papers were sent to Croly Hill plantation, where the Allston family were refugees.

[28] In making selections from the papers as he found them in Mrs. Hill's possession, the writer endeavored to obtain all except the papers of Mrs. Pringle, which he felt might better be treated as a separate unit. These selections he was allowed to retain in his possession until the completion of the present work, when they became, according to Mrs. Hill's stipulation, the property of the South Carolina Historical Society. Meanwhile, Mrs. Hill decided to place the Pringle papers on deposit in the Library of the University of North Carolina, and there they are still to be found. (For a description of them see the *Guide* mentioned in n. 26 above.) Further examination reveals that the latter contain a number of items which might properly have been included in the Allston Collection, but none of these has been considered of sufficient importance to be printed in the present volume. Since Mrs. Hill's death, two small parcels of Allston papers have turned up in the hands of dealers. The first was purchased by the South Caroliniana Library and through the generous action of its director, Professor R. L. Meriwether, has been added, by exchange, to the Allston Collection in the South Carolina Historical Society. The writer was permitted to make a superficial examination of the second parcel but not to make any use of its contents for the present work. For a preliminary survey of the Pringle manuscripts he is indebted to Mr. Frank W. Ryan. [After the present volume had gone to press, the papers of the late Arnoldus Vander Horst, a grandson of Robert F. W. Allston, were deposited in the South Carolina Historical Society. These contain a number of pertinent documents, but they do not appear to be of sufficient importance to justify further delay of publication.]

ords of earlier and later dates, the collection begins in 1809, the year of the
death of Robert's father, Benjamin Allston, Jr., and is concluded in 1896,
when Robert's widow died. The documents are unevenly distributed over
the intervening years; two periods (1824–34 and 1839–49) are inadequately
represented, but with patience a fair degree of continuity may be established.

Allston seems to have kept a rough diary devoted chiefly to plantation
operations, but only a fragment, covering parts of the years 1859 and 1860,
has survived. Portions of the diaries of his wife and of his daughter, Mrs.
Pringle, are also included in the collection but have no great value for present purposes.[29] The relatively large number of account books does not mean,
unfortunately, that the record of financial transactions is complete. In fact,
Allston's own accounts following the year 1841 were lost, probably along with
his factor's records, which were sent into the interior of the state and there
destroyed in the last year of the war. Most of the surviving books relate to
estates that Allston was called upon to settle. Each has its value, but that of
the estate of his brother, Joseph Waties Allston, is outstanding. Covering a
period of twenty-three years (1834–57), it is accompanied by vouchers explaining in detail practically every entry.

The documents selected for printing in the present volume begin in 1810,
the second year in which the collection assumes a definite continuity, and end
in 1868, a few months prior to the sale of Robert Allston's estate at public
auction. Though the papers of later dates touch, to a limited extent, upon
operations on the one plantation that remained in the possession of Robert's
widow, they are not sufficiently significant to warrant publication. Such materials as the account books, the legal papers, and, with a few exceptions, the
receipts have been excluded as too voluminous for a book of any reasonable
size, but generous levies have been made upon all other types of documents.
The criterion that the editor has endeavored to keep steadily in mind, namely,
the value of the record as evidence of life on the rice plantation, has naturally
led to the choice of comparatively larger proportions of the materials relating
to the factors, the overseers, and the slaves.

II. GEORGETOWN DISTRICT

An added significance is given to the Allston records by the fact that their
locale is the Georgetown District of South Carolina. In no other region of the
South Atlantic coast was rice-planting more predominantly the major economic interest; in none was the volume of production greater.[30] It may also
be noted that both the period in which the peak of production was attained
and that in which the decline was obviously in progress fall within the chronological range of these documents.

[29] The former covers the years 1850–52 and 1864–65; the latter, 1861–63.

[30] See data for the rice-producing divisions of North Carolina, South Carolina, and
Georgia as given in *United States Census Reports* of 1840, 1850, and 1860.

In 1826, when Allston was preparing to plant his first important crop, Robert Mills was led to observe that in Georgetown "every thing is fed on rice; horses and cattle eat the straw and bran; hogs, fowls, &c. are sustained by the refuse; and man subsists upon the marrow of the grain."[31] This was doubtless an exaggeration, but the census report for the year 1839 (the first to give figures on the rice crop) shows the Georgetown District producing 36,360,000 of the total United States crop of 80,841,422 pounds of rice.[32] Twenty years later the amount was 55,805,385 pounds, and, although the ratio between the Georgetown crop and that of the country in general had appreciably decreased, the former was still producing 30 per cent of the total.[33] By 1869, the year following the last one covered by the records here printed, production had been greatly curtailed, and it continued to decline in the following years; but as long as rice was planted in the southeastern states the Georgetown District accounted for a proportionately large part of the crop.[34]

The reasons may be found on the map. Four rivers—the Waccamaw, Peedee, Black, and Sampit—suitable to the cultivation of rice, converge into Winyah Bay near the southeastern corner of Georgetown District, and between this point and its southern boundary lies the great stretch of the Santee swamp. Along these streams, in some instances for a distance of as much as twenty miles, lay the "famous rice lands of this district," from which, as Mills said in 1826, "so much wealth has been, and still continues to be, derived by the planters."[35] Here and there the sweep of the rice fields was broken by a spur of high land extending down to the river's edge, but on the low peninsula between the Waccamaw and the Peedee, where the Allstons planted, there was one continuous expanse of tidal swamp relieved only by the intricate network of banks separating one field from another and marking the boundaries between the Waccamaw and the Peedee plantations.

Georgetown District had the type of local government peculiar to Colonial and ante-bellum South Carolina. Created in 1768, it had originally embraced all the territory lying between the Santee River and the North Carolina boundary and extending inland to a line which roughly paralleled the Atlantic shore at a distance of some fifty-five miles; but during the period of

[31] *Op. cit.*, p. 558.

[32] *Compendium . . . . of the Sixth Census of the United States, 1840* (Washington, 1841), pp. 192, 359.

[33] *Eighth Census of the United States, 1860, Agriculture* (Washington, 1864), pp. 129, 185. In 1850 the amount of rice produced in the Beaufort (S.C.) District slightly exceeded that in Georgetown, but by 1860 the latter's lead was recovered (*Seventh Census of the United States, 1850* [Washington, 1853], p. 346).

[34] *The Statistics of the Wealth and Industry of the United States . . . . Ninth Census* (Washington, 1872), p. 239, and subsequent reports.

[35] *Op. cit.*, p. 358.

the Allston papers it was confined to the southeastern corner of this region, the other sections having been detached to form the districts of Marion, Williamsburg, and Horry. Administrative functions were acquired from time to time, but Georgetown remained primarily a judicial division until erected into a county in 1868. The election districts were the three parishes—Prince George Winyah, All Saints, and Prince Frederick's—which had served the Anglican church until its disestablishment in 1778. Each has continued down to this day to be an ecclesiastical unit of the Protestant Episcopal church, but Prince Frederick's ceased to be an election district after 1790. Thus it was that the inhabitants of that part of the district lying to the east of the Waccamaw, that is, All Saints, chose one set of representatives in the state legislature, while those in Prince George Winyah (the remainder of the district) elected another group.[36]

In the second quarter of the eighteenth century, while the provincial government was sending freshly imported Scotch-Irish and Welsh immigrants into the back-country townships on the Black, Peedee, and Waccamaw rivers for the better protection of the frontier,[37] the older settlers of the province were advancing across the Santee into the lower valleys of the future Georgetown District.[38] Recognizing, perhaps at an earlier date than has previously been accepted, that tidal areas were superior to the inland swamps which hitherto had been chiefly used in the cultivation of rice,[39] they quickly established a plantation society in which the number of Negro laborers was unbelievably large. By 1800 the slave population of the district was 12,406, whereas the whites numbered only 2,150;[40] forty years later the whites had added only 43 to their number, but the slaves had increased to 18,274.[41] On the eve of the Confederate War the slaves outnumbered the whites six to one, and the average number of slaves per owner was greater than that of any other district in South Carolina.[42] Even today the number of Negroes in Georgetown is disproportionately large.[43]

[36] The best account of the evolution of the local divisions of South Carolina is to be found in William C. Harllee, *Kinfolks* (New Orleans, 1934), I, 41–62.

[37] Robert L. Meriwether, *Expansion of South Carolina, 1729–1765* (Kingsport, Tenn., 1940), chaps. vii–ix.

[38] The early history of this lower region is still vague. The statement here made is based upon impressions gathered from a study of the land grants.

[39] Henry A. M. Smith, "Hobcaw Barony," *South Carolina Historical and Genealogical Magazine* (hereinafter cited as *SCH&GM*), XIV (April, 1913), 61–80.

[40] Mills, *op. cit.*, p. 567.

[41] *Compendium . . . . of the Sixth Census of the United States, 1840*, pp. 44–46.

[42] *Eighth Census of the United States, 1860, Population* (Washington, 1864), p. 237.

[43] In 1930 the population was 64 per cent Negro; in 1940, 58 per cent (*Fifteenth Census of the United States, 1930, Population* [Washington, 1932], III, Part II, 785; Julian J. Petty, *The Growth and Distribution of Population in South Carolina* ["Bulletin of the South Carolina State Planning Board)," No. 11 (Columbia, 1943)].

Mills attributed the lag of white population to the unhealthfulness of the region: "As long as no measures are taken," he wrote, "to improve the health of the country by reclaiming the rich lands, that lie buried in swamps, this must be the result."[44] The appalling number of deaths reported in the letters of Charlotte Ann Allston would seem to confirm this explanation, but due allowance should be made for such factors as the competition of slave labor, the difficulty of getting products to market, and the inability of small farmers to engage in rice-planting.

Many of the planters went north during the "sickly" season, some to Newport and others to the Virginia Springs. The Allstons did not forego the benefits of brief sojourns at these health resorts, and in 1855 they indulged themselves in an extended tour of Europe; but, believing that absenteeism was one of the greatest curses of the plantation system, they usually spent their summers at the near-by seashore or in the dry pine lands. "These pine-land retreats for the summer," Allston wrote in 1854, "are now frequent for planters on the Peedee, Black River, and Sampit—free from the annoyance of musquitoes [sic] and from oppressive heat at night. The planters of Santee resort chiefly to South Island, where there is quite a village, and a population in summer large enough for the care of a Pastor. At Plantersville, 16 miles from town, the summer congregation consists of about 30 adults. . . . . The planters of Waccamaw retreat to some one of the valuable islands on the Sea Shore (Waccamaw Beach) lying in a direction North and South nearly parallel with the river for 30 miles, about 3 miles from the plantations and separated from the main land by extensive plains of Salt Marsh overflow'd with salt water twice in the 24 hours."

Until recent years Georgetown was the only town of the district. The site on the north bank of the Sampit, some eight and a half miles from the entrance of Winyah Bay, had passed into private ownership as early as 1705. At some time prior to 1732, a well-conceived town plan having been put into operation, it was made an official port of entry. In 1768 it became the seat of justice of Georgetown District, and in 1785 it was made the depository of local records hitherto kept in Charleston. Twenty years later it was incorporated and its government lodged in the hands of an intendant and four wardens.[45]

The only port on the hundred and fifty miles of coast between Charleston and Wilmington, Georgetown seemed destined to become an important center of foreign as well as coastwise trade. Its surrounding rivers were navigable, one of them—the Peedee—for as much as a hundred and twenty miles from the ocean. Yet, after some development during the Colonial period, George-

[44] Op. cit., p. 567.

[45] Henry A. M. Smith, "Georgetown: The Original Plan and the Earliest Settlers," SCH&GM, IX (April, 1908), 85–101; Harllee, op. cit., I, 41–62; Thomas Cooper and David J. McCord (eds.), Statutes at Large of South Carolina (Columbia, 1836–41), VIII, 227–33.

town grew only slowly. Washington, on passing through it on his southern tour in 1791, reported: "The Inhabitants of this place (either unwilling or unable) could give no account of the number of Souls in it, but I should not compute them as more than 5 or 600."[46] Sixty years later the number of whites was 604, the Negroes 1,024.[47] In 1840 there were no business houses engaged in foreign trade, and the three commission merchants had an invested capital of only $10,300.[48]

According to tradition, a shallow harbor and a shifting bar prevented the development of Georgetown's commerce,[49] but closer study suggests that the stubborn resolve of Charleston to control the trade of the southeastern coastal plain may be an additional, if not a more important, reason. While the citizens of Georgetown were dallying with plans for a deep-water channel at the close of the eighteenth century,[50] Charleston built the Santee Canal up to their very back door. From an early time sailing vessels and, later, steamboats from Charleston were plying on the rivers of Georgetown District.[51] In 1860 young Benjamin Allston wrote his sweetheart in Charleston that the railroad would soon bring them closer together. "I hope," he said, "the 'Iron Monster' will [soon] chafe and tramp along the way, waking up the sleeping woods and bringing in his train the life, energy and activity which shall convert the wild places into the happy homes of industrious citizens." It was, nevertheless, almost a quarter of a century before Georgetown completed its first railroad.[52] Long before this, Charleston had tapped its hinterland with a railway running through Kingstree to Florence and Cheraw in the upper Peedee Valley.[53]

Robert Allston sometimes drove his sulky over the sixty miles of road between Georgetown and Charleston, and the stagecoach was always available; but the better part of two days which the journey consumed and the hazards

[46] A. S. Salley, *President Washington's Tour through South Carolina in 1791* ("Bulletin of the Historical Commission of South Carolina," No. 12 [Columbia, 1932], p. 7).

[47] *Seventh Census of the United States, 1850*, pp. cxiii, 1019.

[48] *Compendium . . . . of the Sixth Census of the United States, 1840*, p. 193.

[49] Attention was called to Georgetown's shallow harber by John Drayton, *op. cit.*, pp. 170 n., 207–8. A quarter-century later Robert Mills elaborated this point, adding that "obstructing bars increase as cultivation releases more soil into the rivers" (*op. cit.*, pp. 557, 559–67). Ulrich B. Phillips, *A History of Transportation in the Eastern Cotton Belt to 1860* (New York, 1908), pp. 6, 34, and Leila Sellers, *Charleston Business on the Eve of the American Revolution* (Chapel Hill, 1934), pp. 6–7, accept this explanation.

[50] Drayton, *op. cit.*, Appendix and accompanying map.

[51] This advance of Charleston into Georgetown's back country is best told in Phillips, *Transportation in the Eastern Cotton Belt*, pp. 83–91, 349–55.

[52] The date of the first rail connection is given as 1884 in *Millers' Planters and Merchants Almanac* of that year.

[53] Phillips, *Transportation in the Eastern Cotton Belt*, pp. 349–55. For further discussion of communications see below, pp. 40–41, 42–43.

encountered at the four ferries that must be crossed generally led the traveler to prefer the ocean route between the two towns. Except in time of war, the crops of the Georgetown District were shipped directly from the plantation wharves, or the neighborhood "pounding mills," to the counting-houses of Charleston.

So Georgetown definitely remained in the "shade of Charleston," as Washington put it; but it was not without its importance in the lives of the surrounding planters. Its bank and its newspaper office, the courthouse, and the mother-church of Prince George Winyah were centers of interest. Occasionally, the planters embarked at Georgetown on their voyages to the northern states, and supplies not anticipated in their orders to the Charleston factors might be purchased in its retail stores. Here they maintained town houses, attended the Winyah Indigo Society and the lyceum, and drew their books from the Georgetown Library Society.

III. THE ALLSTON FAMILY

Robert Francis Withers Allston belonged to the fifth generation of the Allston family in South Carolina.[54] His great-great-grandfather, John, had been sent to Charleston in 1682 by his father, a "gentleman of Hammersmith, Middlesex, England," there to serve as a merchant's apprentice.[55] John must have eventually prospered to some degree, for when he died about 1719 he left three thousand acres of land to be divided among three sons and a like number of daughters. He was living at this time, it seems, in the parish of St. John's Berkeley, well within the circle of settlement by which Charleston was then surrounded.

Two of John's sons, John and William, preferred to be pioneers on the new frontier that was opening up beyond the Santee River in the future Georgetown District.[56] Here they are found between the years 1732 and 1739 receiving grants of no less than 6,500 acres,[57] which, not to mention later acquisitions, they in due course passed on to those of their nine sons and seven daughters who survived them. John and William had intermarried with the Belins and the LaBruces; their children formed alliances with the Marions, Simonses, Moores, Atchisons, Watieses, and Rothmahlers, and replenished the earth to such good effect that it has been said that four-fifths of the rice plantations on Waccamaw Neck have been owned at one time or another by their descendants.[58] So numerous, in fact, did the John, William, and Joseph

[54] Joseph A. Groves's *The Alstons and Allstons of North and South Carolina* (Atlanta, 1901) is an exhaustive but not always an accurate genealogy. Elizabeth Deas Allston's *The Allstons and Alstons* (s.l., 1936) gives biographical sketches of outstanding members of the family.

[55] A. S. Salley, "John Alston," *SCH&GM*, VI (April, 1905), 114–16.

[56] Wills in Charleston County Office of the Judge of Probate.

[57] Office of the Secretary of State, Columbia, S.C., "Indexes to Plats."

[58] Henry A. M. Smith, "Hobcaw Barony," *SCH&GM*, XIV (April, 1913), 69.

Allstons become that it was found desirable near the close of the eighteenth century to introduce a variant, or rather to make permanent an earlier uncertainty, in the spelling of their surname, and, ever since, there have been single-*l* and double-*l* Allstons.[59]

Robert F. W. Allston represented the double-*l* branch of the family and was descended from both of the pioneers, John and William; for his paternal grandfather, William Allston, Jr., was the son of John, and his maternal grandfather, William Allston, Sr., was the son of William. Both were planters, but while William, Jr., appears to have been content to live the life of a settled planter on the Rice Coast, his cousin ventured into the more plebeian regions of the upper Peedee River, accumulating lands, later to be estimated at 30,000 acres, but apparently little wealth in other forms.[60]

The sons of William Allston, Jr., were Benjamin, Jr., and his half-brothers Washington and William Moore. Washington was to acquire fame as an artist and make his home in Cambridge, Massachusetts; William Moore went into business in the North; but Benjamin, Jr., remained at home to become a rice planter. In 1788 he married his cousin, Charlotte Ann, daughter of the second William Allston, Sr., and to this marriage were born Elizabeth Ann (1790–1822), who appears in the records here printed as Mrs. John H. Tucker; Charlotte Atchison (1793–1847), the later Mrs. John Coachman; Mary Pyatt (1795–1836), the later Mrs. William H. Jones; Joseph Waties (1798–1834), who was three times married: first to Sarah Prior, secondly to Charlotte Nicholson, and thirdly to Mary Allan; Robert Francis Withers (1801–64), who married Adele Petigru; and William Washington (1804–23), who died unmarried.

Tradition has it that Benjamin, Jr., inherited from his father the plantation on Waccamaw River, known as Brookgreen, now a part of the famous gardens developed by Archer M. Huntington. It is further asserted that Benjamin lost this patrimony by indorsing the notes of a friend.[61] However this may be, he was not in possession of Brookgreen nor was he a wealthy man when he died in 1809 at the age of forty-three. His estate included, it is true, two plantations—one on the Waccamaw several miles above Brookgreen and another on the Peedee—and a hundred or more slaves; but this property was heavily encumbered.

From a date shortly before the death of Benjamin the history of this par-

---

[59] Best known among the single-*l* Allstons was Joseph, governor of South Carolina (1812–14) and husband of Theodosia Burr. It may be well to add for the sake of those whose interest in Theodosia never flags that the Robert Allston papers contain no information on this subject.

[60] The land speculations of this William Allston may be traced in the records of Marion, Marlboro, and Darlington counties.

[61] Susan Lowndes Allston, *Brookgreen, Waccamaw, in the South Carolina Low Country* (Charleston, 1935), p. 18.

ticular branch of the Allston family is to be found in the records from which the selections in this volume were taken. For some ten years these documents are concerned, in the main, with the struggles of the Widow Allston to preserve intact the property of her children. She was not one to bear her burdens with gentle submission. Her letters are filled with complaints—complaints in general of her ill fortune and complaints of the conduct of certain of her children. She felt that, though a girl should marry early, it was a boy's duty to see that his mother was provided for first. Yet Charlotte Ann never shirked her duty. With the advice of her factor, Charles Kershaw, and with financial assistance on occasion from her sister, Mrs. Elizabeth Frances Blyth, who was to prove in other respects to be the fairy godmother of the family, she managed to hold off the creditors until 1819, when Joseph Waties was old enough to take over the responsibility of the Waccamaw place. The mother was then able to concentrate her attention on the Peedee plantation, which had been left to the younger boys, but her troubles were not over. Before she died in 1824, death had already claimed her oldest daughter, her youngest son, Joseph's first wife, and Joseph's little son, who had become the apple of her eye.

One may well imagine that Robert Allston was early impressed with the seriousness of life. He was first taught by a governess; later he attended a classical school in Georgetown conducted by John Waldo, an excellent teacher, he says, until his attention became "too much engrossed by his pretensions as an author";[62] and finally in 1817, at his mother's urging, he entered West Point. It was taken for granted that he would be a planter, but planters, Mrs. Allston felt, should have a profession to occupy them in their spare time and to supplement their incomes. She was undecided whether Robert should be a lawyer and collect fees for settling the many boundary disputes of their neighbors or whether he should study physic and thereby escape the expense of having others treat his Negroes. The boy himself thought of entering the ministry but decided that he was unworthy.

Having failed to reach a decision in this important matter, young Allston did the usual thing; he accepted a commission on the completion of his course at the Academy in 1821. He was quickly assigned to duty with the Topographical Service and for several months was employed in surveying the harbors of Plymouth, Massachusetts, and of Mobile Bay, thus gaining experience which was to be of great value to him as a planter. The next year he resigned with the intention of relieving his mother of her burdens, but, deciding apparently that the income from the plantation, where much of the rice land was still uncleared, must be supplemented from another source, he accepted an appointment as surveyor-general of South Carolina. The duties of this

[62] R. F. W. Allston, *Address before the Members and Pupils of the Winyah Indigo Society . . . . on the 5th of May, 1854* (Charleston, 1859), pp. 14–15. Waldo's *Latin Grammar* was published in Georgetown in 1816 (*SCH&GM*, XLIV [October, 1943], 233).

office interfered seriously with his work as a planter, and, although he assumed the full management of the plantation at the death of his mother, it was not until 1827 that he commenced to plant in earnest.

From the beginning Allston was ambitious for political office. He was much gratified, therefore, by his election in 1828 to represent the parish of Prince George Winyah in the state house of representatives. He was returned two years later, but, having become a staunch advocate of state rights, he was defeated by a Unionist in 1832. Later, however, in the same year, at a special election, he offered for the senate and was successful by the narrow margin of one vote. From this time until 1856 he was regularly returned, and from 1847 on he was president of the senate. After many disappointments he was finally, on December 9, 1856, elected to the governorship by the General Assembly, an office which he held until December 14, 1858. Some idea of the methodical care with which Allston attended to his public duties may be gained from the following statement which he entered in his diary on retiring to private life: "Came home 9th Decr. for the remainder of the month, being the first time in 35 years excepting the year 1827, and a part of 1837, when my wife was ill . . . . , and during this whole time, 4 years as Surveyor Genl and 28 as Representative (4) and Senator (24), I have not lost a day from my seat, with the exception of one week, when dispatch'd on duty to inspect the workshops of the So Ca Rail Road at Charleston, Hamburgh & Aiken & the proposed inclined plane at Aiken." The fact that the General Assembly met in those days for only three or four weeks in November and December and that the governor was not required to reside at the seat of government, except during the sessions of the Assembly, were doubtless factors in making such a record possible.

"My political creed," Allston stated in 1838, "is based on the principles of Thomas Jefferson, as express'd during the discussions in Virginia in 1798 and the subsequent canvass which resulted in his election as President in 1801. I adopted this creed some where about the year 1825 from a conviction of its virtue and purity regarding the peculiar nature of our polity and the character of the elements of this great Republic. Every year that I have lived since has served by its experience to confirm me in the belief that a plain, honest, common-sense reading of the Constitution is the only true one and that in legislating for the government of the United States, nothing—absolutely nothing of authority—should be allowed to precedent as such." There is no reason to believe that this attitude was later changed in any respect. To what he regarded as violations of the Constitution by the northern states, especially of its clauses protecting the institution of slavery, he advocated a vigorous resistance. It was these views that led him to support nullification in 1832, to go as a delegate to the Nashville Convention in 1850, and in 1856 to contribute to a fund being raised to send slaveholders into Kansas. He probably favored united resistance on the part of the southern states; there is nothing, however, to indicate that he doubted the wisdom of separate secession by South Carolina in 1860.

It was Allston's original intention to bring about a reform of the poor laws of his state. With this object in view he studied the systems of other states, but, he explains, "the excitement of the public mind occasion'd soon after by the Protective Tariffs and the consequent contest with the Federal Government so absorb'd all the interest of Statesmen as to put a stop to any further attempt to effect any state reform." Before the question could again be taken up, Allston had convinced himself that, "in view of the habits of living and thinking among . . . . [the] people in the several sections of the State differing so materially from those of the people whose laws he had consulted it was entirely out of his power to frame a better system of poor laws." His interest in social reform, however, was not abandoned. There are many references in his papers to efforts to improve conditions in the South Carolina reservation for the Catawba Indians, to make more ample public provision for the deaf and dumb, the blind, and the insane, and to expand the facilities of public education.

A bill which Allston never tired of presenting had to do with changes in the free school system. Nine years of service as a local commissioner had led him to believe that the public elementary schools would not be successful until they were attended by the children of all classes and not by the children of the poor alone. He further asked for an increase of the general appropriation, taxation within the local districts to supplement state aid, the establishment of a normal school "with a model school attached," the creation of the office of superintendent of education, and the printing of the necessary textbooks within the state.[63] He had the satisfaction of seeing the annual appropriation doubled in 1852, and the city of Charleston at length adopted the second and third of his proposals, but the acceptance of his program in its entirety was postponed until a later day. More immediate success probably attended Allston's efforts as president of the Winyah Indigo Society to direct the school which it maintained for the poor of Georgetown District and as a trustee of South Carolina College, where he maintained a scholarship and on occasion gave a prize for the best historical essay based on original materials.

The South Carolina Historical Society and the Carolina Art Association gave Allston other opportunities to stimulate a "diffusion of knowledge" and an interest in the arts. In 1860 he called the Art Association to the attention of the members of the Secession Convention, suggesting apparently in all seriousness that "an hour bestowed occasionally in viewing some specimen of art . . . . may contribute an agreeable diversion to the minds of gentlemen

[63] The best statement of these views is found in Allston's report to the South Carolina legislature (*Reports and Resolutions of the General Assembly of the State of South Carolina . . . . 1847* [Columbia, 1848], pp. 210–43).

habitually engrossed in the discussion of grave concerns of state."[64] But he was probably most at home in the agricultural societies which flourished in great abundance in that day. Of his local organization, the Winyah and All Saints Agricultural Society, he was president for a number of years. It was at a meeting of the State Agricultural Society in 1846 that he chose to present the fullest statement of his program of school reform, and his *Essay on Sea Coast Crops* was read in 1853 before the Agricultural Association of the Planting States.

For such recreation as he allowed himself, Allston had his neighborhood club, the Hot and Hot Fish Club, where he might bowl or play a game of billiards and refresh himself from its ample store of wines.[65] Thursday was his day for hunting, and there were the dinners of the Indigo Society and Masonic gatherings in Georgetown. Marriage drew him into the charmed circle of Charleston society, and eventually he joined the South Carolina Jockey Club and the St. Cecilia Society, but he seems to have begrudged a little the time spent in the city. "My visit to Charleston," he would say, "like a favorite toy with a child, put every thing out of my head."

Allston liked to think that he put none of his multifarious duties ahead of that to the church. He had his pew in St. Michael's in Charleston, in Prince George's in Georgetown, and, probably, in the little chapel of Prince Frederick's, which stood near the plantation and which he was helping to rebuild when the work was stopped by the war. From time to time he served as a vestryman, and at intervals between 1847 and 1859 he was a member of the General Convention of the Protestant Episcopal church. It was his habit to give financial assistance to students preparing for the ministry, but he did not insist that they adhere to the church of his preference.

Allston had felt the quickening effect of the humanitarian spirit that was pulsing through the America of his day. With a little less of his practical nature and a little more of ardor he would have been at home among the New England reformers, and yet he did not question the morality of slavery. It would be easy to explain this on the ground of self-interest, and, unquestionably, this was a factor in determining his attitude. Few men would invite the destruction of property into which they had put a quarter of a million dollars. He had thought, too, of the race problem which would follow emancipation. Such an "alternative," he said, "cannot be contemplated, namely, the giving up of our beautiful country to the ravages of the black race and amalgamation with savages." But Allston had an additional reason. He believed that the Negro, being what he was and having been brought into association with the white man, was better off in servitude than he could be free. It was the white man's mission to rule him and to guide him to better things. "In short," he said, "the educated master is the negro's best friend upon

[64] Pringle, *Chronicles of Chicora Wood*, p. 23.

[65] The manuscript journal of this organization is preserved in Allston's papers.

earth." To one of his sons he wrote: "Many of the negroes enquired kindly for you. You must try to be a good boy, in order to treat them judiciously and well, when Papa is gone." With some men this course of reasoning would have been plain sophistry; with Allston it was unquestionably sincere.

Allston could have written the "Psalm of Life" had verses come more readily to his pen. He was, in fact, so earnestly occupied with making life "sublime" that he had little time for intimacies of any kind. "There are so few persons," wrote his wife, "who understand and appreciate Mr. Allston that I was quite glad to find one who had." Yet his efforts won rich returns of respect and admiration. James D. B. DeBow felt that such essays as Allston's *Memoir on Rice* had done more "for the advancement of agricultural science than can well be conceived";[66] and James L. Petigru, his brother-in-law, wrote to him during the war: "We have always looked up to you as combining more than any one else, prudence with the other cardinal virtues; and when your troubles are so great as to lead you to complain, it is proof that forethought and discretion are not enough in these days to keep us out of harm." He deserved the tribute which his wife paid him shortly after his death: "His character was very noble. He was strong too and able. No business confided to him was neglected. He was full of resources, an active mind and clear judgment."

There is a tradition that it was the knowledge of these qualities of her suitor that had led Adele Petigru to accept Allston's proposal of marriage in 1832. When one of her sisters opposed her choice with the argument that the beauty and the wit of a Petigru deserved a better fate than that of the wife of a planter who lived both winter and summer in the country, Adele is said to have replied that she had made up her mind to marry Allston because he was "as obstinate as the devil," obstinacy being a quality which the Petigrus lacked.[67] She may have doubted the wisdom of her decision after learning what the life of a plantation mistress would be, for her brother was shortly writing: "The goodness of your heart and your native moderation of mind make me hope that you will accommodate yourself to your new duties with such good will as to preserve that sweet serenity which makes one happy in one's self & diffuses happiness to others"; and she yearned at times to find in her husband the wit and sparkle of her people. Adele was endowed, however, with a character scarcely less sturdy than Allston's. The many letters which she exchanged with her brothers, her two sisters in Charleston (Mrs. Philip J. Porcher and Mrs. Henry D. Lesesne), and two other sisters (Mrs. John G. North and Mary Petigru) who remained at the old family home in Abbeville

[66] *DeBow's Review*, I (April, 1846), 356.

[67] Pringle, *Chronicles of Chicora Wood*, pp. 57–59. Much information concerning the home life of the Petigrus may be found in J. P. Carson, *Life, Letters and Speeches of James Louis Petigru* (Washington, 1920).

show her sharing one responsibility after another with her husband and even supporting the whole burden after he died in 1864.

Of the ten children born to Adele and Robert Allston, five lived to maturity. Like his father, the eldest son, Benjamin (1833–1900), went to West Point, where he was graduated in 1853. He remained four years in the army, serving at various western posts; then he made the "grand tour" of Europe and was settling down to the life of a rice-planter when he was called into the Confederate Army. After the war he returned to planting but under difficulties with which he was unable to cope, and eventually he entered the Episcopal ministry. A second son, Charles Petigru (1848–1922), was too young for military service until near the end of the war. After graduation from the College of Charleston in 1869 he managed, despite the loss of his father's property, to set himself up as a successful rice-planter. Adele (1842–1915), the eldest daughter, married Arnoldus Vander Horst; and the youngest, Jane Louise (1850–1937), married Charles Albert Hill. Adele and Jane Louise have little further connection with the Georgetown District, but a third daughter, Elizabeth Waties Allston (1845–1921), remained to be, like her mother and her grandmother, a woman rice-planter. Left a young widow by the death of her husband, John Julius Pringle, she first purchased White House plantation on Black River and later her father's old homestead, Chicora Wood, on the Peedee. Here she lived and wrote her two books about life on the Rice Coast.

The Confederate War had tragic consequences for the Allston family. The father promptly offered his services in the field, but his sixty years were too many for military duty. He had to be content with the thought that in producing food he was contributing to the cause. His efforts, however, were beset with many difficulties. He must help with the management of his son's and his nephews' plantations as well as direct the work on his own places. The Georgetown District was constantly threatened with invasion, and new ways of sending the crop to market had to be found after the water route to Charleston was closed. For three years Allston struggled with these problems, and then on April 7, 1864, weary with his many labors, he died.

Mrs. Allston quickly assumed control, directing the overseers from Croly Hill, the refuge up the Peedee River to which she had taken her younger children. The next year she had to face the results of the long-dreaded Federal occupation. For a time the Negroes pillaged the plantations at will, but this was not the most serious of her problems. There were heavy debts against the estate. She struggled to meet these obligations. Some of the plantations she rented; others she put under Benjamin's direction, urging him to greater and greater efforts; while she herself opened a school for girls at her home in Charleston. The problem would not be solved. In 1869 the estate was sold at auction. Chicora Wood and a tract of timber land were all that was saved, these being awarded to the widow as her dower. At Chicora Wood, Adele

Allston made her home and planted a few acres of rice until her death in 1896 at the age of eighty-six.

IV. THE ALLSTON PLANTATIONS

The two plantations which figure most prominently in the Allston papers are those which Benjamin Allston, Jr., bequeathed to his three sons. The first was Waverly, located on Waccamaw Neck, in All Saints Parish, some ten miles north of Georgetown. Here Benjamin was living when he made his will in 1807, and here his family continued to reside until the division of the estate in 1819. At that time Waverly passed, according to the provisions of the will, into the possession of Joseph Waties, the eldest son, and would not have been heard of further in the records here printed but for the fact that when Joseph died in 1834 he left his brother Robert as executor of his estate and guardian of his two infant sons, Joseph Blyth and William Allan. For this reason the Waverly accounts, covering the years from 1834 to 1857, which are presently to be analyzed,[68] were preserved in Robert F. W. Allston's papers.

Nothing is known of the early history of Waverly; Benjamin Allston says no more than that it "originally belonged to Dr. Allston."[69] A plat of 1827, however, shows it to have included 587 acres: 150 in rice fields, ranging in size from 10 to 30 acres and located on both banks of the river; 28 occupied by the margins, banks, and ditches of the rice fields; 37 in uncultivated swamp lying along Chapel Creek, which formed a part of the boundary on the north; and 372 in high land, ponds, etc.[70] On the bluff rising above the rice fields to the east of the river stood the plantation house, flanked on the south by Negro quarters and on the north by the barnyard and a mill which "pounded" not only the Waverly crop but also that of many neighboring plantations. Beyond these lay the pastures and those fields that were devoted to the "upland" crops (doubtless the customary sweet potatoes, corn, and peas), both extending to the main road of Waccamaw Neck, where the parish church, with its surrounding glebe, separated a large tract of pine land from the cultivated areas of the plantation.

The second of Benjamin Allston's plantations was situated on the Peedee River three miles, as the crow flies, northwest of Waverly but seven by river and creek. As early as 1819 it was known as Matanzas (more frequently written Matanza), but in 1853 the name, to the regret of at least one member

[68] See below, pp. 44–45, 46–48.

[69] The destruction of the Georgetown District records during the Confederate War has made it difficult, and sometimes impossible, to trace the titles of the Allston properties. Most of the data presented in the following pages are taken from deeds in the Allston papers.

[70] In 1837, however, Robert Allston gives the size of the Waverly rice fields as 250 acres.

of the family,[71] was changed to Chicora Wood, and by this name, regardless of dates, it will be more convenient to refer to it here.

The frequency with which Chicora Wood had changed hands in early years suggests that it had been treated as something of a speculation. Its 922 acres (915 according to the most recent survey)[72] included what were originally four separate tracts and a part of a fifth. One of these, containing 100 acres of tidal swamp on the peninsula between the Peedee and the Waccamaw, and a second of 420 acres of high land on the west bank of the Peedee, immediately opposite the first, were granted in 1732 and 1734, respectively, to John Allston, the grandfather of Benjamin. In 1738 John purchased from William Waties his adjoining grant (made in 1736) of 246 acres of swamp, and ten years later transferred the first two tracts and 150 acres of the third to his son, John. From the second John they passed in 1751 to his daughters, Mrs. Benjamin Young and Mrs. Peter Simons. Mrs. Young in 1764 sold her half-interest to her sister's husband; Simons sold the whole in 1771 to Benjamin and Richard Waring; and, the former having withdrawn from ownership, Richard sold out to John Waring in 1777. Earlier in the same year John Waring had purchased from Benjamin Walker the two adjacent tracts—one of 132 acres of high land and another of 120 acres on the peninsula—which fill out the boundaries of the future Chicora Wood. Walker had inherited these two tracts from his father, James Walker, who had purchased them from Samuel Gobbaille Dupré, who, in his turn, had acquired them from William Poole, a brother-in-law of the first John Allston mentioned above, the original grantee. Waring retained his title for only two years, then sold to Alexander Rose and John Torrans, who are described in the deed as merchants and copartners of Charleston. Rose purchased Torrans' share in 1785 from the latter's widow, and on July 19, 1806, the executors of Rose sold the plantation to Benjamin Allston, Jr.

When the Widow Allston removed from Waverly to Chicora Wood in 1819, she undertook the management of the latter as the guardian of her two minor sons, Robert and William, to whom it had been willed by their father; but, before this trust was discharged, William's death transferred his share in equal parts to Robert and Joseph. Finally, by purchasing Joseph's fourth interest, Robert became in 1832 the full proprietor of Chicora Wood. In the meantime he had begun to assist his mother in its management, and after 1826 he gave it his undivided attention.

Chicora Wood, under the circumstances which Allston received it, was not a rich patrimony. It was heavily mortgaged; a boundary dispute with Wil-

---

[71] Joseph Blyth Allston wrote: "The namesake of the latter [Matanzas] in Cuba is so beautiful that really one might think you do it from shame at being surpassed therein, which is entirely contrary to the calm steady conduct our family motto prescribes."

[72] Made at the instance of its present owner, Duncan C. Waddell, and recorded in Georgetown County, Clerk of Court's Office, Book E2, p. 249.

liam Vereen, the owner of the plantation adjoining on the south, was impending; and much of the future rice land was still in forest. Writing many years later of his early struggles, Allston said with pardonable pride: "His first labour was, under an August sun, with chain & compass, to run out this land and mark out the banks, ditches, and canals. His first planting consisted of one hundred acres, his first crop was the product of 100 acres of rice land badly prepared and feebly worked because of the weakness of his force." For fourteen years his efforts, apart from the time devoted to Waverly, were confined to this one plantation.

The first definite turn in Allston's fortunes came in 1840, when he inherited a large part of the estate of his aunt, Mrs. Blyth, who, like many another woman in Georgetown District, had successfully operated her plantations for many years after her husband's death, as those of her papers here printed will show. One of these plantations, known as Waties Point and located on the outskirts of Georgetown, was left in trust to Allston for his sons and nephews, and with their consent it was sold in 1854 to a "practical lumber man from Philadelphia." The other was Friendfield, a tract of nine hundred acres situated on Waccamaw Neck, nearly opposite the town. This was Allston's to do with as he saw fit, but, possibly because he considered it too far removed from his homestead to be managed with convenience, it was also sold after a single year of planting.

With the proceeds from the sale of Friendfield, Allston appears in 1843 to have purchased Exchange, a plantation of 482 acres on the Peedee River, a short distance above Chicora Wood. This was sold, however, three years later when he bought the much larger plantation (1,219 acres), known as Nightingale Hall, about six miles down the Peedee. To this he added in 1847 the 363 acres of Waterford which adjoined Nightingale Hall on the peninsula between the Peedee and Waccamaw. This, with some 500 acres of adjacent "seashore," acquired about the same time, gave him a tract spanning both rivers and reaching to the Atlantic coast. The combination contained more than three square miles.

The Nightingale Hall–Waterford unit was located at the best "pitch of tide," and the quality of rice produced there was superior; but Allston seems to have continued to question the wisdom of owning plantations separated by any distance from that on which he resided. Accordingly, he several times considered the sale of these two places, and his expansion in the 1850's, with a single exception, was confined to his immediate neighborhood. In 1851 he purchased Rose Bank (477 acres), which he seems to have preferred to call Ditchford or Ditchfield, adjoining Chicora Wood on the north. Two years later he repurchased Exchange, which was located just beyond Rose Bank. Having in the meantime acquired either the whole or a part of Breakwater (acreage undetermined), he found himself with a second group of contiguous plantations which must at least have equaled in size the Nightingale Hall–Waterford unit.

The last two additions to the list of Allston's rice plantations were made primarily with the object of setting up his son, Benjamin, as a planter. In 1858 he purchased Guendalos, which included the plantation of his once troublesome neighbor, William Vereen, and either all or parts of two other places formerly known as Retreat and Holly Hill—a total of 1,253 acres. An option on approximately one-fifth of this tract was given to his nephew, Joseph Blyth, who was now seeking to expand the Waverly property. One hundred acres of rice land was added to Chicora Wood, and the remainder was turned over to Benjamin on the condition that he assume a share of the cost. The next year, in order to supply Benjamin with an adequate force of laborers, Allston accepted an offer by his wife's sister-in-law, Mary Ann Petigru, of her large gang of Negroes. In so doing, however, he was under the necessity of buying her Pipe Down plantation situated on Sandy Island, a narrow high land rising above the Peedee-Waccamaw peninsula a little above Chicora Wood. The effect was to increase his own holdings by the 294 acres of Pipe Down and to add Guendalos to his responsibilities when Benjamin entered the Confederate Army two years later.

Thus had Allston come into possession of seven plantations. The total area was not less than 4000 acres, of which about one-fourth was adaptable to the water culture of rice. Scattered deeds among his papers show that he acquired in addition upward of 9,500 acres of pasture and timber lands. Some of this adjoined the plantations clustering about Chicora Wood; another tract was located on Sandy Island not far from Pipe Down; cypress lands situated on the inland swamp known as Carver's Bay included some 2,500 acres; and there were 3,700 acres more in the Britton's Neck section of Marion District. This last offered a refuge to which the Negroes might be sent during the Confederate War, but Allston eventually decided that he must provide a place farther from the coast. Accordingly, in 1863 he purchased Morven, a plantation of 1,900 acres located in Anson County, North Carolina. Like most of his lands, this was situated on the Peedee River—"the family stream," as Petigru called it, "uniting them by political association as well [as] geographical limits with that country."

In the summer the Waverly folk went to near-by Oakgrove on the seashore to escape the dread effects of "country fever," but the residents on the Peedee plantations were some years in finding a healthful retreat. Allston took his bride first to Canaan, a tract of some 344 acres given him by Mrs. Blyth, which lay on the mainland behind Pawley's Island. Here, however, they were so frequently ill that Mrs. Allston's brother was led to propose "a general emigration from that inhospitable shore, where the enemies of life and happiness are so numerous." Allston next tried the pine land, first at a place not far above Chicora Wood and later at Society Hill, many miles up the Peedee, where he had acquired a tract of 200 acres known as the Steer Pen Spring. This was too far away from the plantation and the "old seashore smell" which he dearly loved; so in 1845 the family went to Pawley's Island, where Allston had purchased 20 acres fronting on the beach and obtained a grant of 54 acres of marsh across which to build his own private causeway. In 1862 he bought a house and lot in the pine-land village of Plantersville, but Pawley's remained the favorite of his summer places.

Charlotte Ann Allston was not infrequently to be found at her house in Georgetown. Robert had a house there, too, but he seems to have made little, if any, use of it. His family paid frequent visits, more frequent in fact than Allston liked, to their relatives in Charleston. It was not, however, until 1857 that a house was purchased in the "capital of the plantations." This was the first year of Allston's term as governor, and, though he might have continued to reside at his plantation, going to Columbia only, as the law required, for the sessions of the General Assembly, he probably felt that he should be both more accessible and better situated to perform the social duties of his office. The result was the purchase of what a kinsman described as "beyond all comparison, the finest establishment in Charleston."

When the Allston property was sold in 1869, Mrs. Allston managed to buy Canaan Seashore and the Plantersville house. These she retained, along with Chicora Wood and the Carver's Bay tract, which had been allotted to her under her claim of dower, until her death in 1896. Benjamin bought Pipe Down for himself and Exchange in partnership with his brother, Charles Petigru, but these soon passed out of their hands. For a time the Allston plantations continued to be planted to rice by native proprietors; then one by one, as rice-planting ceased to be profitable in the South Atlantic region, they were sold to men from other states who maintain them today only as winter homes and game preserves. Even Chicora Wood passed out of the family shortly after the death of Mrs. Pringle in 1921.[73]

V. THE OVERSEERS

Robert Allston's practice of residing at the center of his plantation operations from first "black frost"[74] until late in the spring and within easy visiting distance during the remainder of the year may explain the comparative dearth of overseers' reports among his papers, but it seems more probable that this type of material bulks large among those parts of the collection which have been lost. For only one planting season have these reports sur-

[73] The writer is indebted to Mr. Victor B. Stanley for calling his attention to certain deeds in the Marion Courthouse.

[74] In Peedee parlance "three white frosts make a black frost; that means that all the potato vines and other delicate plants had been killed so completely that the leaves were black." The usual date of the return to the plantation was early November; that of leaving, late May (Pringle, *Chronicles of Chicora Wood*, p. 67).

vived in any abundance, and that was the year following Allston's death, the last months of the Confederate War, when plantation routine was far from normal; but, where more direct evidence is lacking, allusions in the family correspondence, receipts for wages, and like material may be made to reveal much about the men who endeavored, according to their "lights," to translate the planter's ideas into the realities of crops and living conditions among his Negroes.

The simple articles of agreement by which William T. Thompson bound himself in 1822 to oversee Friendfield and Waties Point "in a planter like manner" for Mrs. Blyth suggest that the Allstons regarded as unnecessary the elaborate form of contract known to have been used by their neighbor, Plowden C. J. Weston.[75] Of what little effect the overseer's written promise might be is illustrated in Thompson's violation of the clause forbidding him to keep for himself more than two cows and two calves, the adjustment of which exposed Allston to charges of injustice by his opponent in the political campaign of 1842.[76]

Nevertheless, Thompson must have been a superior man in comparison with the first overseer to be mentioned in the letters of Robert's mother. In 1818 she wrote: "Mr. Sessions asked Cousin Ben to let him stay there again but I told him I would give him his victuals for God sake, but I would not for his services, such as we had last year." She thereupon resolved to manage without an overseer, but the season was not far advanced before she had changed her mind sufficiently to employ John Oliver, "brother of him who married a young woman brought up at Mr. Martins," and Oliver appears to have been still in charge at Waverly when Joseph Waties Allston assumed its management.

On moving to the Peedee in 1819, Mrs. Allston secured the promise of a neighboring planter to supervise the work at Chicora Wood. This arrangement could not have been satisfactory, however, for the next year she employed James Hull to ride to the place twice or thrice a week "to see how they go on," and on Robert's return, in 1822, Daniel P. Avant was engaged as a resident overseer. His letters, written to Robert in the summer of 1823, would seem to indicate that he was not inferior to others of his class, but his merits had already been brought into question. He had incurred Mrs. Allston's disfavor by whipping a Negro, and a little later Joseph was writing: "I do not think your man very stirring and active, and cannot well conceive how he managed to have all the fields in the situation I saw them." For these reasons, probably, Avant was not re-employed at the end of the next year.

Thomas Sanders appears to have been the overseer at Chicora Wood from 1825 to 1830, but he is known only through the receipts which he signed for

[75] Printed in Phillips, *Plantation and Frontier Documents*, I, 115–22, and sometimes cited as typical of the Rice Coast.

[76] See below, p. 257.

wages. His successor, Gabriel L. Ellis, stands out, however, in a clearer light. Entering Allston's service in 1831, he was still in charge in the summer of 1838. He had obviously been a successful manager, for in this year he was allowed to add to his responsibilities not only Waverly but also the planting interests of Dr. William Allston. This may have been his undoing, but it should be noted that Ellis was charged with cruelty in his treatment of Negroes while in Allston's employ and that in the records of Wehaw plantation, where he later served, he is described as a "Bad Man."[77] In all events, he was dismissed at the end of the year.

At Waverly, Ellis had supplanted George C. Gotea, whose term of service dated at least from the year of its owner's death. Ellis was followed by Benjamin A. Tillman, Tillman by G. Savage Smith, and Smith by Thomas Hemingway, who appears to have been in active service up to a few months prior to the termination of Allston's stewardship in 1857. Smith held what was in effect an *ad interim* appointment of less than a season's duration, so that the other two men divided about equally between them the good record of nineteen years of service. Until 1850 these Waverly overseers appear to have been required to supervise the operations of the pounding mill, but after that date a miller was regularly on duty.[78] Henry W. Tilton held this position for five years and was then succeeded by Edwin M. Tilton, whose name and age (he was only twenty) suggest that he may have been a son of his predecessor. The younger Tilton was still at his post in the years immediately following the war.

In the meantime the quality of the overseers at Chicora Wood was noticeably improving. J. A. Hemingway came to Allston in 1839 with a good indorsement. After one year at Chicora Wood he was transferred to Friendfield. When this place was sold the following year, he left Allston probably to set up as a planter in his own right. He may have been the man to whom Allston referred when he wrote: "My own overseer who was with me when you first came down the country is now a man of some capital." It is certain that in 1855 he offered his Negroes to Allston for the sum of $10,000.

William B. Millican was associated with Allston in some capacity as early as 1838, and he appears to have been in charge of Chicora Wood during the season following Hemingway's transfer to Friendfield. In 1842 he gave place to the man who was to remain longest in Allston's service and to contribute more than any other toward redeeming the reputation of the overseer class for shiftlessness and general want of respectability. This man was the

[77] For information concerning Ellis at Wehaw the writer is indebted to Mr. Henry C. Cheves.

[78] David Kidd, whom Allston described as "a machinist from Scotland, of very high character for ingenuity and practical ability" (Allston, *Memoir* in Ruffin's *Report*, p. 19), was employed to rebuild the Waverly mill in 1837, but it does not appear to have been steam-driven until 1850 or 1851.

owner of the curious name of Jesse Belflowers, a fact which should make him an easy subject for the genealogist. Nothing, however, is known of Jesse's origin. None of his early reports has survived, nor is he more than mentioned in the family letters during the ten years following his first appearance in the Allston records. By 1852, however, it is clear that he had won his employer's regard. He was ill, and Allston was "sitting a half hour or more every night & reading for him a chapter and a Psalm." It is now, the latter observed, "if ever, an impression is to be made on poor Belflowers' untutor'd soul." A little later Allston advised his son, Benjamin, to come home in order that he might profit some years by Belflowers' experience, and Jesse was still in his employ when Allston died in 1864. His reports for the following year furnish a graphic account of the chaos produced by the Federal occupation of the George-town District. When in 1866 he followed his employer to the grave, he was buried in Prince Frederick's churchyard not far from Chicora Wood.

Belflowers' entrance into Allston's service coincides with the beginning of the latter's expansion, when additional overseers were presently needed. J. S. Dewitt appears to have managed Exchange during the first period of Allston's ownership. James Kelly was employed as early as 1843. Three years later he was put in charge of the Nightingale Hall–Waterford unit, remaining there until 1850, when he went to California. Kelly was succeeded by William Faulk; Faulk gave place in 1857 to Harman Pitman; Pitman in 1861 or 1862 to Joseph M. Thompson, and Thompson in 1864, apparently when efforts failed to secure his exemption from military service, to W. Sweet, who has left a long series of reports for the years 1864–65. Because of the difficulty of finding overseers during the war, both Thompson and Sweet undertook the additional responsibility of managing Guendalos.

To the task of supervising the plantations centering about Chicora Wood, Belflowers seems to have been equal, with the assistance for a time of a "sub-overseer," but for his outlying lands Allston was under the necessity of employing additional help. He seems usually to have turned to one Elijah Fox-worth. When the North Carolina place was purchased in 1863, he engaged J. C. Yates, a neighboring farmer, to give it a general supervision and Duncan Barrentine to attend to the daily routine.

After the war, W. J. Westbury was employed for a single season at Chicora Wood. The one letter from his hand here printed would seem to justify Mrs. Allston's laconic characterization of him as a "fool." She advised that Negro foremen be used thereafter to direct the work of the freedmen.

The salaries paid by the Allstons and the services which they required from their managers bear out the statement of Professor Phillips that on the Rice Coast "overseers had relatively good wages and exemption from manual duties."[79] A house on the plantation (and in certain instances another at the

[79] U. B. Phillips, *Life and Labor in the Old South* (New York, 1929), p. 307.

seashore), a woman to cook and wash (or an allowance of $40 per year in lieu thereof), and a boy for miscellaneous tasks were standard perquisites. Avant received in money $300 per annum, but his contemporary, William T. Thompson, possibly because he had to manage two plantations at some distance apart, was started at $500 and regularly advanced to the sum of $900. Ellis was receiving $800 in 1838 for his services at Chicora Wood, $400 at Waverly, and $50 per month from Dr. Allston, whose business he was allowed to undertake in the middle of the season. The regular annual wage at Waverly was $400 until the advent of Benjamin A. Tillman, who received $500. The practice adopted some years later of combining in the accounts the items of wages and of hire of slaves belonging to the overseer make it impossible to determine what the salary was for this later period. The miller, however, is known to have regularly received $900 per year.

To what income the overseer might aspire is illustrated by the case of Belflowers. He received in the beginning $300, was advanced to $500 in 1846, $600 in 1849, $700 in 1850, and $800 in 1851. After 1852 his salary was $1,000. With his savings, larger perhaps than those of other overseers because he had no family, he purchased Negroes, whose hire was bringing by 1856 an annual return of $800. This investment was lost through emancipation, but still Jesse was able to leave behind him property of considerable value. When administered in 1866, his estate included fifteen shares in the Bank of Georgetown; a half-interest in a store which he and Benjamin Allston had established, apparently with the object of picking up some of the freedmen's trade; and bonds to the value of $4,500. Against these assets there were claims of only $1,300.

That Robert Allston respected his overseers and the trade which they followed there can be no doubt. In advising one who was apparently a newcomer to the Rice Coast, he said: "Every son should go out & bind himself to a trade or to an overseer . . . . to learn the secrets of success in that employment than which there is none more lucrative. . . . . On Santee the sons & grandsons of Jonathan Lucas who was offered a knighthood by the King for introducing into England a Rice-Mill, they deem it not unworthy of them to superintend the business of absent Planters for a consideration." To two of his overseers (Belflowers and Pitman) he was sufficiently grateful to provide legacies for them in his will, but between these men and their employer there was a barrier which none ever surmounted. They came from the poorer class who were settled in the pine lands of the Georgetown District;[80] their lot in life was hard; and they seldom overcame their handicaps.

[80] Most of the surnames of Allston's overseers are to be found in the Georgetown District as early as 1790 (*Heads of Families at the First Census Taken in the Year 1790: South Carolina* [Washington, D.C., 1908]). Sundry receipts show extensive purchases by the Allstons of timber, shingles, and cooper stuff from these people.

VI. THE SLAVES

Eighteen Negroes were listed in the will of Benjamin Allston, Jr., under the head of specific bequests to his widow and four of his six children. The residuary group, numbering 126 according to an inventory prepared in 1819, were divided, "share and share alike," among the seven heirs. Those going to Mrs. Tucker, the eldest daughter, were transferred, after some swapping with Mrs. Allston, to her husband's plantation. Those of Joseph Waties and those of his sister, Mary Pyatt, which the former subsequently purchased, were employed at Waverly, where they became the nucleus of a gang which was to number 106 when their master died in 1834. Three of the remaining groups—her own and those of her two minor sons—passed under the control of Mrs. Allston, some to be hired out and others to be worked at Chicora Wood. Here, also, were employed at least a part of the third daughter's share until her marriage, about 1827, to John Coachman, a neighboring planter.[81]

To Robert, his father had left a boy named James and a half-interest in two carpenters, Billey and Thomas. His share of the residuary group was sixteen, than whom, his mother assured him, "there are not in this part of the country a Primer set of Negroes." Eight or nine more were received in 1823 from his brother William's estate and seven the next year on the death of his mother. Nine others having been purchased from the latter's estate, he found himself with a gang of some forty-two Negroes when, in 1827, he was ready to give his whole time to planting.

From this relatively small beginning Allston steadily increased his force until it numbered 590 at the time of his death. In 1840 he inherited 58 Negroes from his aunt, Mrs. Blyth[82]—the stroke of fortune which encouraged the first addition to his list of plantations. Meanwhile, as numerous bills of sale bear witness, he had already begun to buy extensively. Most of his purchases were of small lots ranging in number from 1 to 8, but four acquisitions were sufficiently large to have had an important bearing upon his progress as a planter. The first, made in 1828 when he was clearing additional swamp at Chicora Wood, included two groups—one of 48 and another of 16—belonging to the estate of Robert Francis Withers.[83] The second was made in 1851 at the time of the acquirement of Rose Bank, both plantation and the 51 Negroes included in this lot being bought from the same party. The last two extensive purchases were made in 1859. The first, consisting of 41 individuals, was purchased for his son, Benjamin, who began in this year the planting of Guenda-

[81] These and their issue were left to Allston, his sons, and his nephews when Mrs. Coachman died in 1847.

[82] Thirty-nine others were received in trust from the same source for his sons and nephews.

[83] A statement by Allston in an undated biographical note to the effect that he acquired 20 Negroes in this year would seem to indicate that some of these were resold.

los. The second included 116 Negroes and was said to have been made with the same object in view, but in the final settlement the father retained for his own use something over 70 of this group.

With the exception of occasional sales prompted apparently by financial need during the Confederate War, Allston parted with virtually none of his own Negroes.[84] On one occasion he planned to sell a group of sixteen, but his unwillingness to allow them to be inspected elsewhere than on the plantation raised an obstacle which appears to have caused the offer finally to be withdrawn. In managing and settling the estates of others, however, Allston was called upon with a fair degree of frequency to appear as a seller in the slave market. The largest transaction of this kind recorded in his papers was the sale in 1837 of fifty-one of the Waverly Negroes.

This trading in Negroes was not lightly undertaken by the Allstons. "I earnestly pray," wrote the mistress of Waverly after reluctantly agreeing to sell, that "the people may be fortunate in being owned by a good master." Her fears on this score were doubtless removed when her brother appeared as the purchaser, but even at that she could not bring herself to be present when the people were sent away, and in the end she allowed certain favorites to be withdrawn from the sale. Not infrequently the preference of the slave as to who should be his purchaser and the desire of the seller to avoid the division of families were controlling factors in a sale.

The problem of the superannuated Negro was also an important consideration in several of these transactions. The seller of the gang purchased in 1851 was careful to note: "With this family there is the incumbrance of an old man of 80 years, father of Betsy." On agreeing to buy the Pipe Down Negroes eight years later, Allston wrote: "But I do ask to be indulged with the privilege of disposing of O. Conkey to J. W. LaBruce who owns his wife and to have old July (Blind-Hannah does nothing but wait on him) and old Ned, who has been dying every night during the winter with short breath, omitted from the list of negroes to be paid for. They shall be cared for so long as they live, just the same." This request was refused on the ground that one of the chief considerations of the owner in selling was to secure for her old people the advantages of ownership by Allston.

What proportion of the Negroes belonging to Allston in 1864 was the result of natural increase it would be impossible to say. How high the birth rate might have been in certain instances is illustrated by one of the groups acquired in 1828, which had increased from thirty-two to forty-eight individuals in the space of twelve years. This case was probably exceptional, however, for the sizes of the families recorded in the slave lists are not excessively large; but marriage was easy under Allston's regime, even if it involved a change of

[84] A group of eight Negroes sold to Mrs. Mary Allan Allston in 1836 reverted to Robert Allston on the failure of the former to make good the bond given in payment. Another group of four sold to the miller at Waverly was probably purchased with that end in view.

ownership in order to bring the parties together, and childbearing was the order of the day in the planter's family as well as among his slaves. The pathetic case of Doctor, who had three times discovered his wife in "adulterous living," and the decision of "Sammy of Ganderlos" to quit his mate for unknown cause furnish the only records of broken homes.

The number of deaths among the Allston slaves does not support the general belief that Negroes enjoyed almost complete immunity from the diseases of the Rice Coast. Fifteen months after the division, Charlotte Ann Allston reported ten deaths among the 126 Negroes belonging to her husband's estate. Allston says at another time: "I lost in one year 28 negroes, 22 of whom were task hands." In 1861 his overseer was troubled over the many deaths which he had to report, but he added, "I can't help or stop death." The "solemn cadence" indicating that a Negro was being laid to rest in the graveyard of Chicora Wood was not an unfamiliar sound.

Naturally, the planter was eager to prevent deaths and to promote good health among his Negroes. In the description of "every day life on a Rice Plantation" here printed from the pen of Dr. James R. Sparkman, one of Allston's neighbors and for a number of years his plantation physician, the statements concerning the medical care of slaves are not exaggerated.[85] The plantation had its "sick house," and the doctor was in more or less constant attendance. Numerous bills from the latter are convincing evidence that his charges were one of the important items of plantation expense. In several cases the patients were sent to Charleston and placed under the care of those who were considered specialists in the treatment of the particular maladies from which they were suffering.

The Waverly Negroes sold in 1837 brought $725 "round," but this was considered an exceptionally high price. On this subject Allston gave one of his nephews the following advice in 1859: "I would not buy negroes at cotton prices. If you meet with an orderly gang of some planter neighbor or otherwise who would sell you at $500 rather than send away and separate [sic] his people at a higher figure then in such a case you might adventure." On occasion he was willing to pay more for an individual trained to some particular vocation, but in none of his larger purchases did he exceed the figure which he had fixed upon as his maximum.

How Allston's force was distributed among the several plantations in normal times is not known. When the inventory of his personal property was made in the last year of the war, there were 236 Negroes at Chicora Wood and its adjacent plantations, 151 on the Nightingale Hall–Waterford unit, 90 at Pipe Down, 30 at Britton's Neck, 53 at Morven, and 30 at Croly Hill. In addition, there were 100 or more at Guendalos and probably an even greater number at Waverly over whom Allston was exercising a general supervision while their masters were absent for military service.

[85] See below, p. 348.

Field labor on the Allston plantations proceeded under the task system in general use among the planters of the Rice Coast.[86] An able-bodied man with a spade, Allston says, was expected to break up 1,500 square feet (one-thirtieth of an acre) of rice land after the plow had turned it; a trencher, using a hoe and following the harrows, would do three-fourths of an acre in a day. Of sowing, the task in "the Rice region of S. Carolina," he says, "is (150 × 150 feet) a half acre"; but the labor in this case "depends so much upon the weather, whether windy, or moist, or otherwise, it is better not to require any given task." Ordinarily, a woman was capable of doing two or three tasks of sowing per day. How other tasks were made to vary in accordance with the types of labor performed is not revealed.[87] Doubtless the overseer, with due attention to the capacity of the workers and to what was customary on the plantation, fixed the daily stints, and the Negro foremen, or drivers as they were called, saw that they were properly done before dismissing the hands. Whether the working day on the Allston places was calculated to be eight to nine hours in winter and ten in the summer, as was the case with Dr. Sparkman, is not known. Sunday was a day of rest, after the rations for the week had been distributed, and the overseers indicate with a measure of frequency that on Saturday, except during the harvest, they gave "Holerday."

That the work of even the agricultural laborer on a rice plantation was varied is amply attested by the overseers' reports. The greater part of this time, of course, was spent in the rice fields. Here in the fall and winter he either guided a plow behind the lumbering oxen or cleaned the ditches and drains. Harrowing and trenching were his chief tasks during the month of March; early in April, and sometimes later, he was busy with sowing. During the "sprout flow" which followed he was at work on the high land, where the planting of sweet potatoes and corn had already commenced.[88] Some twenty days later, however, found him back in the swamp for the hoeing which must precede the next inundation known as the "long flow."[89] While the water was this time on the rice, some of the hands were again on the high land, plowing, hoeing, planting slips from the potato vines, and sowing peas for later growth among the corn stalks; but others were required to wade through the rice fields, pulling the grass which had escaped the hoe. A period of dry culture now succeeded the "long flow," and all hands turned out for the two hoeings

[86] Ulrich B. Phillips, *American Negro Slavery*, p. 247. On the subject of the labor system and methods of cultivation the manuscripts are supplemented at many points by Allston's *Essay on Sea Coast Crops*.

[87] It was Allston's rule not to plant more than five or six acres to each full hand that he owned (*Essay on Sea Coast Crops*, p. 34).

[88] Allston seems not to have used the "point flow" which on some other plantations was made to follow the "sprout flow" (cf. Phillips, *American Negro Slavery*, p. 89).

[89] Frequently called by other planters the "stretch flow."

that Allston deemed necessary. At last, however, toward the middle of July came the "lay-by," or harvest, flow. Some grass was still to be plucked up and volunteer rice must be destroyed, but for the next seven or eight weeks the tempo of labor was greatly reduced.

The harvest began early in September. A day or two before the rice was fully ripe the water would be withdrawn; sunrise the next morning found the reapers in the fields cutting the grain with old-fashioned sickles. Then, after a day of drying on the stubble, it was tied into sheaves, stacked in the flats, and transported to the threshing yard located on the high-land side of the river. Here it was threshed by machine, then sent to the Waverly mill or to Charleston to be husked and cleaned; or, if it was to be sold in the rough, it was shipped directly to the factor's counting-house. Meanwhile the gathering of the provision crops was in progress and might continue well into November, when it was time to start again the routine of the year.

A group of plantations such as that which Allston had brought together was an industrial as well as an agricultural unit, and no inconsiderable number of the workers should be classified as artisans, mechanics, or, where they were employed in the mill, even as operatives. On his departure for the North in 1838 Allston had left the carpenter inherited from his father in charge of remodeling the plantation house at Chicora Wood. Before his return he was informed: "Thomas says he has done all the Sashes for your House and will be done the Lathing tomorrow, I hope the Bricklayers will soon commence their work." Doubtless some of the twenty carpenters employed in rebuilding the mill at Waverly in 1837 were hired from other planters, but at another time Allston was able to muster a force of eight apparently without great trouble. These carpenters had their shop at Chicora Wood, and the blacksmiths were similarly provided. Whether James, who was apprenticed in 1817 to a cobbler in Charleston, ever overcame his indolence sufficiently to learn his trade and be of use to his master is not known.[90]

For threshing, Allston used the Emmons' Patent Machines, employing in their operation several skilled mechanics. Milling required an even larger force. Of the operations of the mill, Allston wrote:

The mill performs ingeniously enough the finishing process, thus: By steam power, the rough-rice is taken out of the vessel which freights it, up to the attic of the building —thence through the sand-screen to a pair of (five feet wide) heavy stones, which grind off the husk—thence into large wooden mortars, in which it is pounded by large iron-shod pestles, (weighing 250 to 350 pounds,) for the space of some two hours, more or less.

The Rice, now pounded, is once more elevated into the attic, whence it descends through a rolling-screen, to separate whole grains from the broken, and flour from both; and also through wind-fans, to a vertical brushing screen, revolving rapidly,

[90] For details concerning James's apprenticeship see below, pp. 362, 366, 368–69.

which polishes the flinty grain, and delivers it fully prepared, into the barrel or tierce, which is to convey it to market.[91]

The barrels meanwhile had been made by coopers, included among the mill-workers, each one dressing his material and making three barrels per day.

A corps of domestics completes the Negro personnel met with in the Allston records. A wet nurse probably needed no special training in her art, but some of these servants, like the artisans in certain cases, were apprenticed to seasoned workers wherever they might be found. The elder Mrs. Allston, for instance, is found in 1819 putting out Philander, Nancy, and Linda, "the girls to be taught to sew, wash, etc. and the boy to be put to the carpenter's trade." On another occasion a Charleston relative reported: "I have sent Fibby to school to learn to sew. Miss Nell, the distinguished instructress of little nigs has her in charge and I hope will make her a passible [*sic*] seamstress." The butler, who also did service as a valet when the master was on his travels, received the most careful training. Concerning the holder of this office in 1850 and his understudy it was stated: "Stephen went with his master to Nashville and has returned with an increase of folly and levity if possible. We have a very good servant now in Nelson whom you may remember was placed with Lee in Charleston some years ago to learn to wait; he came home this spring and is much more steady than Stephen tho' many years younger."

How wide a gulf separated these classes, one from another, can only be inferred. Belflowers' remark that if Charley did not behave himself better he ought to "Go with the Gange to Work" carries the suggestion that demotion could be used as a form of punishment. That the hope of advancement operated as an incentive to better service even among slaves is revealed in the case of Isaac, who was offered to Allston in 1860 as a coachman for the fancy price of $1,400. "I would like you to have the boy," wrote his mistress; "it would be a promotion for him and I think a good servant for you, and he is willing to go."

The harvest season was followed by a holiday, probably at the time that the year's supply of clothes was distributed, and again at Christmas the Negroes were allowed three days for celebration. Of the Christmas festivities in the year of Allston's election to the office of governor, his wife writes: "The next morning there was a great demonstration, the negroes coming up as usual to wish Merry Christmas and the compliments of the Season, but more than usual to greet their master the Gov. They made a great noise and drank the Governor's health in many a stout glass of whiskey." The merrymaking was less vociferous in other years, but always there was the early morning gathering at the "big house" with portions of rum or whiskey and tobacco, extra rations, and small gifts for all.

[91] Allston, *Essay on Sea Coast Crops*, pp. 36–37.

Allston believed in the efficacy of rewards for extra service and for excellence in the performance of recognized tasks. The coopers were paid twenty-five cents for each barrel over and above the daily quota of three. It is doubtful whether he would have entered into the agreement to purchase hogs from the Negroes if they had not taken possession of his herd, but he is found at other times paying them for firewood, chickens, pumpkins, and honey. The best sowers were awarded prizes, and a bushel of small rice was given to each Negro who had not lost a day on account of sickness during the year. The arrangement for Linda, who had borne twins, to have "milk, etc. & 1/2 work for a year" might be regarded as a reward, but a more sensible interpretation would be that a mother with two babes to suckle needed more of her time and strength than was ordinarily the case.

Where rewards failed, punishment sometimes had the desired effect. "I like to be kind to my people," Allston said; "but I imperatively require of them honesty, truth, diligence and cheerfulness in their work, wherever and whatever it is." The flogging of eight women in 1860 by Overseer Pitman for "hoeing corn bad" illustrates what meaning could be given to the second part of this statement. But the lash does not appear to have been in general use, and the overseer who applied it unreasonably found his authority reduced or himself dismissed. Ellis, for instance, was moved to complain in 1838 that, if a Negro could reach the mistress at Waverly, "she will not sufer me to punish it at tall." This letter of Ellis' contains the only reference to the use of stocks. Confinement of other kinds, however, is recorded with some degree of frequency. The requirement that Thomas and Cupid run the gauntlet for stealing a hog may have been a penalty inflicted by their own people, who had been deprived of their Christmas until the guilty were discovered; but it seems to have had Allston's approval.

Thoughts concerning "a future state of rewards and punishments" may also have acted as a deterrent to misconduct, for the Negroes had ample opportunity to become acquainted with the mysterious ways of their master's God. Benches were rented for them in both the All Saints' and Prince Frederick's churches, and at Chicora Wood they had their own chapel. "The Revd. Mr. Hunter now preaches to my negroes once a fortnight on Sunday," Allston explained in 1859, "& catechises the children as often on a week day." Not satisfied with this, he was offering a certain J. W. Smith ten dollars per week to serve them as lay reader and catechist in alternate weeks. The list of twenty-seven candidates for confirmation at Nightingale Hall in 1857 would seem to indicate that the harvest was not disappointing. How many of the Negroes preferred to join the Baptist and Methodist churches, which were also accessible to them, is not known.

How the slaves responded to the treatment received on the Allston plantations is, like most questions concerning the attitude of the Negro to the white man, only partly revealed. Evidence is not lacking to show that contentment and happiness among the rank and file were the results of an intelligent and humane direction of their lives. One would be rash to read into the record left by Mulatto Joe a complete submission to his fate, but undoubtedly there is acquiescence and the desire to make the best of the situation.[92] Samuel Tayler evidently did not feel that his status as a slave was a permanent impediment to the realization of his nostalgic longings.[93] But there are many indications that even these people who had known no life but that of bondage desired to be free. In 1829 it was necessary to use such severe methods in suppressing a revolt among the Negroes of Georgetown District that James L. Petigru was prompted to write to Joseph Waties Allston: "I am afraid you will hang half the country."[94] Even when Mrs. Allston was recording the Negroes' joyous celebration of their master's election to the governorship, she was impelled to remark that, owing to rumors of insurrection, two of the overseers had "brushed up their guns and ammunition chests etc. and observed and listened, but held their tongues." When the opportunity for freedom finally presented itself in the form of the Federal blockade of the Georgetown coast, some, notably Stephen the valet, were unable to await the issue. At the risk of their lives they made their way to those who would make them free. A few remained loyal to the whites during the orgies which followed the Federal occupation of the district, but many joined in the pillaging of the plantation houses.

But freedom brought disillusionment. Their saviors had no economic program that would lift them out of the plantation system. After a short time they were compelled to place themselves as sharecroppers, tenants, and wage-workers under the control of their former owners. It is not improbable that the disappearance of the plantation in the Georgetown District, which came a generation later, more deeply affected their lives than had emancipation.

VII. PRODUCTION AND MARKETING

On October 17, 1859, Allston jotted down in the fragment of his diary that has survived: "Bro't in the last [rice] at Chicora Wood—Chapel Field. The weather continuing fine the crop is reported well cured & put up in 335 stacks which will probably average 100 bushels = 33,500 besides straw & dirty rice, say 500 B. At Nightingale Hall they finish'd a few days earlier 225 stacks = 20,000 Bushels, probably besides straw &c. God be praised for his blessing on the labors of the year." The fact that the final "turn out" was 51,620 bushels, some 1,800 less than his estimate, probably did not greatly abate his fervency. Allowing 20 bushels to the barrel, the usual calculation, this gave him 2,581 barrels to send to market.

[92] See Joe's letter to his master, below, p. 337.
[93] See Tayler's letter to Elizabeth Frances Blyth, below, p. 339.
[94] Carson, *op. cit.*, p. 66.

This bumper crop, perhaps the largest in Allston's career, was made in the first season in which all six of his plantations came into play. To what extent earlier crops had kept pace with increasing acreage is only partly revealed. An account book kept by his factor during the greater part of the period that Allston's operations were confined to the single plantation of Chicora Wood shows a more or less steady increase of sales. The amount advanced from 216 barrels in the season 1826–27 to 484 in 1832–33 and to 636 in 1838–39. But for the succeeding years no account books are available. It is known only that in 1847–48, the year following the purchase of Nightingale Hall and Waterford, the crop was about 950 barrels and that ten years later, when all the plantations save Pipe Down had been acquired, it was 2,267 barrels. Only one normal season followed the great crop mentioned above; then the war caused all operations to be greatly reduced.

Information concerning the crops at Waverly is more satisfactory. When Joseph Waties Allston died in 1834, the plantation was producing something over 600 barrels of rice annually, but, the property being heavily mortgaged, Robert decided to relieve the pressure through the sale of half its Negroes. The result was a decrease of the next year's crop to less than 200 barrels. By 1841, however, much lost ground had been recovered. During the ensuing decade the average annual yield was 387 barrels; and before Allston resigned his trust in 1857 this had been increased to 535 barrels.

Overseer Avant reported in 1823 that he would make $1\frac{1}{2}$ barrels (about 30 bushels) of rice to the acre, and this seems to have been the average of the plantations on the Peedee River.[95] In later years, however, Allston was able to make a better showing. In 1837 he tells us that the average yield at Waverly was from $2\frac{1}{3}$ to $2\frac{1}{2}$ barrels. A note in his diary to the effect that, in 1858, 370 acres at Nightingale Hall yielded 18,270 bushels would seem to indicate that this record was being sustained. This, doubtless, was the result of the care which Allston exercised in selecting his seed, in fertilization, and in the avoidance of overcropping. About one-third of the rice land appears each year either to have been permitted to lie fallow or to have been planted to such other crops as oats and peas.

In normal years the ancillary products of the Allston plantations were corn, sweet potatoes, peas, turnips, and oats; to these the necessities of the war period added rye, sugar cane, and salt, the last being obtained in fairly large quantities by the laborious boiling of sea water. Concerning the volume of the customary crops the records supply little data until the season of 1859–60, when a notation shows that the "turn out" of corn on Allston's plantations was 3,000 bushels, of sweet potatoes 12,000 bushels, of peas 970 bushels, of turnips 1,500 bushels, and of oats something better than 800 bushels. An entry in the plantation diary to the effect that corn was being sold may be taken

[95] Doar, *Rice and Rice Planting*, p. 41.

to indicate that Allston was able to discontinue the purchases of this important article of slave diet which he had been in the habit of making in earlier years.

The rice crop was marketed in Charleston through commission merchants known as factors.[96] Except for a brief period, during which the Waverly account was held by Alexander W. Campbell, who, until his failure in the Panic of 1837, also served as an executor of the estate of Joseph Waties, the factors who acted for the Allstons were the firm originally known by the name of its founder Charles Kershaw but subsequently called after his successors: Kershaw and Lewis; Lewis and Robertson; Lewis, Robertson, and Thurston; Robertson and Thurston; Robertson, Blacklock and Company; and Thurston and Holmes.[97]

Kershaw was an Englishman who came shortly after the Revolution to Charleston, where he remained active in rice factorage until his death in 1835.[98] The first letter from his hand shows him acting in 1808 as the factor of Benjamin Allston, Jr. On the death of Benjamin in the following year, Kershaw, like Campbell in a later period, took up the duties of an executor in addition to those previously assumed. This arrangement remained in force for eleven years; thereafter Kershaw and his successors served the Allstons as factors only. Differences might be pointed out between the activities of the factor who was also an executor and those of the factor pure and simple, but it would be difficult to show that the zeal of the one was greater in his principal's behalf than that of the other.

The services performed by these agents well illustrate the accepted definition of a factor as one who "could, and in many cases did, do anything which the principal could do through an agent."[99] Not infrequently the planter's children were intrusted to the care of the factor. When, for instance, Robert Allston was leaving for West Point in 1817, Kershaw arranged for his passage from Charleston. "Our city still remains sickly," he wrote to Mrs. Allston, "and although he has been taking medicine for his last illness he may not escape the malignant disorder which now prevails. Vessels are continually going to New York and I could get any of them to call at the Island [Sulli-

[96] The following data on the factor have been presented at somewhat greater length in the writer's article, "The South Carolina Rice Factor as Revealed in the Papers of Robert F. W. Allston," *Journal of Southern History*, VII (May, 1941), 160–72.

[97] These are the principal names under which the firm operated; others were used during brief periods. The continuity is certain in all except the last case; in this, references to certain records of Robertson, Blacklock and Company as in the possession of Thurston and Holmes seem to indicate a definite connection.

[98] Obituary in the *Charleston Courier*, August 8, 1835; Kershaw's will in Charleston County, Court of Probate, Will Book H, p. 141; information furnished by Mrs. G. T. Kershaw, of Charleston, S.C.

[99] Norman S. Buck, *The Development of the Organization of Anglo-American Trade, 1800–1850* (New Haven, 1925), pp. 6–7.

van's Island in Charleston harbor] and take Robert on board." Later, Kershaw sought in vain to gratify the mother's desire to place her youngest son with one of the Charleston business houses. "Merchants," he said, "will not take lads into their stores or countinghouses without their parents find them in everything . . . . it is considered that what they learn in the stores is full compensation for their services." At a later time Alexander Robertson, who managed the Allston correspondence after Kershaw's death, had to report the death of a younger member of the family who was attending school in Charleston. "What I did for our late Orphan Child," he wrote, "was no more than I felt bound to do. Could anxiety and care have kept her, she would now be with us. But it pleased God to call her. . . . . I had everything done as though she was my own and discharged my last sad duty towards her by putting her in our private cemetery in St. Paul's church yard."

In buying and selling slaves, Allston sometimes found it necessary to enlist the services of the regular traders, but negotiations were generally left to his factor. If a Negro was to be hired out in Charleston, or placed at a trade, such as shoemaking or barbering, or put in the hands of a doctor for treatment that could not be had on the plantation, the arrangement was made through the same channel. A Negro boy, James, affords a case in point. He had been sent to Charleston to learn the shoemaker's trade. Kershaw reported in 1819: "I have seen Mr. Black; he will give only ten dollars per month for James to find him, but you must find him in clothes and shoes, pay doctor's accounts and allow for the time he is absent whenever you send for him to Georgetown either at Christmas or any other time. Mr. Black says he is a good workman and capable of turning out work equal to any of his colour, but he is so very indolent that he requires a very tight hand kept over him."

Plantation supplies were regularly purchased through the factor, and, in addition, he was called upon to procure every article that human taste could desire.[100] A shipment made in 1808 included a barrel of apples, a new cheese, a piano, and two kegs of nails. When a woman's judgment was required in the selection of some piece of feminine apparel, the factor's wife was pressed into service. On one occasion Robertson wrote in desperation that his time and that of a friend during an entire day had been spent in vain search of a certain kind of carriage which Allston had ordered and that, as a last resort, he was sending his own as a substitute. Even furnishings for the parish church were bought by the factors, and, when a new building was erected for Prince Frederick's, they were called upon to act as treasurer of the building fund.

Except in cases of large loans the factor was the planter's banker. He carried his client's balance on deposit, using it, as need arose, in honoring

---

[100] The variety is best seen in those account books which have survived and in copies of parts of others. The latter were prepared from the current account book kept by the factor and sent periodically to the planter.

drafts and in making purchases at the planter's order.[101] He bought bills of exchange, gave advice on investments, went into the market to purchase every form of property from bank and railroad stock to plantations, and voted his client's proxy at stockholders' meetings. He is even found on occasion going joint security on the planter's notes. In one respect, however, the Allstons made less use of their agents than a knowledge of the factorage system in the ante-bellum South would lead one to expect. They do not appear to have required the heavy advances between seasons usually regarded as a chronic evil of plantation finance. The average annual charge for interest on advances made to the estate of Joseph Waties Allston was less than $112.[102]

In the final analysis, the factor's most important service was the selling of the planter's crop, for on his success in this depended all other activities. Aided by the newspapers, which carried every conceivable kind of information concerning the condition of the market, the factor watched with eagle eye the ebb and flow of prices and advised his client accordingly.[103] Shipments, as might be expected, were heaviest during the weeks immediately following the harvest in September, but they continued with remarkable steadiness throughout the year. The Allstons were among those who staggered their shipments, with the result that over a period of years the records show sales of some portion of their crop in every month.

Some progress had been made in opening an inland waterway between Georgetown and Charleston like the one which connected Charleston with Beaufort at the southern end of the South Carolina coast, but the rice boats mentioned in the Allston papers invariably followed the "outside," or ocean, route. During the earlier period these were schooners and sloops, commonly known as coasters, capable of carrying three hundred and fifty barrels of

[101] On the subject of drafts drawn presumably by clients whose balances were exhausted, Robertson wrote Allston on November 14, 1858: " 'We don't accept' is the old rule and one that we must adhere to, or we will soon become involved. You, however, know that we don't hold always to it, with old and well tried friends. Only to guard against ——— we must hold out the principle, and trust our old friends will support us in the stand; for it is pretty clear their true interest to do so."

[102] Other planters appear to have been less careful. On May 11, 1823, Kershaw wrote to Charlotte Ann Allston: "We have advanced to one friend or another all our disposable Funds and in place of receiving what we advanced, our Friends were in so much distress, occasioned by the low prices of produce, that in place of being able to return to us what they had borrowed they were in want of further help. It is in these times that our Business becomes very painful, we are compelled to refuse the assistance which we would willingly give."

[103] This included a daily list of rice cargoes arriving and departing, frequent summaries of the same covering periods of varying length, and price quotations and amounts of sales in both domestic and foreign markets (files of the *Charleston Courier* and *Charleston Mercury*). That the newspaper price current was supplied to merchants in distant markets is revealed in letters of F. and C. Winthrop of Charleston to Moses Taylor of New York (MSS in Charleston Free Library).

clean rice or five thousand bushels of rough. Many of these little craft appear to have been of New England registry, having come with cargoes of fish, potatoes, and Yankee notions to the Rice Coast, where they remained to haul rice so long as the season lasted. In the later years covered by the Allston papers the coaster seems to have been holding its own on the run between Charleston and Beaufort, but the steamboat was definitely replacing it in the Georgetown trade.[104]

En route from planter to factor the rice cargo appears to have been protected by no other form of insurance than a ship captain's agreement to make delivery unless prevented by "the Dangers of the Sea and River." Seldom was it insured even after it reached the factor's wharf, for ordinarily it was sold on the day of its arrival. Sales were usually made at auction, for cash or payment within sixty days, to agents known as "rice buyers," who represented merchants in widely scattered markets.[105]

Except for a short period, when he appears to have specialized in producing large quantities of seed for sale to other planters, Robert Allston sold mostly clean rice. The seed rice had been carefully threshed by hand. The clean rice had been threshed by machine on the plantation and husked and pounded either at Waverly Mill or at one of the several great mills in Charleston. After assignment by the factor to one of many grades ranging from "inferior" to "strictly prime" and "choice,"[106] it was packed in barrels,[107] or tierces, of approximately six hundred pounds gross weight.[108] Other planters, however, sold much rice in the rough or unhusked form.[109] Handled in bulk and reckoned by the bushel, this was often preferred by foreign buyers, partly, it would seem, because the grain was thought to deteriorate if kept too long after husking[110] and partly because mills in the markets for which it was destined were eager for the profits from processing.[111]

[104] Elizabeth B. Pharo (ed.), *Reminiscences of William Hasell Wilson, 1811–1902* (Philadelphia, 1937), pp. 18–19. The South Carolina names borne by several of the vessels regularly mentioned in the Allston papers and in contemporary newspapers suggest that the traffic was not so largely in the hands of New England vessels as Wilson says. The types of vessels are indicated in the "Marine News" columns of the Charleston and Georgetown newspapers.

[105] Little light is shed by the Allston papers on the trade after it reached the rice-buyer.

[106] Market quotations in the Charleston newspapers.

[107] "Barrel" was the common term, but "tierce" and "cask" were occasionally used.

[108] On this point, however, the factor advised: "Sales are often helped by the Barrels being heavy and weighing 700 Gro., for all Coastwise freights, and to France, is paid by the Barrel, whether it weighs 650 or 750 Gro. and is oftentimes a matter of consideration to shippers."

[109] The term "paddy," meaning rough rice, which is generally used in later *United States Census Reports*, does not appear in the Allston papers.

[110] If necessary, however, rice could be stored for months and even years.

[111] Ruffin, *op. cit.*, pp. 19–22. Ruffin asserted that the English tariff favored rough over clean rice in order to encourage mills in England.

On the completion of the sale of each parcel, no matter how small it might be, the factor rendered his client a detailed statement known as an "account sales." These vary so little in form that an analysis of one will explain the procedure followed throughout the whole period. On August 4, 1837, Lewis and Robertson advised Robert F. W. Allston of the sale of 69 barrels of clean rice ranging in weight from 621 to 707 pounds and 5½ barrels of "offal" (rice flour and small cracked grains), the total being the product of 1,568 bushels of rough rice pounded in Charleston at Nowell's Mill. Twenty barrels had been sold on July 25 to G. and I. Gibbon at $3.81¼ per hundredweight; the next day 49 barrels were sold to C. Edmonston at $3.87½ per hundredweight; and on July 27 the 5½ barrels of offal were sold at prices ranging from $3.62½ to $3.75 per hundredweight. The gross proceeds were $1,706.89. From this amount the following charges were deducted:

Freight on rough rice from plantation to mill @ 6¼ cents per bushel	$ 98.00
Freight on clean rice from mill to factor's wharf @ 25 cents per barrel	18.75
Mill toll (7½ per cent of gross receipts exclusive of freight on rough rice)	111.56[112]
Factor's commission (2½ per cent of gross receipts)	43.58[113]
Cost of the barrels	28.75[114]
Coopering	7.50
Landing and weighing	7.50[115]
Storage of 5½ barrels of offal	.24
Total	$315.88

The planter's return from this sale was $1,391.01, or 81.5 per cent of the selling price. The remaining 18.5 per cent was distributed as follows: freight, 6.8 per cent; milling, 6.5 per cent; factorage, 2.7 per cent; and miscellaneous charges, 2.5 per cent. When the milling was done at the plantation, this charge was diverted to the planter's account, thereby reducing the cost of preparation and handling to 12 per cent of the selling price. Otherwise the ratio between charges and net proceeds varies little throughout the period covered by the Allston records.

[112] This appears to have been 7½ per cent of the receipts from 69 of the 74½ barrels after the freight on the rough rice and the planter's refund for the barrels were deducted.

[113] This was 2.5 per cent of the gross receipts including the refund for barrels, hence approximately 2.7 per cent of the actual selling price of the rice.

[114] If supplied by the mill, barrels cost the planter 87½ cents each for whole barrels and 62½ cents for half-barrels. In the sale he received a refund of 50 cents for each. The figure above was the difference between the cost and the refund. An effort was made by the planters in 1837 to force the refund up to $1.00, but this failed.

[115] The wharfage rate was fixed by law and was published in the almanacs of the day.

The commissions on the sale of Allston's largest crops probably amounted to $1,600. The factor may have collected an additional $200 or $300 as interest on advances; storage charges probably yielded a small amount; and the planter's balance, which the factor held for periods of considerable length, may have been used to his profit. It would be difficult to show that the factor, unless he was also acting as an executor,[116] took more than these rewards for his services. He may have accepted rebates from the merchants who sold him the planter's supplies, but, if he did, the evidence has been successfully concealed.[117] He charged no commission on these purchases; nor is there any reason to believe that he charged brokerage on stocks and bonds which he bought, or premiums on bills of exchange, or fees of any other kind. On the whole, it would seem that the rice factor was willing to perform many extra services in order to secure the business of selling the planter's crop. He probably had no large capital investment; at the most he owned a warehouse where his office or counting-house was located. If he had to borrow to make advances to his clients, he ordinarily used for collateral the rice that was constantly passing through his hands; but unless he dabbled in other lines—the cause, it seems, of the failure of Alexander W. Campbell—his obligations were never heavy. Robertson summed up the position of the rice factor when he said in 1837: "The accounts today from England are still worse, and more must go. I mean merchants. Factors have no right to fail."

The concluding letters of the factor's series in the Allston papers tell an interesting story of the efforts to divert the rice trade into new channels during the Confederate War and to revive old practices in the years that followed. Upon the closing of the ocean route between Georgetown and Charleston by the Federal blockade, it was proposed to use the inland passage, but this appears not to have been feasible. As Georgetown was still without railroad connections, Allston was put to the limit of his resources. For a time he sent small amounts of rice by wagon to Kingstree on the Northeastern Railway. Finding that the security of $20,000 and the rental of $100 per day that were demanded for a steamboat, which he proposed to charter, were prohibitive, he built lighters which were soon being poled up the Peedee River to Mars Bluff, Society Hill, and Cheraw and, on Black River, to his private station at Salters on the Northeastern. At Cheraw, Duncan Malloy and Son acted as his factor; at Florence, Alexander McKenzie; and at Wilmington, DeRosset, Brown and Company. From Mars Bluff, L. Gilchrist offered the following bit of unsolicited advice: "I hope you may be able to send your

[116] The usual commission in this case was 2.5 per cent on receipts and 2.5 per cent on disbursements.

[117] For information on this point the writer has examined, in addition to the Allston materials, the account books of Plowden C. J. Weston in the College of Charleston Library, and Mr. John de Porry has searched for him the Edward Frost records in the Library of Congress. None of these, however, are factors' accounts.

flats up soon, for if you can get your rice in the hands of men who are true to the *South* it is best." Such was the momentum given to this inland trade that it was continued successfully after Allston's death in 1864, and until the Federal occupation of the Georgetown District brought planting to a temporary halt. After that the trade gradually flowed back into the old channels.

VIII. PLANTATION FINANCE

As might be expected, the financial data in Robert Allston's papers leave much to conjecture concerning the value of his property at any given time. The sum paid Joseph Waties Allston in 1832 for his fourth interest in the Chicora Wood plantation suggests that the land was valued at $32,000; and, if one may accept as a general rule Robert's statement of some years later that one-half his capital had been put into slaves, it might be said that his total investment was approximately $65,000.[118] This amount does not appear to have been much increased until 1840, when, suddenly, his aunt's bequest of a plantation and fifty-eight Negroes had the effect of doubling Allston's fortune.[119]

The prices of three of the plantations acquired during what may be termed Allston's first period of expansion (1843–53) are recorded in an appraisement of his estate. For Waterford he paid $25,000 in 1847; for Rose Bank, $23,100 in 1851; and for Exchange, $25,000 in 1853. The same source furnishes the information that Nightingale Hall and "about 100 Negroes" were purchased in 1846 at $80,000. If in this transaction Allston followed his practice of not paying more than $500 "round" for slaves, the plantation cost him $30,000, and, if one may put down at $11,700 the 117 acres of Breakwater which he added to Exchange,[120] the amount expended for land during the decade was $115,000. Stocked with the number of Negroes which Allston considered necessary for its proper cultivation, the entire property probably represented a value of $230,000, thus raising the total investment to approximately $300,000.

For the long-term credit required for these purchases Allston had recourse at first to the banks in Charleston, where, if necessary, his factor was willing to be his surety; but in later years, having established a reputation for good management, he was able to buy both plantations and slaves with a small cash payment and his bond and mortgage to cover the balance. The readiness with which this paper appears to have been accepted and the facility with which it passed from hand to hand, prior to final redemption, lead one to believe that

[118] No attempt has been made to evaluate outlying timber and pasture lands. These had no great monetary value, Allston considering $1.00 per acre a good price.

[119] The plantation was promptly sold, as pointed out above, but the Negroes were retained with the object, perhaps, of working them on other places which Allston had in mind to purchase.

[120] Mills gives $100 per acre as the average price of rice land in 1826 (*op. cit.*, p. 566).

Allston's creditors were inclined to treat plantation bonds in much the same way as other investors dealt in the securities of a corporation or a business partnership. In issuing these bonds, Allston himself probably did not feel very different from other businessmen who employed this means of augmenting their capital.[121]

Allston endeavored, however, to retire his bonds as rapidly as circumstances permitted. "It has been my custom," he wrote in 1861, "when able, to pay off annually all interest due [the usual rate was 7 per cent] and an average of ten thousand dollars of principal." Unfortunately, the records of Allston's plantations are not sufficiently complete to permit one to say with what degree of success he adhered to this rule in the management of his own affairs, but the Waverly accounts record in detail what he was able to accomplish while supervising his brother's estate, which consisted of one plantation and a mill.[122] When he assumed charge in 1834, the liabilities were somewhat in excess of $50,000. Deciding apparently that this was too heavy a burden to be borne with comfort, he sold Negroes to the value of $43,000. A large part of this money was not collected until many years later; nevertheless, Allston had freed the estate of debt by 1846. Meanwhile he had begun to restore its labor force, ultimately expending for this purpose some $35,000. Twice he rebuilt the estate's mill, converting it on the second occasion to steam power; and, before he withdrew from the executorship in 1857, he had made other capital outlays amounting to $8,000. These investments had caused him to run into debt to the extent of $12,000, but this liability was partly offset by bonds due the estate to the amount of $8,000. Thus it may be said that within a period of twenty-three years Allston had added not less than $50,000 to the value of the property,[123] and this was accomplished while at the same time a relatively small estate was yielding him $13,500 in executor's commissions and providing for the living expenses and education of his two wards.

If the value of the Waverly property could be precisely determined, the data contained in its accounts might enable one to test Allston's estimate that "the profits of a rice plantation of good size and locality . . . . [were] eight per cent. per annum, independent of the privileges and perquisites of the plantation residence," for, having to make an annual report to the court of ordinary concerning his management of the estate, he was careful to preserve a complete record of every transaction. But neither the purchase price of

[121] There is the further suggestion that it is misleading to count those who actually owned slaves as the only persons who had a stake in slavery.

[122] Ordinarily the account books were posted by the factor, who recorded only the receipts and expenditures that passed through his hands. On the difference in this respect of the Waverly accounts see above, pp. 6, 19.

[123] In this estimate due allowance has been made for certain sums derived from the sale of land attached to the estate.

Waverly nor the number of its slaves after the appraisement of the property in 1834 is known, and there is an additional complication concerning the value of the mill. The Waverly data, however, are significant in other respects, and for this reason they are analyzed in Tables 1 and 2.

Up to 1857 there is every reason to indorse Allston's claim that his progress in planting had been "regular and systematic." At that time, however, he began to show far less caution. Some extenuation is doubtless to be found in the fact that he was aiding his son, Benjamin, to become established as a planter, but it will be seen that he was allowing himself to expand his own interests beyond the point of safety. In 1857, being governor and desirous of providing a residence befitting that office, he purchased the house in Charleston at a cost of $38,000, paying less than $2,000 in cash. The following year he bought Guendalos plantation at $75,000 ($21,500 in cash and his bond and mortgage for $53,500). One part of this was added to Chicora Wood; another part was given to Benjamin; and the remainder was turned over to his nephew, Joseph Blyth Allston, with the understanding that Joseph had the option of purchasing it at $25,000. This offer was ultimately rejected, thus leaving Allston liable for the whole amount.

In 1859 arrangements were made to supply Guendalos with laborers. One gang of 41 was purchased at $20,500. These Allston either gave to Benjamin or indorsed the latter's bond given in payment for them. In seeking other Negroes, the father was led, somewhat against his better judgment, to purchase a group of 116, together with Pipe Down plantation, to which they were attached. Forty of these were released to Benjamin in exchange for his bonds in the sum of $20,500, but Allston had made himself liable for the whole amount of $78,000.[124]

These purchases brought forth a mild warning from Petigru. "I should think that you were speculating," he wrote, "if the prices that you are giving for Negroes were not so much more moderate than other people are willing to pay." But circumstances made it difficult for Allston to restrain his hand. During the war he felt compelled to buy Confederate securities. In 1862 he purchased the Morven place in North Carolina at a cost of $10,000, and the next year, when his eldest daughter was married, he contributed his bond of $10,000 toward her marriage portion.[125] The result was that in 1866, when his executors were finally able to turn their attention to the settlement of Allston's estate, it was found that, with accrued interest, the liabilities amounted to $255,000. One-half the value of the estate having been lost by the emanci-

[124] It seems to have been understood that Benjamin would ultimately pay his father's estate the further sum of $15,000 in order to make these gifts approximate in value the legacies intended for each of Allston's children.

[125] To match the sum contributed by her husband's father.

TABLE 1

EXPENDITURES OF WAVERLY PLANTATION AND MILL, 1834–57

OPERATING COSTS

Season	Supplies*	Lumber and Fuel†	Mill Repairs	Overseer's Wages‡	Miller's Wages	Slave Hire	Medical Service	Legal Service	Taxes	Interest on Advances	Interest on Bonds	Miscellaneous	Total
1834–35	$1,446.66	$182.21	$51.00	$234.72					114.39		$4,486.11	$747.19	$7,262.28
1835–36	2,635.68	1,153.18		481.78			$28.79		136.60		3,398.98	389.22	8,332.62
1836–37	2,105.59	90.43	686.05	400.00			159.60	$7.50	204.89	$108.30	3,386.21	2,174.30	9,214.57
1837–38	656.20	1,211.34	1,156.60	385.00			27.50		94.56		1,868.90		5,305.60
1838–39	627.80	949.25		400.00			28.50	1.07	98.10		1,101.33	573.50	3,776.01
1839–40	859.10	729.82					13.93	1.49	56.41		993.70	1.25	2,697.39
1840–41	1,321.99	107.75		1,092.00		$100.00	20.38	1.49	65.28		844.05	400.00	3,687.40
1841–42	1,441.81	550.13		500.00		100.00	117.80	1.00	94.21	83.33	1,088.83		5,019.80
1842–43	1,000.55	245.95	700.00	500.00		100.00	587.27	75.35	78.83	54.95	593.83		3,569.61
1843–44	1,591.86	79.10	300.00	500.00			85.00	34.08	88.43	72.45	–469.58		2,866.80
1844–45	869.67	339.36		500.00		518.75	185.90	16.10	89.11	28.35	280.00		2,814.98
1845–46	1,811.43	810.56	1,845.33	500.00		990.00	262.73	3.48	100.88	16.77	280.00	1,518.50	6,598.64
1846–47	1,255.05	479.29	1,045.00	500.00		275.00	238.07	53.00	94.61			132.00	5,607.07
1847–48	2,235.30	747.16	2,126.83	600.00		733.00	20.00	38.50	108.56				6,702.31
1848–49	1,713.04	1,025.58	4,955.25	85.00		867.00	737.80	3.00	124.81				9,562.56
1849–50	2,207.37	1,372.10	3,076.22	912.50		600.00	287.53	153.57	125.77	236.56			13,164.62
1850–51	4,502.46	2,879.43	5,432.47	745.23	$550.00	880.00	15.38	222.50	173.12	492.78	839.47		18,987.90
1851–52	3,583.86	5,560.28		850.00	450.00	600.00	757.54	4.00	183.16	505.05	839.47	25.00	13,361.07
1852–53	3,610.40	4,079.74	833.88	937.50	700.00	600.00	35.00	76.50	140.24	413.00	839.47		12,988.20
1853–54	3,873.78	6,310.01	1,884.93	1,000.00	2,300.00	1,184.00	806.90	4.00	231.71	454.97	839.47	65.18	18,993.01
1854–55	4,875.80	2,747.25	878.50	1,100.00	580.14	780.00	237.25	4.50	218.31	42.86	839.47	631.98	13,361.07
1855–56	4,976.34	4,839.55	1,792.45	1,100.00	800.00	925.00	6.50	16.00	249.60				15,544.98
1856–57	5,843.13	10,076.37	2,410.58	1,050.00	900.00	1,504.31	1,514.81				1,419.01	188.06	25,171.87
Total	$55,044.87	$47,240.84	$28,300.09	$14,373.73	$6,280.14	$10,757.06	6,174.18	$717.13	$2,871.67	$2,569.37	$24,407.94	$6,846.18	$205,583.20
Annual average	2,393.26	2,053.95	1,230.44	624.94	273.05	467.70	268.44	31.18	124.85	111.71	1,061.21	297.66	8,938.40

* Chiefly food and clothing for the slaves but does not exclude many personal items for the white folk.

† Includes cooper stuff for the barrels furnished by the mill.

‡ After 1847 this includes an undetermined amount paid for hire of the overseer's slaves.

TABLE 1—*Continued*

PERSONAL EXPENSES AND CAPITAL INVESTMENTS

Season	Church Contribution§	Personal‖	Executor's Commission¶	Slaves Purchased	Bonds Paid	Other Capital Investments	Total
1834–35	......	$ 100.00	$ 354.07	......	$ 6,486.63	$ 369.12	$ 14,572.10
1835–36	......	100.00	802.01	......	8,078.00	......	17,912.63
1836–37	$ 200.00	180.00	531.84	......	15,700.00	......	25,926.41
1837–38	......	......	206.18	......	3,500.00	......	9,011.78
1838–39	50.00	522.03	196.34	......	4,580.07	......	9,124.45
1839–40	50.00	473.25	315.41	......	9,300.00	133.00	12,069.05
1840–41	......	200.00	182.41	......	1,996.75	165.00	6,231.56
1841–42	50.00	636.62	211.83	......	3,350.00	......	9,268.25
1842–43	......	591.60	141.74	......	1,483.33	20.00	5,806.28
1843–44	50.00	430.22	179.04	795.00	3,000.00	......	7,321.06
1844–45	200.00	627.38	208.38	2,451.76	......	......	6,302.50
1845–46	125.00	799.08	313.99	......	4,000.00	1,960.00	13,788.61
1846–47	60.00	720.39	627.06	3,720.00	......	3,000.00	12,572.24
1847–48	25.00	768.61	341.56	......	......	......	6,742.24
1848–49	85.00	1,706.15	404.84	......	......	......	8,958.30
1849–50	64.00	2,049.55	381.19	......	......	470.00	12,527.30
1850–51	15.00	2,196.55	1,333.64	9,069.00	......	75.00	25,853.81
1851–52	60.00	1,871.66	992.14	......	......	......	21,910.82
1852–53	60.00	3,317.35	902.22	......	......	620.00	17,887.77
1853–54	75.00	3,728.54	1,175.61	1,696.00	......	250.00	25,828.16
1854–55	280.00	554.88	907.18	......	......	......	15,102.60
1855–56	112.00	286.33	1,043.21	......	......	695.13	17,681.65
1856–57	......	4,287.82	1,733.28	5,657.00	......	1,207.90	38,057.88
Total......	$1,561.00	$26,139.91	$13,545.17	$23,388.76	$62,074.78	$8,965.16	$341,357.45
Annual average	67.87	1,136.52	588.92	1,016.90	2,608.90	389.79	14,841.63

§ For the support of the parish rector.

‖ Chiefly for the school expenses of Allston's two wards.

¶ Includes 2.5 per cent on receipts and 2.5 per cent on disbursements.

47

TABLE 2

Crops and Receipts of Waverly Plantation and Mill, 1834–57

Season	Whole Barrels	Half-Barrels	Bushels	Crop Sales*	Mill Earnings†	Bonds (Principal and Interest)‡	Stocks (Interest)	Sale of Slaves	Sale of Land	Miscellaneous	Totals
1834–35	599	52	……	$ 10,762.73	$ 454.59	……	……	……	……	$1,238.93	$ 12,456.25
1835–36	607	21	……	11,334.04	268.40	……	……	$ 1,564.26	……	906.75	14,163.45
1836–37	189	28	1,985	6,274.11	1,491.37	……	……	25,141.55	……	1,764.38	34,671.41
1837–38	62	25	……	1,738.49	1,242.88	$ 1,128.84	……	……	……	566.29	4,676.50
1838–39	181	15	……	4,581.79	2,721.66	……	……	……	……	……	7,303.45
1839–40	154	26	……	3,971.92	1,717.12	1,307.60	……	……	$5,500.00	83.15	12,579.79
1840–41	373	21	175	7,218.04	911.60	414.24	……	……	……	……	8,543.88
1841–42	407	……	……	7,092.00	798.26	……	……	……	……	……	7,890.26
1842–43	323	……	……	4,163.26	717.82	393.93	……	……	……	400.00	5,675.01
1843–44	441	……	……	5,844.45	540.08	796.84	……	……	……	……	7,181.37
1844–45	543	70	……	8,970.30	633.04	973.34	……	……	……	……	10,576.68
1845–46	438	59	……	10,629.91	775.10	140.00	$ 100.00	……	……	……	11,645.01
1846–47	366	13	510	8,832.47	1,564.73	2,640.00	100.00	……	……	……	13,137.20
1847–48	288	3	……	5,997.22	890.86	273.59	100.00	……	……	……	7,261.67
1848–49	493	7	……	8,553.70	556.30	140.00	100.00	432.50	……	318.00	10,100.50
1849–50§	118	3	……	1,937.92	503.62	560.00	100.00	……	……	……	3,101.54
1850–51	687	1	……	13,177.40	5,041.75	10,503.52	100.00	……	……	……	28,822.71
1851–52	521	3	……	9,842.94	5,664.49	3,140.00	120.00	……	……	……	18,767.43
1852–53	536	1	……	11,591.48	7,251.89	140.00	120.00	……	……	……	19,103.37
1853–54	531	2	……	11,863.02	6,640.94	3,738.00	130.00	……	……	……	22,371.96
1854–55	536	3	……	14,486.59	7,325.53	140.00	140.00	……	……	……	22,092.12
1855–56	312	3	……	8,824.56	13,382.78	2,752.85	130.00	……	……	……	25,090.17
1856–57	609	6	……	15,264.92	15,786.32	1,748.18	120.00	……	……	86.88	33,006.30
Total	9,314	362	2,670	$192,953.26	$76,881.13	$30,930.91	$1,360.00	$27,138.31	$5,500.00	$5,454.38	$340,218.03
Annual average	405	16	116	8,389.27	3,342.66	1,344.82	59.13	1,179.93	239.13	237.15	14,792.03

* Includes small sums received for rice flour not included in crops.
† Mill earnings include receipts from toll and the sale of barrels.
‡ The greater part of these amounts were payments of bonds accepted for slaves sold in 1837.
§ A year of short crops everywhere on the Rice Coast.

48

pation of the Negroes, the value of the remainder in ordinary times would probably not have been greatly in excess of these claims.[126]

All efforts to avoid a sale of the property at the ruinous prices then prevailing were futile. In 1866 there was only $8,000 to be distributed among the creditors. By 1868 this had dwindled to $1,100, and it was decided to sell at public auction. Chicora Wood and an adjacent tract of pine land were reserved for Mrs. Allston under her claim of dower. The remaining property brought approximately $60,000. Thus were swept away the results of thirty years of wise management.[127]

[126] Allston believed that the sale of the Nightingale Hall–Waterford unit and one hundred Negroes would have been sufficient to meet all obligations, exclusive of those which he had assumed for Benjamin. The latter, after making an effort to meet his obligations, went into bankruptcy.

[127] The details of the settlement will be found in the papers relating to the suit of *Allston* v. *Allston* (Charleston County, Clerk of Court's Office) brought for the purpose of expediting the handling of the estate.

ALLSTON FAMILY LETTERS

Charlotte Ann Allston to Robert F. W. Allston[1]

Virginia Sweet Springs[2] September 27 1818

. . . . think of what Profeshion you mean to persue my Dear Robert, and let me know I am so disappointed at Joseph, that I shall not survive if you turn out in the same way. he left Colledge, went into the Army,[3] without my consent or approbation, came Home Engaged himself to be married, gone on the Plantation without saying Mother I am going to do so, what do you think of it if the Plantation was his and clear of Debt, which it is not, bad enough would he find it, to maintain a Family without a Profeshion what will he do, situated as he is, when the Novelty of Matrimony is over, then will he see other young Men of his acquaintance and Age, who has studied a Profeshion and is able to gain themselves and Familys a handsome Maintanance in any part of the World, where they may be thrown, and he after all his Toiling, poor and in no way to Educate his Children, or Maintain them as he would wish, then will he be disgusted with himself, the World, his Wife, his Children, and all he has, and wish he had attended to his Fathers last request, and my Intreaties. think of it my Dear Robert, your Father split upon this very Rock, it was the wish of his Friends, that he should study a Profeshion, and not marry so early he repented when it was too late, and with Tears in his Eyes, he told me on his Death Bed, it was his request to me, to make his Sons study a Profeshion, and not to give them up the Property unless they did so what more can I do than tell you, and persuade you, for his sake, for mine, for God sake, and for your own good to do so had I Burned the Will as he told me to do I might have had more influance, but I did it not, now the Executors are tyard of the trouble, persuade him [Joseph] to take posestion which he has done and I knew not of it, till I heard Joseph tell Mr Tucker that W B Allston and R. F. Withers had persuaded him to do so, me and my opinion thrown out of the Question he persists in marrying Sarah Prior, who is older than your Sister Mary, and has been so often engaged to others, that I look at Joseph with wonder, he never will repent it but once, and that will be as long as he Lives. I write you thus particularly my Dear Robert that you may not do the same—take warning, and be advised by your Mother, not to do as your Father, Uncle Washington, and Uncle William, and as your Brother

---

[1] Addressed: West Point, N.Y.

[2] Where the writer and her daughters were visiting.

[3] Joseph Waties Allston entered the United States Army on June 29, 1813, and resigned on August 31, 1817, having attained the rank of first lieutenant.

is going to do the Mind of Man is never at rest, and hårdly matured at 21, how differantly do we view things this year, to what we did last that love youth has is ardent, but not lasting and it is a Mercy it is so, we alter and have a Priveledge of Improving ourselves and it is Our Duty and Interest to do so. I think you had better stay at West point till next December twelve-month, learn all you can, then choose a Profeshion, study that 2 years in some Healthy Clime, then come Home at 21 [to] see us all, when you will be able to judge for yourself, Protect and Comfort your Mother, Aunt, Sisters, and other Friends, and never be ashamed to enter any Company, or meet your Fathers Enemies or your own it appears like a long time my Dear Son, and as if I do not wish to see you, but that is not the fact, 3 years more will soon pass off, and perhaps circumstances may throw us in each others embraces before that time, but should it not, you will have the con-solations of thinking you acted as your Nearest Friends wished you to do. I shall have many a strugle with Winds, Weathers, and hard Fortune before that time arrives, if I live, if not I leave you my Blessing with which I have but little else to mingle.

Will, Ellich, Mary and Frank, James,[1] tell you howdye they are all home sick Cousin Ben, your Aunt join me in love to you not one word have I heard from William this Summer, why I cant tell, but trust I shall see him in two or three Weeks. Heaven Bless you my Dear Robert is the earnest and Daily Prayer of your Affectionate Mother.

Charlotte Ann Allston to Robert F. W. Allston[2]

Georgetown February 21 1819

Tomorrow my dear Robert is 10 years since your Father Died, and left us to Battle with a Wide and Trying World, and time would fail, were I to Inumirate all my Trials, but God is all sufficant and Mercifull and will carry us through all we look to him.

The Court of Equity set on the first of February and Mr Tucker and Joseph Petisioned for a division of the Estate which was granted, and is to take Place on Thursday next, Mr F and Robert Withers, Mr B Huger, Mr Joseph Pyatt and W Alston junr on the Commishioners[3] the poor Negroes appear in dread I feel for them, but it is evident they all cannot belong to me, with some I have had severe trials.[4] I wrote you a few days ago, and forgot if I mentioned this or not the Court has Appointed me yours and Williams Guardian, but if you think of any one that is more active and can attend better to the Plantation do write and say candidly as you are

1 Slaves.

2 Addressed: West Point, N.Y.

3 For further details concerning the division see below, pp. 367, 370.

4 A list of these slaves will be found on p. 331.

both old enough, but we had not time, after it was agreed on to write and get your Answer, time enough to let the Court appoint whome you chose. Mr McDowel has bought the Adjoining Plantation from Mr Cohen, and I am quite Pleased that we have so good a Neighbour he will nessesarily have to go there often through the Summer, when attention is most wanted, and will no Doubt Direct for us. Indeed he has offered, and I mean to offer him something for his trouble after I hear from you, unless you think of some one who will do better, but my Dear Robert although we have large connections and Able Men connected, yet when that kind of Attention is required, where can we look for it all, all are Interested for themselves, and have not time from Week to Week to attend to anything but their own Multiplicity of Business this by Wofull experiance I know, for our Estate had been clear of Debt long ago had there been proper attention Paid to it, any Active Man with two such Plantations and 130 Negroes would have Doubled its income in 10 years, but alas, what is Friendship to a Man in the Grave, or to his Ofspring the Debts are not paid but we all are to sign a Bond and Mortgage of the Property to Mr Kershaw to whome the Creditors continue to look for payment. . . . .

Charlotte Ann Allston to Robert F. W. Allston[1]

Georgetown April 5 1819

. . . .

Your Sister Charlotte went with me to Marion, also Mr William Hemingway, who surveyed 4 Tracks of Land one of that Number is that that Jones lives on, his Lordship I did not see, but he says he means to hold on, which is Irvins [?] advice. I do expect to have a deal of trouble with those unprinsapled People. I went also to Statesborough[2] which is as far Superior to Marion as Charleston is to Georgetown they are Rich Cotton and Corn Planters, live Genteelly, and of coarse treat people Accordingly. I regret for more than one Reason I have not been there before, but the Fact is my Fathers Lands and Business has been too long neglected to be done now in a [MS torn] and I have been looking forward to the Period of my Sons coming to Age to assist and protect me, but alas that hope is as a Castle Built in the Air, which I see fall to the Ground. Joseph is married has his own concerns to attend to, and I am still Battling with a Wide, Wide, unfriendly World none but God who is the best of Fathers and Friends to look to as for you my Dear Robert I am affraid to trust myself to Hope that I can have or will have you to assist me you are of a far more lively turn of Mind than Joseph and of coarse will not be so inclined to Sedate Business. Williams period is far distant, and I have had the Mortification to hear he will not learn what is to become of me, those who have no Children

---

[1] Addressed: West Point, N.Y.   [2] Stateburg in Sumter District.

would give any thing for some, and those who have them are in constant Dread and Anxiety about them which is my case. Charlotte was compleatly sick of her jaunt says she would not live at Marion for any thing, and means to sell her part of the Plantation. Mary says she will go next and will not sell her part poor Joe[1] has some how offended Jones who says he will Beat him, which will hurt and Displease me very much, as I think it will be only on my account as the People there say, it is because he has an Ambition against me but I think it any thing but Ambition, which if they had, they would certainly act Differantly in every respect. . . . .

Charlotte Ann Allston to Robert F. W. Allston[2]

Oakgrove August 12 1819

. . . .

. . . . we dined with Major Carr, who has undertaken our Marion and Marlborough Business, which I trust we have now in a good way Edward Simons is jointly concerned. I have a troublesome Neighbour in Mr William Vereen [?] on Pee Dee, who has taken Posession of a Field on the Main, Ruined our Pine Land, and now lays claim to upwards of 170 Acres of swamp on the Island, which I shall have a deal of trouble to keep. I ordered Scotland to go in and clear some of it, he ordered him not to touch it, I repeated my order, he is now clearing a Ditch way, and I suppose I shall be sewed, but I prefer it to sewing him. Mr McDowel, Mr Hemingway, and I hope, your Brother will go over tomorrow and have the Line run, after that if I can find some Papers that are wanted I shall not care for him, but I feel sorry to have such a near and Disagreeable Neighbour our crop is not large but good, I pray God nothing may injure it. I mean to send in to Mill near Charleston, as we have but a few hands and a small Barn, and I wish to get the New Land in order for another year. I hope will be for the Best, as I mean it.

I have never receved an answer from you my Dear Robert about what you are to study for a Profession. I wish you would determine my Dear Son.

Charlotte Ann Allston to Robert F. W. Allston[2]

Georgetown March 17 1820

I wrote you some time since my Dear Robert and did not intend to do so again untill I heard from you, but your good old Aunt has called and requested me to inclose you this Bill of $10, with her love, which induces me

---

[1] The slave, Mulatto Joe, who, according to the will of Benjamin Allston, Jr., was to be allowed to remain at the farm in Britton's Neck and, together with his wife, Milley, to receive two cows, two calves, and an annual stipend of $15 "for services to be hereafter rendered." See below, pp. 333, 337, 356.

[2] Addressed: West Point, N.Y.

to write now, tho I have not any news to relate we are all ploding on here much at the old rate Rice fell badly, and that depresses the spirits of the Majority of the People here, whose chief object is to make Rice to buy Negroes and Buy Negroes to make Rice there is so much contention about Property that it keeps the Lawyers Busy, then sickness Keeps the Doctors also Busy, but the Merchant can go occasionally to take a Game of Billiards, and not be Missed out of his stoar the Markets are bad, no Money, no Money is the cry continualy we had 112 Barrels of Rice sold, which brought only $1012, which you know is not enough to pay Tax clothes Blankets and shoes, besides Doctors Bills and other expencies how can we expect to Live, what is to become of us this is what you have heard all your life my Dear Son, and it looks as if we are Doomed to live in this state of fear and hope which no Doubt is for the best, if we had all we wished we would be too [illegible] and never think of another World, which we are Doomed to, and ought to prepare for.

I will send you tho the $300 in June for you to Travel to Boston if you are still in the same mind, and if you make a right use of your Journey it will be money well spent or Laid out, but do write often as we are anxious to hear from you always I am again to go to Marion, set out on Tuesday next if nothing happens their is a great Fresh in Pee Dee from a deal of Rain we have had lately, how I shall get through these swamps, I cant tell my poor old Horses hold out wonderfully, I much fear one day or other they will fail and leave me in the Road. . . . .

Charlotte Ann Allston to Robert F. W. Allston[1]

Georgetown April 19 1820

MY DEAR ROBERT . . . . Mr King[2] said you had sent him a Pamphlet, and enquired very kindly after you he thinks if you will persevere, their is not a more Honorable and Lucrative Profession than Law, but if you want Perseverence, it will be Time thrown away Phisic I think would be of more real Service to you, as you can then save yourself the expence of Doctors Bill on your Plantation, and in your Family, which I trust one day or other you will have, but your Father and Dr Blyth[3] both wished one of you should be a Lawyer which would also save a good deal in our Families. I have just heard from Mulatto Joe, he says Maria and her Colt are both dead, I am sorry for it, but must expect to loose sometimes if I live I expect to hear diffirant Language from you and Eliza, then Confound the Marion Business, if I had a Male Friend to exert himself for me, it would go on very diffirantly

[1] Addressed: West Point, N.Y.

[2] Mitchell King (1783–1862), a Charleston lawyer, who was acting as legal adviser to the executors of the Allston estate.

[3] Joseph Blyth (d. January 3, 1818), husband of the writer's sister, Elizabeth Frances Blyth.

your poor old Grand Father would have been hurt if he could hear it, or thought one of his Children could make so lite of what he thought so highly off, the Property is good, if the People are bad I trust in the Lord it will not be always in so troublesome a state. . . . .

Charlotte Ann Allston to Robert F. W. Allston[1]

Georgetown May 8 1820

MY DEAR ROBERT it is not long since I wrote you, and requested to know whether $50 would do for your immediate wants, but as so good an Opportunity offers as [illegible] I cant let it slip, as the sending Money by the Mail is rather Precarious, so I will wait no longer for your Answer, but inclose you $100 of Thomas's Rice, as our Crop fell short, and the Price Lessened it, I need not remonstrate about Economy my Dear Son, you well know your Property is small and we still in Debt, if you take care and Live within Bounds, it is a very pretty begining, as Thousands begin with Less, yet if you run in Debt that nor as much more will not Suffice.

We are all tolerable well and join in love to you we have commenced a New Crop, and as usual hope for a Better Price I have employed James Hull to ride to Matanza twice or thrice a Week, to see how they go on Joseph speaks of going to the Northward, which I hope he will, as he was so ill last fall, if he stays he will expose himself, and to be so sick again this Fall would undermine his constitution very much if he got over it, and it is not in my Power to go to Matanza as often as is nesessary some one should I am to give James Hull a dollar for every Barrell of Rice that is made over one Hundred Barrels he Lives at Mr Pringles the same side of the Ferry that Matanza is there are 9 Hands for you, 9 for William, 8 for me, and we jointly pay for Scotland and Patty, which makes 28 in all,[2] and we are to Plant 130 Acres of Rice, and 13 Acres of High Land if we do not do better we will be in Debt when you come, which I am trying to avoid I am about to go to Marion again, we form a party Colonel Carr, who has undertaken to settle the Business for us, a Surveyor, Miss Rothmahlar, Charlotte and myself, it is getting so late and hot now I wish it was over my old Mare and Colt is both dead Joe writes me, so I will keep the Filly for you and the Horse for William, if I can, but it will be 7 years Old by the time William is of Age, that wont do if we make a good Crop the Next year, I will get you to Buy me a Well Broken Pear of Horses and Drive them in for me if you come by Land, if by Water, we will see about the best way this is something in the stile of *Building Castles* alas I am where I was before, in Debt and know not how to pay if your Fathers Debts were

[1] Addressed: West Point, N.Y.

[2] The basis of the division of the crop.

Discharged, and I could take up the Mortgage of this House,[1] I would be truly thankfull I paid Mr Wagner for it, but Borrowed the Money from Maria Stone, now Mrs R Shackelford, who has bought a Servant and wishes to get another and to save me I cant get as much as the sum is $800 if it Pleases God to take me, before it is Paid some of you will have to exert yourselves to pay it this Idea is what carries me to Marion, there are in that Place and Marlborough not Less than 30 Thousand Acres of Land, which if we can turn into Money, would releave me much some we have sold some we have Rented out and some we mean to keep I look forward to a time when some of you will be better situated up there, where you can have Health and keep the Crops you make [better] than here, sickly and have to watch every thing that is made, to get it to Market, and hurry from River to Sea every year I think this will be the Last Summer I shall spend at Oak Grove, if your Brother Marries again, which I hope he will[2] the Place is left to him, and I will not live with another Mistress there I mean to go up the Country every Summer and return in the Fall as soon as you come to take Charge of your Property.

. . . .

Your Sister Eliza sends her love to you she has Lost Brutus the Brother of Sary and London, so there are 10 Deaths with the Negroes Since the Division, Charlotte Lost 4, Mary 4, myself 1 and Eliza 1 Heaven Bless you my Dear Robert and direct you in the right way is the Prayer of your Affectionate Mother.

Charlotte Ann Allston to Robert F. W. Allston[3]

Georgetown April 2 1821

. . . .

I have been for a Fortnight at Marion, and Marlborough, have got my Business there in a better train than ever, and I trust if I do not live to enjoy the fruit of mine and my Fathers labours some of *you* will [Mulatto] Joe is quite well, and talks a Deal of you, he says the Philly must start on the Coarse next February, and he must Ride her himself and he will take the Prize for Master Robert he will Bet 20 sheep that he wins, he has a fine Flock of sheep, so there is if nothing happins a fine set out for you to Gameing an Old Rider upwards of 60, so attached to you that he will run the Risque of his Life and Bones in your behalf the Horse colt is a fine one, he is now Breaking him, I expect you will like him lest the Old Mare was Killed last year with her colt in a most Wanton Manner by 3 Dogs who charged her, the other Bay Mare has a fine Horse colt a Week old so I trust you

---

[1] Apparently in Georgetown.

[2] Joseph Waties' wife had died on September 3, 1819, leaving an infant son, Benjamin Allston, to the care of the writer.

[3] Addressed: West Point, N.Y.

wont be Obliged to Walk unless you choose Mary has sold all her Negroes to Joseph, and I have made Chance my Driver at Matanza Old Brutus and Beck have mine and in Town, they with all these Negroes and Mulatto Joe send howdye to you I am making some Shirts for you and will send them soon Mr Tucker sent you a Barrel of Sweet Potatoes, they went down by Captn Toby to Charleston, but by whom they were shiped from thence I have not heard. . . . .

Samuel L. Smith to Charlotte Ann Allston

Waccamaw December 8th 1822

DEAR MADAM   I recd your letter by Harry in answer to mine written you a short time since, and in reply readily admit that my little negroes were to be *fed* at my expence, although at the time I had considerably more offered me for my negroes than you agreed to give, without that deduction being made, which I declined taking as the negroes prefered going to you. My disposition unfortunately for my own interest is too averse to any thing like litigation and I would at any time sooner submit to a partial loss than have any controversy about it particularly where a lady was concerned. As I mentioned to you before I was surprised at hearing that you had not cloathed my little negroes as I thought for the reasons I then stated you should have done so; but I was truly astonished on reading your letter to see what you state in it, that my negroes did not go to your plantation to work 'till the 10th or 11th January whereas I have been constantly under the impression 'til the receipt of your letter that they went on the first of the month for the following reasons which I beg leave to submit to you. I made the agreement with Mr. Shackelford who represented you that the negroes should go to your place on the first of January, Mr. Wilson my overseer whose term of service with me expired at the same time had positive directions to send the people to you on that day, on which day I was given to understand they did go, all except the woman Amey who was prevented by indisposition. I will only add that by my agreement with Mr. Coachman in the sale of my land to him, the negroes were to be removed and posession given him of the premises by the first of January. When I made the agreement with Mr. Shackelford (which was in the month of December) for the hire of the negroes I was sick in bed and continued so 'til after the first of January or I should have gone to Pee Dee and seen the negroes delivered at your place but from the circumstances I have mentioned I thought there would be no difficulty or mistake in the matter, experience however proves that difficulties will sometimes arise let the utmost caution or circumspection be observed. I regret with you that there should be any misunderstanding respecting the contract between us.[1]

1 See below, p. 337, for agreement which occasioned this letter.

O. Potter[1] to Charlotte Ann Allston

[Georgetown, February, 1823]

MY DEAR MADAM   A sad misfortune has happened to Cane while I was in Charleston, he had a scuffle with my little molatto boy and the molatto stabbed him in the foot with a knife it bled profusely I am informed and Doct. Wragg was imediately called and dressed the wound I arrived the next day and Dr. Wragg expressly told me the bandage must not be removed for 14 days and nights, and this order has been complied with, and in the mean time I constantly enquired of Cane if he felt any pain and always received an answer that he felt none or very little yesterday he began to feel a stiffness in his neck at dinner time, and became quite bad with lockjaw by evening the doctor was called imediately and he is no better this morning I believe the doctor thinks he shall be able to cure him but I fear his situation is a bad one he is at my house I [truly] lament the accident but have done all in my power for him since it happened.

O. Potter to Charlotte Ann Allston

Georgetown th24 February 1823

MY DEAR MADAM   Your letter of the 22 from Pedee I have this minute received, and hasten to answer it I much regreat that the price of rice is so low, & also regreat that you feel distressed, But am surprised at your observation relating to what I *think my due* surely you never seriously imagion that I would voluntarily consent to pay anything towards Cain. I was in no way accessory to his death & therefore not liable as I suppose if you cannot this year pay the Estates acct, you may give me a dubill and I will wait your convenience as relates to the woman for a nurse, I think the price well enough for no doubt she is worth that as a field hand, but being a raw field negro will poorly answer the purpose of a nurse, the little nice attentions that are expected to be paid a little chile, she would not understand this sending her down from Pedee has caused however some trouble to your kind daughter, and detained the woman from her work I will therefore prepose paying for this 1/2 months wages, $3, I beg you to accept assurances of my good wishes & regard . . . .

Charlotte Ann Allston to Robert F. W. Allston[2]

Matanza, April 3, 1823

MY DEAR ROBERT   It is two Weeks since I got your letter by Major Bull. I would like to hear often and often Vainly do I wish you had not gone away. I thought by this time to have been back from Marion, but I have not yet gone but think of going next Monday, if nothing happens there has been a high Fresh in Pee Dee for 3 Weeks past, so that I could not go, it

[1] Potter appears to have been a Georgetown tailor with whom Cain had been placed as an apprentice.

[2] Addressed: Columbia, S.C.

is falling now the Wind from the West has prevailed, and hard all March which has made the Tides here low, or emtied the Rivers, so that we have not been prevented one day from Working in the swamp, but we did not begin to plant untill Monday 1 March the Middle Field next to Vareens, finished last night they are now Trenching in the field next to that towards the River I went to Santee last Monday, Returned to G[eorge] Town on Wednesday 26th came from Town yesterday about 2 Oclock found poor Chance extreamly ill, and in less than two hours he Died they say he got up turned out the People in the Morning got out 18 bus Rice went over the River put all in their Tasks, then went to lay out some Ditching for 2 Hands who were over and above in planting, he sat on a Log and said he felt sick, got up to Walk fell down and became cold and depressed up all his Limbs. They brought him Home to the Kitchen and sent for Mr Coachman who did all he could yet none ever thought of sending to me or for a Doctor. I set George off, but before he could have reached the Ferry he died I Blistered Rubed etc but he had no Pulse I dont know who to put in his Place do write me what you think, I have thoughts of Charles or Jacob big Sam is at present, that is yesterday and today, attending to Mr Avant in that way, except Mulatto Joe or George I could not have met with a greater loss, but Gods Will be done I may not live to want any of their Servises, my Heart is sunk, with one trouble after another, and Duned on all sides and not a Dollar will Mr Lewis send me I have writen repeatedly but to no effect, he treats me like a child, 26 bbls sold at $2 3/4, 17 at $2 1/2 I sent the 31 Barrels from Major Wraggs to Mr William Allen he sold it directly for $2.25, and I expect that [$]363 any Hour he thanks me for sending but the other writes as if he thought I cant do without him. If it is possable I will not trouble them again I sent up Andrew with the Philly, he returned two Weeks since, said the little Philly that we got Brother to lead up for us is dead it is indeed wonderfull what can kill so many creatures up there your large Mare has a Sorrel Horse colt, Andrew says it is quite large. I have gotten Mr Tuckers Carriage at $200 got Will to clean up the other Carriage, which I have left in Town to be sold at $500, with the Harness, which cost me 69, the Carriage $600 exclusive of repairs, at different times the Shadd are very plenty now, as I sat in the Piaza last night I heard them playing in the River I wish you could come down sometime the last of April or 1 of May we are all at a loss what to determine about for next Summer, your Sisters ought to go away, they wish me to go too, but what prospects have I with such a Family to get money enough how shall I get the Repairs done at Oak Grove I would be glad for your Aunt to go their with me Mr Vareen is getting better now you ought to attend to this Line between you, as it Sadles this whole Family with the Debts Ben and Ann are quite well, they often speak of you William is still quite idle Heaven Bless you my Dear Robert.

Charlotte Ann Allston to Robert F. W. Allston[1]

Georgetown, June 8, 1823

MY DEAR ROBERT I received your letter a few days since and feel more than I can describe at your not being able to keep a Horse or Servant, my Dear Robert after the Deprivation to us all of your Company, and the continual exertion you are obliged to make, to be so reduced is too bad, but why do I wonder at any thing after all I know we are and have been an unfortunate Family in many Matters for 2 or 3 Generations past, and I have in the midst of Rich Friends and Possessions of Property been poor for years . . . . poor Paris Died on the 30 May, his illness was a painful one and Distressed Charlotte Much, and she is in bad health I have beged Mr Coachman to go over in case of hard sickness and on any disturbance among the People, and should it be of a Serious Nature to send for Joseph, who is to act as he thinks best for us on Tuesday 27 May Mr Avant and Jerrey [?] had a fight. I heard nothing of it till I went to Mr McDowells on Saterday 31, he asked me which of my Negroes Bit Avant, at night I sent for Joe, who told me. Jerrey had a Horn which he Blew for his own amusement, which offended Mr Avant, who asked him what he was doing with that Horn, he said he wanted it, what for, Nothing, he then Ordered him to go in the Barn for the Corn for the Horse. so soon as he got in Avant locked the Door, called to Bob for his Whip, and Mrs Avant with their Dog, the Flail sticks, and they Beat him a long time he scuffleing all the while, he Bit and Avant choaked him twice till his streangth failed, and at last had to send for Geog in the Chappel swamp, who tyed [him], and Avant then gave him 20 or 30 lashes, twice I understand I told Mr Avant that was not the way to do, and that Mrs Avant had nothing to do with the People, nor their Dog, I hope they will do well Mr Tucker says he thinks the two Goose grass Fields are lost past recovery in consequence of that old field robbing them, but Mr Coachman and McDowell say it is beautiful Rice, so I dont know who is right we are generally so unfortunate that I fear the worse Mr [illegible] called to say his Money had not arrived from C[harles] Town yet, but so soon as it did he will pay it to Captn Coachman whom I requested to inclose to you Ten Dollars, and take the Eight to get some Boards from any Raft that passed, for Thomas to finish those Buildings he has Raised Mr Avant said you told him to go into that House till a better could be Built, I told him he had better write to you respecting it, that I could not do more than order Geog to Whitewash the House he is now in.

Joseph said Mr Waddlesworth is about a steam mill up Waccamaw, and applied to him for Thomas and Billy, but he did not know that Thomas was to be blind I hyed him to have him for 6 months, by that time we will see

[1] Addressed: Columbia, S.C.

if it is best to go on, so do my Dear Robert think of it and write to your Brother as you think best, and may God of his Infinite Mercy Bless [illegible] and protect you is the earnest Prayer of your own Affectionate Mother.

Joseph W. Allston to Robert F. W. Allston[1]

Holly Grove July 6th 1823

MY DEAR ROBERT, ... I was at Matanza about a week since just after a very heavy rain of two or three days continuance and found all hands busily employed in planting slips the corn is very inferior there is some pretty decent rice on the Island but it is all miserably grassy, and it is almost too late in the season to have much grassy rice the first new ground on the Island has some splendid rice but it is not regular, and the little field adjoining it would make very pretty rice but it is litterally over run with weeds, at least was when I saw it the field on the main next to Coachmans was ruined by the may-birds; there is scarcely any rice in it, that and the field opposite on the Island will make very little I do not think your man[2] very stirring and active, and cannot well concieve how he managed to have all the fields in the situation I saw them I am afraid too, from what I saw on that day, that either from his ignorance or inattention, your negroes will suffer very much if they should be sickly, which happens not to be the case at present. Beck is a very good nurse but she is a lazy old devil, and will not do anything unless she is made. My own crop is tolerably good the fields to which you allude particularly, would I think turn out very well if they were regular, but some how or other the rice did not come up well. I have not yet heard a word from Mother, I think it is time. Avant informed me when I saw him the other day, that Fraser had taken Thomas with him when he removed to his summer retreat in the Pine land. I presume he must have hired him from Mama, as I have had no communication with him on the subject. I suppose before this reaches [you], you will have seen Mr. Withers and Dr. Heriot at Columbia, if the old mans spirits keep up, Heriot may have a tolerably pleasant time of it, but if he gets below par, god help him. The 4th Inst. was celebrated at their usual parade ground by Capt. Flaggs troop, when things were car[ried] on in grand style, and some flaming p[oliti]cal toasts drank, which you will see if you take the Geo:town paper. I this morning received, under cover from an aid-de-camp of his Excellency, the commission of Deputy Adjt. Genl. of this (47 division) with the rank of Lieut. Colonel. . . . .

[1] Addressed: Columbia, S. C.

[2] The overseer, Daniel P. Avant, whose reports are printed below, pp. 247-48.

Joseph W. Allston to Robert F. W. Allston[1]

Holly Grove September 4th [1823]

MY DEAR ROBERT,   I was truly in hopes to have had no more afflicting tidings to communicate to you this summer, but alas! "in the midst of life we are in death." This has been verified in the case of one of our own family. Our poor brother William is no more. I do not know when I have been more shocked. He sent Andrew down about ten days since for several things which he wanted from Georgetown and wrote me saying that he had the fever every other day, but mentioned it in such a way, and it was so represented by Andrew, as not to create the slightest uneasiness in me he requested me to send him a few bottles of wine which I did, and begged him to come down and stay with us on the beach as I thought a change of air would be servicable. These were the last tidings that I had of him. Last night after dark [illegible] and said that Master William was dead, that the coffin had been brought down from Marion, and was then at Turkey Hill waiting for me. I was at first almost overpowered, but recollecting that it was necessary to act speedily, I gallopped over to Turkey Hill, having got Dr. Magill to accompany me, and then found it necessary to bury the body immediately as it was already very offensive. Mr. Belin the minister who has officiated at all the funerals here this Summer was ten miles off; it was usless to think of sending for him at that time of night, so I had to read the service over him myself. The body was accompanied from Marion by a Mr. Grice who I did not see, but who gave Mr. Avant the following particulars. He says that William had an intermittent fever for some time back and was in the habit of exposing himself, very much during the intermission, riding about the country, and on an occasion not long since, [was] thrown into a ditch on the catfish causeway and his horse fell on him. Mr. Grice visited him on Sunday last and found him worse than usual, persuaded him to have a Physician, and also begged him to remove to the same house where he boarded in the village, and at which it seems a Mrs. Hilling also stays. William went up to the village on Monday Morning in the carriage appeared very much exhausted, when he got there, but soon recovered, and appeared cheerful, but was very ill on that afternoon, a Physician attended him and he died on Tuesday Morning about five oclock. They had a coffin made, and left the court House about three oclock in the afternoon, and by travelling in the night reached Matanza about 3 oclock yesterday, where the negroes had sense enough to direct Mr. Avant to Turkey Hill. He did not mention any of his friends. In fact poor fellow, I question if he was sensible of his danger until within a few hours of his death. He seems to have gone very much in the way of Mr Huger. Mrs. Hilling wrote on Monday to apprize me of his danger, but I did not get the

---

[1] Addressed: Columbia, S.C.

letter until this morning. I am truly apprehensive of the ef[fect] it will have on our poor Mother, it will c[ome] upon her like a thunder bolt, for it seems Mr. Grice wrote to her from Marion. She has not yet recovered from the shock of Ben's death,[1] and this second stroke I am afraid will be too much for her. Give my Love to Aunt Blyth and all our friends.

[P. S.] Genl. Carr is very sick again.

Joseph W. Allston to Robert F. W. Allston[2]

Waverly September 25th 1823

My Dear Robert, ... The crop at Matanza, will from what I have heard turn out better than I expected when I heard from there last week the people were well and they were going on very well with the harvest, but since then we have all received a severe check. On Monday 22d, the weather became very tempestuous, very cold, with a strong northerly wind, and every appearance of an approaching gale; this continued until last night, with more or less rain, when it cleared off and relieved us from the apprehension of a storm; but night before last a most tremendous fresh reached us, and is now, in conjunction with the tides, I am afraid doing great injury. I can only speak of my own situation, as I have not been on any other plantation. At the moment I am writing the water is rushing over all my banks in every direction, I have none of my prime rice cut and it is so ripe as to fall. I will either go or send to Matanza tomorrow or next day and let you hear the state of affairs there.

Fenmore, Mr. Tucker's driver informed me on Monday last, that about a fortnight before your Jack who is working at Sandy Island in place of Joe, was most dreadfully beat on Pee Dee by Swinton, Genl. Carr's overseer, so much so that he had not been able to work since. If I had heard it immediately after it happened I should have gone to Sandy Island, for the purpose of seeing the situation of the Negro as it is Mr. Tucker's overseer is the only white person who can speak to that point, there was another white man with Swinton whose name I shall endeavour to discover and if the punishment was as severe as represented to me, I think Swinton ought to be prosecuted as nothing could justify it. . . . .

Joseph W. Allston to Robert F. W. Allston[2]

Holly Grove September 30th 1823

My Dear Robert I wrote to you on the 25th inst, since which I have received yours of blank date, the Post mark of which was the 20th. I have

[1] The infant son of the writer who had died while accompanying his grandmother to New York.

[2] Addressed: Columbia, S.C.

considered seriously the subject of your resignation next winter; in fact it occupied my thoughts before you recommended it to my consideration, as an idea which would probably present itself to you. I conceive it myself to be a step almost indispensable to your own pecuniary interest, and one which would contribute very largely to the comfort, ease, and consolation of our Mother in her present afflicted and bereaved situation. Yet I am convinced that it would at the same time injure your prospects for public life, although not entirely, yet for a long series of years; in as much as the change of circumstances in the family which will have induced you to resign, can only be explained to a few of your most intimate friends, and would by them be probably deemed satisfactory; but the great majority of those upon whom a man must on all occasions depend for advancement, would either remain ignorant of your reasons, or not allow them the consideration which they merit. The only answer I can give you therefore, is that in my idea, you must determine whether you are to be a public or a private character for the next eight or ten years and act accordingly. I would advise you however, to consult some other friend than myself on this subject before you make a final decision, one on whose judgement you can rely, and to whom you can communicate freely.

I have received a letter from Mother, of the 16th inst, in which she mentions her intention of coming in by land, by the way of Baltimore, Norfolk and Fayettevelle. She contemplated leaving Philadelphia on the 15th or 16th October, and desires that Andrew should meet her on the 25th with the carriage and horses at Fayetteville. The horses are very thin having had no corn all the summer. I have therefore directed Mr. Avant to give out corn for them, and to see that Andrew attends properly to them, and gets them in better order, and I will see to his being off in good time and with proper directions.

I am happy to say that the fresh which I mentioned in my last proved only to be a temporary swell, and the principal inconvenience arose from the extraordinary tides, which still continue to our great annoyance, running over the banks at every flood, and breaking a great many, this too without any apparent cause, it being ten days since the full moon, in fact it is higher this evening on the beach, than it was in the height of spring tides. I was at Matanza yesterday and was glad to find that they had not been interrupted by these tides; they were more forward than I had expected having taken in all the rice except the chapel creek field on the main, and I have still 55 acres out, this was not perfectly ripe and as the corn had not yet been broke in I advised Avant to do that immediately as it was wasting very much in the fields and to let the rice remain until Saturday. I think you will make a tolerable crop; there is some very heavy rice. . . . .[1]

[1] The family letters of the years from 1824 to 1836 are few in number and of little significance.

Robert F. W. Allston to Adele Petigru[1]

Matanza (Georgetown) 30th Jany. 1832

As far as it may be in my power My Dear Adele, I am determined to leave you no apology for delaying that valued communication for which I look so anxiously and on which you know I depend for the fulfilment of my warmest wish.

Your Sister Mrs. N.[orth], I regret to say, could not see me on my arrival in Georgetown, altho' she is better than when you heard from Miss P. I hope for the pleasure of seeing and making a friend of her when I go down tomorrow.

You cannot think how annoy'd I have been at my reception in town and the account of Reports which have been rife in my absence. In going to the city I did not intend to disturb the good people of Georgetown by passing through their town but they, honest folks, concern'd for the welfare of their representative, traced my movement, by means of some passenger on the road, and bruited the matter far and wide. It was settled at once that the occasion of my going to Charleston at this unusual season could be no other than one of love, which determination, by the way, was sufficiently accurate, but this kind of distinction, if it be craved by some minds, is not by me, even altho' it be supposed to result from the standing which our little community have too partially assign'd me.

The World, however, will have its say and will have its curiosity gratified at somebody's expense, it is at ours just now, and the more brief the space we give it for speculation, I think, the better.

I have inform'd my Aunt and Mrs. A. of my happy destiny, the first has said all that the most indulgent friend may be supposed to say who loves me more than I deserve and who is pleased with every body who is pleased with me, but both have reproved me for not bringing them more positive information in naming the day of our nuptials, for this, my love, let me hope that you will compensate by answering me fully and pointedly in this matter, this will conform too with your cherish'd promise, on which more than all, I rely with certin confidence. If you could fix upon the 28th Feby. or 1st of March, at the same time that it would consummate my bliss, this arrangement would add very much to my convenience, and for that freedom of which you are so jealous, I will promise that it shall not [be] abridged on my part till the year of [MS torn] 1833, and you shall, moreover, be the arbiter between us. Do not then, Dearest, deny me the high pleasure of presenting you on my return from Charleston the first week in March.

I have kiss'd that "modest ring," the pledge of a highly-prized affection o'er and o'er again, and now thro' it salute you with my best, warmest, purest love.

[1] Addressed: Charleston, S.C.

John Cheesborough[1] to Elizabeth Frances Blyth

Charleston 12th January 1836

DEAR AUNT   Father is slowly recovering from his long and violent illness. He believes that a voyage to Europe early in the spring, there to remain untill fall will be the surest means of restoring him to permanent health. He has determined that I am to accompany him. I am desirious of turning all my little means into money to vest in Cotton in the hope of making something by it and to vest the proceeds in merchandize to bring back with me. The principal one of my resources for raising money is by the sale of York, whom Father bought from Cousin William for me last winter. I am unwilling to sell him to any one so that he cannot occasionally see his family. I can obtain a high price for him to go to the Western country, but I am willing to sell him to you for several hundred dollars less so that he may be with his family. I am anxious that you should buy him and am willing to take from you $1,000 for him. He is well supplied with tools, as you are so well acquainted with him it is useless for me to say any thing about his character or qualifications as a carpenter. Father will give you a Bill of Sale of him if you determine on taking him.[2]

Robert M. Allan[3] to Robert F. W. Allston

Charleston 6th January 1837

DEAR SIR   When I was in treaty for the 17 Negroes offered me by Messrs. Jervey Waring and White,[4] they wished me to go up to Pee Dee and look at them. I told them it was impossible for me to leave home just now, [that I would] take the Negroes provided they answered the description. Mr. White informed me this morning that he had seen them, and that they did answer that description. If that be the case (and I do not at all question it) you may send them down whenever you please. In order however, to prevent all difficulty, I will give you the idea I have formed of them, and what I expect them to be. In the first place, where the age has been given, without any remarks, the Negro is supposed to be prime. The only one in that list opposite whose name a remark has been made, is "Jacob, 24 prime and ready, but has lost one thumb by bursting of a gun." The injury being from the bursting of a gun, the presumption is that it is his left hand, and that he is therefore able both to use a hoe, and to pick cotton. [MS. torn] on the list is put down at 40, if he does not exceed that age, he is still prime; the eldest of the children at 12, if not younger, she will very soon be able "to take the

---

[1] Son of J. W. Cheesborough of the factorage firm of Cheesborough and Campbell.

[2] York was purchased by Mrs. Blyth (see below p. 382).

[3] Allan was a Charleston factor and the brother of Allston's sister-in-law, Mary Allan Allston.

[4] A Charleston firm of auctioneers and brokers.

field," and even now, will be serviceable in picking cotton. These are the only points upon which a difficulty can possibly arise; and as I said before I do not apprehend any. But after I have seen them should they not answer my expectation, I propose to leave it to arbitration, I choose a friend, and Mr. White, if you will, shall act for you, should they agree, the matter is settled. Should they disagree, they shall have power to call in a third person, whose decision shall be final. If again [MS torn] be at your option either to annul the contract, or to deduct such amount as the arbitrators shall deem correct. I regret the impossibility of my leaving home, but although I do not anticipate the slightest difficulty, have thought it best for all parties, to put you in possession of my views before the Negroes are shipped.[1]

Jervey, Waring, and White to Robert F. W. Allston

Charleston Jany 24, 1837

Sir   Mr. Robert Allan has notified us, that as it has become indispensable to a completion of the Contract, he should go up to inspect the Negroes, or take them according to the Statement furnished, the former, as he States, being unable to do, he declined the purchase of your Negroes it is extremely mortifying to us, that this matter has thus terminated. We hope that in the course of the transaction, nothing has occurred to impress you with the opinion, that we have been otherwise than attentive to your interest we should be glad to be informed, if it be your desire, that we continue our efforts to effect a Sale.[2]

Mary Allan Allston to Elizabeth Frances Blyth

Sylcope Janry 30th 1837

.   .   .   .

Perhaps my dear Aunt, you may have heard that my Brother Robert was in treaty for our people. Mr Campbell after hearing from Brother concluded on Friday last with my Brother for them, he is to give $725 round; in fact it is the only offer we have had for them, I feel truly grateful to God

---

[1] The following note in Allston's hand appears on this letter:

"Jany 13th

"In a personal interview sought by Mr. Allan I stated that I would not leave to arbitration a matter on which my mind was already made up viz, I had determined to sell those negroes at a given price. If therefore they were sent from my plantation at his instance, they were his negroes at that price which was agreed on between him and Jervey Waring and White. It was at his option to see them on the plantation. He had declined doing so. If he desired to be off the bargain and Messrs. J. W. and W. were willing to release him, they had my full consent, but the matter of treaty with him was in their hands." See letter following.

[2] Apparently, Allan had decided to purchase instead a larger group of Negroes belonging to the estate of Joseph Waties Allston. See letter following.

my dear Aunt for the Sale, but at the same time it has caused me great uneasiness for I very much fear still, that he has been induced to give so high
a price merely from their having been ours; I believe I mentioned to you,
that he spoke when at Waverly of doing so; to which I was very much
opposed, for you well know my dear Aunt, my objections, to having money
matters with Relations, and should it turn out a bad speculation I shall feel
it; but I have been induced to yield to the opinions of my Friends, and may
our heavenly Father of his great mercy grant, that it may prove of advantage to both parties. You must excuse this hurried scrawl my dear Aunt,
but it is the first opportunity we have had since I knew of the Sale being
positively concluded on and the affectionate interest you have always
taken, in any thing relating to our dear Boys[1] made me anxious to inform
you of it as early as possible; though I cannot yet say when we shall be at
Waverly, as my dear Brother does not yet know when they will be sent up
for, and I do not wish to be there when the People leave, the making up
my mind to the sale, has been trial enough for me, the hope that it is for the
best supports me, and when I reflect how much lessened the debts of my
dearest Friend will be I feel perfectly resigned, for oh what agony would it
cost me, did I think that any one should suffer from him, one who was so
much respected and beloved during life. . . . .[2]

Carroll and Porter to Robert F. W. Allston

Charleston 22 March 1837

DEAR SIR,   We have been instructed by Mr Wm. Mikell to inform you by
letter that the Negro Girl named Letty purchased by him from you as
Exor Mary P Jones[3] a short time since, has proved to be unsound. She has
been examined by Dr Dill of Edisto who gives it as his opinion that she is
really unsound and that the injury arose from her confinement some years
ago. The Girl is incapable of working and says that she has been attended by
several physicians for her disorder. Under these circumstances Mr Mikell
expects that as there has been a failure of the implied warranty arising from
the sound price he gave for the Negro the purchase money will be refunded
upon the return of the Negro.

Should you decline taking her back and refunding the money, Mr Mikell
instructs us to inform you that he will feel himself obliged in justice to himself
to put her up for sale at auction at the risk of the Estate of Mrs Jones.

You will oblige us by giving us as early information as may be convenient
of your view of this matter.[4]

[1] Joseph Blyth and William Allan, sons of the writer by her late husband, Joseph
Waties Allston.

[2] For further details concerning this sale see below, pp. 384–86.

[3] Allston's sister, the late Mrs. William H. Jones, whose estate he was settling.

[4] See below, pp. 69, 73, 385, 387.

James L. Petigru to Robert F. W. Allston

Charleston 15 Apl 1837

MY DEAR ALLSTON, I suppose Mr White communicated to you what I said to him about the negro that Mr Mikell wishes you to take back. Dr Jervey's certificate throws doubt upon the question; he does not consider her unsound, because her disease is curable. But that opens the door to the whole contest, as to what does or does not constitute unsoundness. As regards horseflesh there is a vast contrariety of opinions, some judges holding that every sickness or defect almost is ground to rescind a sale, others that nothing short of some constitutional, radical infirmity will answer the purpose. Then again if Judges would agree Juries cannot and the whole subject is one of the greatest uncertainity. In these circumstances possession of the fund is of course a great advantage. If Mikell sells the negro at your risk, the most politic thing you can do is to induce the overseer that wanted her at first to buy her now, and give 5 or 600 for her. If she was to sell for anything of that sort the presumption would be almost conclusive that the difference of price is owing altogether to the fall of negroes, and that the plaintiff has sustained no injury. I advise you to lose $100, rather than run the risk of losing more, and to agree with the overseer, that he shall run her up 100 dollars further than he is willing to go, and that you will pay him the difference. . . . .

George A. Trenholm[1] to Robert F. W. Allston

Charleston April 18, 1837

SIR—I had this day the honor of receiving your respected favor of 15th inst. and without pretending to any extraordinary Skill in Banking, shall have much pleasure not only now, but at all times, in a free interchange of views with you, on the subject of your little protegé at Georgetown.[2]

I esteemed very highly the honor of forming your acquaintance at Georgetown, though I did not know whether I was at liberty to think, that it would also be my peculiar good fortune to harmonise perfectly with you, in our respective official relationships to the Bank. There was one ground upon which I was sure however, that we should always meet, I mean that of being, both of us, entirely disinterested in our views. Of this you shall be better persuaded perhaps by and bye, than I can expect you to be at the present moment, since it is very well known that there have been Several Candidates for the Agency of the Bank at Charleston who could not possibly be influenced by any other considerations than those of pecuniary emolument. On this Score however I believe that my House occupies a

---

[1] George A. Trenholm (1807–76), member of the Charleston firm of John Fraser and Company, later secretary of the Confederate States treasury.

[2] Probably the Bank of Georgetown, incorporated December 21, 1836.

position that is perfectly impregnable, in placing the administration of the affairs of the Bank in the hands by which they are now guided, we have accomplished the *only object* which we ever had in view. That we should assume the Agency, was a Condition made with us by the friends whose influence we wielded and we shall to the extent of our ability fulfil the duties we have assumed. But, if our intercourse with the Board shall prove of a character not entirely agreeable to our feelings, or, should the arrangements for the Agency here not prove in every respect perfectly honorable for ourselves, we shall not hesitate one moment as to the step to be taken, but tender at once our resignation to the Board. With the feelings which we entertain for its members individually, of respect and Esteem, and (allow me to add for myself) for no individual there more highly than yourself, this course would be painfully unpleasant to us, but I feel very well assured, that you would yourself be the first to justify us, should we take such a step from feelings of proper pride and self respect.

I discard the thought as much as possible and hope no such emergency shall occur, but if it do, our friends here, who are large holders of Stock would probably be desirous of selling and as it would be in any event our primary object to retain the present administration in office, I would have much pleasure in tendering to you and your friends the first offer of their Stock, indeed I would be disposed in that case to make much better terms for you than for others, so that our present friends might continue to wield the destinies of our little Bank.

I find that I have detained you much longer upon points merely personal to myself, than I am at all justified for having done and therefore throw myself upon your indulgence without attempting an apology.

I now see for the first time and appreciate your motives in desiring an interview between the Board and myself when at Georgetown and regret very deeply having lost an opp[ortunit]y which I now see I might have improved to the manifest advantage of our united interests. I am familiar with the management of the Branch of the Bank of the State at Georgetown and there is no other comment upon its policy necessary than merely to point to the deserted building which it lately occupied.[1] You are entirely and perfectly correct; if the new Bank is to tread in the Steps of the old, its career will terminate precisely where that of the old Bank terminated, the attempt will be abandoned as unprofitable, you say that yr. experience does not suggest the remedy; I think I can give you a simple test, before which all difficulties in the administration of our affairs, will vanish. It is this, to apply every proposition coming before the Board to yourself personally and decide for us (the Stockholders) as you would for yourself. There is not the slightest shadow of difference between our interests as a

---

[1] The Branch of the Bank of the State of South Carolina at Georgetown was closed in 1833 and its business thereafter conducted through an agency.

Bank and yours as an individual. Let us try an example. I will take for instance your *third* proposition, to *wit*, that for the accommodation of the Agricultural portion of the Community 1/4 or even 1/3 of the Capital might safely (I notice however that you don't add here "and profitably") be invested in Bonds duly Secured by Mortgages and on 1, 2 and 3 Years credit and this to be banked on as usual.

Now ask the question of yourself, as an individual knowing your own interests (I presume here of course that you are following the profession of a Banker) wd. you deem such a disposition of your funds desireable? Would you deem it safe or prudent when exposed to daily or hourly calls from your *creditors* to place your *debtors* in a position that would absolve *them* from any demand at all for 1, 2 or 3 Years and then perhaps be amenable only to a tedious suit at law? And what profit would the Bank derive from such an operation? If the Stockholders were desirous of investing their Capital in Bonds and Mortgages what possible necessity could there be for obtaining a Charter for this purpose? A Charter too at an expense of 2 1/2% of their Capital to begin with, and then the expense of a Banking House and sala-ried Officers, all for the purpose of having that done through an expensive Agent which every man could have done for himself without difficulty and without expense. Suppose the Capital all lent out on Bonds and Mortgages, at 7 pr Cent Int. what would the Stockholders get? We have already agreed to give away in Salaries alone 2 per cent on the Capital, consequently the Stockholders could not in that case get more than 5 per Cent for their money. Now, if it wd. prove unprofitable and impolitic for the whole Capi-tal, it cannot be profitable or proper for any part. It is Contrary to the very Spirit of Banking to lend out money on Bonds and Mortgages, I notice that you add "and this to be *banked* on as usual." Here lies the difficulty, there is no possible way in which a sum of money so locked up can be made to yield more than the naked 7% charged to the Borrower. If the Bank has $20,000 of specie in its vaults, you may issue 60,000 of Bills, which at 6% int. is equal to 18 per cent on the amount of specie Capital, and this may be done with safety, only by discounting *short* and available paper, which by constantly recurring gives the Bank an opportunity of Collecting its funds regularly and replacing its specie as fast as it may be displaced by the return of its Bills. If on the Contrary the Bank lend $20,000 for instance on a Bond Mortgage and pay out its Bills, should Specie be Immediately drawn out for the Bills, there is an end of that transaction until (in all probability) the expiration of the Charter and the appointment of our friend Mr. Coachman to wind up our Concerns. I think I hear you ask if the Planting interest is not to be accommodated at all? That is a question that it is unbecoming in me to offer a reply to. In Charleston the Banks refuse all accommodation to those who have not Bank credit to sustain, a Country note for instance must have on it a City name, the name of a

Merchant who must pay it up by 2 O'Clock on a given day or *fail*. My House has always furnished in this way to its friends the accommodations necessary for ordinary purposes. To furnish actual *Capital* to be invested in real Estate, is generally deemed impolitic and unsafe for a Banking Institution, no matter what class of the Community may be the borrower, it is in fact compelling the Stockholder to invest his money in real Estate against his inclination, the property is bonafide his and the Speculation in a great measure made at his risk.

I believe it may be laid down as an axiom in Banking as conducted in this Country that it is intended, not to furnish Capital to those who have not any, but to those who have, to furnish the *means* of *anticipating* the *returns* of their Capital, if you ask in what way this rule may be practically applied in the course of business the answer is obvious, it is by discounting for the Merchant and anticipating the payment of such Notes etc. as have accrued to him in the ordinary Course of trade. The Safety of the Stockholder necessarily requires that in every instance two names of undoubted responsibility should appear on every Note, and all such *business paper* should at maturity be paid up *in full*. The Banks in Charleston have fallen into the Custom of discounting accommodation paper, renewable every 60 days on paying 1/4 of the principal, which I am convinced is in some measure an Evil, be that as it may, yr board will doubtless do the same and I know of no hint I would give upon this point except that of looking with vigilance to the ultimate responsibility of all the parties to such paper. To irresponsible people, unless with most undoubted endorsers, there will not of course be any loans under any Circumstances whatsoever.

To foster the trade of Georgetown, to yield a reasonable accommodation to all classes of the Community under proper guarantees not only for *ultimate*, but *punctual* payment, I consider the primary objects of our Institution, the remuneration to the Stockholders must be derived from individual deposites (which I trust will be respectable) and from their Circulation, in extending which I hope we shall be able to make essential [illegible] here.

The Stockholders in Charleston are of opinion that with a little caution the Circulation may be pushed to $400 M with a specie line of $200,000 making an aggregate of 600,000 with the Capital. They anticipate that the resources of the Bank would exceed the legitimate wants of Georgetown and having furnished nearly the whole Capital they wished to have a respectable portion employed here, in profitable Exchange operations, in maintaining a City Circulation, in availing of opportunities to push it into the interior, and in furnishing the Bank at Georgetown with City funds by means of which its Bills when presented at Georgetown could be redeemed by Checks upon Charleston without paying out Specie.

I wished to give a prompt reply to your Enquiries and have thrown my views together with very little order or arrangement I fear. I trust to yr.

indulgence in this respect. I find I have been voluminous though I wished to be brief and in Endeavouring to be so, have hardly perhaps displayed all the Courtesy towards you that I *feel*. I beg you to believe therefore that all I have said is intended in a Spirit of entire respect and soliciting the favor of a line from you at any time when my services can in any manner be rendered acceptable.

Carroll and Porter to Robert F. W. Allston

Charleston 27 April 1837.

DEAR SIR, Mr White has informed us that Messrs Petigru and Lesesne have given their opinion against his receiving back the Negro Girl purchased by Mr Mikell from you as the Executor of the Estate of Jones. The two Physicians who examined the Girl on the part of Mr Mikell have given their opinion that she is thoroughly unsound; and Mr M. therefore feels himself perfectly justified in offering to return her. Should you therefore decline receiving her, we are instructed by him to give you notice that she will be sold at auction on Monday the 8th May and that he will bring suit for the difference between what he gave and what he realises from the sale.

You will be kind enough to inform us whether we may refer to Messrs Petigru and Lesesne or what other gentlemen of the bar, for an appearance to the Writ on your behalf.

R. W. Gibbes[1] to Robert F. W. Allston

Columbia May 20, 1837

DEAR SIR, I have lately determined to convert my Cotton plantation near Columbia, into a Stock Farm, and to try the experiment of Supplying Columbia with mutton etc. I have good pasturage, and as I intend to plant grain altogether, hope to have an abundance of food for Stock in the winter. I have procured some of the Tuscany Cattle from the Estate of John Middleton, as probably best adapted for our country, and feel anxious to get the Broad-tailed Sheep. John Hume who passed through our town a few days ago informed me that you have the full blood of that Stock. If so, perhaps you can spare me a few ewes and a ram, or if not, you can inform me where they are to be procured. Col. Hampton has the Leicester Stock lately imported, and has lost some of them, they are very fine looking large and round animals, and probably will do well, but I am disposed to think the Broad tailed the best for our climate. Our crops of Cotton look very badly, the prospect is of half a crop, there is such a poor stand. I had planted Cotton but ploughed it up and put in Corn, and intend to abandon Cotton and plant grain for the Columbia market. Will you do me the favor to write me

---

[1] Robert Wilson Gibbes (1809–66), prominent doctor and author of Richland District.

as early as is convenient and say whether you can dispose of a few of the Sheep, or inform me where I can procure them.

We have had a very healthy Spring, and the Doctors are doing nothing in our part of the Country.

Robert F. W. Allston to Mary Allan Allston

1st Oct. 1837

My Dear Sister, My fidelity to my brother's memory, and to the interests of his widow and children, you cannot suspect. But it is very apparent to me that you are far from approving of my management (such as I deem'd best) of my brother's Estate, in which you are chiefly interested. So far, indeed, from approving, I cannot doubt any longer, you are offended by it.

Regarding therefore, my continued connection with that Estate as tending to the prejudice of those interests, which I would preserve, as tending too, to engender in the hearts of my nephews, as well as to cultivate in yours, such sinister feelings towards me as might disqualify me from rendering them any future service should they need it, and which I would not, for countless wealth, have to exist, I have determined to withdraw from the management as soon as the Court of Equity will release me from the Executorship which I have assumed.

To enable me to present my application to the Court with the least probability of denial; I beg leave to suggest, that you, individually, assume the payment of the remaining debts of the Estate, in which suggestion, if you concur, have the goodness to sign, with me, the enclosed instructions[1] to Mr. Dunkin. I have overcome my reluctance to make the proposition by the following considerations, 3d That these debts, which in 1834 amounted to somewhere about $50,000 (Fifty Thousand dollars) are now reduced to $32,531.17 (Thirty-two thousand five hundred and thirty one $\frac{17}{100}$ dollars) against which as an offset, you will hold Bonds and notes to the amount of about $16,500 (Sixteen thousand, five hundred dollars) which will reduce the actual debt to $16,000 or thereabouts. I here assume that the balance of the last years crop on hand, together with the Tolls of the Mill 'till January next, will be sufficient to pay Mr. Kidd the Millwright and all outstanding expenses of the Mill so that, to pay $16,000 of debt and the expenses of your family, you will have a new and valuable Mill unincumber'd and capable of yielding, from Toll, Two Hundred (200) barrels of Rice pr annum, and a plantation[2] of 250 acres of Tide-swamp with negroes (enough to work it according to the plan which I had arranged, viz planting 1/3 (80 or 90 acres alternately) every year, leaving uncultivated the Mill-pond) capable of making, one year with another, Two Hundred (200) barrels more = 400 barrels which @ $15 a barrel are worth $6,000 nett pr. annum.

---

[1] Missing.   [2] Waverly.

2d. For the 2 that when after these debts shall have been paid you are the residuary and sole Legatee for Life.

1st. As you were so dissatisfied with my management of the negroes on the plantation, I should have but little hope of succeeding with any counsel I might give respecting the education of the children.

You will observe that I have not taken into calculation the debt ($4,000) due by Mr. Campbell.[1] The course which I suggest will be recommended to you by other considerations, which will, no doubt, occur to you. One of the most obvious of which is, that we will be enabled thus to close the business of *the Estate*, after which it will be conducted altogether in *your own name* and you can employ such agent precisely as will suit you. You reside on the plantation in winter and quite near to it in summer, and will, I doubt not, do it that justice which it deserves at your hands.

I can only say further that I shall be happy ever to render to you or the children, such assistance as I am able, with counsel or otherwise, should it be acceptable.

I shall continue the management as usual until the change suggested above has been effected, which, I trust, will be done in all the month of January.

With best wishes for your prosperity and happiness.[2] . . . .

Isaac E. Holmes[3] to Robert F. W. Allston

Charleston Nov. 11th 1837

My Dear Sir—Yr letter directed to me at Flatt Rock, together with other letters from my friends, after taking a regular Tour through the states, have been deliverd to me in Charleston, so much for Amos Kendal's regulations! I regret extremely not having recd yr letter during the sitting of the Convention not only as it deprived me of the Proxies you entrusted to me, but as it prevented my corresponding earlier with you upon a subject deeply interesting to our State. As it respects the proceedings of the Convention, you may be informed by the publishd proceedings, a Copy of which, I herewith send you.[4] Now for my own private opinion.

You will perceive that Two important Resolutions have been adopted, 1st The Purchase of the Hamburg Rail Road, 2dly The Commencement of the line of Road toward Kentucky.

The first resolution is essential to the execution of the Work embraced in

[1] Alexander W. Campbell, who was the third executor of the estate. See below, pp. 384, 392, 394, 395, 399, 400.

[2] The difficulties referred to were evidently removed, for Allston continued to act as executor long after the death of his sister-in-law in 1841.

[3] Isaac Edward Holmes (1796–1867), member of the United States House of Representatives from South Carolina (1839–51).

[4] Missing. Probably the *Proceedings of the Stockholders of the Louisville, Cincinnati and Charleston Rail Road Company . . . . at Flat Rock, North Carolina on the 16th October, 1837.*

the second (the Reasons given by Chancellor Harper in his report will convince you of this). But the execution of the second I greatly doubt, both as to its practicability and its utility—if you have read Col Gadsen's letter, you will see the reasons fully set forth. There is no necessity to spend 20,000,000 Dlls to pass the Mountains when by an Union with Georgia Rail Road Companies we can reach the Tennessee River and thus the Ohio. The Delegation at the Convention from Kentucky, was composed of two Gentlemen only. *This* was sufficient to convince me that Kentucky lookd upon the enterprise with indifference. North Carolina has subscribed comparatively nothing and Tennessee thus far very little. In a word, So Ca has subscribed 4 Million 700 Thousand, whilst the rest of the States interested in the work have subscribed only 600 Thousand. What follows; Why! That we ought to apply our own resources to our own Works. Buy the Hamburg Road, unite with the Georgians. Bring into our State the Cotton of Georgia and North Alibama. Transport from the Muscle Shoals on the Tennessee whatever of Flour, Meats and so forth, Ohio, Tennessee and Kentucky may be disposed to send us. I find my paper out, so must stop.

Robert Nesbit[1] to Robert F. W. Allston

Waccamaw Decbr 26, 1837

DEAR ALLSTON   I have Just been informed by Driver Cudjos wife that he Cudjo was murdered last Night by the men on Waverly Plantation they run him through the Mill pond with a boat and overtok him and then comitted the deed he was found on the Bank to Day. I have been a hunting all day and have informed you as soon as I heard it my self they thretten his wifes life likewise but she is within my Premises Yours in haste.

Robert F. W. Allston to Elizabeth Frances Blyth

Saratoga 11th July 1838

MY DEAR AUNT,   I[t] gave both Adelle and myself the sincerest pleasure to receive your letter of the 29th June at this place. We were glad that you had reach'd the Sea shore in safety and trust that you will pass the summer in comfort.

The account of your visit to Canaan and your description of the forlorn appearance of the place excited in us both the deepest emotion, it brought forcibly to mind that distressing summer when you so kindly and with great sacrifice of habitual comfort, came to us there, and bore with us a large share of our troubles and our trials.

Your unmerited kindness towards me and mine together with the great and continued forbearance and indulgence which you have shown to me, has, in a measure, unfitted me for mingling with the world. And it takes a month or two after leaving home before I can realise to myself that I and

[1] A neighboring planter.

mine are in fact no more to the rest of the world than any other body who may happen to come in its way.

We are drinking the waters of Congress Spring with some effect now, 'tho for several days Adelle did not take to it kindly and Rob to this day will not take more than one mouthful, puts down the tumbler and turns his back upon it saying "me dont—want—bad—water." I gave him a ride this morning on a little circular pleasure Rail-Road that is on the hill just above the Spring (ride three times round for seven-pence a piece) and he has promised in consequence to drink a full tumbler tomorrow. He is not well this day or two and I am the more anxious that he should drink the waters. Ben drinks it very readily. He takes one tumbler, A[dele] takes 4 and I 4, sometimes 6 before breakfast beginning at 6 O'clock the rides about the village are pleasant but horse-hire is so high that we do not go about much, there is a fine court-yard attach'd to the house (Congress-Hall) at which we stay, where the children are enabled to run about and play in the shade all day, they have a swing among the trees and there are several other children of several nations and they are very happy. Little Sis. is as fat and lively as she well can be, not a tooth has yet made its appearance, she is very strong and is improving much. I thought at first that the waters did not agree with my wife, her nerves and muscular system are still very unstrung, the day we came up the Hudson the day was hot, and the boat somewhat crowded, she was so much fatigued that I was induced to stop a day at Albany to rest. I am in hopes now tho' that if she will continue to take it regularly it will prove beneficial, with this view I think of remaining a week longer. If A[dele] is then strong enough we will go to the Falls of Niagara. There are a number of persons here but the houses are not at all crowded yet. People come here from all and every region of the country and of every description of character, a family from Philadelphia named McCauley have been very polite in giving us their card and requesting to be informed "when we reach that City." We will not be there till October, when on my way home.

Every body here travels by steam either rail-road or steam boats. Horses are not near as plenty as they used to be when the stages were used. I wish to get a pair when going home, they are however some what cheaper.

I am glad to learn that Sister and her children are well pray give our united love to them. I trust that you may all enjoy this summer that degree of health which is so necessary to comfort. I am gratified too at your account of the crops. I hope to hear by next letter that Mr. Kidd is making his alterations at the Mill. Your letter was forwarded by Mr Laffan from N. York, direct there as usual whenever you are able to bestow an hour on us. A[dele]'s best love and both the boys blessing Rob says "I wish Aunty hab heap cake." I have been obliged to restrict him a day or two past. God bless you, Dearest Aunt. . . . .

John A. Allston to Robert F. W. Allston[1]

Break Water 26th Augt. 1838

DEAR COUSIN,   The prime object of this letter will be explained by two numbers of the Georgetown Union[2] which I invelope and direct to you herewith   the call made by a voter of Prince George Winyaw Was to get Mr. Middleton out which you will see in the last paper has been effected and that too in the Way I at first anticipated. Noncommittal, a writer above him in the Same paper, and whom I believe to be the same man, calls for reasons for your political faith. This is sent for your inspection to determine under your own Judgement whether you deem it right to respond or not   You have still time enough to give a communication publicity before the election.

I am nursing a valuable and very ill field woman of mine today and days previous in a Malignant case of bowell complaint which has been rife on my place for a fortnight past, whilst I understand the neigbourhood is generaly healthy. Yr Place Mr. Ellis informed me today was quite so, our white vicinity is also injoying health   My own family intirely so.

You will of course expect something said of growing Crops. Yours I am told without yet seeing the whole of rice is reputed to be very promising. Provision is inferior. My own crop is fair, and the Rains now in great abundance, which may portend a Storm, but we must hope under god for a pass by this year haveing had so many last year.

. . . .

My Ideas are cramped today from thinking more of my sick than elsewhere or I might give you some local news not however of much interest. By way Dr. Heriot is fairly in the field in All Saints as a candidate, and I am realy affraid from all accounts may be left at home. Magill it is said is loosing ground as head of his clan, and if this is true Heriot will be opposed and beaten. The object has been to get J. W. Coachman again out which I think he will consent to on the Manifesto of Middleton. . . . .

Robert F. W. Allston to John A. Allston

New Port 5th Septr. 1838

DEAR COUSIN   Your letter of the 26th Ulto touching a call for my political faith by a writer in the "Union," I received yesterday on my way to this place. The numbers of the Paper which you were good enough to send me at the same time have not come to hand. I am at a loss therefore, as to the precise nature of the call upon me. It is enough however for me to know that any of the voters of Winyaw are in doubt respecting my political sentiments, and desire in good faith to ascertain them.

In a parish which I have represented in one or the other branch of the Legislature for the last ten years, it will scarcely be necessary for me to explain that my political creed is based on the principles of Thomas Jefferson,

---

[1] Addressed: New York, N.Y.   [2] Missing.

as express'd during the discussions in Virginia in 1798, and the subsequent canvass which resulted in his election as President in 1801. I adopted this creed some where about the year 1825 from a conviction of its virtue and purity, regarding the peculiar nature of our polity, and the character of the elements of this great Republic. Every year that I have lived since, has served, by its experience to confirm me in the belief that a plain, honest, common-sense reading of the Constitution is the only true one, and that in legislating for the government of the United States, nothing, absolutely nothing of authority should be allowed to precedent as such. The constitution itself should be studied as the best Text, and every public man, tho' he will have been benefitted by the commentaries of others, should illustrate his own practical commentary, by application of its principles to the cases as they come up before him. The Constitution of the U. S. declares that "nothing but gold and silver shall be made a legal tender," I believe therefore that gold and silver constitute the only legal currency of the United States; that is, the only currency which Congress have the right to impose and to regulate. For facilitating the commerce of life, Bank bills may become a part and the most considerable part of the currency by being notoriously and promptly convertible into gold and silver. But it is not in the power belonging either to Congress or the State Legislatures to make any citizen receive in payment for a debt due, the bill of any Bank, however constituted, no more than the note of hand of any one of the Directors of a Bank. The note of hand of a Director for $5, or for $500 may pass from hand to hand and be received in payment of debts, the drawer being known to be solvent and punctual, as long as it so passes it is a part of the circulating credits of the country is a component part of the currency, and is as good, for as far as the credit of the Drawer is recognised, as a Bank bill of the same amount.

I believe that Congress does not, and never did possess the right to incorporate a Bank of the United States, and as at present inform'd I would pronounce it inexpedient to confer such a right by an Amendment.

Not to speak of any merit which may be awarded by others to President Jackson, I believe that posterity will bless him more for preventing the recharter of the United States Bank than for any act of his administration. I would not be understood to approve, in the slightest manner, the measure by which he commenced his operations. But, for his veto against the Bank and for recommending a more frequent reference to the standard of value I would justify him with all my heart. I believe that in any country, it is wise to separate the business *of lending money* from the power *to create money*, else to supply the demand for lending to one portion of the community, more money might be created than might be consistent with the good of the whole, because it is notorious that the value of money, like every thing else bears an inverse ratio to its increase. New York would have entitled herself to the honor of furnishing the best paper currency and, at the same time the best

Banking System, if in her late Bank-Law, she had confined the character of the security to State Stock, and not allow'd the deposit of Bonds and Mortgages. The Law works thus, a certain number of stock holders associate for the purpose of Banking, in the city of Hudson, they appoint an agent who goes to the Comptroller and deposits with him by transfer $50,000 in public stocks and $50,000 in Bonds and Mortgages whereupon he receives $100,000 in Bills issued by the State of New York and made payable at the office of the association in the City of Hudson; which office is required always to have on hand in specie not less than 12 1/2 pr cent of the amount of its Bills in circulation.

From what has gone before you will readily understand how I am opposed to connecting the Government with Banks or Banking. Now I am in favor of an Independent Treasury furnishing a Standard (gold and silver coin) by which all paper-credits shall be valued, and leaving the regulation of exchanges in the hands of those whose business 'tis to deal with them. I am aware that the rate of exchange will not be as easy as it was under the management of the National Bank, but I think of this as a great statesman once said of Government, the wheels of Finance may run too easy and smooth, so much so as to make us *forget* that we are riding on wheels and liable to break down.

These are my views compress'd into a sheet of paper, they are written off-hand and dispatch'd without delay. Use them as you think best. Altho I might, with greater leisure be able to change their dress the principles would still be the same. With best wishes for yourself and kind remembrances for my friends. . . . .

Robert F. W. Allston to Rev. C. B. Thümmel[1]

New Port 12th Septr. 1838

SIR, Having heard of you from the Revd. Mr. Dumont of this place, as a gentleman in the habit of teaching, I take the liberty, without introduction, to apply to you on the subject, in which I am much and deeply interested.

If your present avocation does not preclude you, allow me to ask if it would suit you to take charge of a parish school in the lower part of the State of So. Carolina? If yes, Have the goodness to appoint a day certain, between the 28th Septr. and the 10th Octr. on which you will afford me an interview at Albany (Congress Hall) where I will explain further the locality and other circumstances, I shall be in New York, on my way South, at the time specified, and should it suit you as well to come there, I may be found at No. 7, Murray St.

Meantime I will say this much, the planters in the neighborhood of which

[1] Thümmel is described in testimonials submitted to Allston as a former student at the universities of Halle and Tubingen who had been teaching for some years in New York State. He accepted Allston's offer but does not appear to have remained long at his new post. See below, pp. 81, 86.

I write, have among them some 12 or 15 children of both sexes and various ages from 13 to 4 years old, whom they are anxious to have instructed at one school (the instruction heretofore has been private at their houses).

The education is to comprise the English in extent and thoroughly, the French language, Latin and Greek, Music and dancing they are willing to pay liberally for the time and services of one who pleases them entirely. Being actively engaged themselves, in their vocation out of doors, they require, as the instructor of their children one in whom full confidence can be placed in every regard.

The school will be chiefly under the supervision of the pastor of the parish, a young Englishman of good education, excellent temper and devoted to the interests of the protestant Episcopal Church of which he is a worthy clergyman.[1] A house will be furnish'd you among the settlements in winter and one on the Sea side during the Summer months. In a word it is a situation in which a teacher who will render himself both agreable and useful will have no cause to find fault with it, so far as the people are concern'd.

Have the goodness to write me in reply, and as soon as I hear from you, I will consult my friends at home respecting the appointment, before concluding the matter. With this view it is important that I know the inclination of your mind as soon as possible. . . . .

C. B. Thümmel to Robert F. W. Allston

Clinton, Oneida Co. N.Y., Septbr 18th 1838

D SIR, Your favour of the 12th inst. came to hand yesterday, and, according to your request, I hasten to answer it without delay. The offer, contained in your letter, of my taking charge of a parish school in the lower part of S. C. I have duly and maturely considered, and feel myself not disinclined to take charge of the Same, provided that, at the proposed interview, we shall, as I doubt not, be able to arrange every thing to our mutual satisfaction. One or two things I ought perhaps to mention respecting myself to prevent any misunderstandings. They are these, that I am a German by birth and education, but have for the last twelve years resided in this State, and for the last ten years been actively engaged in teaching; further, that I am a married man, with 3 children, and lastly, that Music and dancing, two of the branches mentioned in your letter, are accomplishments, which I do not profess to teach. Perceiving from your letters that you design to consult your friends at home respecting the appointment before concluding the matter I have deemed it best, to mention to you Tuesday, the 9th of October as the day, on which, if life and health are spared I will meet you at Albany, for the purpose of definitely arranging this business. I should be happy to say, that I would meet you at New York but the expenses of visit-

---

[1] Alexander Glennie (1804–80), a native of Surrey, England, who was for many years rector of All Saints Parish. The school was known as the All Saints' Academy.

ing that city being rather more than my purse will warrant at present, connected with circumstances of a domestic nature, have induced me to decide on Albany as the place of interview. Should anything particular, of which I know not at present happen, to prevent me from meeting you at the appointed time and place, I shall, of course, take the earliest opportunity of notifying you of the same by letter, and I hope that in case you should wish an earlier day for meeting me, or otherwise desire to communicate to me by letter previous to our personal meeting, you will favour me with your commands, as a few days previous notice will sufice me so to arrange my affairs here, that I may leave home for a few days.

Robert F. W. Allston to Elizabeth Frances Blyth

Boston 25th Septr. 1838

My Dear Aunt, Being very much engaged the last day of our stay at New Port, Adelle wrote instead of my replying to your last letter of the 7th, the next day we took the stage at 9 O'clock and drove through the Island, a most charming ride by the way, and went to Taunton where the Rail Road took us up at 1/2 past 4 and brought us to Boston by 7. I had engaged lodgings previously, so that we experienced no inconvenience from being late in arriving; but as you say, the boarding is very high. The day after getting here I rode out with Mr. Rogers in his chaise to see Uncle Washington who received me very kindly. I went to the house first (a small brick house in Cambridge port) and was there received by his wife a middle aged, sedate, very respectable looking lady, after sitting a little while she advised us to walk to his painting room if we desired to see Mr. Allston.[1] We did so, this was about 1 O'clock, and found him just warming his room (the weather was a little chilly and quite damp) with a coal fire-place and a stove previous to commencing his days work, tho he had just finish'd his segar, he brush'd a place for my hat (for every part of the room was cover'd with dust, as if it had not been swept in 12 months) drew a chair to the fire-side and commenced again. After some conversation he said "I must shew you something but I have nothing but sketches," he accordingly shew'd me several heads which he kept for his own study, and at length pull'd out from the apparent rubbish the sketch of a storm and shipwreck at sea, very spirited, his seas are always fine, and another Titania's Court, one of the most beautiful conceptions that I ever saw. He then invited me to dine with him in his own way on tuesday (to-day) "at 4 O'clock" said he "you had better come, my ordinary dinner hour is 7, for I like to work up all the day-light before I dine." He then sits up with his friend if he have one and his segar till 1 or 2 in the morning.

He is grown much older since I saw him and lost much flesh, his head is

---

[1] Washington Allston (1779–1843) was Robert's half-uncle. His second wife, to whom reference is here made, was Martha, the sister of Richard Henry Dana.

quite white and venerable, but his noble countenance is placid, mild, and intelligent as ever. Yesterday he call'd here, but unluckily we had gone to ride to the navy yard and Mount Auburn. After dinner his wife call'd to see Adelle, and set a few minutes, she goes with me to dinner.

The drive to Mount Auburn yesterday was a most delightful one. It is a piece of ground of 60 acres about 5 miles from town, which a charter'd company have bought, and keep in delightful order as a burial place. No graves are suffer'd to be dug now in the city; and this place is laid out in beautiful gravel'd walks and serpentine paths among the woods, all along which you see the most expensive and fine-looking monuments to the dead and vaults for burying, the whole is kept very clean and neat by men who are paid for it. The monument on Bunkers Hill is not yet finish'd. We have had several days of bad weather since coming here and as the sun has been crossing the Line, I am afraid that you have had a bad storm at home which must have very much impeded the harvest, if it has not destroyed a part of it. I hope for the best tho.

The children are quite well, and send howdye for you and the boys. A[dele] unites with me in affectionate love to you and sister. The provision crops have been cut short by drought at the North as well as in the South, so I suspect we shall have to live on Rice next summer. . . . .

[P.S.] We go to New York again tomorrow.

Joshua J. Ward[1] *to Robert F. W. Allston*

Brook Green Septr. 28th 1838

DEAR ROBERT Immediately on the receipt of your favour of the 14 inst. (from which I was happy to learn that you were all well) I saw Magill and Heriot on the important subject of the Parish School, they appeared much pleased at the intelligence from you and hoped that you would be able to succeed in engaging the Gentleman and Lady you speak of provided you find on your interview with him that he will suit us and that his Lady teaches music and I am authorized to say that you can offer him $2000. We presume he will be able to get the house at Woodville for his winter residence which we will have to make habitable for him and build a house some where on the Beach for the Summer; give him to understand that he will have to take Boarders.

Miss Catonnett leaves me in November; if you cant succeed in getting a Gentleman and Lady for the Parish, I wish you would have the goodness to look out for just such a Lady as you think will suit me to take Miss C's place and if you can find one write me on the subject.

We have had for the last week very bad harvest weather; rain nearly every day and Oh my fine big rice at Long Wood has been in all of it; and

[1] Addressed: New York, N.Y. Joshua John Ward (1800–1853), proprietor of Brookgreen plantation.

such a litter left in the field you never saw, however today the sun shines on us and I trust for the remainder of the harvest we will get along better; I cant tell you how your crop is, for I have not seen it, but Oliver was over here a little time back when I took him around my Main fields which is fine Rice, the best I have, he said he thought it good for 75 bushels and that it was the best Rice he had seen this year excepting Col. Robert Allstons reclaimed fields; I hope you will succeed in getting a pair of Horses; have you seen any of Colts patent repeating rifles if you have and think favourably of them I wish you would get me one with equipment etc. complete. Doctor Hasell begs you will do the same for him, send them both to Robertson and draw on him for the same.

We have been so far quite healthy in our Parish Mrs. Ward joins in Kind regards to Mrs. Allston.

Abram Cruger to Robert F. W. Allston

Princton N.J. Oct 8th 1838

DEAR SIR   Your favor dated Oct 3rd was not recd. untill Saturday evening last and as there is no mail passes through this place between Saturday and Tuesday morning I have deferred writing untill to day, and shall in reply endeavour to give you a particular and correct description of my horses. They are dark *Yellow Bays* with each a Small Star, no other white except on one foot of the off horse (or rather between the hoof and fetlock) their feet are all black, they are 15 hands 3 inches high, short perhaps 1/4 inch but will measure that full at 6 yrs old, the off horse is rather the coarsest and heaviest boned, they are both large in the arm and chest with a clean flat leg, they are smooth in the hip, tails large and bushy and natural carriage good, they are a pair of round bodied, heavy quartered, quick, active Horses, they were both sired by Alexander, an Imported full *bred English Hunter,* they are *Sound, Kind* and free from *blemish*, all which I am willing to warrant, and can satisfy you as to my responsibility. As to speed, I do not like to speak positively, as I do not wish to represent any thing to you that is not strictly true, I can say however they are good travellers and can I think travel from 10 to 12 miles in an hour with ease, they have been driven but little on the road since I have had them together, having purchased one of them about three months since and he had scarcely been off the Farm where he was raised before I purchased him, they have been used by me principally upon the Farm, to the Plough, Harrow, Waggon etc to give them sufficient exercise and render them kind and gentle. I have on one occasion drawn them about 40 miles and they performed the last five miles of their Journey with as much spirit and life as they did the first and am satisfied I can reccommend them as great bottomed Horses and good performers, they are in fine condition, with flesh sufficient to appear well on for any use, but Sir I can assure you they have never been bitted or pampered in any way, you will see them just as nature formed them. I am not a proffessed horseman my business is Farming and as the various operations of my Farm require my constant and unremitted attention I have not the conveniences or time if I had the experience, to prepare Horses for the Market like those who make it their business. I have no doubt that in a horsemans hands there is great improvement to be made both in their appearance and their Speed. In short I have advertised them as a Superior pair of Colts and in doing so I have only expressed the opinion of every man who has seen them. I live in a retired situation 3 miles from Princeton and have not offered them any where, I have held them at $600, and did not like to take less, but as winter is approaching and it is out of my line of business I will take $550, rather than take them to the City to look for a market.

I will meet you at Henry Smiths Tavern in New Brunswick on thursday of this week at 12 oClock (Noon) You may reach there by the N. J. Rail Road between 11 and 12 and depart by same route at 2. If the weather should prove *very stormy* I will meet you on the next fair day at same hour.

Robert F. W. Allston to Adele Petigru Allston

Columbia 9th Decr. 1838

MY DEAR ADELLE, ... The day after I had the satisfaction to hear also from Aunt Blyth, in her usual kind thoughtfulness. She is much troubled, poor old Lady, in consequence of the protracted illness of her overseer Mr. Thompson. I wish it was in my power to relieve her mind of its anxieties. My residence is too far from her plantation for me to serve her usefully in the management of it, unless she were to confide it to me altogether, and then, I fear, the negroes would continue to trouble her with complaints. Aunt writes me that the scarlet fever is still prevailing in Georgetown, which I regret very much.

To-day we have accounts of the destruction by fire, of Mr. B. Allston's Mill with much Rice. I fear the effect of this disaster on the mind of my poor old friend. The fire must have been owing to some straggling persons stopping near the Mill at night and carelessly leaving fire behind them. Tell Mr. Ellis to keep a sharp look-out for stragglers at Matanza and Waverly, and send them to Jail unless they can give a reasonable account of themselves. I would neither take nor urge any unusual measures of precaution about the house or the plantation, only he must be watchful of every body who comes and goes without unnecessarily asking questions.

Yesterday the new Governor, Mr. Noble,[1] was elected, and will qualify tomorrow until which time, I am sorry to find, he has postponed shaving his beard. He left the chair immediately on his election and Mr. Patterson[2] was chosen without opposition. . . . .

[1] Patrick Noble (1787–1840), lawyer of Abbeville District.

[2] Angus Patterson succeeded Noble as president of the senate.

Higham [?] and Company to Robert F. W. Allston

Charleston So Ca 13th Dec 1838

DEAR SIR   We are instructed by Miss Waring to enquire if you will purchase three of her servants which you know as formerly the servants of Mrs. Huger, viz:

Amy   38 years of age, pastry cook and House servant
Ella   17 "   "   "   her daughter House servant and field Hand
bought of Col. J Ward a year ago at $1000 and
Louisa 4 "   "   "   also a daughter of Amy; and please say what
price you would pay for them. Miss Waring feels under some obligations to make the first offer of them to your neighbour Col J. J. Ward, which I have done by this mail but she, intending to leave here for Savannah *this day week* and being anxious to dispose of them before she leaves, thought there would not be time allowed her to write to you *after* hearing from Col. Ward, should he decline the purchase. May we request the favor of your earliest reply.

Rice dull at $3 3/4–$4 5/8, Rough Rice 90–$1³, upland cottons 10–13 1/2 to 14, S[ea] I[sland] cottons 35–50. . . . .

Robert F. W. Allston to Adele Petigru Allston

Senate Chamber Columbia 15th Decr. 1838

MY DEAR ADELLE, ... Pray tell Mr Ellis to buy a few fat Hogs if they offer themselves, and tell James to make a good pen, floor'd and cover'd but open to the sun on the South side, for my Pigs, and do tell Howell not to feed the Calf on Rice flour. I have order'd up from Charleston some Hay for him, until that comes he must live on straw.

The weather has been finer than I ever knew it at Columbia. I hope we may not have the reverse of this when on the way home. Should the dry weather continue I contemplate a change of my course by going down through Pineville and across Lenud's ferry, as I shall have abundant time to make a visit to Aunt Blyth before Christmas.

I have much sympathy for poor Mr Thümmel in his inevitable embarrassment [MS torn] disappointment, at his inhospitable reception.[1] I hope that comfortable provision will eventually be made for his family, and trust that he will not hold me responsible for his comfort.

16th.   Thus far I wrote yesterday during an uninteresting discussion on the "Bill to prevent the carrying of deadly weapons about the person" between Judge Huger and Mr Gregg. As soon as this was ended I could no longer divert my attention from the business in course. The mail too did not go last night, tonight's mail I hope will take this to Georgetown in time for

[1] Probably on presenting himself to fill the teaching appointment mentioned above, p. 81.

your post on Wednesday. I am just from Church, had the pleasure to hear the Bishop preach, "Render unto Cesar, the things that be Cesar's and unto God the things that be God's." Confirmation was administer'd to some 12 or 15 persons among whom were Proff. Henry and another grey head and Mrs. Taylor and other women, the congregation however was small. Mr. Wm. Barnwell was again at this Church tho' he took no part in the service. Mr. Dawson from St John's Berkley is one of the most regular attendants at this Church during the Session. . . . .

L. M. Waring to Robert F. W. Allston

Charleston Decr. 26th 1838

MY DEAR FRIEND I have taken the liberty of sending Bob, without first knowing, whether it would be agreeable to you to have him until I return from Savannah, in April.

He is a complete house servant if he pleases, and hearing Hynes[1] was in very delicate health, thought Bob, would be useful to you, as well as an *accommodation* to me. I did not wish to gratify him by leaving him at a Hotel, since, he has left me, have discovered *some little dishonest acts*, which accounts for his being desirous of remaining in the City. I will then, request the favour of you, my friend, never to allow him to visit Georgetown, as his temptations there, will be great. Should he be at all in your way have the goodness to request Mr Robertson to send him in the Steam Boat to Mr William B. Bullock Savannah. I hope you will not trouble yourself in giving him clothing should he ask for any, I do assure you he is well supplied a new suit of Black never yet worn I gave him also money, for another pair of Shoes so that he should have no excuse to call upon you. . . . .

Robert F. W. Allston to Adele Petigru Allston

Columbia 12th Decr. 1840

MY DEAR ADELE I return'd to Columbia day before yesterday after an absence of a week and found your welcome letter of 1st here waiting my arrival, together with a host of others on various matters of business. These last I attended to immediately with the view to dispatch them before my mind should become re-engaged in the business of the Senate, and tis well I did so, for as soon as I took my seat again, I found the Senate deeply engaged in discussing the most interesting subjects, two of which had been prepared by my own Committees and none of which had been disposed of in my absence. One of these was my School Bill in which subject you know I have long been interested. Twas a Bill to establish the office of Superintendent of Free Schools, made as simple and isolated as it was in my power to make it,

---

[1] One of the Allston butlers.

but after a discussion which occupied the greater part of the day, it was defeated at 1/2 past 3 this afternoon. The State Treasury is at a low ebb and members are fearful to vote away any money lest they be call'd to account by their constituents.

This absorbing affair (which occupied me until 12 last night) disposed of, I am now seated in my little chamber with a quiet and contented mind to commune with you, and to express my gratification at receiving yesterday your letter of the 5th and this morning that of the 8th Inst, they reminded me of those sweet morning salutations from your own dear self, and I repeated them as the best substitute. Blessings on you my Love and on our little ones. I sincerely trust that, with Louise to cheer you, you will soon forget your cold and suffer it to pass away. You must not suffer your Sister to leave you 'till after Christmas, Porcher and Lesesne[1] will both be up about Christmas to take them all down and Susan will go up with Harriete. Write to Messrs. McNulty and Dozier for Raisins and what ever else you may wish and tell them to charge to my account. You must have mince-pies by all means. I recollected the omission of the candles when in town the other day, and sent a Box up, together with 6 lbs. of currants by the Schr. Matilda, Capt Chadwick, going to J. H. Allston's. My mistake was in sending these instead of raisins. I am sorry I did not know better.

I waited a day in Charleston to see Mr. Gallagher[2] who had gone up to Wiltown to preach on Sunday. It was a relief to my mind to have an interview with him and I was glad to find that it relieved him of much embarassment as to his future movements. He ask'd permission, which could not be denied him, to take a fortnight to make up his determination whether to go to W[il]town (which depends, it seems, upon the vestry hearing from the Seminary of Virginia to which they have applied) or to Georgetown, and attend the Pee Dee Church from there, if the latter be his course, he will be up by Christmas day. He looks much the same as when he left us. His wife is rather a showy woman, pretty and agreable, her sister appears to be more quiet and retired, they have a little boy just running across the floor. I feel very sensibly the awkwardness of his situation, tho' I am satisfied, as he seems to be, that it will have been for the best. During my flying visit I saw your brother twice. He had been to the Chatahoochee and found a bad crop and the overseer dead. He looks well as usual. Pray send 5 yds of white plains over to Kate Harriet's Mother.

[P.S.] You will look for me every day after the 23rd.

[1] Philip Johnston Porcher and Henry Deas Lesesne, husbands, respectively, of Mrs. Allston's sisters, Louise and Harriette. Lesesne was for some years a law partner of James L. Petigru.

[2] J. B. Gallagher, rector of Prince Frederick's Parish (1840–42).

W. H. Fleming to Robert F. W. Allston

Georgetown 19 March 1841

MY DEAR SIR   While in Geo Town I desired to purchase Louisa and her children the property of Mrs. Shackelford and to effect this I enquired of Mr Waterman who would be the advisers of Mrs. Shackelford, I was answered you would be. In the character therefore of the friend of Mrs. S. I address you and presuming from our early acquaintance you would act with that impartiality of doing to others that you would have them do to you, and trusting therefore that this conscientious feeling will have a respectfull attention in the ultimate decision of Mrs. S. and that she as well as yourself can learn from Mr Waterman my private reasons for this request. I will however assure you that I will not make Louisa or her children the Slaves of any human being, and though I am aware by the Laws of this State, they cannot be emancipated, yet any mode that can be adopted to make her condition free will be placed with confidence to your direction and advice. In an effort to contribute to the ultimate happiness of the persons the subject-matter of this communication I hope to be met with a feeling of philanthropy and not tax my purse to an amount to prevent the object I have in view. But let me assure you that I wish all that is fair and just and in saying so I leave this matter to the adjustment of my friend Mr. Waterman.

E. G. Shackelford to Robert F. W. Allston

January 3rd 1842

DEAR SIR   Your kind attention in calling last evening and advising me, has been much dwelt on and with grateful feelings I assure you, but reflect if you please again on the subject, the family is a valuable one, and to sell the Mother and 3 fine Children at the very reduced price that Servants now sell would not be justice to my Children, some time previous to my seeing you I had told Mr Waterman to know positively whether or not the sale would be made at $1600 the answer had not been received, if they can be purchased at that price and taken away would it not be better? and if the sale does not take place she must be humbled. Though I have not determined on what you concluded best, in this matter, withhold not in future your advice, were you to see the Children you would think it a pity to part with them for little or nothing.

Robert F. W. Allston to Adele Petigru Allston

Columbia 10th Decr. 1842

MY DEAR ADELE   Last night [your letter] reach'd me in which is express'd your disappointment at not hearing from me. Indeed my love, I regret deeply that you should have to connect with the recollection of your husband the idea of disappointment in any shape. But if you knew the excitement to which I have been subjected for the last week, you would be at no loss to understand the rapidity with which it has pass'd over my head.[1]

And if I had but something pleasing to say to you, I would write as often as I sleep. Sleepless nights have been my portion 3 nights out of the last six.

Your brother's accidental presence here was valuable to me beyond computation. For he could give, and he found, during the single day which he staid, occasion to give the true version of things, which was necessary to the understanding of my position, in quarters where I never visit.

The new Govr. qualified today, and now that my feelings are relieved by being beaten, which on all hands is ascribed to my pertinacious disclaimer, I can sleep; but the late strenuous effort to bring me out contrary to repeated protestations to the contrary, has thrown me among a number and kind of people whom I never have been in the habit of meeting heretofore. New relations you know are what I am not apt to form. But here I am launch'd upon a sea of political strife and placed in a most conspicuous position contrary to my will. God knows how I shall avoid the numerous snares which surround my post. I look to him for counsel and aid.

Judge Huger is here a candidate for the U. S. Senate. He is opposed by Mr. R. B. Rhett and Mr. Pickens, it is to fill the place of Mr Calhoun after the 4th March next.[2] The election will be a very close one, but I think and trust he will be chosen. . . . .

Henry D. Lesesne to Adele Petigru Allston

Charleston, December 19, 1842

. . . .

Mr. Petigru has been in Milledgeville the last 10 days. In his first letter to me from that place he speaks of Mr. Allston's course in regard to the Election of Governor, in terms so handsome, and in which I, and indeed every body, so fully concur, that I cannot refrain from giving you the extract. Harriette would send love to you and the children, but she has been in the arms of Somnus the last hour.

[1] Contrary to his wishes, Allston had been nominated at the last minute to oppose James H. Hammond in the election for governor and had received 76 votes against the latter's 83. The *Charleston Courier* on December 10 commented as follows: "Hammond is elected. R. F. W. Allston, it is thought, would have won the Executive Mantle, had he not risen in his place in the Senate, and, as I understand, said he was no candidate. His friends ran him, it is said, against caucus, dictation and domination, a close run." See also *Courier*, December 16, 17, and 22; *Charleston Mercury*, December 12 and 17; and Elizabeth Merritt, *James Henry Hammond* (Baltimore, 1923).

[2] The successful contestant was Daniel Elliott Huger (1779–1854), who remained a member of the United States Senate until 1845. Robert Barnwell Rhett (1800–1876) was at this time a member of the United States House of Representatives; in 1850 he succeeded Calhoun in the Senate. Francis Wilkinson Pickens (1805–69) was later (1860–62) governor of South Carolina.

THE EXTRACT

Our friend Allston covered himself with honor at Columbia by refusing the Government, because it was tendered to him at the last hour. It was a delicacy more remarkable than the merit to receive votes enough to elect one. The circumstance that the opposition fixed on him shows that he was considered a man of weight, and his firmness in insisting that he would not take advantage of what might be considered a hasty resolve, not accept a high office without having been regularly placed before the people, shows that he deserves the influence attributed to him. Altho' there was no management in it, yet it would have looked like an intrigue, and been easily misrepresented. And I am heartily glad that he resisted the tempting offer.

James L. Petigru to Robert F. W. Allston

Charleston 5 June 1843

MY DEAR ALLSTON . . . .

I remained at Columbia several days after you, did not leave it in fact till the 28th, and then went to Augusta but did not stay there long. Our friend Carson[1] has met I am told with a great loss. He hired Irishmen and had some beautiful embankment on an obscure stream which is called Back River, and when he settled with them the work came to 6000 Dollars. He was not surprised at this for he supposed he had 300 acres. Last week he got Quash Pinckney to survey it, and it turns out only 130 acres, which raises the price of the land without trunks or inside drains to 50 dollars per acre, over and above the first cost. 200 Dollars for land in high order and well settled would not at this rate be high.

P.S. I really think the less you go about the swamps, and the sooner you turn your back on the plantation the better.

James L. Petigru to Robert F. W. Allston

Charleston 25 August 1843

MY DEAR ALLSTON, Since I received your letter of the 18th I have not been able to make any progress in the history of Gideon Dupont. I have looked at the note 2 Ram. 206[2] and am much disposed to think it fabulous. The water culture of Rice must have been more or less understood from the beginning and the additions that were made to the stock of Knowledge among those who cultivated the grain, were likely to be the gradual results of experience, rather than the sudden accession of a discovery. Besides if Gideon Dupont did present a memorial to the Legislature in 1783 the his-

[1] William Augustus Carson, husband of Petigru's daughter, Caroline. The plantation was Dean Hall, on the Cooper River, now known as Cypress Gardens.

[2] I.e., David Ramsay, *The History of South Carolina* (Charleston, 1809), II, 206, where credit is assigned to Dupont for the introduction in 1783 of the water culture of rice.

torian should have referred to it, and not been content with the putting off upon us at second hand the reminiscencies of Judge Bee. I have in fact sought for the Resolutions of 1783 without being able to find them. In fact the Resolutions of those times were not put forth with the care that is observed now. There are a few Resolutions to the acts of 1784 But I could find only one complete copy of the acts of 1783, and that in the Charleston Library,[1] but not a single report or Resolution annexed. Probably the Clerk of the house or Senate could find the original papers; and if any such exist they would certainly be entitled to notice in a memoir on the subject of this planting.

The family of Gideon Dupont I cannot trace at all. Dr Du Pont whom you knew was the son of Charles Du Pont, Charles had a brother called Gideon who imigrated to Florida during the Revolution. His children came back afterwards. One of his daughters married Augustin Mazyck[?], whom you may remember as a claimant at Columbia, many years. I have engaged Alexander Mazyck to read the note in Ramsay to his father and ascertain whether he knew the Gideon Dupont mentioned there. I have an indistinct recollection of having heard of a Dupont who settled in Chester or York along with old Faucheraud a relation of the Grimkes. The Gideon Dupont who went to Florida could not be the man that Dr Ramsay speaks of, at least it seems improbable. But if he was his family are dispersed in the west. . . . .

Robert F. W. Allston to Adele Petigru Allston

Columbia 1st Decr. 1844

MY DEAR ADELE . . . . While Louise is with you, you will not suffer her to lack exercise. The horses will be profitted by it, when you use them, and you do not mean to use the carriage give Aleck notice that he may drive them in the waggon, hauling tailings, wood or something else. Pray give him word from me too that he must make Joe move both of the big brown horses, every morning, in a walk and trot before they are put into the harness. Pray tell Mr. Belflowers to try to get Mr Geo. Ford to see measured the Rice from No. 12 when it is thresh'd (the same field a part of which he has already seen measured and which took the prize here). I did not, I believe mention in sufficient detail in my last, that the cotton plaids were for the maid house servants, the gray mix'd *cloth* for the men's coats and the Tweed (twill'd) cloth for their trousers. If there is enough of it left I would like a coat of it for myself for going into the mill etc. There were some *ox chains* sent up by the vessel just as I left home pray tell Mr. Belflowers that 1 p. of them he must send to Mr. Dewitt.

. . . . You are quite right to have the Chapel open'd, and go to hear him every alternate Sunday. It is good for the people to assemble themselves to-

[1] The Charleston Library Society.

gether, if it is only to hear the word of God read, and preparation should be made there for the visit of the Bishop of which Mr. Glennie informs me in his note. Has he written to invite Mr. Geer down? You will scarcely have good weather for killing hogs till about the change of the moon i.e. about next Monday 9th. It is now uncommonly warm, cloudy and damp. Do give an eye to Richard's work, make him transplant the large roots and manure them well. Aleck must haul manure for him, tell him not to level the bank on the hill sides at the branch, the rains would only wash away the earth now. Tell Belflowers to move the hogs near to the Barn Yard. My letters do not reach you as quickly as yours come hither, in consequence of the number of documents going into the mail here. . . . .

P.S. Some Demi-johns of Brandy were sent up by the vessel which arrived soon after I left home. Have one open'd, should you want any and the rest put in a place of safety where no candle may be carried. Pray send word to Dewitt to keep the ploughman employ'd in listing ground and grubbing stumps out of the ponds in the field over the road where they cant plough, advise him too to apply to J. H. A. for Col. Read's business. Wall was to have had it had he lived.

Robert F. W. Allston to Adele Petigru Allston

Senate Chamber Columbia 6th Decr. 1844

MY DEAR ADELE   My good true wife! as I anticipated your letter came by the mail after my last to you, you will know how to understand my satisfaction at the moment of perusing it, when I tell you that under heaven it affords me the best antidote in advance against disappointment & defeat and a sure point d'appui in my retreat from public life, regarding your sentiments, so creditable to your heart and character, as the result of a calm & dispassionate survey of our circumstances & my position in life, rather than the furtive conclusion of despair.

At the moment of writing you there came up from the other House Resolutions respecting the agent of Massachusetts recently sent to Charleston which kindled the deepest excitement and led to a debate in which I was obliged to take part.[1] A step has been taken by this Legislature which will raise a great commotion at the North. The new Governor's bed will not be one of roses.

This morning was usher'd in with clouds and rain but towards 10 O'clock the sun shone out & there is an appearance of fair weather again.

I attended the party of Mrs. Ellet and a very pleasant and well conducted one it was. Nothing was handed but at 10 the company were usher'd up

---

[1] The allusion is to the visit to Charleston of Samuel Hoar in an unsuccessful attempt to compel the abandonment of the practice of imprisoning free Negroes among the crews of Massachusetts ships during their stay in the port.

stairs to a well spread table where the ladies and others were help'd stand-ing & soon after which I retired[1] W. G. Sims and Mr. Holmes the authors were distinguish'd as guests. There was another party at the College yester-day evening. Mrs. Monk is looking well in deep black and behaves with propriety, last night there was music. I did not reach the party till after 9 O'clock, having dined with Col. Manning at 5.

12.[o'clock] The hour is come at which the two houses are to elect a Governor. In preparation for it you see I have been communing with you, my best treasure! whose support and counsel I shall need, even more, if I should be elected than if I fail. You must remember that you have more influence with me than any human being. Never, therefore, suffer yourself to advise your husband without due consideration & enquiry previously into the facts. The Senate are now absent voting, I will endeavor to keep you inform'd. May God rule the issue for the good of my Country, and if greater re-sponsibility is to be thrown on my shoulders, sustain me with his Grace which only will be sufficient.

Our Federal relations are critical to a high degree, I would give the revenue of any 10 negroes I own if your brother thought with me now. In a certain event I shall have constant need of the best legal advice, from a sound orthodox constitutional lawyer. Aiken 63, Seabrook 39, Buchanan 28, Allston 24. This you will say is a very poor beginning; I agree with you. 2d Ballot—Aiken 74, S. 45, B. 21, A. 21.
3d "   —A——81, S. 53, B. 2, A. 24.[2]

This will indicate to you the uncertainty of elections and the anxiety neces-sarily incident to them in the minds of those engaged in them. I trust I may be permitted to yield with good grace & especially with resignation. Mr Aiken is elected as you perceive, so I will come back to you and look at home entirely for my comfort & my business & leave fame to others, who are more of fortune's favorites. . . . .

Robert F. W. Allston to James H. Hammond[3]

Waccamaw Beach near Georgetown 24th July 1846

DEAR SIR I had look'd forward to the mid summer meeting of the State Agl. Society with a good degree of certainty, for the occasion to acknowledge

[1] Elizabeth F. L. Ellet (1818–77), author of *The Characters of Schiller* and other works, whose husband, William H. Ellet, was at that time professor of chemistry in South Carolina College.

[2] Allston failed to record four scattering votes which made a fourth ballot necessary. The successful candidate was William Aiken (1806–87), who later (1851–57) was a member of the United States House of Representatives.

[3] Original in the Library of Congress. Hammond was the proprietor of Silver Bluff plantation on the Savannah River. He had been governor of South Carolina (1842-44) and was later to serve as United States senator (1857-60).

your polite attention in sending me a copy of your valuable letter on the uses and application of Marl.[1]

I read the pamphlet soon after receiving it with great pleasure and much profit. I am glad to see regarding its value that it has been incorporated among the publish'd proceedings of our State Society.

Allow me, at the same time, to tender you as your fellow-citizen, as a man whose pride and pleasure it is to be able to appreciate your meirt, my congratulations on the ability and success of your Masterly letters to the abolitionist of Scotland.[2] As a planter, also, representing others who like himself, have half their Capital invested in slaves, my warm and grateful acknowledgements for inditing & publishing the said letters.

I do not hesitate to speak of them and to you *now* because they never can be class'd among the ephemeral productions of the day; but will be found hereafter among the papers elucidating the history of the State, the character of her people, and the spirit of her institutions.

My acknowledgement indeed would have been offer'd earlier & at the proper time, but for the circumstances in which I found myself placed before the public of which you are one, and which can never obtain again.

I beg leave to congratulate you on the taste for which you have given your preference i e, the life & pursuits of a Planter which if view'd aright, regulated by the principles of Religion, that highest Philosophy, enlighten'd and aid'd by Science, affords both the means & opportunity to do as much good, and contributes to the true dignity of man, the elevation and just influence of his character, quite as much as any other avocation whatever.

Robert F. W. Allston to Adele Petigru Allston

Senate Chamber Columbia 24th Novr. 1846

My Dear Adele Yesterday I was absolutely preoccupied until night or I should have told you of an accident in coming to Columbia and at the same time of our deliverance and ultimate safe arrival at this place late on Sunday evening.

Soon after leaving Orangeburg Depot, the passengers in the 2d Car of whom I was one were surprised and terrified at finding it jumping and thumping along at the usual rapid rate, and instantly they were running hither & thither in utter confusion & agitation. The Car we were in together with the one in the rear had been displaced from the rails & were rapidly going to pieces the last one was after a minute detach'd with violence much broken. We had no means by which to communicate our danger & extremity to the Engineer in charge of the locomotive in order that he might stop its

---

[1] Published in 1846.

[2] Letters to Thomas Clarkson, published in 1845 in two South Carolina newspapers, the *Carolinian* and the *Mercury;* reissued the same year in pamphlet form; and reprinted in *The Pro-Slavery Argument* (Charleston, 1852).

killing velocity, both Conductors were in our Car, and the passengers even in the Car immediately before us were ignorant of our risk, the axle tree[?] in front broke in two, the floor was at every jump breaking upwards, and in a minute more or less the front part of the Car must have come in contact with the sleepers of the rail road, and have been dash'd to atoms, our danger was thus imminent when providentially the Engineer discover'd the Car in the rear which had been forced loose, & stop'd to recover it. When, of course our jolting ceased, and we were greatly relieved and I trust grateful for our deliverance.

I did not leave my seat as I knew of no refuge, one passenger jump'd out and most fortunately escaped the loss of a limb from doing so imprudent a thing. We all crowded into the unhurt Car, and I was fortunate in getting a seat, after an hours standing, which I retain'd to Columbia where we were landed between 7 and 8 O'clock It was 9 however before we got home and had dinner.

Last night I call'd with our Mess on the Govr. and Mrs. Aiken She is grown quite stout and look'd by candle light better than I have seen her, enquired for you.

I suppose that their design is to astonish the natives with a great display on the close of his Gubernatorial term.

I trust you are all well.

Do ask Porcher to call at A. E. Miller's Office and get me 2 copies or one of Prof. Shepard's "Analysis of Rice" and send up to me by some one who may be coming. . . . .[1]

Robert F. W. Allston to Adele Petigru Allston

Senate [Columbia] 10th Decr. 1846

MY DEAR ADELE Our boys, God Bless them! set out this morning, it had been raining early, & did rain hard afterward, but the sun is now out, a beautiful [illegible] and all nature rejoices in the [illegible] wholesome atmosphere.

Chancellor Johnson,[2] who is now our Governor, chose today for qualifying instead of yesterday, and I would not detain the boys. They would eat nothing before going, Stephen told me, but took with them a supply of crackers and cake. I trust they will reach you in safety. I instructed them to summon William and to pay a visit to Mr Coates the Teacher,[3] pray remind them of it in order that it may be done forthwith. Mr. Coates you know usually goes into the country in December.

[1] Probably Charles Upham Shepard, Jr., *Analysis of Rice Straw, Chaff, etc.*, reprinted in *Supplement to the Proceedings of the State Agricultural Society* (Columbia, 1847).

[2] David Johnson (1782–1855).

[3] Christopher Coates (d. 1856), a native of England who was conducting a private school for boys in Charleston.

I think of sending them to him, after conferring with him here. I am inform'd that the French language is taught at his school to the classes. This will determine me. They will be boarded by Mr. Coates. They may ascertain therefore what they will be required to bring with them.

The inaugeration of Govr. is just over, the old man, in the presence of a bevy of beauty, the wisdom and the politics represented by the Bench and the Legislature, was very much embarrass'd. He dwelt much (some thought unduly) on the exercise of the pardoning power. [Illegible] present did me the honor to express a wish that I should occupy the same position 2 years hence. Gov. Johnson was much moved, when he refer'd, towards the close, to the motive to be ascribed to the Legislature in his election.

Judge Butler[1] has resign'd his seat on the Bench and expresses his determination to accept the proffer'd seat in the Senate of the U. States, the way he came to be elected was something after this manner. Genl. Hammond who was proposed to be elected by a number of persons in consequence of his letters on the subject of slavery, [is] very odious to [illegible] party in and about Columbia, and those who sympathised with them nominated Judge Butler; and by the aid of members who did not sympathise with Mr. Calhoun together with his personal friends, and the odium which, in spite of his ability, attach'd to Genl. Hammond succeeded in electing him by a handsome majority. I voted the other way myself, not having been enlighten'd as to his conduct 'till the day after. The Judge now Senator, call'd at our Mess the evening of his election, and express'd himself very satisfactorily (after being inform'd that we had voted [illegible]). Your brother is, of course, gratified at this result, as I announced to Butler that evening. He will scarcely be in Charleston before Christmas. . . . .

Robert F. W. Allston to Adele Petigru Allston

Columbia 24th Novr. 1847

MY DEAR ADELE, It is now a week since I left you and I am desirous to hear from you. I wrote you on Saturday from Charleston, and last night sent to the office, but Stephen return'd empty-handed. I am entirely alone at my desk and have made good use of my time these three days, preparing my papers for the Society, for the Patent office and my address for tomorrow night. I cannot but think it fortunate for me that I have been so much alone, for altho the Society is now reduced to a mere skeleton, I yet would be much gratified to be well prepared. Last night my Report on the Free Schools was read before a small audience. I had it printed in Charleston and it will be distributed tomorrow to members at their seats.[2] I flatter

[1] Andrew Pickens Butler (1796–1857), United States senator from South Carolina (1846–57).

[2] The report was read before the State Agricultural Society. It was reprinted in *Reports and Resolutions of the General Assembly . . . . 1847* (Columbia, 1848), pp. 210–43. See below, p. 443.

myself it will tell sooner or later. It has had already this good effect viz to rouse a Committee which was appointed in the House last winter to their duties.

25th at night 11 O'clock   I was interrupted in the foregoing last night and as Col Edwards has join'd me since I have no opportunity to close it during today. I sit down to do so now in hopes it will be in time for the mail to-morrow, just as Judge Butler & W Gilmore Sims have left us. They walk'd home one with Edwards & the other with me from the meeting of the Agl. Society, & sup'd with a great deal of pleasant and witty colloquy, both doing me the honor to say that I acquitted myself creditably tonight.

There was but one Lady present. My audience was small but very in-tellectual, the knowledge of which chill'd me somewhat and I have no idea that I deliver'd my address quite so well as I did before you who constituted my audience the only time before. I have excused myself a moment for the purpose of reading your letter which Stephen brought from the office during our absence.

.   .   .   .

I have not recd Mr Belflowers report, do remind him to plant rye with the rains and that he can get seed from Mr. Tillman for any place where his gives out, the same can Mr. Kelly. . . . .

Robert F. W. Allston to Adele Petigru Allston

Columbia 16th Decr. 1849

MY DEAR ADELE   I have got to find my only time for writing now that the Session draws to a close, is on Sunday, the only day on which the laborer rests. My hands were already full enough when I was appointed one of a committee to investigate certain charges against the President & Directors of the Bank. Yesterday we sat upon it till 4 1/4 O'clock. Your Brother was, thro' Telegraph, retain'd to defend the Bank, and came up on Thursday, the very day you left. . . . .

Send a boat to meet me in the Waccamaw River. Order about the Hogs as you think best as to killing. I hope they will not be lost this year tho' the weather here is just such as may bring about such a result. The condition of things in Congress is the topic of universal conversation. During 12 days the House of Representatives have ballotted for, without having elected a Speaker, of course there can be no organization, and no business done. This difficulty & the excitement consequent upon it, will serve to assure our Northern friends of the feeling which pervades the Southern Country on the subject of slavery. I should not be surprised if they were to break up all & come home. The Pee Dee Country propose to send me [among] others as a Delegate to Nashville next June to consult on the subject in Convention. I would be pleased if some one more able could be selected. I dare not recommend Col. Williams. Dr. Smith or J. D. Wilson will probably be selected as another.

Unless the Northern people now come to be reasonable people, Revolution will be unavoidable. It were better to settle the matter now than leave it to our children.

Ben may remain in ignorance of the present state of the political atmosphere for me. As long as the Acadmy at West Point exists, I wish him to remain and complete his course. I received from him a letter, same day that yours came, written with apparent care, tho' his spelling still requires correction.

Last night I could not go out of doors to the Senate Session, but I ventured to go to the concert given by Strakosch and Biscaccianti under the same roof. It is the only recreation I have had since my arrival here.

Bishop Andrews preach'd in the Methodist Church this morning. My friend De Treville who went to hear him says his subject was "domestic relations" the duties of Husband and of Wife. Discussing the topic this evening in the Ladies parlor, whither I stroll'd from my room & sat half an hour, I advanced the opinion that the influence of woman was greater in a Republic than elsewhere, this led to an animated conversation as to what is the influence of woman; in which Mrs Whitaker (Lady Miller) took quite an active and conspicuous part, her husband is here reporting for the Courier, the proceedings of the Legislature, a man of letters, but very odd. He came to Carolina a Unitarian & is now I understand Swedenborghian.

Joseph was to have dined with me today but he is disabled from having worn boots too tight, his foot is quite swollen Stephen says, I will send him tomorrow a phial of Opodeldoc. I cannot see him before Wednesday I fear. His last monthly Report has no unfavorable marks. So you see, my dear, our boys are all improving, thank God. How we should try to remember the Holy injunction "be not weary in well-doing" ye shall reap if ye faint not. Heaven grant that all may yet be well with them, and I have a faith that it will be so.

Upon this pleasing promise you may dwell until you drop to sleep, then perhaps to dream of Honors from men, and favors from women for them, and last of all perhaps you may dream of me. What toy do you suppose would suit me best? that was quite a philosophical thought, true and just. Truth is the highest Philosophy, and Philosophy is higher than Poetry. But I shall weary you, so Adieu— . . . . .

Adele Petigru Allston to Robert F. W. Allston[1]

Beach 4 June 1850

MY DEAREST FRIEND,   Your two letters, one from Atlanta, the other from Chatanoga I had the pleasure to receive yesterday, when Aleck brought the grits. I was glad to find you had got on so successfully, and am sure you must enjoy the travel, the scenery, the mountain air, and the cold spring water, and even the extravagant talk of your host exceedingly. I shall be happy if you get no cold, or other ailment.

When I wrote you this day week Bessey was sick, which I fear may have caused you much anxiety. She had no return of fever that night, but rested well, consequently I went to Matanza Wednesday and attended to all I had to do there, it proved a very favorable day for such an excursion. James steered the boat. I held the large umbrella and did not find it warm, arrived at Matanza at 9 o'clock. I had the wine drawn off, 10 dozen bottles and a small demijohn, the corks gave out which made it necessary to use the demijohn. I looked at the young poultry of which there is a pretty parcel.

I left there at 5 Oclock, the sun was overcast, an umbrella was not necessary. I reached the causeway at sunset, having had an agreeable day and not feeling fatigued. We have had a great deal of very cool weather requiring fires and a great deal of rain until last Saturday when it cleared. I drove to Canaan Saturday afternoon. Mr and Mrs Glennie had not moved, some of their servants were there. A great part of the way the road was like a creek running with a rapid current. I never saw so much water in the woods, but I dare say it has dried a great deal since as there has been no rain.

Joe commenced yesterday going to Mr Platt for an hour, from half past 3 to half past 4 in the afternoon, and I believe he is desirous to study, but his constitutional laziness is a great barrier, he says his memory is failing him. Carie North's example has a decided influence upon him, and she is really a *student*. She gives Adele 2 lessons in music of an hour each day, then she practices 2 hours herself, then she gives 2 hours to reading history, and 2 hours to reading and writing french. Then she offered to teach Joe french and he reads french to her which she assists him in translating and pronouncing 1 hour daily, all this she does without dilly dallying between whiles for 5 minutes in the day. I fear it is too much, and that she will not improve in looks by her sojourn on the Beach if she continues it. She tells me Johnston first put her in the way of regularly dividing her time, and of not losing any while going from one to the other. She is not at all gay, but quietly cheerful, appears quite content, enjoyed the bathing greatly the only day we have been able to go in the surf, it has been so cool and damp I thought they had best not go, indeed the weather did not permit it. I hope her influence upon Adele will be altogether favorable.

[1] Addressed: Nashville, Tenn.

I was quite shocked last night to see by the papers the death of Col Elmore,[1] it is really awful. Our poor Govenor will be in a state of infinite perplexity, will Mr Meminger[2] now attain the height of his ambition? What will be the fate of Mr Clays compromise? It would seem to me it could not pass either house. They will probably wait to see what is the spirit that actuates the Nashville convention. God grant your deliberations may be wise and harmonious. It does appear to me the Missouri compromise ought to be the line, and to encroach upon that is to break their former pledge. You see by this I have read some of the papers, tho I do not feel that I know a great deal about the merits of the case. I really fear Mr Clay is a traitor to the South, but I'll say no more, enlighten me as to what is likely to be done. I see a wonderful account of a mysterious personage in Paris, professing to derive his commission and power from our Savior and another that a french chemist has discovered how to make diamonds. We surely live in the latter days.

We have seen none of our neighbors as yet the 2 Mrs La Bruces called, but we were out, no one else has called. Carie Joe and Adele have taken a ride on horseback since we have had a beach in the afternoons. The horses have improved. I sent Alick to see New York. She is better but not fit for use. Hamedy could not finish the house for want of stuff, the frame is up and shingled, he had no boards to enclose it, he and his hands left this Saturday.

Mr Belflowers report from 26 May to 1st June 4 ploughs going all last week, Sam and the pregnant women working in the potato field, the rest of the hands howing rice at Waterford, on Tuesday 28 he dried Myers field and nos 12 and 13, freshet falling, on Thrusday 30th finished hoeing Waterford and flowed all the rice there, on friday 31 all hands picking grass in no 10 Matanza, Saturday 1st June, gave holiday, rained on Wednesday Thursday Friday and Saturday, both Eves infants dead, Hagar with a bad foot, Booie with a bad foot from a cut, no one very sick.

Mr Faulks report 26 to 1st, I do not understand as well, he says hoed rice with all hands every day, and mentions which fields, Saturday he says 17 hands in potato patch, and the same day flowed corn field, head and Middle 22 acres, 40 acre head an Middle Dandy Dolly is better, and he thinks Rebecca's child better, tho some of the bones have come out of the head, no body sick, the wheat has taken the rust, the rice crop looks well.

Mr Hemingway says, 2nd June I have finished hoeing the whole of the Island, and have put long water on it, hoed out one field on the main, and picked out one, coopers making barrels all of the last week, sick 7,

[1] Franklin Harper Elmore (1799–1850), who had qualified as United States senator from South Carolina on April 11 and died May 28, 1850.

[2] Christopher Gustavus Memminger (1803–88), later secretary of the Confederate States treasury.

but none very sick, and all better. This is all of the reports. We have not yet had any beef. I suppose it will commence this week. Mr Belflowers sent to know if I *wd* have Mondays beef sent over. I shall leave it for the plantation use. I have heard nothing farther of the Lamb party. Peter works on the causeway but gets on slowly. I shall send George to help him next week. The canal requires to be deepened in places, it has filled up considerably. I hear the cows and calves at Waterford are very poor. I charge Nelly not to oppress them but to milk lightly, among the articles from Charleston I see a coat for Scotland, shall I send it to him?

Our children are well. I was obliged to keep them up a good deal on account of the weather. I walk the causeway every morning after breakfast, and stroll upon the beach and sandhills in the afternoon. Alick has given us fish nearly every day, but not very choice ones, today he has brought a whiting and a sailors choice for the first.

Adieu dearest friend, I fear my letter is scattered and uninteresting, if so it is the fault of the head. All send love, and kisses.

Robert F. W. Allston to Benjamin Allston[1]

Nashville 7th June 1850

MY DEAR BEN,   I write you again from the Western Country, this beautiful region of middle Tennessee where I have been this week past confering with gentlemen from Virginia & Georgia & Alabama & Mississippi & Arkansas & Texas & Florida & Tennessee & So Carolina respecting the course of legislation in Congress on the subject of the Territories acquired from Mexico by the close of the late war. I have found here a noble body of intellectual men, among whom are some sterling characters, men who are to be relied on in any emergency. Oh how beautiful it is, to meet with in men, and how grateful, to associate with reliable virtue, virtue & character which without offensive arrogance or forward pretension, is here found by your side when most needed. Modest in itself it never reminds one of a service which may have been render'd.

I have been much pleased especially with Judge Tucker of Va. half brother to John Randolph of Roanoke, Judge Colquite of Geo. Genl McDonald of Geo. Judge Goldthwaite and Fitzpatrick and Walker, and Campbell of Ala. Judge Sharkey & Smith & Boykin of Miss. among many other gentlemen of worth and ability. I have been looking too at River farms in the neighborhood, and at the Hermitage the residence of Genl. Jackson up to his death, now belonging to Andrew Jackson (né Donelson) whom he adopted as his heir and who has assumed his name. The Tomb of the old General is an object of interest to every citizen who comes to Nashville. It consists of 3 elevated marble steps rising from the garden to a circular stone platform

---

[1] Addressed: West Point, N.Y.

12 feet in diameter in the centre of which is a plain modest obelisk & on each side a tablet, one inscribed to Genl. Andrew Jackson born in 1767 died 1845 the other with a lengthy inscription to his wife who died in 1828, the whole is cover'd by a circular kind of dome supported by grecian columns. My old classmate Major Donelson (nephew to Mrs. Jackson) with whose accomplish'd family I had pass'd the previous evening was my [illegible]. He was moved by his visit having been 5 years absent as Ambassador in Germany, and I touch'd with kindest sympathy, did not attempt to detain him beyond a casual survey.

This is a beautiful and very fertile country. The soil produces corn in much larger quantities than we can make, but chiefly the farmers cultivate the pasture grasses, and feed on them stocks of cattle, sheep, hogs, horses. I visited on friday a farm of 5000 acres, on which were work'd but 9 negroes where an abundance of corn is made for every body & every thing, and where there are to be seen grazing 2000 head of sheep in separate flocks of 1 or 200, 100 head of cattle, 30 jennies with their foals, as many blooded mares to foal and 60 mules. I rode through the forest and saw them feeding on blue grass up to their knees or reclining under the shade trees.

They are building a Mail Road from here to unite with the Georgia road to the Atlantic, at the Tennessee river, which will be finish'd in about 2 [illegible]. We shall then be able to ride to Charleston in two days. . . . .

Robert F. W. Allston to Adele Petigru Allston

Cincinnati 5th Octr. 1850

MY DEAREST ONE,   When I wrote you hurriedly the other night I was surrounded by noisy crowds of [illegible] strangers & expectant Agriculturists the music of the Ball room (a grand Ball, given in honor of the State Fair) adding to the confusion of sounds and the Ball itself detracting much from the comfort of the house. It occupied me long therefore hurrid tho' it be and was not revise'd (tho ordinarily, I never revise my letters to yourself, but it should not be omitted even in writing to my bosom friend, my better half, when I attempt to recount travelling incidents and material facts) so pray let me see it when I again have the pleasure to embrace you. . . . .

An affection of the eyes next day reminded me & that only of their undue exercise. They breakfast here at 1/2 past 8, at which hour the Convention meets daily.[1] After reporting myself, and sitting 2 hours, finding that nothing of importance was embraced in the programme for the day, I took my leave and rode up to the exhibitions of the State Fair. Thro' clouds of dust & immense throng a ride of half an hour brought us to one of the prettiest and best arranged scenes of the kind, where I remain'd with all my eyes till 1/2 past 5. The ground selected for enclosure was a plane of gentle accliv-

---

[1] The General Convention of the Protestant Episcopal church.

ity for about 700 feet then broken by a ravine through which traversed a small riverlet enclosed for the benefit of the numerous stock of all kinds, the whole being cover'd with a fine sward of blue grass which was a great relief after the dust of the ride, around & within this enclosure were arranged the numbers of Short horns & Devons the Merinoes, Southdowns & Saxons, with Shepherd dogs too, the Berkshires, Woborns, horses [illegible] & colts which were competing for premiums. At various points nearer the centre of the area were exhibited the various mechanical inventions the agricultural implements & produce, the fruits & flowers and floral creations in great profusion, the fruits & *dahlias* in great perfection. Here were some red potatoes as large as any you have received from Matanza, what this flavor is I dont know. Under a Tent of immense size, "a circus tent" were assembled the Committee of the Agricultural Board of the State who awarded the premiums. Having purchased a badge for $1 instead of a ticket for 20 cents, I was priveleged to go every where. Here I beheld groups of people here & there & individuals all about reclining in as many different attitudes and postures on the inviting, soft, green carpet of nature. Yielding to the invitation of my weary limbs, I too rested, until the crowd assembled to hear the awards, I join'd the throng nearest the stand, & heard the awards & also a good popular speech from Govr. Wright of Indiana who insisted that this country should no longer be call'd "the West" Cincinnati was "the centre of the Union, and as a Kentuckian once said in London when ask'd as to the bounds of his confederacy; they are, 'to the East the rising Sun, to the North the Aurora Borealis, to the W. the procession of the equinoxes and to the S. the rest of creation.' " He appear'd a hardfeatured, plain, animated man of 45 without a cravat & not much dignity but as if accustom'd to his business.

From all that pass'd I learn'd that this is the Fair, in Ohio, that is held under the auspices of a Board of Agriculture appointed for 5 years and furnish'd with funds by the State, and that Indiana is disposed to do likewise. The cattle here, some specimens at least, are finer than I have seen elsewhere, the french Merino & saxons were good some of the former yielding near 20 lbs of fine wool. The horses are finer than I have seen elsewhere, the best specimen came from Kentucky.

In the evening I attended by invitation the Horticultural exhibition, the grapes & apples remarkably fine by the way a large orchard of apples 10 acres in full fruition which I saw on my way hither & never saw before, is one of the richest and beautiful of rural sights at 8 O'clock an address was deliver'd by E. D. Mansfield, a former Class mate of Capt Brewerton's at the point. It was flowery like his subject and statistical also, but the concourse was immense and his voice not strong nor well managed so he did not give it all. He pass'd several times but as he did not recognize me I did not recall myself at 9 1/2 I retired and slept comfortably. The bells were ringing the fire alarm, and a distant part of the City was blazing when I went to bed. It would seem to be the City of fires. . . . .

Robert F. W. Allston to Adele Petigru Allston

Charleston 22d Novr. 1850

MY DEAR ADELE, ... Mr. Barnwell & Mr Rhett got to the City yesterday & at a dinner given by the City to Genl Hammond he recounted the occurrences & incidents at Nashville recently. I am sorry to learn through him that my friend Donelson acted a conspicuous part in promoting the disorder of the galleries in the midst of which the Convention adjourned. It is mortifying & it would have been more so had I been present on the occasion.

I presume that some portions of the press will be still more condemnatory of me now that the Nashville Convention has actually adjourn'd in time for members to reach Columbia for the Legislature.

They have asserted the right of a state to secede, and recommended the convocation of a Southern Congress to meet next year at Montgomery Ala.

Our Legislature will doubtless convoke a State Convention which will entertain the question & provide for the sending of Delegates to the expected Congress.

I anticipate some trouble at Columbia, but it is no more than the common lot. I trust at least that time will do justice to my [illegible] in the estimation of most of those who now are disposed to condemn me. . . . .

Robert F. W. Allston to Adele Petigru Allston

Columbia 25th Novr. 1850

MY DEAR ADELE, Amidst a large crowd, and an immense train I arrived here on Saturday evening late & quite well. On my way I encounter'd two of the Delegates from Nashville returning to their homes, who gave me an account in detail of the disgusting procedure of Col. Donelson. My collegue Genl. Hanna was taken ill while crossing the mountain, and is now lying ill at Genl Jamison's house in Orangeburg. I went down to the Depot last night in hopes to meet him coming up but instead, I met Judge Cheves & Col. Dubose, both just from Nashville & charged with a lecture for the absentees, of which however I dont admit myself to be one, as my place was supplied. And as I told them, it was unquestionably my duty to be at Cincinnati, having an alternate for Nashville. It is in the religious conventions of the several denominations that the subject of slavery has been previous to the present year agitated with most effect. And because it was not mooted in ours, I am not therefore to be condemned in being there. The opposition to me is strong and the excitement considerable; and to make it doubly mortifying to me, they have set up "the jew Moses"[1] against me. It is meet that I should be mortified, no doubt, God's will be done, if I am defeated, I shall try & believe it is for the best. Perhaps if I were elected President of the Senate, it is possible I might have to resign my Chair to fly to you. I trust no such necessity will exist indeed, but my heart has been very anxious about you having seen you suffer so much the few days before I left home.

I am interrupted & must now go down to the State House. I will inform you this evening of my success or defeat. Middleton also has warm opposition for the Speaker's Chair.[2] It is highly probable that we cannot both be elected. I have not stir'd out of my quarters except to go to Church and have not broach'd my own name to any individual.

9 O'clock   I exchange congratulations with you Dear heart. I was elected handsomely today 27 to 14 and only seize a hasty moment now to say so to you. I am engaged in appointing the Committees to-night & shall not get through with all my eyes will bear. So you must wait upon a few days. James Simons is elected Speaker of the House.

We give a dinner to Mr. Cheves tomorrow. . . . .

Robert F. W. Allston to Adele Petigru Allston

American Hotel 11 O'clock P M
Columbia 27th Novr. 1850

MY DEAR ADELE, ... Your brother is here retain'd to contest the election of Senator of Richland District a case which has excited a great deal of personal feeling and even hostility.[3] He has accepted the place of Dist. Attorney of the U. S. It is generally believed that no other lawyer in the State dare venture to take it.

Tomorrow night we are to listen to the Eulogy by R. B. Rhett of Mr Calhoun. Both Houses are draped in deepest mourning. The appearance of the Senate Chamber in sable impress'd me very solemnly on entering it at 11 O'clock on Monday for the first time. It [at] once occur'd to me as proper, in the event of my being elected President, to make some allusion to it. I cannot tell whether it was well done or meagre, for I have not review'd my remarks except so far as to write them out for the press. The Govr.

[1] Franklin J. Moses, member of the South Carolina senate from 1842 to 1862 and father of the later "scalawag" governor of the same name.

[2] John Izard Middleton (1800–1877), a member from Allston's district, had been speaker of the previous house.

[3] Petigru represented Joseph A. Black, who was protesting the return declaring James H. Adams elected to the senate from Richland District. A new election was ordered, but Adams was again successful.

recommends a square of land to be bought and a monument to be thereon erected to our late great Statesman. The Legislature have appointed friday 6th Decr. as a day of fasting, humiliation, and prayer throughout the State. A sermon to be preach'd and services held in the Capitol. There is here a very determined Spirit evinced; & recent accounts from Georgia, the result of their elections for the State Convention, show much of an opposite feeling there. God help us.

I hope I may be able to acquit myself of my responsibilities. I feel however, that my tastes are not suited to the times even as they were in 1830–32.

Altho' sensible of the compliment convey'd in my election on Monday receiving 27 votes out of 41, I feel also very sensible of the rebuke given in the 14 negatives no more than 3 of whom may be said to have been personally hostile to me. It is good for the inner man to be chasten'd sometimes. It cures vanity.

I have just received an offer for Nightingale Hall thro' Mr. White. Shall not I sell it. . . . .

P. S The Commencement will take place on Monday next. It is then I generally take cold. Our members of Congress are all here with Mr Cheves and most of the Nashville delegates. 12 O'cl[ock].

Robert F. W. Allston to Adele Petigru Allston

Columbia 5th Decr. 1850

DEAREST WIFE . . . . The sentiment which you express in relation to public affairs will be that of the Legislature, unless our young men, hurried on by some rash, bare-faced & exciting act on the part of the Government shall precipitate matters. We shall recognise a Southern Congress and provide for the State being represented therein. Genl Means will be elected Governor probably,[1] Tho' Pickens is a formidable competitor just now. I wish'd it arranged so that Pickens should not run, as he will be beat and I do not like that, looking to his service at Nashville, but I am afraid his friends are too sanguine of his success to withdraw his name. I must vote for Means, tho' to say truth I am not content. He is an untried man, fond of popular favor, and very successful in commanding it. If his judgement is not very sound he may often lead us astray. He possesses however, one element of success, which is very important to a Governor of somewhat a facile turn. He has the power, namely, of commending himself to the counsels of wise & good men. In 4 days more the matter will be settled as far as our new Governor is concern'd. Means is not much known out of the State. . . . .

[1] John Hugh Means (1812–62) was elected.

Robert F. W. Allston to Adele Petigru Allston

Columbia 27th Novr. 1851

MY DEAR ADELE   I have given within a meagre account of the chief sight seeing in Charleston which may serve to interest the children.[1] I went to the opera twice, the singing was tolerable only, I enjoy'd it however, tho' not very well. . . . .

I received since coming here an offer of Dr. Jarvis' pictures from his Exor. Pray look over the catalogue at home & see if there be any worth $500 in your estimation. Tell Dr. Sparkman I send him a Paper. Kiss the children Good Night.

[ENCLOSURE]

Power's Eve stands upon a pedestal some 2 1/2 feet high as does the Greek Slave. The statue is 5.6 feet high, the size of a rather tall woman, and represents one just fully develop'd, standing on one foot, the leg of the other being slightly bent at the knee, barely enough to exhibit a variety of muscles in several functions. An apple, the forbidden fruit, is held in her right hand up to her right breast, two others, attach'd by a leaf from the tree are in the left hand, which depends naturally beside her. The head reminds me of the other prize statue, both having in them something of the Venus de Medici. The bust is not as large, indeed, I think, the figure is not as large as the "Slave," the proportions, the subject, the composition, the tout ensemble, are more pleasing. I can imagine nothing more chaste & beautiful. The Tempter, after having wound himself partially around the broken trunk of a tree beside her, discovers the remainder of his scaly length along and around the top of the pedestal forming a border to it. In this design there is much of originality. On the whole I deem it the most satisfactory statue I have ever seen.

There were exhibited at the fair some beautiful specimens of ingenuity. Among the rest, specimens of native cameo carved out of Sea Shells by the Miss Withers, 2 female busts also painted on canvass by two sisters believed to be the same.

The show of machinery was pretty good. An improvement on previous years. Lebby's pump for cleaning canals & draining land with a 4 horse-power engine raised 4 1/2 feet and discharged, by estimate, 2400 gallons pr. minute. A curious straw cutter from Geo[rgia] (Columbus) of which Mr Hatch is the agent in Charleston. A neat little specimen too of the hydraulic ram by which for every foot of elevation water could be raised 3 feet, if you can submit to a loss of 3/5 for wastage.

[1] The writer had evidently visited the fair of the South Carolina Institute, Max Maretzek's Italian Opera, the exhibition of Hiram Powers' statue of Eve, the "Poultry Exhibition at Hatch's Hall," and, possibly, Robinson and Elred's Southern Circus, all of which were in progress in Charleston during the latter part of November (*Charleston Mercury*, November 19–27, 1851).

At the same time with this fair was exhibited at another place a great variety of poultry. Fowls of all sorts and sizes from the little booted bantum up to the "Moley" and "Shangai" Monster, as tall as a turkey but more clumsy, ranging in price from $5 up to $100 each. Here several varieties of Pheasants were shown, among the rest the Golden and also the Silver Pheasant. They have tails as long as Charley's arm, and the birds not bigger than a pullet. The Penguin, and Penguin duck were among the curiosities, 2 specimins of coos and 2 pairs of the most beautiful summer duck.

In the same street a little higher up, over the way was to have been seen the "hairless horse," a good sized well built horse without a particle of hair on him except the beard.

Robert F. W. Allston to Adele Petigru Allston

Columbia 29th Novr. 1851

DEAREST ADELE .... Mr. and Mrs. John Witherspoon, David Williams & his wife, his sister Serena & two other young ladies of their party, are among the arrivals today; together with neat little sweet little Mrs. Chesnut, whose husband[1] is just now, owing to the result of the October election among the most prominent men in Columbia. Lacking issue, poor fellow! his Father keeps him hamper'd, much under what, might be construed, his displeasure. He is one of the Cooperation party, and is of course of the majority. His party have met twice but have accomplish'd nothing even with the experience and aid of Mr Cheves. They meet again tonight & have been trying to get your brother to join them.

The members of the Legislature of the Secession party met in caucus only last night, they number'd 85. They did me the honor to invite me to the chair on which occasion I ventured to utter a sentiment which I found to be unpalatable, the day before, to some members. I have hurriedly written out my remarks & send them for your inspection.[2] Keep them as it is possible I may have to refer to them in future. I was inexpressibly gratified to find, in the course of the evening, that the caucus seemed disposed to yield to the suggestions made by me. If they do, the State will be united again in less than 12 months. But there are ambitious and restless spirits on both sides, and no one can tell what may yet be the consequence of their aspirations. . . . .

---

[1] James Chesnut, Jr. (1815–85), at this time a member of the South Carolina House of Representatives and later (1858–60) United States senator. His wife (*nee* Mary Boykin Miller) is remembered as the author of *A Diary from Dixie*, edited by Isabella D. Martin and Myrta L. Avery (1905). The Chesnuts, Witherspoons, and Williamses were related families of Kershaw District.

[2] Omitted.

Robert F. W. Allston to Adele Petigru Allston

Columbia 1st Decr. 1851

A beautiful bright day for the Commencement but the young men in procession were noisy and ill-behaved opposite the Capitol while waiting for the two houses to form in rear of them. The Exhibition was a good one. The Mississippians were both extensively applauded, both indeed acquitted themselves in a manner worthy of applause. Wm. A. Goodman tho' feeble from the effects of recent indisposition deliver'd in appropriate manner a very good short address on the Union of Science with Labor. Our friend J. B. Allston who was suffering somewhat from hoarseness and could not therefore give full effect to his voice, was more influenced by diffidence than others of his associates. He pronounced a good speech on Firmness of Purpose with good emphasis, but rather too rapidly to give it credit for all the merit it is doubtless entitled to.

Mr. J. A. Chalmers closed the exercises of the day by a speech on Democracy in which in alluding to the political attitude of Virginia, Georgia, Alabama and Mississippi he mourn'd over the fact that South Carolina too had resolved to "co-operate with them all in submission" in a humorous style which produced roars of laughter as well as thundering and repeated applause. Some of the present majority in the State looking daggers the while. A part of his duty also was to pronounce the Valedictory address which he did in a manly appropriate style, alluding touchingly to the infirmity of the late President Preston,[1] feelingly to the severance of Dr. Thornwell[2] from the College & the benefits which it derived from his instruction, and very handsomely to the indisposition of his classmate Elliot (1st honor man) which had disabled him for performing his part (the Salutatory addresses in latin).

The address of the acting President Dr. Leiber as the Senior Professor,[3] was able & appropriate but was not distinctly heard in consequence of his foreign accent. It will read well, he pay'd Goodman an unusual compliment by alluding with commendation to the subject of his speech. Several incidents served to remind the auditory of the regretted absence of Mr. Preston who it seems is but 57 years of age as I learn'd today from his former class mate, Wm. Cain of St. John's Berkley.

2nd   Last night the Commencement Ball came off very well. The managers acquitted themselves creditably and there seem'd to be more decorum than

---

[1] William Campbell Preston (1794–1860), former United States senator (1833–42) from South Carolina, had been president of the South Carolina College since 1845.

[2] James Henley Thornwell (1812–62), Presbyterian clergyman, had resigned as chaplain and professor of sacred literature but, as stated below, was about to be elected president.

[3] Francis Lieber (1800–1872), the German-born author of *On Civil Liberty and Self-government*, had been professor of history and political economy since 1835.

usual observed. The ladies retired about 1 O'clock and poor Joseph went home very hoarse. William was there, but I saw little of him in the general mélé. Miss Howe was among the ladies & danced whenever invited, she enquired for her relations the Nesbits, is here with Dr. Gibbes family and is to spend the Xmas holidays with some friends in St. Stephens Parish. Seeing she was fond of dancing, and finding that she was disengaged on one occasion by seating herself beside me as I was conversing with her Aunt, I led her out just as the dance commenced immediately after which supper was announced. Judge Wardlaw[1] was the only representative of the Bench present. Our nieces acquitted themselves very satisfactorily. Caroline made an impression on some new acquaintances, and doubtless Minnie did also. One of the prettiest girls was Miss Sparks from Marlborough, but poor child she was laced up like a wasp, her cousin from Society Hill made himself known to me. Serena Williams would not go to the Ball.

11 1/2 O'clock at night, Your brother & I have just return'd from the College having sat 4 hours. Revd Dr. Thornwell has been elected President and Dr. Reynolds[2] to fill his place. The first a Presbyterian, the latter a Baptist clergyman. I think it is a mistake to have any Sectarian Clergymen, at the head of the College. But the general voice is otherwise.

I went up to see Joseph a few moments before meeting the Board of Trustees, he is sick but not in bed as he ought to be, I prevail'd on him, however, not to meet his classmates at the annual supper to-night. He & his associates have to make up $350 for the Ball I am told.

Robert F. W. Allston to Adele Petigru Allston

Columbia 10th Decr. 1851

MY DEAR ADELE, ... I have received, from the Exors, Dr. Jarvis' catalogue, which is now in the hands of Mr. John Preston, the most liberal patron of the Arts.[3] I must strain a point and lay out $1500 or 2000 here, such an opportunity will never occur to me again. What say you? I have been expecting to hear from you on the subject.

By the way there is a treat in store for me presently. I wish you were by to enjoy it with me. Powers has sent his "Greek Slave" here to be exhibited on his account before it is finally disposed of; and Mr. Preston has proffer'd the exhibition at the same time in the same room & on the same account his "Eve." It would be worth a journey hither and I wish indeed you could come.

---

[1] David Lewis Wardlaw (1799–1873), at this time a circuit judge.

[2] James L. Reynolds, elected professor of belles lettres and elocution.

[3] John Smith Preston (1809–81), brother of William Campbell Preston, at this time a member of the South Carolina Senate.

Senate Chamber.   Before assuming the chair and entering upon the labors of the day I must tell you my impression on first seeing the two statues together. I look'd in, on my way hither, & found the Preston brothers, Mrs. W. C. Preston & a few others at the opening of the exhibition. It is due to truth & candor that I begin by recalling my opinion of the comparison, as express'd to you from Charleston, where I saw the "Eve" alone. The abundant light perhaps, still more, the ample room, in which the latter was seen, caused the illusion that it was smaller, and juster in proportion, than the one which we saw in each other's company in N. Y. The "Eve" is the larger statue, the fuller figure, the woman—5.6 1/2 feet in height the "Greek Slave" is the smaller, more delicate figure, the maiden 5.3 feet in height. I have come from a transient view of these masterpieces of Art with a feeling of indescribable satisfaction. It would require a great deal to make me angry today. You understand me I believe.

Mrs. Preston claims for her husband the merit of patronizing Powers. She got up a subscription for him to go to Europe whilst they were in Washington, and one day when speaking of it in a large drawing room she declared she had $1500 subscribed for him, this was overheard by her brother in law John Preston who step'd up to her & beg'd that she would say no more about it to gentlemen, as he had determined to send Powers abroad on his own advance of money. The next day she went to Power's Studio when he was then engaged working her bust. She told him of this generous determination of Mr. J. Preston and that she was authorized to say so to him. She says his hand was arrested, his eyes fill'd with tears; he turn'd from her and walk'd to the window, over-looking the Valley of the Potomac, threw up the sash, and look'd out, in silence for a moment then recovering himself he return'd to his work exclaiming, The dream of my life accomplish'd in an hour!

It is thus that he went to Europe, he who was a Vermont boy, and went, a Stone-Mason, to Cincinatti, he who is now one of the first of living Artists.

I wish they could place the Statues in the Hall of the Library of the College, one at either end of that magnificent Hall, with its tall ceiling would be very fine.

10 P.M.   I have written to you by snatches, as I always have to do, when I inflict a long letter, or rather whenever I succeed in giving you one. I have just got to my room, and on my way in company with Dr. Simons, look'd in upon the Statues by candle light one turns with admiration from one to the other, in each perceiving beauties of the highest order. The "Greek" is of a size more consonant with that of women of the present day & of a delicate finish in limb rarely to be met with in nature I suspect, the hips are larger in proportion to height than those of the other, as are also the paps by candlelight. The head & face of the "Eve" are superior to anything

of the kind I have ever beheld, and the tout ensemble is not larger than what may be justly supposed the size of the first woman. . . . .

Robert F. W. Allston to Adele Petigru Allston[1]

Matanza 2nd Feb. 1852

MY DEAR ADELE   Friday was a calm, bright, beautiful day, the sun rose a minute or two before I reach'd the wharf in company with Joseph, and a large ship had just, (in full sail, but without wind) drifted past its rays as they were reflected, vividly, by the glassy surface of the water. The sea was comparatively still, and I was grateful for this. I who never go to sea without realizing in some degree a penance. I was far from being happy when leaving you, and altho' I had pass'd the night chiefly without sleeping, I did not lie down during the day; but fixing my eyes upon the paper which I read, I was occupied until (a short space it seem'd) after passing the Georgetown Light-house, dinner was announced. We reach'd the wharf at 2.30 a.m., stop'd nearly an hour and got to Mr. Anderson's Mill at 4 O'clock. Not seeing my carriage I became satisfied that my note of Monday had miscarried. I was about crossing the fields for the purpose of walking over to Nightingale Hall where I could get a conveyance, when in the Barnyard I met Mr. Anderson himself. He beg'd me to use his carriage, which had already been order'd to take Toomer Porter up to Dr. Sparkman's. Of course I did not slight his civility. So after a little Mr. Porter and I set off together. As his object was to reach Dr. Flags on Waccamaw, he came to Matanza, went to Waverly with me next day & from thence up the river.

I went that night, after ordering supper, to see Mr. Belflowers, who, although in the same spot & posture in which I left him, seems to have acquired a larger stock of patience, of which indeed, he is destined to have much need, poor fellow! While sitting with him his chimney took fire, excessively dry as it was, this was cause for alarm. God knows what would have become of him, had the house taken fire.

I sent an active fellow on the house-top with a pine-top to brush off the sparks, then pumping a blanket until it was wetted applied it to the fire-place. Happily no damage ensued, except to the blanket, which had daylight burn'd through it.

One of Molly's little girls "Elsy" was taken that day with ulcerated soar throat & died at daylight this morning. As I write, I hear the solemn cadence which bears her to the grave.

Every one here is hunting or shooting today tomorrow, and next day. I will join them on Wednesday, if possible & meet the club on Thursday. Friday is my day for the Indigo Society, and the same or day after for Mrs. Lance's Estate. I improved Saturday, the day after my arrival, in looking

---

[1] Addressed: Charleston, S.C.

over Waverly & the Mill. Today I went to the Hall, returning to dinner at 6 O'clock I found 3 men waiting, who all, of course, shared my spare-rib & small Rice.

I left the "Views of Venice" together with two little pamphlets civilly put in my hands by Mr. Cogdell, on the toilet wrapt in a newspaper, I hope you have taken notice of, and return'd them.

Yesterday Mr. Hunter's congregation was small. F. Weston's family were gone to Waccamaw to hear Bishop Payne of Africa. The sacrament was administer'd. I miss'd you from my side. There is a Holy beauty, most attractive to me in the spectacle of two persons so intimately connected, in one spirit of repentance & humble reliance on a Common Savior, bending the knee before this sacred feast. Did you mark the collect of the day? I did. The Epistle might be read with profit by our Son. I recommended to him "Don Quixote." . . . .

Robert F. W. Allston to Adele Petigru Allston[1]

Matanza 7th March 9 O'clock 1852

MY DEAR WIFE   I have this moment return'd from Mr. Belflowers' solitary house where I have been in the habit of sitting a half hour or more every night & reading for him a chapter and a Psalm before retiring myself. On tuesday he had an awful turn; for 15 hours it was doubtful whether he could survive. His sick leg was very much twisted and in great danger. He sent for me at 3 O'clock when at dinner, with a guest from Marion. I order'd my horse immediately & was there at 3.30 and until 8.30. I return'd, took my tea and was about going to bed, when he again sent for me. I went at 10.30, had to send for Dr Sparkman and remain'd with him (the Dr. also) until 8 O'clock next morning. He was in great extremity so that neither of us rested the head that night. He is better, but has been desponding since, is always cheer'd by my visits, which I make daily at such an hour as will suit my business best, i e when night comes on. At church today, Elizabeth said to me "Uncle you are alone. Wont you come to see us in the evenings? I wish to talk to you about our boys." She does not know that all the day light is consumed by me without the loss of a half hour after 8 O'clock, and when I can see no more to read or write, I order my poney & go on this mission. It is now, if ever, an impression is to be made on poor Belflowers' untutor'd soul.

I will go and see Elizabeth tho', some time this week. But here comes your missive inviting me to Town. It is well Mr. Faulk thought of sending it up this evening. Tomorrow I must go to Waccamaw and I could not have been able to gratify you, had I not received your letter tonight. I have forthwith given the necessary orders and if the servant does not fail to wake

[1] Addressed: Charleston, S.C.

at Cock-crow, your turkey & guinea fowls & ham will be on board the morning's boat. I hope they will reach you in good order. I will send you some eggs by Wednesday's boat, they cannot be prepared now. I am afraid I will not be able to present myself, but will endeavor to be in readiness, and if Belflowers mind is sufficiently clear and firm by tuesday night I will leave the homestead at 4 O'clock in the morning & join you in 12 hours.

What you say of William gives me much concern, nous verrons.

I enquired for bacon today for plantation rations. Mary look'd & told me there were but 2 crowns (I gave one to Thomas yesterday, & have used none myself) and 6 chines. Of course I told him not to give them out, as they were not enough.

My former correspondent Randall, of Merino-sheep memory, and attache to Mr. Van Buren, has re-open'd his correspondence. Having been elected Secretary of State of New York & being thus exofficio Superintendent of the Common Schools, he writes to inform me of the fact, and to proffer his attentions in the way of educational Statistics, a pamphlet respecting which accompanied his letter. . . . .

Adele Petigru Allston to Mrs. R. Hamilton

Chicora Wood May 19th 1853

MY DEAR MRS HAMILTON   I received yours of 12th inst yesterday and hasten to answer your inquiries about Miss Ayme.[1] She has lived with us as governess to our two little girls two years. We part with her now because we go north and will be absent 6 months probably moving from place to place under which circumstances it is vain to expect School to be regularly taught. We decided therefore to make a merit of necessity and give the girls a holiday. Miss Ayme is engaged for the next 6 months to a family in this District and will return to us next winter. She has received $500 per annum the last two years. She teaches all the branches of an english education: Music, drawing, french, italian, and the rudiments of latin. We chose her as a teacher on account of her ability to teach correctly what she pretends to teach. She is not a fast teacher, but is in the main a good one. She is withal a simple-minded honest-hearted woman.

Hoping that your daughters whom we remember with much pleasure are well and that you may all have a pleasant Summer. . . . .

Robert F. W. Allston to Adele Petigru Allston

Columbia 27th Nov. 1853

MY DEAR ADELE,   I arrived quite safe last evening after a very dusty ride on the Cars. Our good host had reserved a snug room for me which I trust

[1] Mary Ayme, who continued to correspond with the Allstons after her return to her home in England.

will be found comfortable when the weather changes. The day before leaving the City my friend Belin accosted me with an enquiry for Miss Ayme's whereabouts. He desired to apply for her & enquired what sort of an inmate of the house she was as a member of the family. I told him she was in Georgetown at Mrs. Lester's, but I did not [know] this until I met John Ford on the Steam boat coming down, that she would be at Chicora in a fortnight's time as, at her request, you were to send for her on 3d Decr. but how long she would remain I could not say as she was desirous to change the climate, etc. That she was under no engagement to us. As to her qualities, she was altho' a little curious & fond of talking, she knew her place and would give no trouble if she was made to understand that you were aware of it. That she was honest & conscientious, a good teacher of French, speaking it well, and of the rudiments of Music. A well-read woman & fond of reading. In teaching English prefering English to American Geography, fond of good living, not exacting delicacies so much as a plenty of substantial fare, especially fond of hot cakes at breakfast and etc. all of which you know. Says Belin, our table is none of the best, pray say nothing to her of my having named her.

John Ford mention'd that Miss Ayme received a letter in the summer about Katy to the effect that she would be with Mrs. Magwood for a month or for some given time, after which she was to see & remove her. The Fords offer'd to have her fetch Katy up, but she declined to have her *in her room*. Soon after we came home Miss Ayme went to Georgetown with the purpose as they understood, of going to Charleston to see after Katy and were surprised to find her still at Mrs. Lesters. Some time in the summer she received a letter from Mr Baynard of one of the Islands near Beaufort, describing his situation, size of family (3 or 4 daughters) and desiring to negotiate for her services. To this letter she declared she would not reply because the postage on it was not prepaid.

I hope all my things are here safe. I have not yet open'd the box containing the sword for Col Huger. On enquiring of the Governor if he had heard aught of Capt Stewarts', he said yes, it had arrived the day before, "but in bad order the head is broken off."[1] You only can conceive my mortification & annoyance at this. It must be fix'd here, but in the present state of my occupation what anxiety, what care it adds! I had eaten nothing since 6.30 yet I had no relish for the dinner they sat before me. I shall account with his Excellency tomorrow, pay him over the balance in my hands and let him do the rest. I have to prepare a letter to him on the subject of the Industrial exhibition, which must be imperfect, and I find I must copy over my lecture to be sure of being able to read it.

A number of the "Temperance Advocate" will come to you (I believe

[1] In 1852 the General Assembly had authorized the presentation of swords to Colonel Benjamin Huger and the late Captain James Stuart in recognition of their services in the Mexican War.

it is still among my papers) freighted with a report of the most horrible cruelties & feindish brutality that ever disgraced the columns of a public journal. The catching by dogs and murderous killing of a runaway negroe by some men from this district. The case was tried in Walterborough before Judge O'Neal who has publish'd it. Pray if you meet with it, dont let your children get hold of it nor Mary O'Shea.[1] One of Miss Ayme's failings is to bruit such a thing. One of her favorite subjects last summer, Ford told me, was the courtships & liaisons, or some such things, of the Princes & Princesses of Europe. He says she frequently talk'd about such things to the no small scandal of his rustic good wife, the daughters being present. I apprehend she may have received injury last summer from having too little to do. No French, no music teaching. She had better have taken Emma Heriot than to have had nothing to do that was worthy of the name of employment.

. . . .

I believe I got all your things I hope they will please you. Among the crockery you will find, to be carefully handled, a glass case for the "Prodigal Son," have it placed. The rug will come to you from King St. as nice a one could be had in the City, a little too much yellow. I was sorry to find it had taken every bushel of my rice which has been sent to market so far to square my accounts in the Counting House. I shall pay no debt before Jany. . . . .

Robert F. W. Allston to Adele Petigru Allston

Columbia 4th Decr. 1853

MY DEAR ADELE   The unwelcome pressure of one extra care is at length removed from my mind. I read my essay last night before a small assemblage[2] and as soon as the Association adjourn'd, I repair'd to my seat on the Board of Trustees of the College, where we had to elect a Professor of Mathematics in place of my poor friend Williams, who was so valuable a friend to Joseph when at College. He has over work'd himself without due recreation, and is broken down in both mind & body. He resign'd ten days ago, and is preparing for another world. Prof Gibbes of Charleston College was chosen to fill the vacancy.[3]

We have had three excellent addresses deliver'd before the association viz by Revd Dr. Bachman on "Natural Science as Connected with Agriculture," Mr. H. W. Ravenal on "Botany in Aid of Agriculture," and by Revd. Dr Lipscomb of Alabama on "the Development and Progress of

---

[1] An Irish nurse employed by the Allstons until her return to her native country in 1854.

[2] *Essay on Sea Coast Crops* read before the Agricultural Association of the Planting States. See above, p. 3.

[3] Lewis Reeve Gibbes (1810–94) does not appear to have accepted the appointment created by the resignation of Matthew J. Williams, for he remained at his post in the College of Charleston until 1892.

Southern Mind."[1] Yesterday the gentlemen strangers dined with Col. Preston (there was a great display of silver). This is the only attention which has been shown them in Columbia. Dr. Daniel of Georgia enjoyed this entertainment very much, so much indeed that he went to sleep & snored aloud in the middle of my reading.

. . . .

The Coast Survey in Georgetown is under the charge of Mr. Boutelle, (young Huger is with him) who has obtain'd my permission to pitch his tents at the Point, the field there being a fine place to observe the heavens he is to ascertain the latitude & longitude of that point. He was up here yesterday and tells me Mrs. Boutelle is to go up with him this week (tomorrow). Some of their things will be in my house, but they will occupy the Tent. Should you go to Georgetown at all, pray dont omit calling on her even with Hardtimes or Amy's introduction. Meantime, send them a piece of Mutton when you have a quarter to spare. I dont know who she is.

Pray say to Mr. Belflowers that No 10 Rice sold for $4 1/4. I hope he and Mr Tilton will be able to keep up my brand "Chicora" which now has the opportunity to establish itself in the market. Nightingale Hall has establish'd itself fairly. I hope the two together will enable me to pay off, this winter, the mortgage to Moultrie. . . . .

Robert F. W. Allston to Benjamin Allston[2]

Chicora Wood 21st April 1854

MY DEAR BEN   I have pleasure in acknowledging your letter under envelope with your power of Atty to me all right. Joseph has sign'd the Title, and I am now arm'd at all points, so as to prevent any pretext for delay in complying with the terms of sale. I sold the Point[3]—the old Point where the Mulberry stood, of my childhood—to a practical lumber man from Philadelphia David Risley for $9,000, one fourth cash. This 1/4 I turn over as Joseph's portion for him to travel upon to Europe if he likes, or expend in purchasing a Farm in Marion District, where he proposes to settle & practice his profession, one fourth payable in one yr from date, this shall be William's portion, and the balance in 1856, this shall be yours when you need it after that date. I did not reserve the Lot as you desired as it would inevitably have injured the sale, and everybody thought my demand (the price) upon the stranger was exorbitant without. Besides, he is to put up Saw Mills (4) there and [illegible]

---

[1] The speakers were: John Bachman (1790–1874), professor of natural history in the College of Charleston and co-author with Audubon of the *Vivaparous Quadrupeds of North America;* Henry William Ravenel (1814–87), planter of St. Johns Berkeley Parish and authority on American fungus; and Andrew Adgate Lipscomb (1816–90), Methodist clergyman of Montgomery, Ala., and later (1860–74) chancellor of the University of Georgia.

[2] Addressed: Jefferson Barracks, Mo.   [3] Waties Point plantation.

Turpentine Distillery on the other side, so that it would no more be habitable to me.

It is astonishing to see the impetus which this negotiation of mine has given to the demand for property in Georgetown. Mr. Weston has sold his home I hear tho' as it is for a distillery, I think he might have consulted with me, so as to let all the lots be disposed of together for as I said before I cant remain in that quarter of the Town after Saw Mills & distilleries shall be at work. . . . .

P. S.   This is my birth-day. I have number'd 53 years God be praised.

Adele Petigru Allston to Carie North[1]

Waccamaw Beach July 11th 1854

MY DEAR CARIE   . . . . My letter to your Mother was just concluded when our little community was thrown into great excitement by the appearance off the beach of an English vessel,[2] a large three masted bark, with her flag at half mast and reversed, which are both signs of distress. Your uncle was gone to Chicora but Mr and Mrs Glennie were dining with me, we looked at the vessel thro' the telescope, could see the people on board and everything very plain, but could only wonder what was the matter, for a high sea was running, tho the weather was fair and the wind moderate. Just as we were going to dinner three men presented themselves at the door perfectly wet; their story was soon told, they belonged to the bark off the beach, one of them was her captain. They were from Havanna, and bound to Cork in Ireland, laden with 900 hogsheads of molasses; when 2 days out they encountered a storm which injured their vessel, they sprung a leak, and it became necessary to work the pumps incessantly, on the 5th day the yellow fever broke out among the already fatigued crew, 2 had died, 2 were then ill, all were unable to work. The Capt had therefore taken 2 Sailors in one of the boats to come ashore, the Sea was so high their boat was capsized, and they swam for their lives. The Capt added that he then had the fever on him, and would be thankful for dry clothes, and medical aid. I gave him the dry clothes, and sent him into what used to be Joe's room to put them on, after that sent them up to Doct Hasel for advice, with the direction to go into Mr Barnwells house, as it was fortunately vacant. Mr. Glennie wrote a circular and sent round to the neighbours. The next morning early the bark was run ashore at high water. The sick were attended by Doctrs Hasel and Post. The Capt's case proved not to be yellow fever, in a few days he was well enough to get a vessel up from Georgetown and have his cargo transferred, his vessel pumped out and towed away by the Steamer Chuck. The sick were sufficiently recovered to go with the vessel except one, who is still in Barnwells house.

[1] Daughter of the writer's sister, Mrs. Jane G. North.

[2] Identified elsewhere in the Allston papers as the "British barque Aquatic."

Our Beach was thronged while all this was going on, and more vessels, and steamers came to our shore than have been here before. The atmosphere of this little Island has been unusually pleasant, soft and balmy air, and lovely nights, tho sometimes warm after going to bed, the surf bathing I enjoy. Your uncle is as well as usual, takes all the exercise he did 20 years ago. . . . .

Adele Petigru Allston to Benjamin Allston[1]

Beach 20th Sept 1854

My beloved Son   . . . . Since I wrote you last we have had a great blow, Storm. It commenced on the 7th inst and lasted until the night of 9th. The tide was higher than has been known since the Storm of 1822. Harvest had just commenced generally and the damage to the crops is immense. From Waverly to Pee Dee on the 8th not one head of rice was to be seen above the water, not a bank or any appearance of the land was to be seen. It was one rolling dashing Sea, and the water was Salt as the Sea. You will see at once that the crops must have been terribly injured. Many persons had rice cut and stacked in the field, which was all swept away by the flood. Your papa had none exposed in that way for he apprehended high tides from the state of the moon, and prepared as far as possible for it. Mr J J Middleton had 40 acres of very superior rice swept away, a total loss, and many others suffered in the same way, tho' not to the same extent. On Sullivan's Island many houses were washed away, and many hundreds of people took refuge in the Fort. No lives were lost. I know nothing of what occurred there except from the newspapers. I do not correspond with either Mrs. Carson or Mrs. King, and do not know how they individually fared. Your uncle was at Badwell whither he had gone a week before to visit aunts Jane and Mary.

The yellow fever is very bad in Charleston and of a very malignant character. When I last heard Aunt Harriette's Son James was ill of it. As I have not heard within the last week I trust he is better. . . . .

Adele Petigru Allston to Benjamin Allston[1]

Beach 3rd October 1854

My dearest Ben   I wrote you a fortnight ago, and tho I have nothing new to relate I still take up my pen to say how do ye do.

You know how one day passes like another here, and how quietly we live. For a month past we have been kept in a state of great anxiety by the prevalence of the Yellow fever in Charleston in its most malignant form. It has committed terrible ravages. When I last heard, a week ago, our relations were well, except aunt Harriett's family. She and James and Hal had all had the fever. Hal more violently than any of them. He had been desperately

[1] Addressed: Salt Lake City, Utah.

ill, but was better. Aunt Louise's family were well but she says they were almost an exception in her neighbourhood, as all suffered more or less. I am sure you will be sorry to learn that our neighbour Mrs. Read has lost her eldest child that bright and beautiful girl Anna, whom you no doubt remember. She was Adele's dearest friend her earliest friend, the only playmate she had in all her early childhood; she is as you may suppose a good deal affected by it. Anna fell a victim to the prevailing fever. I tremble for our friends. If they all escape we will have great cause for gratitude to a merciful God. Brother had not returned from Abbeville when I last heard.

I accompanied your papa to Chicora Wood last Thursday and had the ill luck to fall into the river. It happened in this way. I went with papa to look at a field of rice ready to be cut, and when returning we landed a little beyond the barn yard. Your papa steering, Nelson and Francis rowing. We came up to the bank broadside of the boat, the tide was high, and the boat stood nicely for us to land. Papa call'd to Nelson to put out his oar to steady the boat, which he did, but just as I was in the act of stepping on the bank Nelson removed his oar and the boat swung round, the water was deep, I was wet up to my waist, and a good deal agitated, fortunately I had a change of clothes at the house. . . . .

P. S.   We see by the news papers that Capt Arthur Mayer of the Steamer Nina has fallen a victim to the fever in Charleston. He is a great loss.

Robert F. W. Allston to Adele Petigru Allston

Columbia 8th Decr. 1854

MY DEAR ADELE   . . . . You have seen the account of the fire here. It occur'd about an hour and a half after I had dispatch'd to the Post office a letter for you address'd to Georgetown. It was on the square directly over against my lodgings the whole of which, excepting 3 small houses, was burnt. It was a very imposing sight. Our house was full of women, and such a scene as they presented was confounding and distressing. They were not quieted until all their baggage was moved to the head of the stairs and they were assured that the proprietor had prepared waggons below to move every trunk away as soon as there was any real danger near the house. Then each woman took the arm of some one of the numerous men around, and paraded the balcony until the fire abated and it became cold out there. They then retired and one by one went to rest about daylight. I pack'd up all my things & was ready to move the moment the wind should change to the Eastward, remaining steadily at the N. West, at daylight I lay down again but could sleep none. You may imagine how poorly prepared, I was, after dispatching business actively for four & a half hours the day after to figure (5 O'clock) at the handsomest dinner of the season given by Preston to Govr. Manning. A magnificent feast it was, beginning with a bad soup served in silver tureens we had salmon trout from the lake, bass and whiting from the sea, a saddle of mutton from England (butcher'd there) capons from N. Y. Pheasants from the N W. Canvass back from the Chesapeake and such beautiful desert & creams as you may best imagine. I tasted only one and will endeavor to describe it to you when we meet, which I trust will be ere long, and in pleasure. You will have to come with me next year if we live and make the acquaintance of some of these people. I will engage rooms at my lodging house here, in time, or take a house, as you prefer. I think you may be better off at lodgings if you dont find them too public. Time enough to talk about it.

. . . .

I think tho you had better send up word to Mr Belflowers by the Nina to make the first killing of hogs, first good weather. I hope Mr Robertson has sent up 3 barrels of lime and 2 barrels of plaister of Paris for the beach house. . . . . .

James L. Petigru to Robert F. W. Allston

Charleston 3 April 1855

MY DEAR COLONEL,   I congratulate you on the restoration of Peace. As long as the war in the East continued humanity mourned the waste of human life, in battle and in sufferings worse than death. Nor could I ever feel sure that we would not be drawn into the vortex as long as the elements of Society were so agitated. Now I hope that for the rest of my time at least there will be peace. And perhaps the good fortune of the Empress in giving an heir to the new empire, may not be unimportant in the same sense. So I am glad of that too, tho man for man I prefer the Bourbon to the Bonaparte.

However this is not to the point. We have to examine the title of Phoebe.[1] It seems that Henry M Parker is the seller. He married a grand daughter of the Haskell, and so the property no doubt came that way. The woman is much younger than you suppose. She says she is 32, and she certainly does not look like 42. It will be a long time before her children will earn wages. I am afraid you will be rather shocked by the light complexion and fine features of the eldest, more in conformity with our ideas of an Western Odalisque than of one of the labouring class. I think the price is high, $1200, tho Mr Capers asseverates that he was on the point of closing with Dr Haig at the same price. If the title is examined today, and [illegible] on them, the woman can go tomorrow.

[1] Note in the hand of Allston: "Phoebe is the daughter of my old and faithful man Thomas (Head Carpenter) who has no child belonging to me. Hence my willingness to gratify him in his declining years, I would freely give him freedom if it would help him. I believe he does desire it."

P. S. . . . .

I am happy to think that your rice obtained the prize. It is not only a personal compliment but it does credit to Pedee, and I hope Pedee will appreciate it.

Robert F. W. Allston to Benjamin Allston[1]

Washington 25th May 1855

MY DEAR SON . . . . I hope you will need no money before the next crop comes to market but if you should, draw on Robertson & Blacklock directly, for your own account, they will do the needful for any small sum. I counsel you to avoid acquiring either the habit of extravagant living or the reputation in the service of commanding a large purse. You ask'd to have a servant put to be train'd as a gentleman's servant, I have not done so, as the only place at which I could feel confidence in placing a boy is Lee's at the club house, and this is all fill'd. In looking around however, there is not one of your boys or girls either but will lie, and I would not take the pains or lose the time to train one who can not be depended on for the truth. I have assign'd to your service either Page (Pirce) or his brother Thomas as you shall choose, boys with both of whom it is worth while to take pains, truthful and honest, but high temper'd. Joe is the same but if you prefer him it can only be a temporary service, either of the others shall be your own.

27th   I have seen the President, who says when you arrive here, he will see you. I told him you would give him faithfully a general resumé of the occurences at Salt Lake City during the winter so far as they bear upon the Mormons, but take care not to fatigue his ear with unnecessary information, or such as can be of no avail to him in administrating the Government. The Secretary of War will introduce you. If he does not think of it you will remind him, as being at my request. You will be the most recent arrival from that alien population, be not agitated but give your information simply plain & distinct. We would gladly get you to go with us to Europe, but, it is not to be accomplish'd.[2] I fear I shall not be available to go with you any more. Duty, the path of duty is the path of safety. As long as your heart is in the service sufficiently to retain you there, act up to the duty of the service, but pray do not yield when you return to the Missouri country, to all the savage indulgencies by which you will be surrounded and with which you will be tempted. Lose no opportunity to cultivate Geography in its large sense and Geology.

We have nothing from you since 29th Feb. I sent you by express another copy of the Hireling and Slave.[3] . . . .

[1] The address is missing. Benjamin Allston was in the army at this time. On March 28 his address was Salt Lake City; the following July he was at Fort Lane, Oregon.

[2] Allston, his wife, and eldest daughter were about to depart for Europe.

[3] William John Grayson's proslavery poem, published in 1854.

Robert F. W. Allston to Adele Petigru Allston

Columbia 4th Decr. 1855

Much to my surprise a young man one of the Professors in the arsenal academy here applied to me on Saturday for a Copy of my "Eulogy on Calhoun"[1] and he wishes it forthwith. Will you therefore, essay to find and send me a copy? You must put 2 blue stamps upon it, or it will not come by mail.

Now about finding one. If you do not pick up one among the loose pamphlets in the gun-room or elsewhere, you will find one in my Study upstairs in one of the several parcels (wrap'd up) near the fire-place, on the floor, and by this time cover'd with dust.

I have been reading with much interest the news from Oregon by the California Steamer in the "Mercury" of yesterday. Thereby, you will see that our poor fellows have had some hard fighting to do on the Columbia river. God grant our son may be supported to do his part and may pass thro' the trying ordeal safe from harm as well as honorably. But we should try and prepare ourselves for accounts which may number him as well as others among the wounded & crippled or missing in such a savage warfare. God forbid! I am writing him.

The College Commencement yesterday was very beautiful. The day being fine, and this, President Thornwell's last appearance, the procession was very full, and the Chapel, large as it is was crowded to overflowing. The exercises were quite as interesting as usual, and the President's address to the graduating class remarkable. All the Scholarships except my own were represented by young men exhibiting promise of future distinction. There is some obstacle in the way I suppose but am not yet inform'd. Dr Leiber [Lieber] is to wait on me this morning, & I presume he may be able to enlighten me.

11 O'cl.   Dr Leiber says that President Thornwell has not troubled himself about my foundation, because it is intended to benefit the Episcopal Church. Professor McCay has this evening been elected President of the College, very much to the mortification of the learned Leiber.[2] It is a Presbeterian dynasty. But I sincerely hope it will be successful and insure to the College an increase of prosperity.

The weather today is colder & I trust you feel secure about the bacon. You had better have all that are ready slaughter'd next week when the weather shall be favorable.

Have not you heard yet from Joseph. He must have written. Pray tell William to write and let me know what Mr Hemingway has to say about

---

[1] *Eulogy on John C. Calhoun, Pronounced at the Request of the Citizens of Georgetown District, on Tuesday 23d April 1850. By Robert F. W. Allston* (Charleston, 1850).

[2] Charles F. McCay, professor of mathematics and mechanical philosophy. Lieber promptly resigned.

himself & the business & the new overseer etc. I have not heard from Mr. Belflowers, I hope he sends some aid weekly to Mr. Faulk who is repairing the Waterford banks. . . . .

James L. Petigru to Robert F. W. Allston

St Michaels Alley [Charleston] 10 Jany 1856

MY DEAR SIR, The enclosed is Mr Burt's letter[1] containing Miss McDuffie's offer of Cherry Hill, which is in compliance with her promise. I did not tell her who it was that I meant when I asked her for the refusal of the place, and told her that I spoke on behalf of a friend.

It would give me as much pleasure to see you at Cherry Hill, as to be the Master of any other place. But the price partakes of the effects of an inflated market. McDuffie gave poor Noble only 6000 for it; and Mrs Noble did not even get her Dower. But it is also true that my friend William Calhoun always said that Cherry Hill was a better cotton plantation than the great Flat woods place, where the negroes are. Now if you like to set a foot on the Savannah River side and possess the handsomest seat in South Carolina, by many times the handsomest, and rejoice the Spirit of Adele's great Ancestors in the contemplation of the elevated place to which his posterity have attained in the land where he was a stranger and a sojourner you have only to drop a line to Mary; and who knows but that when Ben returns with the merits of a gallant soldier, a way might be discovered for settling the debts, that would make it like Mercy in the Merchant of Venice, a quality equally pleasing to Debtor and Creditor. Indeed in such a case it would be difficult to say who is Debtor and who Creditor.

But if you have no idea of such a thing I will write to Mary and let her know, that she and Ben are to be happy, if they ever are happy somewhere else. . . . .

J. H. Means to Robert F. W. Allston

Buckhead [Plantation, Fairfield District] Jan 15th 1856

MY DEAR SIR You will no doubt recollect a conversation which many of us held at the table of our mutual friend Mr DeSaussure on the subject of the Kansas difficulties. In that conversation we all agreed that Kansas was most probably the ground upon which the great battle for slavery would be fought, so that we ought to do something for our friends who were so gallantly fighting for our Institutions there, by way of sending them aid in men and money. I remember also that you and others said that you would give a negro to any good man who could be trusted who would emigrate to Kansas, so that I told you I would furnish the man. In a conversation last of all in your room in Columbia I told you that I had found it much more difficult to furnish the "man" than I at first supposed it would be. Yesterday I received a letter from a very worthy (but somewhat desperate)

[1] Missing.

young man in my District stating that he was anxious to go to Kansas and bear his own expenses, provided he could get 20 men to go with him. He also states that he has but little doubt but that he can raise that many or even more men. From the daring character of this gentleman he is the very person to send upon such an expedition, and I look upon him as being perfectly reliable. He states also to me that many of the persons who have expressed their wilingness to go are too poor to bear their own expenses, and begs me to meet him at the Court House on the first monday in February to try and arouse our people to the necessity of giving aid. I see by the papers that a meeting of the Citizens is called for that day I have no doubt myself that the company can be raised, and that our Citizens will do something towards raising a fund for their support, but whether an adequate sum can be raised or not I do not know. After I had received the letter alluded to I thought of the conversation with you and my present purpose of troubling you with this communication is, to ask you in case such a company is raised what can you and your friends in your District do for it by way of furnishing funds. I need not trouble one of your intelligence by dwelling on the importance of such a movement. In fact I know your opinion too well on the subject to suppose that you needed any thing from me to fire the ardour of your zeal. Will you do me the favour to let me hear from you at your earliest convenience, and if you would let me hear from you by the first Monday in Feb I would take it as a favour. If you write in time for me to get your letter at the time indicated, please direct to Winsboro, if not direct to Buckhead.

I hope you have had a more pleasant time than I have had since your return home. We have had nothing but rain sleet and snow since Christmas. The ground has been covered for 12 days three inches thick with ice, the thermometer is now standing below freezing point and I do not know when the ice will melt. There is a slight thawing every day from 12 till 3 oclock but at night it freezes again. All work is effectualy stopt except getting warm, and even the negroes are sighing for something to do.

Robert F. W. Allston to J. H. Means[1]

Chicora Wood 21st Jany 1856

MY DEAR SIR   I have just received your letter, which to be sure is better late than never. You will be at no loss, my Dear Genl, to understand that I hoped to hear from you before the beginning of last summer. Our conversation took place in Decr. 1854, soon after Mr. Atchinson pass'd thro' Columbia, on which occasion I undertook (in the hope that some of the gentlemen present would be induced to follow our example) if you would find a proper man to go as a settler to Kansas, I would pay his expences there and give him $50 in pocket there to start with, or something to that effect.

[1] Copy written on the back of the letter above.

Since coming home I have sent $100 to Major Buford, whose advertisement to raise 300 men to start 2nd Feb from Eufaula Alabama I noticed.

And I am happy to have it still in my power to transmit to you herewith an order for a similar sum, which I entrust to you under the circumstances you mention, to place in the hands of some citizen who will do the cause good service.

Robert F. W. Allston to Benjamin Allston[1]

Chicora Wood 28th Jany 1856

MY DEAR SON, ... And you are now in the latitude of Montreal north of Oregon City how does the Thermometer range? Mr Glennie keeps a regular meteorological register for the Smithsonian Institute with which I put him in communication, so that his uniform scientific attentions are fully appreciated.[2] I keep no more a register since Kelly has left me, being no more regular enough in my habits. But I dare say you will do so when you come home. I wrote to Kelly (James) at Sacramento City last Spring, but have not heard of him in two years.[3] Enquire for him.

. . . .

I am glad you have an opportunity to see that fine new country, Oregon, about which Washington Irving in his work entitled "Astoria" wrote so pleasantly many years ago. This name was given to the book in compliment to the patron of an expedition to the Columbia river many, many years before it came into the posession of the United States. John Jacob Astor a millionaire merchant (twice told) of New York sent out a party with a considerable store to trade in that country at his expense or possible profit. Washington Irving was the historian of this adventure or expedition & he call'd his book "Astoria." Col. Fremont, too who has just had his immense tract in California "Mariposa" worth $2,000,000 confirm'd to him by the Federal Court. Col. F. wrote an account of his exploration of that country & has now recently publish'd under the authority of Congress a map which now lies before me. The Cascades & the Dalles are between you and Wallah-Wallah which from all accounts has been the scene of much suffering and disaster to your comrades of the army. God bless you my Son and guard as well as guide you through the arduous path of duty which lies before you! I have written to the Adgt. Genl at Washington soliciting your appointment on the Western Boundary Survey in one capacity or another. I agree with you of course in your preference for actual scientific employment. There is nothing mentally (perhaps nothing morally) improving in your present life, and we must improve or deteriorate as life advances. We must keep steadily in view the great end of existance, and strive unceasingly to prepare ourselves

[1] Addressed: Fort Lane, Ore.

[2] Copies of these records are preserved in the College of Charleston Library.

[3] One of Allston's former overseers.

for it. You speak of Genl Wool with all his consequential brusquerie what a wreck he is, and how disappointed of his ambition. Genl Scott! the first soldier of the present day in the field, disappointed of his ambitious hope and derogating from his high & venerable & heroic position to discuss with the law-officers of Government the paltry allowance of back-pay for his new distinction. Genl Garland broken in constitution, dyspeptic & testy. The Col of every Regt. of Artilery & Infantry except the new ones super-annuated, self-indulgent and yet with many of their juniors unfit for any other mode in which to earn a livelihood! Such are the scenes in present life to which the progress to the highest promotion in our service opens a vista. Genl Gains died an imbecile, the catastrophe having been hasten'd by his Government repudiating his patriotic but unlawful call for volunteers to aid in repelling the invaders of Texas. A call which now, but for the warning of this example, Genl Wool would gladly make on California & Oregon! provided our accounts of the prowess and appointments of your savage foe be not exaggerated. We all wish you were with us. Belflowers is getting old a little as well as some others, and it would be well for you to profit some years by his experience whilst he is still active & capable, provided you ever intend to plant. Craighill was with us at Xmas & seems to have taken quite a serious turn. He admires the classics, and I offer'd to carry him through our College at my expense, if he desired to accomplish himself in that way. He declined respectfully, but was not communicative. I suppose he has written you since. Joseph is still in Paris, he was no better when we left him and it was evident his Spirits were affected by his lingering rhumatism. The same post brought a letter from him to us, he does not mention his health, but seems to concern himself in unravelling the future of the powers of Europe, and our internationel relations with them. I doubt not the Hudson's Bay Company keep your Indians well supplied with ammunition, our relations with England being at this moment much complicated, and the head of British Ministry being a mortal enemy to peace and to this "plebeian" Country.

1st Feb.   The advice & opinion of Louis Napoleon will materially influence the opinions & action of the British Ministry. The Association of Austria & Sweden with the Western Allies will probably reduce Russia to terms, demoralized as their troops are by repeated defeats. Should the terms proposed induce peace between the European powers, America may expect some hot work yet for the Army and Navy. Joseph opines that the year 1856 is big with important events to be develop'd more fully before its close.

Yesterday we had a meeting of the Winyah and All Saints Agl Society, at which our venerable President presided, and afterwards at dinner produced 2 very old and fine bottles of wine. Mr Tucker is now 76 years of age. He kill'd a deer last week. He is getting infirm. We had the company of

Capt Petigru & Mr J. Walter Philips to dinner. The Capt goes again to Washington next week. Mr Phillips you may remember seeing some years ago at Canaan he now resides on the Mississippi but makes us a visit every two or 3 years. He stop'd here last night. I have received the Report of the Secretary of War from the Department but have not time to read it, as my letter to you, if not dispatch'd tomorrow will be too late for the earliest Pacific Mail-Steamer Isabel sails from Charleston to Havanna on the 4th and 19th of every month, by this conveyance our letters are taken to the Cuba where they are mingled with those of the great mail from N. Y. to California & Oregon. I hope it will reach you safe & in reasonable time. We all feel anxious, but I trust you, as with all I hold most dear, to a good & merciful God, our Common Father & friend! In the night of the 15th Jany towards morning I dream'd that I heard you call me "Pa." It wak'd me up & so strong was the impression that I raised my head to look about the room!

The Indians are getting troublesome again in Florida, Lieut Harstuff's detail near Fort Drum were dispersed, 4 kill'd and he narrowly escaped with his life.

William is gone to N. Carolina to escort hither your cousins the Miss Norths' now on a visit to their Sister, Caroline. Joseph beg'd me to keep his Father's Estate together another year in order that he may not be compel'd to come home. I agreed to do so with William's consent first obtain'd. Will goes to Waverly occasionally sees Bob Nesbit in a hunt, a fishing (they are getting up a shad-net betwixt them), stay a night or two and then returns to us. He has no establishment there yet.

All the negroes send how'dye for Mas Ben. It has been very sickly with them & I have lost 5 good hands within as many weeks.

P. S. The Abolitionist are getting troublesome every where. Congress cannot organize. Kansas is the scene of bloodshed, with more to do—And England threatens a War! Do you ever meet with Bishop Scott? He knows very well who I am. He went to Oregon from Georgia. Make yourself known to him should you be thrown in his way. I would gladly send you a servant if I could. Employ a Chinese if you meet with a good one.

I sent you 2 or 3 Pamphlets to Bernicia or San Francisco. Grayson's "Hireling and Slave." Charly is reading his lesson now and sends you howd'ye, so does Jane.

J. H. Means to Robert F. W. Allston

Buckhead Feb 8th 1856

MY DEAR SIR Your letter containing a check on Messrs Blacklock and Robertson for $100 was duly received and will be paid over to the Tresurer of the Company that is to emigrate to Kansas as soon as it is organized. The day upon which the meeting was called was so inclement that it was impossible to keep the people in the Court House, so very little was done except to appoint a Committee to raise subscriptions. Seventeen men are enrolled already, and many more are willing to do so. We will send a Company I think of 20 men, with $4000 to support them, which sum is about 1/2 the amt of the taxes of our Dist. I do not know that we will raise that sum, but we will try. If every body would act with half the public spirit you have shown in this matter, there would be no difficulty about it. . . . .

E. B. Bell to Robert F. W. Allston

Graniteville Feb 11th 1856

RESPECTED SIR   As a young Charlestonian and Carolinian I throw myself upon your charity and generosity, by the advice of many friends I was induced to advertise and appeal to my native state for aid to organise a company of Emigrants to proceed to Kansas. Depending on my appeal not being in vain I have organised and accepted men and made arrangements to start on the 30th March, my appeal to all intents and purposes is a dead letter, but I have gone so far that I cannot honorably withdraw and I would now rather bend my knee as a suppliant than retract, if one leading man in the state (like yourself) would start the ball in motion, I know that the Patriotism of the state would soon follow. If you have already subscribed as much to the cause as you desire can you not solicit from your citizens a purse for my company, or a letter from you that I may publish will help the cause, I can give abundant recommendations of my abilities.

[NEWSPAPER CLIPPING INCLOSED]

HO! FOR KANSAS.

At the solicitation of many friends I will proceed to organize a Company of one hundred men, to proceed to Kansas, about the last of March.

This pioneer band needs the aid of the moneyed citizens. They go to a far off country for the purpose of securing homes and at the same time to defend Southern Institutions. They appeal to their native State for aid with the hope that their appeal will not be in vain.

It is impossible that the people of South Carolina can hear without emotion the news which daily comes to us from Kansas. The long and bitter animosities have at last ripened, and slavery and abolition, the North and the South, confront each other in armed and deadly war. The issue has come, and to the people of the South, and of this State, to each and every slave-holder, the question addresses itself: What shall we do for Kansas? Shall we look listlessly, tamely on, while our friends, surrounded by the hosts of Abolition, are risking their fortunes, perhaps shedding their blood in our behalf? Can we do nothing, give nothing of our abundance in such a cause?

We trust that these questions may be answered in a worthy and liberal manner. Let Patriotism and State pride, and Southern spirit, be expressed in some suitable, practical form of aid for Kansas.

E. B. BELL

House of Representatives
31st December, 1855.

Capt. E. B. Bell.—DEAR SIR: In reply to your letter of the 28th, I must first repeat my proposition. The pledge was to give an hundred dollars to each company of *one hundred men* that might go to Kansas under pledge to remain *two years*. Whenever you organize a company of an hundred men and *start* for Kansas, I will pay to your Treasurer the amount pledged. If my colleagues are not called upon to contribute to companies which may be raised in their own Districts, they authorize me to say that each will contribute handsomely to the aid of your company.

Your intention of appealing through the press to the spirit and patriotism of the people of the State, is admirable. There are men scattered all over the State also who are willing to go, but not in sufficient numbers to form a separate company in each District. Come out with your publication, and when you get one hundred men, solemnly pledged to go to Kansas, I feel authorized to pledge the South Carolina Delegation for *two hundred and fifty dollars*.

You will certainly have the hundred dollars from me, whenever you are ready to move with an hundred men. Or should you fail in getting the full number of an hundred men, then you may call on me on the day that you start for as many dollars as you have men under pledge to go and to remain two years in Kansas.

Yours truly,
P. S. BROOKS.[1]

Robert F. W. Allston to Benjamin Allston[2]

[March, 1856]

MY DEAR BEN .... You ask my opinion of Kansas affairs? We are raising men & money here to counteract the effect of the Northern hordes sent there by the East Emigration Aid Societies. All Saints parish has raised $3000 & I suppose Winyah will do as much I have [given] $100 to Major Buford, 100 to Major Herbert & $230 here. The destiny of the Kansas as a State will be determined by the result of next October Elections & our purpose is to have Southern Settlers in the Territory sufficient to vindicate their privileges at the Poles and to defend themselves against the hired myrmidons

[1] Preston Smith Brooks (1819–57), member of the United States House of Representatives (1853–57) from the Edgefield section of South Carolina, adversary of Charles Sumner in the notorious Brooks-Sumner incident.

[2] Addressed: San Francisco, Calif.

of the N E. These last have met (in Decr last) voluntarily in an irresponsible Convention at Topeka, form'd a Constitution & elected State officers to go into operation this month (4th) and if sustain'd in this, they meant to apply under it for admission to the Union as a Free Soil State. This was so flagrant a dis-respect to and usurpation over the establish'd Territorial Govt. that President Pierce issued his proclamation against all disturbers of the Peace and order'd the troops at Leavenworth to act on the requisition of Territorial Governor in maintaining order. God knows what will come of it all, if Congress should decline to sustain the President, which seems to be the temper of the House. He receives violent abuse in both Houses. We are disposed to fight the battle of our rights with abolition & anti-slavery on the field of Kansas. If beaten there, altho' it may be fought repeatedly elsewhere unexpectedly, irregularly and tragically, yet reflecting men cannot fail to perceive that in such case our prestige of equality in the Union will be lost forever, and we must prepare for organization & defence out of it. For the worst Tyranny which is known to mankind is that of king numbers weilding unrestrain'd power which would be the case, in that event, with the Northern Section of the Un. States. The computations of intricate calculation have proved the impracticability of emancipation by deportation, and the other alternative cannot be contemplated, namely, the giving up of our beautiful country to the ravages of the black race & amalgamation with the savages. Pinckney Alstons son John is going to Kansas next month to set up as a surveyor. I yet hope for the best, but we are sorely press'd and boldly villified at Washington, in Massachussetts Vermont & N. York! I could not contain myself in Congress, I would not therefore go there.

It is rather probable I may be elected Govr. next Decr. and if elected I have promised to serve. Tho' God knows I would be better off at home. The novelty of the position & my ambition for it have long ceased, but on being appeal'd to by my constituents & by my friends of the PeeDee Country, it would have been selfish in me to decline. If my stand before the public on a late occasion (against the National Convention for nominating a President, proposed here by B. H. Wilson) should be condemn'd in the State, I shall be opposed and probably defeated. It will be of little importance any way. . . . .

My Son, you speak of my commanding you to come home, and you will obey. It is long since I have commanded you to do anything but that which is right in the sight of God our Common Father. To him you are responsible as well as I, and as you must render account to him for all you do, so you must endeavor to know his Will, in order to do what is right. Do me the simple justice to remember what pass'd between us when you said nearly the same thing to me at home. "If you say I must resign Sir, I will resign." No my Son I will not say so, I have a plenty of work for you at home & you shall be well paid for attending well to it. But you wish to join the Army your heart is in it. Go and make acquaintance with the world. When tired of roving, and of the alternately exciting & indolent life of garrison & the field, or when you see its emptiness & unprofitableness, then come home & help us. You can have enough to do & will find a Home. Welcome. I promised to place the first one of you that is married at Exchange merely for a residence until the owner shall take it. I have made my Will & you are all provided for. But I wish to invest $100,000 before it is divided even after my death.

Pray lose no opportunity to study Geology and Botany in that fruitful country, fruitful in Specimens at least. You can make a small herbarium in the Spring wherever you may be, and send or fetch it home, with a brief memoir. . . . .

[P. S.] Jesse Belflowers takes this to the mail in the morning. Write whenever you have an opportunity and express your mind freely to your Father who lives for his Wife and children. You cannot write too often. Cary, Minnie and Louise North with half a dozen others will be here during the Month of April. Adele is really a fine girl no[w] 16 and well grown and accomplish'd for her years. She and Bessie wrote you under my last envelope.

E. B. Bell to Robert F. W. Allston

Graniteville March 3rd [18]56

DR SIR Yours of 23rd Feb came to hand yesterday, it had taken a trip to Greenville or I would have recd it sooner. I expect to start about the 25th of this month. Allow me to return you my sincere thanks for the Liberal donation. I shall use it economically and shall render a faithfull statement of my disbursments. I shall be happy to give you a statement of our condition after we arrive there. I am determined to carry one Hundred men if the Funds will allow me.[1]

Robert F. W. Allston to Benjamin Allston[2]

Chicora Wood 29th May 1856

MY DEAR SON . . . . We are moving today and I have just sat down a moment to acknowledge your letter & let you know our movements. I will finish another letter to you [illegible]. It is Bessie's birthday (11 years old). She and her sister will be at school until the last of June, then they will come to us. They are both growing and improving much and are made almost too much of by our friends in the City. I wish we could have them at home with a finish'd Governness, But this is a person so very difficult to find. . . . .

---

[1] Bell is reported to have recruited thirty men with whom, on March 30, he joined the Alabama party (above, p. 127) headed by Major Jefferson Buford (see J. B. McMaster, *History of the People of the United States*, VIII, 240–43).

[2] Addressed: San Francisco, Calif.

I believe we shall not have War with England except it come by means of the citizens and subjects of the two Powers becoming entangled & fighting in Central America. Under other circumstances the two peoples will not [illegible] a War.

. . . .

I knew nothing, of course of your having been unfortunate in a tender passion. It is no more than has happen'd to your Father, among many other honest men, I know it is hard to bear with equanimity. But Providence knows what is for our good, better than we do. Let this reflection assure you completely, and bide your time. If you are to live the domestic life of a Planter, no one of the Ladies (however beautiful, accomplish'd and agreeable) whom you meet with in the Army, I mean daughters and connexions of Army famlies who are accustom'd to move from Post to Post and from City to City, will ever be satisfied and happy in it. So "look well before you leap." The old saw is "marry your neighbors daughter" if you wish to content & be content. But we have no neighbors daughter whom I would be pleased to see you wed. Miss Mary Pringle seems to be the only one who is brought up with due regard to habits & education. Elizabeth Weston is quite too lax in her notions of education & her girls are not the thing for you & their Father is quite too indolent to find out the right way. You can never marry a first cousin. But you will [have] a plenty in this State & Virginia from among whom to choose after proving by long association her temper, habits, health & vigor of mind and body. For Gods Sake, "dont marry in haste to repent at leisure." Your Sisters can give you many hints when you come home as to the habits and character of their school companions. Col. Nauman has a daughter at school with them But here I am at the end of my sheet.

P. S. . . . . Charles & Jane are well & happy at the idea of going in Rainbow over to the Sea Shore. I hear their Merry voices under the [illegible] Tree as I write. They are on the way not to miss Ma when she moves down to the boat. Ma is giving books to be pack'd and is looking about generally, being the predominating spirit. She wants me to go to Congress instead of being Govr. but the bear gardens of Washington are not at all to my taste. I wish to retire from public life entirely. God give me grace to prepare for another world and for accounting in his presence!

Robert F. W. Allston to Adele Petigru Allston

Philadelphia 19th Oct 1856

MY DEAR ADELE   Yesterday as the Convention[1] did not sit after 1 O'clock I took the cars at that hour for Lancaster & made a visit to Mr. Buchanan who with Miss Lane (in mourning) enquired particularly & kindly for you.

1 General Convention of the Protestant Episcopal church.

I sat some 2 hours, took tea, and then return'd towards this City half way to Dawningtown, near which place lives a farmer with 7 children named Wm. Hasell Wilson[1] who was expecting me for the night. I breakfasted with his family this morning in Quaker style (he married (Miss Miller) into a Quaker family) and came down by the only train which runs on Sunday, expressly to receive your letter which I have been looking for these four days. I heard from Mr Belflowers 3 days ago (date 11th) that he had finish'd the 9th and he says nothing more except that all are well, that the Barn-yard is not as full as last year, that he digs no potatoes except for the children, as they turn out only 1 bushel to the row of 1/2 acre. He is an economist decidedly.

. . . .

Mr. B[uchanan] is in full flesh & high spirits (for him) (he is blest you know with enviable equanimity) relying confidently on the success of his party and indeed I have never seen the actors of that party to such advan-tage as on this excursion. Judge Woodward of the Supreme Court & other men of substance were discussing within my hearing in the Cars yesterday the question of Slavery in Kansas as fearlessly & fairly as it could be done in Carolina, more calmly however. Mr B[uchanan] ask'd me a good deal about the prominent men of my State. Manning & Pickens both have been to see him & he intends to return their visits in January next which month he pro-poses to spend in Carolina if elected, making Charleston his Head Quarters. I warn'd him not to count too confidently on Tenessee, but he says Cave Johnson assures him weekly of a large majority there, as Donelson V. Presi-dent on Fillmores ticket has become quite intemperate and exposes himself in his efforts to advance his cause. He is a renegade from his old party & I am not surprised at his losing influence. The Whig vote is strong in that State. . . . .

Adele Petigru Allston to Benjamin Allston[2]

Chicora Wood January 1st 1857

My dear Ben   I wrote you last from Columbia giving an account of your father's election to the office of Govenor.

I remained in Columbia 10 days and then returned to Charleston where I stopped 3 days with your dear aunt Anne, (with whom Louise North is passing the Winter) and then I took the road home, bringing Charles and Jane with me, leaving Adele and Bessie with Madame Togno.[3] I reached home Saturday before Christmas, and busied myself in having curtains put up, and various little arrangements made, mince pies prepared and cake

[1] A former South Carolinian. See Elizabeth B. Pharo, *Reminiscences of William Hasell Wilson (1811–1902)* (Philadelphia, 1937).

[2] Address missing; Benjamin was in California at this time.

[3] R. Acelie Togno, who conducted a school for girls in Charleston.

made and iced, all of which was completed by the time your father came, which was not until the evening before Christmas. He and Joe came up in company. The next morning there was a great demonstration, the negroes coming as usual to wish Merry Christmas and the compliments of the Season, but more than usual to greet in their Master the Gov.

They made a great noise and drank the Govenor's health in many a stout glass of whiskey. Many were the inquiries made after Mas Ben. All were well and in good spirits. We went to church after we finished giving out such little matters as are always given out at this season. Joe and Will went to Waverly to see Christmas given out to the negroes there, but returned here to dinner. Mr and Mrs Hunter[1] came with us from church and were the only strangers we had at dinner, company out of the family I should say. I never knew a more quiet Christmas. Accounts had been received here and in the State generally of an effort at insurrection in Kaintucky and Tennessee. It was represented as being very general and well organized, and caused a good deal of anxiety, tho very little or no talk, as every one felt it should not be the subject of general talk. Belflowers and Oliver (the overseer at Waverly) brushed up their guns and amunition chests etc. and observed and listened, but held their tongues. No signs of organization or of serious discontent were observed as far as I am aware of. Your Papa changes his overseer at Nightingale Hall this year. Faulk who has lived there the last 6 years goes away and Pittman goes to that place. I hope Pittman may prove a good mana[ger of the] negroes as well as a good planter, he has a high reputation. . . . .

Adele Petigru Allston to Robert F. W. Allston[2]

Chicora Wood May 17th 1857

MY DEAR FRIEND   Your anxiety about the freshet may be laid aside. It is receding very decidedly and William wrote me by Billy that on Friday, owing to the west wind Mr Oliver could scarcely get water to flow the necessary fields. It has certainly done no damage here. The worms that really seemed to threaten destruction to the upland crop, the negroes tell me, are beginning to *slack*.

. . . . I gave out cloths to the children Saturday (yesterday) shall to the grown people this week, and go to Nightingale Hall the 22.

William writes me the cloth fell very short at Waverly, 800 yards was the quantity ordered. I wrote Will to calculate as nearly as possible the number of yards given out, and then calculate how much more he wants. He says he has given out to 78 children. I should not be surprised if it does not hold out here. I think it was 139 who took not counting boys such as Tony and Moses.

[1] Mr. and Mrs. Joseph Hunter, the former the rector of Prince Frederick's Parish (1848–62).

[2] Addressed: Charleston, S.C.

I think it would be as well for you to order 100 yds of cheap calicos, not lower priced than 10 or 11 cents very good may be had at that, and the cheaper are not worth any thing. Paul did not bring any box from Frasers, he brought only a basket of stale [illegible] bread.

Stephens wife Lizzie is getting worse and worse. I do not know what is to be done with her, if some regular employment cannot be found suitable to her I think she will lose her senses from these tempers. I am very sure she ought to leave this yard where her example is unfavourable. If she was in a house next to old Thomas perhaps he would acquire some influence over her. . . . .

Monday morning We rose in health this morning. A good deal of rain fell last night. It is still cloudy and threatning this morning. 20 men from Nightengale were here the greater part of last week, and are to continue here until Tuesday evening. I wrote you of Pinset being left over the river until his wife came and brought him over last Wednesday night. I found on enquiry that Driver Sam had gone to meeting at Thomas house, and Tim *says* he was staking a flat. I think Hamedy ought to go to the Beach the 21st or 22 at the farthest. We ought to move before you come home as I do not think it would be well for you to pass a night on the plantation after returning; tho the weather is still very cool. I think it would be as well for Adele to write to Madame Chovin Rue Roisomere to send her three evening dresses. That is if Lemon would undertake to be the medium of communication and you would give her the needful. I suppose $200 out of which he should get her from Desprice one dozen pair gloves. It would be necessary for Adele to write to Madame Chovin and send a dress body and the length of her skirt, and limit her as to price.

I hear the Ashe lot that has the small house on it is to be sold, Miss Ashe being dead. Suppose you look at it the situation is certainly very fine. You ought to take some step about a house if we are to have one in the Winter. And I do not abandon the idea of bringing Adele out for all dear Ben says to the contrary. She will be in her 18th year, and has been pretty steadily at school. I have no doubt as to the propriety of the step. That is if she is to be introduced at all. It is time for me to go to the childrens lessons.

Henry D. Lesesne to Adele Petigru Allston

Summerville, June 18, 1857

DEAR SISTER ADELE, Your mentioning me in connection with the Dehon Mansion[1] in your letter to my wife I will assume as my warrant for the privilege of writing you a note, brief it should be, for the Yankee clock on my simple mantel is on the stroke of 12. The house will be for sale sooner or

---

[1] This house, which the Allstons eventually purchased, is known as the Nathaniel Russell House and is located at 51 Meeting Street.

later, at the latest not more than a year or 18 months perhaps hence, I think. One of the two acting Exors., with whom my conferences have taken place, is disposed to advertise and sell at once. The other has faith in the brilliant anticipations for Charleston of which we have lately heard so much, and thinks it would be better to wait a while. If his view prevail, they will endeavor to rent the premises for the present, and will expect a sum equal to the interest on the estimated value of the property with taxes, insurance etc. added. One disposed to hire on those terms might have it immediately, or it might be purchased at once by one willing to give the price they hope to obtain. It is, I think, beyond all comparison, the finest establishment in Charleston. It was built without regard to cost, not by contract, but by day's work of the best mechanics, and cost $80,000 or more. When Mr. Russell made his will, his fortune had become impaired, and considering that neither of his children could afford to take it at its true value, he directed that in the division of his Estate it should be set down at $38,000. The Exors. have not decided yet what price they will ask, but the assessed value in the Tax Office is $30,000; and it is the rule to assess property for taxation lower than its supposed market value. I think they expect to get something between $30,000 and $40,000. The Hopley house[1] will cost Mr. Adger, when his improvements are completed (it is said) $45,000. And I think this is in every respect a very preferable establishment. I would be delighted to see you in it, and will take great pleasure in doing every thing I can for the Governor and you in the premises. . . . .

Henry D. Lesesne to Adele Petigru Allston

Summerville July 2, 1857

DEAR SISTER ADELE, I duly received your letter, and Mr. Petigru has showed me one from the Governor to him saying he would be willing to give $30,000 for the Dehon Mansion. I communicated this to Dr. Dehon, and to-day he and his brother called on me and informed me that they had fixed the price at $38,000, which happens to be the sum at which Mrs. Dehon took it in the division of Mr. Russell's estate, according to the provisions of his will, of which I will annex an extract. They promised to furnish me with the dimensions of the lot, and if they do so tomorrow I will give them to you in a P. S. I suppose you would not make such a purchase without an inspection of the premises being made by the Governor or yourself, and I think that after such an inspection you would at any rate say that if any establishment in Charleston is worth the price named, this is.

I was not exactly in earnest, as you suppose, in saying I might arrange to live summer and winter in my Summerville house. But I *would* sell my town

---

[1] At 32 Legaré Street, now more generally known as the Simonton or Sword-Gate House.

house for $20,000, and hire one until I could find a suitable smaller house which I might purchase. I have found it a delightful residence, but it is entirely unsuitable to my fortune, and therefore I have never been quite at ease in it. To have nearly the whole of one's estate invested in his Dwelling gives him a false position, and must subject his family to distress as well as mortification when he is removed, and the income they have enjoyed goes with him. In the price named I would include some things which are peculiarly adapted to the house, such as the Gas fixtures, carpets in the Hall, drawing room, dining room, and chambers in the third story, and perhaps some other things which I do not now think of. . . . .

July 3. Dimensions of the Dehon lot, about 130 feet front, by about 224 feet deep.

Extract from Mr. Russell's Will. "As I am well persuaded that the price which my Mansion House cost with the premises in Meeting Street ought not to be the rule of valuation, to prevent difficulties, and I hope dissatisfaction in the valuation of that property, I have concluded to prescribe the sum at which it shall be valued for the purpose of a division, and do hereby affix thereto the sum of thirty eight thousand Dollars; as to all the other property the persons appointed are to exercise their judgment in point of true value."

I just now met an energetic neighbor, who lately purchased the house next to mine, who informed me that he is getting up a memorial to the City Council to improve Tradd St. by grading and Mac-Adamising (not paving). The circumstance which would cause me some regret at parting with my house would be the loss of the cistern. While many have been dry, and others contained disagreeable water, ours has always supplied ourselves and several friends with an abundance of pure water.

Robert F. W. Allston to Benjamin Allston

Executive Department Charleston 17th Jany 1858

DEAR BEN . . . . You speak of the difference in appearance of the Rice at Chicora and N[ightingale] Hall. It is notoriously so, the young rice below never promises as well as that above, but when it heads out and matures, being less blades, but with full ears it turns out well if it is to be treated well, so dont be discouraged by appearances. Let Dr Sparkman send for and have his Buck lamb, it [illegible] you or I have not mention'd it to Pitman. I write and endorse it to you. Dr S is to have one of the lambs (a buck) saved for my eating.

Mr Weston is quite right to buy Waterford it is so necessary to complete the embellishment of his residence, Hagley,[1] my birth-place, that situated

[1] Hagley plantation was situated on Waccamaw Neck immediately north of Allston's Waterford property.

as he is 5 or $6000 should not deter him from adding it to his premises. His grounds will then be magnificent. If there was any chance of my ever owning Hagly, no money could buy Waterford from me, only $4000 divide us. It shall be kept open certainly until the canal be cut on the Island. Advise Leander to do his work more briskly wherever Mr B[elflowers] puts him. If he improves decidedly, he will probably be put back, but dont tell him so. Both you and Will are mistaken as to the value of the Mill, ask Mr Weston what his was valued at, which he has leased it upon at 10 pr cent. As between the brothers, the offer of Joe is very well, if you add the cost of the stave and hoop-machines and their buildings thereto, say $9000 with the alternative to sell or buy. I am sorry to hear of John Tillman's illness. He is a valuable citizen. When you go through the corn now be mounted, a field of tall corn is hotter than a cane-break. As soon as the Oats or Rye is cut have some slips planted with first rain, the June slips always do best. . . . '

Robert F. W. Allston to the Kansas Executive Committee[1]

Executive Department [Charleston] 18th Feby 1858.

GENTLEMEN   I acknowledge your politeness in sending me a card for the complimentary dinner to be given by your association to Mr. Carr of Kansas;[2] and would certainly be with you, if by my presence, I could aid your purpose in forwarding the views of Mr. Carr and those with whom he acts. But considering that I might rather mar the hilarity of the festive occasion, I ask that you will allow me to decline joining you at dinner. Be assured, however, of my sympathy in the demonstration of Kindness with which your guest is honor'd in the reunion with his former associates at the bar, and with the companions of his boyhood. I beg that you will assure him also of my Sympathy in the struggles for independence which he and his friends in Kansas have made and have so gallantly sustain'd.

I do not hesitate to express such sympathy but do it with the greater freedom because of the efforts which have been made and in making by persons who have been entrusted with authority in that [illegible] Territory, to prejudice the public mind against the party whose cause he has espoused. And because of the extraordinary Steps which have been taken by certain able Statesmen greatly distinguished in the public estimation the tendency of which is North and South to degrade the labors in Convention of that party, and to neutralize the patriotic design of the Federal Executive as express'd in his recent message to admit Kansas into the Union as a State under the Constitution last adopted. The promoting [?] result of the Lecompton Convention is exhibit'd [by] the gratifying spectacle of Massachusetts

---

[1] Copy addressed: Charleston, S.C.

[2] Joseph P. Carr, who had been recently elected a member of Congress from Kansas in vain anticipation of the admission of that territory to the Union under the Lecompton Constitution.

and Carolina acting harmoniously together in doing what they deem to be right under the terms and in the Spirit of the Federal Constitution.

Robert F. W. Allston to Benjamin Allston

Meeting St. [Charleston] 3d June 1858

DEAR BEN   You were quite right in ordering the best seed for planting over. I am much disappointed in this account of Mr. Pitman's management and vigilance. He should forfeit the value of the seed wasted. I have never but once had to plant over a field at home and once at Friendfield when Hemingway was sick, this last I traced to its cause *too deep a flow in the "sprout"* and I doubt not this had something to do with the failure at N.[ightingale] Hall, whether or not it argues a want of due attention and judgement. It is too late to plant over. The rice must be push'd forward from the start and throughout by water, and then the product will be very materially diminish'd by Rice-birds, if not destroy'd. You had better make Mr Pitman sensible how incumbent on him it is to send to market some 5 or 600 bushels of wheat, or you will feel sensibly the effects of a short crop of rice next year, notwithstanding the 70 acres of fresh land at Waterford. I fear Trim has forfeited his half.

Fortunately you are quite independent of Mr Weston and his path. The stables on the other side are better for horses every way. Thomas and Abram can sleep over one of the stables and do their cooking any where and keep their things on the beach. Do not contend with him and dont speak to him of Waterford unless he first mention the subject. I have no objection to your explaining my estimate to Dr. Post who doubtless will allude to it. He was the first person to communicate Mr. Weston's desire to own the Eastern or All Saints portion of the tract, the price of which I put at $15,000. He said he thought Mr Weston would willingly give $12,000 for that portion after I had named the foregoing price. The Doctor is very communicative and very insinuating and deferential. You will find him and his wife both agreeable, but bear in mind, he was raised in this city, is familiar with its street habits and is the familiar and convenient friend and somewhat dependent on Charles Alston, Mr Weston and Mr. Middleton.

In course of time I desire to throw farther into the Marsh, my (back) road possibly as far as Mr Westons, I dont know his location, but the labor cannot be spared until the canal is cut at Waterford and the bank made up on the main.

By last boat I received a Report from Mr Tilton at Mill but none from Chicora. However I dont need this if you will give me an abstract. If George is not satisfactory send him to Tilton to work as a Carpenter and agree what shall be paid for him pr. month. If he is steady, he can catch fish for you daily and build at Canaan 1 lime kiln in June and 1 in July.

We are all gratified that you have dismiss'd your cold and are getting on well with William. When you become accustom'd to it you will find it a regular and rational mode of life, far better suited to a planter than that which I am now living both morally and physically.

I go tomorrow at 10 O'clock to meet the School Teachers at the public school and will take Charles and Jane with me and ma if she will go.

Benjamin Allston to Robert F. W. Allston

Beach June 4th 1858

My dear Father   Yours of 3th inst has just been received and I hasten to answer it. Pitman sent up at once for the rice and fortunately found enough already thrashed out to answer him and he finished planting on Wednesday last. The Wheat is quite ripe and will be cut on Monday. I fear we shall loose much of it, in one way or another. I went over to Chicora on Tuesday, Bellflowers sent the boat for me and knew very well that I was coming, but I saw nothing of him, neither did I get his *report*. Why I do not know. He was over the river I saw Collins and gave him the instructions which I intended to give B. about the hay etc. I am afraid you will not get much, as Pitman said he could put up none. Why the preserves did not go down was because Bellflowers neglected to tell Mary, she has them. I should not be surprised if I sent down Linda and the little black mare soon by Prince, if he can be spared. I will try and attend to all that you desire. I have just returned from Club where we spent a very pleasant day Dr. Hazel was quite facetious, and thinks my name is handed down to remotest posterity by being mentioned in Abbots P. R Survey in Oregon. George has conducted himself pretty well thus far, not very many fish to be sure, but enough I shall set him to work at the Kiln. Why Bellflowers sent for lime I do not know. Mr Weston has the plats and says he will send them home at once, says that he is sorry that you and he did not agree about rice land that you value it much higher than he does. He mentioned the thing first of course. So I suppose there is an end of the matter. I intend getting the plats and riding over the lines getting him to go with me if I can. His road works very well much better than I supposed it would and I have not moved my horses, and I shall not do so, if with any degree of comfort I can get on with them here. Thomas thus far has behaved very well. I do not vouch for his continued behavior. Hern Tucker is cutting his road on back beach and invites William to meet him on Monday and find out the line between them. I see that you will be compelled in the course of time to let the road pass through your premises, as the others, or be esteemed very unaccomodating and unhospitable. Such is evidently the wish of many now. I of course shall not pass any without your sanction. If ever your Causeway is made passable for wheels, and that road be cut it will be the thoroughfare of the Island to the Main Have you seen a letter that I wrote to Risley upon the receipt of one of his. I sent a copy to Joe. That is what takes him to Charleston I think. I am tired of his shuffling and evident desire to stave off the debt, as long as possible. I want the money. I have just received another letter from McRae saying that the Certificates of shares would be sent on the next steamer, and assuring me that all was right, etc. Property worth $500,000.00 so he says. I wrote to him per last mail saying that the money should be sent to him upon the receipt of the certificates, also I wrote to Jas. E. Calhoun asking him to ascertain what the character of the company was and of its President, McRae. A copy of both letters I have. I am full of confidence that it will eventually turn out right.

I am much obliged to Mother for her kind letter, and would answer it if I had the time but I understand tonight that the Boat leaves Waverly at 6 a.m. and I must be over there in time to see her. If she goes further up the river tomorrow very well but if she goes down to Georgetown at once I am much afraid you will loose your provisions, lamb etc, as it will not be possible to have them ready so early, as I told Pitman yesterday at noon she would pass. I shall tell Tilton about the sheep skins. . . . .

Robert F. W. Allston to Benjamin Allston

Meeting St. [Charleston] 8th June 1858

DEAR BEN . . . . It would be convenient to me to part with Waterford or a portion of it. But having laid out upon it so much of my energies and my peoples labor, I do not think I am extravagant in my estimate of its value. Mr. Weston's father bought the place Hagley so very cheap that his son can afford to pay a full price to complete his premises and it is only a full price. I have repeatedly been inform'd that the former owner of Hagley, Col John A Alston, learning that his father would give $300 an acre for the property, anticipated him and paid that price or very nearly. If Mr. W. is willing to give $12,000 for the main as Dr Post told me he was, he can submit to my estimate of the island surely, which is only a little over $200 an acre.

The Statue of Washington is come and Mr Hubard[1] the artist is with us occupying your room. He is a small inferior looking man but agreeable. The statue is to be set up in the centre of the orphan-house yard, near the statue of Pitt.

[1] William James Hubard (1806–62), a native of England, who made several copies of the Houdon Washington in the capitol at Richmond, Va., one of which South Carolina purchased. Allston later reported to the General Assembly that it would be cared for in Charleston until the completion of the new state house in Columbia. It now stands at the Gervais Street entrance to this building. For information concerning Hubard the editor is indebted to Miss Helen G. McCormack.

You must bear a great deal with Jesse Belflowers, he is a man of few words, of fix'd habits and those solitary. You will rarely meet with him on so large a place, for he is always circulating and no one knows where to find him. The negroes dislike him mortally on this very account and will not fail to get up a disagreement and jealousy between him and Collins. I think Collins will show it this summer I have never required him to wait for me, but to attend to business as it came in his way. Having his report weekly I had no need to question him. What you wish Mary to attend to, tell her yourself or send it to her on paper. She will have it read to her. It will be an advantage for you to have the benefit of B's experience in going over the crop, but you must humor him, he is a crooked stick. The trunk minder will always find you out and is full of information if you will take pains to develop it. If you give him too much of leading questions he will be apt to mislead you. . . . .

Robert F. W. Allston to Benjamin Allston

Meeting St. [Charleston] 25th June 1858

DEAR BEN .   .   .   .

[June 28] The only message which I remember having given you, was to Mr Tilton, namely to say that I had left with Jas. Adger and Co an order to Mr Tighe of Richmond for a larger grain Separator (Solmon's) to be used as a chaff-fan. He doubtless has written a particular description of its proportions etc very properly. I drew out the description for an order here and had Jo Blyth Allston to copy it, in order to familiarize him with the instrument its uses and cost etc. Mr Tilton will reserve a small parcel of Ro[ugh] Rice in order to test it (should it come) before entering upon the Toll-business of the Season. I hope you are both well.

. . . . Let James select 4 good hams of this year and 2 old ones, have them pack'd in a neat box in dry chaff and direct to me by next boat. I will send them by him [Hal Lesesne] to the Atty. Genl of England to whom I intend to give him letters. As the box will receive a new address here, let my name be placed near the upper corner to the left. Pray let me know the numbers on the papers of seed, which I gave you for Mr. Glennie. I gave one to Mr Middleton to present in Georgetown to Dr. Prior which I think was A No 65.

.   .   .   .

Great are the preparations for to-day. It is the anniversary of the battle of Fort Moultrie, now made a Holiday, and devoted to the memory of Calhoun. The day open'd with clouds, a light shower has pass'd and now there is some promise of sunshine. The Genl Staff will assemble at Head Quarters at 2 O'cl to lunch and hence we will move at 3 O'clock to join the procession under escort of the Dragoons. Look at the programme and you will see how imposing it must all be. I shall wish very much for my charger, as, I am to review the troops of the Brigade on Monday next at 6 O'clock A.M. all this was quite unexpected. Col [illegible] and some others are in Town for the purpose, and next Wednesday Evening there is to be given by the Ladies a Promenade Concert at Institute Hall for raising funds for defraying the expenses of today. Your Mother has intimation that she is expected to go and to contribute flowers and refreshments. I dont know if she will go, except merely to indicate her presence, but the flowers will and refreshments. The Military band from the U. S. will contribute the music.

. . . .

P. S.   When you read Sim[m]s description of the battle of Fort Moultrie, cut it out and put it into your scrap book.

Benjamin Allston to Robert F. W. Allston

Waverly July 7th 1858

MY DEAR FATHER   I have just received your letter for which I am much obliged. The boat did not come up last night, and goes down as soon as finished taking rice, moreover I have a sore hand, which tho' better than it was is not well, therefore my letter must be short. I send you Belflowers report. The week has been spent in hoeing rice you see, no rain having fallen the corn and potatoes bid fair to be consumed by the heat, and no slips could be planted any where. Sunday made three weeks since we had had any rain. On Monday however it fell nicely while we were at Musterfield blowing some too, and it has rained with but little interruption ever since mostly a fine soaking rain, just what we most needed. God is Good and gracious. Let us thank him. There was a full attendance on Monday of the people. Reed, Wilson, Dozier, and Brewerton Jr. who has come out for the Legislature were the speakers. There was no oration proper. The people did not seem much excited by the speakers and Brewerton Sr. was the only one who applauded at all. His Son made a poor figure.

I did not go up to Watchesaw on Saturday, on account of my hand being much swollen. I remained at Plantersville Monday night with Heriot. You were frequently asked for by your friends on Monday, and were handsomely toasted by John Tucker, he will not speak, tho' he will it is thought head the ticket. Yesterday Belflowers was planting slips in the field on left of Avenue, today he plants the oat field, in the corn field. The rain is very propitious thus far, it will give the corn new life. I did not see the rice yesterday, but was told 'twas looking well. Pitman has been sick, and I am afraid he has lost another child on the plantation. He seems to be not very careful to the children when sick. . . . . .

J. J. Flournoy[1] *to Robert F. W. Allston*

Athens P. O. Geo. Dec. 1858

Hon Sir: When the white men of the Slaver, Echo,[2] were arrested, it, beyond all doubt, was a clear case of "engaging in the illegal slave trade"; and how the Jury, at Columbia, S. C. could bring in "No bill," on so obvious a *true bill* fact transcends all my ingenuity of apology for them on any other principle, but the conclusion that they have committed *perjury* (*a common thing, now among juries*) and that if they but had justice, they would be branded on their forehead with the ignomeny.

Sir, the slave trade procuring Africans into any American country, now diabolically sought to be into the Southern department of the U States, in the sequel in the view of Philosophy, only creating an amalgamation of blood with the Place of the accursed Home, having their father's doom; making Americans in the long run no better than Spaniards and Mexicans, who are, it is well known, of Moorish taint. this Slave trade is a heinous inequity, and subject to the abhorence and condemnation of every rational mind!

Does not incorporation with the blacks obtain even now. Look at the North; does she not legalize marriage, in which, while no white man weds the black wench, negro rascals are but too glad to marry white women. Do not many of our pretty white girls even now, permit illicit negro embrace at the South, [illegible] how much Woman is for [illegible] and amalgamation? We have as many of these black devils to manage now, and *keep from our women*, as we can, and to add by reinforcing them with new recruits from Africa, is the last degrading diabolism that can be effected.

Do you believe Sir that Slaves will exist *forever* in our country? I know better. Already the North in spite of Sewards *insane* apprehensions about Slavery absorbing them (he didn't believe himself, he only wanted to stir up Northern blood against the South) is the resting place of free negroes, who has the leave to get white wives. And Slavery will never never recommence there. At least not African Slavery. Already in Kentucky, Missouri, Virginia, Delaware, Maryland, and parts of North Carolina, Tennessee, Georgia (by my own observation here) the idea of continued black Servitude is scouted. And in the next or succeeding generations the liberation of our negroes will be seriously capitated   Mr Hammond was as foolish when he

---

[1] John Jacobus Flournoy (*ca.* 1800–1879), erratic Georgia advocate of the expulsion of the Negro from the United States.

[2] The "Echo" had been seized and brought into Charleston Harbor in the preceding summer. The vessel was confiscated and the Negroes returned to Africa, but the captain and the crew were later acquitted.

proclaimed the perrieniality of Slavery in the South, as was the villian Seward, when he said it would go North if not stopped South.

Why you South Carolinians and Georgians are running like mad-caps after the *ignus fatuus* of such small-sighting reasoner as Hammond, etc. But never will for your lives see Deaf Flournoy as he is 'Nor imbibe a salutary light from his ever widely luminating mind.'

Well, It can be helped. "Whom the Gods intend to destroy, Etc."

I do not believe it seems that Liberty in the fallen condition of man, is ever to be his inheritance in one 99th part that it belongs to Despotisms! *The Earth is too cursed for it, yet.* Nothing but trouble is man's lot, "for a time and times." And only some Monarch *to tease and worry him.* Our fathers, I fear made a mistake in supposing the liberty they fought, bled, and died for, would *abide* with their sons! The only legitimate Government looks as if it is Monarchy. We have elements of ruin to the Union and the constitution; and the second farce will be a military rule, and a Monarch! Our negro Slavery is bad enough in its place to lead to this direful catastrophe. And our Juries are nearly all perjurists and damned rascals! They do not feel, as the people or they are any responsibility to God for their freedom, "as above the responsibility of Monarchial subjects, and are sadly, thus, "found wanting!"

There are two things necessary to be done to secure and prolong liberty. It is to abolish the Trial by Jury as a failure and a nuisance, if not to punish them when they perjure themselves. And to send packing off, by Expulsion, the negroes, who are about fit to stay here, free or bond, as you or I can swallow *prussic acid!*

Unless these be done, our men of fore cast had better be making up their minds to see that we are getting bad fame with [illegible] as fathers, that supinely bequeath to their children grievous curses!

I am yours, always sorrowfully, considering Etc, Etc, Etc.

N. B.   Dick Yeadon, and Dan Trezevant, knows me like a pea.

P. S.   Juries are to find *facts*, whether adverse or not to their own prepossessions and not to let go facts and qualify their verdicts accordingly to circumstance or public opinion. As they fail here, so they are no more *Juries;* but a set of Partizans.

Note   I always make my argument, when I adduce any strong, cogent and logical, comprehensively covering all grounds, but am always, frankly, open to conviction; and would be exceedingly rejoiceful, did, in a fair and full contest, any gentleman overthrow my assumptions. But alas, none seem to be able to so do. I have the reputation of being absolutely unanswerable. But I don't like to be, if I am in error, and only supported by greater adroitness and acuteness of ingenuity. I would meet any advocate of the retenence of the *negroes* here, (I dont say "slaves" I am not at present engaged on a controversy with *institutions*, but on a *Race;* "negroes" therefore is the best term to *designate* with the strongest argument he can offer, that of Divine Authority for the institution of Slavery, and with the [illegible] on the Subject.

If but the Africans be gone, I would not seriously object to enslaving the wild Indians, who cost us so much. So the curse *in* Ham be gone, Shem may dwell with us and no fear of the evil of such amalgamation. So you see I am rather a prosecutor than otherwise; but the subjects and the unmitigating evil of incorporation!

God allowed Slavery in the Patriarchs and regulated it by Moses. Why? Because his Law or will was not fully promulgated to the Patriarchs. And his allowing it by Moses was to deter incorporation, and become of the contrariety of the people's hearts as in [illegible].

Is this not so, when we saw what construction the Almighty put on Noah's prophecy against Esau, *who was ever unrepenting.* Instead of directing the Hebrews to ensnare the countries for servants, he commanded their total extirpation! and rebuked saving any alive! as see chapter 2 of Judges, first verse. So if God authorised Negro or Hammonian association among us He would have allowed it in Palestine. But as it was not, [illegible].

P. S.   Are Juries vital? are Judges incorrupt? Hear Janius—"A pure and impartial administration of Justice is, perhaps, the strangest bond to secure a cheerful submission of the people, and to engage their affections to Government." So many corrupt Juries are weakening American attachment to their country. The 12 that tried the Slaves, are but a sample of the rest of American Juries, who prevent Justice on every thing throughout the Union, more or less.

James L. Petigru to Adele Petigru Allston

St Michaels Alley [Charleston] 21st Decr 1858

. . . . It is time nearly that Sister Anne should hear from the Boys, for my words were that the Governor would expect an answer by Christmas. She is as much in the mind to sell as ever; whether she will sell if the boys oppose may be doubted; but I am sure it is not their interest to do so, for she would not thank them for thwarting her wishes. I have said nothing more to her about the Abbeville negroes because I told her from the first that she might include or reserve them. And I mentioned to you that Philip Sarah and Hannah would be reserved, tho their services if they are willing may be secured. If the Governor had a strong preference for the Abbeville property she would probably assent; tho as it is, I infer that she would like to keep it longer, and disposing of Sandy Island at once.[1]

[1] The reference is to the purchase by Allston of the Pipe Down plantation and slaves from his wife's sister-in-law, Mrs. Mary Ann Petigru. See below, pp. 149, 352, 353.

Johnston is talking of going to pay Jo a visit but I prefer trusting this to the mail.

Tell the Governor I have heard from Moses that he is a Trustee in place of Lieut Carn. As ill news travels fast, you no doubt know already the fate of the Blue ridge.[1] McGowan says with truth in a letter I have just received, the Parish system is defended on the ground that it assures the State of a certain number of enlightened liberal members in the Legislature. But when we see them voting with the narrowest views, and the allies of a contracted selfish policy we are constrained to doubt whether Parish influence is worth preserving. . . . .

James L. Petigru to Robert F. W. Allston

Charleston 29 Decr 1858

MY DEAR GOVR. . . . . Thursday morning [December 30]—So far I had written when interrupted, I have seen Sister Anne, and also the note you wrote to Johnston.

With respect to Pipe Down, she complies with any thing you choose. But she has susceptibilities about the people. She has told them they are sold to you and has claimed their thanks for having kept in view her promise to give them a good Master. That they would pass to your heir was what she hoped and expected for them, but she did not expect to convey them to the Heir but that he would receive them from his Ancestor, with the responsibility (whatever that may be) that attaches to what is inherited. She wishes therefore that you would not insist on any change, as she accepted the proposition in your name it is not unreasonable that she wishes to retain the advantage of dealing directly with you. It is not to be supposed that she is wounded or hurt by your advancing Ben with these negroes nor putting them on Westons place nor doing with them as you please; but she thinks she ought to secure to them what she promised by putting their fate in your hands.

There are 3 negroes in town. A mother her child, and nurse at Henry Lesesne's. The mother was lent to Harriet as a nurse, they will be returned probably very soon.

Your views about the stock meet her entire concurrence. She writes to her Nephews by tomorrows boat, to co-operate in giving full effect to the agreement, and meeting you for that purpose directly. In the meantime I enclose a letter for Josh, which you will send to him for greater despatch. . . . .

[1] The defeat in the General Assembly of a bill to provide additional funds for the Blue Ridge Railroad.

Alexandre Nattemare[1] to Robert F. W. Allston

Agence Centrale des Echanges Internationaux

Paris, January 3d 1859

DEAR SIR, A most severe sickness which, for several weeks, prevented me from attending to any business, is my only apology for having delayed so long acknowledging your Kind letter of November last inclosing a Bill of Exchange of £61.7.3 for the expences of our Agency during the elapsed year 1858.

Please to receive my most Cordial thanks, not only for all your Kindness for the System of exchange and its humble author while Chief Magistrate of your noble State, but for your liberal contributions, as planter, of Seeds and plants you forwarded but unfortunatly not received yet.

I trust Dear Sir, that although retire[d] from public life our intercourse will not be interrupted and that the Medals[2] and other testimonials of esteem and high appreciation of your efforts for the improvement of Agriculture etc. will not be the last I shall have to transmit to you and that our next agricultural fair will be enriched by new specimens of the territorial riches of South Carolina, and of your successful experiments in improving them.

The Imperial and Central Societies, of Agriculture, Horticulture and Acclimatation will receive with great gratification, and are ready to pay due attention and justice to your Communications, as well as to those that may reach them from other planters or Agriculturists from South Carolina.

The elementary books I addressed to you were procured at the suggestion of the Hon. Mr. Calhoun, Secretary of Legation here, for the use of a Standing Committee appointed or to be appointed to investigate the Educational System of Europe and see what parts of the Same may be appropriate to your own.

May I beg of you to be kind enough to call the favorable attention of your Honourable Successor towards our noble cause of the intellectual union of nations, and secure to it the Continuation of the generous patronage bestowed upon it by all his predecessors ever Since 1849.

In the hope of receiving soon a letter from you informing me that you are preparing Something for our next Agricultural fair. . . . .

[1] The writer signed himself as "Agent of S. Carolina for international literary exchanges."

[2] Probably prizes won by Allston's rice at the Paris Exposition of 1855 and at an exhibition the following year.

Robert F. W. Allston to Joseph Blyth Allston[1]

Chicora Wood Jan 13th 1859

MY DEAR JOE, The terms of payment for any bond you may give us, you can arrange to suit yourself within 7 years $20,000, the balance may be made payable by a separate bond two years after. I have been over the ground since, as far as the head of Bullens Lake and it occured to me that the 3 fields on Long Creek and along the Guandelos line will suit Ben better than you to work (if ever he gets at them) and that I had better rescue the Sand Knowl bluffing on Long Creek both for sand and for a Mill site (it is the spot which was selected by me years gone by for Mr Fraser to build a Mill on). So that we will divide Bullens on the Tucker tract, and make your bonds for $25,000, if you are still of the mind to take it, making the line such as is indicated by the dotted line upon the rough sketch enclosed herewith.[2]

Hearing that Mr. F. Weston was very moody at the place having miss'd his hands I had them all to dine with us, and offer'd him the purchase to be shared with you. He declined saying the debt would be too heavy for him. Now my dear Joe I must commend you to the like consideration. Do not involve yourself too much, so that a disaster such as Chisolm's or an epidemic among the negroes (I lost in one year 28 negroes *22* of whom were *task hands*) might embarrass you for life. I would not buy negroes at Cotton prices. If you meet with an orderly gang of some planter neighbor or otherwise who would sell you at *$500* rather than send away and separate his people at a higher figure then in such case you might adventure. But I would not give more unless I had the money to pay down and without being indebted for it. I am just now considering such a negotiation with Dr Foster whom I met on Tuesday at the appraisement for divisions of the Heriot Estate. You ask me about the Heriot negroes. They are generally good negroes having never been abused. But I presume the gang at large has been culled Orinoca is a smart intelligent Driver but tricky. He was sent to Dr. Sparkman by Dr Heriot in his life time. You will see the printed list and understand that I would not pay for them more than $500 and at a long credit. . . . .

Robert F. W. Allston to Sarah Carr[3]

Chicora Wood 17th Jany 1859.

MY DEAR YOUNG LADY Far from having any thing to excuse in the application which you make to me, I am pleased to see, by the terms of your note and the practical manner in which you have described the embarrassment,

[1] Copy.

[2] Missing. The reference is to the option on a part of the recently purchased Guendalos. See above, p. 22.

[3] Copy.

that the daughter of my former friend proves herself so capable to aid her Mother in business. Acknowledging my disposition to assist you in this praise-worthy effort, I yet am apprehensive lest, in my declining years, it would be presumptious to undertake the management of an insubordinate Slave, where previous misconduct ought to be punished, before he can be transfer'd to me as his owner.

I like to be kind to my people but I imperatively require of them honesty, truth, diligence and cheerfulness in their work, wherever and whatever it is. I do not think your Mother's man would get on well with me unless he could answer to the above qualifications. And it is a principle with me to face and defeat trouble if it come in the discharge of my duty, but never to make trouble for myself. You will see therefore that I have determined against the purchase of your Mother's man, tho' I could employ him if he was an honest fellow.

With thanks for your kind wishes I reciprocate them heartily for your welfare.

Joseph Blyth Allston to Robert F. W. Allston

Charleston Jan 18th 1859

MY DEAR UNCLE   I purchased the Harietta[1] gang of negroes to day at $575 round being $35,075 in all. Doar had previously offered $550 round. It is more than I should pay but the winter is passing with little prospect of their selling for less and the Waverly mill would perhaps be benefitted more by an increase of hands this winter than at any future time. The terms are 3000 cash balance within 7 years. I shall go up on the Steamer on Thursday receive the negroes at Harrietta and thence to Waverly. Frederick Rutledge had bought the driver which is a great drawback. There are 61.

I saw Mr Petigru tonight he will probably write you tomorrow but bid me say to you that if the Foster negroes are those which Mrs Withers paid Read and Wilkinson $10,000 apiece for, the title is clear.

With regard to E. F. Allston I know of no legal remedy that you have to hold the negroes being only security My advice would be to notify Mr Betts by some one or more persons who could bear testimony of the notice that you understand E. F. Allston intends leaving the State and that if he allows the negroes mortgaged to him to leave the State without satisfying the bond and mortgage you refuse to pay you have a right to insist that Betts should urge his claim upon the property and satisfy himself out of it.

If you can spare time dear Uncle in the midst of your business to advise Will as to the best manner of making room for the 61 negroes I shall bring up it would greatly oblige me. I think the academy out buildings might be used.

[1] Harrietta plantation, on the Santee River, which had been acquired in 1858 by Stephen D. Doar.

Aunt Adele and the others arrived to day and look so well as to speak more strongly than words in favour of country life.

Robert F. W. Allston to Adele Petigru Allston[1]

Chicora Wood, Saturday night, March [1859]

DEAR WIFE, Your note has been read to Mary, who, with a low curtsy "Do tell Miss heap a tanke for the frock, likewise for the letter Sir." Some Turkey Hens have turn'd up at Ditchford and she will send six Molly has but 3 left. There have been no capons made, except "of Dunghill fowls." Mary reports tonight 10 dozen Eggs put up to go over Monday out of which 2 Doz duck Eggs, from Barnyard, "6 last-fall chickens" and a small supply of butter. The clothes will be done up and sent down when ready.

Ben's rested field was finish'd today. It will be a Study for him to gain experience by when he comes up, remembering its condition, let him look at it now, tight as a jug and ready for the trenching hoe. I deemed it best to stop work on the rested field before the house ("Landing field") the Season being too far advanced. If I could have procured the hands from Pipedown early in January, this now would be in as fine condition as the other. But as it is, the surface is cover'd with the green of water weeds and there is too little space betwixt this and planting time to take the "sour" out of it, 1/4th of the good seed would be lost in it, and the work can now be better bestow'd elsewhere. I will have 50 spades in the line-ditch on Monday Tuesday and Wednesday after which he must do his own ditching and planting.

I made an effort to see my neighbors today. The Hunters were gone visiting, and E. Weston to Waccamaw. The day was charming and the atmosphere along my banks freighted with the perfume of Jessamine, especially along the Ditchford Avenue, which was so shady and quiet I linger'd leisurely and agreeably. Indeed I was happy, until I met with an ox which had been abused by John and turn'd out of the cart. This quite upset me because of the poor animal, and because of the penalty which I had to impose. Puss, for the first time, pays me a visit tonight and is domiciliated on the rug. I do not lie down till 11, and then I sometimes would not but that my eyes fail. One of the advantages of this lonely life is that the evening psalm and the morning chapter *en Francais* are not neglected.

Apropos of the foreign language, if Adele desires to continue her Italian she may try M. George as a Teacher. It cannot be said that I paid for a quarter in advance, but the truth is I lent him $20 stranger as he was, and left his due-bill with R[obertson] B[lacklock] and Co. You must form an opinion of the man. He seem'd to me modest and gentle in his demeanor, but found little difficulty in asking for money. He will of course desire a further supply from somebody.

[1] Addressed: Charleston, S.C.

The ginger nuts will be sent in Wednesday's boat.

I enclose with this a remarkably full and detail'd account of the late horrible affair in Washington.[1] Sickles is the man who, by his conduct at Mr Peabody's dinner in London in 1854, produced the coldness between his principal Mr. Buchannan and the Banker. What an awful end of ambitious aspirations after influence in the political and fashionable world!

I will now address myself to sleep, after saying my prayers to the Good God, who I humbly trust will overlook or rather forbear my faults, render me content in my retirement, and bless and keep you and our little ones.

Robert F. W. Allston to Adele Petigru Allston

Waverly Mill 11th March 1859

MY DEAR ADELE   I have the pleasure to say Ben reach'd me safe yesterday. We breakfast together today and went to the Guendalos ditching then I left him at 10.30 to come hither. I have been to the seashore where the N[ightingale] Hall hands are clearing out a canal and working the causeway. The Bridges are giving way and a good deal of work to be done there, but it made me sorry to see the condition of Canaan (the dear old place where I first had the happiness to know you were to be a mother where we have been bless'd and in so many straits help'd each other). The house that old Paul lived in is half strip'd of its weather boarding the stable ditto. The sashes of the house a good deal shatter'd and the grand front steps about tumbling one side. The house is firm and greeted me with the well-remember'd old sea-shore smell agreeable to me. Tho some disrespectful fellows had been roasting oysters in the fire-place. Such things were never seen there before now. I permitted Mr. Tucker's overseer to go into the house last summer at his particular request and I presume this has given a licence to his negroes to go there, the most lawless set I have had to deal with these and the Barnwell's. Well I have just come to the Mill and while expecting the steamer with papers perhaps a letter, I occupy myself thus. It is now 5 O'clock. I brought over a bucket of butter (no bucket went the last trip, it seems Milley had not enough, and Mary omitted to inform till today we must make the [illegible] therefore to Capt Davis) and the trunk with the girl's clothes (the key to which is enclosed) all could not get in, and none of Charles', but Phebe put in 3 pieces of her new work for Adele and 4 for Bessie, being all that were done up.

Lavinia has been put in possession of her new work. Mary exhibited some turkey Eggs [illegible] Is not it time to set the turkey Eggs? I would not take away any more.

I must leave you now to look for my dinner. . . . .

[1] Missing. The reference is to the killing of Philip Barton Key by Daniel Edgar Sickles on February 27, 1859.

A. Sachtleben[1] to Robert F. W. Allston

Charleston March 15th 1859

DEAR SIR, Your favor of the 8th inst was duly received, also the Sketches of Washington Allston, sent by Mr. Perkins of Boston arrived last week. I would have done myself the pleasure to reply before this, had I not desired to wait till after a meeting of the Art-Committee, in order to report to you, as you wished it, the opinions of the gentlemen composing the Committee in regard to Mr. Allston's Sketches. But as on Saturday afternoon no quorum was formed, I can only give my own impressions, which however, I fear, are of very little value.

I think that very many of the Sketches contained in the volume are exceedingly beautiful, especially some of the groups and single figures from "Gabriel Setting the Watch," and from "Jacob's dream." Also the Sybil is very fine, the group of Dido and Anne, as it should be, of purest classical taste and the "Fairies leaving the Seashore" very happily and delicately conceived and executed. Altogether the volume is such, that I do not wonder that judges like Retsch and Cornelius have spoken of it in high terms of approval. We shall take good care of the work, it is however perhaps best to mention now, that the book has been slightly injured (in the margin and cover) on its journey from Boston to this city.

I regret that you were prevented from favoring us with your presence at our first anniversary. The celebration was in every respect creditable and successful, and reflected much credit on the committee appointed to superintend it. Mr. Middleton's address was admirable, and Mr. Hayne's poem very fine, as far as I could hear it, for Mr. Hayne was, in consequence of indisposition, not in good voice and could not always be distinctly understood throughout the Hall.[2] You will however soon have an opportunity of judging yourself of the literary efforts of Messrs Middleton and Hayne, as both will be printed.

As soon as the pamphlet is issued I shall not fail to mail a copy to your address, though the same will no doubt be done by the chairman of the Committee of arrangements.

Alexius M. Forster to Robert F. W. Allston

Friendfield March 15th 1859

DEAR SIR Your note of 9th inst. I received yesterday evening.

I am now passing the Waterfield Seed Rice through the Fan and Skreen and it will be ready for you at any time after today. I am sorry to say how-

---

[1] Charleston teacher, active member of the Carolina Art Association and later (1877–98) professor of Greek and Latin in the College of Charleston.

[2] These speakers were Nathaniel Russell Middleton, president of the College of Charleston, and the young poet, Paul Hamilton Hayne.

ever, that the quantity will be not more than half what you want. In whipping it off, too much rice was left on the sheaf, and then the winnowing, fanning and skreening have reduced the quantity to about 500 Bushels. There was more light Rice than I expected, caused I suppose, by the overtopping when the plant was in barrel. I regret this deficiency both on your account and my own. What there is, however, is in prime condition, never having been wet, or damaged in any way.

I do not remember ever having heard of Levi being ruptured. I certainly was not aware of it at the time of selling him, or I should have informed you. The fact of his never having complained of this affection, and his never having been in the Sick-House five days in the year since I have known him, makes me surprised to learn that he is so affected. I sold him as a sound negro; and if he really be the subject of Hernia, I am willing to arrange the matter to your satisfaction I can examine him; or I will take the declaration of the Physician of your neighbourhood.[1]

Revd Mr Mitchell says he will accept the appointment to deliver the anniversary address before the Indigo Society.

Robert F. W. Allston to Adele Petigru Allston

Chicora Wood 16th March 1859

MY DEAR ADELE . . . . I will send over tonight a bag of peas, a box of Eggs and whatever else Mary may have; and will send Minda in the boat. She suffers from prolapsis Uterus which renders her weakly in comparison with what she used to be. This winter she has been very ill, and has been some months obstructed, is now swelling, tho' not laid up I prefer to send her down to recruit she is very steady, honest and intelligent. If you choose to have her taught to work she may learn something this summer. I shall want her in the threshing Mill next winter.

I regret that I fail'd to think of asking Adele if she wish'd to pursue Italian when M. George applied to me for money. She might have profited by my advances to him, if I were gifted with any sagacity. Mrs Pringle with her daughter is pursuing German with intense assiduity. She took a lesson before breakfast in Charleston and has here a teacher domiciliated, ie a german woman to talk with her. I dined with Read on Monday. Pringle told me this at dinner and further, that he never invited an Englishman to his county seat unless "he knew him."

The birds are vocal now and active as the season progresses and the Jassimines are abundant and perfume the air, the Dog-wood is in blossom. Indeed a ride into the woods is charming provided you find a dry place to ride. . . . .

[1] Levi was one of forty-one Negroes purchased from Dr. Alexius M. Forster in January, 1859; see below, p. 351. For further details concerning his illness and the treatment which he received see pp. 157–58, 160, 416, 450, 451.

P.S. I have sent Conky to J. W. LaBruce who owns his wife, Mrs. La Bruce desired to have him.

J. W. LaBruce to Robert F. W. Allston

Ruinville March 18th [1859]

DEAR SIR   I received your note by Conky saying I could have him, I am willing to take Conky and take care of him as I have his wife, he is old and I dont think will be able to pay me in work for it, but if you will let him come, I will be much obliged to you.   they as you say are many old people at Pipedown which was one reason John and myself did not go in debt for them, I am much obliged to you for the Acorns.

James L. Petigru to Robert F. W. Allston

Broad Street [Charleston] 1 April 1859

MY DEAR ALLSTON,   I will send by Jo the Deeds for Sister Ann and you to sign. Also the plat of Pipe Down and the deed of Robert Heriot commissioner to Mary Ann Labruce. That same Mary Ann is a real Labruce, meek and unbending. All you said about Conky and all I could add to it was just thrown away. No strict constructionist could have more horror at a liberal construction of the Pact or Compact than the aversion which she maintains for any modification of the letter. I thought to promote an equitable construction by bringing Public Opinion to bear on her judgment with evidence of the usage. But I am driven to confess that I did not find a Broker to agree with me in the opinion that if I buy a gang at so much per head none are counted but those that are or are likely to be of some value. And I believe I applied to every body but Capers and Heyward. I hope that [illegible] after all the price is not extravagant, but with the number of mendicants in the population the acquisition is not as good a bargain as the purchase of Louisiana. Adele will tell you all I could say about it. . . . .

Robert F. W. Allston to Benjamin Allston[1]

Charleston 28th May 1859

DEAR BEN, J. J. Pettigrew[2] has come to take leave of us, he may meet with you, if not this will be mail'd somewhere so as to reach you, only to say that the boy's name who was kill'd by Lightening was William (Hannah's son) Francis was with him and severly burn'd   He is doing well.

They finish'd planting 24th. Levi came down last week but I have not seen him and he was sent forthwith to Dr. Porcher who has said nothing to

---

[1] Address missing. Benjamin Allston was at this time in New York about to depart for Europe.

[2] James Johnston Pettigrew (1828–63), cousin of James L. Petigru, author of the report to the South Carolina General Assembly opposing the reopening of the African slave trade.

me on the subject. I fear tho' you will have a hospital bill to pay of some size, and nothing done. Toby is nearly well again the instrument having been removed. I received from Dr Forster a note respecting Levi again. Having heard he was dead, he requested me to deduct from the year's interest whatever sum was right for his unsoundness which he knew nothing of etc. I will respond to him today. Levi must remain in the City until he is dismiss'd by the Dr. or until fresh orders come from you to R[obertson], B[lacklock] and Co.[1]

Rice has gone down flat again, the demand having been speculation. It must revive, if the war continues so I have directed the N[ightingale] Hall Rice to be sent in its turn last.

Should you go to Haarlem in Holland, do not fail to visit the garden of the Widow "Aban Eaden et Fils" where we bought Hyacinths, Tulips etc. I have just received a card from them containing a catalogue of their flowers and plants; but I can order nothing this year. I will give it some circulation however. It is the 2nd or third they have sent. . . . .

If you have my communication suggestions of a monument to Calhoun over his grave pray send it to me, or if you have not destroyed it, say where I can find it. . . . .

P. S   I advise you to keep a Diary journal of (not every day travels but) interesting events and good thoughts, of which when you write you can give us a summary Keep cool and look well about you. Do as others do in general and avoid any appearance of singularity.

Robert F. W. Allston to Benjamin Allston

Charleston 10th June 1859

DEAR BEN,   I send you a letter from our Army friend at St. Louis. Major Van Dorn reports another Indian fight with the Comanches. Fitzhugh Lee badly wounded.

Mr Pitman's last report is to 4th June on which day Patience was safely deliver'd. Hoing Corn and Rice all the week. Weeds and rushes bad. Rice small. Upland wanting rain, everywhere. I have advised Joe to stop the Mill until August and clean out the crop in this dry time when the Rice market is so unsettled and dull. His brother William Allan came down in the last boat and is staying here. Last Monday we attended the funeral of Mr Tucker who refused nourishment 2 days before, he said he wish'd to die. He has left Litchfield to Henry, Willbrook to Hyrne and some unclos'd land. The Pee Dee Settlement to John, Joe and Daniel and the House in Town to Mrs. Weston, his *single* daughters to live there always, to Anne 5 negroes and $15,000, poor Anne has done her part very faithfully by him. . . . .

[1] See above, p. 157.

Ma came down safe from Abbeville last Saturday. She will tell you all about Charles. I do not think we shall get to the Beach before the last of the month. It is so dry everywhere I would not move now as long as the cistern holds out and there are few musquitoes. Many cisterns are empty, dry and wiped with a towel. The dust here is distressing. I have had your shoe-measures fitted at $1.10, and will send down your mare as soon as I reach home, perhaps sooner if I can dispatch William or Stephen tomorrow, he shall go, as I expect to go up the Wando River with Mr Robertson and some friends on a visit to his plantation pr Steam boat it will be a good chance to give him a lift. A great and unusual sensation has been created here by the announcement of the failure of the ancient, strong and liberal house of John Fraser and Co. in which Mr Geo. A Trenholm is Senior partner. Money to the amount of 1/2 a million has been offer'd to him by the Banks, but their liabilities surpassing $1,000,000 he promptly determined like an honest man to "*stop*." He has sold his negroes at $650 deliver'd in Jany and every thing else that is perishable and is off to Liverpool in order to save all that may be possible. This and the cause of it, has made money very tight, and it behooves every body to be very cautious how they spend it even in the way of business. William Allan Allston had to come down to make arrangements for the sale of his bank-stock. I am still in arrears at the Counting house over $9,000. More I apprehend than the remainder of my crop will liquidate. . . . .

Robert F. W. Allston to Benjamin Allston

Guendalos June 12th 1859

Sunday 12   Al. Grist, peas, and pork
   13   Hoe'd Rice
   14   Do.
   15   "
   16   "
   17   " Rainy P. M.
   18   " and Planted slips in the Missing places in potatoe field. 2 visits from Dr Heriot to Betty's child. Mr Tilton was here yesterday looking at Mill. 3 plows going. Sick James 2 days, Dinah 2, S. Hagar 5, Hannah 1, Anthony 1. old Minus is dead.

Very Resp.

H. Pitman

Dear Ben,   I made the above copy of Mr. Pitman's Report as soon as received, but it has been damaged by the rain beating into the window. Nevertheless being legible still I will not withhold this very sheet   as I write a gentle breeze comes in at the same window freighted with the perfume of the poppinac, sweet flower which has been blooming near six weeks. . . . .

Yesterday I was much moved by seeing your old man Levi standing in the Street at Dr Porcher's gate. He look'd very badly and as I stop'd [on the] opposite side to look at him he gazed with such a wistful, doubting look, that I cross'd over to where he was and enquired about him if he had been cut etc   No, they said he could not bear it now, and he was failing in strength, reduced in flesh and yellow in the eyes. I sent a message to tell him to come round to where there are at least more familiar names intending to speak to Dr. Porcher, but he has not been here since. If he should be attack'd here with any fever, it would most likely carry him off. He wants "to go home bad." . . . .

I sent for Dr Porcher to speak to him about Levi who when he came to the yard could eat nothing. I was out when he came, but your Mother spoke to him and he said plainly "Levi had better go home, he is not doing well." Only yesterday the Steam boat went up and will not go again until we go next Wednesday 6th July. Meantime we will try to take care of him here. Tho' when a negroe gets off his feed, it is rather a bad business. . . . . Reports just come down rain every day last week. Cut oats 20th. 6 sheep came from Mr. Grier. Betty's child ill.

Mitchell King to Robert F. W. Allston

George Street [Charleston] Wedr night 29 June 1859

MY DEAR SIR   I have this moment 10 1/2 P.M. received your note of this evening, and I hasten to acknowledge it that my acknowledgement may reach you at as early an hour tomorrow as possible.

It gives me pleasure to say that my manuscript is still in my possession, and that I shall assuredly obey your wish by leaving out of it the passage which you desire should be omitted   My sole design in writing it was to do justice and honor to you in putting on record the fact that you years ago earnestly recommended to the adoption of our State, the system of Education which is now received with so much well deserved favor, a fact which, I respectfully think, ought not to be forgotten.

My unhesitating acquiescense in your wish will, I believe, necessitate the omission of the notice of Dr. Irving's address, and I shall really be glad to have my report made as much briefer as possible. I rather think that I should not have noticed it, had I not desired to record a fact which I deem highly honorable to you.

It would give me great pain to have anything in my report that would be in the slightest degree unpleasant to you, for I pray you to be assured that I am in all sincerity. . . . .

P. S.   Before the visitors of the schools separated this afternoon I made an engagement with one of our body, the Rev. Mr Burd I think, to meet him at the Courier office tomorrow at 11 A M to put my manuscript into his hands.

Catharine M. Moore to Robert F. W. Allston

July 15 1859

DEAR SIR Will you excuse the liberty I take in writing to you so often I look upon you as my friend and therefore hope that you will pardon whatever is wrong about me of which I feel there is a great deal

I wish to beg you to favour me with some catechisms and Sunday School hymn Books about nine of each I have commenced a Sunday School with the children that go to School to me I feel that I am deficient in many ways but I will exercise what talent I have in trying to make a Serious impression upon the minds of those dear children who do indeed need instruction Dr Sparkman has shown much to those Smiths I told him that they never went to church and their excuse was they had no clothes so he has given them all clothes now they Say they intend to go to church Dr Sparkman also supplied me with testaments for my Sunday School I told him that I intended to ask you for the other Books I knew that you would be willing to give them please to send them as early practicable for I need them very much Another Book I have been wanting is the memoir of Mrs Sarah Louisa Taylor if you have it and can Spare it I would be very glad if you would give it to me also a Mitchels Geography to acompany the Atlas you Sent me also if you have a Mitchiels biblical and Sabbath School Geography I would be very thankful for them please excuse me for troubling you so often humbly yours.[1]

Robert F. W. Allston to Blue Ridge Railroad Committee[2]

Waccamaw Beach 11th Aug. 1859

GENTLEMEN It would afford me much pleasure to unite with the citizens of Pickens District on the 19th Inst in exchanging congratulations upon the substantial progress which has hitherto been made by the managers of the Blue Ridge Rail Road I find myself however precluded from such an indulgence.

I offer you my own hearts congratulations and encouragement for what they are worth. Living on the shore of the great Atlantic, it will afford me sincere gratification to know that the well-proportion'd Tunnel has been completed, and that the company is pressing the work forward into Tennessee.

I deem the completion of the Road due to the Independence as well as the interest of the Commonwealth, as may be infer'd from what has been said by me in a public capacity.

I own no Stock in this or any other road, except a few shares in the So Ca R. R. about to be transfer'd to another enterprise nearer home. Here it is

---

[1] Allston wrote in his diary: "Sent 2 Methst Catechisms and some other books to Catharine Moore to help teach the Smith's children in Sunday School out on Mill Pond." See below, p. 451.

[2] Copy.

due that I should say this is owing to no distrust of the utility and benefit of Railway enterprises, but to the fact that I have no funds to invest. All that I am worth lies in So. Carolina, and is invested in lands and negroes; the annual income from all which is pledged before it is realized. And I had no hand in projecting the Blue Ridge Railway unless indeed the suggestion made in Nashville in 1850 may have given some direction to the enterprising capitalists of the day.

It occur'd thus and I mention it to show in what light of importance to the State I have ever regarded the completion of this Road, since its first commencement.

It happen'd that I was present, at the meeting in Memphis when the Memphis and (Charleston) Chattanooga Rail Road Company was organized. So, when committees were appointed thereby to apply for a charter to the Legislatures of Tennessee Mississisippi and Alabama I ventured to suggest that those Committees be authorized to enlist the influence of those States with the State of Georgia to obtain a license for the So Carolina R. Road to cross freely the Savannah River and unite with the Georgia Rail Road at Agusta else they could not be sure of reaching Charleston without impediment. In the year succeeding, namely in June 1850, learning while at Nashville that the Legislature of Georgia had shown no favor to the application on this behalf, I express'd my opinion of the policy which should govern the communication by Rail Way of Tennessee with Charleston in these words "Turn the Savannah River" i e go around the main stream.

Certainly such a design seems to me to have influenced, in part the projection of the road through the Rabun Gap, tho its first Western terminus be nearer to Knoxville than to Chattanooga.

In any event let us all who can, give it a lift forward. For without it, the inhabitants of Carolina, are at present dependent on the interests of the Georgia Rail Roads for a passage to the West. All persons who are familiar with the history of the So Ca R. Rd. will remember what obstructions it used to meet at the Savannah river near Augusta, and how heavily the Company has been tax'd for the privilige of building its own viaduct a privelege which they never succeeded in negotiating, I believe, until the ground was broken under your charter.

Be assured gentlemen of my earnest desire to see your great work carried forward to successful completion. At the same time, accept my acknowledgment of your civility together with my best wishes for the agreeable success of the occasion which prompts you.

Benjamin Allston to Robert F. W. Allston

Pawleys Island June 18 1860

MY DEAR FATHER I am sorry that I did not discover your note yesterday until after I had despatched my letter, otherwise I should have mentioned it and thanked you for it as I now do. I went to Chicora today and gave all the directions you desired me to give. Toney has not yet made his appearance, though I do not know if the McRae has yet arrived. How he could tell you that I sent him back for my saddle, is what I can scarsely understand, as he must know that I did not see him at all, and the Capt. and I think Mr. Murrey both told me that, upon being told by them to attend to the horse, he replied that he was not going, but came down to put the horse on board. I saw a good deal of your rice today, most of Chicora, all looking well, the corn also They were harvesting oats today, all well, except one girl whose name I do not remember, who Mr. Belflowers fears is going into dropsy. At Guendalos all going on well, except that Pitman unnecessarily took off the two primest hands today to send me our horse feed, which being in no wise my intention quite put me out. He does some strange freaks sometimes. I did not see him, as he went to town but I shall see him on Wednesday next, if all goes well, and will tell him what you say. I am glad to hear that you are coming up on Tuesday next. I find it dull work living here alone, true my neighbours are all very kind in their invitations etc. but I miss the home folks much. I have not brought over Margaret, as yet, for I do not know what the accomodation will be when you come up, or how much service she would be to the family. I would like her to be with her husband as I suppose you would desire him to be with her and if she could be useful to Mother in any way I would be glad to bring her.

Elias is quite sick again, but I trust not dangerously so, and Stephen I keep pretty well occupied in one way and another, also old Toney, and, the result is that I sometimes have no one to call upon for small things This is a matter of no consequence however and it only gives me an opportunity of doing somethings for myself. My horse was brought over today, and with usual wisdom, boy Frank brought with him only the clothes on his back, which were of course his newest.

Where will you desire to land, at Waverly I supposed until Mr. B[el-flowers] told me today that you landed last time at Hagley, if you can let me know what you desire I will try and meet it. There is wanting, flour, coffee, green tea, and loaf sugar, of the three first we are destitute I sent down for 25 lb. of flour to G[eorge]town today which will last us some little while. There is nothing else that I learn from Mary.

Mr. B. has not yet planted slips but is preparing. I hope the rains will not desert us too early. I will keep this open for tomorrow night. Tuesday night—I have just returned from the river the steamer went up without landing anything and I waited for the rain to cease until nearly dark when seeing no prospect of it I started homeward, thinking it were better to get wet while there was light than to tumble about in the dark. I got quite wet, that is my legs, my body being protected by my coat, and no letters for my pains. Of course I know that there are letters for me but that does not mend the matter. I am not able to reply to them. I came home at once and took all the ordinary precautions, and do not think that any ill effects will result therefrom I go over to the plantation tomorrow, and again on Saturday. Toney has just reported himself, and, I think he had best go to the river, at least until you come up. There are enough here at present to take charge of the horses. I have John here thinking you might come up today and would find him useful. I shall now keep him here until you do come, when you can dispose of him as it seems best to you. I am very glad to hear of your early coming up as I feel quite lonely sometimes. . . . .

Robert F. W. Allston to Benjamin Allston

Charleston 18th Aug. 1860

DEAR BEN   . . . . I hope the work on our Rail Road will be finish'd smoothly. I heard some talk in Town of the road being required in January next. If this be the fact, I pray you say to Mr Lee frankly and at once that the necessary work on the plantation will forbid my undertaking any more, unless by good management we can finish the *6th section* which has been progress'd with as far as the Rice-field. But let the part we have been working on be finish'd before harvest so that it may be turn'd over, and Mr Pitman or yourself can receive for me a certificate from the Engineer of the value of the work and receive the work itself. Otherwise we may be call'd on to repair damages. You may talk to Pitman freely about it. He is intelligent and enters readily and heartily into the views of his principal. I spoke to Mr Bostwick about letting my servants with their horses and carts get shelter in bad weather at the house where he lives. He said yes, they can get it so pray tell Joe to go and ask for it civilly when Mr B. is at home which is only at night and get him to show him the place that he may not interfere with anything unaware. . . . .

Robert F. W. Allston to Benjamin Allston

White Sulphur Springs 29th Aug. 1860

MY DEAR BEN   I was glad to get your letter this morning and to learn that all is well so far. It would be a great mistake for Pitman or Belflowers to postpone the harvest until the 1st Septr. In 3 weeks thereafter much of their rice would be shelling in the field, and before the close of harvest still more. It is indispensable, when using water freely in the cultivation of the crop, to lose something in quantity in the first cutting, in order to save a great waste in the later bulk of the harvest. But the overseers do not realize this and are too apt to postpone the day of readiness. I shall be disappointed if my harvest does not commence today at one place and tomorrow at the other.

Tommy would not have been abandon'd by his hands on Sunday, if he had not set them the example the first Sunday they were to remain there, and in doing this he has given me reason to think less of his qualification as a Driver than I was disposed to.

The first element in the compositon of one in authority is to obey orders and conform to instructions notwithstanding the privations necessary. Daniel possesses that element and some few others, but he lacks energy, ready intelligence and satisfactory accountability which the other has.

. . . .

Certainly Joseph can have the rest of the Rail Road Iron if he desires. He is using a part of it now together with the wheels on which the car is convey'd, which were taken on condition that they be replaced by others whenever they be needed at Chicora. I hope the hands will be suffer'd to go home on Saturday 25th; but I think the carts ought to be employ'd steadily, until the filling up to be done by them is finish'd. I hope and trust Mr Pitman wont get sick. Tell all howd'ye for me, and enjoin strict attention to these 3 points, 1. Take up the Rice clean off the field, 2nd. Carry it into the yard *dry*, 3d. See that it does not overheat in the stacks. The watchman can find out the stacks that are heating, by the stacks smoking too long after day light.

. . . .

Good luck to you and the harvest, remember there is a great contrast of extremes in the mid-day sun and the dews of September and October. The one is sickly, the other is chilling. They ought to be avoided. Take your meals regularly and temperately and I trust you will pass safely thro your first harvest.

Robert F. W. Allston to Benjamin Allston

Wh. Sulphur Springs 6th Septr. 1860

DEAR BEN . . . . I am glad the harvest has not been postponed. Tell Mr. Pitman, where his banks are good at N[ightingale] H[all] to cut the ripe rice and stack it in the field, especially the fields that are to be falloe'd next year. In doing this the task at Savannah River [?] is to cut 1/2 acre and tie and stack a 1/2 acre for the day's work. Stack it well in the field, and not move it, till ready to thresh it. Then in dry weather it will be moved and thresh'd the same day.

I am gratified that your party on the 29th were pleased with the crops, and found a satisfactory entertainment at Chicora. Adele tells me you had Rice-birds! I am sorry to hear of Rice-birds. I lost by them over 3000 bushels of Rice last year at the two places. I hope the harvest-weather may be good. Tell Mr Belflowers he need not move the Pipe Down main Rice until he is ready to thresh it. Let me re-iterate to them through you, "harvest clean." Look out for the weather between the 22nd Septr. and the full moon. I trust Mr Pitman will be done by that time. I presume your election will be very quiet and you must submit to being advanced to the responsibility of a representative before you are ready for it. Not so quiet in the City. Patrol duty should not be neglected, tho' the duty ought not to be done too annoyingly unless vagabond whites render it necessary. I am sorry to see that the scenes of arson and lynching enacted in Texas have been threaten'd in Alabama. . . . .

I shall be disappointed if the work undertaken and in hand at the R Road does not yield me $1,500. The whole ought to be worth $3,000 at least.

Robert F. W. Allston to Benjamin Allston

Wh. Sulphur Springs 10th Septr. 1860

MY DEAR BEN   In the last Georgetown Paper which reach'd me, I perceive that Mr Weston has been nominated for the Legislature. The foregoing[1] I venture to send you as suggestive of the spirit in which you should meet it. In this I doubt not you have anticipated me, but I will not withhold the offering, tho' satisfied of your disposition to do what is right and if Mr Weston is put forward by the Citizens and voters of Winyah, in good faith to retire and bide your time.

I regret to see by the same paper the death announced of one of my strongest friends on black river C. B. Cumbee, who would have been a friend to you. Whitman too on the same river is dead.

We are just on the move for the old Sweet and will go to Point Comfort I think before or about the 1st of October and return to Charleston as soon as it is safe. I intended to be in the City on the 15th to leave the Children at school, but the yellow fever rumors will prevent that. If the fever becomes bad I will get you to send for us to Kingstree. We will write you further from the Sweet. Stop my letters and papers at Georgetown, and let no more be sent here. . . . .

[1][INCLOSURE]

MR. EDITOR   In response to certain queries address'd to me, amongst others in a late number of your paper I take leave to say, that were I a member of the Legislature, it would afford me pleasure to advance the views of those interested in the Georgetown Rail Road in procuring an amendment and extension of their Charter, and to contribute in any other way in my power to forward the wishes of the Corporation for the completion and successful operation of the Road.

It is owing doubtless to my nomination for the honor of a seat in the House of Representatives that I have been enquired of upon a matter of special local interest such as the Rail Way, it is right that the opinions of your Representatives should be known to the constituency. Upon matters of general policy and the details of legislation, where opinions have been form'd they may be utter'd also, and be open to discussion but I think it better to send our Representatives to their post of duty, unpledged, and free to exercise their best judgement, based, upon the light within their reach, on questions of interest as they arise, provided we can rely on their honesty and fidelity.

I take occasion to say this much, as I deem it important to keep a Representative man under a constant sense of his individual responsibility.

Now for the nomination, sensible of the honor intended, and, free to express my willingness to take my turn in serving my fellow-citizens, whenever it may be in my power to do so, I beg leave on this occasion, to unite the expression of my preference for Mr. P. C. J. Weston with that of your correspondent of the 5th inst, and to withdraw my name from the canvass, if Mr. Weston's consent to serve Winyah can be obtain'd. The parish will be better served by him, who has acquired already much experience in the House, who is a ripe Scholar and in whom I have every confidence, to whom therefore, I shall be gratified in being permitted to defer, in the ensuing general election.

Robert F. W. Allston to Benjamin Allston

Richmond 6th Octr. 1860

MY DEAR BEN Arriving here last thursday I determined as the weather was very unsettled to remain over to Monday. We were detain'd in Staunton a day after visiting the cave not by the weather but by a desire to remain and greet Mr. Yancey[1] who was to address the Democracy there on that day. We were quite repaid for the delay (tho' it caused us to lay over here 3 days) by the treat in popular oratory of which he gave us a good specimen. Adele *mere et fille* and I repair'd to the armory at 2.30, which was soon fill'd up, and he commenced a little before 3 and spoke until 5.30, then answer'd questions from an impracticable Douglas man till 6. The whole of the Western Virginia has a majority divided betwixt Bell and Douglas, but they are making masterly efforts here to either fuse, or draw off enough Douglas men to secure the Electoral vote to Breckenridge and Lane. Almost every village in Rockbridge and Rockingham Counties has a flag with Bell and Everett inscribed on it flying at a mast-head. They seem to have no idea of the principles for which we contend, and of the disastrous consequences which must flow from a triumph of the Seward party. They go for the men who were associated in interest and sympathy with Henry Clay the Hero of Western and Middle Virginia.

Mr Hunter[2] is here and address'd the Democratic Citizens last night near two hours very ably and sometimes eloquently. I went to hear him and had taken a seat with the rest on one of the back benches when I was recognized and after the committee came in and had taken their seats on the stage, one of them was sent down to invite me among them, being there I was call'd upon before the meeting adjourned and of course acknowledged the compliment done to So Carolina in their civility to me. Adjourning with the Executive Committee I closed the evening with them. They are re-

[1] William Lowndes Yancey (1814–63), Alabama secessionist.

[2] Probably Robert M. T. Hunter (1809–87), at this time United States senator from Virginia.

gretting and many are ashamed of the action of the Legislature last Jany. declining Carolina's proposition for a conference. It was a most senseless and I fear a fatal step. Such a conference is now far more necessary now than it appear'd to be last year when it was proposed. Govr Wise's idea is not to secede from the Union, but to take the Union along by taking the Federal City and Treasury. I wish he could put this in a practical form and so I told the meeting last night. It will require material and hearty aid and co-operation of both Maryland and Virginia. If we leave them the Treasury, the Archives and Offices, they having the prestige of office and the semblence of Authority will have incalculable advantage over us. Our only trust is in the Lord who sees and knows all things.

Last Monday morning I despatch'd Stephen with a pair of large grey horses from Lexington. I hope he will reach home in safety. I wish them to be driven daily by Alek and kept in the harness many hours so as to be pre-pared for service by the time your Mother returns. If they answer for her carriage I can dispose of the white tail horse "Bill" if any body wants him. He is very hardy and serviciable and quite safe I think in the Sulky or buggy. I bought a cream color'd horse at the Springs for Adele to ride and I have sent him home by a man named "Price" with authority to sell him, his back being too round for the side-saddle. He is 14 hands high rather slender but with fine loins white mane and tail and canters well, if not sold on the way he will be left at Hockadays for sale 5 years old. I dont know what H. will ask, being a fancy horse and only for the saddle. Both of these horses would show well in cavalry and do good service. How does your troop progress? From this I send Phebe home with some extra luggage which is in the way. She will go directly up in the Steam-boat and after a day to see her child must go to work. Tell Mary to get the roll of Homespun cloth out of the press in the entry upstairs and have Lavenia cut out a pair of trousers for me and a pair for Charles and let Phebe make them. If Mr. Pittman is still at the summer house she can go there daily and ask Mrs. P. to teach her to use the sewing machine and keep it in order. Send her down to the City again with William on or about the 25th with some supplies of grits, Potatoes, chickens, Eggs and 2 hams, not forgetting a bushel of Middling and 1 of Small Rice fresh butter and a little lard. Alek had better take the new horses down too, if they are all right and let them become used to the City forthwith by land, in that case Andrew will be wanted in Charleston. Nelson will find enough to do at home in the grounds. Neither he nor Phebe nor Lavenia have anything to do with the home inside unless wanted by you or summon'd by Mary, until we move. This on account of responsibility. They all understand it I suppose and I only mention it out of caution to you. You will not move till 1st Novr. then after that we will be glad to see you in the City and hear all the news from home. I hope I shall find a parcel of Rice from both places in market before that to be follow'd up rapidly by 2 or 3 more. When the fresh comes down and the highland crop shall be [MS breaks off at this point].

Robert F. W. Allston to Charles Petigru Allston[1]

Chicora Wood 8th Novr. 1860

MY DEAR BOY, I have arrived at home safe thank God, and find my people pretty well in health, and doing well. They have thresh'd a little rice and are now getting in the corn and potatoes which will both yield a fair return. . . . .

Many of the negroes enquired kindly for you. You must try to be a good boy, in order to treat them judiciously and well, when Papa is gone. Strive to think justly, to act wisely and diligently.

. . . .

In one of your letters, you speak of the "minute men." These are volunteers all over the State who profess to be ready at any moment to obey the Governor's orders, should their services be needed. I hope this volunteering will not have the effect to disturb the school. Do not be alarm'd at the rumors of Wars, but attend closely to your studies. The best service you can now render your Country, is to attend diligently to your studies of school, and thus qualify yourself to act wisely and efficiently, when you grow up to be a man. If you are wanted otherwise you will be call'd for. When does Mr Porcher's school break up? on what day? write word as soon as he determines. You shall have your money in time, if the mails dont fail.

Stephen (whom I have just dismiss'd to go to bed) tells you howd'ye. I sent him home from Virginia with a pair of big horses for Ma's carriage. Then he brought home the 3 boys whom I had in Sumter. They are now here. Harry has grown quite tall, the other two are still short but smart. They practise in the piazza every morning about breakfast time.

. . . .

A Drover was here today with mules to sell, but I could not buy any, having already spent all the money I could afford in buying horses in the mountains. Do not ask for Typee, but fetch your saddle and bridle. . . . .

Robert N. Gourdin to Robert F. W. Allston[2]

Executive Chamber, "The 1860 Association."
Charleston, 19th November, 1860

MY DEAR SIR In September last, several gentlemen of Charleston, met to confer in reference to the position of the South in the event of the accession of Mr. Lincoln and the Republican party to power. This informal meeting

[1] Address missing: Charles was a pupil at Willington Academy, Abbeville District, at this time.

[2] A printed circular.

was the origin of the organization known in this community as "The 1860 Association." The objects of the Association are,

1st. To conduct a correspondence with leading men in the South, and, by an interchange of information and views, prepare the Slave States to meet the impending crisis.

2nd. To prepare, print and distribute in the Slave States, tracts, pamphlets, etc., designed to awaken them to a conviction of their danger and to urge the necessity of resisting Northern and Federal aggression.

3rd. To enquire into the defences of the State and to collect and arrange information which may aid the Legislature to establish promptly, an effective military organization.

To effect these objects, a brief and simple Constitution was adopted, creating a President, a Secretary and Treasurer, and an Executive Committee, specially charged with conducting the business of the Association. One hundred and sixty-six thousand pamphlets have been published, and demands for further supplies are received from every quarter. The Association is now passing several of them through a second and third edition.

The Conventions in several of the Southern States, will soon be elected. The North is preparing to soothe and conciliate the South, by disclaimers and overtures. The success of this policy would be disastrous to the cause of Southern Union and Independence, and it is necessary to resist and defeat it. The Association is preparing pamphlets with this special object. Funds are necessary to enable it to act promptly. "The 1860 Association" is laboring for the State and for the South, and asks your aid.

Robert F. W. Allston to C. Williams

Chicora Wood 25th Decr 1860

DEAR SIR   In response to your note of yesterday, I beg to say that all my negroe men should be at the Service of the State, if needed and available But it would be worse than needless to send to Georgetown or beyond, any but those who will be reliable hands who will do good work without giving trouble.

I will order *ten men* to be ready, whom I hope will be found such, to be sent to such place and at such time as you will please to indicate on your assurance of some competent person to direct their work, protect and care for them in case of sickness etc They will be accompanied by a capable head-man who will aid in their work on its being laid off for him and pointed out. They will be furnish'd with plantation provisions for *one week*. You will please inform me whether any further rations will be provided for them on the ground. Please inform me as fully as you can.

P. S.   I sent your notes to Mr Weston Drs. Sparkman and Heriot and enclose herewith Mr. W's note to you. Sorry I did not see Col G.

Mary Petigru to Adele Petigru Allston

Badwell December 27th 1860

MY DEAR ADELE . . . . We give the time to the Servants and call on them as little as possible, they are very quiet more so than usual I think. There is to be a wedding here to-night quite a great occassion Ned one of Andrews sons to Susannah one of Eves daughters the preparations are ample. George and Diana are engaged but prefer putting it off till Spring. George brought in a note from Jones proposing to hire him on the same terms next year and as I can do no better I will send him back, Jones gets a great deal to do at the village and I hope will be able to pay me up in Jan. for the year $160 and while on the subject dear Adele, I would say if you are in the same mind about purchasing Isaac for a coachman, now is the time, this farm is so unprofitable that I have determined not to keep him any longer assisting to make food and clothes alone. I ask'd the boy if he is willing to be sold to you as coachman he said quite willing, as well he might be, he has proved himself so far, an uncommonly good and valuable servant, honest and trustworthy. I put his price at $1400, it has been frequently said he would bring 1500, therefore I hope you will not think it too much as they sell here even now, it would not be thought so, but if you have changed your mind about it, or made other arrangements, we will just drop the matter and say no more about it, and I will not be disappointed or troubled. Sister Jane is quite willing for me to dispose of him, I therefore make the proposal. I know the unsettled state of things makes a difference, and you may think differently from what you did last winter, be assured dear Sister I will be satisfied whatever decision you may come to on the subject.

South Carolina occupies a critical position and a very unenviable distinction I think, in being first to break the Union. What greavous wrongs had she to complain of more than all the rest! . . . .

Jane G. North to Adele Petigru Allston

Badwell Dec 29th [18]60

MY DEAR ADELE, I intended to write you before Xmas, but interruptions happen even here, and I was obliged to forego the pleasure. The subject of the boys delay is old now, but I would just say in reply to your comments on the subject, that I concluded that my opinions upon politics, and perhaps on other subjects were considered demoralizing, and hence the terror, especially I thought so, as Ben did not write; but with your letter came his also three weeks old. I was very much pleased to get it, his sentiments are firm and well expressed, and I have no doubt there will be room enough for the Faith which inspires to heroic deeds thro' many a dark day to come, for my part, I must ever regard with amazement the temerity which could break up this august government, and not recoil from an act involving the well being of Millions, and the glory of the nation, but these ideas are only fit to be ridiculed, perhaps ere long may lead to the stake, or at the least as a favour to confiscation. I feel too much to write or talk so return to silence as usual.

Mary is anxious to realize more for Isaac than she has done last year or is likely to do this, and told me she wd offer him to you as a coachman. I entirely approve her doing so and wish you may take him. I can testify to his good character and capability. I have never known a finer young servant, he was 25 in Augt he is well made and active, just suited for such employment as you design, looks like daddy Tom, and it would be agreeable to you (I should think) to have one of the old stock, of course the interest would be all that Mary would want, and is certainly the best bargain she has offered. I would like you to have the boy, it wd be promotion for him and I think a good servant for you, and he is willing to go, has no wife, but will take one next year at Mr Bretts should things remain as they are, decide at once, and write for I think Mary will hire him out if you do not take him. . . . .

Robert F. W. Allston to Benjamin Allston

Charleston 24th March 1861

DEAR BEN   Your Aunt Jane North going up to Waverly tomorrow morning, I am induced to write a line by her. They were all with us to tea last night including Mrs. J. L. P[etigru] in all her glory and full of the reminiscences of her youth. The pleasure of this re-union was enhanced by an unexpected but agreeable visit from Genl Beauregard with Capt Hartstene of the Navy and Capt Ferguson of his staff, so the whole family had an opportunity to make his acquaintance. He is of the Provisional Army I understand, as contradistinguish'd from the permanent and does not intend to remain in the service, as I heard today, soon as matters shall be settled.

It is believed by those who have the position to judge that the troops from Fort Sumter will depart in the Str Marion for N. Y on Wednesday. The Govr has been shuffling with them in the hope that through impatience Anderson would evacuate of his own accord, as he did Fort Moultrie, or we might commit ourselves by demanding and enforcing a surrender of his forces. Capt. H. who went down there Thursday night tells me the officers are indignant at the neglect of their Government and freely speak of the advantage we enjoy in having so much better a President than they have. He told them that if their Government did not soon withdraw the troops we would be obliged to turn them out. There is beginning to appear much suffering and privation among families in town of the soldiers on duty whose revenues are materially diminish'd and curtail'd by absence from their vocations these three months. I trust their relief is near at hand. Then what will J. L. P[etigru] do? I think he must go abroad.

I cannot leave the City until the harbor shall be restored to the State. Supposing that to be in the course of this week a carriage load will leave next tuesday 2nd April and if you will send the carriage to Kingstree. You can mention this in case you leave home, the servants and luggage will go up day after in the steamer. Or better will go at 11 Tuesday night and take the carriage at the Depot right on. I suppose Aleck will be sent up first.

I go today to dine with Genl Simons to meet Genl Beauregard and others. Your Uncle dines Govr. Pickens and lady, he did not invite me soon enough to secure my presence. I shall probably entertain them both [before] going into the country therefore I shall need the mutton and Ma's last Turkey. If you can get Molly to send a pair of Guinea fowls and James a roasting pig or two by the return of this boat or by the boat Friday (to be put on board the day before) we shall be able to wind up here respectably on Easter Monday.

Benjamin Allston to Robert F. W. Allston

Guendalos, March 31, 1861

MY DEAR FATHER . . . . The Bishop arrived last evening and preached today. Adele and myself dined with the Hunters today and there I took the Bishop and wife, and Mrs. Hunter in his carriage with my horses and he took Adele in his buggy, and we went to N[ightingale] H[all]. The Bishop spoke a short while to the people, and then confirmed *Daniel* the driver. It was quite an impressive scene and new to them doubtless.

. . . .

Mr. Weston is to come over on Friday evening here, and go with me up to Small Hopes on Saturday, where there is to be reviewed the "Carver's bay Rifles." Our Company is invited to be present, and also to assist in furnishing the dinner. I think we should make an effort to be present in force, although many of us will be in the midst of planting. I have asked Mr. W. to remain with me until after Tuesday and witness our Quarterly Parade which comes off on the 9th.

I hope that you will be able to bring us some definite news about Fort Sumpter, I concluded that it would have been in our possession some days ago. It is high time that we should have it, or we shall cause much suffering, which is apt to engender discontent at home.

The planting is progressing.

I will not be able to commence before Tuesday. I have gotten the seed for my first planting from N[ightingale] H[all] upon Pitmans voucher that it was better than mine, 80 odd bushels I wish twenty five bushels of strickly prime seed to plant two acres with. Do you know of any or hear of any in town. There must be no volunteer. . . . .

Benjamin Allston to Robert F. W. Allston

Head Quarters Morris Island April 14, 1861

MY DEAR FATHER   You will before receiving this have heard the glorious, and astonishing news that Sumter has fallen.[1] The impregnable fortress has been forced to yield in a bombardment of less than thirty six hours and not a life lost in the encounter, so far as I have been able to learn. Such a "bloodless victory" has never yet been recorded in the pages of history, and it is inconceivable, how among the many balls that fell among our men, none were injured. One indeed was struck in the back by a 32 pd ball, knocked down but arose uninjured. Our men have behaved with remarkable courage, coolness and untiring energy. And those few who worked the batteries, have gained for themselves a very lasting fame, while their behavior will inspire and encourage all the others in a remarkable degree. We have all had hard and diligent service, sleepless nights, and during Friday night particularly so. A fleet was off the bar, and to all appearance, intended coming in that night, but a violent gust of wind and rain, during the early evening, with succeeding darkness and a heavy sea, made them, I suppose, determine not to do so. They might have, with some risk, run in some boats between three o'clk and day light. I was very anxious that night. I was up the whole night, and could not resist the belief that they had taken advantage of the lull in the storm. But it turned out afterwards not. That night was a very hard one on the sentries, being much hard rain, and heavy squalls. The fire on the Fort was continued during the night at intervals of 20 to 30 m., until day light when all the batteries opened a brisk fire, the ships seven in number all together, seemed to be in the positions of the previous night. About 8 a.m. (I being sent to give some order to the companies relative to the entering of the ships into the harbor, for we all expected that they would make an attempt on us) I heard a wild shout from the men about me, and looking towards the Fort, I perceived it was on fire; it gained with great rapidity, and our Batteries seem to have become excited by this circumstance and the rapidity of fire increased with the flames. I arrived at the Hd. Qrs. soon after, and I never saw such a scene before. Major Whiting, who I before told you was the dominant spirit, and indeed he has been the life and soul of the work on this Island, was very much distressed, almost to tears, the sight was most painful, for we supposed that they must all smother or burn. Capt Manigault, (Arthur) was very much distressed, his face pale, and his frame trembling with the violent excitement. He thought the firing should cease, but the U. S. flag still waved, and moreover no one there had any authority to order the firing to cease; so it continued tho' orders were sent to maintain the former rate of firing. In course of time the flames

---

[1] The writer had served during the bombardment as a member of the staff of Brigadier General James Simons, stationed on Morris Island. For another account of the action see below, pp. 416–19.

seemed to abate, and an occasional gun boomed out against Fort Moultrie, showing that in spite of the flames within and the firing without they were still not disposed to yield passively. Soon there was an evident explosion, then another and after sometime the flames breaking out anew, another heavy one throwing up pieces of timber etc. After all of this they ever and anon fired their single gun, and their flag still waved. The fire soon after this broke out again and consumed the other Barracks, and about 1 oclk, the flag staff was shot away. A flag of truce was soon after sent over, by the hands of Col Wigfall, and shortly a white flag was seen waving above the blackened and smoking ruins, the firing ceased 2 p.m. and in one to two hours the scene appeared as calm and quiet, with the exception of the smoke, as if a great conflict had not been raging. When the fire broke out in the Fort, it was the general opinion that the fleet would at once move to his support, and orders were at once sent to all commanders to get all their men ready for action. But, shame be to them, they did not move, tho' they could witness the whole action. The indignation excited in the camp was intense, by this, to us, dastardly conduct.

It was supposed that Major Anderson would remove from the Fort that day, that we would occupy the Fort that night. But this was not so, and he remained quiet until today when preparations were commenced for his departure.

Monday Morning—10—The Isabel, which we understand he has chartered to convey him to N. Y. refusing to go in the vessels which failed to support him when in such distress is just now leaving our harbor, and I suppose will convey him to N.Y. . . . .

Adele Petigru Allston to Mrs. Joseph Hunter

Charleston 15th May 1861

MY DEAR MRS. HUNTER   I was sorry not to see you again before leaving the country. The conversation with Mr Hunter on the occasion of our visit that 2nd of May, the last time I saw you, was so painful and mortifying that I cannot describe how it depressed me.

You and Mr Hunter have of course a perfect right to your opinions and preferences. But that you should side with the North in its present attitude of bitter hostility to us, is inexplicable to me, all that we ask being political separation, to be allowed to govern our own Section in our own way, anyone who believes in the principles of self government, who admits the justice of the principle for which we fought in the war of the Revolution, cannot object to our movement now.

When we left the government of England, we left an ancient government and a parent country. How much more clear the right to withdraw from a government we assisted in creating when the guarantees which induced us to join it have been violated, ignored, trampled upon. I conscientiously believe our cause the cause of constitutional government in opposition to the will of a mere majority, which sets at defiance all written law. I cannot understand the madness which makes the North engage in a war upon us, whom they have professd to pity and deplore as the plague spot. Still less can I understand how you who have sojourned among us for 15 years nearly can join the [illegible] cry against us because we ask to part company in peace, and to enter into treaties for mutual understanding and good neighbourhood.

Every act of Lincoln's administration has shewn the spirit of a usurper, a cunning plotting crafty usurper, thinking only of his party platform in place of the constitution, by which alone the union could originally have been secured by the observance of which still it could alone be preserved.

The dominant party speak insultingly of preserving the union by war, none but an absolute monarch could use such language with a show of justice.

But why should I write to you thus. You and Mr Hunter have both spoken of the North as "our side." I write thus simply to express my sincere opinions and feelings and to tell you that believing and feeling as you both do, I conscientiously think you ought not to remain another month in the Southern Country.

This I meant to have told you if I had seen you again. I have felt too sincere a regard for you since I first knew you, not to act towards you with frankness and straight forward sincerity.

I shall always feel an interest in your welfare, and a lively sentiment of friendship for you and shall always be glad to learn of your prosperity and happiness, and that of your children.

I omitted to leave with Nelson the $5 for the Theological Student which I promised Mr Hunter. I enclose it now. I will be glad to hear from you, if only to say you have received this.

Adele Petigru Allston to Robert F. W. Allston

Charleston 3 June 1861

MY DEAREST FRIEND   I wrote to you in a great state of excitement on Saturday, caused by yours received that morning saying you would remain on the plantation until the 13th, and then join us here. The imminent danger attending such a course impressed me most painfully, and I wrote instantly. If it was unadvisedly I trust you will pardon it. I cannot describe how unhappy I am at the thought that you should be exposed to such a danger, and from no cause but the inconvenience of moving to the Beach. I hope and trust you have thought better of it and that you have either moved to the Beach or are on your way here. I think there is risk in coming from the plantation here now, and it would involve the necessity of being careful for 20 days. But to remain on the plantation and come down the 13th would be going against all experience.

Surely my dear this is not a time when anyone man should needlessly expose himself to danger, how much less one so important as you are to your section of country and to your family. In case of invasion you are the only man in all that region who can be looked to as a leader, or a director of the movements of others. It seems to me that every man who can bear arms should be drilled earnestly, and armed in the best way possible. All these things you understand better than any one else. I have often said you would make a great General. I have no wish, Heaven knows, to see you compelled to prove this true. But who can doubt now that a dreadful struggle is at hand. I went to see Cousin Lynch yesterday evening after church. She was shocked at the thought that you should remain on the plantation until 13. Said she prayed you not to do so, her nephew spoke quite sensibly on public affairs. She suffers a great deal.

. . . .

I received this morning a letter from Caroline Pettigrew asking us, you and I, to make use of Cherry Hill for the Summer, in the kindest and most generous terms. Gov Pickens and Dr Gibbs called yesterday, the Gov said he had received a dispatch from President Davis urging him to have Johnstons Regiment formed on their own terms and sent on as soon as possible. I heard from others that the Govnr's of all the Southern States had received orders to send on as soon as possible every available man that could be mustered into service to Virginia. Everything goes to shew that the nature of the contest there is most serious, not to say *desperate*. Oh my beloved do not expose your precious health or life. I have always had great confidence in your prudence but to remain on the plantation until the 13th June is greatly imprudent.

[P. S.] Adeles cold is better tho' she looks not well. Jane has a cold, but has gone to school. All send love in large measure.

Sarah C. Williams to Adele Petigru Allston

Asheville July 10th [18]61

DEAR MRS ALLSTON, I have just heard from my sister Jane that Gov A. had been enquiring of Mr S. Evans about a summer house in our neighborhood. I write to offer you our place, Croly Hill, where we have passed several summers since Oaky Hollow was burned. The house was built 30 years ago, and has never been painted since, it was occupied for some years by the widow of Genl Williams, and afterwards was lent out, and rented out and occupied by overseers, before we took it, so it is very *shabby*, still it has a pleasant parlor and two very airy tho small chambers in the second story, two garret rooms which served us as lumber rooms. There are 4 rooms down stairs with fire places 2 above, 2 log rooms connected by an uncoverd passage with the house, a piazza in front with shed rooms at each end. The outhouses are poor. You are very welcome to it if you should desire it.

There are pine bedsteads in it, and some other things. You can have the use of our garden at the Factory and get milk from there as we did, or take a cow or cows as you please from the plantation. My son George is at home and will be very glad to do any thing for you. There is no other house in the neighborhood that would answer for you, it is about 1 1/2 miles from the Factory and the same distance from the church about 1/4 mile from Jane's and quite near a house rented by Mrs Martin (Betty Evans) for the summer. We came here ten days ago and find the climate very pleasant. There is a good Hotel they say in Asheville. We are 4 miles out housekeeping. I feel better, tho' Sam not well.

Robert F. W. Allston to Adele Petigru Allston

Richmond 15th July 1861 .

DEAR ADELE   . . . . I paid my respects last evening to the President who looks very feeble and to Mrs Davis who call'd me "Mr Aiken" and enquired twice after you. Mrs. Chesnut, Mrs. Wigfall, Mrs. Preston, Mrs. Trott and her visitor were in her drawing room in the course of the evening. Mrs. Davis has not lost any flesh since you saw her and is as animated as ever. She moves about, receives and talks, as in a triumph, and is strong in having her country women about her as a sort of court.

. . . .

My visit here, as I supposed, has proved bootless, office-hours from 9 and 10 O'clock to 12, and then surrounded by crowds of expectant waiters on the favors of those in power. I should make a poor courtier. I cannot stay here idle; and as Ben's horse is not yet come, I will make an excursion to some of the frontier posts, and see what may be seen at the risk of being caught in a skirmish. Genl Mansfield has taken the place of Genl Patterson, and is repairing the Viaduct across the river at Harper's ferry, and the Rail Road generally, when that is done the communication of the enemy will be open from Baltimore to Ohio and the West. This is against us, but it cant be help'd.

Mrs. Gaines has just arrived, having stolen off to N. York she travel'd by the Lakes to Louisville the past 5 days. She is full of talk and some sensible talk, but she look'd soil'd and shabby. If you were here you would get out of her all she knows about Washington! Mrs. Singleton with her daughter is going with Mr Barnwell to assist in nursing the sick in the hospital at Culpepper C. H. I promised to send some Rice there for the sick so I have enclosed an order to R[obertson] B[lacklock] and Co and hope they will get some down ere long, or get a few barrels in exchange for as many of mine when it shall come, they are in need of it now. She beg'd me to say to you and your daughter, that Flannels, socks and old clothes generally will be acceptable, this you can mention to some of your neighbors, and possibly, you may among you make up a parcel and direct it as in my order, with a paper inside address'd to Mrs. John Singleton a good many Carolinians are said to be there with measles and pneumonia. Mrs. Hopkins has been there and to Yorktown and she says the Virginia women are kind to the sick in their neighborhood, but they dont know how to fix a hospital nor how to manage with funds to keep one going. She has an ambition to be at the head of every thing useful even the commisary no Department more useful, and few more negligently conducted, by the way. Good Bye.

Robert F. W. Allston to Adele Petigru Allston

Piedmont Va. 20th July 1861

MY DEAR WIFE I brought with me in my pocket this sheet and envelope which I have the pleasure of using in addressing you, having first yielded the pen to Ben to use a half sheet found in the port folio of the good people who have kindly taken care of me and mine here. And knowing too how grateful to you all will be the appearance of his well known hand, he superscribes the envelope which I trust will bear to you safe our joint essays. Having finish'd my talk about the coast of Carolina with the President I started for Winchester where Ben's Regt. was station'd and where a battle was daily expected. On approaching the Mannassas junction I heard all about the little fight of the day before a mile or two beyond Fairfax C. H. the retreat order'd by Genl Beauregard with the loss of a cannon and the burning of the C. H. etc. on arriving we learn'd of their advance and our retreat from Centerville dropping a few worthless clothes with the design to draw them into a crescent-shaped entrenchment which he had just completed. It succeeded and the action had continued that day from 9 to 5 1/2 [illegible] 12 to 5 all you have heard ere this by Telegram. But falling in with the confidential agent of the government who had to go [to] Genl B's Head Quarters with despatches I learn'd the result thro' him from Col Jordan viz that the enemy "had retired badly hurt 900 kill'd to our 70 kill'd and wounded." That night I came in expecting to be in at Winchester about the time of the battle there but learning from the aforesaid agent Mr Dan Ratcliffe confidentially late of Washington, that Genl Johnston would have orders to move down rapidly to the support of Beauregard, Genl Patterson having been moved down the Potomac slyly, I stop'd here with a kind family and met Ben yesterday, they have taken good care of us (20 odd breakfasted here this morning) and as they are waiting for the cars (10,000 men have gone and the road is still lined with 10,000 more) I have the satisfaction to see something of our son and his Col., a gentlemanly western man. I left my trunk in Richmond but do not regret it as a clean Shirt is more than a Sunday luxury here. I am loth to leave the neighborhood before the battle is over, it is a very critical one, but I know not how I can manage. The water in Richmond has affected me much and the water here and the sweet milk, is very grateful to me, but I cant remain here, if the country were safe and you were all here, I would be very glad. This is the line of the debateable ground about equidistant, 35 miles from Martinsburgh, Harper's Ferry, and Manassas. Genl Scott designs to break up the Congress in Richmond [illegible] the simultaneous attacks. If the enemy will not slink out of the way, our troops will endeavor to pursue their advantage, and if they can reach Arlington and dislodge them, bombard Washington from that point, God knows what will be the result of this consummate strategem of the wary Scott. But we hope for the best, and have good reason to hope, if we can only have a fair field and reasonable notice. I must break off now to go down before the [illegible] takes the cars. If I have anything to add I will endeavor to give it him. Ben has not got the Blankets, nor the letter enclosing Joe's, nor mine from Richmond in which unfortunately I enclosed yours.

God bless you all. Keep a good heart and pray for the right. I will come to you when ever I can or my funds give out.

21st   As we could not get off yesterday I did not mail this, after transporting about 10,000 troops, one of the conductors went to sleep and broke [?] an Engine on the road so as to make it impassable till today. All was reported quiet below up to last night, but every one believes an important engagement to be at hand, unless Scott orders some deeper stratagem than we can fathom. I have been in the midst of a bivouac of soldiers for 3 days they occupy 3 miles of the narrow valley of the Manassas and its tributary without the sign of a tent and now without cooking utensils. Having made a forced march to this point they are to be transported hence by Rail there are 9 or 10,000 yet to go. I will go along for a day or two until the battle is over, if my strength be not too much exhausted. This condition of my bowels is a great trial. Try and keep well and cultivate an even temper. I brought up news papers, but they dont care about them. Tobacco and Spirits are their greatest treats and coffee and good water their greatest necessities. This country abounds with beef cattle of the very finest. A man drove up to the P. O yesterday with 2 fat oxen. They were both shot down and used up in short order. It requiring 2 beeves for every Regt. and there came by 20 Regts. Ben is in command of his just now. I am enabled to help him some, tho' I must give him concern when I leave these good people. William was very glad to see a familiar face.

Robert F. W. Allston to Adele Petigru Allston

Camp at Mannassas Junction 23d July 1861

DEAR ADELE   We arrived here yesterday morning very early, but too late to participate in the great battle which was fought the day before. We brought 5,000 men who had been waiting at Piedmont two days for transportation if they had arrived in time, the enemy could have been driven into the Potomac. It is thought, as it is, that they have left Alexandria for fear of pursuit. Stewart pursued them as far as beyond Fairfax C.H. and took down the U.S. Flagg there and brought it in. They have left their dead and wounded lying all about the woods, many of the latter have been brought to our Hospitals, indeed they are bringing in to this moment wounded and prisoners. Captain Ricketts is one of the latter and Capt Wilcox the notorious commander of the Chicago Zouaves. But as soon as I got out of the cars I learn'd among other things that Genl Smith, with whom I had sup'd the night before at Mrs. Edmonds and Genl Bee and Henry Middleton were mortally wounded, with pack on my back I at once push'd thro' the mud (it was raining and rain'd all day) 3/4 of mile to their quarters, where Bee was suffering awfully, shot thro' the lower part of the stomach, he recognized me and ask'd for Ben who could not then leave his Regt. (they have been order'd on an outpost of the Battle field and I must try to see him today). It is one of his last lucid moments. I went the 1/2 mile further to the Quarters of Hamptons Legion and found that Lt Col Johnson was kill'd on the field that Middleton was provided for in a house on the field of Battle 5 miles off. Capt [illegible] and the Surgeon were gone after them, that A. Heming and Green and Smith from Georgetown were slightly wounded so, after giving them an encouraging word I came back and remain'd with the gentlemen in the room until Genl Bee died peacefully (His body in charge of Capt Hill goes home this morning) almost his last words were "push on, push on," as if urging his men, some of whom I am sorry to say required to be urged. It was then 12.30 and after looking thru the hospital again I trudged back thro' the mud to find Ben if possible But there was no sign of any of them, they were order'd in advance to do duty. Prisoners are still coming in and wounded in all sorts of fashions and there is poor accommodation for them the rain not ceasing until in the night. They are burying our dead with salutes of infantry, and the air resounds with the noise. I will add to this if I can.

8 O'clock   I have been on the battle field today on my way to Ben's Regiment and such a sight I trust I may never see again, near 700 bodies are still lying exposed and nearly as many horses. Our men are obliged to go out and bury some it will take the rest of the week, and nearly all the homes within 3 miles are fill'd with wounded which until tonight none [?] had medical attendance. Ben was out on a Picket guard at a church where there are 200 yankee wounded and I have not seen him, but I saw William and got a bite at his tent, and I saw Middleton who seems to be better and he takes his confinement so patiently that I trust his lungs will heal, he is shot thro the lungs or thereabout and is reclining with a chair under his back so that he breathes with ease and I think the lung will heal. He is well cared for as well as can be in a large room with six of his corps, the other rooms are fill'd with yankee officers and soldiers among whom is Capt. Ricketts, Adele can mention this to her friends to their common relief. He said he

was [illegible] attended by 2 of his comrades, I could do nothing for him. I will return to Richmond and get a clean shirt, tho I could spend the summer very comfortably in the Piedmont hills.

Robert F. W. Allston to Adele Petigru Allston

Out Post of Genl Johnsons Division
Hospital at Swoley Church, on Bull Run 25th July 1861
MY DEAR WIFE AND CHILDREN,   Ben and I both wrote you from Piedmont. We were in company with an Army of 18,000 men many of whom wrote to their friends. The Post Master, in whose hands I placed my letters, told me that he had thus 3 bushels of letters in the office to mail, which he intended to devote the succeeding day, this was 1 O'clock at night. I wrote again from Mannassas 2 days after the battle, it was a very fatiguing day to me so was yesterday when I found Ben out here bivouacing under a white oak tree where I slept beside him last night, and went thro' the hospitals with him this morning. Tis a post of horror and responsibility as well as of exposure and hardship. This is the place at which Genl McDowell with the advance column of his army cross'd Bull Run at 4 O'cl Sunday morning and march'd up stealthily on the flank of Evans and had decidedly the advantage until 12, when they expected the reserve under Tyler across the Stone Bridge 2 miles off from here, Beauregard however had had 10 acres of creek Swamp clear'd so that the road could be commanded for a mile by the heights on our side (where at Evans' quarters he had establish'd a Telegraph) and the large trees were fell'd across the road, the reserve was so delay'd in clearing the road for themselves as to give time for our left wing to come up viz Bee's and Smith's brigades and Jackson's (arrived only the night before from Winchester) and Hampton's Legion all which drove them back and with others retrived the fate of the day and render'd it glorious tho bloody. Well they retreated this way and that way and every way in the greatest confusion leaving 280 of their wounded and dying in this church and the adjacent buildings. On tuesday morning at daylight Major Allston was sent out here with 400 men to guard the approaches, with 30 prisoners and see that the wounded are duly cared for by their own people if they come; by ours, if they do not. I am sharing with him, his greenwood lodging whilst he remains thus seperated from the army. It is a revolting duty to go thro' the hospitals, but many of the poor devils listen earnestly and with soften'd features to a kind word some are stolid silent and unaffected, others swear awfully and recklessly. This morning as I came forth from the Hospital I was surprised by the Revd Dr Andrews who lives near Harpers Ferry and came down to offer ghostly counsel to the dying. Mr Lyon too of Richmond came out today with his brother-in-law Lieut. Penn-Stewart of Johnson's army greatly distinguish'd himself in the pursuit and has been made a full colonel.

My diarrhea is very exhausting today, but as long as the rice lasts I can keep up and observe for Ben in his absence, until the command be order'd to march. Then I will retire to Richmond where I hope to hear from you. Having no horse I will not attempt to march with them. Frank and Gerald arrived safe last Monday, very much to our relief.

I saw Middleton again on my way here, but feeling convinced that he prefers to be waited on by his comrades, Ford and Thomas, I did not remain long, he is rather better but not out of danger. You will perceive I write on the enemy's paper. The troops have not ceased to fetch in spoils near 200 muskets and cartridge boxes were sent in from here today, this is 9 or 10 miles from Head Quarters. Oh I long'd for a drink from Chicora Spring as I came out of my nest this morning. The water in every Spring is soon muddied by the troops, they are so many. Dr Andrews says Genl Patterson has cross'd the Potomac at Harper's ferry, having apparently relinquish'd his design upon the valley of Virginia. He says thousands of manacles (hand-cuffs) have been captured from the enemy, and his eyes dilated and glisten'd as he added, "I never agreed with South Carolinians, but I see you were right in your estimate of these people. I can hardly believe my own eyes and understanding." The Dr. is a learned and excitable person but is very slightly demonstrative ordinarily. Said he "Maryland is fast coming round to secession, so is Kentucky and Missouri." He came to where we slept, I offer'd him the only camp stool and sat on a box they feed the horses in, the same on which I now write. Said he, you sleep here? yes and "you so brave and cheerful, the men are of your little [illegible] there are men there worth $100,000 and I saw them last night sleeping with their feet to the fire, cover'd only with their blankets and up to the time for sleep they were singing songs and psalms. . . . .

P. S. I understand Middleton is not as comfortable today. Another man from Charleston says the enemy have taken off some 200 negroes.

A. M. Manigault[1] to Robert F. W. Allston

Camp Marion Septbr. 20th 1861

DEAR SIR Yours of the 8th I received as I was about starting on a visit along the coast, and since my return my time has been much occupied, or I should have answered sooner. The system of signals you speak of is important, but would cost much to carry them out, as only careful and intelligent men, could be employed and they would have to be stationed on the shores of the Wynyah Bay, in an unhealthy country at this period of the year. I suppose you allude to telegraphic signals. When the works at South Isld. and Cat Isld. are completed, and if there be any reserve force in its neighbourhood, I shall adopt one, to any point, where intelligence may be gained,

---

[1] Arthur Middleton Manigault (1824–86), in charge of the defenses of Winyah Bay and Santee River, later adjutant and inspector general of South Carolina.

or reserves etc brought up. In the meantime I have a detachment of cavalry, on duty at So Isld., and a guard in the Light house on North Isld. to give any information of the appearance of vessels. One or two mounted men could convey intelligence to the Main portion of the Regt. in 2 hours, I have also applied to General Ripley for the use and entire control of a light draught steamer, for this post, which requisition he has complied with and a steamer is now on her [way] to me, from Charleston, with her I will be able to move a force of 3 or 4 companies, to any point of the coast threatened, and by taking in tow, flats, lighters or small boats, a very considerable force, may speedily be moved either to the entrance to Winyah Bay, or to any point on the Waccamaw River, as high as Conwayboro. I have also suggested to Genl. Ripley, that one or two companies of Cavalry should be placed on the coast, north of North Isld, as a coast guard. Altho they may not be able to resist a landing in force, still they might annoy an enemy and rapidly convey intelligence throughout the country, and in this way afford means of providing a sufficient force to meet and attack them. I do not think from the nature of that coast, the small size of the inlets, and comparitively shallow water on the bars, that any serious demonstration will be made, by our enemies North of Winyah Bay. The seising of the Post, erected for its protection, and the control of Georgetown and the adjacent waters, would give them, also the control of all the different rivers emptying into the Bay, including also the North Santee River, and if they could once possess themselves of the point mentioned, they could carry out any plans, for holding or destroying Georgetown and all property on the different rivers, with greater ease at less expense, either in life or money than by making a descent on an exposed coast, where their shipping would continually be in danger, and their land force liable to be cut off from its supplies.

The inference is, in my humble opinion, that this point should be carefully watched, the works thoroughly and efficiently constructed and armed, as it is the most and almost the only attractive point (not excepting Bulls Bay) North of Charleston. I only regret that we are to be furnished, with guns of small calabre, 24 par. [?] being the largest size. I wish that yourself and others of influence, could prevail on the Authorities to Supply Ord[nance] of heavier metal, I know that there is a great scarcity of heavy Guns, still I think a few might be secured. I have urged and shall continue to urge it.

The Bouy on Long Beach, I think drifted there, from Georgetown Bar, I have no idea that it was placed there by any of the vessels of the Federal Navy. It was sunk by my orders, since which time I have thot that its position one of accident, its being opposite and near to fresh water pond, argues nothing, on examination (personal) I find several of them, one or two on a large scale, and offering every facility the same as the one alluded to, indeed they seem to be peculiar to our coast.

I should be glad to see you in our camp at any time that you may feel inclined to honor us with a visit.

Henry D. Lesesne to Robert F. W. Allston

Charleston, Sept. 26, 1861

DEAR GOVERNOR, How are you in these "times that try men's souls"? Uncertainty and suspense are very oppressive to the nervous system, and we are sorely subjected to those trials at the present. I try to comfort myself with the belief that our chosen Rulers have good reasons for their apparently supine course, which it would not be proper to make public, and I think I would succeed, but for the clamor and exciting talk which one hears at every turn, and reads, not in every paper, but in the Mercury *ad nauseam*. That, I confess is a trial which I find it hard to bear patiently. And it is strange, almost everybody disapproves, but no one does anything to check that mischievous print. I wrote "A word in Season" in last Saturday's Courier, with that view. But not wishing to provoke bad feelings among ourselves at such a crisis, I suppose the admonition was too gentle to merit the Editors notice. At any rate we have grounds for an abiding trust in a power which cannot fail. How opportune was the arrival of the Bermuda with her invaluable cargo of Blankets, arms, munitions etc.! It has diffused joy through the community.

I returned to-day from the Bible Convention held at Orangeburg. It closed its deliberations at 10 last night, and they indeed constituted a refreshing episode at this time when all are so sorely tempted to give the rein to feelings which are not in accordance with the teachings of our Master. Some short speeches, spontaneous outbursts, which followed the business, and the prayer which crowned the whole work, were indescribably delightful. The Convention appointed Delegates, and invited the Societies in the other C[onfederate] S[tates] to appoint Delegates, to a general convention, for the purpose of establishing an Agency to take the place of the great Central one which heretofore existed at N. Y. It is certainly remarkable that it should have fallen to the lot of our State to lead the way in matters of State, War, Church and Charity. . . . .

James L. Petigru to Robert F. W. Allston

Charleston Decr 1861

MY DEAR GOVERNOR, Nothing has given me so strong a sense of the sad times upon which we have fallen as the representation of your embarrassment. We have always looked up to you as combining more than any one else, prudence with the other cardinal virtues; and when your troubles are so great as to lead you to complain, it is a proof that forethought and discretion are not enough in these days to keep us out of harm. I have not any right to speak for Sister Ann but there is no chance of putting her negroes at Cedar hill, for it is let to Hill and Crosier for four years to come. But surely it is better not to move the people if it can be avoided at all. It is true the Edisto people and Islanders have done so, but it is at an immense sacrifice. And Mr Mathews has burned his rice, and between the destruction by fire and by the Enemy there is little or no difference to the owner; tho a great deal to the other party. But if the Enemy would take the rice and nothing else, it seems to me the negroes had better remain; one crop may be destroyed by a storm but if the Plantation is left the loss may be recovered. I have no idea that the Yankees desire to take the negroes away. It is preposterous. It would not be possible without a vast number of ships. And where wd they carry them? The notion of taking them to Cuba for sale might suggest itself to an individual here and there, but could not be done with the consent of the abolitionists nor without it. If however you find it necessary to remove your own people, it would well become our friend to think of it. Cherry hill would offer a safe asylum, but where is subsistence to come from?

I have a letter from Johnston. Nothing it contains gave me so much pleasure as the account he gives of Ben. He overheard a conversation between two of the Alabama Regiment he commands, who were remarking that he was thought strict at first, and he was strict; but not more than the service required, that he had done the Regiment a great deal of good, and is one of the best officers in the South.

It is supposed that Butlers expedition is intended for Bulls bay, and if so it may be looked for soon. God help us! Let us hope for the best. But what is the best? Perhaps, that Beauregard may whip McClellan, and overrun the whole North, and make Jef Davis Emperor. If he and McClellan stand face to face eating up the substance of the country, it will not be long before famine is added to Insolvency.

You may observe that I do not expect any order from the Confederate Government to remove the negroes, for they gave none at the South; and they would be afraid of taking the responsibility; for such an order would give the Planters a claim for damages.

My work is returned by the want of Printers who are all in Camp that are fit for duty. But for Gen. Trapiers condescension the work would have absolutely stopped. I will go to Columbia someday this week with a few sheets. . . . .[1]

E. L. Bowman to Robert F. W. Allston

Charleston, Dec 27th [18]61.

MY DEAR KIND FRIEND . . . . The night of the 11th was indeed an awful one.[2] The fire commenced in a quarter of the town so distant from us, with the wind bearing it in a contrary direction that for some hours we apprehended no danger; but, about midnight the wind, then increased to a gale,

---

[1] As code commissioner of South Carolina Petigru was preparing the work later published under the title *Portion of the Code of Statute Law of South Carolina, 1860–62*.

[2] The great fire of 1861 destroyed a large section of lower Charleston, north and south of Broad Street.

veered suddenly round, and bringing a actual sea of flame surging over upon us with such frightful rapidity, as left little time for preparation. But our friends were very kind. Mrs. Parker sent her carriage to convey us to a place of safety with her son James to be our escort, and Mrs. Roper and Capt Childs were with us the greater part of the night giving all the aid in their power, and with such efficient help every thing might easily have been saved had it been possible to procure carts in time, but vehicles of every description had been appropriated hours before the fire extended to Broad Str, and it was not until — O'clock in the morng when our roof was in flames, and we had left for the Arsenal that Capt Childs succeeded by indefatigable efforts in procuring 2 drays, just in time to bring away our beds, house linen and clothing. Papers and plate we took with us. The standing furniture etc was nearly all consumed, but we are thankful so much has been spared, and that we and our household are unhurt.

Though deeply grieved for the desolation of our already afflicted city, yet, through the Mercy of God, I felt neither fear nor fatigue throughout that dreadful night, and the girls were calm and collected, giving all the help they could.

Very gladly would we have availed ourselves of your kind offer dear Robert, if we had not already found refuge in the vacant house of our good friend Mr Roper whose family are in Camden, and he as one of the Home Guard, and much engaged in business seldom spends more than an hour at home. One more move we propose to make next week to Statesburg there to remain D. V. until the fate of Charleston is decided. . . . .

Robert F. W. Allston to Governor F. W. Pickens[1]

Chicora Wood 13 Jany 1862

DEAR SIR, Living in a district in which no steam Cars rejoice our eyes, rather remote from the busy world, excepting the business of preparation for War on the Sea Coast, I have not desired any public office whatever. My neighbors however desiring me to assist in the drill of our beat company, I am willing to do a humble part in preparing for defence. And your Excellency having done me the honor to appoint me a member of the Provost Marshal's Court for this district, I will endeavor to perform my duty therein. My friends spoke to me in Columbia of the chief office of that court. Respectfully to them, I declined it, as one imposing active duty unsuited to the habits of three score years; I am grateful for your consideration in naming me (if in the Court at all) for the lesser duties of a simple member, in which capacity I will try to be useful to the Community in which my property lies. I would be glad to receive from the Executive any hints which might aid in the organization and [blank] of such a Court, new entirely to me. I can only liken it to the old fashioned County Court, but

1 Copy.

clothed with far greater power. I presume however that Dr Parker has already the benefit of your ideas, as he was lately in Columbia. It were needless therefore to trouble you further, oppressed as you are with the cares of Office. Be assured of my sympathy, and do me the kindness to present me respectfully to Mrs Pickens who will permit me to offer the regards of my family including my son Major Allston who has just left us for Cavalry Service at Norfolk. He came a week ago from Centreville, on sick leave, his face and eyes quite jaundiced. He would be happy to be called to a regiment in Carolina but is of the opinion that the decisive battle must be fought on the Eastern or Western frontier.

Robert F. W. Allston to James H. Hammond[1]

Chicora Pine-lands (near) Georgetown 26th July 1862

DEAR SIR   Dependent upon our own efforts for the manufacture of Molasses as well as Salt, I am trying to make both. Beginning to succeed with the latter, the vandal Enemy, last week, broke up my Salt boilers, stole 2 boiler heads and wantonly scatter'd the Salt into the Sand.

My Sorgho is not yet ripe, when it is I desire to know how to proceed forthwith, so as to lose neither time, or material in experimenting. With this view I beg you to give me the benefit of your experience, a statement of the best method of boiling the juice, the length of time, the time for putting in the lime, (and quantity) whether before, or whilst boiling.

In preparing Sugar from the Ribbon Sugar Cane, the quantity of lime is, I believe, 1 to [illegible] parts of lime and is put in before boiling. Your experience I understand is full, and I am sure it will afford you pleasure to put me in possession of it, as fully as your leisure will permit, both as to the making and keeping of the syrup of Sorgho, a Chinese Sugar cane. The other uses of this cane I believe are confined to fatting cattle and hogs.

See what paper we are reduced to in the country off from R R. transportation!

P. S.   I write thus, tho' the enemy be in, and commanding our waters; I may be broken up, in the midst of the harvest of half a crop of Rice and 3 acres of Sugar cane.

By the way how much Syrup may be expected from an acre of cane? I have never before turn'd my attention to it.

W. L. Morse to Robert F. W. Allston

Effingham S. C. Oct 10 [18]62

DEAR SIR   Yours of the 3rd Inst, came to hand last night in regard to the contents, I am living at Effingham on the N[orth] E[astern] R[ail] R[oad] attending to the Agency of the Road here, and acting Post Master, but I

---

[1] Original in the Library of Congress.

could have you a boat built at prety Short notice, and especially so if you can furnish me two or three hands, that has the use of tools. write me imimediatly the size boat you want, the plan also. you can have any sort you want if we can procure Spikes and bolt-Iron. you can have a small boat of 75 ft length built at from 450 to 800 dollars one 100 ft 16 or 17 ft Beam, from 800 to 1600 dollars, the plan or quality of boat has much to do with the price. you could have what is called a flat Boat, with open deck, 75 ft long 14 or 15 ft Beam, culed only in bottom for about 350 dollars. you however will have to decide for yourself, and if you propose to build you had better procure Spikes Nails and bolt rod iron in Charleston or George-town. I will allow you for hands a fair price, and will if I build for you be glad to git them as hands are scearce here.

Adele Petigru Allston to Benjamin Allston

Plantersville 30th Oct [18]62

MY BELOVED BEN Your precious letter of 10th written from Harrods-burgh, telling of your wound was received just one week ago. God be praised for your preservation which seems to me almost miraculous. I would have written to you immediately but that I feared you might be in the hands of the enemy and no letter would reach you. I wrote you on the 3d and on the 19 and 20th inst and if you are now at Knoxville as we hear the army is, those letters will give you all recent news of us. I was very much relieved two days ago by a note from Dr Parker informing us he had just received a letter from Frank telling him you were doing well and travelling with the army in an ambulance without seeming to suffer much. This was a great comfort to me. He also mentioned that Dr Nott had seen you, of which I was very glad.

Your Father left us more than a week ago to look for places to remove his and your negroes to. He returned last night having looked at many places and having concluded the purchase of one in North Ca[rolina] on the route of the R R that is to be. Morven is the name of the place. It is on the Pee Dee in Anson county, 12 miles from Cheraw. There are 1900 acres and some improvements. The owner lives in Mississippi, the price is $10,000. We consider this a fortunate arrangement. I am sorry to say your Father came home with a bad cold and much worn, and he found us all ar-ranged for a party. All the inhabitants of this village and the acquaintances at the camp were invited to pass the evening with us. Such parties have been given by all our neighbours, or rather, some of them. The Westons Tuckers and LaBruces had given many. Adele and I concluded we ought to shew a social disposition by extending an invitation ourselves. The camp is to be removed from its present position to-morrow, and be placed some 8 or 9 miles from us, so we could not put it off. Another reason was LaBruce Mortimer is here on a visit to his uncle Josh LaBruce. He received a wound in his right hand at the battle of Sharpsburgh, is still unable to put his arm in his coat sleeve, but is very well and fond of dancing. He has behaved well thro' all our hard fought battles: has been in 8 great battles, and innumerable skirmishes, was promoted to corporal for gallant conduct, has never asked for leave or furlough, and endured all the hardships of the common soldier. He is just 21, his birthday being last Sunday. I wished to shew him some attention as he leaves in a day or so. If the company had not been here your Father would have gone to bed at once, but you know his spirit: he stayed up to the last and looked at the dancing with interest. I was very much afraid he would disapprove of the whole thing, but the only thing he found fault with was that there was not supper enough, that I ought to have had two turkeys and two hams, and every thing in proportion. Last monday night Mrs Joe Tucker had a party which kept up quite late. The Westons were there of course. The next morning their surprise was great to hear that their head carpenter and 18 others of his finest, most intelligent and trusted men had taken his family boat, (which had been since May in the piazza of his old house, being too large to be gotten into any lock up house, no door would admit it, and it required 20 men to move it,) at an early hour after dark and made their escape to the enemy. There are many circumstances connected with it that makes it very painful; and shews quite a widespread feeling not only among Mr Westons people, but through the neighbourhood. Plowden Weston arrived at Mr Francis Westons that evening. He came to see us the next morning. His service in the army has made him greatly older, but I think has improved him otherwise. He thinks he will return after the Legislative Session is over. There has been a glorious fight at Pocataligo, and Coosawahatchie. Joe received two flesh wounds, they did not confine him to bed.

Milly and Mary send love and howdey to you. God bless and guide you my beloved. Charly has been confirmed and received the communion.

[P. S.] Mrs Williams offered us Croley Hill. We accept it and will pass the winter there if obliged to leave here. John Tucker is still ill. I fear not able to do efficient duty.

James L. Petigru to Adele Petigru Allston

Summerville 31 Oct 1862

This morning I said to my self, today I'll write to Adele, and before I came out of my room they brought me the packet containing both your letters. You may be sure I was glad to see it, and the sight had no tendency to weaken the intention that I had mentally declared. First as to Ben, it was really a relief to know he was only wounded. So long an interval since I had heard of his whereabouts, indeed I believe the last account I had of him was from Col McGowan at Abbeville, that there was room for all manner of things to happen; and I hope that he has paid now for the experience of a soldier having been taken prisoner and wounded, so that if he even meets with no other adventures he will have a biography of his own. Joe too has his scars to show, he was twice wounded at Pocataligo, in the arm and a flesh wound below. One of the Heywards told me he saw him the next morning walking on the platform at the Depot at Pocataligo with his arm in a sling, which relieved my mind from any apprehension for him, and a letter from Jane confirms what I thus heard. Abram has arrived from Badwell but instead of stopping here, proceeded to Charleston. I have sent for him as I want to see him before he goes; but as he had not made his appearance this morning, I am afraid I will not see him nor have the opportunity of doing something in the way of relief for the great privation which they sustained on the Rail Road in August. Hamlet gives Abram an excellent character. With Caroline and Mary's George, Hamlet had three carpenters under him. They thoroughly repaired the China Grove house, with new sills, new roof, shutters to the windows, under pinning and banisters to the piazza. They put a new roof on the Kitchen at Badwell repaired Janes Cotton house and built and completed a house for Silla one of my people, and finally put up a house for Gilfoil on a piece of land which we paid Mrs Jones for, where Gilfoil was placed as a Tenant by brother Tom, to secure the Title which was not marketable. But we took it of Mrs Jones to help her, there being a dozen who had the same right as she. They had only raised Gil's house but Jane sent Abram at my request; in fact I believe he ought to have been sent the first instead of the last of this month. I hope the Governor has not been impeded in his operations by the want of him, and should he be in turn wanting force in that line I will send Hamlet to him with pleasure. I dont wonder that the Governor has gone up the Pedee instead of coming to our side. The Pedee is the family stream uniting them by political association as well [as] geographical limits with that country. But it would have been to all of us the source of much joy and gratulation if he had set up his tents in Abbeville.

The spirit that our people have shown in all encounters with the enemy goes far to redeem the rashness that has ruined so many, and is likely to ruin more. But the praise of fortitude which they well deserve really entitles them to the respect of the world. How much longer we are to suffer the process of impoverishment and reduction, nobody can tell. But one thing I feel sure of, which is that when the fate of Maryland Kentucky and Missouri is settled, either to go with the North or the South, the quarrel will be so much nearer the end. But still the Mississippi River and Western Virginia will prove a sore subject of difference. To speak now of myself. I have had a fortnight of much suffering. It is two weeks since the trial of Major Lowndes by an Alien Enemy commenced. My feelings were wrought upon in a high degree and in returning on Friday evening (17th) I forgot myself so far as to sit for near an hour in a draught of fresh eastern wind. The consequences exceeded any thing I ever suffered in that line before. I am now much, indeed a great deal, better; but still unfit for business.

I am delighted by Allstons consideration for Sister Jane. The two barrels of salt will be a great blessing. I am only afraid of their being stolen. How were they sent? by Kingsville or by Charleston? I think you are happy in such a friend as Mrs Williams. I sympathize in your recourse to History. I am reading the Pictorial History of England. One of Johnston's books. The reign of George the third. Find many things in it applicable to the present times. But small is the relief that History gives to Charles Lowndes for instance, a model of a good master, whose nigs are leaving him by scores. And our friend Mr Vanderhorst too has lost 40. Bessy and Jane are too young to feel how much distress there is. May they continue in the same happy ignorance! Adieu, my dear Sister, remind Allston of my thanks and Addy of the parental affection of her Uncle.

[P. S.] Dean Swift in his Journal to Stella, dilates on blots as marks of a warm and open heart in the writer. But I am ashamed of them. And can only excuse them by the shaky condition to which my cough has brought me.

Adele Petigru Allston to Elizabeth Allston

Plantersville 11th January 1863

MY DEAR BESSIE . . . . Every thing here remains as usual. Your Father is less disposed to move than he was, and is preparing to plant a crop here. We all thought after the battle before Fredericksburgh that the war might terminate soon and we might be spared the trouble and expense of moving, but the political horizon is again overcast and know not how much longer this most wicked war may be urged against us. . . . . Your Father will be going to Morven about the middle of this month and I think Adele Charles and I will go at the same time to Society Hill I do not know that we will set up our tabernacle there, but it is necessary to look after our furniture which was sent from Charleston as well as what went from Chicora and see what is there and in what condition. We then wish to go to make a visit to Aunt Louise and to your Uncle; for the latter purpose we would go to Charleston, and visit him from there. I really long to see him, and am anxious to go, would like to go this week. But your Father is thinking of hiring Waverly Mill from Joe, and if he concludes to do so I fear it may detain us. Of course all these plans are subject to alteration by the military operations of the enemy. If they succeed in their attempt on the North Carolina R R and upon Wilmington it would throw us into a state of confusion and I do not know what we would do. How I do wish your Father had moved Ditchford house out here. If we only had a tolerably comfortable house we would be content here, but we are wretchedly housed. The one fire place smokes terribly. . . . .

Robert F. W. Allston to Adele Petigru Allston

Plantersville 26th March [18]63

DEAR WIFE I reach'd a lonely home last night, and sup'd upon 2 of the Eggs and the piece of ham which you put up with some Rice and potatoes, but I found a comfortable bed which after dispatching 2 letters to my mail, I enjoy'd with a thankful heart till 7 this morning. Now I see a firm roll of butter on the table and with 3 eggs sent with it by Milly I shall make a hearty breakfast. Peter is exemplary in obedience and willingness to learn but I am afraid Saml. has spoil'd my horses, by galling them and not adjusting carefully the harness. Attempting Tuesday night to get to Mr Shaw's they stall'd in the deepest place in Thorn Creek and I had to hire 2 hands of Salters to pull out the Carriage, which I left in the broad Road and return'd with servant and horses to Salters' at 11 O'clock. Next morning the harness being better adjusted (it is very poor and ragged) they drew off without any trouble and never perform'd better. I call'd and sat more than half an hour with Mr. Shaw who is feeble and grunting. His present trouble is about "feeding the people" the Presbytry is to sit there next Tuesday and all the week his house will be full and he has no wheat flour. I told him [to] send up to you and you would let him have 25 lbs. I wish you would send him that much, or at any rate the bag full that I left with Adele, direct it to Kingstree care of P. B. Mouzon. Miss Betsy came into the parlour and found a chance to tell me without their hearing that her best cow Bremen is dead chok'd in the stall. I suppose they fed her on cob-corn instead of meal and peas. I go to Waverly today and will add a P. S if possible. You had better get John Williams to buy the horses and get a receipt for the money and if he can get another good one from the old man for Sam. I will pay the money I want to let the little mares [illegible] and get their bruises well. Nothing but flour and tailings to feed on.

7.30 P M I have just dined and take time to add a few lines. Poor Joe has another negroe very ill. I went to see what chearing words I could to her. Dr. H. says th[at] all the things his people took in the boat, attempting to reach the Blockades have been wash'd up the Club-house Creek, he therefore supposes the hands were drown'd. That is not my opinion. They were in an [illegible] life-boat which might fill and have things wash'd over board but would never sink. The negroes send howdye to Missess. Molly offers this evening 4 Doz Eggs. I will send you some beef Saturday if possible.

Robert F. W. Allston to Adele Petigru Allston

Plantersville 10th April 1863

MY DEAR WIFE After reading the very gratifying account of the repulse of the iron-clads in the[ir la]te attack on the Forts in the harbour of Charleston, I feel impel'd to write a few lines by W's servant if only to congratulate you upon the auspicious event. God be praised! But the end is not yet. Their blood being up they will try it again. May it Please God to enable us to repulse them, on every attempt by sea or land.

J. W. Williams has sent for Ben's buggy, the servant who takes it up will be the bearer of this. He gets it cheap, as things are going, $350 was I think the cost of it, 500 could not now bu[y the same] thing. Appropos of sales you enquire what Brass is to do. I sent him up to split Rails, and told him upon his repeated failure that he must go to the vendue table, whenever he could not do this. Now if any one about you is going to Charleston, give Brass a new shirt and send him to Robertson Blacklock and Co. to be turn'd into money, forthwith. It is the best thing to be done with Brass. There must be no fuss about it, or noise, or notice.[1]

Stephen got back a half day later than I expected. He spent all the money I gave him and $5 [more whic]h I paid him from the bill you gave him, old Brown (the jew) charged him $8, for the oil. He did not give it very properly. He engaged it to me at $5, and that's the reason I sent for it. I have a plenty now. Got 30 lbs. of lard from Mrs. Davis. The old man, her husband, died last week. I will not be long after him. . . . .

Van R. Morgan to Robert F. W. Allston

Naval Station Marion, C H, S C. April 13th 1863

SIR,   I have not had an earlier opportunity to reply to your letter, in which you say that you will charge the Government *ninety* (90.00) Dollars a month for the 2 men and 2 boys now employed at the Navy Yard at Peedee Bridge. I will accept your offer and ask that you will hire them to me for three months, with the privilege of keeping them longer, probably six months.

If you wish your servants to return home, occasionally, I will let them go, provided you sustain the loss of time in making such visits. If it were nearer, it would be a matter of no importance.

We will pay you monthly for the hire of your negroes and have the pay already dew now ready for you.

Robert F. W. Allston to Adele Petigru Allston

Plantersville 18th July 1863

DEAR ADELE,   Your last letter came today in which you ask if I intend to move Ben's negroes? It has given me, all along since being disappointed of my purchase in Darlington, much concern that I am [not] provided with a place for Ben's negroes. I would take them up and build potatoe cellars for them in the Sand Hills near one of John William's spring branches, if he would allow me the privelige to do so, and to plant the old fields where Ladrus is. I know no better thing to do. Yet it may not be agreeable to the

[1] For report concerning the sale of Brass see below, p. 426.

Williams, and they are kind enough every way. My own will more than over-stock the farm at Morven. The flats are engaged moving off Rice from the Mill. Nothing else can be moved just now except a little salt.

I have directed Stephen to go up and see where the box of silver dishes and covers has been stored the past year.

Do tell Ladrus [to] plant it largely of Peas again soon as they have done with the slips. Rain here every day. In moving about so I am aware that I must neglect somethings and overlook many things and perform my duty imperfectly. God grant me health and memory for my duties. I am anxious now about William's boat with 160 Bbls Rice, on the River for William's Barn. It is old and the river rising. I am in dread of some accident. It is his old boat and not hard to sink.

I send Stephen up to keep him employ'd. I am to be back here the 1st Aug.

God bless you all. I go to-morrow to pay for some corn at Jeffries Creek and expect to take the Cars Tuesday evening, for fear they may not suffer Nelson to go into the City.

Robert F. W. Allston to Adele Petigru Allston

Plantersville 25 Oct. 1863

MY DEAR WIFE   Yesterday I spent in Town riding there and back in the rain, paid my War Tax $1236.12 said a word to the Enrolling Officer for Joe's Miller and Ben's Overseer and return'd to dinner about 5 O'cl.[1] It was dark before I got through. On my way home I sat an hour at Weston's and walk'd home, a little light-headed last night and this morning. No church today Mr and Mrs. Glennie gone to Waccamaw. Severe change in weather. Mrs. Sparkman has given birth to her 6th son, doing well, Doctor in full practise. I go tomorrow to Britton's neck for two days to take account of the porkers there and Joe's boat will leave sometime Tuesday with 8 porkers for you 6 in one pen, 2 in another. (Tell Ladrus to prepare 2 pens for them in time, and give them as much corn as they can eat, with a boll of Hickory ashes, charcoal and salt, on side of which they will lick and twill keep them healthy. They should be fed a month with advantage before they are large and fat enough. However you can kill one or two of the fattest next cold change.) 10 young turkeys 2 old ones for N[ightingale] Hall. My tin paper boxes, boxes of books, some furniture, Atlas, Ben's wardrobe containing clothes and your little book case, which I hope will go safe, also 2 coops of chickens, 2 more geese for Morven. All these I have order'd, having ap-pointed to go to Brittons Neck, I cannot see them forwarded. Besides a cask for the Neck Joe takes 11 casks of salt 5 of which will be landed at Mar's Bluff if the people want it 2 for J. Witherspoons and 2 for Ed. Evans. I will take their corn another time, 2 at the Barn, one for Gandy, you had better

[1] For details of the procedure followed in applying for the exemption of overseers see below, pp. 277–79.

let him haul his 100 bushels of corn at once, if you can put it away. I have sent 50 bushels of Rice flour for your poultry etc and pigs, also 50 for Morven tho' Barrantine undervalues it. Louisa, Maggy and family go up to the Farm. Doctor asks permission to go in order to recover from his faithless wife his blanket and things! He says he caught her in adulturous living 3 times, the last time he knock'd her and she swore against him roundly. So he told me this morning in a very subdued voice and manner. I shall not object if you send her out of the yard.

I breakfasted with the Shaws and was inform'd Mrs. Cobart announces an approaching marriage between the President N[orth] E[astern] Rail Road and the widow Parker in her neighborhood. I wrote Charles yesterday not to come down this week, but the week after, let Paul drive him down in the little wagon after taking the carriage to have top put on. I am sorry to disappoint him but mules are all engaged hauling wood and the crop and the only draft horses are my little ponies going with me every day. Next week I will look for him with Paul and the blacks, and will have him to superintend the making of sausages. Do let Paul fetch Mary's bucket which took eggs and the boxes and the big white oak basket and the piece of Oznaburghs from Morven, the coops can be sent better by the boat. The girls are all asking about Charles. Why has he not come? and I am afraid they will turn his head when he does come. Adieu and kiss them all for me. I hope your Rye patch is sown and fenced and will succeed finely.

P. S.   If Sam goes up do tell him to enquire after the barrel of Rice for Anne Tucker at Midway. It has fail'd to reach her. She is in need of it. The bottle of Ink is for Morven. The Hogs are from Auba's crawl who says tell [illegible] and send in some ground-nuts.

Robert F. W. Allston to Adele Petigru Allston

Plantersville 2nd Novr. 1863

MY DEAR WIFE,   I have written to Mr. Weston for leave to take Ben's bond out of the hands of his agents. Sparkman says he is a very sick man. I have written too to Ben. The Govt having establish'd a special mail from Meridian Miss. The address is "Shreveport, La., via Meridian, Miss.," with 40 cents postage. So only one should write at a time and send a full letter (1/2 ounce). I have sent his letter with the foregoing address and I think some of us will hear from him now in the course of ten days. Joe carried up 27 Turkeys, more than I intended you to feed. The old ones may be kept for breed, 8 hogs not fat enough till Decr., chickens etc. Ben's wardrobe with his clothes and a great many things which I forget now. Stop at Croly whatever you wish, and what you think ought to stop and send the rest on to No. Ca taking a list of what you do stop. Bessie can do this. Send back the coops and tell Joe to ask for a rope at Mr Witherspoons at Hunt's Bluff. I dont wish to take the corn from thence just yet.

I received yours of 30th. Dr. Smith is a little crooked. He gains the law on this occasion and you must get some barrels from Coker before hand. Keep your horses and cows fit. They are easier kept when fat and more satisfactory. The white ox was in fine order when he started from here, very coarse food serves him, but a plenty shucks cut up and a little flour. I have to go to Town today and tomorrow, shall stay at Dr. Forster's, so tis well Charles is not here yet. But for this I would go to meet the President. We are trying to devise a plan to add to the fund for the Relief of soldier's families. Ned Moore was carried to jail yesterday as a deserter, goes to Columbia. William has got his exemption from the Medical on their opinion that he has permanent cataract threatening blindness. They are to occupy Mrs. Guerrard's house for the winter without locks! Frank Heriot is loud mouth'd against the S's and says Wm. E. S. applied for his sister Em. but shall never get her with his consent, "got too much of the blood (poor blood as it is) already." I have reason to believe there is much scandal dealt in here. F. W. H. says every body has been borrowing from him and never returning, till he is obliged to move away to Sandy Island. All the negroes seem to wish you home many send howd'ye. The crop is light. I am glad Adele is better fix'd.

P. S.   Ancrum goes up tomorrow to carry 10 sheep to Mr. Wilson. If the old man dont want them, he can leave them with Ladrus if he finds difficulty in driving them and take on his cow and calf. I regret very much the discouraging accounts from Abbeville. Her passing away will be another warning to me. God grant I may be ready, as she is.

Robert F. W. Allston to Adele Petigru Allston

Plantersville 11th Novr. 1863

MY DEAR WIFE   Charles is so taken up by his horse, gunning and visiting, that I must not wait longer on him to write for me. But on this bright frosty morning (your birth-day as well as I am inform'd) I sit down since breakfast to say, tho' hurriedly, Good morning to my Treasure-Keeper, and to our joint Treasure. I am glad to think you must be all well enough to enjoy this fine weather. Ah! I am check'd by the reflection that our country suffers and is in danger of devastation. Perseverance is the quality in which as a people, we are inferior to the Northern feinds. If we fail with them, it will be due less even to their superior preperation than their pertinacity and endurance. But God forbid that we should fail, the idea is intolerable. Tis sad, however and sorrowful to see that some of our people are giving away. Christian, they tell me (a man for peace on any terms) has been elected in Anson No. Ca over Ashe, and Witherspoon over McQueen in So. Ca. I dont condemn Witherspoon but the ground of the opposition is for peace. I am for Peace as much as anybody, but Peace on honorable terms only, first of all our

Independence. God grant us power to win it, and grace to administer it worthily and wisely. . . . .

Alexander Glennie to Robert F. W. Allston

Plantersville Dec 29th 1863

MY DEAR SIR   I want to address you on a subject that has given me much concern not for myself but for others Can you not make some move whereby our clergy may be enabled to purchase provisions at a price within the reach of their salaries. I do not know it but I fear their has been no increase of salary and if not how can they meet the wants of their families. My suggestion is entirely disinterested for from the great kindness of the people here and among them none more kind and thoughtful than yourself and of those in our own Parish I can with truth say that as far as provisions and salt are concerned we have not in the *least* felt the pressure of the times. When I think of all the comforts we have, wood for the cutting, plenty of provisions and even if we have to buy at a cheap rate my heart goes out to those who I know are filled with care and anxiety about these matters. You will not I hope think I have gone out of my place and had we been sufferers from the high prices I would not have addressed you but as I feel I can do it without one selfish feeling I have ventured and hope you may communicate with other members of our Church and see if something cannot be done to enable the clergy to get provisions at a rate to suit their salaries. I know you feel a deep interest in all connected with our Church and surely this is a matter of interest that the clergy should be relieved from this great anxiety as to meeting the necessities of their families. My kind love to Mrs Allston and the girls and with the best wishes of the season wishing you all a happy-New Year.

Adele Petigru Allston to Benjamin Allston

Croley Hill   31st May 1864

MY DEAR BEN,   Yours of 12 inst was received this morning. Your letter to your dear Father written you say on 6th has not been received. You have probably before this received the sad tidings of our great bereavement. Your Father's death has made as yet not much change in our outward circumstances; but oh! how great a change in our feelings and real condition. The negroes have behaved remarkably well, and all things go on with their usual order. I saw a good deal of your people while we, Bessie Jane and I, remained at Chicora. I gave out meat for them and medicine, and good words just as I did to those at Chicora and Nightingale. Quash was sick with swelling. I sent him a bottle of medicine a few days ago which I hope will relieve him. Wallace and Toby continued poorly, but I hope will ultimately recover. All of them asked after you, and begged to know when you would come home. I told them I thought you would be here about the time the rice begins to turn yellow and hang its heads, and I begged them to let you find a good crop. This I told them to keep up their hope and heart. You must not my beloved pine for home, or dwell too much upon it. Such a state of mind will unfit you for your duties there. Remember that the honour, the good name of our House now rests upon you. Nerve yourself for every duty, prayerfully and most earnestly. A few days before the commencement of your Father's illness some one expressed the desire that you should return. He exclaimed with emotion, God forbid! and when asked the reason he said Ben's duty is there and I should regard him as a disgraced man were he to lose the situation he holds. He should devote his every faculty to the discharge of his duty there. You must not think I am greatly distressed by the new duties of my situation. As yet they are not arduous and the good behavior of the negroes has been comforting. I am Executrix, you and Mr Lesesne are the original Executors. When he added the codical to his will he named Alexander Robertson as addition[al] Executor. Charles is also to be one when of age. Mr Belflowers will remain in charge of Chicora Wood as long as he lives. Our dear Charles is not well. He had an attack of indisposition while at home which I considered quite serious. It detained him from school a fortnight. Your Uncle Henry's health is so bad he can do nothing for us except as a law adviser. Mr Robertson has just lost his Son Alick, he was killed in Va a few days since. I do not know that he will qualify on the will. But I trust we will get on with moderate success. The condition of things just now is terribly critical, may God help us. It is said Genl Whiting has disgraced himself by drink recently, and failed at Petersburgh to support the attacking party to the great hazard and loss of our soldiers. Joe and Charley Porcher were with the attacking party, and were both wounded, reported slight, but we know only the newspaper account. Before this reaches you things must be better or worse. I thank God that you have escaped. May His protection be with you. May He bring you safely home to us in peace. But do not think of home in any other way. Give your whole heart to your duties. Avoid all things that you find a snare to you.

I will write to Ellen.[1] Your Father said to me at first, write and invite her home, tell Ben to send her, but I said, no her place is there, to be a comfort to Ben, and a nurse in case he is wounded or sick. I hope to go tomorrow to Morven, to see the negroes crop etc there. Our neighbours the Williams and the Evanses continue as kind and neighbourly as possible. They all expressed interest in your marriage, and in your wife. . . . .

Adele Petigru Allston to Colonel Francis Heriot

[July, 1864]

DEAR SIR I wish to consult you about the condition of things at Chicora Wood. You know all the circumstances of Stephen's desertion.[2] You know

---

[1] Ellen Stanley Robinson, whom Benjamin had married in Austin, Texas.

[2] On the subject of Stephen's desertion see below, pp. 289–90, 291, 294, 315.

that his wife is Mary's daughter and that she is the third of her children who have gone off. Thomas and Scotland her sons were young men, and Tom the carpenter who went off with all of his family as Stephen has done, was her brother. It is too many instances in her family for me to suppose she is ignorant of their plans and designs. She has been always a highly favoured servant, and all her family have been placed in positions of confidence and trust. I think this last case should be visited in some degree on her. I do not think she should be allowed to retain her position in charge of the house with the keys etc unless she can prove her innocence. May I beg you to give the matter your attention, and aid Mr Belflowers to come to a conclusion in the case. I think the police of the District should take such cases in hand and hold the near relations, parents etc, responsible for the ill conduct of the younger members of their families. It might have a good effect. Mr Belflowers is not young, and he must require aid. At the same time I think the effect would be better if it were understood to be the police of the county. If you will give this subject your calm consideration and aid Mr Belflowers with your counsel, I will be greatly obliged to you. It is important to do nothing rash, nothing inconsiderate, nothing ill judged, but something ought to be done.

I had a very satisfactory letter from Lieut Wm Elliott, and I feel that Mr Sweet will be allowed to remain until the end of the year at least. Hoping you will excuse the trouble I give you.

P. S.   It seems to me important that our consultations and investigations and plans on these subjects should not be spoken of in presence of servants or others but that the utmost secrecy should be observed. If in giving this case your consideration you come to the conclusion that Mary should be removed from the care of the house and premises I think she should be immediately sent off the plantation. Mr Belflowers might send her to Grayhams turnout with a ticket to go on Railroad to Cheraw to the care of D Malloy and Son. No child should be allowed to go with her. She has a son and grand children at Morvin.

Henry D. Lesesne to Adele Petigru Allston

Cedar Spring, Oct. 30 [18]64

MY DEAR SISTER,   I wrote you on the 26th with the R. R. Receipt for the Keg of 4 penny Nails. I went to the Factory day before yesterday, and the agent told me he was bartering for Rice at the rate of one for five, so that you would have to give 500 lbs. of Rice for the keg of Nails (100 lbs.) I told him it did not seem to me to be equitable, but he affirmed that a Mr. Legg of Spartanburg had lately bought rice in Charleston at 20 cents per lb., making five pounds worth $1, the value of a lb. of Nails. I will inform myself of the market value of Rice, and endeavor to have the matter arranged on terms of justice. Or can you give me information of its value where you are, which would be a more proper standard. I am now going to ask you to take some trouble for me which I do with reluctance, but I know you will sympathise with me in the subject matter. The expenses of the Cedar S[prings] Institution[1] have increased so much, owing to the cost of supplies, as to raise some doubt whether the Legislature will grant the appropriation that would be necessary to keep it up. The dispersion of the Teachers and pupils, and closing of the House would be a calamity, which those only who are familiar with the establishment, and know the blessings it imparts can fully appreciate. To aid in keeping it open is an object worthy of the attention of the benevolent. You have many such persons around you, and they are large producers of corn. Corn is one of the heavy items, and is always scarce and exorbitant in this region. Can you negotiate with some of your worthy neighbors for the purchase of 500 or 600 Bushels? If that can be accomplished, the next thing to be considered is the avoidance of transportation, which may be managed thus: Let the corn be delivered to the nearest Receiver of Tax in kind, and his receipt be taken for it, as "from Newton F. Walker Steward of the S. C. Institution for the Deaf and Dumb and the Blind on account of Tax in kind." With that Receipt Mr. Walker will be able to get the like quantity of corn from the Receiver at Spartanburg. I find that I am writing on an appeal to the humane,[2] which was very successful, and I will take it as a good omen. There is no hurry about receiving the corn, but it is desirable to secure it as we are about to make up our Reports for the Legislature. If you could get 100 bushels in my name in the same way I would be glad. . . . .

Charles Petigru Allston to Adele Petigru Allston

Chicora Nov. 9th, 1864

DEAR MAMMA . . . . I have not been able to get Mr Belflowers to start the mill as he is anxious to get the corn in. The corn crop looks pretty well here but I am afraid that both Guendalos and Nightingill have made rather short ones, but I have not told Mr Sweet so. He is not so careful in measuring as Mr Belflowers but on the whole does very well better than I had expected. He spoke to me yesterday about staying another year and said that he was quite willing to stay if we wanted him and the state would let [him], he is over age for Confederate service. I told him that we would keep him and try to get an exemption and told him that he had done very well this year etc. I think you will have to give him the wages that Mr Thompson received i e $600.

[1] The South Carolina Institution for the Deaf, Dumb, and Blind, founded in 1849 and placed under state control in 1857.

[2] A printed appeal asking aid for the Lunatic Asylum at Columbia.

There has been some difficulty in getting the boat up then her repaired but I hope will be able to do it this evening and I hope that by the time the rice is ready for her she will be finished, though it will be slow work with the hands we have here. Mr Sweet told me yesterday that he thought that it would be no harm to move Frank and his family, but I dont think it feasible, just yet at least, his wife (Frank's) came to me the other day to ask for her children which are at Briton's I told her you would be down this winter and would then tell her. I will send Tony and Iris by the first boat, and if Joe's is not ready I will send Williams. Will is to be married on Tuesday quite privately at his house and is then going with his bride up to Black River, but I should not think that he would stay there long, it would be very lonely for just they two. I think that you had better come down and give out clothes and any little thing you may have for them even if you do not stay. Some people think that we will have a raid here this winter about Christmas. The Westons are to move tomorrow if it is good weather. . . . . Have you got the whiskey yet from Pamel? send some by Paul. The salt boilers are to start on Monday to picking mirtle berries. Goodbye, love to all send some of that lard by Paul we will want it. I am afraid that you will have to send for a gallon of oil to Wilmington or some where.

Charles Petigru Allston to Adele Petigru Allston

Chicora Nov 16th 1864

DEAR MAMMA   I received your letter this evening. As to Frank and George I dont think that they need be delt with as harshly as you propose not at present anyway. I believe that the report about George was just an attempt of the salt boilers from Nightingill to either displace George or else to break up the whole thing and come home. For upon questioning Abraham from whom they say they got their information he says that George never had any such conversation with him and that he does not think that George has or ever had any notion of going. There is no fault to find with Frank it is his wife who created the suspicion by something she said. Paul arrived safely with the things but has been sick ever since, Mr Belflowers gave him something which he said stopped the pain but he is sick again today. There has been no rice pounded yet, indeed none thrashed, so I will not wait to have it pounded but send it in the rough. I have heard some talk of an agreement which Papa made with Mr Iserd to pound this crop and if it is so I think it would be best for us to send the rice there for as long as Tilton is at Waverly nothing but hard feeling will be gained by sending there. I am glad to hear that you have an offer for Nolen [?] almost anything would be better than the present arrangement, and there is one advantage in his being so [illegible], the conscription will let him alone. The people about here seem to anticipate trouble here this winter, so that I think it would be as well to move as much provision away as possible. I do not think that the boat will be done before next week, so that the last of next week or the first of the week after is as soon as you can expect me, for I wish to see the wine safely stored on board and the boat push off from the warf before I start I will come up in the Sulkey I think. . . . .

Adele Petigru Allston to W. M. Junno

Society Hill 1st Dec 1864

CAPT WM M JUNNO   I received a few days since a circular from the office of subsistance to the rice planters of South Carolina.[1] I am very willing to sell half our crop to the government. The overseer estimates the whole crop at 10,000 bushels. I desire the crop thrashed and deliverd as soon as possible and have given such orders to Mr Belflowers. I wish you to send an agent to receive the portion for the government. It may be stored in the barn on the plantation as long as you desire and every care will be taken of it that is taken of our own, but we must deliver it at once. The half of [the] crop which we return will be removed out of the District of Georgetown as fast as we can. Please let me know when you will receive the rice, and whether you will desire it to remain in our barn, or will remove it. Address your answer to me at Society Hill.

James R. Sparkman[2] to Adele Petigru Allston

Plantersville Decr. 7th 1864.

MY DEAR MRS. ALLSTON,   In view of the enhanced price of every thing, the Medical Society of this, as well as of many other Districts throughout the State, resolved two years ago to double their charges. During the last year the very large advance in the price of Horses and of grain necessary to sustain them, found the medical men entirely unable to live at the rates agreed upon, and they again met as a Society, and resolved to regulate their charges according to the price of grain and forage leaving it to each individual to do the best he could in arranging with his patients for the means of living. In Williamsburg the medical charges are 5 times the old rates. So in Charleston, and most of the other Cities. I am exceedingly reluctant to adopt any rates that, with some, might prove almost prohibitory. I am too well aware that all classes are suffering severely the privations incident to this cruel war, and that in sickness the distress and affliction is tenfold compared with what we have to endure in ordinary health. After mature deliberation, therefore, I have concluded to continue the *old rates* of charging for all *past and future* services to those who will furnish to me grain or forage *at old prices*. In a large number of cases this proposition has been readily accepted, as fair and just, and the easiest way to arrive at a rate of charge satisfactory to all parties. Especially does it seem just and equitable to the agriculturists.

[1] See below, pp. 316, 429.

[2] Dr. James R. Sparkman (1815–97), proprietor of Dirleton plantation.

I am willing to receive Corn, Rice, Peas, Potatoes, Fodder, Pork, Mutton, Lard, Butter, Eggs, in fact, any and every thing that will enable my family to live, and feed my Horses. Few are aware of my embarrassment, and I would not allude to them, but in justification of the course I have concluded to adopt, I have not made one grain for market since 1861. My negroes removed to Clarendon, so far from being self supporting, in the simple item of *bread* have cost me Thousands per year. The last Spring with a view to remedy this condition I risked the removal of a portion of them back to the Rice fields. The result has been entirely unsatisfactory. The Birds have been so destructive that I have not made my provisions, taking all the Rice into account in addition to the upland crop. I must purchase provisions to carry me through the next year, and if I have to pay eight and ten times the old prices, it seems to me not unreasonable that my bills should be multiplied accordingly. As before stated I am disinclined to this. I prefer being *supported* by contributions of grain etc., and if there are any who think this unreasonable or unjust, they have only to bear in mind that the Government is so monopolising that private individuals are almost debarred the privilege of purchasing even for their families, tho' in some instances they may be willing to pay three or four times the Government schedule rates.

The fact is, at old prices, one years entire practice, will scarce pay for one Horse and Sulkey at their present valuation. I merely wish to live. My profession has positively not been able to supply horses, vehicles, and harness necessary to carry it on, and the expense of feeding my Horses has been for two years past, entirely beyond my receipts.

The proposition to attend at old rates, for grain or provisions of any kind at old prices is general and will be tendered to all who wish my services for the future, or are willing to settle bills of this year in this way. I beg therefore that you will do me the favor to say at once if my proposition is accepted by you, as I must have provisions for the next year, and wish to secure them at once. I shall be very happy to include Col Ben Allstons interest with yours if you feel authorised to act for him.

With my kindest regards to the young Ladies and the assurance that I am most sincerely etc.

E. J. Means to Adele Petigru Allston

Commandant's Office
Naval Station, Marion C[ourt] H[ouse], S. C.
Dec. 19th 1864

MY DEAR MADAM   Your favor of the 17th came to hand a few minutes ago, and I hasten to reply. When you spoke of hiring Joe's wife near the Navy Yard I thought that it was in consequence of his having applied to you to do so, and spoke to him about her, so as to find out what sort of a servant she was. The reasons he assigns for not wishing her here, are, that she is attending to what little property he has at home and if she is brought away it will all be stolen. He has applied to me for permission to go home Christmas and as Mr Murray the Constructor at the Yard informed me that Gov. Allston had authorized Lt. Morgan to allow them to go home three or four times a year, I consented to let him leave next Friday, to remain till the 1st of Jan. I will not let him go tho' until I hear from you. Gibert, and in fact almost all of them have asked for permission to go, but I will await your answer before letting any of them go. By writing as soon as you receive this, I will receive a letter from you by Friday, or Saturday morning at any rate. Please write immediately and let me know what you wish me to do in relation to their going, or if you wish me to let them go on Friday, it would be best perhaps to send me a Telegram from Florence. Mr Deacon the Paymaster of the Station has just returned and I will send him over to Society Hill next week to settle the amounts due from the Negro hire. The shoes I got for $50.00 pr pair.

Jane Pringle[1] to Adele Petigru Allston

White House 15th Jany. [18]65

DEAR MRS ALLSTON   I hear you have abandoned the idea of coming to your plantation which Mary and I deeply regret. It is quiet and calm here, whether merely the lull which precedes a hurricane you know as well as I.

Meantime one goes on as if there really were a next year coming. I write to ask your permission to send my people next spring or summer to Pawley's island to make salt for plantation use. The settlement they had on Mr Pyatt's seashore came to an end by the untimely death of our mule and the overseer suggests Pawley's island as a point that could be made subject to his personal supervision and as in all respects more convenient for the purpose than the site chosen by the last overseer, if you have objections state them frankly, if not it will be a neighborly accommodation for which I shall be greatly obliged.

The White House negroes are come back and I only wish I could also have brought home the Greenfield people who are now the only ones left in the interior but prudence in provisions is a cardinal duty at present, and they must be kept away unless run out from Mrs De Veaux's which seems not improbable.

I have charming letters from the boys in V[irgini]a in such contrast with our utterly demoralized condition here. They are burning to get to Ca[rolina] for the fight and Butler has twice applied to return with his regt. and thank God been twice refused by Gen. Lee who says he cannot spare them.

---

[1] The widow of John Julius Izard Pringle, of Greenfield and White House plantations. One of her sons, to whom she refers as being with the army in Virginia, later married Mrs. Allston's daughter, Elizabeth.

My dear what is coming! I try to screw Mary[1] up to my own opinion which is to stop quietly here and try by our presence to save something, instead of going on the rampage refugeeing *where?* that's the question, shew me a safe point and I'll go tomorrow, but no such happy Valley exists in the Confederacy and I prefer the attitude of the Roman Senators when the Gauls found them sitting in their places to a sheep-like headlong flight into perhaps a worse danger and a nearer fate. What are you going to do?

Elizabeth[2] to Adele Petigru Allston

Friday March 17th 1865

DEAR AUNT   I wrote in much haste yesterday not wishing to keep your Boy and uncertain if I could get any one to take it down having no horse and but few servants about only a part of Phoebe's family in such haste I omitted much that would interest you. Mrs. Pringle I suppose will write you, I hear she has suffered much having had three visits in one week one at midnight four Negroes and White men that Mary fainted away and she hated to recover her. The Pyatts went at once to George Town leaving every thing Toney having not a change of clothes for her infant and I hear has not a servant. Her house was given up to the Negroes at once. Mr H A Middleton was ordered to G[eorge] T[own] his house and buildings burned a faithful Negro got him a change of clothes which he hung on a stick across his shoulder Mr. Gailliard offered him a horse which he refused I hear he was met by the Enemy who took his Hat and Clothes from him. Dr Parker went off at once and his place was destroyed. Mr. G[illegible] broke the Oath of allegeiance and can therefore give us no news. Mrs G is with him but wants to get away. The Wards fortunately got off in time to Marlborough. I hear Mr. Wm Trappier is in prison. The Revnd Mr Trappier was long in prison and threatened with hanging for poisoning the Wine he gave them and his [illegible] Son with him who was made to testify against his Father, he is again at Liberty but his family have been stripped of every thing and the faithful Servants who wished to remain with them were carried off by force. They would starve but for Mrs Lance who sends them provisions secretly at night. The George Fords were burnt out some time ago and lost almost every thing they moved out here to the FitzSimmons house. They have now had to move out and Mr FitzSimmons has broken his Arm by his Horse falling on him. Mr. LaBruce has had to go off to join our Army. Mr Reese Ford was put under arrest for 5 hours not allowed to speak, his Bacon and provisions taken from him because a Negro Boy complained that he had switched him (he had not touched him). They have all gone off no one knows where without a change of clothing I hear

[1] The writer's daughter.

[2] Possibly Elizabeth Blyth Weston (nee Tucker), daughter of Allston's sister, Elizabeth Ann, and John H. Tucker.

they had 9 Trunks and were not allowed to take them. Mr C Alston has been gradually moving and has gone today with his family as the house Servants refused to wash for and wait on them and he could hardly get provisions from the plantation all their Negroes have come down from Williamsburgh and gone to their old homes and he says there are no provisions down here for them. Mrs. LaBruce is anxious to go to Poplar Hill but her people refuse to move her. The first week they divided out our land and wanted to root up our beautiful Wheat and Oats and Rye and pulling down fences and would have no driver our Overseer went off at once. Capin Morris of the Chenaugo and Lieut Whitehead called and promised that nothing of the kind should happen again and told the people they must work in the usual manner and make more than provisions as they must trade with them and they would bring them all sorts of things and now they can buy all they want in G[eorge] Town, we just sit down here nothing to do with our own place and in daily fear of a Cavalry Raid as we hear a large number of troops have come in a barge of Negroes been sent off. Most of our principal young Men have gone. We all unite in much love to you all Pray for us. The Sparkmans talk of going away and the Glennie's too. Mr. Glennie is thoroughly disgusted. The Hagly Negros went to the Parsonage and took his bedding etc. They want to go to England and Captin Morris says in the course of time he will send him. We shall feel for [him] indeed when he leaves us. Jane Read and ourselves have determined to stay for we have no Provisions elsewhere, and know we cannot move any now. You will wonder that three Men could do us so much harm but the Man [illegible] passed himself off as Col Stoddard who we knew was the Officer in Command in George Town and whose written promise we had to harm no one who behaved themselves. I am so sorry to hear of Joe being a prisoner and hope Adelle may soon hear good news of her Husband. The Charles Alstons have gotten the George Fords to live in their house to protect their things left. The Glennies are going very soon and I think will go with the Sparkmans till they can arrange to leave the Country. I wish you could have told us some news we are shut out from the world hear, hear nothing of what is going on. What we gather in G[eorge] Town is unfavourable to us but they say they have heard no news for some weeks. Mr Alston['s] Servant came on saying his young Master could not get to Charlotte and that my George was not there but had gone on to Tennessee and that Gen Lee was retreating there.

P. S.   Charles went off the first night comes back in a few days saying he had been made a Corporal that they took him prisoner because he could not tell where our Silver was, he lives in idleness and we look on him as a spy and think he has influenced the people badly, he is to be a Preacher and Teacher. Harry, Joseph, Beaver, Washington and Thomas remain faithful

and promise we shall not Starve ..
incur much ill will thereby. Charlotte ha.
out yet. Charles took down my Secretary and
the whole of my furniture, large presses too large ..
pieces and every book carried off many torn and strewe.
the Secretary locked and the keys taken off and now I have got ..
less for they wont give up the Keys. [Illegible.] Carpets were cut up   .o
squares right off she has not one left.

Adele Petigru Allston to Colonel Brown[1]

[March, 1865]

I find myself under the necessity of appealing to you for justice and protection, to do so I must trouble you with my story.

The 24 of February I left my home Chicora Wood plantation on the Pee Dee river 13 miles from Georgetown to attend to some necessary business here and place my youngest child at school, intending to return to the plantation in, at most, three weeks. Before my little matters here were arranged I learned that on the first Sunday in March two of your soldiers accompanied by Sam Johnson and others went to the place, broke open the doors, (tho they would have been opened for them if they had asked) went over the house, took all they wished and then told the negroes of the place to help themselves and do as they liked. Consequently not an article was left in the house, neither bed or sheet, table or chair. The banisters to the staircase broken down, every lock taken off, and the doors taken off their hinges. Then the meat house and store room were plundered in the same way, and I learn further that on a subsequent day you went to the place and divided or caused to be divided among the negroes all the cattle and stock.

I feel confidence in appealing to an officer of the U S army for redress for such grievances. I wish to return to Chicora Wood; it is our home. Will you give me a safe conduct for myself and daughter, and protect us from ill usage? All our horses have been taken except a pair of brood mares, old and feeble, I fear if I go down I may have them taken also and be left with no means of moving except on foot.

I acquiesce readily in the freeing of the negroes, but surely our other property should not be taken from us and a portion of the crop should come to us as rent for the land planted.

I am a widow and Executrix of my late husband's Estate, most of my children are minors. If you will be so good as to write me a note and assure me of protection I will at once return to my home.

You will I trust pardon the trouble this long note gives you.

[1] Copy. Colonel Brown was in command of the United States forces in Georgetown.

Adele Petigru Allston to Captain Morris[1]

[March, 1865]

Being temporarily absent from my home the first week in March, I am now warned that I will be exposing myself to outrage and injury if I attempt to return there without securing your good offices.

I have learned with great regret that my house at Chicora Wood plantation has been robbed of every article of furniture and much defaced and injured also all my provisions of meat, lard, coffee and tea taken. That we are left without a bed or blanket and that all these necessary things are distributed among the negroes. I apply to you and to Col Brown for a protection for myself and daughter in returning and also the restitution of the furniture and stock divided among the negroes. I am the widow of R. F. W. Allston. My eldest daughter Mrs. Vander Horst is residing at this place at present. My other two daughters are minors the youngest at school here I acquiesce entirely in the freeing of the negroes but surely our other property ought not to be taken from us. I trust we will be allowed rent for the land. We have no other means of living.

I send this note to Mr Sweet overseer on one of our plantations I have not heard from Mr Sweet since I left home the last week in Feb. but I hope he is still at his post.

I wish an assurance that we will be allowed provisions from the plantations as heretofore, protection from injury or molestation and that my pair of poor horses will not be taken from us.

Jane Pringle to Adele Petigru Allston

White House 1st April [1865]

MY DEAR FRIEND You are the comfort of my life, since through you only do I hear of and hold communication with what I love best on earth. The N[ightingale] Hall overseer brought me yesterday the welcome packet of letters which covered one from N. C. of 12th March, all well. I have enclosed an answer to Susan so if you hear of an occasion let her know that it may go forward. I hope if you and Bessie decide to come here after reading the very disagreeable account I shall have to give you of things, that you will immediately drive to this place and stay quietly here till you put yourself clearly in possession of the situation, which you are so far from understanding that I hate to enlighten you, but it is no moment to disguise the truth. I fear that your absence from this part of the country bars your claim for the present to any of your property. This question I am told will hereafter come up and at the end of the war be decided and acted on by the U S. Govt. The only drop of comfort I can give is that the land will not be given

[1] Copy. Captain Morris was in command of the "Chenaugh" in Georgetown harbor.

to the negroes. They are to be given only the Sea islands where even the Yankees allow they neither work nor get a living but just hang on as suckers. Those who have remained on their plantations can claim them and will probably establish their claim and meantime I am sustained in the ground I took at the moment of the Emancipation of the blacks on this place, "The land is mine you can either leave it or pay 1/3 crop as rent." These conditions having been acceded to by the negroes (I hear without an idea of complying with them) they will now be compelled to pay me. All your furniture has been taken not only by your own negroes but by troops and hordes of blacks who like vultures hung round the plantations here and by their numbers overawed the negroes and got the lion's share of the booty, mostly from Geo. town. Yr woman Lavinia claimed and took all the furniture in the Plantersville house. As to the cattle sheep and hogs these were I know ordered by Col. Brown himself to be shared among the negroes on each absentee place. Those residing in Plantersville covered what was in and about their houses there but their plantation property was not respected. Of course this is all wrong but who is to make it right. Had you staid at Chicora Wood it wd have no doubt protected the property but it is too late now either to go back over the past or even to regret it. Your daughter and yourself could not perhaps have endured what I supported Mary through. When I tell you what I told a Yankee Capt. yesterday you will form some idea of what I suffered "Sir, had I had poison in the house on those two days (of the great orgy) I should probably have given it to my daughter and taken it myself, for I despaired." You did what you thought right and best, you went to yr children at Croly Hill, do not reproach yourself for acting according to yr instincts. You are all safe and have saved that place. As to property it has become impossible to assume or feel any responsibility about it. Had I had a place up the country I should have fled there gladly, this is my only home and we clung to it with the blind tenacity of insects. We have, by absolute miraculous interposition at first, weathered the storm and now we have received a full protection for "the Pringle estate" but at first no Capts. held out their hands and we battled defenseless 2 alone. You say you "acquiesce in the freeing of the blacks," but you evidently use a form of words which carries with it no relative idea of what is covered and comprised by the freeing of the blacks. If you come here all your servants who have not families so large as to burthen them and compel a veneering of fidelity, will immediately leave you. The others will be more or less impertinent as the humor takes them and in short will do as they choose. *Here* I have over them the abiding fear of the Yankee Capts. who go out and speak sharply to them and sustain my authority, but you are too far up to depend on the frequent visits which they make here and without which I believe a residence among negroes would be humiliating and impossible. Your negroes are I hear perfectly insubordinate, the men at "the upper plantation" and the women at N[ightingale] Hall have behaved like devils. At N[ightingale] Hall the women turned in and killed the sheep and acted in a frenzied way Mr. S[weet] told me. To talk of getting back these sheep which they have eaten, you see is quite idle.

Capt. Creighton now gone North told me that "Mrs. Pettigru on Sandy Island had immediately written to the fleet and obtained a protection for her property." It is believed that this is *a negress* and that the property she protected is yours. I give you the Plantersville version, this property might be restored to you perhaps. I warn you however not to stir up the evil passions of the blacks against you and your family if you wish to return here. The blacks are masters of the situation, this is a conquered country and for the moment law and order are in abeyance. As to a protection for Bessie and you it is quite unnecessary for your personal safety as far as the Yankees are concerned. You do not run the slightest risk. Nor do you from the negroes unless you try to dispossess them of the property they have seized. In that case any so-called protection from Georgetown not backed up by a guard day and night would be inefficient. The negroes would force you to leave the place, perhaps do worse. I have not been in my negro street nor spoken to a field hand since 1st March. The only way is to give them rope enough, if too short it might hang us. No outrage has been committed against the whites except in the matter of property. It is I know extremely difficult to "remain inactive" as you say, but whether it is worth while actively to stir up a nest of hornets is the question!

Grisett that deserter and thief came and stole all my poor horses, including Tom Thumb and little Nell. We drive mules and hide them every night.

I repeat, if you wish to judge things for yourself come to me and decide then after deliberation what course to take. But mind, don't rush to Chicora Wood and commit yourself by any expression of determination or menace.

I don't believe any one will be found responsible for the cotton, it will be claimed as rebel property and lawful war spoils, perhaps it is. The question of servants is the pressing one here. Miss Trapier is cooking and washing the Chas. Alstons were left alone and went off to Columbia. Mrs. Read fears that after the 60 days during which planters were bound to feed the blacks all the servants in Plantersville will leave. She told Mary that at a ball in Georgetown the whites and blacks danced together. The blacks had a large dinner party on Dr. Sparkman's place last Sunday and got drunk and have invitations out for a picnic. Dr. S. and Mr. Glennie left in disgust after an interview with Capt. Stillwagen on board the Pawnee. I believe now I have told you every thing, bad enough. Mary sends a great deal of love to Adele and Bessie.

Adele Petigru Allston to Jane Allston

Plantersville 1st August 1865

MY DEAR JANE .... We will break up at Croley Hill in Oct or Nov but where precisely we will fix ourselves for the future is uncertain. I hope we may be guided for the best. I hope you bear the necessity to do a great deal of your own work cheerfully, and that you help Adele all you can. I can never feel kindly towards Nelly again. She has gone to the farm and set down with all her children on Milly. She takes in washing from Mrs. Read and gets as much as she can do. I have not fed either her or her children except Clarrissa who is about as formerly. Phebe gets into an ill humor occasionally and *jaws* me, but on the whole she is very good. I have agreed to give her $50 a year and Aleck the same, but Aleck has been gone for a week and I think he will possibly not return. Ben's Frank is with us now, so that we do not miss Alick. Poor Kitty is stone blind, and as I hear Ned is in a miserable and hopeless condition you see I am without a horse to depend upon. I shall probably have no need in future of a coachman. Toby goes up, he says to marry Daphney. He can help pick peas and get in the crop. I will feed him for his work while there, and Dianna the same. She can be of service in many ways besides nursing Margaret I will feed her for her services. Toby has been serving a mess of officers in Charleston as cook, and getting nominally $16 per month, but I provoked him to tell me how much they had paid him, and he had received only $15 in money for 3 months services. I told him that was $5 per month; he said "They will pay me when they come back, they have gone to the north and had not the money to pay before they went." Possibly Mr and Mrs Evans may not like to see Toby and may forbid his going there. He is a free man and must go as he pleases. Charles consented to let him drive the wagon up yesterday was Charles's birthday. He invited the young people of the Reads and Westons to pass the evening I gave them a bottle of Champaign and a poor cake. I long to see you and Adele very much. You must devote yourself to Adele for the present. Study to anticipate her wants. Do not let her have to worry with house keeping, or sweeping etc. We hear that Helen Alston has to cut wood and bring it in from the woods, cook and wash and labour in every way. Willie and William cook and wash and do every thing, he milks and sells milk 2 quarts a day. He is much improved in health.

Adele Petigru Allston to Benjamin Allston

Croley Hill 10th Sept 1865

DEAR BEN I received your letter by Billy. I do not understand your conduct. It grieves me very much. You act with great precipitation, and feel no hesitency in undoing regulations made by your father, and that had worked well. The allowance to the negroes up here was arranged by him with great care.

I hope you will go and look at the house Mary Grice has chosen to return to, and you will see there was good reason why your father moved her away, and intended to remove the house, as it is an *improper* place for a family to live. In the midst of the field and too near the Barnyard. There ought to be no *excuse* for negroes hanging about the Barnyard. Mary deserted her post in the hour of danger. I did not send her to live with Betty but I do insist that as she went there *of her own will* she remain there until some other plan is made than sending her to the Barnyard. That house must be pulled down and used for the repairs and the fences of Chicora yard. If you consider a moment you must know Marys children are thieves, notorious. Their opportunities at the Barnyard will not be lost. Belflowers is cowed by the violence of the negroes against him and is *afraid* to speak openly. He is trying to curry favour. His own morals are impaired by the revolution, and he always required *backing* as your father expressed it. *You* must tell him what to *do* and *support* him in carrying it out.

I gave the order for the Izard negroes to get full rations, because they planted and worked the crop, and took food from the Izard barn until August. I ordered 6 quarts to Chance and Eliza and Solomon because they came down after the crop was planted and nearly done worked, and besides had behaved *extremely ill* in No Ca. and are such *bad people* I would rather not have them on the place. Chance did refuse to go in a flat to take fodder to Exchange. What ever order I have given I have had a reason for. I never rescinded an order or regulation of your fathers except when the circumstances which called it forth were changed. I ordered Short to give the people the Rye as allowance. You ordered corn purchased as much as they wanted. It is to be paid for at one Dollar per Bushel. We are allowed 80 cents for what you arranged with Coker about. Belflowers told me he thought the corn crop would be very short. How do you propose to feed mules and hogs etc? I conclude in giving out allowance at Chicora you gave as much as every body claimed or wanted. The conduct of the negroes in robbing our house, store room meat house etc and refusing to restore anything shows you they *think it right* to steal from us, to spoil us, as the Isrealites did the Egyptians. Yet they can ask nothing from you you are not prepared to grant. You certainly take a very inadequate view of our condition. But if we were ever so well off your conduct in rescinding your father's and my regulations with the precipitation of a child empowered for the first time to give orders, would fill me with dismay. I suppose you do not *design* to do wrong. Your education was military you ought to know how serious a matter it is to act as you have done. It is a rule with wise men, when at a loss, not knowing the bearing of things, to *do nothing* until informed. I have no hope of making any impression on you. I spoke of the pain your conduct towards Antony gave me. It is all alike. You *consider* nothing. If you had gone to look at the place Mary wished to go to, and had found out that it had not been occupied since old

Sam died, and was not to be again surely you would not have sent her there. Billy came to me for his allowance while at Chicora saying he was working for you I gave it to him. He demanded Rice which I could not give as it is out, not enough to go round, in consequence of it having been doubled the last month. Margaret announced last night that Billy brought her word her brother William will be at Graysons Cross Roads for her tomorrow. She has behaved very ill. Will reach you safely I hope.

Adele Vander Horst to Adele Petigru Allston

Chapel St [Charleston] Sep 20th 1865

DEAREST DARLING MAMMA . . . . Think of Mr. John Prestons good fortune $400,000 of the money for his L[ouisian]a estate had been paid before the war the other $600,000 became due during the struggle and Mr Burnside deposited the sum with an English firm in Liverpool, and now the entire Preston family have departed to Europe there to establish themselves Mr. Preston pere saying this is no country for a lady to live in. Things here are quieting down very much I believe and the chief of the Freedmens Bureau Capt Montate wishes to get a place on Cooper river. Arnoldus says your house can be repaired for $150 or thereabouts, the roof is mended and it is the walls that require repair now. It will be much better for you to occupy it and have your supplies from the plantations and the family together as much as possible, the children at least instead of being scattered in the endeavor to gain something of a finished education. Mrs. V. says the two Rutledges, Lize and Lullie, are going to open a school this winter I know not how true this is, but there must be many women quite as competent who will be obliged to do something of the sort. Mr. James Conner[1] is spoken of for the next Mayor a military man being earnestly desired and one who will conscientiously do his part. . . . .

Benjamin Allston to Adele Petigru Allston

Plantersville, Oct 10, 1865

DEAR MOTHER   Here I am apparently as far from my purpose of reaching Charleston as before, but I have been hoping to hear from you or see Charles by this time, thus far we have heard nothing. I went yesterday to Georgetown, and not seeing Joe Ford, knowing his mill had been out of repair, I sold the rice for two dollars pr bushel and the offal. There is of course a margin of considerable proportion between this and $13 pr hundred, but I would rather make a sure gain, than risk too much, so having your sanction, I acted. It may have been better to have held it, but I did not like leaving it, while I went to Charleston. The corn crop has been divided, and the

---

[1] James Conner (1829–83), brigadier general in Confederate Army and later attorney-general of South Carolina, but never mayor of Charleston.

negroes at last begin to realize how lamentably short they are, some of them at least do, and with the decrease of the military force here I am not at all sure but some effort might be made upon the rice, when they begin again to want bread, which many of them will do. So soon as it is shipped I shall fix a day for my departure, probably next Monday or Tuesday. I will go by Kingstree I think. I wish to see Sam. McCorrison has gone I settled with him yesterday in time, giving him a due bill for 57 bush rice at Chicora and 22 1/2 at Guendalos, being the result arrived at by estimating the crop in the yard. It does not near reach his expectations. Falk I offered to hire for Guendalos and Pipedown occasionally for the remainder of year for $50.00 and his bread he engaging his own servant, he broke off from it because I would not agree to feed and have cared for his mule. I have not been to Pipe Down since Charley was there with me. I will go soon again, or send B[elflowers] on to see how matters stand. He must do all that is necessary there. We pay him a large price and he must earn it, by exerting himself. I go to Nightingale tomorrow. . . . .

Adele Petigru Allston to Adele Vander Horst

Guendalos 15th Dec 1865

MY DEAR ADELE . . . . I think our school will be a success.[1] I wish Mr Bryan to write some notice of it, graceful and flattering, and have it put in the Savannah and Augusta and New Orleans papers. I wish notice of it put in all the leading southern papers. We will do our best to deserve success.

I brought Charles here to get enough money to send him on. The remnant of rice in Joe Ford's Mill not having been pounded as promised, Ben tried to borrow the amount in Georgetown but without success. I now think I will give up the idea of the Institute unless we get the rice and sell it very soon. In case he can not go to the Institute I will endeavour to send him to the Va University when we can get the means.

The negroes are as unsatisfactory as possible, the prospect ahead discouraging. The poor nigs have certainly deteriorated very much in *appearance and manners* in the last year or 8 months. They are without shoes or clothes and tho' I see plenty of shotes and swine of various kinds nothing that looks like the comfort of former days. Our prospect for meat is poor indeed.

I fear Milly is tired being good and faithful. She appears discontented. It seems to me she wants the whole of the stock, the profits of it at least. Ben drove me to N[ightingale] Hall this morning, the nigs are doing very bad there, cutting all that beautiful pine forrest your poor father prized so about their new settlement. We found 30 beautiful trees felled and some hundreds of small ones. I stood up and gave them a tremendous scold, and

[1] The writer's school for girls was opened at her Charleston home on January 1, 1866.

told them they should be endicted and had Ben to write down their names. But it is all vain. I see no hope; the nigs are so numerous and we have no redress. There are not any who are willing to engage for another year. They still wait for some great thing 1st Jan. . . . .

Sarah C. Williams to Adele Petigru Allston

Factory Jan 17th 1866

MY DEAR MRS ALLSTON, ... At the plantations all is quiet. Most of my negroes have remained and have gone to work under the new contract with great zeal, they are to have one third of everything grown, and if they make five bales of cotton to the hand they take half of the cotton. They have agreed to pay the Doctor four dollars a year each one for his services. We pay the overseer a tenth. My son put 50 rows of cotton for the highest task, they enter themselves as full or half hands as they please and draw shares accordingly. They feed themselves we gave them a gallon of molasses each and a months allowance of meat to start them, for which they seem very grateful. Strange to say most of my Son's negroes left him, to his great mortification, but now they are returning and one offered to pay $50 to be allowed to return and was allowed. None of my house servants went. Cornelius came and begged to be taken back as he was before. Serena took him gives food and clothes pays Doctor's bill and gives $2.00 a month. I do not know of any servants who would suit you [illegible] Ellen [is] Constance's maid but her husband is a rogue and she has two children to keep. . . . .

John E. Allston[1] to Adele Petigru Allston

Brooklyn Mch 13 [18]66

DEAR COUSIN Yours of 4th (Postmarked 7th) was recd. yesterday 12th and am glad to find that my letter reached you as was merely from a paragraph from a newspaper that I learnd that the widow of Ex Gov. Allston was teaching a school in Charleston, which was the first intimation I had of my Cousin Robert's death and as newspapers often make strange mistakes, thought the only possible way of finding out was to address you as I did. My wife and self having been looked upon as Southern sympathisers and myself often threatened at the beginning of the war with Fort Lafayette, hanging etc were obliged like many up here of our friends to be cautious, though my wife was and is much more bitter than I am; however it's past and am satisfied all will go well if the Radicals in Congress will restore the South her rights etc. You give too much credit to me for what I did, it belongs equally to my wife and rather more so, for the practical aid came from her, I unfortunately, though willing had not the means to do any thing and the instant she heard of the situation of the poor fellows at the

---

[1] Son of William Moore Allston, half-uncle of Robert F. W. Allston.

battery Ranock [?] went immediately to the Bank though the weather was intensely hot, drew the money and was not satisfied until it was in the hands of a gentleman of our acquaintance whose moderation she could trust, better than my hearty Allston temper. I cannot but say that this feeling on her part gratifies me exceedingly. Your blood would run cold at the tale of neglect of some of their Prisoners in this same city of N York, but thank God as soon as it became known friends were found to mitigate their sufferings. I notice what you say concerning your children and trust all will go well with them, let them and you keep up a good heart and hope for the best. I give below the prices of different articles of Dry goods and Groceries as I obtained them yesterday though the state of the market is so unsettled that they vary daily, particularly Sugar, though I think in dry goods at any rate there would be a saving of fully 50 pr ct. from your prices, when you order, please state the kind of goods and number of yds. required for dresses also as to the gaiters, whether of kid, prunella, satin francais (which last my wife says is good for nothing now a days) whether with heels or without laced or buttoned, also if the foot is narrow or full. Calicos are from 22 @ 25¢ pr yd light summer Lawns 30 @ 35 [illegible] 30 @ 35¢ other muslins 25 @ 60¢ [MS torn] Gaiters vary from 3 to 5 Dolls Dble soles something less for single soles. The Silk wraps vary so much it would be best to state about what price.

Sugar Brown refined B and C 14 1/2 15 1/2¢ lb a Bbl weighs 200 lbs a Hhd would weigh as much as 12 to 15 hundred

Green Tea from $1.00 1.05 1.10 1.15 1.25 per lb.

Black   ''   95 to 1.20 pr lb

Coffee 30 to 40¢ what kind do you use, Rio Havanah or Java? So much for business, now to family affairs, as to ourselves we have no children our only child for whose loss my wife is still inconsolable a lovely and intelligent girl died nearly 9 years ago at the age of 16 and half years her name was Anna and I never dare mention her in her mother's presence. My poor sister is still at the Asylum at Providence, Washington is in N Yk doing nothing as usual, Uncle William Rogers is well at the age of [illegible] and was inquiring of your husband and self [here the MS breaks off].

Benjamin Allston to Adele Petigru Allston

Guendalos March 26, 1866

MY DEAREST MOTHER . . . . I am surprised to see you think of paying the taxes on the house in town out of your school fund, also to clothe the children. Do not do this Mother, it is not necessary nor just nor required. Please to bear in mind what I before wrote you, "keep your school expenses and money separate and distinct from any of the Estate's affairs." Should matters culminate disastrously to the Estate, (which I trust may be avoided) you would then have a separate and distinct fund for yourself. The children are entitled to their *education*, their *clothes* and *subsistence* from the Estate, and all the taxes should be paid from the Estate's money. What you receive from the Estate over and above their provisions may be justly charged against you, but this will not be an equivalent for the other expenses. Do my dear Mother bear this in mind and keep matters distinct, or you will find yourself so complicated that you will not know how much you may have made or lost at the end of the year. What is true of the children is also true for you and you are entitled to the same things. The Court will give you this I am sure, and will designate a specific sum for each purpose. Were we sure of the result you might place your earnings at the use of the Estate to endeavor to clear it up, but even then it should be in definite sums and for a difined object, thus you will gain all you desire and keep things clear also. The furniture from Georgetown will go down by the next trip of the boat, consigned to Ed. Thurston, look out for it. Mr Risleys absence prevented it being sent before. We have had a sudden change, and I fear will lose some lambs, which are here on the rice fields. Be not desponding dear Mother, and try to divert your mind from Dwelling constantly on debt and money. Even should we lose the most of our property, your dower will be secured to you, and riches are not the essential of life, dear Mother pardon me for attempting to offer words of counsel or advice, but they are easier given than performed, and I feel that I am so often deficient in matters that I can advise very clearly about, that I do not think I have any right to advise anyone, yet I know that we can work to more advantage suffer less wear and tear, when our minds are not harassingly bent always on one topic. "Contentment is great riches" saith some one of the inspired writers, and it surely aids us much to do all we can in the right direction and trust in God to work out the end, if He wills either way, we must be satisfied that it is right. . . . .

Adele Petigru Allston to Benjamin Allston

Charleston 22nd April [18]66

MY DEAR BEN   . . . . I agree with you that the tax had best be paid. I suppose you could give an order on Thurston for the money. As to the income of 64 there was none. The rice 100 barrels or nearly that, was taken with the boat, Joe the former cook, being in command at the time. The taxes to the Confederate Government had been paid, the tax in kind and others also, and they had taken every thing available up to the time of your fathers death. The taxes and interest would leave no income. I am truly grieved at the report of Mr Belflower's illness. I scarcely hope for his recovery. He is old and his constitution much shattered and enfeebled. He is one of our *true* friends, and a link connecting us with the past. He is a great loss. His knowledge of all our land and the negroes as well as of the best process for planting. . . . .

I think I learn from her [Mrs. Willard] that you offended some U S officers who went to Guendalos to attend to some business for you, and met you just going to drive Ellen out, and instead of being invited into the house and told to await your return, and have their horses put up. You merely told them you could not attend to them that day, they must come the next day. They returned to Georgetown, and never returned, and hence I doubt not all your trouble with negroes. The negroes obey Willard and the officers of the Freedmens bureau implicitly. . . . .

Monday night 11 P M . . . . I have had the kindest letters from John E Allston of Brooklyn N Y. Chancelor Lesesne is in Spartanburgh. I never see Mr Miles, but I am sure we ought to pay what debts are necessary to be paid and the interest on those about which there can be no dispute, and if $1000 or 1500 could be allowed for the support of the family it would be a great help to us. We will try to get things arranged when you come down. If you could buy beef and mutton and poultry for us it would be a great help. I am forced to stop sending to market.

. . . .

Good night. Tell Milly and Nelson and Bob howdy for me. Also Caroline.

P. S.   If Mr Belflowers is alive give my very kind regards and good wishes to him, and ask if I can get any thing for him.

Benjamin Allston to Adele Petigru Allston

Georgetown May 22nd 1866

MY DARLING MOTHER   . . . . I have not been over the crop at Chicora or Pipe Down yet, but reports are good. I visited N[ightingale] H[all] yesterday, and find 204 acres planted with 50 more to plant, this is doing very well, considering the Rice does not yet look as well as I hoped to see it but I trust as soon as we can get to hoeing it it will improve, rapidly there are some 70 acres of corn planted there, which is very grassy at present, but will I hope be reached in time. At Chicora there are 175, and Nelsons 22, making 197, planted they will plant there in all about 236 or 240 acres. The corn looks very well, about 70 or 80 acres, not measured exactly at least I have not the exact measurements now to give you. The sheep are already sheared there and will soon be sheared at N[ightingale] H[all] when I will I hope bring the wool down with me, boat after next say. There are no old peas, all have been used both at C[hicora] W[ood], N[ightingale] H[all], and Guendalos. Do ask Charly to send me a sheep bell, he can have one made if he cannot buy it. I can get neither shears nor bell in this slow town. I will bring you a mutton when I come down. If you can discover any lover of fine cattle, you had best offer to sell a fine bull. My bull has whipped the big brindle one, and one of the two had better be sold, the brindle from his superior size and better appearance, will bring most money, tho' I would be quite willing to sell mine. Either of them should bring at least $200 I should think. Mentioning Rice alone I should have said that I estimate nearly 200 planted at Pipe Down, where we shall plant 204, then when we consider Holly Hill of which I know nothing now and the Exchange counting as over 1400. I hope to look up a little next year. The Agent recently employed, Mr. Westbury, left two days after my departure and has not yet returned.[1] I expect him every day. Mr. Verner too is going, so that I shall have to look out for some one there. The Small pox has not yet completed its work. I lost my head *plowman* and Billy head Carpenter is now sick. Harry has been sick with it and I doubt not more will have it, this pulls us back not a little. Almost every one is now drawing on us for corn and we shall be obliged to buy before long, very shortly indeed. In paying out money [MS breaks off at this point].

Joseph Blyth Allston to Benjamin Allston

Georgetown June 3d 1866

DEAR BEN   By day before yesterday's mail I received a letter from Miles and the amendment of Bill and copy of Exhibit and have written him in reply. He will doubtless shew you my letter. It seems likely to raise the question of the validity of debts for negroes between you and the Estate and will be of great moment to you. In fact practically your entire property rests on that question. At the same time it seems likely to put the entire facts of the Governor's intentions more clearly forth and I think he is right in filing the Amendment. By this Agreement it would seem that not only the Bond for $6000 but your liability on the Bond for $14,500 as between yourself and your father rests on the basis of debts for negroes. As the question of the validity of these debts is raised in the Bill and as the Estate is as vitally interested therein as you are individually I take it for granted the Executors will consent that the costs be paid by the Estate. I would like to know from Miles concerning this.

This matter is of such moment to you that I do not like the sole responsibility of conducting it. While I think that a great deal can be said against the collection of negro debts my opinion as to the Law is by no means positive against them. On the contrary Precedent so far as it goes is in their favour. There is the fear too lest my attention being drawn more particularly to this point may lead me to neglect other points of more practical importance which a person viewing the subject from another standpoint might perceive. It would therefore be really a relief to me if you were to engage other counsel with me. Conner is almost the only lawyer in Charleston who has not expressed to me a decided opinion in favour of the collection of these debts and is one with whom I could work most pleasantly. Should you retain him I will go down and consult with him before filing the answer.

[1] See Westbury's report below, p. 329.

I have as yet had no time to study authorities only getting Miles letter last evening but it may be a question whether to plead or demur to the Jurisdiction of the Court on the ground that the emancipation of negroes was an act of the U. S. Authorities and the question as to whether within their Constitutional powers one for the decision of the U. S. Courts. If you retain Conner suggest this to him.

At any rate ask him for me to tell you where you can get the best *Precedents of Equity Pleading* and bring it up with you. I have also asked Miles to send by you a conveyance to Uncle as Exor of Ten acres of land on Pawley's Island. Wilson and Dozier concur in the opinion I have already expressed to you that on the facts as yet known it were idle to attempt to set up the Will of Bellflowers. Dr Parker gave me your message about house on Pawley's Island. I shall see Col. Smith to-day and offer it to McCusky to-morrow. But you do not mention the rate of rent so until I hear from you I will offer it at what you at first asked $160 and repairs. . . . .

Adele Petigru Allston to Benjamin Allston

Charleston 26th June 1866

My dear Ben . . . . I am glad my little presents were well received by the freedmen and women. I dare say Milly fears that I mean the dress as part of her pay for her services. If I am to pay her $5 per month the butter will be dear to me. I think the estate must pay her I would be willing to advance her something. She ought to make it by the sale of the skimmed milk etc. Speak to her about it, $5 per month is too much to give her unless she makes it pay. I am glad Mary was pleased with the apron. I did intend to send the tin box with some hats trimmed to suit the taste of the freedwomen, for you to put in your store, but the hurry and excitement of the boarders leaving etc prevents our sending them this time. We will by the next trip of the boat. Adele will come to stay with us a month, after the boarders all go.

Can you send me a boy of good character? As to the overseer or agent, it is evident he is a fool, but keep your own council. Do not talk much to him, and not at all about him either to black or white. I had a visit from Wilson the other day who said he wished to return to his family. Binky is his wife. He is not yet mustered out. Phebe left and so is James. . . . .

Adele Petigru Allston to Benjamin Allston

Charleston 3rd July 1866

My dear Ben Yours of 25 came duly to hand, the butter came the trip before. I return the box by this boat and will be glad for a fresh supply. I think we had best not sell butter in the neighborhood; it does not pay. If I had more than enough I could sell it here to more advantage. Let Haris have 6 yards of the twilled and 6 of the shirting, and let Stepney have 6 yds of the twilld. I dare say I did promise it him, tho' I do not remember it.

I must be more careful about promising, in future. I have seen Philip only once. He reported his wife as no better. I advised him to employ Dr Porcher, who would not charge him except for the medicine he might furnish. Negroes are generally in a very excited and turbulent state in and about town. There have been several riots, and some loss of life. I hear this afternoon that Mr Ben Rhett has been shot to day on his farm. It is common to brick bat white people in the street at night. It is impossible to say where it will end. . . . .

Adele Petigru Allston to Benjamin Allston

Charleston 14th Oct 1866

MY DEAR BEN . . . . Tomorrow my school will open and I will have my hands full. A letter from Gov Bonham says just as he was setting out with his daughter he had such representation of the prevalence of fever here that he decided to wait till he has notice that it is safe to come, and a letter from Mr Devereux says great and unexpected pecuniary losses put it out of his power to send his daughter to me this year. I have had no new applications. I wrote to Mr Devereux saying I will dispense with the payment in advance in his case if it will aid him. I fear the school will be smaller while the expenses are greater than last year.

I will be glad to get the potatoes, and hope also to get some butter by the next boat. If I can will send the chicken coop to be landed at Keithfield.

Arnoldus wants a pair of oxen. I am sure they can be spared without taking too many from the estate Adele ought to have some advantage of the stock. So I wish you to tell Bob "Miss Adele wants a pair of good oxen to plough her nice fields," and ask him to choose a pair for her. I wish you to engage Charles Robinson either for yourself or for the estate. He is such a good hand with stock, and knows how to manage oxen. I think you had best engage all the labourers you can.

Charles would probably be willing to bring the oxen down for Arnoldus for a stipulated reward. I wish you to give Daniel at N[ightingale] H[all] the worth of the 6 eggs he presented me. Do not forget this, a bit of bacon or something from the estate.

Arnoldus planted half cotton this year, it turns out good cotton, but he says he will never plant another seed of cotton, it is such a difficult preparation, and the rice negroes dislike the tedious preparation necessary for it very much, then the tax on it is a draw back. He has tested it fairly. . . . .

Adele Petigru Allston to Benjamin Allston

Charleston 5th Nov 1866

MY DEAR BEN Yours of 29 Oct came safely also the two bags of grits and 2 of potatoes and one of turnips. As there was but one bushel of grits in each bag, why should it not have been all put in one bag, as one bag would have held it? Do not think this querulous. I only ask the question. The things were

all good, very good the potatoes are keeping well. Also the turnips and
are more to me than you can imagine.

I am glad the corn is divided. It is very small, but every little helps, and
if we can get our living off the estate we will be thankful. The corn and
potatoes grown at N[ightingale] H[all] were always particularly good. The
potatoes that rotted so badly had been put near the boiler on the boat, and
that caused their immediate decay. Bob is mistaken about my having selected
a heifer to be sent to me. I only enquired about that young cow, as one that
was given to me as a calf. I will take your selection; by all means send me
the Red heifer. Bob had a fine pea crop; perhaps he could pay part of the
price of the twilled homespun in peas. I would be glad to get a few bushels,
or even one bushel for table use. I do not wish to reduce the labour needed
on the plantations, and when I express a wish that Arnoldus should get a
yoke of oxen, I only wish him to get them after the estate and you are supplied, and I knew there ought to be enough for all. Have them divided out.
Say 16 for Chicora; 16 for N[ightingale] H[all], 6 for Pipe Down and 6 for
Holly Hill. Then surely there will be a pair or 2 pair for your use and one
pair for Arnoldus. Arnoldus has not yet returned. As soon as he comes I will
write you about it. I do hope you may succeed in getting labour. With a
view to that I am in favour of giving some extras, such as a beef etc to the
plantation, provided they abstain from stealing and work tolerably. I am
sure you will do the right thing, and I hope you will get labour. It will be
greatly to your honour to save the estate, which can only be done by planting
largely. Negroes have sense; and a good supply of oxen, and kind treatment
will I hope secure a large number. Have the young men who went into the
army returned? There were a large number. July, Walker's Son, Gabriel,
Son-in-law to Bouie and Minda, Dave Alfred's Son, and a great many
others. I am in favour of killing all those young hogs this winter except the
sows you keep for breed and the boars, pigs born in January make very good
bacon in Nov. I raised a number at Croley, that was their age when killed,
better bacon I never had. Have you sowed Rye? It is high time to have it
in the ground, if you are to have pasture for lambs. Oats too are better for
being sowed full early.

I am glad you have a good hog from George.

. . . .

I hear there is a Rich man from the north enquiring about lands in Georgetown and country around, and that Nightingale has been enquired after.
Now be careful how you name a price for that place. It is the best land.
If Holly Hill and Bullins Island could be sold it would be a good thing. Some
good crops on those places would give them a name in market. If we can
work out the debt it is our great interest to do it, and sell all waste land. I
hear lumber has gone down and those who put up mills have lost by doing so. . . . . .

James R. Sparkman to Benjamin Allston

Clarendon Dist, Novr. 23d [1866]

DEAR BEN, ... There is however great restlessness and uneasiness manifested by the negroes throughout the State, and they are evidently awaiting
some development of import. In this section not one has as yet made arrangements for the coming year. They positively refuse to contract, and I think
I can foreshadow serious embarrassment to themselves, and also the whites,
by this tardiness. *Compulsory* labor seems to be absolutely necessary. But how
to enforce it is the difficulty. They can be forced by law *to contract* but how
to enforce their labor is not yet determined, for neither hunger nor want
can stimulate them to any reasonable effort. Unless something is done
promptly, on the 1st Jany the season for preparing the lands for a crop will
pass by neglected; and every day's delay will only tend to increase the
difficulty likely to arise in 1867. Two successive failures to make a provision
crop will inevitably bring about a most desperate condition of the country.
Want is always a fruitful source of crime, and with such a population as the
Negro race, suddenly transformed from servitude to idleness, and wonted
indolence, without the compulsory application of labor, I can see in the
future nothing but ruin to all classes. God grant that all my fears may not
be realized, but they oppress me by day and by night, and hang upon me
as an incubus not to be shaken off.

I was in Manning yesterday at the Congressional Election. The race
between Kennedy and Dudley close, in *the Village*, Dudley one vote ahead.
Cant say how it will turn out in the District Vote. Whilst there, I was invited to a *secret conference* on a matter of the gravest import, and which I deem
it my duty to place before you. Three of the most respectable citizens gave
information of an insurrectionary movement, wide spread, and terrible in
its plot. All the male adults and children were to be massacred, on a given
night between this and Jany. All the aged white women were also to be destroyed, but females between certain ages, to be reserved for servile and
licentious purposes. The information was derived from conversations among
assemblages of negroes who could be heard but not seen. The listeners could
not identify the parties in conversation, so as to establish upon oath their
identity, but an affadavit was made setting forth the general facts by one
party, and two others deposed as to their concurrence in the statement
from what they considered corroborative testimony. The thing is generally
credited and organizations are being rapidly formed to meet the contingency.
A copy of the Affadavit is to be served upon the Govr. and the Town Council
of Manning being already privy to the facts. I trust the matter will easily be
circumvented. It is unquestionably true, that suspicions or apprehensions
of similar organizations or plots exist throughout the State, and all in authority cant be too vigilant. As far as the thing was discussed among the negroes,

on the occasion when they were overheard, it seems that they were not to rise and assemble at any given rendesvous, or rallying point, but each house was to be attacked simultaneously, and particular individuals to be dispatched by certain detailed parties for each particular locality. The most important feature in the case is *the belief* that certain white and black disbanded soldiers of the U. S. forces are in complicity. The officers and garrison at Sumter are not to be relied on; and yet it does not do to say so. The citizens generally would not shrink to take the matter in their own hands, if the Yankees were out of the way. As it is they are not disposed to ask any interference from the Yankees.

I give you the information just as it has been developed here. It is worth your while I think to scrutinise as closely as possible all gatherings in your neighborhood, as there may be an understanding with other districts. Something corroborative of this view arises from the fact that many Yankee stragglers are passing to and fro, and usually spend the night on places where there are no white residents, or in the negro quarters with the negroes where they might be suspected of the whites. They come and go, *incog.* but messages are frequently left with negroes for other plantations, showing at least an extended acquaintance. A case of this kind came under my observation but two days ago, the man claiming to reside in Darlington and taking a most circuitous route to get there. He left a message (altho' apparently a stranger) for some negroes on an adjoining place, that "*he was getting on very well.*" This looked fishy.

I hope you are getting on well. I have matured no plans for the future. I am bankrupt and can only await the Executioner as calmly and resignedly as in my power, which, with my large family, is no easy matter. Having spent all of my manhood on P[ee] D[ee] with a pleasing recollection of past intimacies and associations, and indebted to the partiality of many departed friends for whatever professional or personal claims I may have upon the confidence of that community, it is to me a source, I do assure you, Dear Ben, of constant grief and regret that I am not there with you all, to battle shoulder to shoulder against the storm that is upon us. Circumstances uncontrolable brought my family here. Imperative has been the necessity of here remaining, up to this period. With a thorough knowledge and appreciation of my circumstances I have not been able to return to the low country. To go now would be *to starve.* I have nothing left but my profession, but that is non productive from the necessities of others. On my last visit I found the scarcity of provisions so great that I failed utterly in engaging even enough corn for my family, and with nothing for horses, to practice would be simply impossible. Gladly would I return to Plantersville and make P[ee] D[ee] my *home* until gathered by the side of those now sleeping at Prince Fredericks, if I could see the way of living. Up here my embarrassments are many, but an abundance of *fuel* is a comfortable reflection with the scarcity of winter before us. I dont expect *one* of my people here to remain with me after the first Jany. They all have a preference for the Rice-fields, and an estrangement of three years has only made them the more eager to get back. The Ladies of the family have no expectation, but to pass through the ordeal so many others have undergone, to wait upon themselves, cook, wash, sweep, sleep soundly, and awake from their slumbers to realize that, "all is vanity, and vexation of spirit."

Write me at Columbia, if I can do anything for you.

Adele Petigru Allston to Benjamin Allston

Charleston 27 Dec 1866

MY DEAR BEN . . . . I am sorry to say stealing is common. The chickens Nelson sent me, I had fed and kept until they were really fine Christmas night 15 were taken out of the yard. No one can tell any thing about them. Since my illness I find poultry more agreeable and wholesome diet than beef.

I am grieved and disappointed that the crops turn out so badly of course there has been prodigious stealing. I do not think the people have earned a beef except it be the Pipe Down people. Chancelor Lesesne and I disapprove the agreement with the overseer. We can not afford high wages, and I think we had best employ negro agents. Philip has done better than any other agent we have employed and is the cheapest by far. Negroes will soon be placed upon an exact equality with ourselves, and it is in vain for us to strive against it.

Exercise your best judgement in choosing a negro agent. One belonging to the plantation or a stranger, but one of character Richard will not do. He is not *open*, he professes one thing and acts another. His children too are utterly faithless except it may be Hines. Did Haris get the pair of shoes?

You must remember I have not had any Rice yet. I will require 2 barrels of good quality cracked Rice and 2 barrels of small rice for my years supply, and I would like one barrel good whole rice sent to Mrs Williams.

Let the 4 barrels rice for my family use be taken from the different places part from Chicora, part from N[ightingale] H[all] and part from Pipe Down.

People say rice will be higher by and by, but storage here is too high. We had better sell as the rice is ready. I wrote to Milly but have heard nothing from her. I will be glad to have a mutton as soon as you can send it provided the weather continues cold. I would be glad to get some Sausages and feet, but do not deprive yourselves to send to us. Mrs. Genl Woodbury told me Washington Woodbury cheated his own mother; but I dare say he is as good as any one you can get to act for you. It might be as well to advertise the Marion land for sale in the Marion and Georgetown papers but it is not probable that at this time we can get a suitable offer $3 per acre would be very good. Let me know how much Nelson's field made to the acre. I had hoped to feel strong and well before this, but am sorry to say I feel weak and good for nothing. . . . .

P. S. I have grits enough to last one month I think. Send me no more for three weeks. I have purchased a new piano from New York $500. When I ordered it expected a larger school.

Oliver H. Kelley[1] *to Benjamin Allston*

Washington D. C. April 18, 1867

DEAR SIR Yours of 12th just received. I had your name recorded as I felt satisfied you would well represent your state in such a work and should you lack enthusiasm at any time, a visit to our mutual friend Mrs. Pringle, would give you inspiration. I consider her one of the most enthusiastic ladies I met on my southern trip.

The work we are commencing upon is one of magnitude and will require much time to perfect the arrangements necessary to put it into complete working order. We shall need suggestions from those interested in all parts of the country, as it will not be sectional in its character. I enclose you completed list of the Vice Presidents and Secretaries[2] all of whom we believe will freely express their views and any suggestions you may offer to me will be most cheerfully submitted for consideration.

The South needs a large influx of population for you have vast tracts of land that should be under high cultivation with crops suited to your climate. It was the object of my trip South to make a complete report upon the Agricultural resources and capabilities of the South, but the Commissioner smothered the whole of the report of the work that was furnished to him, though a mass of matter I collected I still have in reserve and as soon as we succeed in getting rid of him and a good competent man in his place I hope to resume and complete the work in which I feel a deep interest.

Regarding the method to pursue to secure immigration, the advantages should be made known in Europe and in the North and the most liberal inducements held out backed by assurance that they will be faithfully carried out.

Once get the tide of immigration set towards the south and you will have no difficulty in securing a good class of people to open farms, build towns and populate the country. The south lacks population, the immense plantations comprise too many acres idle that should be under cultivation. In our Western States where Government sells 160 acres for the small sum of twenty dollars after a residence upon it of five years, that quantity of land is considered land enough for one family and if properly cultivated it yields a good return.

[1] Oliver Hudson Kelley (1826–1913), founder of the Patrons of Husbandry.
[2] Missing.

To secure lively immigration it is all important first to restore quiet and secure representation in congress, in the present unsettled state of affairs it will be impossible to induce any active immigration South, but as soon as harmony is restored you will speedily see a favorable change in this respect, while if lands are offered at reasonable rates they will find ready customers.

When lands are held by individuals a portion should be offered on very reasonable terms to actual settlers who by their improvements will enhance the value of that adjacant. The same plans used to encourage immigration to the west can readily be adopted in the South and our association will give as much attention to one portion of the country as to another. We propose to perfect our arrangements this season and secure a charter from Congress in December. Andrew Simonds Esqr. President of the National Bank in Charleston is Vice President for your State whom if you are not acquainted with, this will serve as a letter of introduction and you will find him a gentleman you can appreciate. I will enclose a letter of introduction to him.[1]

Let me hear from you often and I shall be pleased to publish in Northern papers any matter you may favor me with.

My kind regards to Mrs. Pringle and also to Col. Smith if he is yet at Georgetown. I often call to mind the pleasant visit to your plantation and last evening was reading over the copious notes descriptive of your buildings, machines etc. which you furnished me with.

I am pleased to learn from your letter that matters are more cheering than last year at this time. As soon as we are reconstructed I trust all will move smoothly.

John A. Wagener[2] to Benjamin Allston

Charleston, 4 July 1867

DEAR SIR: I have just now returned from Newberry and find your letter on my table. I shall mail to you today the pamphlet you desire and also another, that refers to the subject of immigration. Your plan of a factory is a good and sensible one and I am delighted that a gentleman in your section of country should be willing to make the effort. Whatever scheme you shall fully determine upon will be forwarded to our agent with instructions to bring it to the notice of such capitalists, and manufacturers, as it would be likely to interest. I think, I perceive, that you have already reflected well of the subject and understand it. I only wish to suggest, that you prepare a full and comprehensive scheme, with a statement of all the advantages and

---

[1] Missing.

[2] John Andreas Wagener, a native of Germany, who emigrated to Charleston in 1833. He was later (1871–72) mayor of Charleston.

facilities, that you and those interested can offer, etc., not forgetting, that a capitalist will [illegible], unless the chances are all in favour of success.

[The following notes in Benjamin's handwriting appear on the back of this letter:]

Let us take a machine capable of producing 1000 lbs of no 20 yarn per day as a standard, from which any other estimate may be made, taken from DeBow of February, [18]67, page 178, second table $54,346.

Suppose the months from October to March inclusive only to be employed in [the] running of the Factory, the others being used to cultivate their own crops, this would give 156 working days excluding Xmas and New Year; and would be equivalent to 156,000 lbs. of yarn, which would be the product of about 733 Bales of 250 lbs wght. which would be 183,250 lbs of cotton, wh. exported from Ch[arles]t[o]n for instance at .01c pr lb. would be $1832.25 at same rate of transportation the yarn would be less $272. This exclusive of all interior freights, see DeBow Feby. [18]67, p 175 par 2nd.

Then there is at a profit of .01¢ pr yd on [illegible] sheetings, a clear profit of 25% on Capital invested see ibid (Apl and May), [18]69, p 468. Now the advantages of buying and manufacturing at least up to yarn, by your own agents I presume and no one will dispute, the saving will be quite important, considering the number of intermediate agents, all of whom have their pick and pull, with corresponding chgs, to say nothing of wastage and dirt, which let us estimate at $100.00, an amt. quite within the mark.

Then there is the Govt. tax of .12 1/2 pr lb. wh. may be varied by our fickle masters but I do not think abolished, amounting in this instance to $4581.25. Adding these together we have $4953.25, saved on 733 Bales which is alone over .09% on amount for machinery.

I again beg you to come and see what we propose, and aid me with your counsel and experience. Mazyck and I will take pleasure in showing you everything and the country.

John A. Wagener to Benjamin Allston

Charleston, 13 August, 1867.

DEAR SIR: Your valued letter of the 3d inst. was duly received. I am now every day very much engaged in preparing another pamphlet for distribution in Europe and in our Northern states. I should be glad to insert your prospectus, if you could succeed in time in any definite organization or certain plan. I am very desirous, that a Society for Immigration and other useful public objects should be instituted in every district. In your case and with your views, I think, I should endeavour to induce a meeting of the landowners of the vicinity at once. Let them form a company. Let Mr Mazyk put a valuation upon his site and buildings and such of his adjoining lands, as he will spare. Let as many other planters, as can be induced to join, put in as much of their lands as are contiguous, as they will, at a low valuation. This may be their stock. It is not money, but it is money's worth. Supposing you commence with a nominal capital of 150,000 dollars, in shares of $1000. A has 1000 acres vald. at $2, gives him two shares, etc, he makes the title of his lands to the company and the company gives him two share certificates. Then let these lands be laid off in small tracts and fairly appraised. Let them then be offered for sale at a figure below the appraisement. This will give you three chances: 1. If your company desires to make the venture for profit, you can probably purchase the machinery on a liberal credit and you can easily for a good salary obtain the services of a competent Superintendent. 2, Your shares will be in a form, which is marketable, where lands in themselves have no acknowledged rate. And the shares being once in the market will be an advertisement of the lands and an encouragement for settlers. 3, If you, as I believe you to be, are truly desirous of the good of the State and development of your section, you will in this manner have cheap lands to draw immigrants and employment for a large number, that are not agricultural, besides instituting a branch of pursuits, which is of inestimable value and in this manner perhaps inducing others to follow the example.

I am very much engaged and cannot therefore fully elucidate my views. My belief is, that immigration is our first necessity. That will of itself develop our resources in agriculture. Manufacturing is another necessity, only second to the first. Both can be accomplished by our planters, if they will heartily join hands after it. Let politics go to Old Harry for the present. Let the Devil rule for a while, as rule he must, but the day is very near, when, if we get immigrants and factories, the old regime will return to all their power and influence, to be exerted probably with more beneficial results for our noble State, than heretofore. I do not despair in the least, but I do want to put our house in order, not for the day of our dissolution, which is now, but for the day of our resurrection (regeneration, when Charley will have his own again,) which is not far off. Let me pray you then, to have your meeting and agree upon some organization, put that into working order, and let me help you, to give it life and prosperity. It will be impossible for me to accept of your kind invitation, but I mail you today my address at Newberry, which explains some of my ideas. I have to do all my own work and my correspondence is very large. I should indeed be proud and gratified as an adopted but not less a sincere Carolinian, if one of your old and honored name would work out the development of your district, which is susceptible of great prosperity. If you can accomplish your association in time, I would like to have from you for insertion in my pamphlet a full report of your wishes and prospects. If you will write me such an article, I will insert it. Or if you wish it, I will make up one from your letters. I would rather however have you do it after organization, if you can effect one. Describe your plan, its advantages and probable results, the capacities of your section of country and the inducement you have for immigrants in cheap lands, their capacity and salubrity, facility for market and the disposition of your people to welcome, aid and assist the industrious stranger. In making up your prospectus bear in mind that no capital is ventured without fair prospects of liberal returns and that no man will emigrate anywhere, without a chance of improving his condition. State then, how much cotton your section will produce under ordinary circumstances for manufacturing with spot you have in mind, what facilities you already have for the establishment of factories and what will be required to complete them and put them into operation, what will be the probable result, how many acres of lands you have pledged and for sale, and at what prices and conditions and their locality and capacity, what are the general advantages of your section, fish, game, etc., etc. You must not become tired of your effort nor disheartened and you will surely succeed in your aims.

Benjamin Allston to Charles Richardson Miles[1]

Plantersville August 17 1867

DEAR SIR   A short time since I wrote you that I purposed to use the [illegible] in paying (usual allowance) for the preparation of some portion of the land for another crop.

I now desire to say that in the main this will not answer. I cannot get the land prepared in this way. If there is any purpose to plant the Estate another year, and I would advise it, now is the time to prepare the land. Many negroes are out of food and work and can be hired, at say (in provisions mostly) 50¢ pr day. I desire very much that you would consult the Creditors or their representatives. Of course I mean after advising with the Executors, and let me know what to count upon.

I shall be unwilling to pay now for preparing land, and then in January to contract for a portion of the crop. If we pay now, which seems the only way in which the work can be secured, we must pay throughout the year. This will be cheaper in the end than the contract or share of the crop system.

I have secured the hands on one place to go to work now, preparing lands etc, under the contract system, continuing simply this present contract on to '68, and agreeing to advance them provisions, to be returned from the crop.

This is what I hoped also to have done on Chicora Wood but it is what the negroes will not consent to. If therefore you can secure the money by advancing on this year's proceeds, I believe we can remunerate ourselves at least to a degree for present losses.

To do this all of the money which shall arise from N[ightingale] H[all]

[1] Miles (1829–92) was a Charleston lawyer who was acting as legal adviser to the executors of the Allston estate.

crop must be returned to the entire Estate for the year 1868. Or a loan must be effected.

I am very desirous to know in time, as I am daily receiving applications for work from good hands.

I think the system pursued by Mr Hazard on Santee, by Mr. Ford on Black River, which consists of their own tickets given weekly for so much and redeemable at specific times offers the best prospects for getting work from the Negro and saving the expenditure of the planter of any. Trusting to hear from you at an early date. . . . .

Oliver H. Kelley to Benjamin Allston

Washington, D. C. Sept 6, [18]67

MY DEAR FRIEND   Yours of 30th ult has been received   I owe you many apologies for not writing before but I have been waiting to hear from the P. M. at Georgetown, and putting off writing from day to day, though that ought not have prevented my answering your previous letters. . . . .

I can comprehend your situation and hope the time is not far distant when a more prosperous state of affairs shall exist. You say you have numerous ideas you would like to see inaugurated, be free and tell me of them, promulgate your views. Some of you must come out boldly, with new and enlarged ideas and it has seemed to me that *you* are the proper one to take the lead. Let me have your views and anything I can do to enhance their value I will cheerfully. I can present them to leading ones here who will cheerfully consider them.

On the reorganization of political parties in your section, what is there to prevent your being a leader? By cautious movement in laying a good foundation, you certainly can make yourself popular. You see what is wanted, the whole social system of the South is changed, and you can come out boldly with new and enlarged views, sentiments that will meet with favor in the North. If the Negro predominates in your district and their vote is to carry the day, make yourself popular with them and *get their votes*, the color of the votes is of little consequence so long as good sensible white men are elected by them.

Never mind the apathy and nervousness of your neighbors, go in for *number one*.

I expect to resume my appointment in the Dept of Agriculture the coming week. Should any opportunity offer there, where you can be servicable, I assure you I shall bear you in mind. It will evidently soon be a more ponderous institution than now and need a much larger force to propel it. We can tell better what can be done soon after Congress meets.

I am as intimate with the present acting commissioner as two friends can be and he is inclined to favor my views.

I believe old Newton destroyed all the Abstracts of my report that I sent him while South, they are not to be found or any rate as yet.

After I get fixed and at my old work again, I propose to run down and see you, sometime during the winter, then we can talk immigration, politics and everything else to our hearts content.

By the way, where is your old friend Col. Smith (I think it was) who took me to your house? I have not heard a word about him since I left Georgetown.

I often think of your Pine forest and your steam engine in the Rice Mill, and I believe if I was proprietor, I would turn the main floor of the Mill into a Saw Mill when it was not needed for threshing, and make it bring in something. The land being level to the Pine, a timber track could be laid, and the logs drawn in by mules on small cars, then put the sawed lumber into flat boats and run it down to some point where it could readily be loaded on vessels and sent North. I consider your Pine land worth more money to you than all the rice lands you have in your neighborhood. It may be you do not see matters in the same light I do, but I assure you it is poor policy to let a 15 horse power Steam engine lay idle ten months out of the twelve.

A portable Saw Mill could be put up in that large building where you had so many fan mills, and only use half of the main floor and be propelled by the engine where it is. I do not know what the mill itself would cost, but can find out, perhaps $500.00 set up.

I think you have a magnificent chance to make money in the lumbering business, equal if not superior to any I saw while South.

If I remember right, there is also a steam engine on your Mother's plantation. You see with us "Yanks," when we see available power lying idle, we have an itching for making it work and we consider it is as poor policy to have a steam engine idle as a stable full of horses.

You must not take offence at my free suggestions, but they have passed through my mind hundreds of times since we parted. I expect you will get up some morning, completely revolutionized and resolve to build a manufacturing town on the river bank. Such a chance as you have would soon be seized upon if it was in the North. Dont sell your Pine lands. Pine lumber is getting scarce in the North, particularly in the vicinity of New York and large quantities are now shipped from Michigan for that Market. If I am correct I think your Pine is worth 50 or $60.00 per thousand feet, in N. Y. and Phila., it cannot cost more than 3 to $5.00 per M. delivered on the river bank all sawed. Somebody makes a profit. Every acre of Pine you have is worth fifty dollars at least for the lumber alone as it stands.

I trust this will find you well and enjoying yourself, as soon as the P. M. fills that blank we will try to complete the P. O. matter.

Oliver H. Kelley to Benjamin Allston

Washington D. C. Oct. 10 [18]67

MY DEAR FRIEND,   Your very interesting letter has just been received. I have not time to answer you tonight, but drop you this to beg you to keep up your courage. "There is yet a God in Israel." The elections all through the North are going with tremendous Democratic majorities and all will yet come out right. The Congressional plan of reconstruction has proved a failure, and the people are determined that peace and quiet shall be restored. What we want is the Union restored and I believe the good men of the South will do all in their power to aid in restoring peace. Ohio and Pennsylvania have led off with tremendous victories. In November the balance of the States will vote to stand by the Constitution. All this hubbub has been created by the Radicals in hopes to secure the next President but it will be labor thrown away. Seems to me I would go into the Convention but as an Independent man. They will be in session sometime of course and during that time the whole face of things will likely change from what they now are. Congress will be in session in six weeks and will be very apt to change its course of action entirely, seeing that the people of the North are against Radical measures.

Again I say take courage. The *people* at the North are not more desireous of being *ruled* by the nigger than you are in the South, but you are surrounded with them and the sudden outburst of popular feeling against them evinced at these late elections may have a tendency to make the darkey uneasy.

I will answer your letter at length in a few days.

[P. S.]   I will look after your Georgetown P. M.

Theodore G. Barker[1] to Benjamin Allston

Charleston October 10 1867

DEAR ALLSTON   I have delayed answering your letter in order to get some of the results of the Ohio and Pennsylvania Elections. The reports are that in all the Elections where the question of negro suffrage was submitted the proposition has been rejected by very large majorities and the principle of "white supremacy" been signally triumphant at the polls. The Democratic gains have been very large in Ohio, and even in Pennsylvania, where the question of negro suffrage was not voted upon, the Republican vote has been seriously deminished and Democratic majorities been secured in many counties. I regard the result as most important and salutary, and am encouraged again to hope, that the government of the Southern States will not be allowed to pass into the control of negro representatives after all.

[1] Theodore Gaillard Barker (1832–1917), Charleston lawyer, later prominent in Hampton movement to restore native white supremacy.

The evidences of a marked change in the public sentiment of the Northern masses are sufficiently striking to be a most potent warning to Radicalism and to strengthen the hands of the President, who is opposed to negro suffrage, and will save the white governments in the Southern States, if he possibly can.

I have not been able to ascertain the opinions of those who differ with me on the subject of reconstruction, because I have not discussed the subject. I have not heard "the Convention" mentioned in Charleston since you were here.

As to my own views on the subject I can only say that I look with sorrow on every act of our people which can be construed into acceptance or voluntary acquiescence in the Military Congressional Reconstruction. Participation in any shape or form whether by *useless Registration* or hopeless efforts to control or influence the Convention are to my mind terrible mistakes. If the South had stood off in quiet solemn protest by having nothing at all to do with the whole business, we would have, I really believe, been at this day clear of the danger of negro voting and negro juries. By registering, we have lost the force and value of our protest, and led the opponents of negro suffrage, at the north, to believe, that it was not so horrible a thing after all. We have delayed the awakening of the sentiment in the Northern masses against negro elevation, which would have come to our rescue in time to sweep away the whole programme of Congress. These convictions have grown on me and I cannot believe that any good can come of our mixing in negro politics, or intermeddling ourselves in the business of establishing a Liberian Republic in South Carolina. Let the negroes alone, give them the necessary amount of rope, let them have their representatives, *all black*, in the Convention, let their ignorance, incapacity, and excesses have full scope and accomplish its end; dont attempt to modify it, with white sauce; let it be all black, and it will soon cure itself. The problem of reconciling in practice the dogma of "governments resting on the consent of the governed" and "all men are born free and equal" with the fact of negro incapacity for self government is a problem of Yankee creation, the solution of which is *their* responsibility not *ours*. Then why should we help them to solve it. You say for the sake of peace and good order. I would suggest a policy which seems to me to promise far better fruits, stand off and say to the negroes, *that it is their affair*, advise them to select the most reliable of their own people, in whom they (*not we*) have most confidence; counsel them how to act, but dont attempt to influence them, *dont become their candidate*, and the sooner they get into a muddle, in politics, and the Science of Government, the sooner will we reach *the inevitable End*, viz, to have the reins of Government taken out of their hands by white labouring men, their natural enemies and rivals. I give their negro government a lease of life of very few months (if so long).

I have heard of the subject of our people being candidates for the Convention being discussed in very few places. Octavius Porcher of Abbeville has been trying to acquire an influence with the Negroes and they say has succeeded in getting them to nominate white men to represent them in Convention, and contemplates accepting the place. I respect the earnest purpose which would actuate a man of refinement and sensibility so far as to induce him to undertake such a work, but I believe it will do as much good as Mr Glennie's preaching to them before and during the war did in Christianizing their natures. In spite of white representatives mixing with them in Convention they must break down, and before six months are over we will have a white Convention called in the States of the South for the purpose of establishing a new constitution. It is a serious problem but I must believe that our true policy is to stand aloof altogether. I cannot bring myself to acquiesing in the horrible business of negro elevation. In the name of my race I protest against it! He is not a citizen by law, is not entitled to suffrage, is not the equal of the white man! By accepting the position of his representative I would feel that I was acknowledging all these points, and keeping Puritan-Yankee lies afloat. By keeping him and his race politically at arm's length I feel that I am true to my race and to civilization, at any rate I am not sanctioning a vile precedent or making a mockery of representative republican government, by dancing a political jig with Sambo. I will not live under a negro government, still less under a mixed republic. I will leave my home when it comes to that. In the meantime I await the time when the Yankee Army will protect white *citizens* in voting, for a *white* Convention.

F. W. Pickens to Adele Petigru Allston

Edgewood 22 Nov. 1867

My dear Madam   I recd yours sometime since, but I am so worried out of my life by constant calls and attention on the miserable freedman, that I have no time to call my own. If I had the means I would escape to some place of quiet, but as it is we are obliged to stand and bear it all.

It will afford me the greatest pleasure to do any thing I can by way of urging and recommending your school, for I know and feel that it is just such a place as a genteel young girl ought to go, but then my dear madam, there is no one who can afford to go any where. The country is in hopeless poverty and ruin, and I fear must get worse. We had all hoped that this abundant crop year would bring with it some means for our poor disheartened people to struggle and do something for themselves by way of education at least. But now the price for cotton does not pay taxes, and wages of labour and cost of transportation I assure you it costs now 16 cts a pound to raise and take one pound of cotton into market, and this is the best price for it. Besides the wretched Military Bureau gave orders to freedmen to retain cotton on plantations until every cent is paid them, although their wages are not due until 1st Jany. All this, discourages and disheartens all white men so that if a man, even the best of us, can have potatoes, and grits and meat, and keep out of the hands of the Military and the negroes, he is doing well this winter. It requires the closest kind of management to support one's family now. Then we have so many objects of necessary charity in old negroes, and poor disabled white soldiers and helpless families all through the country, that a man has not a cent beyond his immediate demands. God grant that our country may be saved from total ruin! I think there is a prospect of change for the better. But things are in a very critical situation financially and politically. All society stands now like a cone on its Apex, with base up. The least jostle is liable to make a total overthrow of the whole structure. Such a state of things cannot stand, for it never has in any age or in any country as a permanent structure I think, by May next, we will begin to see light, and we will at least begin to know what to expect, and to try and adapt ourselves to it. At present all any one can hope for, is to try and support oneself for a few more tedious and oppressive months. We are bound hand and foot, and our only policy is to keep quiet and *silent*, and be ready to take advantage of circumstances as they arise. Then we must meet our fate, whatever it may be, like men and like Christians. I cannot but think that Providence has nothing better in store for us, at least I hope so.

I do not write to depress or discourage, but with a desire to develope the truth to a lady of your distinguished standing and information so that those you influence may know truthfully our situation. I do not despair, for I have great faith in the final uprightness and sturdy virtues of our English forefathers and the blood they have infused throughout our country. In England, under James II, and Charles and Cromwell, they lost their liberties and seemed sunk permanently, and yet their great endurance and worthy virtues brought them out, and they recovered all they lost, and gained more permanent guarantees. It may be so with us. I pray God it may be.

Mrs Pickens begs her kindest remembrance. We have suffered tortures, but we both bear up wonderfully.

Oliver H. Kelley to Benjamin Allston

Washington D. C. Nov. 30 [1867]

MY DEAR FRIEND, You must pardon me for neglecting you so long, an extensive correspondence has crowded me much of late. While I was travelling in the South I saw the unhappy state of matters and also saw plainly that the political parties never would produce a harmony of feeling. I was satisfied if all could come together as farmers and planters and keep the great interests of agriculture uppermost we could get under the vine and fig tree and wave olive branches with some meaning. I then conceived the idea of getting up a great National order and last August commenced the work. With half a dozen good friends here I set at work and already have a little army of correspondents in fifteen States. To convince you of the popularity of the movement, over two hundred of the enclosed slips[1] have been sent out and only one letter has yet been received that was opposed to it, and that was from Saco, Maine! About the first of January we hope to have the work complete and commence organizing "Granges." As one black ball rejects a candidate I fancy there will not be many "fancy colored" members. But I must answer your very interesting letters of Oct. 28 and Nov 22nd.

Politically you must be convinced by this time that the revolution in public sentiment is as I predicted. At the North Negro suffrage has played out, and as to impeachment of the President that has played out also. Congress has commenced hauling in its horns and a more amiable disposition will be shown towards the South. In fact I shall not be surprised to see all the States represented before the 4th of March next. Of course you can see that all the oppression comes from the extreme Radicals who have been aiming to secure the vote of the Negro to help elect a Radical President, but I doubt very much if there is the least shadow of a chance. It must be a conservative man who can secure the popular vote of the North. Very likely Grant will be elected. If so I believe he will do justice to the South.

Your last letter relative to the fruits and enclosing a meteorolgical table is very interesting and I handed the same to my friend Saunders who was much pleased with its contents.

Your idea of going to California may be good, but do you think by going West you are to get rid of the Negro? I think not. As I saw the South, and observing the progress of enterprise, there is much more in Mississippi and Louisiana and Texas than on the Atlantic Sea Board. Wages are higher on the Mississippi than in your state. In Alabama the Whites were encouraging labor to leave Georgia and in Georgia they were coaxing the darkey from South Carolina. As you are not importing the Negro, you will soon see them getting scarce in your vicinity. "Westward the star of empire takes its way," the natural course of immigration is West. As they leave you the White immigration will come in, and I venture to say in ten years your Negro population will be so meagre as hardly to be noticed, immigration and disease will take them away. The enterprising ones will go to California if they learn of its inducements, and if you are anxious to get rid of them you can tell them of the *blissful abodes* in store there for them!

I hardly think you will find any more agreeable climate all things considered than you now have. I would counsel patience, all will come out right in the end. Dont be alarmed at poverty, it's merely a misfortune and no disgrace. Obstacles are merely opportunities to encourage us to diligence and when we overcome them and meet with success then we appreciate that success. Dont get discouraged. I am glad you are to remain on the old plantation another year during that time no doubt you will be successful and

---

[1] Missing.

more pleasing prospects present themselves. We have at last succeeded in having Col. Horace Capron[1] of Illinois confirmed as Com. of Agriculture which is a good move. I doubt if I get South this Winter as matters now are I must go to my home in Minnesota as soon as I get the work of our order complete. I do not like to be away from my wife and little ones so much. I have not seen the pamphlet you refer to upon the Negro.

Benjamin Allston to Ellen Allston[2]

Guendalos Jany 12, 1868

MY DARLING NELLIE . . . . The day of its [her letter] arrival (Friday) was the day appointed for the Sale of my effects,[3] and during the morning I was much exercised. Only the perishable articles such as belong to plantation, no household articles were sold. Learning that the sale was to take place I wrote to Miles in Charleston, to send me authority to purchase certain articles, such as oxen, flats and boats, to enable me to carry out a contract I had made with these people on behalf of the Estate, but got none so on the day of sale I determined to buy certain essentials myself. I found the utmost consideration manifested for me, on the part of all present, and as soon as it was known that I desired any article no one bid at all. Sparkman did the bidding for me; I did not bid at all. I have since written to the parties most interested in Charleston, to know upon what terms they will allow me to plant Guendalos. If they do not reply to me, at a very moderate rate, I shall again sell the articles I bought, and run the risk of being brought up before the Court, for a non fulfilment of contract; which I desire to avoid, and therefore make this offer. I do not like the idea of risking all my salary this year in *rice* and negroes, but, I wish to keep my contract. I will give you a sample of what I bought. A flat $25.00, the cow, Mary $20.00, 1 yoke of oxen $50.00, Rice $1.40 pr bush, peas $1.31 pr bush. I do not think I can lose at such prices even if I have to sell again. Blacksmith tools $5.00; I paid nearly $100.00 for them little more than a year since. In about a week I will write you the result of my application. I sincerely wish I had you here to assist me with your Counsel and general aid, my dear wife, but this cannot be, I trust I may be inspired and guided to act rightly and for our interests. M. A. Cusher bought Bess for $60.00 and Jane for $20.00. I feel rather nervous about trying the Rice again, but I do not exactly see how to do otherwise. Should all things go smoothly I would do well at it, but should there be again a failure, lackaday, it would be hard indeed. I have Sam Benjamin for Foreman, he was my old Driver, and in this I am better off than heretofore. You will be apprehensive of the result, and may fear the result, even

[1] Capron (1804–85) was commissioner from 1867 to 1871.

[2] Addressed: Austin, Texas.

[3] The result of bankruptcy proceedings.

as I feel, but we must trust to Providence. . . . . I am sorry yet pleased that you should find all the country looking so much like S.C. Say what I will, I have an affection for my old home wh[ich] will manifest itself now and then in spite of me, and it wld please me if you could share it. If the towns are growing rapidly as you say the country must be improving especially where a stream of Immigrants are coming in. Should we ever succeed in reestablishing prosperity in this country, we will do well also. I think the time will come but how long—who can tell? It is well to have more than one string to pull, and this is secured by your now being in Texas. California as you are aware is the place of all I shld desire to go to. Tams and myself have had long talks on the subject. He thinks this country (and with some shew of reason) will ere long be again prosperous and valuable. . . . .

Harry has just been in to see me and says that he was told by Paul a few days since that I was to make Bynah work the garden and that he did not say anything but if I would only feed him and give him a piece of ground for himself he would work the garden. He would work it for nothing before he would let any other people come &c, &c. Professed much respect for me &c, and I really believe felt it. I agreed with him. I wished him to cook and garden, but this he could not, would if he knew how but did not, and I did not insist. I must get rid of Bynah or Becka or both. . . . .

Adele Petigru Allston to Caroline Carson[1]

Charleston 13 April [18]68

MY DEAR CAROLINE   From the time I read your beautiful inscription for your Father's monument[2] (I saw it first in the *News*), I have desired to write to you and express my admiration of it. I think it really worthy of the subject, and I can say no more to express my appreciation. It seems to me in your father's own style and spirit.

Yesterday, Easter, Bessie, Jane and I gathered flowers, Lemarks cloth of gold and souveniers, made them into a wreath, a cross and a bouquet and laid them on that hallowed spot. We then saw the monument up for the first time. We regarded it with admiration and emotion. The lettering is beautifully done, and seems to bring out the sense and truth of the inscription. I congratulate you on this work, worthily, nobly done. Your mother told me of your design some time ago. I begged her to say to you, I would gladly bear part of the expense. I understood that you declined it. No one could possibly owe more to another than I to your father.

I see now how wise you were to leave this country. The ruin is almost universal. Last year, and the year before our school did as well as I could expect. This year it has fallen off so as to discourage me greatly. It really does not

[1] Address missing. Being opposed to secession, Mrs. Carson went in 1861 to the North and later to Europe.

[2] To James L. Petigru, in St. Michael's, Charleston.

make enough to pay the teachers employed. Bessie would like to get a situation as governess. Arnoldus took Adele and the two little girls to Ashepoo a fortnight ago. They are in a negro house, the dwelling having been burned. Adele writes cheerfully. The birds sing as sweetly, and the flowers bloom as gaily as ever, and those who are very young will not, I hope, feel the dreadful ruin as elderly people must feel it. Charles is much grown, and is good looking. He stands well at the College, and is a very good, blameless boy. He is respected and liked by his friends. Jane is considered pretty. She has the most beautiful complexion possible, and her features are not bad. She will be prepared to take part in the school next winter as a teacher, if we shall be able to get our school. I cannot tell you how the falling off in the number of my pupils mortifies me. I conscientiously think my school a good one, a very good one. Mlle Leprince is admitted by every one to be a most admirable teacher of French. I suppose I have offended the prejudices of the people, tho' in what way I do not know. I would be glad to get boarders from the North where the climate must be unfavourable to delicate girls. If I could get 15 or 20 boarders from elsewhere I would be able to continue my school next winter. Mrs John Laurens is teaching a boarding school, and all her relations, the Frosts and others, exert themselves very much in her behalf. A great deal is done in that way. Mrs Mason Smith is teaching a school without advertisement or notice, and a great many others. So I ought not to wonder at my diminished number.

I am happy in my children. Ben's character is excellent. He is employed this year as manager of the estate. He has gone into Bankruptcy. The estate will be wound up next winter I presume. I am to get my dower, the sixth of the landed estate. That is all any of us will have. If we had friends who would loan us money I dare say the plantations will sell very low; and we might buy some of it in. But we are very much alone. But for these debts which your Uncle Allston incurred in the latter years of his life we would be very well off. He had been successful all his life in planting, and did not apprehend the revolution.

Dear Caroline I hope your trip to Europe may prove successful, and your health be restored. I have been grieved to hear of your sufferings. I hope this long letter may not have wearied you.

I regret that my younger children will never know you except thro' others. They send love to you.

That God may bless you and give you the light of his countenance is the earnest prayer of your affectionate Aunt Adele.

Adele Petigru Allston to Benjamin Allston

Charleston 16th April 1868

MY DEAR BEN Yours of 11th with the turkey, the 22 cooters and the keg of rough rice and eggs came safely to hand Monday evening, in a hard rain.

I thank you my beloved son for your consideration and kindness. I rejoice that you have lost your chill and fever; and do hope you may not have a return of it. Chills and fever have been very unusually prevalent. I thank the Sparkmans for their attention to you. I think of your loneliness with much concern, but a *man* must be a *man*, and not easily sucumb. There is always danger in such a lonely life of being tempted to solace oneself with stimulants. It is a temptation that strong, and even good men have yielded to. May the good God give you grace to resist all evil enfluences.

I forgot to mention the butter in enumerating the things received. It was most opportune, as we were just out. It is very good. I hope your servants improve. How does Dave conduct himself? I am sure his mother will instruct him to steal everything he can. I would be very glad [if] he could raise himself to respectability. I was much attached to that family, and would be glad for them to do well. Charles and James Lesesne, and Arthur Mazyck and two or three others, went to Kiawah for a fortnight to hunt and fish. Arnoldus offered them the use of his house and bedding. They had a charming time. Took their supplies of bacon, lard, flour, etc. Margaret cooked for them, and made herself very satisfactory. James told me he thinks her the most capable servant he ever knew, and so civil. Quash also proves a good, faithful, intelligent agent to Arnoldus. Margaret's judgment was right, tho' her morals were bad, when she decided to abandon Joe, and replace him by Quash. Joe must be a poor degraded wretch.

Charles reports the negroes at Kiawah working well under Quash, and behaving with respect, and even defference to them. Tell Margaret's mother that she, and her children are well, and doing well. . . . .

Benjamin Allston to Ellen Allston[1]

Guendalos Apl 16, [18]68

MY DARLING WIFE   It is raining as if the Heavens were coming down, and vivid flashes of lightening play between almost continuous rolls of Thunder. I have just escaped the storm, have been out all day trying to get men to do their *duty* in voting against the constitution submitted by the Radical Convention. I have been repulsed in two instances. Frank Weston, at whom I am not surprised, because he is a "coota" generally and loves inaction for its own sake, and because he is an obstinate creature prone to take the reverse side of almost any question presented to him, still it annoyed me, the other Fishburne, from whom I am last come, disgusts me. He promised Sparkman and myself, only on Monday last that he would vote, that he thought every one who could, should vote etc., now he tells me he has been thinking well on the matter and deems it all a farce, no use to vote, etc. I am so disgusted that I cannot help writing it to you, for whom it can have

[1] Addressed: Austin, Texas.

no earthly interest except so far as I am interested. I may say to you what perhaps I would not be justified in saying to others, that I consider Fishburne totally without principle, and now, "on the fence" politically. I would not give two straws for his "say so" one way or the other. You may think this harsh, but it is not drawn from this circumstance alone. There are some private ones of which you are aware and this is the second time in which in a political matter he has, *falsified*, I do not use too harsh a term, his word. Mark what I say now. Should this Party succeed in erecting a Government, with any success, Fishburne will be one of their Candidates for Office at the next elections. I will now leave this subject, and have in future as little as possible to do with the subject of these remarks. . . . .

Adele Petigru Allston to George Peabody[1]

Charleston 18 July 1868

DEAR MR PEABODY   I received in April 1867 from Gov Aiken a kind remembrance from you in the form of an order on Duncan and Spearman for five hundred dollars ($500). Your kind recollection of me was most gratifying and I should have written to tell you so at the time, but understood you had already gone to Europe. I do not know that you have returned, but I feel impelled to acknowledge your kindness and express my grateful sense of it.

Nothing was ever more grateful to me than hearing, thro' Mr Aiken, of your kind inquiry about me. I believe it is not often that persons in great adversity are sought for by friends of more prosperous days and pleasant recollection of old acquaintance renewed and refreshed by acts of substantial kindness. Yet it is such examples that enoble and dignify human nature.

On the termination of the disastrous civil war I was left in great distress. My honoured husband had been taken from us by death the year before. I was thus deprived of his great ability in affairs at a time when they were most needed. The sudden emancipation of the negroes, and the effect it produced upon them, rendered our estate entirely unavailing. My three youngest children were to be educated, we were entirely without means even to live. I decided to open a school, hoping in that way to finish the education of my two daughters and to obtain the means to send my son to the Charleston College. I hoped also to be able to lay by something to enable me to purchase a house when ever the estate of my husband should be sold. The two first years I accomplishd as much as I expected to do, but this year has been the worst we have known. The loss of crops, and other disasters, prevented many persons sending their daughters to school. Our school has been smaller, and the pay worse.

It is probable the estate will be up the last of this year. It is to our interest

---

[1] George Peabody (1795–1869), founder of the Peabody Educational Fund.

probably that it should be. I am to get my dower, one sixth of the value of the land. The condition of the country is such that it is possible the land may sell for one tenth of its real value. In which case it would be to our interest to buy it in. I want a friend to advance me the means to pay the cash part of the purchase. Would you my dear friend aid me in this way? My eldest son is residing on the plantation and has been managing it since the war. He knows its value. I will not desire to buy the place if it sells for any thing near its real value. But it would be grievous to me to see it go to strangers for a mere song, while we would be left in absolute poverty. We would pay you 6 pr interest on the loan, and give you the mortgage of the property. You will I am sure pardon this application. I felt it due to my own feelings, and to the sincere friendship you have expressed for me, to place the situation before you. If you can aid us you will impart a ray of happiness and hope to a family in distress and perplexity, and have our sincere and grateful thanks. Mr Alonzo J White is my business friend here. I expect to leave Charleston in a few days to pass 2 months in the Pineland near the plantation. If you will give me a few lines addressed to care of Alonzo J White, Charleston, So Ca. it will be sure to reach me.

I am, dear Mr Peabody with a grateful sense of your kindness, and with sentiments of high consideration

P. S.   I find I have omitted to name any sum as the amount I would probably need. Ten thousand dollars in currency would be as much as we would wish. I would not take the risk of a larger sum.

OVERSEERS' REPORTS AND OTHER DOCUMENTS

An Overseer's Contract, 1822[1]

South Carolina, Georgetown District.

Be it remembered that it is hereby agreed between Mrs. E. F. Blyth on the one part, & William T. Thompson of the other part, in manner following, that is to say, that the said William T. Thompson agrees, from the first day of January eighteen hundred & twenty two, to the first day of January eighteen hundred & twenty three, to oversee the two plantations of Mrs. Blyth, one of them at Waccamaw, & the other at the Point, at the entrance of Georgetown River, and the negroes, stock, barns, & every species of property of Mrs. Blyth thereon, in a planter like manner, with care, skill, fidelity, sobriety, & ability, & more especially with moderation & humanity to the negroes, & to exert himself to the utmost of his power for the interest of his employer, & the said Wm. T. Thompson further agrees, that he will in no instance strike a negro with a stick, & in case of any uncommon occurrences on either of the said Plantations, which in the opinion of him the said Wm. T. Thompson might call for the exercise of severity, he will in no event use it, without first applying for, & obtaining the sanction of Mr. B. Allston, or Mrs. Blyth, or of Mr. Keith, & that should he violate any part of the above written agreement, he may be discharged from his employment In consideration whereof, Mrs. Blyth agrees to pay to the said Wm. T. Thompson, at the expiration of the said term, the full sum of Five hundred Dollars, & to allow him for the year, a negro woman to cook & wash, & a negro boy to wait on him In witness whereof the parties to these presents have subscribed their names hereto this 15th day of January 1822.

WM. T. THOMPSON
ELIZABETH FRANCES BLYTH

Witness
JOHN MCFARLANE

[RENEWALS]

We agree to abide by the above agreement for another year from first January 1823 to 1st Jany. 1824.

We agree to abide by the above agreement for another year from the first of January 1824 to 1st Jany. 1825, saving only that the compensation instead of being Five hundred dollars as above shall be Five hundred and sixty dollars.

---

[1] Overseers' records are not abundant in the Allston Collection. With the exception of a few trivial items, all that are now to be found are included in this section.

We will abide by the foregoing agreement for another year from the 1st Jany 1825 to 1st Jany 1826. The compensation above mentioned being Six hundred dollars, instead of Five hundred and sixty as above. The said William T. Thompson keeping for his own use, on the plantation at which he resides, two cows & calves, and no more, and not keeping or raising any Geese as heretofore.

The foregoing agreement is still of force for the year ending 1st Jany. 1827, the compensation and restrictions last above written continuing also the same.

Geo. Town 1st Jany. 1827.

The above stipulations by consent of both parties will continue in full force 'till the 1st day of January 1828, the compensation only to the said William T. Thompson, being increased from Six hundred dollars as above written to Seven hundred dollars pr annum.

7th Jany. 1828.

The foregoing agreement & stipulations will continue in force for another year to 1st Jany. 1829, excepting only that Mr. Thompson shall be paid for his services duly rendered, Eight hundred dollars.

3d. Feby. 1829.

The foregoing will continue of force till the 1st. Jany. 1830, Mr. Thompson's wages being the same as last year Eight hundred dollars.

Georgetown 7th. Jany. 1830.

The agreement of last year is continued till the first day of January (1831) next, with the foregoing stipulations.[1]

Georgetown Novb. 23d. 1831.

The foregoing agreement, will continue by mutual consent, till the 1st. January 1833, the stipulations therein mentioned being in full force.

Georgetown November 30th 1832.

The foregoing agreement will continue by mutual consent, until the 1st. January 1834 the stipulations therein contained being nine hundred dollars $900.

1st. Jany 1834

The within agreement is continued for another year, namely till January 1835, under all the stipulations therein, except that Mr. Thompson's compensation shall be as last year Nine Hundred dollars.

Geo. Town, Jany. 1835.

The within agreement holds by mutual consent for another year viz 'till Jany. 1836 under the same stipulations and with the same compensation as last year.

[1] The omission of a renewal for the year 1831 is explained by another copy of the contract covering that year. Except that it shows Thompson's compensation to have been $800 in 1831 and $900 in 1832, this differs in no important respect from the copy here printed.

Georgetown, Jan. 1836.

The within agreement holds by mutual consent for another year say to 1st. Jan. 1837, under the same stipulations and with the same compensation as last year.

Georgetown, 7th Novr. 1836.

The foregoing agreement is hereby renew'd for another year, say to 1st Jany. 1838, under the same stipulations & the like compensation as last year.

The foregoing agreement is continued for another year viz from 1st. Jany 1838 to 1st Jany 1839 under the same stipulations, and with like compensation as last year.

Daniel P. Avant to Robert F. W. Allston

So Carolina, George town District, Augt 9, 1823.

Dr Sir/ I & family are well at present   now hard sickness among the negroes   the women lies up a great Deal But not much the matter   I have not herd from Flora since I sent her Down   I expect to hear this Evening I am pushing on with my Ditching & other plantation work that I named in my the other Letter   my Rice is Beginning to hang & Turn yalow   the field by the Barn that got so Ruint By the Birds has improved vary much as to the chapel field that is a vary nice field of Rice   it is about too feet & half high & thick anough where the logs was above [?] the land   we have vary heavy Rains   in Deed I am afraid too much so for the good of the crops By your mothers Request Before she went north I have hired thomas to Mr Benj'n Fraser at $25 per month commenceing the month on the 23 of June   he sed he wanted him for too or three months   he is still working there yet   after your mother left the plantation he finished the poltry house that he was working on & then Raised the frame of the Dairy before he went to Mr Frasers   I have sent out to git cooper stuff on Wednesday last I am going to provide cooper stuff for 250 Barrels   I want a grindstone   the one that is here is worn so small the negroes cannot sharpen their Tools they have to go to Mr Coachmans & to Mr Vareens to grind them   the Sheep is all here & looks vary well   the cattle is here & looks well   Mr Hamblin came here a few Days ago & clamed that Brindled cow that was over the River so late with the caff   I told him that I could not give her up & more than that she is not Exactly in his Mark   their is a Difference of a small under Bit   she is in his mark all to the under Bit   I ast him after shewing him the under Bit if he was satisfyed & he would not say   he first offered to swair to her   But after Shewing him the under Bit he went home   there is of that Bulk of Rice that lay in the Barn 112 Bushels heded up in Barrels its of an infeir quality   your mother never let me know what to Do with it the physic Salce is out & Rheuburb & the julop is a most out & Powder & shot   the Birds & crows is vary Bad on the corn & the Squaril on our new ground Rice   They cut it Done vary much & the summer Ducks is vary thick.

Daniel P. Avant to Robert F. W. Allston

So Carolina, Georgetown District, Augst 16, 1823.

Sir/   I have to Turn out on munday on the rodes to work the hands is Done geting heden[1] & will cummence on monday to geting staves the Big newground & 15 acker Betwen it an the River is hangin & is vary yallow & is Exelant Good Rice clear of voluntier[2] that 15 acker field with that Larg crick that plaged us to stop that cannot Bee no Better Rice jest yearing out the 14 acker field in frunt of your house & the field Beyond is as nice Rice as I Ever saw But the volunteer Rice is Ruined it I think from what I can see ove it that they will loose about three or four hundred Bushels at the lowest calculations the too Goose Grass fiels is not so good By my Gudgment I think they will make a Barrel & a half to the acker & not more the field By the Barn still improves & also the chapel field It is Beginning to Shute & year out & is very Good Rice the negroes is all well at present But Cretia she is sick But not much the matter, a little feve & pain in the hed they have quit laying up a little to what they Did a while Back I herd from flora last friday she Gits now Better Guy told me the potatoes looks likely Enough to be good the slips[3] Groes vary well the corn some parts is vary Good & some parts again is vary inferier the peas is vary likely & with out too much Rain will bee vary fine I have got to line Bank with the Ditch way & the Ditch with in too or three Day will git the senter Ditch too I cannot find any line ove the crick at all I Traced it from in frunt ove the line Bank to the edge of the crick But never can Discover any line on the other side I have stuck too stakes on the Bank & lind them together & Gon over & cleared the Ditch way by them & keep them strate with the line Bank & I'll have to Keep a line of Stakes behind us to go strate.

William T. Thompson to Robert F. W. Allston

Monday morning, Oct 27th, 1837.

Dear Sir I was quite sick yesturday and all last nite. I took a dorse of lobelia and feel much better this morning. I sent the boat Over last evening and Mr Warterman has sent you a note when he will send the vessil up. I rote to Mr Porter to git all the papers and Leters for your self your Aunt Coln. Ward & Mr Heriett, and he only sent one for Mrs Blyth leter & one paper for you. he beged in a note that I would send back this morning & he would send all that had arrived, which Caused me to keep frank untill this morning. Mr Glenning [Glennie?] says he sent up on saturday all he had by old footy.

---

[1] Probably heading, for barrels.

[2] Rice growing from grain left in the field, a cause of much trouble to the rice-planter.

[3] Sweet potatoes growing from cuttings rather than seed.

I will now give you a list of my catle, to wit, 8 cows & calves 16

2 dry cows	2
3 hieffers	3
4 Steers	4
1 Bull	1
Hed	26

As I said before I was willing to take bank shares at par, with the insta[l]-ments all paid, but not willing to take them and pay the ballance dew on them Because I would be paying a way what I ought to Receive.

Gabriel L. Ellis to Robert F. W. Allston

March 3, 1838.

DEAR SIR   I over took Some of Mr Sp[a]rkmans men in the Roaad this Evening coming home frome the Muster feild and took one of them and give hime about 25 or 30 lashes for the ofencence of Runing of Mr A Wilsons gig whele out of the Road and there was Six or Seven of them in companey and this man Said that he was in charge of the Rest of the companey If I have comited and ofence that is worth notice I think that Mr Sparkman had beter Say nothing about my being So cruel as to charge me with being So cruel as to Say that I would Keep a Negro locked up if I had the fellow in confinement I would turn him out from your note of this Eve for your Sake altogether as for Mr S. Saying anything about my conduct with Negroes I think he had beter Say as lite as posible I am Sorry that you have ben troubled about it therefore I make this apoligy on your act. not on act. of Mr S. I would rather convince Mr S. of his Erer in a personal conversation I am willing to Stand any thing like a law Suit that Mr S may think proper to enter against me for my misconduct. I there fore hope you will Excuse me for being So Explicet about the Circumstancse.

William E. Sparkman[1] to Robert F. W. Allston

March 4, 1838.

DEAR SIR   Five of my negroes have been getting out Rails for me for the last few days on Judge Dunkins Land, and on their return home this evening were overtaken by Mr Ellis just opposite his house. Four of them he sent home but detained the foreman and took him to his house for what purpose I am at a loss and as Mr Ellis is a man I would studiously avoid having any communication with I have thought proper to address you he being in your employ. The negroes had no Ticket as I did not think it necessary. If Mr Ellis has any charge to alleage against any of my servants there is certainly a gentlemanly course to persue, if it is merely to indulge his spleen against me, will you do me the favour to investigate the matter.

[1] A neighboring planter.

Gabriel L. Ellis to Robert F. W. Allston

Matanza, June 10, 1838.

DEAR SIR the people is all well at both places Except old Joe. the Dr. has Salavated him other ways I think he is beter. the Mill Pounded 113 Barrels in May. your lot of Rice that I Sent to Mill is done. it has made 49 Bls of Prime and 4 of Small grain I forget how maney of Midling. Dr. Allston has not Sent yet I have put 800 Bushels of the Est[ate] in Mill. the Mill comenced pounding it last Friday Dr. Magill wrote to Mr. Single-ton[1] that he Should not Send any more Rice until august or September the wier for the Brushing Skreen is Six feet long Six peices 14 Inches wide. Your thrashing Mill axel betwen the Jurnals is 3 feet 5 Inches long lenght of the Jurnals 3 Inches sise of the Jurnals 1 Inch and 5 Eighth lenght of the End for the Nut for the Band 8 1/2 Inches Sise of the flanges 8 Inches in diameter the hole for the axel is 2 Inches leaver 3 Inches from the hole to the out Edge of the flanges Seser arrived home last Monday with your Sadle horse Very Badly foundered he is geting Some beter but he looks very bad yet he can hardly walk yet he has falen off very much we had good Seasons here last Saterday & Sunday and Monday the upland crops begin to look verry well the oats is short but I think that they will fill tolerable well. the corn in verry promising at this time all but the peice back of the old Barn yard that I had to plant over last Saterday and it is Jest come up if the Season is faverable for late corn it will be tolerable good if not it will be worth but litle of course the Potatoes is good. the prospect of the Rice crop is at this time beter than we have Ever had take it all together. we have now only 160 Bushels of corn on hand and Mr. Oliver thinks that he will want the 61 Bushels that we borrowed of him this year. the corn will last till about the 20 of July. Mr. Waterman is seling his corn at 1 Dollar and 23 cts per bushel. I write this to you so you may buy it there if you think best to do so. I beg the faviour of you to find out what Bricks will be likely to be worth in Charleston next winter and let me know by doing so you will confur a faviour on me.

William Allston to Robert F. W. Allston

P Dee, 19th June, 1838.

MY DEAR COUSIN, Since your absence from here, I have been compelled tho' very reluctantly to separate from and to discharge Mr. Gotea[2] from my services and that too in consequence of his continued irregularities. I lament the Circumstance very much and would not have done so if I could possibly have avoided it. And I now find it impossible for me to continue here for the Summer without jeopardizing my life. In vain do I look around me for friends to assist and advise me. The more I think of my Situation here

[1] Isaac Singleton, assistant overseer or miller at Waverly plantation.

[2] George C. Gotea, former overseer at Waverly.

after an absence of 12 or 14 years the more it harrasses me and at times I feel as if I should become deranged. My health is declining, my System waisting, without appetite and Sleep and I know ere long I must terminate my career, unless I can get to the Mountains in time to escape Disease.

Situated therefore as I now am, my only alternative My Dear Friend, is to make my appeal to you. If you were at home I am conscious you would most readily and at once accord to my petition, to permit Your Manager Mr Ellis to superintend my place until my return. He passes by twice a week, is in excellent health, Is an excellent Manager and all his concerns are prosperous and flourishing. It is to me My Dear Robert the greatest favour you can possibly confer upon me. It will enable me to escape to the Upper Country before I fall a Victim here. And I hope and trust it can not prove injurious to you, as Mr. E. now goes by twice a week. I hinted to him and stated my situation to him but he declines doing so without your appro-bation and I therefore write to you upon the Subject. You know My Dear Robert and all my other friends are of the same opinion and the older I get the more sensibly I feel it myself, that to remain here a Summer will be Suicide. And as I shall be compelled to remain unless I can get a responsible Agent I hope and trust our Ties of Kindred and our former Friendship will plead my Cause and enable you to grant My Request. Mr. Ellis declines writing to you lest you might Suppose Emolument was his object, and if he did obtain your permission his only object is to prevent the sacrifice of my life. I feel very much indebted to him for his Intentions and hope My Dearest Friend I shall hear from you favourably and by the Mail if this should find you in Charleston, or wherever it may find you. I hope My Cousin Self and family are all well.

Gabriel L. Ellis to Robert F. W. Allston[1]

Matanza, June 20, 1838.

DEAR SIR   I Received your leter of the 10 Inst. on 16 Inst. your horse is geting beter   I went to town to see Mr Kidd on Monday. he is to meet me to day at 11 o clock at the Mill to comence the work. I have sent Thomas & Jorn over to the Mill as you directed me to do. I saw Mr. Waterman and priced his corn. he will take one dollar per bushel in town if taken in 10 Days and he will Deliver it at the Plantation at one dollar and 6 1/4 cts. Mr. Olivers corn is growing short he says that he will want all the corn that we have borrowed from them for the 2 last years. that is 161 bushels. Mr. Waterman thinks that in a months time that he could not furnish the corn for less than $1.25 cts per bushel which will be about the time I shall want it. Mr. Oliver says that he wont want his before that time   do write me what I shall do about the corn arangement. your Rice that was in Mill is shipt 53 1/2 Bbls. the People is all well at both places. the crops looks tolerable well

---

[1] Addressed: New York, N.Y.

the Litle Island is verry prity now and would make a fine crop if it was not for the Volentier but there is more of it on that land than I have Ever seen on any other land the big Island has improved a good deal it has thickend up and looks as if it was a tolerable stand of Rice the Potatoes at Waverly is as fine as I ever saw at this time of the year. the corn dont look so well over there. the crop at Matanza is a fair one all to gether. Myersfield and the old field next the crick is as prity as I ever saw. the other old field is not so good the stand is not good in the first place and then the wier grass & Rushes make it look bad I send Mrs. Shackeford 10 Bushels of Rough Rice to day I have to send Ceaser with the mules and waggon to carry it. do let me know if you want the Mares at Waverly put to any Horse or not and if to any to what one. the bay Mare has a fine horse colt it is about 4 weeks old. Delier has a child at Waverly and Venes has one here.

Gabriel L. Ellis to Robert F. W. Allston[1]

Matanza, July 6, 1838.

DEAR SIR   the People is all well at both places Except a few cases of Diarrhoea not dangerous the children is verry healthy. the crop at home is I think the best we have ever had altoghether at Waverly it is tolerable the Litle Island is good the other is not as good as I could wish the upland crop is fair at both places except the oats which is sorry. Hines went with 2 of your sheep to Dr. P. last Monday came back yeasterday and fetcht 2 others a yew and Ram lam which is a verry fine lam in deed. I Received a leter from Mssrs L[ewis] & R[obertson] the other day by the Vesel directed to you which I thought was about Plantation business which I opend it contained a Receivep from Paul & Brown for somthing over the Rice of $300 which I have put up safe and will keep it until you Return unless instructed otherways by you. the windows of the Chappel I have neglected to measure and it is now after 9 o clock P.M. I will give you the dementions in my next. we had a fine diner on the 4 Inst at the Muster field a plenty of Brandy & Champaign which gave some trouble it made Dr. Sparkman and S. C. Ford Esqr. fall out with Colo. Carr for some language which Mr. F used to the Colo. he struck Mr. F for which had like to have given a good deal of trouble to hush up. I am not sure thet they are done with it yet. no Oration. I hear of no other Candadates for the House of Representatives than the following Col. Belin & Col Carr and J. Z. Midelton Esqr. and none for the Sinate but yourself. I understand that Mr. Dozier says that there shall be no other for the Sinate. I have had to send all of your Rice to Mill to keep her from stoping I have shiped 21 Bbls to day the balance will be done about the midle of next week. we have pounded and shiped all of the Est[ate] Rice 132 Bbls went in the Wacamaw to day. the Mill

[1] Addressed: New York, N.Y.

done 156 Bbls in June. Mr. Frasier has aplyed to me to day to pound his Rice which I have wrote to him I would do Dr. Magill nor Dr. Allston has not sent any Rice to Mill since you left here. the Neighbours is all well except William E Sparkman who the Dr. says is quite sick Capt Allston told me that he was agoing to write to you some days ago. him and his family is well my family and self is well. I am glad to here you all arived safe in New York and are all well.

Gabriel L. Ellis to Robert F. W. Allston[1]

Matanza, Agst. 4, 1838.

DEAR SIR I have Received your leter of the 30 of June. Mssrs Lewis & Robertson has sent me 311 bushels of corn which I Received the 2 Inst. I have Returned Mr. Oliver 161 which is all that you was dew the Est[at]e of Dr. P. Weston the provisions at the Este has given out and I have wrote to Mr. R Thurston for 50 bushels of corn for Waverly. Mr. Ivey has not fecht the Raft of Cooper Stuff yet. I have had to send the flat to town 2 times for Bbls to keep the Mill from stoping. the Schn. Wacamaw is atending the Mill and there is no white man in her when she comes up to the Mill Capt Tobey stays at the Island Mr. Thurston has wrote to me to ship by her although I wrote to him that Capt T did not come up in the vesel and no one to give a receipt for the Rice put on board. he wrote to me that you told him to write me that you had Rather the Mill stop than for me to ship any Rice by any other vesel than the one he suggested Mr. H. Frasier has sent 2461 bushels of Rice to the Mill and he is vext because I told him that the Mill arangements was that the vesel that atended the Mill was to carry all the Rice that she pounded he sent no Bbls. there is 70 Bbls of his Rice done. Mrs. Blythes Rice 2900 bushels has jest come to the Mill Dr. Magill & Dr. Allston has sent no Rice to Mill yet. Dr. Allstons will be Ready by the time Mrs. Blythes is done. the tides has ben Verry low the Mill has done only 125 Bbls in July and keep Very low yet so low I can not get water Enough for the Rice the Rice crop at Waverly is jest tolerable good about 50 or 55 bushel Rice if no axident the provision crop was Verry promising some time ago but the dry weather has hurt it much we have not had a good Rain since the last of June until yeasterday and to day. we had a small Rain on last Monday week on which I planted slips but they all died or nearly so I have planted them over to day. at Matanza I planted 7 acres of slips in June which is likely the balance is a bad chance the corn has a fine groth but I think it will be a poore turn out for the July dry weather the Rice crop at Matanza is a good one beter than has ever been since I have ben here Myers field is the best Rice I ever saw by far I think. the two old fields on the canel is fine Rice but not so good as Myers field. the new ground is good. the balence is as good as common the Negros keeps

---

[1] Addressed: New York, N.Y.

Verry healthy no sickness of much importence Sammy has spraind his Right wrist which seems hard to get well I have got Dr. Sparkman atending it and Hagers child I think that Hagers child will not be Raiesed it is broke out all over with ulcers. I dont know what is the mater with it nor the Dr. is not sirten what is the mater with it the Negros at Waverly keeps tolerable healthy also old Celler is dead she was no better as I could see when she com from Charleston than when she went down they sent some Medicine with her to take before she took all of it Mrs. Allston[1] sent and caried her over to the sea shore where she died the Neighbours is all well at this time young A Ford is dead I have not ben able to seell any of your horses nor your sulkey. the Chappel windowes is 6 feet 7 inches Long 2 feet 11 Inches wide.

Gabriel L. Ellis to Robert F. W. Allston[2]

Matanza, Sept 16, 1838.

DEAR SIR   I Received your leter the 1 Inst and would have writen to you sooner but on acount of sickness I had the fever for 10 days but have got up again Mrs Ellis is now verry sick the Dr atending her and has ben for the last week. Mr Millican[3] has had a sever atact of Bilious fever he is a litle beter but the Dr has salavated him our child is quite unwell has fever every 2 or 3 days it is teething. the People keeps healthy all but the children several of them is sick Nanys Ben is I think so low that there is litle or no hope of its recovery Betys William is quite sick also though I think there is some hope of its geting well with good nursing. the carpenters is done the Piaza at the south End of your house and has weatherboarded a part of the old & put in blinds in the other part they are done the thrashing Mill all but some litle fixing about the Rakes & Bands they are done the flats they are done the front Piaza of the house in town but nothing Else Thomas says that he will comence Shingleing your house to morrow I have had to furnish them with 10 thousand Shingles he says when he is done your house he will be Ready to comence the Sick house and he dont know where you want it put. I would rather have it if it suits your aprobation near my house on the path that goes from my house to Thomases on that oak Ridge please let me know in your next leter where it must be put. I comenced cuting Rice on the 13 Inst and fetch home yeasterday the Rice crop is a Verry good one if I have good weather to get it in the yard the weather is now fine the Provision crop is sorry it is so through out the neighbour-hood. the Peas looks promising if there is no wind from this time they will turn out tolerable. Waverly. the Mill in Agst Pounded 151 Bbls the People there keeps healthy all but Lidia who I think is playing Posom Mrs Allston

---

[1] Mary Allan Allston, the mistress of Waverly.

[2] Addressed: New York, N.Y.

[3] William B. Millican, another overseer.

has taken her to the sea shore the mill will have as much old Rice to Pound as she can do until November if Dr Magill sends all of his Rice to her he writs me that he has 4000 Bushels & Dr Allston has 2000 besides 1700 Bushels that is in Mill now comenced on it the 13 Inst. I would like to know if I get out 2000 Bushels of your Rice before the Mill is Ready to pound it if I had not beter get a vesel and send it down in the Rough while Rice is seling well. the Rice Crop at Waverly is about a fair one Neither Verry good or Sorry. the Birds is Verry bad there now but the Rice is amost too forward to do it a great deal of damage. the Litle Island would make a verry fine crop if it was not for the Volentier in it it looks like it was one third Volentier the Provision Crop here is a litle beter than at Matanza in acordence with the strength of the land I comenced cutting Rice here on yeasterday. things goes on very badly here Mrs Allston has divested me of so much of my authority and the Negroes is aware of it that I can not Manage them as they aught to be if one Runs away and goes to her she will not sufer me to punish it at tall breaks of out of the Stocks & Barn she sends it back with a virbel mesage by the same Negro to Mr Singleton for him to put it back in the stocks if he dares which is the case with Water who Run away for nothing not Even a cross word from Mr Singleton nor the Driver which I will Explain more fuly when I see you there is 70 head of young Turkeys at Mantanza Amy got the calico sent her by her Mistress one quilt done and another a most done. do fech me a pair of good Razors when you come and you will oblige Your Sincere Friend and your obt servt

[P.S.] when I here of your Calfs & Pigs has got to town I will send for them & have good care taken of them

[P.S.] I could not get a turnip seed only some old ones at Congdons which I have had planted they have not come up yet Colo. Hamlee has not sent the seed Rye and there is none to be had in the neighbourhood the dry weather blasted all in this section I have writen to Lewis & Robertson to send up 10 Bushels by the first opertunity I look for the Vesel the first wind she has been gone 4 weeks and it is time for her to be back.

J. A. Allston to Robert F. W. Allston

17th Nov, 1838.

DEAR COUSIN,   Mr. Hemingway[1] tells me that he is in treaty for the management of your plantation next year and is Desireous to have charge of Dr. Allstons also, a previlege He says that you offered to Mr. Ellis. I can with propriety and in Justice to Mr. H say that he can from his undivided attention to business do as much (*at least*) as Mr. Ellis or any other person, in his line, that I know of.

---

[1] Probably J. A. Hemingway, who entered Allston's service at the beginning of the following year.

Business yesterday and bad Weather today prevents my spending some hours with you, more time, more time has been my want through Life and does not diminish as my gray hairs increase.

Return of Property on Matanzas Plantation, January 1, 1839,
by Gabriel L. Ellis

	Bushels
the Sheave Rice of Nos. 3, 4, 5, 6, & 7.	3745
the Sheave Rice from one of the Stacks of Nos. 9, 10, & 11	214
Sprouted Rice in South End of the Barn	105
the Seed Rice in the loft of the Barn	97
the Dirty Rice in the North End of the Barn	350
Corn in the old Barn about	100
Peas in loft of New Barn about	150
Oats in Do	100

7 pits of seed slips 2 Do Eating ones
3 Mules & Waggon 2 ox carts 1 horse Do
6 yoke oxen 4 yokes 2 ox chains 4 ox Ploughs
2 horse Ploughs & 2 pair truss chains
6 Sets horsegear for the thrashing Mill
About 5 Bushels Salt about 15 or 20 gallons Molases
part of a gug of whiskey about 10 Bushels of Walnuts
About 3 fifths of a large Hogshead of hand Tobaco
4 Rice Flats 3 in good order 1 worth but litle
4 boats 2 good padling boats one not worth much
one old 4 oard Rowing boat
foder in the loft of old Barn Hay in the Shed of Do
58 head of cattle including the 12 oxen & one durham Bull 2 Burkshier pigs at the Barnyard 3 Shoats at the Negro Houses in charge of old Pompy — head of Stock hogs at the Farm, 18 head of fatning hogs at the Barnyard 39 Round Stacks not thrashed,
1 paper of opium 1/4 Vial James powders 1 Vial Soda 1 paper of assafiotida 1 Vial Tartar Emetic 1/2 Vial Calomel 1 Small paper of Campor 1 Small paper Pink Root 1 paper of Magnetia 1 Bottle of Wix Mustard 2 Snuff Botles Cream Tartar 2 Do Rhubarb 2 Do Jalap 2 1/2 Botles Spirits Turpentine 1 Botle of Swains Panicia 1 Box Scals & weights 1 Set Tooth drawers 1 thum Lancet 1 themometer Barometer 2 thirds of a good Large Box Glauber Salts 11,300 Shingles in the old Barnyard 2 Bbls Tarr 36 5 Inch hoes with handles about 50 lbs oakum 2 Rice seives 2 1/2 gallons Mill oil in gug 3 Emty Dimajohns 2 gugs Do 4 Bushels Midling Rice 5 Do Small grain 2 Do Small Rice Verry Derty 1 Keg Large Nails 30 lbs Shingling Nails in a basket 1 flat Bar Iron 2 feet long 1 Squar Do 8 feet long 1 Rice Hook 1 grubing Hoe 12 Trenching Hoes 7 Spades 2 axes 1 Brand

R.F.W.A. at Waverly Mill 1 Patent Hoister for hauling timber 28 Baskets 14 lbs of Mill [illegible] Wier Steel 1 Tin quart 2 Bushel tubs one 1/2 Bushel Do 1 Peck Do 1 wooden quart.

the following Named Negroes has not ben Sick during the year 1838 1. Y. Buie, 2. H Peter, 3. Dennis, 4. Joe, 5. Jack, 6. John Blk, 7. Abram, 8. Sally, 9. Y Pompy, 10. Trim, 11. Edy, 12. Rose, 13. Thomas, 14. Stephen.

January 1, 1839

Lie[u]t Thos Petigru dew 30 bushels of corn for borrowed corn and Potatoes. the Est[at]e of Dr P Weston 10 bushels of Rice flour borrowed not Entered in the Plantation Book.

Robert F. W. Allston's Reply to Charges of Unfair Treatment of Overseer William T. Thompson, 1842[1]

A CARD

"Nothing extenuate, nor set down ought in malice."

The following narrative is given unwillingly—It is forced from me, however, by the ill-advised efforts of evil disposed persons to distort the facts of the transaction therein refered to, and thus to use them for the sole purpose of injuring me in the estimation of my fellow-citizens.

After leaving the employment of Capt. Vaux somewhere about 1822 or '23, I believe, the late Wm. T. Thompson was employed by Mr. Benjamin Allston, or Major Keith as overseer to the plantation of the late Mrs. Blyth, at which place he remained in the same capacity till the day of his death in the year 1838.

When he came to live at this place, as I am informed, Mr. Thompson possessed nothing more than his house-hold furniture, personal apparel and perhaps a horse. I mention this not to his discredit, God forbid! but as a fact necessary to the understanding of the matter in hand. The plantation was then tolerably well stocked with cattle, sheep and hogs. In the course of several years this stock began gradually to diminish, and a new stock to show itself on the plantation with the ear mark of W. T. Thompson. This latter stock increased steadily and throve well, until at length it came to be a rare thing for the plantation stock to furnish either a beef for Christmas, or a yoke of steers for breaking; and it came to be rather a common thing for Mr. Thompson to furnish both the one and the other *for a consideration*, from his own stock.

[1] A broadside on the back of which is penciled the following explanation: "In 1842 when opposed late in the summer and violently by the late Col. Peter W. Fraser. Two of his warmest advocates were B. A. Wilson, a relation or connection of Mr. Thompson & Saml Kirton—Both now my friends. After being printed the card was suppressed at the intercession of E. Waterman, Ordinary, who undertook to put a stop to the scheme of misrepresentation and upon that condition being fulfil'd, I consented that the card should not be issued."

For many years previous to his death, Mr. T. raised his own bacon on the plantation, having none to buy—whereas not a year brought its winter round, that Mrs. Blyth, the owner of the plantation, had not to buy hogs for bacon, and often from Mr. Thompson himself—and I have no knowledge of her using in the space of time refered to, as many as twelve bacon hogs annually.

Yet there were always cattle enough belonging to the plantation to require the services of a negro man exclusively to mind and herd them, together with Mr. Thompson's. So too, there were always hogs enough left to Mrs. Blyth to require the exclusive labor of another negro man to herd and to feed them together with Mr. Thompson's, and to require feed from the barn. During the greater part of this time, Mr. Thompson was with his family, alone on the plantation, of which he had, after the death of Maj. Keith, Exor. of Dr. Blyth's estate, entire control; Mr. Benjamin Allston only going over once or twice, when some pressing difficulty in enforcing or regulating discipline rendered it necessary as the friend of Mrs. Blyth.

I never presumed to give an order, nor had I any thing to do with the management of the place, (although I passed and repassed through the plantation to and from Georgetown occasionally during summer) until the death of Mr. Thompson, when as the friend of the proprietor, and at her desire, I looked into the arrangements on the place, and attended the appraisement and sale of Mr. Thompson's effects there found.

I discovered that the greater number of Cattle, far the greater number of Hogs, and all the Sheep were regarded as belonging to Mr. Thompson, and were in his mark. On meeting with Mr. Atkinson, the Executor, I mentioned to him some of the facts recited above and suggested the propriety of leaving an adequate stock of each kind on the plantation. This was acquiesced in, and the overseers of the two adjoining places Mr. Capps and Mr. Thomas, I think, were chosen by Mr. Atkinson himself, to make an equitable division of the whole stock, that is Mrs. Blyth's and Mr. Thompson's put together— the result of which was that 20 odd head of cattle were turned out for the proprietor, *four* of which, I know, she had paid Mr. Thompson *forty dollars* for, the year before; as many more, I believe 25 or 30, were appraised and sold as Mr. Thompson's property, and for the benefit of his estate. Out of the number reserved for Mrs. Blyth I requested Mrs. Thompson the widow (who was not interested in the proceeds of the sale) to select two cows and calves for herself, and accept them, which she did.—Forty odd head of hogs, of all sizes, were left on the plantation, *fifty* head of hogs or thereabout were appraised as Mr. Thompson's property and sold for the benefit of his estate. Seventeen head of sheep (ewes and lambs) were left on the place I think; *eighteen* head of sheep were appraised as the property of Mr. Thompson and sold for the benefit of his heirs. I write from memory, having no documents by me—any inacuracy as to numbers may be corrected by reference to the Ordinary's Office where both the appraisement and account sales are doubtless of record. This co[urs]e was suggested to my mind by a regard as well to the univers[al] principles of justice, as to those of policy which should govern the [r]elation of proprietor and manager in a domestic view. It is the i[nter]est of every proprietor that the manager of his property shoul[d live] well, and be comfortable; that he should thrive, and add to [his wor]ldly estate, but not at the expense, and to the detriment [of his] employer in any manner, or in any degree.—If the manage[r (MS torn) thr]ive, provided he be allowed to keep a stock, his emplo[yer (MS torn) sh]ould thrive by the same care, and if the proprietor's in[terest (MS torn)] attended to, and his affairs flourish, the affairs of his [MS torn] improve also and his interests be promoted by the [MS torn] influence of the employer's prosperity. Their interests [MS torn], justly considered: and can, in no honest, or common [MS torn], be regarded as antagonistic.—Besides, on consulting the [agreem]ent made by Mr. Thompson on becoming overseer of that plan[tatio]n I found among other things, that he was to keep *two cows and calves and no more.*[1] Mr. Thompson's salary for the last year was *nine hundred dollars*, every dollar of which was paid to his Executor, besides a small bill of sundries. His heirs ought rather to be grateful that this course was adopted, for if the case had been carried into court, I do not believe that one half of the wages would have been awarded to them.

It is not voluntarily that I have recured to this matter—far from it. I would that the dead should rest in peace. I would not be the one to disturb his memory.

But it has been spoken of freely of late by persons whose interest it is to create among the people an unfavorable impression against me before the October election, and has been busily bruited in various quarters, for either malicious or political purposes; connected, doubtless, with misrepresentation. It is therefore incumbent on me, however disagreable, to present a plain statement of the facts in this connexion.

Having done so, I now submit to the sober judgment of the people, appealing to candid and unprejudiced minds to decide, whether the course which I pursued in the premises, was not due to the relation of friend and agent, in which I stood towards the proprietor, herself unable to look after her affairs—due alike to the general practice and the general policy of the district—and due to a considerate regard for the reputation of the deceased: not forgetting his previous services.

R. F. W. Allston

[1] See above, p. 246.

William Faulk to Robert F. W. Allston

Nightingale Hall, May 21, 1854.[1]

Sunday 21th   Corn Meal & Tobacow

Monday 22th   Hoad the potatoes   Sent 20 hands up to Chicora Wood 1 Lamb Kild by James   Reseav [i.e., received] 1 quart[er] of Beef 71 lbs   Head & Pluck[2]   Sent to the Beech 9 Bushel of Oats 2 Bushels of corn Meal

Tuesday 23th   20 hands up at Chicora Wood   the hands have hoad rice in Crickfield

Wednesday 24th 20 hands up at Chicora Wood   the hands have hoing Rice in Crickfield & line field   Reseav 1 quart[er] of Beef (68 lbs)   Head & Pluck   flood East Waterford

Thursday 25th   Finish hoing line field 12 acor & the rest of the hands hoing in Newground Middel

Friday 26th   Finish hoeing New ground Middel & Head   4 hand in 40 acor head   flood Crickfield Line field & 12 acor   Reseav 2 Barrels of Fish by Hardtimes   Giv Sutherlin his Cloth & fo[r] the Children

Saturday 27th   Hoad Rice in 40 acor head & Middel   Reseav 138 lbs of Beef from Chicora Wood   Sent Frank to Georgeton withe the letters   Sickness   Zelph is Complaining of head ache L. Andrew feve & Headache but he is out to Work   Presillar Complains of Paing in her Side   Minde Complains of Paing in he Chest   Diannah has a Sweld face cosed by a gumbile [i.e., gum boil]   Flood Newground head & Middel on Saturday Night

[P. S.]   Frank has got a Pig to Rais

J. A. Hemingway to Robert F. W. Allston

Chiney grove, May 7, 1855.

DEAR SIR   If I was to sell those Negroes to you   what time wood you want them the most   I have my crop planted and I cold not spar them tel after Ï harvis my crop   I cold Let you have them In novemb or at January Just as you see fit   I wood Let you have them for 10 thousa[nd] Dollars from on[e] to ten years Credit paying Inters Anuly   I wood Not take no amount for them but as I tole you my helth Is such that I am not abel to atend to bisness and I will sell out as soon as I can and move of   I have not seen A well day sinse I see you, I hate to parte with the negroes as thare is all yong and prim and sote me very well but oing to my helth I wood dispos of them

---

[1] It should be noted that the overseers sometimes dated their reports the first day and at other times the last day of the period covered.

[2] The heart, liver, and lights of the beef.

I must ask you one favor Mr John E. Vereen [w]ho Is Living With me at this time oing to his helth Last year he cold not take bisness but have got harthy agen and wishes to take bisness for the next year   will you be so good as to asist him in gettin Bisness by so doing you will Much oblige me, hope you have got thru planting and have a find stand.

Harman Pitman to Robert F. W. Allston

Nightingale Hall, Dec. 1st, [18]57.

DEAR SIR Excuse my troubleing you I have today an offer of 1200 Dolls for my services next year. will you be so kind as to let me go unless you can see wherein it will be to my interest to remain the place can pay over 2000 Dollars & all energetic men who have lived there (from all I learn) have retired when they left which induces me to believe it is an agreeable situation. Money induces me to beg this favour of you, yet will not think hard or become the least indifferent to my duty if you refuse being bound. Should you consent to let me off & wish will endeavor to get a suitable man for you. please let me hear from you at your earliest convenience & you will much oblige. . . . .

H. A. Middleton[1] to Robert F. W. Allston

Georgetown April 15 1858

DEAR SIR,   Mr Pitman (now I believe in your employment) has refered me to you for a character. Will you do me the favor to inform me of those qualities which he possesses, which may be in favor or against him. What his merit as a planter, as a manager generally, as an attendant upon the sick, his temperance, in short everything you shall think valuable in an overseer. Also, (if you have no objection) what wages you have allowed him.

The planters are so mutually interested in the character of men, as overseers, that I ask this information without scruple.

Robert F. W. Allston to H. A. Middleton[2]

Executive Dept. Charleston 16th April 1858

DEAR SIR Your note of enquiry concerning Mr. Pitman is received on the eve of my departure for a military tour. And I proceed at once to respond to the questions you propound, So far as they may be answer'd affirmatively, or in his favor.

I have found him a man of even temper, firm and careful of the sick. He is civil and temperate as to ardent spirits. He is a man of character, and has had experience enough to make him a good planter. But I have not been enough at home to test by observation and experiment, his real ability as a

---

[1] Henry Augustus Middleton (1793–1887), of Weehaw plantation.

[2] Copy written on the back of the preceding inquiry.

planter, since his coming to me. I am not satisfied with my crop last year, but I dont know that any one is.

I gave Mr Pitman $1,000 pr An. My Son has the general conduct of Nightingale Hall and Waterford conjoin'd this year and he will receive the same wages from my Son. I deem him a good agent and Should be sorry to part with him.

Report for Chicora Wood Plantation, July 18–24, 1858[1]

Sunday the 18 July	gave Allowance of grits & Peas & Pork 100 lbs & Punished Jacob B[illegible] 39 strips
Mounday the 19 July	All Hands Working rice No 4 & 5 & 2 Chicora Sam Shelling Corn Guy & Anthony in Shop 3 Carpenters went to Waverly to Work Clarasa Went to Work this Day
Teusday the 20 "	Part of hands in no 6 the rest in no 7 Flat Went to Waverly For Col Allston things the mill grinding 2 Weeks Allowance Punished Jackson With 25 Strips
Wenesday the 21	the People Hoeing rice Rabit island & Myars Field 4 Boys Hoeing Bank Flat Came from Waverly Mosses & 2 Boys came with Wood & unloding of it Gentlemen Walked Around the rice Guy Comensed to Pull Down the Brick Woork
thursday the 22	All Hands Hoeing rice Chicora Myars Field And no 12 & no 13 mosses & 2 Boys Cleaning up Engine yard Elsy Miscaried Guy & Anthony in Engineroom Sam mooving tailling
Friday 23	6 Hands in 5 Acre at Landing · the other Hands in by Parts of no 11 & no 14 & no 9 & no 8 Mosses & 2 Boys Cording Wood Sam mooving tailing
Saturday 24	gave Holerday
	Sick Peter [illegible] 3, Susan 1, Sucky 5, Janr 4, F Maria 2, Lidia 1, Amy W 2, Mary 2.

Report for Chicora Wood Plantation, July 25–31, 1858[2]

Sunday the 25	Had Service Mr Evans Preached in morning in the Evnig gave Allowance grits & Peas & Pork 100 lbs
Mounday the 26	rose Confined Boy Hands Hoeing rice in Ditchford 6 & 5 & 4 Guy & 3 Boys taking Down the Brick Woork Carpenters geting out Flat Stuff Sam Picking Potatoes

---

[1] Probably prepared by Franklin Alfred Collins, who was serving this year as "suboverseer" at Chicora Wood.

[2] In the same handwriting as the preceding report.

Teusday the 27   the Hands Hoeing no 3 & 4 & Exchange old Fields Mr Pitman Cam up & Went round With me Sam Picking Potatoes Flowed 4 & 5 & 6 Lay by Flow

Wenesday the 28 All Hands Hoeing Ditchford no 1 & 2 & the Exchange old Fields 3 Plows Comensed Plowing Slips Sam Picking Potatoes

thursday th 29   Hands Picking grass [in] need for any No. 10 3 Plows Plowing Slips Sam Picking Potatoes I Punished A stranger on the Place 19 Strip

Friday 30 July   All Hands Picking grass in need for any in no 8 & no 9 & no 11 & Low Places Sam Picking Potatoes 2 men Comensd turning Land Carpenters Bin All Week Flat Stuff

Saturday the 31 All Hands Halling up Slips Carpenters geting Flat Stuff Guy Working in Shop
Sick Lidiar 6, Mary 6, York Mary 2, George Emer 3, B Elizabeth 3, Sucky B 6, Jacob B 2.

Harman Pitman to Robert F. W. Allston

Nightingale Hall, May 6, 1860.

DEAR SIR

S 6.[1]   All Grist Peas rice & Pork. Mr Hunter[2] here

M 7.   Trenched L. M. & thined & moulded corn.

T 8.   Planted L. M. & . . . . .

W 9.   Sent 15 men to Chicora. thinned & moulded corn & cleaned wells.

T 10.   Thined & moulded corn.

F 11.   Finished hoeing corn & hoed potatoes. Ground & cracked cobs.

S 12.   Give people [holiday]
Frank sheered sheep this week.
Sick Waley 2 days, Juddy 1, C. Thomas 1, Salina 1.
Flogged for howing corn bad Fanny 12 lashes, Sylvia 12, Monday 12, N Phoebee 12, Susanna 12, Salina 12, Celia 12, Iris 12.

Obituary of Overseer Thomas Briton Hamlin, 1860[3]

Departed this life on the 9th May, 1860 at the residence of his son-in-law, B. Marion Grier Esqre. Thomas Briton Hamlin in the seventy second year of his age.

[1] Sunday, May 6.

[2] Probably Joseph Hunter, rector of Prince Frederick's Parish, 1848–62.

[3] Accompanying this sketch, which is in the handwriting of R. F. W. Allston, is a note to the following effect: "Gov. Allston knowing him as well or better than many others we request that he will announce his death in the *Christian Advocate* and *Pee Dee Times* and oblige B. M. Grier and others."

Born on the 15th October, 1788 and exhibiting early in life a passionate fondness for hunting he lived a life of hardy exposure. For many years he devoted himself faithfully to the duties of an Overseer. But latterly he settled with his promising and thriving family in the pine lands of Georgetown District where, without anyone to say him nay, when disposed to roost a Turkey or trail the deer, he pass'd the remainder of his days, an honest independent and dutiful eitizen, a faithful friend and good neighbor. There, he gave all his children away in marriage and saw them settled. Then gradually relinquishing his habits of successful wood-craft (He loved the native forests in which he was wont to roam in pursuit of game, and he loved too their almighty creator) his constitution yielded to the effects of incessant toil and exposure, from early dawn till night, and with a consciousness of the end awaiting him, he breath'd his last calmly, under the watchful care, and in the arms of his children, at peace with the world, and I trust with his God.

The writer knew him well. Possessing all the sagacious and generous qualities of the Forrester, there was no citizen-soldier more earnest, and efficient when on duty patiently enduring, perseveringly active, and intently watchful than he.

Harman Pitman to Robert F. W. Allston

N[ightingale] H[all], May 15th, 1860

DEAR SIR   Yours respecting the beef & C recd & I send you 2 B. grist 2 B. potatoes 1 B. peas Mr Lawtons Buck & one mutton 2 quarters beef one tongue 1 can strawberries 6 pigeons 12 chickens 5 cooters 9 Doz. & 5 Eggs

None of the people much sick Mr Weston was not willing for the building to be joind to the summer house. With beef have done as directed. the chickens verry small but the best I could get could not get the fowls to send. will try to get more chickens by nex week or soon after hoping all may arrive safe & in good order. . . . .

Overseer's Order for Medical Supplies, 1861

Chicora Wood, 27 Jany, 1861.

Medisens

1 Dozen Bottles Sarsaparilla   10[1]
2 Bottles No Six   75
2 Bottles Paregoric   75
1 Bottle Sweet Spirits Niter   50
2 lbs Rhubarb $3

[1] Prices added by another hand.

2 lbs Hippo $3
6 lbs Epson Salts   8 cents
4 2 oz. Packages German Wormifuge   25
2 Ounces of Laudnum   20¢.
1 lb Magnesia   50
1 Ounce of Callomel   12 1/2
4 lbs Casteel Soap   20¢.
1 lb Allum   10¢.   ⎧ 2 ounces of
1 lb Borax   37 1/2   ⎨ Camphorated   18 3/4
4 lbs Soda   25   ⎩ Dovers Powders
4 Ounces Douvers Powders   18 3/4
6 Gallons of Castor Oil   1.60
1 Bottle Sweet Oil   50
10 Gallons Coal tar
1 roll Blister Plaster   75

JESSE BELFLOWERS

Overseer's Order for Tools, etc., 1861

Chicora Wood, 27 Jany, 1861.

A Bill of Tools for Carpenters

5 Broad Axes	@	$3[1]	2 Smoothing Plains	1.00
3 hand Saws	@	$2	1 Box axes	14.
3 Squares	@	.50	6 Boxes Soap	
2 four Plains	@	1.50	1 Dozen Scrap Spades	$12
2 Jack Plains	@	1.25	1 Dozen Corn hoes	6.00
3 f[l]at Adze		2.50	1 Dozen 7 Inch hoes	7
2 1 1/2 Inch Chisels		.75	1 Dozen 5 Inch hoes	5
2 1 Inch Chisels		.62 1/2	1 Dozen 4 Inch hoes	
2 hatchets		.87 1/2	A Suply of Molasses	
3 Jack plains Irons		.75	200 lbs Tobacco	
2 1 1/2 Inch Augers		1.50		

JESSE BELFLOWERS

Harman Pitman to Robert F. W. Allston

Nightingale Hall, Apr. 25th, [18]61.

DEAR SIR   I send you a sample of the rice which the enclosed certificate[2] mentions. The land on which it was grown rested from rice in 1859 but grew a crop of oats and peas. Was plowd last week in January 1860. Rice planted

---

[1] Prices added by another hand.

[2] Missing.

18th April, howd 22nd May, 1st June and flowd 9th June the water continued to harvest except changd grass pickd 5th July, cut 17th Sept. and rain prevented taking in the Rice untill the 21st.[1]

Jesse Belflowers to Robert F. W. Allston

Chicora Wood, 8 Sept, 1861.

Sunday 8   Rain Gave Allowance of Rough Rice
Monday 9   Cut 3, 4 & Part of 5. Lifted Nos 1, 2, 6 & Pict Grass Patty P.
               d Confind boy
Tuesday 10   Cut 7 & the Balance of 5 brough in 1, 2 & 6
Wednesday 11   Cut 9, 11 & 14 brough in 3, 4 & Part of 5 Clarisa Confind
               boy Recd 4 Boxes Shoes from Lynch & Co
Thursday 12   Cut 8 & Some in 10 Brough in 7 & the Rest of 5
Friday 13   Rain Pict Grass then Lifted the Rice on the Stubel Tyed &
               Stackd 9, 11, 14 30 bushel flour [Recd] 7 Bails cloth 1 Box
               1 do Seed
Saturday 14   Cut 10 and brough in 8 the Carpenters at Sundray Work
               all week
               Sick Paul 4, Sicpio 6, Anson 2, Jackson 4, H Mary 2,
               Sony 2, Isobil 4, Caty 2, N. Suckey 6.

Harman Pitman to Robert F. W. Allston

Nightingale Hall, Sep. 8th, [18]61.

DEAR SIR

S.   8[2] Al. grist Potatoes & beef.
M.   9   Cut & Stackd rice E[ast] W[aterford]
T. 10   " W. W. & taken in rice E. W.
W. 11   "   "   "   "   "   "   "   "   "
T. 12   "   "   "   "   "   "   "   "   " & W.W.
F. 13   Taken in rice E. & W.W.
S. 14   "   "   " W. W.
         recd turnip seed. also 1 paper Carrot. Sent 5 barrels rice to Capt.
         Hening for the relief Association. Carpts. at flats. 3 hands at the fort.
         Sick Iris 3 days, W. Patty 2, Andrew 1, Marie 4, Judy 3, Carliner 1,
         Phillis 1.

[P. S.] All Waterford rice on the yard.

---

[1] Added in Allston's handwriting is the following note: "Prize Rice: This measured by E. Foxworth = 80 1/16 bushels pr acre, 15 acres: Another measured by H. A. Bruerton made 75 bushels pr acre, 12 acres."

[2] Sunday, September 8.

Harman Pitman to Robert F. W. Allston

Nightingale Hall, Sep. 15th, [18]61.

DEAR SIR

S 15[1] Al grist potaters & beef
M 16   Cut rice Pint field & pl. turnips 40 A. Head
T 17   turnips 19 A. & pl. turnips high land
W 18   Cut rice L. f. & taken in P. f.
T 19   "   "   "   "   "   " 19 A.
F 20   "   "   "   "   "   " L. f.
S 21   "   "   Cap field H "   "   "

Carp[en]t[er]s at flats Recd from W[aterford] Stock 1 beef of Mrs Izards 25 pounds oakum loaned last year. Sold Mr N. P. Belin 12 B. rice

Sick M. Murrier 6 days, Peter 6, Lenna 2, Lena 1, Zilpha 1, Silvy 1, B. Nancy 2, Iris 2, O Diana 2, Beck, Charles 1, S. Patty 2

P. S.   This place is calld on for 3 more hands to work on the fort they are ready & will go down tomorrow A.M. unless you object if so please let me know so they can be stoped.

J. Alston Reynolds to Robert F. W. Allston

Savannah 28 Sept, 1861.

DEAR SIR   I have invented a machine for planting Rice or other grain, but principle adapted to the planting of Rice.

It is my intention to offer the use of the machine to the Rice planters for the next planting season, which I can safely say that the machine can do as good or better work than any negro can do and will plant from 14 to 16 acres per diem with the use of 5 hand in attendance of it, the machine trenches sows and covers at the same time and can open plant by taking of[f] the covering apparatus, the machine is so constructed that by two leavers that the trenchs can be made from 1/2 Inch to 5 inches in depth. It is constructed for one horse or mule but from the size of the machine I find it two heavy for one animal therefore it is my intention to put them up for two animals.

I have tested the machine to my satisfaction and to the satisfaction of several Rice planters and they have expressed perfect satisfaction so much so that I have sold several of the machines.

Dr J. A. Huger who is an extensive rice planter has perchased several of them and told me to use his name as refferance to the valuation of them or said machine.

If any time you go to Charleston you can call at Messrs W C Bee and C[o.] you can see a lithograph of my machine.

1 Sunday, September 15.

Perhaps you have forgotten who I am as I left the Waccamaw in 1854 and came on this River with Dr J. P. Screven and done business for him untill his death in 1858 which time I have been doing business since for two of his sons Capt John and Dr. T. F. Screvan bothe of them told me I can use their name as refferance to the capability of my invention.

Your overseer Mr H Pitman can tell you who I am, I will state that I am the son of Henry R who left the oaks plantation on the Wacamaw River in the year 1835 and was succeeded by Ralph [illegible] I will onely say that the machine will recomend itself whenever it is tried by any person or persons. please to let me hear from you as soon as possible.

P S   for farther particulars you can address me Box 661 Savannah   I will give you any information you may require, also you will do me a great peace of kindness to inform the planters that you may chance to meet that I have a machine that will plant their rice either open or cover planting and will sell on reasonable terms.

Harman Pitman to Robert F. W. Allston

Nightingale Hall, Oct. 3rd, [18]61.

DEAR SIR   Yours of the 1st inst recd & have wrote Mr Green who is likely at S[outh] Island. Saw him last monday A.M. he said he was going & wished to see me (before he left) at Planters Ville. I am more than sorry to have to say Robin died Tuesday P.M. was taken Sunday P.M. I saw him Monday A.M. & attended to him late that evening   he said he felt better as I told you. Tuesday morning he was walking about in the piazza said he had no pain but felt weak. about one O clock P.M. was calld to him sent for the Dr but he died between 2 & 3 oclock & before the Dr came. So many deaths trouble me greatly but I cant help or stop deaths. Keith-field Mill will pound the rice   Mr Daget sent me word & will send for it in a few days. Mr Thompson[1] sends me word the circular saw will cost 800 to 1000 Dollars   Mr Eason of Charleston makes them all complete ready to go up & if you get one & wish he (Mr Thompson) will put it up & run it untill the hands understand how to manage. I intended nameing business for next year last Monday but for want of time did not therefore as it is growing late in the season & not being certain of seeing you nextm onday think it necessary to write. So far I see no prospect of business to manage with yours & must beg you to aid me in secureing something to manage with yours or larger business to which I can move at Jany   would prefer remaining with you if satisfied & business put with yours to give a satis-factory salary, & also would wait for money (except enough to cover current

---

[1] Probably Joseph M. Thompson, overseer at this time at Guendalos and later also in charge of Nightingale Hall.

expenses) untill rice sells. I am compelld if possible to increase salary yet am reluctant to leave you while I can give satisfaction.

Jesse Belflowers to Robert F. W. Allston

Chicora Wood, 27 Oct., 1861.

Report

Sunday 27   Give half allowance of Grist & Potatoes

Monday 28   20 hands on the Rail Road   4 Ploughs Going   the Rest of the hands Picking Peas

Tuesday 29   4 Ploughs Going   the Rest Picking Peas

Wednesday 30 4 Ploughs Going   the Rest Picking Peas

Thursday 31   5 Ploughs Going   6 hands to Waverly to move   the Rest of the hands Picking Peas

Friday 1   Rain   Picking Peas Part of the Day   Raind   Pict Burrs the other Part of the day

Saturday 2   Picking Peas & diging Potatoes   to much Water for Ploughing Sick   D Abby 3 days, Tyra 4, T Mariah 4, Hagar 6, Binah 6, Lit Hariott 3, Eve 6 Last Week & 4 this.

Jesse Belflowers to Robert F. W. Allston

Chicora Wood, 6 July, 1862.

Report

Sunday 6   Give Allowance of Grit Rice & Peas

Monday 7   All hands Picking Rice   Sent to Brittons Neck 3/4 bushel Salt to Mrs. Bath one bushel & two quarts Salt.   Rough Rice in flat to Brittons Neck 500 bushels   Hamaday 24 lbs Nails

Tuesday 8   All hands Picking Rice

Wednesday 9   All hands Picking Rice   Matildas Child died   Georges Salt 2 1/2 bushels

Thursday 10   All hand Picking Rice   Boston to Mrs Williams

Friday 11   Rain   20 hands hoing younge Corn   the Rest of the hands hoing Rice

Saturday 12   All hands Planting Slips

Abrams Salt 11 1/2 bushels

Guy not yet done the boillin

Tom says William Started up the River this Morning with 40 barrels Rice

Sick   N Suckey 6 days, lit Hariott 4, B Hariott 2, Hagar 6, Scinda 2, P. elisabeeth 4, Lit Elisabeth 6, Rachel 4, Jubiter 6, Jane 4, Susen 4, Sam 6, Tobey 4, Billeys Lizzei 2, Betty 4.

Jesse Belflowers to Robert F. W. Allston

Chicora Wood, 13 July, 1862.

Report

Sunday 13   Give Allowance of Grist Rice & Peas
Monday 14   All hands Picking Rice Sawney Got Back
Tuesday 15   All hands hoing Rice N Minda Britton Neck
Wednesday 16 Rain All hands hoing Rice Georges Salt 6 bush
Thursday 17   Rain All hands hoing Rice the People Got back from James Island
Friday 18   Rain All hands hoing Part of the day then Planting Slips 6 hand sent to Waverly in flat Peter Got home from Britton Neck
Saturday 19   Rain All hands Planting Slips Recd 100 bushels flour Boston Got back

Salt B Boiler 7 bushels Lit Boiler 10 bushels Pot 3 bushels—Let E. P. Coachman have 6 Bushels Salt. Let Mr. C. G. Capell have 4 bushels Mr. Brown one bushel for one bushel flour Let Mr. Hemmingway have 6 bushels Let Mr Plouden have 6 bushels—

Coachman   6 bushels
Capell   4
Brown   1
Hemingway 6
Plouden   6
Mrs. Roberts 1/4

Sick Clarisa 6, Harriett 6, P Elizabeth 5, Mary 5, W Mary 5, F Mariah 5, Rachel 6, Mary Ann 6, Jane 5, Doctor 1, Scipio 3, Tobey 3, Pheonix 6, G Minda 6, Sony 4, Susen 3, M Tobey 2.

Jesse Belflowers to Robert F. W. Allston[1]

Chicora Wood, 27 July, 1862.

Report

Sunday 27   Give Allowance of Grits Rice & Peas
Monday 28   loaded a flat with Rough Rice 600 Bus the Rest of the Men Working in the Pine land the Woman Picking Rice 2 hands Sent up to meat flat with Provisinons Rachels Child died
Tuesday 29   Rain Men Working in Pine land the Woman Picking Rice
Wednesday 30 Rain Men Working in Pine land the Woman Picking Rice Paid to Gov Allston $60 dollars

[1] On the back of this is written: "Salt to soldiers' families."

Thursday 31   Rain Men Working in Pine land the Woman Planting Peas & hauling up Slips

Friday 1   Rain Men Working in Pine land the Woman hoing Peas

Saturday 2   Rain Men Working in Pine land Woman hoing Peas Sarys Child died

Georges Salt	5 1/2 bushels
Mrs. F. P. Carliles Salt	4 quarts
Mrs. J. W. Powell	5
Mrs. J Turner	6
Mrs M Goud	7
Mrs Albert Evens	8
Mr A. Evens	6
Mrs J P Goud	6
Mrs Mary Sandars	9
Mrs Sarah J. Owins	5
Marion Goud	8 Paid for

Sick Suckey 6 days, Hagar 6, Rachel 6, Sary 6, Binah 4, Lit Sollomon 4, Page 3, Sandey 4, Susen 4, S Nelley 4, Abby 5, Scinda 4, Caty 4, Amey 6, Wrenche 4, Jane 3, Dinah 4.

Jesse Belflowers to Robert F. W. Allston

Chicora Wood, 17 August, 1862.

Report

Coly Child died

Sunday 17   Give whole allowance of Rice

Monday 18   Men cutting wood the Woman hauling up Slips 2 hands Winnowing Rice

Tuesday 19   Men cutting wood Woman hauling up Slips Scinders Child died Hooping Cough

Wednesday 20   Rain Men Working Causway at Farm Woman carrying away the Sand from the Pits Loaded flat with Rough Rice 495 bushels

Thursday 21   Rain Men striping fodder Women Chopping Weeds 2 hands sent to Kingstree with oxen & cart 3 bars Iron 19 hed of Cattle Sowney Got back

Friday 22   Rain Men Working on Causway at Farm Woman Picking Volunteer Rice

Saturday 23   Rain Men Working on Causway at Farm Woman Picking Volunteer Rice Elsey Locked up 2 nights

Georges Salt	6 Bushels
Macks Salt	6 Bushels

Sent to Plantersville 1 1/2 bushels

Sent Georgetown   4 bushels
Let Mr. Lyirly have 2 bushels
Sick Abby 6 days, Scinda 6, Wrenche 6, Celia 6, Susen 4, Lucey 6, lit Hariott 4, Lit Sollomon 4, Gabrel 4, doctor 4, Suckey 6, Celiann 2, Cato 5, Margret 4, Jnanney 4, Clrisa 2, Clarinda 4.

Jesse Belflowers to Robert F. W. Allston

Chicora Wood, 24 August, 1862.

Report

Lit Elisabeth Child died

Sunday 24	Rain Give Allowance of Grist & Rice
Monday 25	Rain Men sent to the Seashore Woman Picking Volunteer Rice
Tuesday 26	Rain Woman Picking Volunteer Rice
Wednesday 27	Rain Woman Picking Volunteer Rice the Men Got back from Seashore
Thursday 28	Rain Men ditching on the up land the Woman Picking Volunteer Rice
Friday 29	Rain 5 Men Working on Planters Vile Road All the Rest Striping fodder
Saturday 30	Rain Charles sent to Stur pen the Rest of the hands ditching turning flat striping fodder & takeing in & suning fodder

Georges Salt   4 bushels
Macks Salt   6 bushels
Salt sent to Britton Neck 3 1/2 bushels
J. E. Williames   1 bushel
to Georgetown   2 bushels
Mrs. Martin   1 bushels
Mrs. Mc Connal   1 bushels
Paid to Gov. Allston $20 dollars
Sick Maryann 6 day, Ancrum 4, Jacob 4, Albert 4, flander 4, Jobe 1, Wrenche 6, Rose 1, Liser 2, Abby 6, Lucy 6, Lit Harrot 6, Charioty 6, Caty 6, January 3, Phillis 3, Benkey 3, Claisa 2, fanney 4, Lit Elisabeth 3, Sancho 4.

Jesse Belflowers to Robert F. W. Allston

Chicora Wood, 5 Oct, 1862.

Report

Sunday 5	Rain Give Allowance of Grits & Rice
Monday 6	Rain Mill Going the Rest of the hands Gleaning

Tuesday 7	Men Picking Peas the woman hoing land for Rye the mill moveing Rice fetchd 2 loads of from Pipe down
Wednesday 8	6 hands threshing Peas the Rest Picking Peas brought 2 loads of Rice from Pipe down
Thursday 9	Rain Mill Going 1/2 day the Rest Picking Peas the hands at Pipe down Picking Peas
Friday 10	All hands Planting Rye & Shelling Corn Picking Peas at P. down
Saturday 11	Rain Cut Rice at ditchford & dug 1/2 Allowance Potatos

Georges Salt	6 Bushels	
Macks Salt	11 Bushels	
Wiltchers Salt	6 Bushels	
Mr. Magill Salt	4 Bushels	$32 dollars
Mr. Humphry	2 Bushels	$24 dollars
My Self Salt	10 Bushels	$80 dollars

Sick Rose 4 days, Amintir 4, Toney 4, Phillis 4, Mopy 4, Mary 5, Hagor 6, Elley 4, Pheonx 2, Isabel 6, Frances 5.

Jesse Belflowers to Robert F. W. Allston

Chicora Wood, 12 Octobr, 1862.

Sunday 12	Rain Give Allowance of Grit & Rice
Monday 13	Rain Cut Rice & lifted Rice
Tuesday 14	Rain Cut all day
Wednesday 15	Cut Rice tied & Stacked
Thursday 16	Cut Rice tied & loaded flats
Friday 17	Cut Rice and loaded flats
Saturday 18	loaded flats tied up all & stack all
19	loaded two flats with Rough Rice one Thousand Bushels

Salt sent up River for self	10 Bushels
Mrs. North	9 Bushels
Mr. Edwards	1/2 Bushels
Mr. Jhonson	1 Bushel
Mr. Thos. Tiler	3 Pecks & 4 qut $7 dollars
Georges Salt	4 Bushel
Wiltchers Salt	8 Bushels
Macks Salt	10 Bushels
Sick etc	

Jesse Belflowers to Robert F. W. Allston

Chicora Wood, 19 Octo, 1862.

Sunday 19	Give Allowance of Rice & Potatos
Monday 20	hands sent off to Work on R. R. the Rest of the hands fetching in Rice sent by Boston one Bushel Rye

Tuesday 21   fetching in Rice Boston got home
Wednesday 22 fetcht in the last Rice
Thursday 23   the hands diging Potatos and Cleaning up the yeard & Shell-
               ing Corn Boston started Back to Kingstree
Friday 24   Mill Going the rest of the hand Carrying out Straw
Saturday 25   Mill Going the Rest of the hands carrying out Straw the
               Pipe down hands Picking Peas

               Georges Salt   6 Bushels   Paid to Mr. Allston $25 dol-
               Wiltchrs Salt   7 Bushels   lars Paid to Bob $8 dollars
               Mack Salt   10 Bushels   for a cow
               Mr. Keels Salt   10 Bushels

               Mr. Michal Hill Salt 9 Bushls one qut for one Bail of Cotton
               Weighting   476 lbs left with Mc Kenzie at Florence
               Sick Mary 4 days, dapheny 4, Tyra 4, Nelley 4, Elizabetch 4,
               Chariety 4, Jane 6, Binah 4.
               Recd by Boston 100 lbs Cotton also by Stephen 8 sides of
               leather 4 Barrels W Lucey 6.

Jesse Belflowers to Robert F. W. Allston

Chicora Wood, 2 Nobr., 1862.

Report

Sunday 2   Give Allowance Rice & Potatoes
Monday 3   All hands Picking Peas
Tuesday 4   All hands Picking Peas
Wednesday 5   Rain Mill Going Pipe down hands Geatheing Corn
Thursday 6   Rain dug half Allowance Potatoes
Friday 7   All hands Geathering Corn Joe & William Got back
Saturday 8   All hands Geathering corn

               Salt to Britton Neck   one bushels
               Salt to N[ightingale] Hall three Bushels
               Salt to Pipe down   one Bushel and one Peck
               Wiltches Salt   6 Bushels
               Georges Salt   6 Bushels
               Macks Salt   7 Bushels

               Sick Lit Harrott 6 days, Hagor 6, Binah 6, Clarisa 3, B
               Hariott 6, Wrenche 5, Lit Elisabeth 4.

Joseph M. Thompson to Robert F. W. Allston

N[ightingale] Hall, Nov 9th, [18]62.

DEARE SIR

S 2[1] Al. Rice and Potatos
M 3 *Shipped up Black River 655* Bu of corn and level Reye ground
T 4 thrace Rice

[1] Sunday, November 2.

W 5   thrace Rice
T 6   Pl Rye in the yard
F 7   Straw Slips
S 8   "   "

E Tilton 3 Bushels of Rye
D Mcdonel 2528 cwt Fooder
Sick   W Paty 2, L Pay 1 day, T. Bety 2, Judy 3 day.

Jesse Belflowers to Robert F. W. Allston

Chicora Wood, 9 Nobr., 1862.

Report

Sunday 9   Give Allowance of G[r]ist & Rice
Monday 10   All hands diging Slips
Tuesday 11   All hands diging Slips & loding flat with Seed Slips 250
                 Baskets sent 3 Boxes in flat 2 [illegible] for Hamaday 2
                 Barrels Salt
Thursday 13   All hands Picking Peas
Friday 14   All hands Picking Peas
Saturday 15   finishd Picking Peas
                 Sent on Monday by Tom to Brittons Neck 30 bushels Rough
                 Rice & Part of a Stack of Sheefe Rice & fild up with Straw
                 Sent 4 Cow hides
                 Georges Salt   4 Bushels
                 Wilthers Salt   7 Bushels
                 Macks Salt   9 Bushels
                 Sick W Lucey 5 days, Esey 6, Scipio 4, Mosses Came home
                 from Peters flat by N[ightingale] Hall flat Sick one hand at
                 Mrs. Roberts

Jesse Belflowers to Robert F. W. Allston

Chicora Wood 16 Nobr. 1862

Report

Sunday 16   Give Allowance of Gr[i]st & Potatos
Monday 17   All hands harvesting Corn
Tuesday 18   All hands harvesting Corn
Wednesday 19   Rain All hands harvesting Corn
Thursday 20   dug whole Allowance Potatoes
Friday 21   All hands diging Slips
Saterday 22   All hands diging Slips
                 Sick Scipio 6 days, Henry 4, Caty 1, Patience 4, Mosses 6
                 Macks Salt   13 Bushels
                 Wiltchers Salt   8 Bushels
                 Georges Salt   6 Bushels
                 L. W. Nesmith   10 Bushels $100 dollars.

An Overseer's Contract, 1863

Mem. for the year 1863 Duncan Barrentine is to oversee the Pearson place in Anson County No. Ca. and mak Mr Allston's interests his own to have the use of a cow when she calves and have his horse fed and worked in the crop when not otherwise in use. He is to find his own bread and meat and receive for his services at the end of the year $400.

J. C. Yates to Robert F. W. Allston

[Anson County, N.C.], January the 11, 1863.

MR ALSTON SIR   I will in form you that I have soald sango and his fambly to Mr Roper for ten thousand you will find the money in the Chewraw Bank I seen Mr Hargraves in surch [of] the papers of the liles [?] land he finds that they can make it wright and I have Boug[ht] the land I am to pay them five thousand dolliars at April coart wen they make the title and the other five the 1 day of January next theay will give me A Bond for title and I will give them one for the money whi[ch] will draw am writing tomorow at Mr Hargraves offis I have nothing more at this time when you Receive thes few lines please wright to me.

J. C. Yates to Robert F. W. Allston

[Anson County, N.C.], March the 25, 1863.

MR ALSTON SIR   I have conclude to take theme negros home you pleas send them as soon as you can as I have conclude I can take cair of them at home when you send them wright to me and I will meat them in chewraw I could not hire you A wagoner negros hire at apr one hunderd and 65 dolliar for nine months the prise was so hi that I did not hire I can git you A good Bugy for two huderd dolliars if you wante it at the price write to me and I will git it I have paid Mr Bullaion for yor Corn I can not git you eany Bacon heir at A fair price Bacon is selling at 75 cents per pound I have nothing more at the time preasent I will do all i can for you heir the negro proppert[y] of N C has to Be valiad next monday.

Edwin M. Tilton to Robert F. W. Allston

Waverly Mill, May 28, 1863.

DEAR SIR   I sent on 27th inst by new pole boat (40) forty Barrels for Capt T. D. Hogg Charlotte N. C. Sent weights to Messrs Robertson, Blacklock and Co. mentioning about the (10) Barrel over engagement requesting arrangement about the price, weights given in line by themselves

have sent for Society Hill C. Coker & Bro   40 Bbls brand Allston
have sent for Cheraw D. Malloy & Son   60 Bbls brand Allston
   "   "   "   "   "   "   "   "   1/2 "   "   R.F.W. Allston

above all whole [Rice] the 1/2 Bbl Long grain Rice *all weighed marked on Heads*
for Mrs [MS torn] [Soc]iety Hill 1 Barrel Small rice
"   "   "   "   "   1 Keg Rice flour
for Mrs Sarah Williams   1/2 Bbl Long grain Rice
"   "   "   "   1 Box (small) Rice flour
"   G. W. Williams. . . . . 9 Pots [?]

the Salt he would get at Chicora
as boat was to have a good load did not send any but whole Rice above.

[P. S.] the 40 and 60 Bbls from the Atkinson Rice Black River 2604 Bushels
turn out (large Barrels): Allston 114 ⎫
             " S.   5 ⎬ 125 Bbls clean Rice—3 Bbls small rice
            " S. G.   6 ⎭
(he has 1000 to 1500 bushels [MS. torn] to sell) at same price [MS torn]
Capt Allston request [MS torn] arrange to Hire his boy Owens as Blacksmith
to Peedee gunboat managers he is here can go up at once.

Affidavits concerning an Overseer's Services in Wartime, 1863

State South Carolina Georgetown District

Personally appeared before me Francis W. Heriot, a magistrate, Joseph M.
Thompson who upon oath states, That he is the overseer of Hon R. F. W.
Allston upon his Nightingale Hall plantation and has been thus employed
from January 1861 to the present time. During the present year he also became overseer of Col Ben Allston, Confederate Army, on his Guendalos
plantation Pee Dee.

Sworn to before me this 26th day Aug. 1863
F. W. HERIOT *Magistrate*

Nightingale Hall 26th Aug 1863

This is to certify that Joseph M. Thompson my overseer at this place is
also overseer at *Guendalos*, where there are about one hundred negroes the
property of Col Ben Allston of the Confederate Army, now serving with
Genl. E. Kirby Smith, beyond the Mississippi River. That after reasonable
delay, and diligent enquiry, having fail'd to procure a satisfactory person,
I employ'd my own overseer J. M. Thompson to look after the police of my
son's plantation above named. He has been with my people since January,
1861, and I trust will ensure the police and government of Guendalos as well.
If J. M. Thompson can be spared from the conscription, it would be a satisfaction to retain him in his present employment. It would contribute materially to the Police of the locality in which he resides.

Witness—
   F. W. HERIOT
   JA R. SPARKMAN

Petition for the Exemption of Overseers from
Military Service, 1864[1]

State of South Carolina, Society Hill, 5th. January, 1864.

To the Hon. Secretary of War   The memorial of the undersigned
R. F. W. Allston Rice-planter on the coast of Georgetown District respectfully sheweth—That in April next he will be 63 years of age—that since
1861, his services in the army having been (tacitly) declined by the President,
he has devoted himself to the production (as theretofore) of Rice, Corn and
potatoes their preparation for, and transportation to market as the best
service he could render to his country, being out of the army, was to contribute to the general subsistence. The transportation of his produce by water
up the river Wanee (Black River) the Great and Little PeeDee to a Rail
Road Depot is superintended by himself. The cultivation of the ground
(viz his own and that of Col. Ben Allston's (his son) now serving in Genl.
E. K. Smith's Army beyond the Mississippi) in S. Ca. is attended to, within
hearing of the Enemy's guns, by *Jesse Belflowers* 57 years of age at Chicora
and *Jos. M. Thompson* 21, Col. Allston's overseer at Guendalos for whom he
has already paid to the Government through its enrolling officer in Georgetown the commutation of $500, prescribed by Act of Congress of May 1863.
In *No. Carolina*, where in Anson County, he has provided a Farm for refuge
of his people from the Coast in case of necessity, and where his negroes, in
the intervals of labor on the Farm are constructing a portion of the Coal-
field's Rail Road (a Road intended to convey Coal from the extensive
Coal-fields of No. Ca. to the cities of Charleston and Columbia So. Ca.
I beg leave to refer to the Hon. Mr. Memminger Secretary of the Treasury
for information as to this important work) the work on the Rail Road as
well as on the Farm is superintended by *J. C. Yates* a neighbouring Farmer
47 years of age

The preparing of Rice for transportation to market is attended to, at
Waverly Mill belonging to Capt. J. Blyth Allston of the 27th (Gaillard's)
So. Ca. Regiment, by *Ed. M. Tilton,* engineer and miller about 30 years
of age.

For the security and proper police of his negroes together with the direction of their labor in producing, preparing and transporting his produce of
grain which is the present business of your memorialist for himself and as
Agent for his son Col. Ben Allston of the Confederate Army the presence at
their respective places of residence, of the several persons named herein,

[1] Endorsed in R. F. W. Allston's handwriting: "Copy of memorial to the Hon. James A.
Seddon, Secretary of War, Jany 1864. This was enclosed in a letter and envelope to the
Hon. John McQueen, requesting him to see that it is presented and attended to and the
response forwarded to me at this place 7th Jany. 1864." For the addition of this document
to the general collection the editor is indebted to the late Arnoldus Vander Horst, of
Charleston, S.C., a grandson of R. F. W. Allston.

with the aid of their skillful experience is absolutely necessary. Your memorialist earnestly prays that the Hon. Secretary of War, in view of the useful service they are rendering to the Army and the Community in producing subsistence (so very scarce and indispensable as it is) will furnish him with the necessary Document from the proper office in the War Department which will authorize and require the enrolling officer or their respective commanders (supposing them to be conscribed for the service) to detail them for the agricultural service at home in which they are now most usefully employed.

Namely—   Jesse Belflowers (57) Overseer at Chicora on PeeDee
               Jos. M. Thompson (21) Overseer at Guendalos, Col. Ben Allston's plantation $500 Already paid for him.
in
So. Ca.   Ed. M. Tilton (31) Engineer and miller at Waverly Mill, the property of Capt. Jo. B. Allston of the Confederate Army

and in N. Ca. J. C. Yates (47) Overseer of the negroes working on the Coal Field's Rail Road, and also of the Farm which provides for them subsistence.

Your memorialist may be permitted to mention as some evidence of the useful service rendered by them, that during the past year, besides subsisting his own people, contributing to the support of soldier's families in his District, somewhat to the Revd. Clergy also, and paying near $5000 in taxes; he was enabled to supply the State of No. Carolina with 300 tierces of Rice, the State of South Carolina with over 169 tierces of Rice, and the Confederate Government (Army and Navy) with over 130 tierces of Rice netting each 600 lbs. weight. That he is now delivering at the Rail Road Depots at Society Hill and Kingstree 500 tierces of Rice by order of and agreement with C.S.A. Commissary Simons of Georgetown—all at a price within the schedule fixed by the C.S. Commissioners for the State of So. Ca. In addition to this he has been enabled to furnish Salt for the supply of his own people and also to distribute at various prices, to persons in the interior 400 to 500 bushels— All which (saving the Enemy) he expects to do the coming year, if his Agents be detailed to aid him as heretofore under providence.

The Waverly Mill, the property of Capt. Jo. B. Allston is a regular Toll Mill, at which much other Rice is prepared for market and to License which the Confederate Tax Collector has been duly paid.

All which is respectfully submitted by

R. F. W. ALLSTON

J. C. Yates to Robert F. W. Allston[1]

[Anson County, N.C.], Jan 27, 1864.

DEAR SIR I drop you a few lines Informing you that I have Secured the Bond for the liles land and have possesion of the Same The Boat Reached

[1] Obviously written for Yates by another hand.

Cheraw last Saturday Evening We are Indeavouring to Unload her as fast as we can The Mule in question is in prety good Order but was cripled by a kick from Some of the Mules in the hip We want 2 more horses for the farm and One for my Self to ride if you can Spare the horses we wil Send down after them and if the Mule dos not Improve we wil Send her down when we Send after the horses as I think it not best to put her on the boat in her present condition We will raise the frame of the Saw Mill Tomorow and we can not Spare the carpenters Until the Saw is Started I have Bought the crank and all the Saw Mill gearing of Henry Digs as I thoght it better and as cheap as to take the Iron and have them made the ploughs wil Start on the farm next week we have open land Enough for 10 ploughs after Sowing all our Small grain we have about 75 Aces of new ground now cut down let Mr Barentine hear from you Immediately whether you can Spare the horses as we want them at once to work.

J. C. Yates to Adele Petigru Allston[1]

Anson Co, N C, April the 28, [18]64.

Mrs Allston I received your letter of the 21 to day and was very glad to hear from you I had the sale of the Land last perchased by me Posponed untell the 4 of June I have been looking for the Execeutor hear I can do nothing hear agreeable to the laws of this State untell he comes the Death of your Deceased Husband Stops my Agency hear I have no mony belonging to the Esstate in my hands but I am Paying out my own mony for the use of the Farm and I am Afraid that I will not be able to get Permishion to carry on the Farm untell the Crop is made I beg you to try some of your Friends about Society Hill to see if you can get A lot of Corn if it is so the Executor can not come please write an I will come down an see you the government is pressing Horses Mules an Negrose in this State I am holding them off untell I can see the Execeutor thear is A State Tax dew hear that must be Paid you will pleas send me some Sheep Shears to Sheer the Sheep the Negrose is all well on the Farm I am doing the best I can for you hear fail not to let me no in time concerning the land.

Duncan Barrentine to Adele Petigru Allston

Mill Creek, N.C., May 24, 1864.

Mrs. A. Allston According to your Request I drop you a few lines by Paul Informing you that the health of the Negroes is pretty good No Sickness of a Serious character Among them at this time As it Regards Provisens I can not tell what we are to do We have not more than Enough corn for this weeks Allowance and I cant buye Anny I do not know what Mr Yates is doing I have not heard from him in Some considerable time

P. S We are geting along Pretty well with our farming Interest One of Our Mules is Dead The Impressing Agent has taken my horse frome me.

[1] Written for Yates by another hand.

Jesse Belflowers to Adele Petigru Allston

Chicora Wood, 26 May, 1864.

DEAR MADAM   I give you a daily Report

Thursday 26   all hands Mashing trenching & Sowing Rice

Friday 27   all hands Mashing trenching & Sowing Rice   the River has Commenced falling

Saturday 28   the Pipe[down] hands hoing Rice   the Rest of the hands trenching Sowing Rice & hoing Potatoe   Paul arrived to day. he delevered to me your Letter one Coat & Some May Apple Root [?]

Sunday 29   Gi[ve] Allowance of the damage Rice & [MS torn] barrel of Pork in the Smo[ke] House [MS torn] out to be only a half barrel

Monday 30   the Pipe down hands hoing Rice.   the Rest of the hands hoing Potatoes & Corn   Stephen delevered to me to day the Harnas and Slay

Tuesday 31   the Hands hoing Rice & Corn.   Lavenia Goes to Nightingale Hall to day

Wednesday 1   the hands hoing Rice & Corn.   Mr Sweet has Got one flitch & Gammon.   he will git half allowance of the damage Rice next Saturday and a half allowance for My Self will be all   Stephen I think is Runing a bout a grate deal   I think he has been a bout Planters Ville the most of time Since he come down Withe the Harnas & Slay   I have 47 Acers of Rice to Plant yet as Soon as the Water gits low enogh to Get at the land.   the hundred & fifty Acers of Rice that I Could not Git the Water of in time is Verry Much thind out. theare is Still a talk hear of a Party giting up to Go off. We are all on the look out.   I have not Sent the wool down Yet.   have told Mary to take Care of the umbrela.   the People all Seames to be Quiet With the exception of Some 4 or 5 of the younge People which is suposd to be in the Party Consernd.   Mosses & Elsey has [pa]rted   have no Sick [MS torn] one little [MS torn] which is a worme Ca[se].

W. Sweet to Adele Petigru Allston

N[ightin]gill hall, 1th June, 1864.

DEAR MADUM   I Receive your note Safe in hand and I went over to see mr ford twice But he was not at home   I will goe over and see him again before I Rigth you again or as quick as I can see mr ford see him about the Rice for mr gooch   all is getting on quite well

N[ightin]gill hall

may 26th 39 hands hoing Rice 2 Planting Rice 7 hands trashing Peas 2 hands Plowing 3 hands on the flat had quite a heave[y] Rain and wind in ater noon 1 hand Repairing the warf 1 sick

may 27th 41 hands hoing Rice 3 hands Plowing 3 hands trashing Peas 4 Planting corn 2 sick

28th 35 hands howing Rice 6 hands cuting leaks[1] 6 hands Planting corn 3 hands Plowing 1 sick

30th 36 hands howing Rice 6 hands cuting leak 6 hands Planting corn 3 hands Plowing 1 sick

31th 35 hands hoing Rice 8 hands cuting leaks 6 hands Planting corn 3 hands Plowing 2 sick

1th June 36 hands hoing Rice 8 hands cuting leaks 3 hands Plowing 10 hands Planting corn None sick

[Guendalos]

26th may 15 hands hoing corn 2 hands flating wood 2 Plowing 5 sick

26th [sic] 15 hands hoing corn 2 hands mending Banck 2 Plowing 5 sick 6 minding Birds

27th 15 hands howing corn 2 hands mending Bancks 2 Plowing 5 sick 6 minding Birds

28th 15 hands hoing corn 2 mending Banck 2 Plowing 5 sick

30th 18 hands hoing corn 3 flating wood 2 mending the warf 2 Plowing 3 sick

31th 18 hands hoing corn 3 hands flating wood 2 hands mending warf 2 Plowing 3 sick

1th June 18 hands hoing corn 3 hands flating wood 2 hands mending warf 2 Plowing 3 sick

W. Sweet to Adele Petigru Allston

[Nightingale Hall, June 8, 1864]

DEAR MADUM I have seen a Bout the Rice at mr fords Belonging to mr gooch But mr waterman have sent and taken the Rice away your woman seriener came Down to me on 31th of may But she has no cotton to spin un til she can get fillin to weave you will Pleas send some cotton soe I can make her and her girl spin when she has no weaveing to Doe all is giting on well soe far Pleas let me Know if you left aney Bacon for ganderloss for the negroes to have feast onse a month

N[ightin]gill hall

2th June 38 hands hoing Rice 9 hands cuting leaks 3 hands Plowing 6 hands Planting corn none sick

[1] Probably stopping leaks in the banks.

3th June   38 hands howing Rice 9 hands cuting leaks 3 Plowing 6 Planting corn 1 sick

4th June   39 hands howing Rice 9 hands cuting leaks 6 hands trashing
Peas 3 hands Plowing 2 sick

6th June   41 hands hoing Rice 3 hands Plowing 6 hands Planting corn
5 hands Rakeing trash 5 sick

7th June   43 hands hoing Rice 6 hands hoing shugar cain 5 hand Raking
trash 3 hands Plowing 4 sick

8th June   all hands shucken corn and trashing Peas had a very heavy Rain
all Knighth and Raining until about 1 oclock 4 sick

W. Sweet to Adele Petigru Allston

N[ightin]gill hall, 8th June, 1864.

DEAR MADUM   hester ask me to Righth to you and let you know about her
children in Britens neck she says that her uncle Will sent her word that
her children ware suffering for something to Eat that they do not get Enough
to Eat and the he can not Doe aney Beter with them as he has soe many of
his one to feed she Begs you to let her Bring her children home

you can Doe as you Pleas about it I hope that you will not think hard
of me for Rigthing to you for hester.

ganderlouss

2th June   12 hands howing corn 6 hands flating wood 2 hands Plowing
2 hands mending Banks 3 sick

3th June   12 hands hoing corn 6 hands flating wood 2 Plowing 2 mending
Banks 1 hand mending fence 3 sick

4th June   12 hands howing corn 6 hands flating wood 2 Plowing 2 hands
mending Banks 1 hand mend fence 3 sick

6th June   21 hands hoing Rice 4 Picking Potatoes 2 Plowing 8 half hands
mending Banck 3 sick

7th June   17 hands hoing Rice 8 half hands mending Banks 6 Picking
Potatoes 2 Plowing 8 sick

8th June   all hands shucking corn 5 sick

Jesse Belflowers to Adele Petigru Allston

Chicora Wood, 8th June, 1864.

DEAR MADAM   this is My daily Report

Thursday 2   the hands at Pipe down hoing Rice the Rest of the hands
turning land

Friday 3   All hands Mashing land

Saturday 4   the hands Mashing trenching & Sowing Rice ditchfield Sammy taken down Verry Ill With Bilious Penumonia

Sunday 5   Give half Allowance of damage Rice & Grist

Monday 6   All hands Mashing land
Tuesday 7   All hands Mashing & trenching
Wednesday 8 trenching & Sowing Rice Will finish to day Planting Some
             hands Picking Rice Sammy Still Quite Ill Good Many
             Others in the house to day the boy Charley is behaveing
             badly had to Give a Switching to day Phillip has got his
             Piece of Meat We are haveing to much Rain for the upland
             Crop I have not heard Much a bout the Party that Was
             to go off I have Written Mr. Wallas telling him not to let
             Stephen Come down aney More With out orders the Rice
             that I mention in My last Report has a good deal of it floated
             and the land is Poluted With Rushes I will be in it next to
             try and Clean it out the Rye is just Ready to Cut, the Oats
             is just begining to Ripen if Charley dos not behave Better
             then he has bin doing he had better Go With the Gange to
             Work thear has bin a nother Steamer Run a Shore & Burnt
             near to Mr Middletons house on the Beach & a nother
             Capturd the Same day Still Raining

P. S.   have let Mrs. Tindal have 4 bushels of Salt.

Jesse Belflowers to Adele Petigru Allston

Chicora Wood, 9 June, 1864.

Mrs. ALLSTON   yours of the 9 inst has been Recd I have done but two days
Ploughing since my last Report. theare has been so much Rain and the land
so weet I Could not Plow since done Planting I have Cleand out two feild
of Rice hauld up the Potatoes and Cleand out the Sougum I give the
People last Saterday as holaday the weet Weather has Set the Corn back it
is not looking So Well the Rice Crop is not loocking Well either I have
Made inqurys a bout fright for the Boat but theare is none to be had at
this time have given Joe a ticket to day 15 inst to go up to Society Hill
the Black Mare has had a Colt but it only lived one day and a half Sammey
who was so verry Ill when I last Wrote is gitting Well theare has been no
more hard Sickness since have used all of the damage Rice have not heard
any thing more about the Party that was to go off but Some of the People is
hardheaded and doant want to be managabel I have not Sent for Stephen
as you will see in my last Report that I wrote to Mr. Wallas not to allow
him to Come down any more Without he was Sent for if you still wish
him let me know and I will send for him Hagor & Sary is doing nothing if
had some Cotton I would make them Spin I Am Glad you have let me
Know what to do with the eggs Molley brough me 6 Dozen the other day
which I have taken my self theare has been one or two Application for
Buter Please let me Know if you will sell and if so let me no the Price I

heare of no Sails of Salt or Rice I am hoing Rice yeasterday & to day I think it would be best to let Gilbert & Joe Come home in July as theare is but one Carpinter heare that Can do any thing much the Harvest flats will have to be Repaird & the threshing Mills will be to over hall & if theay do not Come some othe[r]s will have to come I doant think theare is any danger of theare Going a way I do not Know What theare hire is Gilbert & Carpt Joe—Joe the Black Smith, Daniel, Josiah, Lias, Brister thease I think had best Stay. Brister I no is to Stay untill threshing time I have got from the Boat that Beachd and burnt 700 lbs of Iron which is Worth Something While Writing I Can heare the Bombardment Going on at Charleston the Weather Clear to day have no Cradles Like wis no saw up to the 15 June '64.[1]

Jesse Belflowers to Adele Petigru Allston

Chicora Wood, 16 June, 1864.

MRS. ALLSTON   Yours of 16 inst has been Recd. since my last. I have hoed out 60 Acers of Rice hoed 40 Acers Corn Cut Part of the Rye & have Pickt out 40 Acers of Rice the Plughs has Gone over 30 Acers of Corn the Corn Crop has faild Very much since the last Rains and is looking badly the Rice Crop is also looking badly the River Keeps so high that the Water Cant be Keept to any gage and the Consiquence is the goose grass has got the better of it My last Planting is Very much thind out by not being Abel to git the Water of[f] it has floated up on the top of the Water the Oats will be Ready to Cut in a day or to now which will turn out well to the quantity of land Planted all quiet at the yeard the Pople with some fiew exseption [are be]haveing Very well Sammy is gitting well [fast] no More Very hard Sickness Some fiew Worme Cases the People at Pipe down has the mumps or some thing Very much like it the Salt boiling gets on Very Slow the Pans have all given out. I have had one Set of them Mended & have the others over hear now. Guy is mending them. the turn out of Salt for the last Month has not been more than 20 bushels Chickens Sold from Mary 30 head and 3 Dozen eggs. from Molly 14 head & one Dozen eggs. from Jacob 10 head fifty five head in all at one dollar per head the eggs at one dollar pr dozen the Wool that Came down from N.C. 75 lbs. only 30 lbs was due Government for tax. I will save something like 40 lbs of Wool Joe did not Carry any Rice to Mr. Gilchrist Peter says that him & Prince Caryed up two loads each but thay doant Know what time the last load Went I doant no the date my self Peter says that Mr. Gilchrist lives on little Pee Dee in Marion District near the Wilmington and M[anchester] Rail Road I will try and Git the wright statement of the shipments of the Rice & let you Know in my next Report.

June 22th 1864

[1] I.e., the report is concluded on this date.

W. Sweet to Adele Petigru Allston

N[ightin]gale hall, 18th June, 1864.

DEAR MADAM   I have Bin taken as a conscrip Being Beteen the age of 45 and 50 the Enroleing oficer of Georgetown I ast him for a Detail of some 25 or 30 Days until I could hear from you he told mee that you could clame me as an overseer for the Esstate of gov allston and col Ben allston under too heads one to gave the Bacon and Beef that you can not Doe under the other head of the law you could have me Detaild as an overseer on the 2 Plantations 60 Days at a time if no longer I think my self that you had Best get the advice of some lawer on the mater you will Pleas let me hear from you as sune as Posible as he has Requested me to let hime Know what you will Doe By the first of July I will Be 49 the first Day of January next the law that mr allston clam me unde[r] the 5 five hundred Dollars act is nul and voyed and I Know have to Be clame[d] under the last act mr Sam Sampson is the Enroleing officer in Georgetown I will have to goe in to camps By the 15 of July if you Doe not get me oof I have to Report again By 1th of July

P s   my crop is Doeing Prety well considering the heave Rains that has Bin.

W. Sweet to Adele Petigru Allston

N[ightin]gale hall, 22th June, 1864.

DEAR MADUM   I Receive your note of th16 safe in hand and I allso Receive the Botle of medison Safe By Pall toby and quash is Boath fat quite harty and gon to work wallis has got much Beter so he can get out to work on the up land trim is a litle Beter than he was when you left. the Rest of the negroes is all prty well and geting on well no[t] much hard sicknes Since you left I have not Bin able to see aney thing about the stock on wacmaw on the accont that I can not get a horse. I have Just cut the Ry and the oats is not fit for cuting yet as thay are not Ripe I Exspect that I will have to use the Ry to feed the negroes with as my Provisons is geting very short. I have Receive one half alowance of the old Rice from mr. Belflowers if you Doe not wish me to use the Ry for Provisons you will Pleas let me Know.

N[ightin]gale hall

16th June	all hands hoing Potatoes 3 hands Ploing 4 sick
17th June	all hands hoing corn and Potatoes 3 Plowing 3 sick
18th June	all hands hoing corn 3 Plowing 3 sick
20th June	39 hands hoing Rice 4 hands hoing corn 3 hand Plowing 4 sick
21th June	19 hands hoing Rice 6 hoing corn 16 hands cuting Ry 3 Plowing 5 sick
22th June	41 hand hoing Rice 6 head hoing corn 3 Plowing 1 sick

ganderloss

16th June	23 head hoing Rice	3 Plowing	4 sick
17th June	24 head hoing Rice	3 Plowing	3 sick
18th June	24 head hoing Rice	3 Plowing	3 sick
21th June	23 head hoing Rice	3 Plowing	4 sick
22th June	24 head hoing Rice	3 Plowing	3 sick

Jesse Belflowers to Adele Petigru Allston

Chicora Wood, 23 June, 1864.

MRS. ALLSTON   Since My last I have been Picking Rice it will take Me this Week to Git the Rushes out the Rice I have not done any hoing. have Cut the Oats & Rye. the Ploughs has Gone over 40 Acres of land the Crop is looking Badly the land being So Weet & then 2 Week dry hot Weather has turnd the Corn yeollow Peters flat left hear on the 11 July 1863 for Mr. Gilchrist which is the latest date I Can find have lost an infant 8 days old With Lockjaw also have lost Bettys youngest boy from Wormes Molley is Sick with fever no other hard Sickness at this time the last 15 hot days has injurd the Garden some I sent to Mr. Sweet 7 lbs of Cotton & 215 broaches of fillin. George had done Very well in Salt for the last two Weeks I hope he will do better as soon as Can get the other Pans mended from Britton Neck. Mr. Wallas has sent me word that the Hogs is all dying up & thinks is from the want of feed but I hear of Hogs dying elsewear I think it the same disease that Kild up So many Hogs last year the Peopl is quiet Some of them is a little hard-headed Give meat on the 26 inst had a light Rain on the 27 inst. Mr. Tilton want to Know if you will hire him the Coopers and also wants to Know if will let the Boats attend the Mill as thay have been doing thare is none of the Genttlemen that would be willing Pay River freight & that would be no Proffit unless you Got the clean Rice to carry I Give you my opinion on it. the Mill has her full Tole and is Bound to furnish barrels & even if you Got the freight an acident might hapin and Cost you a gratedeal more than the freight would Come to. I think best to do our own freighting & turn as much of the men forse in to ditching as Possiabel as theare has not been any diching done on the Plantation for the last six years and the land is so much out of order that it is impossible [to] make a full Crop Please let me heare from you on this matter the best Plan is to have as little to do with the Mill as Possiable have got Mr. D. H. Smiths Recipt for the 30 lbs of Wool which is the tax in Kind & have 47 lbs of Wool left of the Parsel that Came from N. Carolina.
29 June 1864

W. Sweet to Adele Petigru Allston

N[ightin]gale hall, 29th June, 1864.

DEAR MADUM   I Receive your note and the Paper safe in hand and I went and seen connel harriet [i.e., Heriot] and he attended to it for me and I taken the Papers to mr Sampson this Day and he told me that he would Doe his Best for you and that I must come Back home and Be quiet and attend to my Business and that he would let me know after a while all a Bout the mater that he had found out that the five hundred Dollars had Bin Paid and that he would try and make that Stand

all is going on Pretty well   no hard sickness and the crop Doing Pretty well.

N[ightin]hale hall

23th June	all hands hoing Rice 4 hands Plowing 4 sick	
24th June	all hands hoing Rice 3 hands Plowing 4 sick	
25th June	all hands Beading corn and Planting Peas 3 Plowing 2 sick	
27th June	all hands Beading corn and Planting Peas 3 Plowing none sick	
28th June	all hands Beading corn and Planting Peas 3 [Plowing] none sick	
29th June	all hands Beading corn and Planting Peas 3 Plowing none sick	

ganderloss

23th June	all hands hoing Rice 3 Plowing 4 sick
24th June	all hands Beading corn 3 Plowing 2 sick
25th June	all hands Beading corn and Planting Peas 3 Plowing 2 sick
27th June	all hands hoing Rice 3 Plowing 2 sick
28th June	all hands Beading corn and Planting Peas 3 Plowing 3 sick
29th June	all hands Beading corn and Planting Peas 3 Plowing 3 sick

W. Sweet to Adele Petigru Allston

N[ightin]gale hall, 6th July, 1864.

DEAR MADUM   I have had 2 women confined at ganderloss since you left Emmer was confind with a girl child on 15th June Pacients on 4th of July with a girl child   Boath of the women is Doing well and like wise thare children. you Rote to me that you wish me to let you know how the Ry and oats turnd out   I have not quite finish trashing the Ry But will have it all trash and meashurd out and let you know when I send you my next Report   the oats I will not Be able to trash until I am Done with my Rice. as for my Provisions I Know that I have [been] as careful with them as I could   I have got 60 Bushels of corn 25 of Peas and one hundred of Rice   I Doe not think that it will hurt the negroes to gave the Ry   have it ground up in to meal and mix the Ry and corn to gave half of Each though I will not Doe soe with out your Request. the negroes are all loacking well and get on well   soe far noe hard sickness   they all wish to Be Rememberd to you and family about the cloth mrs Sweet has not Bin able to get the cloth in the lume until last Saterday But if noth[ing] hapens I think that she will get it out By next tuesday But I Doe not think that your woman Serenier will Eaver [illegible] I will let you know.

N[ightin]gale hall

30th June	all hands Picking Potatoes 2 Plowing 4 sick
1th July	all hands Picking Potatoes and takeing Ry 2 Plowing 4 sick
2th July	all hands cuting oats 2 Plowing 3 sick
4th July	30 hands Planting Peas 10 head trashing Ry 2 Plowing 2 sick
5th July	32 head hoing Rice 10 trashing Ry 2 Plowing none sick
6th July	36 head hoing Rice 8 head trashing Ry 2 Plowing 1 carpinter
	7 Days Repaing a house none sick

ganderloss

30th June	all hands cuting oats 3 Plowing 4 sick
1th July	all hands cuting oats 2 Plowing 3 sick
2th July	all hands cuting oats 3 Plowing 2 sick
4th July	all hands listing up slip land 3 Plowing 4 sick
5th July	all hands Planting slips 3 Plowing 5 sick
6th July	all hands heading up corn 2 Plowing 4 sick

Jesse Belflowers to Adele Petigru Allston

Chicora Wood, 6th July, [18]64.

MRS. ALLSTON   Yours of 26 of June has been duly Recd since my last. I have got the Rushes out of the Rice and am now laying by the up land Crop & Planting Peas. have Planteed 7 Acers of Slips. the Crop up on low land is looking badly. the Corn will neaver git over the weet Weathe[r] that we had three Week ago it has improved but it will not be what it Promisisd at one time. Prunels Colt is looking well. Pronel & the Black boath has had the Chance of a nother Coalt. Marva Also has a fine horse Colt. Bess has none & is a little uncirtin if she will have one the Boiss [?] is taken Lavenas hogs at the farm. Bob Tells me that he has lost 4 Shoats. Harry Gives me Plenty of Vegetables I was in the Garden to day. he has a fine Prospect of Water Mellons. We have had a fine Rain. the Garden is looking Better. I have Sent Mr. Sweet the two Pieceses of Bacon for N[ightingale] H[all] and one Piece for Guendal[o]s Richard has got his Piece. Esau was hear some ten day his farther Reported to me that he had leaf to Come dow[n] to see them. I did not no aney better until I Recd your letter. nether did philleip I have Sent Jack to Carry him back to Sam Mr. Smith has brought the Cloth that he has to Weave the Provision is holding out Pretty well yet I sent Tom on last Saturday to Brittons Neck for Stephen & told him to come down on monday. Well on Monday Morning tom got Ready to start. he Cauld on Stephen who Comp[l]aind of being sick Tom went back a gain and Stephen Was absant Lizzie told Tom that Stephen said he Could go on that he would take his Boat & Come on Tom did not waite any longer. So monday night Stephen & his Wife & Children & Tonny left for the yankees.[1] Mr Wallas mising him on a Tuesday Morning took a boat Came down and let me Know. he say theare is no boat mising and dos not no wheare Stephn got a boat not Knoing what Stephn might do I was on Watch all last night. I feel the affects of it to day. no hard sickness at this time the People all Semes to be quiet. Molley has lost most all of hir younge Poultry. Hanah at the farm has lost all of the yonge turkeys

[P.S.]   Kittey has not done any Ploughing.
6 July 1864

W. Sweet to Adele Petigru Allston

N[ightin]gale hall, 13th July, 1864.

DEAR MADUM   my Ry has Done very well I think I have had it clear out and measherd 95 Bushels and I Doe think that it would [be] Just as well to gave to negroes for allowance for I had a little ground for myself and I find it very nice for Bread. my crop of corn and Rice and Potatoes is Just tolerable. I Doe not think that I will Be able to get the Bull fat for summer for he Does not faten well But will mak a fine Beef for chrismuss I will send over to water-ford on next thursday to see if I can [get] any cows over thare I have no hard sickness mrs Sweet has you[r] cloth out and Serinier goe up to chicora on saterday

P S   I supose that mr [Bel]flowers will let you know that one of your men that started to the yankeys has come Back the Boy toney came to mee on last friday morning and I taken him up to mr Belflowers and left him thare at work I Doe not Know much about the Boy But I think that you had Best take him and his family up to noth carolina I Did not wish to Put him in the hands of the military Powe[r] the Rest of the gange that ware to goe with him and Stphen is all caugth and in Jail all Exsept Stphen and his family
    Pleas let me Know if I must give out the Ry or not.

[Nightingale Hall]

7th July   37 head hoing Rice 8 head trshing Ry 2 Plowing none sick
8th July   37 head hoing Rice 8 head trashing Ry 2 Plowing none sick
9th July   all hands taking in oats and listing up slip land 2 Plowing none sick
11th July all hands Beading corn 1 Plowing 2 hands Repairing Wining [?] house none sick
12th July all hands Beading corn none sick
13th July all 29 head Beading corn 7 head faning [?] Ry 3 Planting Peas 4 sick

[1] See above, p. 199.

ganderloss

7th July	all hands Beading corn 2 Plowing 2 sick
8th July	10 head hoing Rice 10 head taking in oats 2 Plowing 3 sick
9th July	all hands hoing Rice 2 Plowing 3 sick
11th July	all hands hoing Rice 2 Plowing 3 sick
12th July	all hands hoing Rice 2 Plowing 2 sick
13th July	all hands hoing Rice 2 Plowing 2 sick

Jesse Belflowers to Adele Petigru Allston

Chicora Wood, 13 July, 1864.

MRS. ALLSTON   Since my last I have Cleand out fifty Acers of Rice & have Nearly laid by All of the Corn & Planted Peas. the Plowing is Nearly All done. have Some Slip land to Plough up yet it looks like a bad Chance for a Slip Crop the Slips that I have Planted is Not More than a half a Stand   the Weather has been So Cleare & Hot that thay have di[e]d. on 11th inst We had a Good Shour of Rain to day but not enough to Plant Slips the Corn has improved a little but Will be a Short Crop the Rice Some of it is looking tolerable Well and Some is not looking Well Lavenia will move back to the farm on Saturday next theare is no boddy Verry Sick. I Am not well my self. I have taken a Verry bad Could and am fealing badly. I exspect it is from being out So much at Night last Week I Can see since Stephn left a goodeal of obstanetry in Some of the Peopl. Mostly mongst the Woman a goodeal of Quarling and disputeing & teling lies Toney has Come back and I have him at worke have not Punishd him this is [his] Storry he Says that Stephen foold him that Stephen Came down hear on Sunday after hearing that he had to Come down & went back on Monday Morning after Tom had left & says to Toney that he had been down to me & that I told him he must fecth his family down that you did want them to go up with him and Cauld Toney & told him that I said he must help him down & to make a hury that he had to be at Kingstree by such a time Toney says that he though it all Reight and he did not no any better until thay got down to the Plantation & found that Stephn was going by he then said to Stephn you are going by the Plantation & Stephens answer to him was this that is nothing to yo. I am going to the yankees & you have to go to Toney says he Knew that Stephn was armd & was afraid to say any thing to him so thay went on & lay in Bullins lake all day tuesday & that night thay went over to Oatland Plantation & theare he left Stephn & went down to Waterford & laid by theare until thursday night when he got a chance to get one of Mr. Middletons flats & got over to Waterford Island thare was 4 other Negros that went from this side of the River. one from Mr. Weston one from Tucker two from Capt. Read & 4 I think was Going from Oatland Mr. Hyman got the wind of it on Wednesday night and Capturd all but Stphn

& family now the Question is this wheather Tony left on his own accord or got frighten & left and Stephn has not been heard of since I hear that thay did not lay by in Bullins lake. if I can find that to be true it will Prove that Tony was willing to Go. I will do my best to find out wheare thay did stay you will Pleas let me Know what is [to] be done with Toney. Some thinks that he ought to stand his triall.

Adele Petigru Allston to Jesse Belflowers

16th July, 1864.

MR. BELFLOWERS   Your last report is received today. I am very much concerned about the escape of Stephen and his family. I am inclined to believe Toney failed in some way to get off, and came back rather than be captured. How did Stephen and family come to get off when the others failed? Do you not think he is hid or was hid somewhere? I would give a great deal to have Stephen captured, not that he is so valuable, but for the moral effect. I wish Toney hired to the Government to work on the fortifications until the war is over. Do not let him return to his family or have any communication with the negroes, keep him confined until you send him off. I think it necessary to take some farther steps. If you could get a small military force, or the patrol and have Mary's house surrounded and searched, and James likewise at the same time you might find out something more. He, Stephen, no doubt left what he could not carry, with them, to get at some future time. I think Mary and James should be taken up and sent to some secure jail in the interior and held as hostages for the conduct of their children. And they should understand that this is done by the police of the country, who require that the older negroes should endeavour to influence the younger ones to order and subordination while this war lasts, and that they will be held responsible for the behaviour of their children. For this course to have the best effect it ought to be universal, and ought to be required by the police of the country. I wish you to show this letter to Col Francis Heriot and consult him as to what course he thinks best. If he thinks it best to make an example among the old people whose children have deserted, then let a cart or wagon be ready as soon as the search of the houses is over, and Mary and James sent off. They might go to Morven, tho I should dread their influence there. Some place of confinement would be the best for them but if nothing contraband was found in the search then they might be sent to Morven; letting them understand they would have to remain there until the end of the war, and desertion or rebellion in any of their children would be laid at their door. If this is done let them not have a day or an hour on the place after it is fixed on. Let them have no communication with any of their family except in presence of a white person, and put their children who have never learnt to work at once to learn. I have named Mary and James. If in your investigations you find Auba implicated pursue the same course towards her or anyone else. You would take the keys at once from Mary and James and take care of them. It does not seem to me reasonable or right to leave negroes in the enjoyment of privileges and ease and comfort, whose children go off in this way. I am persuaded it is done with their knowledge and connivance.

W. Sweet to Adele Petigru Allston

N[ightin]gale hall, 20th July 1864.

DEAR MADUM   I Receive you[r] not[e] safe and I am glad to hear that you . Receive my Reports safe I hope that my Reports is as you wish them if thay are not Please let mee know I will see those Gentlemen about Pounding Rice and let you Know when I Righth the next time I think that I will finish Planting slips on friday at N[ightin]gale hall I have weather for Planting slips light showers Evey Day for the last 4 Days the crops lwocking Just tolerable the negroes is all lwocking Pretty well and Doing Prety well noe much sickness a mong them the negroes all wish to Be Remberd to you and family. I Did not think to say to you that the girl Juely at ganderloss fel Down the other nigth and Broke he Rigth colerboan But she is Doing well and out at work know I will send the chickens and [illegible] for you By the Boat when she comes up. I am sory to say to you that Boath the sows that Belong to the Plantation is Dead and is not a Breading on the Place on[e] Dide with old age and the othe[r] with some kind of sickness in the throat I think that I can Buy one for you But Doe not like to By one until I could hear from you if you wish mee to Get one for you you will Pleas let mee Know when you Right to mee again

Ps   Pleas let mee Know if I must [send] Susanah children By the Boat.

N[ightin]gale hall

14th July	all hands hoing Rice	none sick
15th July	all hands hoing Rice	no[n]e sick
16th July	all hands hoing Rice	none sick
18th July	all hands Planting slips	1 sick
19th July	all hands Planting slips	2 sick
20th July	all hands Planting slips	4 sick

Ganderloss

14th July	all hands planting slips	2 sick
15th July	all hands Planting slips	3 sick
16th July	all hands Planting slips	3 sick
18th July	all hands Planting slips	2 sick
19th July	all hands hoing Rice	4 sick
20th July	all hands hoing Rice	4 sick

Jesse Belflowers to Adele Petigru Allston

Chicora Wood, 20 July, 1864.

MRS. ALLSTON   Yours of the 11 inst has been duly Recd. since my last. I have layd by all the Corn and Planted all the Peas and all the Slips exsept Red Seed. have them to Plant yet While doing the up land Work. the pipe down hand has been imployed in the Rice all the time   Verry little improvement in the Corn Crop   the Rice some of it is looking well   With the help of the two hundred bushels of Corn at Mr. Weather Spoons I will be abel to make out a Cooper Shop   it would be well enough to make your own barrels Provided theare be a fair deduction made on the tole. I think wheare barrels is found theare ought to be a deduction of at least five per Cent allowd and all the offold [i.e., offal]   I doant think theare will be much demand for barrels   I have not made any inquery about Stavs & Hoop Poles yet of Course it will be high   no nails no shingles   if I put up a Shop it will have to be a Verry Coarse one. Will have to Cover it with Pine bark   if you say build one I will put it up   I will look round next week and see what I can get staves & hoops at and let you Know   I will have to do some worke to the Boat as soon as that is done. I want to sende her up so as the hands can git back for Harvest   Carpenters as Gilbert & Joe cant come down. I will try to do the best I can with what is hear   Roger Jackson & Billey I think had better stay wheare thay are   Hamaday would not do much if he was to come down Lavenia has moved up hear   she has nothing to do. theare is [no] Cotton for to spin. I have some idea of Giveing her some sewing work to do until we get some Cotton   I have Toney at work   I think he tells the truth   the pople all seam qui[e]t   no hard sickness   at the same time theare is a Great many in the house   Harry has Given me 4 Water mellons   his Garden is in Good order   have not heard any thinge more of Stephn he must have got through the Pckits and is gone   I hear that Dr Hasels man has lost a boat one that he had to cut marsh in   I have not got cleare of my cold yet. What shall I do with Toney he seams to be satisfide and under the beleaf that he will be Punished   let me hear from you.

W. Sweet to Adele Petigru Allston

N[ightin]gale hall, 3th august, 1864.

DEAR MADUM   I Receive your very welcom note of 24th safe in hand   I will finish hoing over my Rice for the last time on saterday at N[ightin]gale hall I finish on ganderloss on last saterday   my crop is lwocking tolerable well on Boath Plases Rice corn Peas and Potatoes   my Rice is Just comense shwoting out its head   I Doe not think that I will Be able to comense harvest oun til the middle of September   the Rice cropes is all very Backward soe far as I have seen   your Block of yarn made 23 yards of very Prety cloth. I have no very hard sickness among the negroes   those that ware soe sick has all got Beter

and gon out to work all Exsept trim he is stil Pretty sick I had to call the
Dr to him on yesterday the negroes is all geting on Pretty well soe far and
all sends howday to you and family Driver Sam on N[ightin]gale hall told
mee to Beg you for a shirt for him if you Pleas for he was out of shirts. this is
the last sheet of Paper that you left with mee to make out my Reports on.
the negroes are all Beging very hard for clothing But I told them that thay
must wait until you came home in the fal though thay seem Pretty Bare for
cloths though cloth is very hih and I think that thay can make out until you
come home in the faul. hannah has not Done much at Raseing Poltry she
has fiu turkeys and a fiu gines [i.e., guineas] and a fiu chickesne.

N[ightin]gale hall

28th July	all hands hoing Rice 3 sick
29th July	all ha[n]ds hoing Rice 2 sick
30th July	all ha[n]ds hoing Rice 2 sick
1th august	all hands hoing Rice 2 sick
2th august	all hands hoing Rice 4 sick
3th august	all hands hoing Rice 5 sick

ganderloss

28th July	all hands hoing Rice 2 sick
29th July	all hands hoing Rice 3 sick
30th July	all hands hoing Rice 2 sick
1th august	all hands hoing Peas 2 sick
2th august	all hands hoing Peas 4 sick
3th august	all hands hoing Peas 4 sick

Jesse Belflowers to Adele Petigru Allston

Chicora Wood, August 3th, 1864.

MRS. ALLSTON   Yours of 24 inst has been Recd since my last Report. the
hand has been working in the Rice, going over it for the last time. I see in
the oldest Rice some shooting out. the Corn is filling out rite well. the Peas
doant look well, have taken the Rust & a Good many have died the Potatoes
look well the Slips do not look well I have not seen Mr. Tilton yet he
is on black River I think I can get as many staves as I want at ten dollars
pr M. Please let me Know if you can get Boards from the Mill in No. Ca
for the heading I have Recd a letter from Robertson & Blacklock saying
theare is one hundred barrels of Rice at Salters turn out, which is Reported
to belong to Government but are disposed to think that it belongs to the
Estatee. I have writen to Mr. Shaw askeing him to find out a bout it and
let me Know I also inclose theare letter to you People all well & Quiet had
a fine Rain 2 inst have let Mrs Ex. Parker have two bushels of Salt Mr
Tyler has not brought any Honey hear yet.

W. Sweet to Adele Petigru Allston

N[ightin]gale hall, 10th august, 1864.

DEAR MADUM   your leter of the 31 has Bin Receive safe and I will atend to Every thing that you have Rote to mee to Doe I finish hoing Rice on last friday and I have Bin hoing slips and Peas Ever since I will finist hoing slips and Peas about tusday next the crop is lwocking tolerable well trim is litle Beter I have no hard sickness on Eather Place I have not Receive the Bags as yet But will get them in a fiu Deays I would Be very glad if I could get the corn that you ware to let mee have for I will not have Enough Provisions to last mee to September if I Doe not get some sune you will Pleas send mee the Key that Belongs to the Stor Barn at ganderloss as I would lik to Put my Syrup in thar when I Boil it. if you are not going to send toney off in the up cuntry you will Pleas let mee take him home with me to N[ightin]gale hall the negroes are generly well and thay all send howdy to you and family.

N[ightin]gale hall

4th august	all hands hoing Rice	no sick
5th august	all hands hoing Rice	no sick
6th august	all hands hoing slips	no sick
8th august	all hands hoing corn and slips	no sick
9th august	all hands hoing corn	1 sick
10th august	all hands hoing Peas	3 sick

ganderloss

4th august	all hands hoing Peas	1 sick
5th august	all hands hoing Peas	2 sick
6th august	all hands hoing Peas	2 [sick]
8th august	all hands hoing Peas	4 sick
9th august	all hands trashing oats	4 sick
10th august	all hands hoing Peas	3 sick

Jesse Belflowers to Adele Petigru Allston

Chicora Wood, 10 Augst, 1864.

MRS. ALLSTON   Since my last Report theare has nothing transpierd worth notice. We have had a dry hot week Joe arrived hear on the 4 of this inst. by him yours of 31 July was Recd saying you wisht a beef a dry Cow. theare is none that will do. I have sent a 2 1/2 year old Steer in Place which ought to be up by Saturday if nothing hapens to them on the way I find more work to do to the Boat than I thought. I have had to stop work on her and make two Mills for Guendalos & N[ightingale] Hall to Crush Cane am now cokeing Boat. Will try to get her done this week soon as done I will start her up I do not hear of any fright and have not heard aney thing from Mr. Tilten have worked the Slips and find that I have to do some more Picking in the Rice have some Rice nearly all shot out. I will send jugs by the Boat for the oil but I think if you can git a barrel you had best do so as Guendalos & N[ightingale] Hall will want oil. I not it is high the Mills cannot work without it. the People is all well & Quiet Phebe sends howdey to you Lavenia is Gone to the farm

[P.S.] the Boat that is commenced I think if the work is well advanced it woul be advisabel to finish her than to let the work be lost, but if not let it a lone until a more Lasiese [i.e., leisure] time.

W. Sweet to Adele Petigru Allston

N[ightin]gale hall, 24th august, 1864.

DEAR MADUM   I have tride to make out my Repourt and send to you But it is about all that I can. my self and Daugther has Boath Bin Down with chil and fever since saterday and I am not able to sit up to Rigth.

N[ightin]gale hall

18th august	all hands hoin Peas	1 sick
19th august	all hands oan the Road	1 sick
20th august	give all hands holady	
22th august	all hands striping Blades	1 sick
23th august	all hands striping Blades	1 sick
24th august	all hands striping Blades	2 sick

ganderloss

18th august	10 head makeing Banks 28 head hoing slips and Peas	5 sick
19th august	10 head making Banks 28 head hoing slips Peas	5 sick
20th august	10 head making Banks 30 head hoing Peas and slips	4 sick
22th august	all hands striping Blades	4 sick
23th august	all hands striping Blades	7 sick
24th august	all hands Striping Blades	7 sick

Jesse Belflowers to Adele Petigru Allston

Chicora Wood, 24 August, 1864.

MRS ALLSTON   Since my last I Recd your letter by Peter who arrived safely home on the 19 inst I got through with the Rice and have the woman hoing Peas the men have cut wood for the threshing Mill & now have them ditching have let Mr. Sweet have a sow from Auber he is also geting Corn from the farm I Shall Commence giting fodder to morrow & will Commence makeing molases next week Joe Blythe Allston told me that theare was Salt at Salters turnout & he would order it from theare for Mrs. Petigru & Miss North Iris is in a Condition that she would be of no use in the havest I think it best not to move her down I think from what I can learn from Britton Neck that they have a short Crop Joe left hear on the 18 inst in two week time he ought to be up to Society hill the People all Quiet, but have a greatdeal of sickness. Auber is quite sick I have had the fever three days the week I am trying to stave it of with quinine Paul leaves hear to Night for Society hill with the Pears

[P. S.] We must have some oil for the Mill as thare is some Parts of the machenry that must have oil Leard will help some by mixing some oil with it.

W. Sweet to Adele Petigru Allston

N[ightin]gale hall, 31th august, 1864.

DEAR MADUM I Receive Boath of you[r] last notes By Peter and the one of 23th of august I have had the lock taken of the storbarn and a Key made to it and the lock Put Back. I had not Receive aney leter from Dr Preston nor Did not Know that Rose was at Salters Station until I Receive yours of 23th I then sent Rigth for her But thay had not Return as yet I think that thay will come home to Day. I will Get the corn at the farm from mr [Bel]-flowers But that will only Be Enough for 2 allowance for N[ightin]gale hall mr [Bel]flowers says that he Dose not think that thare is over 50 Bushels. I will Get it to morrow as I have sent frank ove[r] to wacamaw after the stock and he has and Reports to mee that he can not find one cow over thare to save his life he was gon 5 Days I am working on my flats and I Exspect to Begin my harvest on 10th I have had several cases of fever Prety tite cases since I Rote to you last some at ganderloss and some at N[ightin]gale hall Minder and 3 or 4 of the children at ganderloss has Bin quit[e] [sick] But all is Beter 3 or 4 children at N[ightin]gale hall But all is Beter at this time you Rote to mee that you would like mee to git some whit[e] Pirson at ganderloss I have Bin trying to get some one to goe thare since June But it is very hard to Get aney one at this time I will stil Doe my Best I would Rather have some white man thare if I can [get] one But the me[n] is all gon in to Service Sue at N[ightin]gale hall was confind on 27th with a Boy child. my self and family has all Bin quite sick with chil and fever But all is up soe thay can set up none able to Get out But my self and I not able to Doe much as yet while I am Rose and susanna has Got home Rose is stil quite sick. the Rice Birds and Duck is very Bad on the Rice I have mad[e] some forhundred Bushils oats at ganderloss But very letle Ry onley 12 Bushels of Ry I have Receive the sow from chicora.

N[ightin]gale hall

25th august	all hands striping Blades	1 sick
26th august	all hands working slips	1 sick
27th august	hands working slips	1 sick
29th august	all hands hoing Bancks	1 sick
30th august	all hands trashing oats	2 sick
31th august	all hands trashing oats	2 sick

ganderloues

25th august	all hands striping Blades	3 sick
26th august	all hands striping Blades	4 sick
27th august	all hands striping Blades	4 sick
29th august	all hands striping Blades	2 sick
30th august	all hands striping Blades	4 sick
31th august	all hands working shugar cain	4 sick

Jesse Belflowers to Adele Petigru Allston

Chicora Wood, 31th August, 1864.

MRS. ALLSTON   Yours of 22 August has been Recd Giveing the turns of Pounding & by Paul I have Recd. yours of 29 August Mr. Sweet will get the Corn from the farm Says that will not be enough to do him I cant speare any more as I have only another days Grinding, which will last me to the 18 of September, and then I will have to dig Potatoes & use the flat & dirty Rice we have had a Sever wind hear which has blew down all Sugar Cane I am now boiling Syrup am about half done Gitting fodder I think I will Cut Rice on the 10 of Septbr I have not been abel to see Mr. Tilton yet I think you could sell your Hoopoles Verry Readley, also the boards for heading I am Very Glad to hear that Col. Ben Allston is exspected home soon. I have mist the fever and am feeling Verry well now Good many sick Childern the People all seam Quiet I am haveing all of the mashed Cane hauld to the Hog Crale, which thay seam to be Very thankful for it.

W. Sweet to Adele Petigru Allston

[Nightingale Hall], September 7th, 1864.

DEAR MADUM   I am Geting on with my shugar cain as fast as I can though I will not Get thru Before saterday I will Begin to cut Rice on Boath Plantation I will [try] to work my shugar cain the Best way that I can I think that I will make something over a barrel at ganderloss I cant tel Exactly what I will make at N[ightin]gale hall as yet for I have Just Begun. I Receive 52 Bushels of corn from mr Belflowers I have had to Brak in some of my corn out of the field to allowance with on Boath Plantations I am giveing half allowance of Potatoes to the children on Boath Plantations. I have made 200 and 50 Bushels of oats on N[ightin]gale hall. when I trash out my Ry in the sumer I trash it over Barrels By hand I then made 95 Bushels since then I have trash over the straw and few oat stalks and with what I had trash out Before it all has turn out one hundred and 60 Bushels. I have had a great deal of feaver among the negroes on Boath Places since I Rote to you last. Pleas Exscuse my Bad Righting for I am quit un well and my family like wise.

N[ightin]gale hall

1th September	all hands trashing oats and cleaning Barn yard 1 hand 21 Days Repa[ir]ing wining house and trashing mill steps 2 sick
2th September	all hands cleaning Barn yard and striping Blads 2 hands Picking Peas 2 sick
3th September	all hands cleaning Barn yard 1 sick
5th September	all hands cleaning Barn yard and working shugar cain 4 sick
6th September	all hands hoing Bancks and grinding shugar cain 4 sick
7th September	all hands hoing Bancks and grinding shugar cain 4 sick

ganderloss

1th September	all hands hoing slips and grinding shugar cain 5 sick
2th September	all hands hoing Barnyard and grinding shugar cain 4 sick
3th September	all hands hoing Barnyard and grinding shugar cain 4 sick
5th September	4 hands on the Road the Rest hoing Barnyard and grinding shugar cain 3 sick
6th September	4 hands 5 Days on the Road the Rest hoing Barnyard and grinding shugar cain 4 sick
7th September	all hands hoing Barnyard and grinding shugar cain 4 sick

Jesse Belflowers to Adele Petigru Allston

Chicora Wood, 7 Sept, 1864.

MRS. ALLSTON Since my last Report I have got in all of the fodder now thrshing the oats have made two barrels of molasses & am boilling for the third the men is working the Road this week have fixt the well in the yeard Paul is feeding Kittey & Bill on oats I have 20 Acers of Rice land turnd with the Plough Lavenia Begs Verry hard that if anna is to go to work that you let her Come down and work on the Plantation with Rest of the hands that she doant wish her to work with Bob I think it best to I have made out Cotton enough to Keep her Spining and can still do so as the new Cotton is opening will cut Rice nxt Saturday the 10 have good maney sick Children yet the pople all seame to be Verry Quiet at Preasant

Mr. Tyler has been down since my last he says that he has had the honney Ready for a longe time but did not no you weare in want of it or he would have brough it down he says the Crop at Britton Neck is better than last year, but doant think they will make enough to last them the year Toney will go [to] N[ightingale] H[all] and help havest theare.

Jesse Belflowers to Adele Petigru Allston

Chicora Wood, 13 Sept, 1864.

MRS. ALLSTON Since my last thear has noth[ing] new transprd. the sick is all better have got all of my flats Ready for havest I did not cut Rice

on Saturday. the tides being very high and the Banks leakey I could not get
the water of the land I cut on a monday & will have in the yeard to day 52
Acres will cut to morow thursday at Pipe down & will ty & stack theare as
it is to far to cut & make a load in the day have made 373 bushels of oats and
good oats at that the Rye will not turn out more th[an] 22 bushels the Cata-
piller or the Army Worme has taken to the Cotton and will not leave a leaf
on it the birds is very bad on the younge Rice I am fearful that thay hurt it
a goodeal have made 3 barrels of molases I think I will make two moore or
very near it I am feeding the Hogs on the seed of the Cane. thay are verry
Poor bob has Got up what Hogs he has that is fit for Bacon as thay did
incline to stray off & was likely to lost People all Quiet & Chearful.

W. Sweet to Adele Petigru Allston

N[ightin]gale hall, 14th September, 1864.

DEAR MADUM I comence my harvest on last saterday on Boath Plantations
the weather is very fin for harvest so far I will Bring some Rice in to the
Barn yard at N[ightin]gale hall to Day and at ganderloss to morrow. I think
that I will make about 2 Barrels of Syrrup on Each Place I finish grinding at
ganderloss to Day I will not finish at N[ightin]gale hall until the last of
next weeak. litle Dianah was confind with a boy child on the 9 I am very
sorry to say to you that one of Prisilia children a boy name July Dide on 12th
with fits a[nd] fever I have had a grea[t] deal of fever among the children
But not much among the grone negroes. old Rose is Stil quite sick mr Belflowers sent toney to mee on friday last I have concluded to let toney wife
stay whare she is for a while as I understand that she is Pregnant and will
not Be much survice in the harvest if I am Rong for soe Doing Pleas let
mee know. the negroes all sends thare love to you an family my self and
family is very un well.

N[ightin]gale hall

8th September	all hands hoing Bancks and grinding shugar cain no sick
9th September	all hands hoing Bancks grind shugar cain no sick
10th September	all hands cu[t]ing Rice grinding shugar cain no sick
12th September	all hands harvesting grinding shugar cain 3 women with sick children
13th September	all hands harvesting grinding shugar cain 3 women with sick children
14th September	all hands harvesting grinding shugar cain 1 woman with sick child

ganderloss

8th September	all hands cleaning Barn yard grinding shugar cain 4 sick
9th September	all hands cleaning Barn yard grinding shugar cain 3 sick

10th September   all hands harvesting grinding shugar cain 2 sick
12th September   all hands harvesting grinding shugar cain 2 sick
13th September   all harvesting and grinding shugar cain 2 sick
14th September   all harvesting and grinding shugar cain 2 sick

J. C. Yates to Adele Petigru Allston

[Anson County, N.C.], September 17th, 1864.

MRS ALSTON   I Will inform you I came Home at the 10 instant and found my attention needing at Home I have Ben very Bissy saving my foder sins I came Home I have Ben to yore Farm twise Mr Baringttine has saved A fine Crop of fodder theay Will commence making Molass tuesday next I expect to Be with them too days u[n]till I get them started Wednesday next is giving in day at Marion I have Drawn up A list of all the Propitye except yore House furtinety I shall not give it in u[n]till I see you as I hope to see yu shortly at the farm The Sessors [i.e., Assessors] Promi[sed] to Weight one me u[n]till I see you thire is som of the furniture Box up and I could not Draw A Correct list of it the govinement Agents wish to Hire the Carptners I wish to no Whither theay Will Be need to finish the Boat or not Mr Lesesne Wroght to me to send him the Reseite fo[r] the Money that I paid for the Lilse land the Reicite Was intered one the Back of the Bond and I Could not send it to him With out sending the Bond the Bond Was need in Coart the clearking Master has now got A order from the Coart to Make the title for the land when you Come up I Will hand you the Bond and the Recitte for the land.

Duncan Barrentine to Adele Petigru Allston

[Anson County, N.C.] Sept 18, 1864.

MRS. ADELE ALLSTON   I send you a few lines by Frances We are all as Well as Usual Anna is Improving We are Clearing New ground Next Week We are going to pull Our New ground fodder the cane Will be to geather and Make Up this comeing in Week the carpenters are all Imployed at home at this time I sent down by the Boat 80 lbs of Wool I kept back the Tythe Wool 9 1/2 lbs a few days Since I had to give in Our Wheat Oats Rye and Wool as Tax in kine Next Wensday I have to give in Our confederate tax Whitch Imbraces a greate Many things as you are Aware I Supose I am at a great loss how to proseed with it I Send you a list[1] of what I have to give in the Mill is runing Ocasionly as we have Water Mr Yates is at home Sela is Weaveing geting Along pretty Well I think I Will send the Barrels as you Requested to the Rail Road Next Teusday.

[1] Newspaper clipping: "Confederate Tax Notice."

W. Sweet to Adele Petigru Allston

N[ightin]gale hall, 21th September, 1864.

DEAR MADUM   I finish grinding my shugar cain at ganderloss on last weddnesday I have very near 2 Barrels of syrrup I finish at N[ightin]gale hall on
monday last and I made about 2 Barrels of molases at N[ightin]gale hall
Stephen got home on monday knighth I have had the Dr to see him and
the Dr says that he think Stephen will sune Get up he has given mee some
medison for him Rose is Beter some times trim is Beter and then he Gets
worse again for some 2 or 3 Days then he is up again the Dr is at work on him.
I have had 2 women confind at ganderloss since I Rot you Sammy wife Serenah
and minder Serenah on 13th minder 16th I am sorry to say to you that I
lost another litle negroe at Nigh[tin]gale hall since I Rot you the Dr ware
cald to the child it was Sealier least Boy. the weather has Bin very Bad for
harvest since last Sunday I have not Bin able to Doe aney thing about my
Rice since last Saterday until to Day it has [been] Raining Every Day
since Saterday until this Day I have got 4 flat loads in the yard at N[ightin]-
gale hall and 2 at ganderloss. have Receive 70 Bushels of corn from mr Belflowers for N[ightin]gale hall and 35 for ganderloss that came Down By the
Boat I have allso Receve 14 Peases of Bacon for N[ightin]gale hall and 7 for
ganderloss making 175 1/2 for N[ightin]gale hall and 107 for ganderloss I
would like you if you can to Get a Pair of shoes for trim as he is with out
aney I gave an old Pair in the spring But that are worn out.

N[ightin]gale hall

15th September	all hands harvesting and grinding shugar cain	2 sick
16th September	all hands harvesting grinding shugar cain	2 sick
17th September	all hands harvesting grinding shugar cain	1 sick
19th September	all hands harvesting grinding shugar cain	3 sick
20th September	all hands gleaning fields	4 sick
21th September	all the men cuting wood all the women Picking Peas	5 sick

ganderloss

15th September	all hands harvesting	2 sick
16th September	all hands harvesting	2 sick
17th September	all hands harvesting	2 sick
19th September	all hands harvesting	2 sick
20th September	the men Diching women caring straw in the field	1 sick
21th September	the men Diching women carrying straw in the field	3 sick

Jesse Belflowers to Adele Petigru Allston

Chicora Wood, 21 Sept, 1864.

MRS. ALLSTON   Yours of the 11 inst. was Recd by Joe. he arrived her[e] on
Saturday night last and delivered one hundred and 27 boards which measurd

2125 feet, & 700 hundred hoop poles the Corn from Mr. Witherspoons &
the Corn from Ladrus was put to geather boath Parsels only measured 365
bushels of Cob Corn, which Gives only 182 1/2 bushels of Sheld Corn I cannot tell how much Mr. Weatherspoons Corn fell short, unless I Knew how
much Ladrus put a bord. I Keep 100 hundred bushels of it, Mr. Sweet 75
bushels Eveans Corn turnd out 22 1/2 bushels let Guendalos 32 1/2 bushels
so the whole only Gives 207 1/2 of Cheld Corn I have only 52 Acres of Rice
in the yeard yet. have all of the Rice at Pipe down cut down & the most of
tyed & Stackd theare been no weather this week to handle Rice. it has
Raind every day since Sunday and still looking like Rain no boddey very
sick. have one little Girl that is very Punny all Quiet

a List of Bacon Give out for haverst. Guendalos 5 hames one Gammon
one flitch N[ightingale] H[all] 10 hames 2 Gammons 2 flitch I Keep for
h[a]rv[e]st 28 Peceses I divided in this way—I Plant 400 hundred Acres
I take four Piecses N[ightingale] H[all] Plants 225 Acres takes 2 Pieces
Guendalos Plants 100 Acres 1 Piece
So you see I have divided it by the acers

P. S.   the Boards I Keep for Plantation use Paul says it was your orders to
feed own oats Since Receveing your letter I have stopt Giveing them.

W. Sweet to Adele Petigru Allston

N[ightin]gale hall, 28th September, 1864.

DEAR MADUM I Receive your note By Jany and would ansered ite when
I Rote you Before But I ware sumond to goe after some yankeys Prisners
that had got a way from florrance [i.e., Florence] and had got Down this
low on thare way to thare gunboats 2 of them stole my Poaling Boat out of
the Barn yard from tom on the Knigth of 19th But ware caugth on wacamaw on 27th and I have got her Back safe. as I ware going to ganderloss on
last friday I taken up one of the yankeys Just at the bank of the Road above
mr charles allston Plantation and I taken him to Jail. I have got my Exem-
tion from General Garlington I am Geting on Pretty well with my harvesting considering how much Bad weather we have had we have had some
Prety gwod weather since last saterday I have got one hundred acars cut
Down and the most of it in the yard at N[ightin]gale hall and about sixty
at ganderloss I have had a gwodeal of fever among the negroes lately.
But nothing very sirious at this time. I have never seen the like of the Duck
for the season in my life as thare is at N[ightin]gale hall I can not Keep
them out of the field Doe all that I can it appiers that thay will Eat up
all of the Rice and Knothing to shwot them with the negroes wishes to Be
rememberd to you and family Stephen and Rose is Beter trim is about
the same.

N[ightin]gale hall

22th September   all hands harvestin   4 sick
23th September   all hands harvesting   3 sick
24th September   all hands harvesting   2 sick
26th September   all hands harvesting   4 sick
27th September   all hands harvesting   4 sick
28th September   all hands harvesting   3 sick

ganderloss

22th September   all hands harvesting   4 sick
23th September   all hands harvesting   3 sick
24th September   all hands harvesting   3 sick
26th September   all hands harvesting   2 sick
27th September   all hands harvesting   1 sick
28th September   all hands harvesting   1 sick

J. C. Yates to Adele Petigru Allston

[Anson County, N.C., October, 1864.]

I Was gone frome Home three Weaks the trip Worsted me very much I Went Before the Medicale Board in Wil[min]gton and got A dis Charge and I should not got A Discharge if it had not Ben for A friend I Can now attend to my Bissnes at Home I Will inform you that there was too Disearts Cought in yore Farm yestarde and I Deliverde them to the enrolling offesaer theay was south Carilneia [i.e., Carolinians] I have not seen Mr Chilson sins I Came Home A Bout the Mill [illegible] I Wish to see you and get yore advice Before I Praseed eany futher I think it Will all Be strateed up Wen I see you if it is so that you Cant Come up shortly pleas Wright to me and I will Come down.

W. Sweet to Adele Petigru Allston

N[ightin]gale hall, 5th october, 1864.

DEAR MADUM I Receive yours of 29th safe in hand yesterday morning I will send you a list of the grone negroes when Paul comes up I am not able to say to you when I will have Rice Ready for the mill or when I will Be Ready to goe to trashing for I have no oil and the mill is in very Bad order I am not Done harvesting yet for the weather has Bin soe Bad that I could not Doe aney thing hardley to wards cuting Rice or aney thing Else for it has Bin Raining Every Day si[n]ce last friday until yesterday I am not able to say what the Rice crop will turn out. I think that I will finish harvesting at ganderlos next weeak if I have gwod weather and I will finish at N[ightin]-gale hall on the weeak after if nothing hapens I could have some Ducks

Kild and send them to you By Paul But I have no shot or Powder nor caps toney is Doing very well soe far I Keep him watch Prety clost I stil have a litle fever a mong the negroes But not as much as has Bin I see that the negroes is to Be Return in 2 or 3 clases you will Pleas let mee Know how you wish mee to Doe a Bout them for the taxses Return must Be made By 20th of this month my self and family is much Beter.

N[ightin]gale hall

29th September	all hands harvesting	4 sick
30th September	all hands harvesting	4 sick
1th october	all hands harvesting	3 sick
3th october	all hands gleaning fields	4 sick
4th october	all hands gleaning fields	5 sick
5th october	all hands harvesting	5 sick

ganderlos

29th September	all hands harvesting	1 sick
30th September	all hands harvesting	2 sick
1th october	all hands harvesting	2 sick
3th october	all hands Puling Beens	3 sick
4th october	all hands gleaning fields	4 sick
5th october	all hands gleaning fields	4 sick

Jesse Belflowers to Adele Petigru Allston

Chicora Wood, 5 October, 1864.

MRS. ALLSTON Yours of 29 has been Recd. the day that I was to have writen to you, after Returning from the Barn in the morning I was taken with a sick stumach, and from that to a Vommiting as shuch I was not abel to write the Prospect of shoes is Verry bad. all the good hides was sent up the River. I do not Know to who to tan 12 good hides & one for my self the hides that Will has to tan is the hides that come from the Sea-shore, and Verry badly damage at that, 7 of them and two good hides from hear. So the Prospect look Verry bad for 200 pears of Shoes and with-out Shoes theare will not be much work done this winter, and it much wanted. it will be almost useless to Plant Rice when the land is in such bad order I would have finishd harvest this week all to 40 acres if the Weather had been good it will take all of next week to get in the Rice if the Weather is good I doant think I will start the threshing Mill before the first of No-vember I doant think Mr. Tilton will be Ready to Pound before that time have heard from Britton Neck this week all well Wills leather is not done taning have sent Binah up theare to wate on Abbey & Iris have given one half allowanc of Potatoes. thay turnout tolerabel well I inquird after Wills Hogs, but learnt but verry little a bout them—the Condition nor the Number of them I have hired the Cooprs to Mr. Tilton at 30 dollas a month & feed them I done this to Keep them from being feed at the exspence of the Estate this will be aded to theare hire a[t] the Rate of what ever Corn is selling at I will send you up 2 Cows as soon as I git in all of the old Rice I[f] thay can be Speard. Will send by Paul the Jugs for oil & one for the Whiskey, he will be up on Saturday night or Sunday morning have lost the little Girl Clarisa that so Puney she is one of Billeys Childern We have had Rain every day since last Saturday done Boiling Molases. made 3 barrels & a fiew Gallons over I see now that I boild down a little to much it Verry thick Molases People all Quiet & no hard sickness

[P. S.] I Supose you have seen that the War taxes has to be Returnd by the 20 of this month must I make Returns for N[ightingale] H[all] or will Mr. Sweet do it, also Guendalos.

W. Sweet to Adele Petigru Allston

N[ightin]gale hall, 7th october, 1864.

DEAR MADUM   I send you the number of men women and half hands all seperrate

35 men with Stephen and toney
48 women with Susanna
8 half Boys . . . . . . 8 half hand girls

Susanna Begs that you will send her close in a bundle By Paul if you Pleas.

Jesse Belflowers to Adele Petigru Allston

Chicora Wood, 10 October, 1864.

MRS. ALLSTON   Yours of the 4 inst has been Recd haveing some Repairs to do to the Waggon it took one day longer than I exspected so I could not start Paul be fore to day the 10 I have sent by him 3 Canns for oil & one Jug one demijohn, 2 locks & screws & the Blue stone that is all that I have I Gave you the amount of Cloth that will be Requiried to give the grone hands an out side suit will take 1509 yeards

to Give them a Shirt	522 yeards
for the Children	350 yeard
will want Shoes	174 Pairs

Mr. Tylar has brough the honey it looks to be in Good order as it so late in the Season I have not sent any of it the Weather is good I want to get in all the Rice this week all so the younge Rice I will gave a list of the tax Returns in my next Report the Pople all well & Quiet.

W. Sweet to Adele Petigru Allston

[Nightingale Hall, 12] october, 1864.

DEAR MADUM I finish harvesting at ganderlos on 12th I will finish at N[ightin]gale hall on saterday 15th and then I will Begin to geather in my corn and Peas on monday 17th my Rice is Just tolerable my Peas I think will turn out Pretty well on Boath Plases my slips lwock Pretty well But I Doe not Know how thay will turn [MS torn] take in my crop as quick as I [can] on Boath Plases I have no[t] much sicknes among the negroes thay all seem to hold up Pretty well Exsept Know and then some of them is in the house Rose Stphen and trim Beter

P s Rebeca and Judy at N[ightin]gale hall Beg mee to say to you that t[h]ay wish to have husbans if you Pleas one of the men is from mr W trapers [i.e., Trapier] the other from mr Pringle at the whit[e] house I can not allow them to have husbans of[f] the Plantation with out your consent if you are willing for them to take husbans you can Rigth me if not let me know Boath of the men has Brougth gwod Recomindations. crismus is the nam of the man that Judy wants from mr trapers and Damond is nam of the man that Rebeca wants from the whit[e] house. [MS torn.]

N[ightin]gale hall

6th october	[MS torn]	
7th october	all hands harvesting	[MS torn]
8th october	all hands harvesting	[MS torn]
10th october	all hands harvesting	4 sick
11th october	all hands harvesting	5 sick
12th october	all hands harvesting	4 sick

ganderlos

6th october	all hands harvesting	3 sick
7th october	all hands harvesting	2 sick
8th october	all hands harvesting	2 sick
10th october	all hands harvesting	2 sick
12th october	all hands harvesting	5 sick

J. C. Yates to Adele Petigru Allston[1]

[Anson County, N.C.], Oct 12th, 1864.

DEAR MADAM I have Settled with Mr Chilson for the mill; we according to your request choosed a Gentleman apiece to Settle the difficulty as to the mill and am Sorry to say that neither of them would act and we finally concluded to settle the matter between ourselve which I hope will be Satisfactory to you. We have also Chosen a Couple more if you feel that you had

---

[1] Obviously written for Yates by another hand.

rather that   as we think will undoubtedly will try to Settle the matter Between us. Said Chilson paid me (3593.75) Thirty five hundred and ninety three Dollars and Seventy five Cents   you will please find Enclosed the Sheriffs Receipt for Taxes of 1864 it being four hundred and Six dollars and Eighty seven Cents   also paid one 100.00 Hundred Dollars for thredd or Cotton Yarn leaving a Remainder of 3086.88 Three thousand and Eighty Six dollars and Eighty Eight Cents which I have this day Paid in the Bank of Cheraw S. C   when you Receive this money you will please Send me your Receipt for the Same that is said money   I have also recd. 1150.00 Eleven hundred and fifty dollars for the wouk of the Carpenters which I will Send you a list of in my next letter it Being from Arnold and Cooley.

W. Sweet to Adele Petigru Allston

N[ightin]gale hall, 19th october, 1864.

DEAR MADUM   I finish harvest at ganderlos on last thursday and at N[ightin]-gale hall on Saterday and I comense takeing in my corn at Boath Plases on monday   the hands Did not much on yesterday for it Raind all day or very near soe   I think that I will finish with my corn some time next weeak and then I will Pick my Peas oan Boath Plases   we have had some 2 or 3 Rigth smart frost stil the Potatoe vines not Kild   I will Doe my Best and take in my crop as quick as I can soe that I will Be Ready for trashing Rice   I will have to have ligth wood for trashing and I will have it [to] By for thare is no ligth wood on the land to cut But I Doe not like to Buy until hear from you   I am sory to say to you that faney little child Dide on 15th   it was not sick more than one or too Days   no[t] much sickness Exsept some children   mr Belflowers and my self went to georgetown on yesterday and Return your and col Ben taxses   mr Belflowers will gave you the statement of the taxses   I would like to see you very much in deed on some Particular Business though I will see you when you come Down home   I have several negroes that I think you had Best move when you come home   I will tel you about Every thing when I see you.

N[ightin]gale hall

13th october	all hands harvesting 4 sick
14th october	all hands harvesting 4 sick
15th october	all hands harvesting 3 sick
17th october	all hands Braking in corn 2 sick
18th october	all hands trashing corn 3 sick
19th october	all hands Picking Peas 5 sick

ganderlos

13th october	all hands harvesting 2 sick
14th october	all hands cleaning up the yard 4 sick

15th october   all hands given holly Day no sick
17th october   all hands Breaking corn .1 sick
18th october   all hands trashing corn 2 sick
19th october   all hands Braking corn 3 sick

Jesse Belflowers to Adele Petigru Allston

Chicora Wood, 19 October, 1864.

MRS. ALLSTON— Since my last I have got in all the Rice exsept the late Rice that is cut down but not brought in yet the Rice Crop is going to be short I have made tax Returns—have Returnd from Chicora Pipe down & N[ightingale] Hall Negroes 403 head, Leaveing out 28 head from Chicora Wood & 5 head at Pipe down & in same Pro[por]tion at N[ightingale] Hall Also have Retund 600 hunderd Acres of Land Planted in Rice & all the lands that is Planted in provisions, all the Stock Cattle Sheep Hogs Goats Horses & Mules. Carts & Waggons 400 bushels oats Rye 112 bushels and Bacon that was on hand after the 17 February 170 lbs Wool, hoes Axes Spads Plough Plough Gears and 1300 bushels of Corn 1500 bushels Rice I can see in the last two weeks some change in the Pople thay doant seem to care to obay orders & Jack the Drive[r] is not behaveing write he doant talk write before the People Ben has been Col F. W. Hariet with a Complant with out any Provecation that I Knew nothing a bout it until he came to me with a note from him Peter left hear yeasterday with two Cows & Caves for you. if nothing hapens to him on the Road ought to [be] up with them Saturday I Pict Peas two days I could start the Mill next week but the Corn & Peas is wasting Verry much & I think it would be best to get it in Some People hear is of the belefe that an attac will be made on Georgetown and if that should be so, the Negros will all Go to them or Pretty much all, for we have no force hear to prevent them I was told yeasterday that theare was some 7 or 8 Vessels laying at the Bar some two or 3 inside I have been sick two days the People all well

[P. S.] I have ingaged Mr. Tyler to work up the Leather in Brittons Neck at 62 1/2 cents pr Pare, which he will take out in provision. we will save more by it I think for if the leather comes on the Plantation to be worked up one third will be Lost Mr. Tyler finds thread & wo[r]kes at the old Price and I am to let him have middling Rice 5 dollars per 100 lbs.

W. Sweet to Adele Petigru Allston

N[ightin]gale hall, 26th october, 1864.

DEAR MADUM I Receive yours of the 20 safe in hand and I will Doe the Best that I can I think that if had the mill in order that I would Be able to Begin to trash on monday weeak But I have neither oil or aney Packing yarn and the mill Bands is very much out of order as the most of thime is very old and Roten though I will Doe the very Best that I can. I have no Enginenear for ganderlos thare fore I can not Begin to trash thare until I Get the Enginenear home you Rote to me to have Spining Done I have But one Pair of cards and no cotton on Either Plais I Doe think that it would Be Rigth to have Spining and weaveing Done on all of the Pleantations and as for Shoes I am unable to say what to Doe about them Exsept you had leather then you wont have them though I have seen Shoes with wodin Botums and cloth tops that is the tops ware made out of canveas which seem to ware Pretty well I am sorry to say to you that Stephen has got worse since I Rote to you last though the Dr is tending of him I have a gwodeal of sickness a mong the children. But not much with the groan negroes. mr Belflowers and my self has made the tax Returns the Best that we could. 1 have 12 head of meet hogs for the Plantation on N[ightin]gale hall and 2 at ganderlos I will Put them in the field as quick as I can get the Provisions out and I will atend to Planting to Ry as sune as I can get oaf the corn and Peas. the negroes all sends howdy to you and family Mrs Sweet stil has the fever Every Day and I can not Brake it on her.

N[ightin]gale hall

20th october	all hands takein in corn and Peas 4 sick
21th october	all hands Picking Peas 3 sick
22th october	give all hands holiday 3 sick
24th october	all hands Picking Peas 2 sick
25th october	all hands Picking Peas 2 sick
26th october	all hands Picking Peas 3 sick

ganderlos

20th october	all hands Picking Peas 2 sick
21th october	all hands Picking Peas 2 sick
22th october	all hands Puling corn 1 sick
24th october	all hands Puling corn 1 sick
25th october	all hands Picking Peas 3 sick
26th october	all hands Picking Peas 3 sick

Jesse Belflowers to Adele Petigru Allston

Chicora Wood, 26 October, 1864.

MRS ALLSTON   yours of 20 inst has been Recd   Since my last I have got in all of the Rice. I am now Picking Peas. I will have to git in all of the up land Crop as it is wasting I will have to work on the Boat before she can be loaded with Rice. She leaks Very bad in the Bottom. I learnt from Joe wheare the 12 hides went March had them to tan Joe tells me that when he was up theare the last time that he did askt a bout the leather and was told that it was all Rotten I am truly Sory for it. I had one in the number that I

Paid a big Price for to make Shoes with Cloth & Wooden Soles it will take a great many tax made for the Purpos with Round heads so that thay will not cut through the Cloth if the leather was not lost it be best to take it for Bottom & the Cloth for the tops. Good Canvast would make Very Good Shows with leather bottoms if you can Git the Cloth & tax I will put James at it. Dr Flagg has movd from Planters Ville I have put Lavenia theare to take care of the House & the furniture Bob has Got in his Crop of Corn & Peas he has Kild a learge Bair I have not Planted any Rye yet but will as soon as we have some Rain. I have not heard any thing from Brittons Neck since Mr. Tyler was down. I do not see any signs a moungst People like Going to the yankees unless the inmey should make a Raid up hear then I think a good meny would Go. I think it would be well to send Toney up to N. C. as soon as his wife is Abel to go.

I hope Peter got up safe with the Cows the Cooprs went to waverly mill last Monday the 24 the People are all well I am better my self

P. S I think you had better sell the Goats. the old Buck is becom to be Very savage & thay are Very mistchivious, that is if you can git a good Price for them I want to Plant a field of oats in the Swamp & thay will destroy them I have not Put up any Hogs yet, as I have nothing to feed them with yet I am giveing them all the Potatoe Scraps to Keep them a longe and as soone as I can git some Rice winnowed out I grind some into flour for them.

Duncan Barrentine to Adele Petigru Allston

Morvin N.C., Oct 26, 1864.

MRS ALLSTON· do you Remember a conversation betwen me and you in refferance to Sawing a bil of lumber for Mr Buchanan the time before the last when you were up You Instructed me not to run the Saw and then you Said I had better Saw his bil as it was a large One he Now Wants it Sawed betwen 12 and 15 Thousand feet Charles[1] when he was up Told Phenix not to Saw Anny more at all Only for the Plantation he did not mention it to me at all I do not know what to do About it. Wil you Instruct me Immediately in refferance to the matter We are geting in the crop pretty fast all is as well as usual I have to Send 2 hands to Work on the fortifications at Wilmington Next Monday last Monday Night Was a Week ago Soloman and July Stole One of Mr Martins hogs.

W. Sweet to Adele Petigru Allston

N[ightin]gale hall, 2th november, 1864.

DEAR MADAM I finish takeing in my corn and Peas at ganderlos on 29th and on N[ightin]gale hall on 1th I have comence Diging my slips at ganderlos on monday I comense Planting my Ry at N[ightin]gale hall to Day But it

---

[1] Charles Petigru Allston.

has Raind very near all Day I will Begin with my slips at N[ightin]gale hall as sune as I can Get thrue with Planting my Ry I will have to trash out my straw Rice By hand Before I Begin with my slips as to Get straw to Put over them in the field Before I move them up to the yard. I am very sorry to say to you that Stephen Dide the very Day that I made my last Reporte to you. his mother Begs if you Pleas to send his things to her By the first Boat that goes up as she wishes them for his child as he Did not Bring aney thing Down with him. I would Begin to trash Prety sune if I had oil and Packing yarn But I have neither nor Even leather to mend the Bands with I had Rote to mr tilton to come and see the mill Befor I Receive your leter But he has not come over to see the mill yet no[t] much sickness Exsept a mong the children I have a goodeal of sickness a mong litle children the negroes all sends thare love to you and family.

N[ightin]gale hall

27th october	all hands Picking Peas	2 sick
28th october	all hands Picking Peas	1 sick
29th october	all hands Picking Peas	1 sick
31th october	all hands Brakeing corn	1 sick
1th november	all hands Braking corn	2 sick
2th november	a Raney Day and all hands in the house apart	

of the Day the Balance of the Day Planting Ry

ganderlos

27th october	all hands Picking Peas	2 sick
28th october	all hands Picking Peas	2 sick
29th october	all hands Picking Peas	2 sick
31th october	all hands Picking Peas	3 sick
1th november	all hands Diging slips	4 sick
2th november	all hands trashing Peas	4 sick

Jesse Belflowers to Adele Petigru Allston

Chicora Wood, 3 November, 1864.

MRS. ALLSTON   Since my last I have finishd Picking Peas & commencd Breakeing the Corn but have to stop on account of Rain have sent 6 hands to Battery White to Work. I hear that George the Salt Boiller is makeing arrangements to go to the yankees, have just heard it, have not had time to make any investigation yet. the Report has come from N[ightingale] Hall the Hogs is dying have lost 25 head yonge Hogs & some two or 3 that was intended for Bacon Mr. Tyler sends me word that leather is not tand, that it is just put a way in the Seccond bark have dug Part of the Slips which has not turnd out well. the Pea Crop has turnd out little better then I exspected the People all well & Quiet, but a great Complaint for Clothes & Sohoes Milley will move down as soon as I can Get in the Corn.

Jesse Belflowers to Adele Petigru Allston

Chicora Wood, 9 November, 1864.

MRS ALLSTON   Since my last theare has nothing Perticler occurd. I am giting in the Corn as fast as I can. the Weather Keeps so damp & Rainy that I cant [get] a longe as fast with it as I ought. Charles is well pleased with the Corn thinks that I will make more Corn then N[ightingale] Hall & Guendalos boath   I think I will make 1600 hunderd busheles   I have Broke in some that has turnd out 22 bushels per Acer and some that only turns out 10 bushels to Acer. the Slipes will be to dig next & then I will be Readey to start the Mill. Joes Boat will be to Cork intirley through. the old Corking being done with Cotton & it is comptley Rotton. I am Gitting Ready to haul her up so that she can be well Corked. I have not heard any thing more from George. Charles has given them ordes to Geather Murtle Berys next week. We are all well. the People all Quiet at Presant.

J. C. Yates to Adele Petigru Allston

[Anson County, N.C.], No[v] the 10, 1864.

MADAM   I have Ben to yore platation to day the Negros are all weell one the farm and are geting one very slow in gethern up the Crop the corn is turning out Beter than I expect theay will Be A thousand Bushels of corn maid one the farm the govnerment is pressing Beef catle heir theay call one me for cattle from yore farm I let them have too A litle pided Bull and A small Red Stir the Agent is to Return me the hids [illegible] has got har Clot out and are needing thread to weave Mr. Baringtine is sowing the small grane theay have gethered all the corn except the new grown I think in an other weak I can have the moste of them clering land.

W. Sweet to Adele Petigru Allston

N[ightin]gale hall, 16th november, 1864.

DEAR MADUM   I finish Diging my slips and Potatoes at N[ightin]gale hall on saterday last and I will finish Bancking the[m] up on friday I have sent 4 men up to the farm to cut ligth wood for the mill thay will cut for one weeak then I will send up and hall the wood Down to Sypres creek and Put it in the flat and Bring it home. I will finish Diging slips and Potatoes at ganderlos a Bout friday or saterday I have Put 2 hands to Plowing at ganderlos and will Put 3 to Plow on N[ightin]gale hall sune as I can Get wood for the mill I will goe to trashing Rice on Booth Plases I see something working among some of the negroes on N[ightin]gale hall that I Doe not like I have notifid your son of the case and I think that thay had Best Be Remove as sune as Posible But you had Beter Be quiet about that is frank and his family you had Best make frank Bring the yong horse that is at N[ightin]gale hall up thare and have that for an Exscuse that you wish him to take care of the horse as he under stands moving him Beter than aney Pirson else he and george and george wife at the see shore I am Prety sirto[n] will goe sune for Every thing is working Right to gether with them and you Best Be very quiet how you move theme take oaf frank first and then his family next Doe not let oan that you know or think of such a thing.

N[ightin]gale hall

10th november	all hands Diging slips	1 sick
11th november	all hands Diging slips	2 sick
12th november	all hands Diging slips	1 sick
14th november	all hands Bringing in Potatoes	1 sick
15th november	all hands Bringing in Potatoes	1 sick
16th november	all hands Bringing in slips	1 sick

ganderlos

10th november	all hands Diging slips	2 sick
11th november	all hands Diging slips	4 sick
12th november	all hands Diging slips	4 sick
14th november	all hands Diging slips	2 sick
15th november	all hands Diging slips	3 sick
16th november	all hands Diging slips	3 sick

Jesse Belflowers to Adele Petigru Allston

Chicora Wood, 16 Novbr., 1864.

MRS. ALLSTON   Yours by Paul has been Recd. to geather with 6 Peceses of Cloth 2 Cans of lard one demijohn of Whiskey one Bottle Castor oil 2 Bits of leather & nails I have finishd gitting in the Corn & will finish diging Slips to morrow. thay doant turn out well. Will Start the threshing Mill Monday if the weather is good. I have got the Boat hauld up. She doant need any wood work done. only wants a though Corking. Milley has moved down to the Plantation. have the Cows & Caves in the fields. I have three Plough Going in the Rice fields. have sent to Brittons neck for the Leather to make Soles for the Cloth tops Shoes. from what I can learn a bout George Going a way I think it not so. Abraham says that George is allways Verry cearful a bout his boat, and that he on hearing that Stephen was Going, that George made him hide his boat every night I have sent 9 shoe measurs which is for the Boat hands, 3 more for the Plough men & five others, Riechard Jack Milley Abram & Phillip. We are all well & the People all Quiet, But much Complaint for Shoes.

W. Sweet to Adele Petigru Allston

N[ightin]gale hall, 23th november, 1864.

DEAR MADAM   I finish takeing in my Potatoes at N[ightin]gale hall on last thursday and I have [been] up to the farm and had 24 cords of wood cut

and this weeak I have had to send 3 carts to hall the wood Down to the flat
which I have sent up for the wood I have got 6 men cuting Pine wood on
the Plantation I comense trashing out my straw to Day with the women and
half hands and I will Begin to trash with the mill as sune as I can Get wood
and oil I am not quite Done takeing in my Potatoes at ganderlos I have
finish Diging them But not Done Bancking of theme and the weather is soe
very cold that I can hardley Get aney thing out of the hands for thay have
no shoes and quite Bare for cloths that I can not Drive them as I wish to Doe
will has Bin up to chicora helping cork the Boat for the last 6 Days & will
wife Phillis was confind on 10th with a Boy child and walleys wife grace
Di[e]d on 19th grace is the old woman that has Bin sick for 2 years she
was a Dead Exspense to the Place.

N[ightin]gale hall

17th november all hands Bringing in Potatoes 2 sick
18th november all hands gleaning fields 2 sick
19th november 6 men cuting wood the women half hands gleaning fields
                1 sick
21th november cold and Raney all day hands in the houses 2 sick
22th november 6 men cuting wood the women and half hands Puling corn
                stalks 7 men haling wood 3 men on the flat 3 sick
23th november 6 men cuting wood the women half hands trashing straw
                4 hands halling wood 3 on the flat 3 sick

ganderlos

17th november all hands Bringing in Potatoes 2 men Plowing 3 hands
                Boiling salt 2 sick
18th november all hands Bringing in Potatoes 2 men Plowing 3 hands
                Boiling salt 3 sick
19th november all hands Bringing in Potatoes 2 hands Plowing 3 hands
                Boiling salt 3 sick
21th november cold and Raney all day hands in the houses 3 sick
22th november all hands Bringing in Potatoes 2 hands Plowing
23th november all hands Bringing in Potatoes 2 hands Plowing

Jesse Belflowers to Adele Petigru Allston

Chicora Wood, 23 Novbr., 1864.

MRS. ALLSTON I have got in all the Slips. thay have not turnd out so well.
it has been Rainey for three days. will start the Mill today. the Weather so
Could that I dont get more then half work. I have Recd a Circuler[1] from Mr.

[1] Printed circular from Wm. M. Tunno, captain and A.C.S., Office of Subsistence,
Charleston, to the rice-planters of South Carolina, October 12, 1864. This states that the
Confederate Government requires one-half of the year's crop of rice for the subsistence of

Tunno wanting to Know if I will sell one halfe of the Crop which I have inclosed to you so that you can see the[re] what thay say you will Please write to me immeadly and let me Know so that I can write to him. I will Put the whole Crop at boath Placeses at ten thousand bushels. We will have to sell or it will be imprest. I have got the leather from Brittons Neck 26 Pieceses & will commencee the Shoes at once. I have heard some more fresh news a bout George. would it not [be] best to brake up the Salt boiling and send him and his wife up to N.C. farme or take him away and put some one else in his Place. Wiltcher I think would do well at the Salt boiling. We are all well & Qui[e]t at Preasant. Please let me hear from you about the Rice for Goverment.

W. Sweet to Adele Petigru Allston

N[ightin]gale hall, 30th november, 1864.

DEAR MADAM   I have Receive your 2 last leters 19th and 26th I will goe up in the morning and see mr Belflowers a Bout Gorge and if he thinks Best for mee to take him to columbia I will Doe so stil I am quite un well But at the same time I will try and Doe the very Best that I can for you in Every Respect that I can I have Receive 21 shirts 29 yards of white homspon 50 yards wollin 1 gallon whiske 1 can oil. you Rote to mee that you wish mee to stay with [you] the next year I am willing to st[a]y with you for what mr thompson ware to stay for 6 hundred Dollars But I am not willing for my horse to goe to the office as he has this year I hope that you will Be satisfide with what I have Done for you this year for I have Doe the very Best that I could for your intrust and for the col. I Doe not know Exact what I will Doe for a cwock until you come home as hester has to goe away though I will Doe the Best that I can until I see you I hope you will come at chismas. will and his 3 hands went to his Boat on monday morning. I would like to if I must send my Rice to the mill to Be Pounde as fast as I Get it trash I think that I will try and Begin to trash on monday if I can. I Doe not know of aney Boats carring frait up the River. I have got 10 or a 11 hogs to kil for the Plantation hannah has 7 young turkeys and 3 or 4 yong gees. Doe knot know what to Doe for cloths for the negroes at ganderlos nor shoes as thare is no leathe[r] for that Place.

N[ightin]gale hall

24th no[vember]	3 men halling wood 3 on the flat 9 cuting wood the women trashing Rice 8 half hands Puting wood in the flat 2 sick
25th no	6 men halling and flating wood 8 cuting wood 8 half hands Puting wood in the flat women trashing 3 sick

the army, that the price at present fixed by the state commissioners is $4.00 per bushel, and that purchases will be made wherever practicable and impressments resorted to only when necessary. Information is sought respecting the size of the crop. See above, p. 203.

26th no	6 men halling and flating wood 8 men 8 half hands cuting wood and loding the flat the women trashing 2 sick
28th no	6 men halling and flating wood for 6 Days 8 men 8 half hands cuting and Puting wood in the flat the women gleaning fields 3 sick
29th no	8 men 16 half hands cuting and loding the flat with wood the women gleaning fields 2 sick
30th no	6 men 16 half hands cuting and loading the flat with wood the women gleaning field 2 sick

ganderlos

24th	all hands Bancking Potatoes 4 sick
25th no	all hands Bancking Potatoes 3 sick
26th no	all hands Bancking Potatoes 2 sick
28th no	all hands Bancking Potatoes 2 sick
29th no	all hands Bancking Potatoes 4 sick
30th no	the men Ditching the women and half hands gleaning fields 4 sick

Jesse Belflowers to Adele Petigru Allston

Chicora Wood, 30 November, 1864.

MRS. ALLSTON   Yours of the 23 & 26 has been Recd I am Truly sorry to hear of the loss of the Horses & Wagon. I have sent to Mill one thousand Bushels of Rice which will be pounded by thusday night. I am threshing all I can to send up in the Boat which will start up on Saturday Morning the wine is all Ready Pact up. Franks Wife and Children & Toney will Go up in the Boat the 38 yeards of White Cloth will cut out 96 pears of Shoes single & half that number cut out duble I have let Mr. Sweet have 50 3/4 yeards fild with wool & 29 3/4 yeards of Coas homespon from the house & 21 Readey made Shirts one Gallon Whiskey & one Can off the leard for the Mills I will have to send to town next week Corn Peas Potatoes & blads which is the tenth or tax in Kind. will have 14 or 15 hogs to Kill. have lost the Cow that Peter Brought down I cannot find out how many hogs Will will have to Kill. I estomate the Crop off Rice at 8 thousand bushels hear & at N[ightingale] Hall, which is a Verry low estomate, though it turning out Verry short. Capt Rece wants to Know if you will scell the Pile driver engine. it cost 900 dollars in 1857, or he will exchange a Smaller one with a Corn Mill attachd to it. We doant need a Corn Mill you can let me Know if you will sell it or not if you sell what is your Price for it Cost in 1857 900 hundrd dollas. or you can writ to Capt Reece, Post Quarter Master Georgetown All that I no a bout George Going enemy or all that I have heard a bout it has come from N[ightingale] Hall by Mr. Sweet. he gets the news by the hands that is boiling Salt with George perhaps it would be best to send him a way I think your Plan of Sending him is much the best. I can furnish the money is Charles Gone in to active servis I am Sorry for him We are all well & Quiet.

W. Sweet to Adele Petigru Allston

N[ightin]gale hall, 7th December, 1864.

DEAR MADAM I have seen mr Belflowers and he thincks that we will try george a litle while longer I have sent up hester and her 3 children and toney from heare on the Boat and I gave them 3 weeaks allowance to Each one which I hope thay will Reach you safe. I see that the goverment has De-manded one half of the Rice that is made on the Plantations and have orderd us not to move aney of the Rice soe I Doe not know what to Doe a Bout [it] until I hear from you I have no flower to feed horses hogs or oxen I have not Begun to trash my Rice yet But will Begin on monday if nothing Prevents more than common. I have sent my tiths of corn Peas Blas [?] Potatoes from Boath Plases Down to georgetown for the goverment mr Bel-flower and my self the hands came home frome the Batry on monday I Beg the favor of you to let mee have a cow to gave milch for mee if you Pleas as the one that I have got is quite Dry and Doe not gave any or soe litle that it is hardley Enough to goe in to our coffee. I think that you had Best try and Get shoes from cheraw for the Drivers and Boat hands if you can and if you thinck Best I will send you thare meshures when I Rigth again. Sammy at ganderlos has left his wife Every thing is Geting on Pretty well.

N[ightin]gale hall

1th Dece[mber]	6 men 8 half hands cu[t]ing and flatin[g] wood 6 men hall-ing and flatin[g] for 6 Days women turning land 2 sick
2th December	the women turning land 6 men 8 half hands cuting and flating wood 2 sick
3th December	women turning land 6 men 8 half hands cuting and flat-ing wood 2 sick
4th December	the women turning land 4 men 8 half hands cuting flating wood 3 sick
5th December	the women turning land 9 men 8 half hands cuting and flating wood 3 sick
7th December	the women turning land 9 men 8 half hands cuting flating wood 2 sick

ganderlos

1th Dece[mber]	all hands turning land 3 sick
2th December	all hands turning land 3 sick
3th December	all hands turning land 3 sick
4th December	all hands turning land 3 sick
5th December	all hands turning land 4 sick

W. Sweet to Adele Petigru Allston

N[ightin]gale hall, 14th December, 1864.

DEAR MADAM   I Receive your leter of 7th safe in hand and I have Bin up and seen mr Belflowers and had a talk with him a bout george he says that he think george is all Rigth and that he will not goe to the Enemy soe I have let Every thing Be quiet. I have Just Begun to trash out my crop of Rice to Day with the mill mr trapiers mill Pounds for the 20th same as waverly mill Dose I would like to Know from you if I must send all of the Rice to mr traperes mill or onley the half that goes to the goverment I am very sorry to say to you that I lost Stephe[n's] little Boy last Saterday he had neither father or mother he has Bin lingering for sometime thare seem to Bee som Diseas a mong the sheep for I have lost som 2 or 3 very lateley I send you up shoe meshers you will Pleas Get the shoes for the name negroes as thay are oblige to have shoes Dri[ver] Daniel Dri[ver] Sam Plowman Peter Dick and new trim. I have got one very fine Beef for N[ightin]gale hall But I have not got one for ganderlos nor I Doe not Know whare to Get one from I see that Dr Sparksman is Bringing cards up to his Place seling theme out for hogs and if you wish to By som hogs you will send me some 20 or 30 Pair of cards and I will Cash [?] Pair for one hog the cards has no Backs to theme I have not got my hogs fit to Kil yet But when I Kil them I will have Every thing taken care of for you I allso send you the shoe mesher for the Boat hands.

N[ightin]gale hall

8th Dece[mber]	8 men 8 half hands cuting and flating wood the women turning land 2 sick
9th Decem	9 men 8 half hands cuting and flating wood the women turning land 3 sick
10th Decem	9 men 8 half hands cuting flating wood the women turning land 3 sick
12th Decem	9 men 8 half hands cuting flating wood women listing land 2 sick
13th December	9 men 8 half hands cuting flating wood the women listing lands 3 sick
14th December	5 men flating wood the Rest of the men and women trashing Rice 3 sick

ganderlos

8th Decem	all hands turning land 3 sick
9th December	all hands turning land 4 sick
10th December	all hands listing lands 4 sick
12th December	all hands listing lands 4 sick
13th December	all hands listing lands 4 sick
14th December	all hands turning lands 3 sick

Jesse Belflowers to Adele Petigru Allston

Chicora Wood, 14 Decbr., 1864.

MRS. ALLSTON   Yours off the 7 inst. has been Recd. I was delivering tax in Kind last Week which pervented me from Writeing as usual I have only threshd out two thousand bushels of Rice yet. Guy has been working on N[ightingale] H[all] Mill for last ten days I have got out a part of my Seed Rice I doant think I will do any more threshing with the Mill until after Christmas. Joes Boat left hear on the 4 of this month with 40 barrels of Clean Rice and 900 hundred bushels of Rough Rice in Bulk & 14 Boxes of Wine, Hester Children & Toney All of which I hope will arrive safe I doant think theare is any danger of George Going a way he was over hear the other day & begd me as the myrtle berrys was so Scearse that thay could not do any thing at it and askd me to let him go to boiling Salt a Gain. I told him to go at it. If Betty Joes Wife if she is favored to much she will become another Lizzie. We will have 18 hogs to Kill, but thay faten Verry slow. I have a Potion of up land Listed up & have four Ploughs Going in the Rice fields. My Root Potatoes will last until January. I have not used any of the new Corn yet the turn out of Rice sent to Mill one thousand & fourty two Bushels turnd out 50 barrels of Clean Rice, 3/4 barrel Small Rice & 60 bushels flour or thus 120 Bushels of flour. Gives me 60 bushels flour 1 1/4 Barrels of Small Rice & 3/4 barrel S. Rice I had to fetch back the Potatoes as theare was no tax in Kind on them I Supose you have heard of the Steamer Caroline has Runing the Blocade & Come in to Georgetown safe no boddy Verry sick. all Quiet.

W. Sweet to Adele Petigru Allston

N[ightin]gale hall, 21th December, 1864.

DEAR MADAM   you Rote to mee to Get in all the salt that ware Due you for wood that has Bin cut on you lands and Rote to Ganeral trapier overseer for the salt which was 50 Bushels and he Rote mee that he could not Pay mee the salt But would gave mee one hundred Bushils of Rice But I Doe not wish the Rice it is all most out of the question to get aney salt from them for thar is 3 of them Boiling salt on your lands and I cant Get salt for the use of the Plantation and when I Doe Get aney it is more trouble than a litle and if I ware you I would stop them from cuting wood and Boiling salt on the land for thay think hard to gave the salt and thay are cuting up the land Prety Bad from what I can see and hear. I have got a leven hundred Bushels of Rice trash out at N[ightingale] hall and a Bout nine hundred at ganderlos I have onley had 5 Days trashing at N[ightingale] hall and 2 at ganderlos. I have lost the old mule sue that wase on the N[ightingale] hall Plantation Driver Daniel wife Binke was confind on 19th with a Boy child. all seems to Bee Geting on Prety well at this time I have 2 negroes at ganderlos that is Prety sick Wallis and old Sary I have had to call the Dr to them I have no[t] much sick at N[ightingale] hall. the negroes all Begs to Be Rememberd to you and family if you have made aney arrangements for to keep mee out of service and to stay with you on your Plantations Pleas let mee know By the firs of January as I have to Reporte on the 2 Day of January.

N[ightin]gale hall

15th December	all hands trashing	3 sick
16th December	all hands trashing	2 sick
17th December	all hands trashing	2 sick
19th December	all hands trashing	2 sick
20th December	all hands turning land	6 sick
21th December	all hands turning land	4 sick

ganderlos

15th December	all hands turning land	3 sick
16th December	all hands turning land	2 sick
17th December	all hands turning land	2 sick
19th December	all hands trashing Rice	3 sick
20th December	all hands trashing	3 sick
21th December	all hands turning land	6 sick

Jesse Belflowers to Adele Petigru Allston

Chicora Wood, 21 Decbr., 1864.

MRS ALLSTON   I hope Joe has got up by this time. theare will be no more Rice pounded until after Christamas. theare will be no hogs fat enough to Kill before Christmas. Will only have one beefe for Christmas & Some Rough Rice Flander has Kild one hog out off the fatning Pen I got a Part of the hog that he Kild. Mr. Wallas Writes me the Mill is done in Brittons neck or that he has done all that he had orders to do. he Says theare is no house over the Mill & wants to Know if he must Put one over it. he also Says that Mr. George More has worked 26 days. Mr. Lowrimore has worked 18 days & himself has worked 28 days. he dos not Say what thay charg per day. Mr. Tyler has sent down a Reel Looks [to] be Verry well made & Counts Correctly. Paul told me that theare was Cards at Society Hill when he was up theare with Backs at 10 dollars & with out Backs at 5 dollars if so Please send me 4 Pairs with Backs & ef theare is none with backs send me Some with out backs Harry is Cleaning up in the Garden & Burning Stuff got 7 Pannels of the Garden burnt We are all well & Quiet Jacob is Laid with Rheumatism.

Jesse Belflowers to Adele Petigru Allston

Chicora Wood, 27 Decbr., 1864.

MRS. ALLSTON   Since my last I am Sorry to have to Say to you that Tom the man that cut Wood at the Seashore Come home last Saturday evening

Verry Sick he died last Night he was Sick six days at the seashore. he had every thing done for him that Could be done for him Isabel is quite Sick now. last Friday Night was verry Could. She lives in her Father house by her self and I Supose she had no Wood, and did not go to any one elses house. Next Morning she was nearly Speachles and is Verry Sick. I think that some of her toes is frost bitten We had a Verry fine beef for Christmas & a dull Christmas & a quite one Jacob is Still Suffering with Rheumatism he has it in boath off his legs I exspect that theare will go a load of Rice from N[ightingale] Hall to Mill in fiew days, and when Pounded, wheare will you have it sent. Please let me Know & to whom you will have it Sent to. the threshing will go on as soon as the weather Clears up I exspect to Kill some hogs in a Week or 10 days time have lost another Cow. she has faild to eat or that is but Verry little since she has been in the field Hanah at Pipe down Says she is willing to go up to Society Hill & Spin We have had a great deal of Rain this Week & is Raining at this time and the River is Riseing. I hope that it is not a going to be Verry high old hanah at the farm Come to me the other day & wants me to move her down to Chicora. Says that you did Prommis to move her down. I have not done so & told her that I could not do it until I heard from you. am geting a long Verry slow with the Shoes git but 12 pears a Week Hope Joe has arrived safe.

W. Sweet to Adele Petigru Allston

N[ightin]gale hall, 28th December, 1864.

DEAR MADAM I have not trash aney Rice since I Rote you last on the account that the mill got out of order But I will sune Begin to trash a gain I will have the mill Ready By monday to comense trashing I am sorry to say to you that Wallis and old sary is quite sick at ganderlos I have no sickness on Either Exsept those too Every thing is Geting on Pretty well soe far Exsept that the negroes is grumbling about close and shoes thay all wish to see you come home very much. I would like to see you very much my self on the account of those men Boiling salt on your waterford land for thay Boil salt and it is more than I can Doe to Get salt from them not Enough for the use of the Plantation the Estate of trapier has Bin Boiling since august and I have got 5 Bushels of salt from them I would Be very glad if you could make some arangments to take this yonge horse from N[ightingale] hall as I have no Pirson that can manage him Properly. I think that I will have out a lode of Rice By the last of next weeak.

N[ightin]gale hall

22th Dece[mber]	the [men] cuting leacks women turning land 3 sick
23th	the men cuting wood the women listing land 2 sick
24th	the men cuting wood women listing land 2 sick
26th	given holeday for 3 Days

ganderlos

22th Dece[mber]	all hands carring straw in the field 3 sick
23th Dece	all hands carring straw in the field 3 sick
24th Decem	all hands listing land 3 sick
26th	given holeday Day

W. Sweet to Adele Petigru Allston

N[ightingale] hall, 4th January, 1865.

DEAR MADAM   I Receive Boath of your last leters 21th and 29 safe in hand I have Proseeded with the Paper that you sent to mee I seen col harriet yesterday and he taken the Paper and said that he would atend to it at onse for mee. hester left hear Pretty well and I hope that she has Rech you safe Before Know Pleas let mee Know if I must sel the cards that you send to mee. I have not Done much at trashing at N[ightingale] hall on the account of the Engin not Being in gwood order But will get to trashing again sune I have no Enginnear that is worth aney thing mr Belflowers let gim come and starte the mill But he has to trash at chicora and at ganderlos and can no atend to all 3 Plases mr Belflowers has Bin very Kind to help mee. I am trashing at ganderlos this weeak. I could not By a hog for the negroes at ganderlos and I had up 6 in the Pen for the Plantation and I gave them one of theme. Wallis and old Sary is stil quite sick yet and also andrew at N[ightingale] hall exsep them I have no hard sickness I would like to see you come home which I hope you will Doe sune.

N[ightin]gale hall

29th December	the men cutin leaks the women turning land 4 sick
30th December	the women listing land the men cuting leaks 2 sick
31th December	the wome[n] listing land the men spliting Rales 2 sick
2th January	all hands trashing 3 sick
3th January	the women turning land the men cuting leaks 6 sick
4th January	the women turning land the men cuting leaks 9 sick

ganderlos

29th December	the women listing land the men Ditching 4 sick
30th December	the women listing land the men Ditching 4 sick
31th December	the women turning land the men Ditching 4 sick
2th January	all hands trashing 3 sick
3th January	all hands thrashing 4 sick
4th January	all hands trashing 5 sick

P s   Wallis Begs that you will let his son come and see him if you soe Pleas.

Jesse Belflowers to Adele Petigru Allston

Chicora Wood 4 Jany 1865

MRS. ALLSTON   Yours of the 21 has been Recd. I am Sorry to say to you that Isabel Died the day after I Wrote to you. I have Kild 4 hogs & will Kill 5 or 6 more in a day or two. Guy is threshing at Guendalos and I am getting out my Seed Rice. if nothing hapens to the Mill he will finish threshing theare this Week, or come Verry near finishing theare, & by that time I will get out my Seed, & then I can go on & finish threshing. the Steamer Caroline Cargo was not for this Place it was discharge in town & taken up Black River. theare was no Sugar to be had. Some of the Sailors had some to Seel at 9 dollars pr Pound. She is now up Black River loading with Cotton I have Put another hand in Toms Place to Cut wood for the Salt boiling. l have just Sold 50 bushels of Salt to Dr. Fishburn at 15 dollars pr bushel. theare is no hard Sickness on the Place at this time & all Quiet. I see that Mr. Sweet has orders to Go & Kill all dogs belonging Negros.

W. Sweet to Adele Petigru Allston

N[ightin]gale hall, 11th January, 1865.

DEAR MADAM   I have very near finish trashing at ganderlos I have not more than one Days trashing with the Exseption of my seed Rice that I will trash out as Sune as I can Wallis and old sary is stil sick But Wallis is Beter sary is no beter Susy at ganderlos was confind on 7th Some pirson Kild the sow from her Pigs that minder had at ganderlos on 10th and I found her on yesterday morning as I went up I have a gwoodeal of sick on Boath Plases But non[e] very sick with the Exception of Wallis and sary and andree and charriety thay are all Beter I think that I will Begin to trash at N[ightingale] hall on tuesday or weddnesday next mr Belflowers has let gime come and mend the Engin for mee I would Be very glad if you could let mee have one carpinter and one Enginnear on the too Plases for this year for I have several trunks to work on Boath Plases and I have no carpinter and it is more than abram can Doe to atend to all of the Business or more than gime can Doe to Run all the mills I wold have Rote to you Befor about them But I thought that you would come home sune and I would see you my self But I can not Get oan with out on[e] carpinter and one Enginnear.

N[ightin]gale hall

5th January	the women turning land	the men cuting leaks	6 sick
6th January	the women turning land	the men cuting leaks	5 sick
7th January	the women turning land	the men cuting leaks	5 sick
9th January	the women turning land	the men cuting leaks	4 sick
10th January	the women turning land	the men cuting leaks	4 sick
11th January	the women turning land	the men cuting leaks	4 sick

ganderlos

5th January   all hands trashing 4 sick
6th January   all hands trashing 3 sick
7th January   all hands trashing 3 sick
9th January   all hands trashing 4 sick
10th January   all hands trashing 8 sick
11th January   all hands turning land 7 sick

J. C. Yates to Adele Petigru Allston

Anson Co. N C, January 12th, 1865.

Mrs ALLSTON   I have seen Mr White and got the amount of your tax   your tax is Six hundred and ninety three dollars and twenty five cts to be paid in Bonds   he will not take eny Bonds for less than a hundred dollars   I received your Note to day and the Boat Was to leave this Evening   I will send July down to you on monday   I received one hundred and sixty eight bushels of good Rice the whole amount five hundred and seventy seventy bushels of good Rice   Mr. Cox has taken Brutus on Teusday   We received all the damaged Rice   Pedee River is Six ft higher than it ever has been known   the Logrounds is covered from 10 to 15 ft in water   at this time the Creeks is so full that Peaple can not pass.

W. Sweet to Adele Petigru Allston

N[ightin]gale hall, 18th January, 1865.

DEAR MADAM   I Receive your last leter with no Date to it   I am glad to hear that hester and her children got to you safe   I am trashing at N[ightingale] hall this weeak   I think that I will Be able to send up some to the mill sune   I am very thanckful to you for the loan of the cow   I am Geting on Prety well considering all things the cold weather and the hands with out shoes and cloths   I Beg that you will let mee have Judy child from Britens neck and selianah from chicora as I wish them for nurses. I have no[t] much very hard sickness   Wallis sary and andrew is much Beter   charriety is out. I have not Kild aney hogs yet for I have not aney fat Enough   hannah lost 4 of her yong turkeys on chismas Eave Knigth   some Pirson Broke open the house on the Back Part and taken them   my family has Bin quite sick But is a litle Beter to Day   I am turning lands as hard as I can   the weather is very cold and Prety windy. the negroes all wishes to Be rememberd to you and family.

N[ightin]gale hall

12th January   the women turning land the men cuting leaks 4 sick
13th January   the women Burning stuble the men cuting leaks 3 sick
14th January   the women turning land the men cuting leaks 3 sick
16th January   the women choping Banks the men cuting and flating wood
            4 sick

17th January   all hands trashing Rice 4 sick
18th January   all hands trashing Rice 4 sick

ganderlos

12th January   the women turning land the men Ditching 4 sick
13th January   all hands trashing seed Rice 4 sick
14th January   the women Burning stubles the men Ditching 5 sick
16th January   all hands trashing seed Rice 5 sick
17th January   the women turning land the men Ditching 6 sick
18th January   the women turning lands the men Ditching 6 sick

Jesse Belflowers to Adele Petigru Allston

Chicora Wood 18 Jany 1865.

MRS. ALLSTON   Yours of the 10 inst has been Recd. I Am Sorry to say to you that Kiah is ded. he was Sick 14 days & had every attention Paid to him Mr. Wallas has been down and says that him self and the other men that worked on the Mill wants provisions for theare work he says thay charge old Prices for work & wants to git Provisions at the old Prices. thay Ask a dollar pr day for work the Mill is grinding and he says when thay have a head of Water will make 2 bushels of tole Corn a Week he says Tommey has not made Provision enough to last them Guy is yet at N[ightingale] H[all] I will be oblige to stop to thresh at home as my Straw is gitting short. the Sheep is looking verry well, but the Cows dos not look well. Mr. Sweet has not got the Cow yet Paul has not got the younge Horse up yet. theare is Some Work to be done to the old Stabel before he can be Kept in it theare is a little boy that has got a Very bad Abses on his thigh had a nother boy got his Knee dislocated & has been suffing a Goodeal theare is no boddey Sick to day exsept 2 infant Children I am turning land as fast as I can it looks as if theare is a big freshet comeing down I heare off a goodeal of Sickness in the neighborhood Please let me Know if those me[n] are to be Paid at old Prices it will take 75 bushels of Corn I supose if thay are not Paid at old Prices thay will charge high Prices for theare work I have got out fifteen hundred bushels of Seed Rice the Potatoes is done I have just Sheld the first Corn off the new Crop to day also let me Know if you want any more Rough Rice sent up by the Boat next time All Quiet.

J. C. Yates to Adele Petigru Allston

[Anson County, N.C.], Febuary the 24, 1865.

MRS ALLSTON   I drawed five thousand dollars from Mr Malloy to pay for the Liles Land and the party was redy to Receive the money and Mr Ashe could not draw the Deed for the lack of a copy of your Husbands Will You Will please get Some Lawyer to examine the Will and let me know to whome the Deed Shall be made and what form it shall be given and give me the names of the hiers as I wish to pay the mony over at once You will pleas answer this by the Boy Tony. I have written to you twice since you left and have had no answer they are getting on at the Farm as well as you could exspect except Charles and Jo has broke in the Smokehouse and stole four pieces of meat Mr Cox has your Shoes redy the Enemy has not interrupted us yet they are makeing great preperation to meet Sh[erman] [MS torn] Charlotte [MS torn].

Jesse Belflowers to Adele Petigru Allston

Chicora Wood, 18 March, 1865.

Mrs. ALLSTON   Yours by Tobey has been Recd wishing to Know of me if I thought it safe for you to move down I do not think so and would advise not to attempt it for the Pople have behaved Verry badly & I do think if you had been on the Plantation that you would have been hurt by the People I have been Compeld by them on the Place to give up the Barn Key or to suffer from theare hands I would have moved a way but have no means to do so as I have give up the Key thay appeer to be a little moore Recconcild to wards me on Sunday the 5 of march two yankeys come up & turnd the People loose to distribet the house which they did, taking out every thing & then to the smoke hous and Store Room doing the same as in the house & took the Plough oxen & Kild some of them the Pipe down People done this the hogs in the Pen is Kild & all the Stock is taken a way the horses is all taken a way. some of the People owns some of them. the Pore mules has been Road to death all most after this the People have Puld down the mantle Pieces Broke them to Pieceses, taken of all the doors & windows, Cut the Banisters & sawd out all such as wanted and have taken a way the fenceing a Round the yeard, brok down the old Stabel & the Carpenter Shop. Bens two Colts is gone the Robers has made a clean sweep in Britten Neck, taken all the Rice & every thing the People had even to theare dogs, Salt & Cotton Joes load of Rice has gone to Georgetown he says the yankeys took him at the uper mouth of Bull Creek but that is Verry doubtful in fact I do not belive it. no other Plantation of People have done what thease have done Bob has three bales of Cotton & two barels of Rice and some meat. the People say thay mean to have it theare is 2 barrels of Rice & one bale of Cotton in the barn but how Longe it will be theare I cannot tell.

Jesse Belflowers to Adele Petigru Allston

Chicora Wood, 20 March, 1865.

Mrs ALLSTON   Since I Closed my Letter the yankeys has bee[n] up and have taken all the Cotton. thay are to be up shortly & divide the Stock to the People thay tell the yankeys every thing all the yonge men & boys have gone down to them to go in the army & some have left Wife & Children and gone the Rest are doing nothing I am not allowd to say any [thing] a bout

Work and have not been to the Barn for the last five days Jacob is the worst man on the Place, then comes in Scipio Jackey Sawney & Paul

P. S   Most all of them have arms.

Jesse Belflowers to Adele Petigru Allston

Chicora Wood, 2 April, 1865.

MRS. ALLSTON   Yours by Jack has been Recd I am Sorry to say to you that I doant wish to go to N. C. as [it] is gitting late in the Spring & that theare is no horses or mules left on the Place to work, and it would be some time before I could git up theare. Brittons Neck is a Place I doant lik. So I will try to Stay wheare I am until theare is a chance for me to git a way. I am getting old and would Reather go some wheare to some quit Place & make my own Bread, tho I am a thousand times oblige to [you] for your Kind offers I understand that some 6 or 800 hundred Colored troops arriveed in town yeasterday and more is exspected to arrive in a day or 2. Part of them is to go to Kingston and the other Part to go up the Waccamaw River. those names I put down in letter to you by tobey do dont say any thing a bout it to aney one of the Peaple. Ladress is down hear. I have not seen him. he has told Paul and many others that I had writen to you all that was done & who was the worst ones. thay are just Ready to eat me up for it. I have seen Randam Jackson Frances William and Brutus

the Peaple have divided the Cattle. But Col. Brown says thay must all go to geather and that Horres must mind them and Molley must milk them & Give the milk to the children the negroes still go on in puling building to Peicies thay have broke in to the Brick Church and taken out all the board that was left in it Puld down the Club house & the two little Barnes up Chapel Creek that belong to Ben the houses that William Put up over Chapil Creek, the Pitman Summer house & the Summer house on the Exchange have cut away the banisters in ditchford house. I hear that thay have made the attempt to Ripe up the floor in Chicora House I have not been down theare in 2 Weeks thay have Kild some of the Goats & som 2 or 3 Sheep Molley & Guy has sold off all the Poltrey or that is thay carred them to town doant say that I said so the People the way that thay Work will not make them Bread. go out at 10 Oclock come in at 12 Oclock. and the Corn & Potatoes that have been Planted is not half done no Rice Planted yet. I have to Pay Nancey for what little I have done

[P.S.]   it Looks Verry hard to Pull ones hat to a Negro.

W. J. Westbury to Adele Petigru Allston

Chicora Wood, Pee Dee, June 8th, 1866.

RESPECTED MADAM   I hope you will not consider it presumtious in me in the absence of your Son, who has seen fit through the influence of my friends, to place me here as your agent, to write you a few lines relative to the condition of things in general at your old and venerated homstead.

I am glad to inform you that the labourers, with a single exception, has treated me ever since I have been on the place with marked respect Sivility and Kindness, and I am persuaded to think that I have been Successfull in exercising a wholesum influence over them, this far.

On this place they have been standing up to the work in point of numbers Remarkeabley well for the past two weeks, not everaging absent more than three per day, out of over forty, they work from four to five hours per day, and during the time they work with a goodeal of spirit and animation. I think we will be safe in setting down the Value of their Labour at about one half that it was in time of Slavery, that is they do the Work about half as well as it ought to be done, but with this half Work, if we bring to their assistance *good* Management Kindness and Discretion, we will yet realize more from them, than we had a hope or a write to expect, some time previous to this, particularly when they have been so much demoralized by their ennemies, as well as our one [own?]

With regard to the growing Crops, I am sorry that I cant focast more favourabley, but for the present bad appearance of the crop particularly the Rice, I am obliged to attribute, more to Bad Management, than to the amount of labour performed. While your Son is energettic, Diligent and persevering, to say nothing of his frequent absence, we must admit, has not yet attained that practical experience so requisite to the Judicious Management of a Rice crop, in fact, I have been planting Rice for near a half Century and I am free to say that I learnt as much about the application of Water to the Rice, the last year as I did the first. I am now controling the water on several fields which was not too far advanced before I got here which are Looking very well, and I think will yield well. With all I am quite hopefull, and am inclind to think, that the influence I will be able to Exercise over the negroes now under contract will be the means of inabling your Son to increas his contracts to a large extent next year. The negroes are now left to their own Judgement, to act for the better or worse for themselves, and, will as a matter of corse, seek good Management where ever it can be found the most wanting [wanton?] scen[e] that my eyes has beheld since I have been here is the Destruction and depredations done to your house, but the negroes appear actually to be ashamd of having it spoken of now, and not one will own having anything to do with it.

There has been one Death among the negroes here resently, Nelsons Mother, who I am told was a great sufferer for some time prevous to her Death. We are done planting excepting one field of Rice which will be planted by the 16 inst. this is late for planting Rice, but I supose could not be avoided under existing circumstances. I have planted Rice as late as the 23d of June, and by pushing the Rice by high cultivation made 40 Bus per acre.

SLAVE DOCUMENTS

APPRAISEMENT OF SLAVES BELONGING TO THE ESTATE OF BENJAMIN ALLSTON, JR., 1819[1]

Name	Value	Total		Name	Value	Total
Maryann	800			Little Charles	1000	
Brutus	150			Sue	800	
Beck	500	2050		Bella	500	
Mariah	350			Betsey	400	4001
Letty	250			Micah	300	
				Nelly	1	
Prince	1			Minus	1000	
Venice	150					
Grace	800			Chance	1000	
Affee	200	2351		Lizette	800	
Pierce	100			Jacob	1000	
Diannah	800			Esaw	800	
Prince	200			Jimmy	700	5251
Cupid	100			Daniel	400	
				Frank	300	
Scotland	1500			Ceasar	100	
Patty	800			Nanney	150	
Lydia	500	3500		Esaw	1	
Daphney	400					
Sarah	300			Big Joe	800	
Lisette	800			Lucy	600	
				Toney	700	
Big Sam	900			Hannah	700	
Dido	800	2250		Stephney	600	5800
Satira	500			Sharper	300	
				Bess	800	
Paul	500			Adam	200	
Nancy	700			Hager	100	
Venus	700			Bob	1000	
Dido	400					
Little Sam	1100	4850		Tommy	1000	
Betsey	800			Cretia and Inf	900	
Clarinda	500			May	400	2900
Paul	100			Eve	300	
Peggy	150			August	100	
Johny	100			Sheba	200	

[1] See above, pp. 28 and 51.

APPRAISEMENT OF SLAVES BELONGING TO THE ESTATE
OF BENJAMIN ALLSTON, JR., 1819—*Continued*

Little Joe	1200	} 1300	John	1200	
Satira	50		Jane	700	} 3700
CudJoe	50		Peggy	800	
			Henry	1000	
Philander	50				
Charity	50		Jacob	900	} 1100
London	1000		Will	200	
Brutus	500				
Sary	800	} 4300	Friday	500	
Philander	600		Monemia	800	} 1700
Nancy	450		Wallace	400	
Linda	350				
Sylvia	300		Caty	600	} 1300
Cinder	200		Binah	700	
			Cinder	700	
Scye	100		Phoebe	800	
Flora	700		Jim	800	
Murriah	800		Hynes	500	
Tom	1000	} 4400	Richard	500	} 5200
Beck	800		Bob	300	
Stella	600		Rose	800	
Gabriel	300		Leander	500	
Delia	100		Abram	300	

Delia	100[1]	Jack	800	Cato	1000
Boatswain	1000	Tally	900	George	1000
David	300	Quash	300	Fortune	500
Simon	800	Leander	900	Dingo	1
Little Sam	200	Sampson	200	Old Tom	200
Big Charles	600	Sandy	200	Smart	1200
Junius	1				

[1] A second list supplies the information that these last nineteen were unmarried and implies that the grouping above was according to families.

CHARLOTTE ANN ALLSTON'S SHARE OF THE SLAVES BELONGING TO THE ESTATE OF BENJAMIN ALLSTON, JR., 1819

No. 3, Mrs. Charlotte Allston's Lot[1]

Chance	1000	Caesar	100	August	100
Lizette	800	Nanny	150	Sheba	200
Jacob	1000	Esau	1	Tally	900
Esau	800	Tommy	1000	Fortune	500
Jimmy	700	Cretia & infant	900		———
Daniel	400	May	400		9551
Frank	300	Eve	300		

19 negroes 9551 under 28—9579 No. 4 will pay No. 3 $21, and Mrs. Charlotte Allston on account of Milley will pay $7 to herself.

A true copy from the original certified by Rob Withers.

AN AGREEMENT TO EXCHANGE CERTAIN SLAVES, 1819

February 27th 1819

John H Tucker and his wife Elizabeth, agree that Mrs Charlotte A Allston shall have the use of Sary her two Youngest children Sylvia and Cinda, and the future issue of Sary, during her life time; Mrs Allston paying their taxes and finding them in cloathing and victuals. It is agreed that the elder children of Sary, Philander, Nancy and Linda are to be put out by Mrs Allston, the girls to be taught to sew, wash etc., and the boy to be put to the carpenters trade, from and after which they are to return to the service of their owners the said Jno and Elizabeth Tucker or their heirs.

Mrs Allston agrees that she will consult with the said Jno and Elizabeth Tucker with regard to the persons with whom these children are to be placed. To work in the room of Sary, Mrs Allston agrees to give during her life Boson to Jno and Elizabeth Tucker and at her death, Boson shall be considered as her property, and Sary with her present and future issue shall return then to John and Elizabeth Tucker as their property received at the division of the Estate of Mr Ben Allston Jun.

> JNO. H. TUCKER
> ELIZABETH A TUCKER
> CHARLOTTE ANN ALLSTON

[1] Comparison of this with the foregoing list shows that at the division of her late husband's slaves Mrs. Allston received two families and two unmarried individuals. Their appraised value being slightly less than the amount to which she was entitled, she was to receive the difference in money. The curious requirement that she pay herself a part of this difference "on account of Milley" was probably the commissioners' way of saying that under the terms of the will Milley was the common property of all the heirs (see p. 53) but that her services were being assigned to Mrs. Allston. Unfortunately, the other "lots" are missing.

It is agreed that Mrs Allston shall keep Philander at his trade untill he is 19 years of age and Nancy and Linda untill they are 15 years old.

[AMENDMENT:]

February 16th 1824

It is agreed between Mrs Charlotte Allston and John H Tucker, that Joe shall be received in the place of Boatswain, and that from and after this 16th day of February 1824, Joe (generally called Little Joe) is, and shall be considered the property of Mrs C. Allston, and in his place, Boatswain, is, and shall be considered the property of John H Tucker.

It is further agreed, that as Boatswain was working in the place of Sary, that Mrs Allston will pay or cause to be paid to John H Tucker for the hire of Sary, the sum of Sixty Dollars anually, as long as she may keep her.

JNO H TUCKER
CHARLOTTE ANN ALLSTON

LIST OF SLAVES RECEIVING CLOTHES AT FRIENDFIELD AND WATIES POINT PLANTATIONS, NOVEMBER 8, 1819

Drivers Primus, and Sam, Carpenters Chambers, Brass, Lilly, Sandy, Tom, Coopers Sam, Lane, long Scipio, Sunderland, Wilson, Scipio, Ben, Primus, Sye, Dick, Jimmy, Andrew, Willy, Jacob, Job, William, Peter, Harry, Tom, James, Adam, Titus, Richard, Moses, Israel, Robbin, Winter, Matthias, Rachal, Lucy, Dido, Elseys Lavenia, Sary, Nanny, Ginny Silvya, Sally, Prince, Maryann, Rose, Molly, Minta, Julatta, Myrtilla, new Rachal, Pendah, Cilla, Leah, Milia Phillis, new Lavenia, Fanny, given away Judy, Affy, Venus, Clarinda, Bob's Rachal, Phebe, Clarinda, Barberry, old Sabina, old Hector, old Sye.

Children

Binkey, William, Archey, John, Mary, Gallatia, Maria, Sam, Frank, Alexander, Toby, Sampson, Jimmy, Nelly, Sammy, Nero, Willy, Andrew, Beck, Mark, John, Sary, Harry, Alfred, Cuffee, Guy, Elsey, Hardtimes, Robert, Peter, Hagar, Frank, Tommy, Phillis, Dead Sally, Friday.

Clothes given the Negroes at the Point

Driver Jack, Thomas, Amos, Hardtimes given away Abram, Jacob given away Washington, Johnny, Bina, Charlotte, Julia, Aimy, Elizabeth, Becky, Dido, Eve, Mindah, Phebe, Tenah, Cate, Peggy, Mary, Murria, Massy, Esther given away Betsey, Harriet, Will, Ellick, Henery, George, Joe, Stephen, Herculus, Philander, Jack.

Children

Mary, Abigail, Catto, Phene, Adam, Massy Dead, Cuffee, Philander, Johnny, Joe, Lenty, Rose, Scipio, Dianna, Peggy, Abel, Daphne, Joan, Tenah.

LIST OF SLAVES RECEIVING SHOES AT FRIENDFIELD AND WATIES POINT PLANTATIONS, NOVEMBER, 1819

Driver Jack, Thomas, Amos, Hardtimes, Abram, Jacob, Washington Johnny, Bina, Charlotte, Julia, Aimy, Phebe, Mindah, Elizabeth, Becky, Dido, Tenah, Eve, Peggy, Mary, Murria, Massy, Will, Stephen, Herculus, Ellick, Henery, Chambers, Brass, Lilly, Tom,

Driver Primus long Scipio, Cooper Sam, Sunderland, Wilson, Scipio, Benj Primus, Sye, Dick, Saxe, Jimmy, Andrew, Willy, Jacob, Harry, Job, William, Tom, James, Adam, Driver Sam, Titus, Moses, Israel, Winter, Robbin, Sandy, Peter, Matthias, Richard, Driver Rachal, Ginny, Sary, Rose, Minta, Lucy, Dido, Lavenia, bobs Rachel, Julatta, Pendah, Silvya, Cilla, new Rachal, Nanny, Elsey, Judy, Maryann, Molly, Leah, Affey, Sally, Melia, Myrtilla, Venus, Fanny, new Lavenia, Clarinda, Phebe, Prince, Clarinda, Phillis.

March 1820 Paid tax for 160 Negroes

LIST OF SLAVES RECEIVING CLOTH, SHOES, ETC., AT FRIENDFIELD AND WATIES POINT PLANTATIONS NOVEMBER 15–17, 1820

Cloth given to the Negroes at Friendfield, November 15

Drivers Primus, Sam, Coopers Sam, Saxe, Carpenters Chambers, Brass, Lilly, Tom, Harry, Jimmy, Long Scipio, Willy, Sunderland, [illegible], Primus, Andrew, William, Wilson, Sye, Job, Dick, Sandy, Adam, Tom, Moses, Ben, Titus, Jacob, Scipio, Richard, Israel, Robbin, Matthias, Prince, William, Philander, Joe, Peter, Hector, Rachal, Lucy, Dido, Levinia, Elsey, New Rachal, Minta, Julatta, Clarinda, Eve, Phillis, Mindah, Myrtilla, new Levenia, Nanny, Molly, Maryann, Fanny, L Dido, B Rachal, Venus, Silvya, Bindah, Rose, Jinny, Sary, Leah, Affey, Sally, Melia, Phebe, Sally, Clarinda, Will, Primus.

Blankets given same time

Driver Primus, Rachal, Brass, William, Sunderland, Eve, Jimmy, Harry, Jacob, L Scipio, Dick, B Primus, D Sam, N Levenia, Sye, Willy, Ben, Ginny, Levenia, Tom, Dido, Rose, Nanny, Silvya, Molly, Gulatta, William, Saxe, Myrtilla, Fanny, Leah, Titus, B Rachal, Job, Affey, Venus, Elsey, N Rachal, Andrew, Maryann, Richard, Robbin, Minta, Sary, Phillis, Mindah, Moses, Clarinda, Sam, Phebe, Peter, Prince, Lucy, Clarinda, Sandy, Wilson, Sally, Melia, Scipio, Leah, Nero, Adam, Israel.

Children had Clothes

Mark, John, Friday, Hagar, Johnny, Senty, Rose, Nero, Willy, Andrew, Beck, Juliet, Ellick, Archey, Sam, Frank, Gallatia, Maria, John, Mary, Luno, Fanny, Nelly, Sawney, Taby, Harry, Peter, Phillis, Joan, Frank, Elsey, Hardtimes, Robert, Tommy, Cuffee, Guy, Sampson, George, Joe, Toby.

Shoes given out at Friendfield

Drivers Primus, Sam, Adam, Venus, Brass, Dido, Phillis, Pendah, Philander, L Scipio, Matthias, Sunderland, Levenia, Israel, Andrew, B Rachel, Sandy, Sary, Melia, Phebe, Rachal, Juletta, Richard, Scipio, Nanny, Nurse Rachal, Peter, N Tom, Jimmy, Dick, Eve, Ginny, Fanny, Wilson, Myrtilla, Sye, Moses, Robbin, old Primus, Dido, Chambers, Maryann, Cooper Sam, Jacob, Lucy, Rose, William, Saxe, Willy, Affey, Clarinda, Mindah, Sally, Minta, Harry, Titus, Molly, Elsey, n Levenia, Silvya, Ben, Leah, Job, Tom, William.

Clothes given out to the Negroes at the Point 17th November 1820

Driver Jack, Bina, Thomas, Julia, Amos, Charlotte, Hardtimes, Aimy, James, Cilla, Washington, Elizabeth, Tenah, Beckey, Johnny, Winter.

Children had Clothes

Dianna, Peggy, Abel, Binkey, Scipio, Mary, Abigail, Catto, Alfred, Frank, Phene, Adam, Cuffee, Grace, Philander, Jack, Daphne, Tenah.

House People had Clothes

Mary, Peggy, Mary, Massey, Harriet, Esther, Stephen, Hercules, Ellick, Henery, Murria, Cato.

The Point and House Negroes had Shoes

Driver Jack, Bina, Thomas, Julia, Amos, Charlotte, Hardtime, Aimey, Becky, Elizabeth, Washington, James, Cilla, Lilly[,] Tenah, Winter, Johnny, Mary, Peggy, Mary, Massy, Stephen, Herculus, Ellick, Harriet, Esther, Will, Clarinda, Primus.

Blankets given to the Negroes at the Point and House

Driver Jack, Bina, Thomas, Julia, Amos, Charlotte, Hardtimes, Aimy, Becky, Elizabeth, Lilly, Tenah, Cilla, Washington, Winter, Ellick, Peggy

friendfield—112   Tax P'd in 1821 for Negroes
Point   — 45
___
157

AGREEMENT TO HIRE CERTAIN SLAVES, 1821

31st Decr. 1821

Memorandum of agreement between Mrs. Charlotte A Allston and Mr Samuel Smith, for the hire of sixteen Negroes whose names are, Harry, Caesar, London, Christmas, Southerland, James, York, Toba, Marcus, Amey, Hannah, Bettina, Yannakee, Violet, Sary, Flora at the price of Seventy five Dollars each, Mrs. Allston is to give each of the aforesaid Negroes, one suit of Winter and one suit of Summer Cloths, and a pair of shoes. Mr. Smith is to be at the expense of feeding and clothing the children of the aforesaid Negroes. The term of hire is to be one year, and to commence from their delivery to Mrs. Allston.[1]

A SLAVE LETTER

Mulatto Joe to Robert F. W. Allston

September 23 1823

DEAR MASTER   I have seen the letter you wrote to Mrs Hillen and will inform you that all the people at the plantation is very sickly off and on three or four sick every day and I have been very sick since the death of poor Master william and am now getting a little better, the crop is a very good one but no house to put it in as the house that Mr Foxworth was a making is not shingled yet and I have no place to put it as such I have not gathered it in this will inform you that your colt is a fine one but is not paid for there is 7 dollars due for your colt to Mr Frase and 5 to Mr Stone for last years colt. do tell Mrs Blythe howde for me and remember me to all friends and I am dear Master

your Servant

MALATTO JOE[2]

SLAVE BILL OF SALE, 1828

The State of South Carolina

Whereas the Honorable the Court of Equity in and for the Eastern circuit of the Said State on application properly made to them Did order the Master in Equity to Sell and dispose of a certain Trust Estate of William and Sarah Allen [Allan], consisting in part of Thirty two negroes at the time of the Sale thereof and required as secuirty from the purchasers thereof a Mortgage of the said Negro Slaves, and whereas William Hasell Gibbs Master of the Honorable the Court of Equity for the eastern circuit did cause a sale of the Said Negro Slaves to be made agreeable to the terms and condition of the order of the said court, *And whereas* at the sale so made one Robert F. Withers became the purchaser thereof and in compliance with the

---

[1] See above, p. 57.   [2] See above, p. 53.

terms of said Sale so made as aforesaid did on the 19th day of March 1816 execute his Bond for the payment of his purchase and as required for its better security and payment gave his Mortgage of the Said Negro Slaves together with the future issue and increase of the females, *And Whereas* since the purchase of the said Robert F Withers, The Honorable the court of Equity has appointed H. M. Haig as Trustee of Sarah Allen *And Whereas* since the appointment of the said H. M. Haig as Trustee as aforesaid by virture of the power contained in the Mortgage of the Said Robert F Withers he has caused to be sold at Public Auction the said Thirty two Negro Slaves in the Said mortgage named together with the increase of the females Born since the date of Said Mortgage which made the number in all Forty eight, in order to Foreclose and satisfy the said Mortgage. *And Whereas* at the Sale of the Said Negro Slaves one Robert F. W. Allston was the highest bidder and became the purchaser thereof

Now Know all men by these presents that I H. M. Haig as Trustee of Sarah Allen for and in consideration of the Sum of Thirteen thousand two hundred Dollars to me in hand paid at and before the sealing and delivery of these presents by Robert F. W. Allston the receipt whereof I do hereby acknowledge have bargained and Sold and by these presents do bargain and sell and deliver to the Said Robert F. W. Allston the following Negro Slaves (To Wit) Pompey, Clarinda, Lydia, Laross [?], Ancrum, Henry, Zacharia, Trim, Matthias, Elizabeth, Ely, Ancrum Jr., Pompey Jr, Jack, (Saley and an infant, Celia) George, Cinda, Nanny, Sandy, Will, Jacob, Peter, Auba, Betsey, Stephen, Hannah, Phoebe, Hesther, Sarah, Hagar, Hester and an Infant not yet named, Booie, Hagar, Moses, Laminar, Eve, Marian, Roger Caty, Celia, Lawdon, Harry, Joe, Booie Jr., Sawne, & Billy, with the future issue and increase of the females—

To Have and to hold the Said Negro Slaves before named and the future issue and increase of the females unto the Said Robert F. W. Allston his executors administrators and assigns to his and their own proper use and behoof forever. And I the Said H. M. Haig Trustee as aforesaid for myself my executors and administrators, the Said bargained premises unto the Said Robert F. W. Allston his executors administrators and assigns from and against all persons shall and will warrant and forever defend by these presents.

In witness whereof I have hereunto set my hand and seal. Dated in George Town this first day of February in the year of our Lord One thousand eight hundred and twenty eight and of the Independance of the United States of America the fifty second

Signed Sealed and delivered in the presence of—
The words "not named" being erased in the Seventh line from the bottom—

H. M. HAIG
Trustee for Sarah Allen

JNO. G. NORTH
State of South Carolina

Georgetown District—Personally appeared John G. North Who being duly sworn makes oath that he was present and saw H. M. Haig Sign Seal and deliver the within instrument of writing for the uses & purposes [?] therein expressed and that he signed his name as Subscribing witness thereto—

Sworn to before me this 18th day
of February 1828
    M. S. M. HARDWICKE   *Regr*

South Carolina. } I do hereby certify the foregoing Bill of Sale to be duly
Georgetown District recorded in Book K. pages 605, 606. & Examined this 18th day of February Anno Domini 1828—By

                  M. S. M. HARDWICKE
                  Regr. M. C.

A SLAVE LETTER

Samuel Tayler to Elizabeth Frances Blyth

Mobile, Sept. 2, 1838

MY DEAR MISTRESS I have been in this City about three years, and belong at present, to Mr. Saml Jaques, merchant. I was Sold for $1,900. He is remarkably kind and gives me a fair opportunity of making pocket money. But Still my mind is alway dwelling on home, relations, and friends which I would give the world to see. As times now are, I Suppose I may be purchased for about 10 or $11 hundred dollars. If you my Dear Mistress, can buy me, how happy I would be to serve you and your heirs; I beg you will write me how all my relations are, and inform them that I have enjoyed uninterrupted health since I came here. Remember me also to Sarah, my ma-ma, and Charlotte, my old fellow servant, and Amy Tayler.

I would be glad to belong to my young Mistress, Mrs. Parker, in case you Should not feel disposed to take me. Please Address me, "Samuel Tayler," Servant, care of Mr Saml. Jaques, Mobile, Ala.

          Most respectfully your Servant,

                  SAMUEL TAYLER

P.S. There are many people, Black and White here from Geo Town, that gives me Some Satisfaction.

LIST OF SLAVES RECEIVING WINTER CLOTH AT FRIEND-FIELD AND WATIES POINT PLANTATIONS, 1836

Name	Yards	Name	Yards	Name
Watchman, Tom	6	Lucy	5 1/2	Liza
George	6	Luner	5	Mary
B Robert	6	L Fanny	5	*Will*
L Robert	6	L Alcy	5	*Mary's*
Cooper, Sam	6	B Alcy	5	Peter
B John	6	Nurse Racheal	5	Alfred
Abel	6	B Dydo	5	*Matillah*
Andrew	6	Grace	5	*Sealea*
Billy	6	Maria	5	*B Alcys*
L Sam	6	Venus	5	*Harriet*
L John	6	L Dydo	5	*Graces*
Marke	6	L Clarenda	5	Peter
Moses	6	Sally	5	Toby
Friday	5	Minder	5	*Moses*
Prince	6	B Elizabeth	6	*Clarenders*
Minders Joe	6	L Elizabeth	5	*Zelpher*
Mathias	5	L Rose	5	*Sallys*
Sunderlan	6	Flora	4	Dick
Sawney	5	L Menah	5	The Baby
Johnney	5	Murrier	5	*Moses*
Cuffey	6	O Fanny	5	Sealea
Tommy	5	Silvy	5	Nancy
Jimmy	6	Fillis	5	*Norage*
T Philander	6	Hannah	5	*Murriers*
Peter	5	Nelly	5	Gilbert
W Phlander	6	Pinder	5	Nanny
Israel	6	B Menah	5	*Clarasa*
Brass	6	Molly	5	*Tenahs*
C Primus	6	M Mary	4 1/2	Eliza
Old Witt	6	Old Rose	5	Abygal
Lilly	6	Binky	5	*Sharlott*
Wills Joe	6	Phebe	5	*Mollys*
Chambers	6	Affey	5	Selina
Old Sipeo	6	Jane	5	Prince
L Sipeo	6	O Sary	5	*Jim*
Old Harry	6	Nurse Clarender	5	Binkys
L Harry	6	Ackamo	5	Silvy
Driver, Sam	6	Sollomon	5	*London*
. . . .		Jack	4 1/2	*Affeys*
Young, Racheal	5	Scy	5	Will
Gean & Mary	5	Guy	5	*Jones*
Matillah	5	L Primus	3 1/2	Pegy
Levenia	4 1/2	L Tom	3 1/2	Beck
Dafney	5	Ben	3 1/2	

The number of yards give out is 523 1/2 for 1836.

LIST OF CARPENTERS HIRED TO REBUILD
WAVERLY MILL, 1837

This is Mr. Kidd's estimate of the value of the carpenters, Novr. 1st 1837

Thomas	Pr. month	$30	Worked	16 months and		25 days	
Hamida	" "	20	"	8 "	"	2 "	
Tom	" "	20	"	14 "	"	20 "	
Alfred	" "	5	"	7 "	"	26 "	
John	" "	10	"	7 "	"	13 "	
Daniel	" "	20	"				
Jacob	" "	14	"	1 "	"	17 "	
Lonon	" "	14	"	1 "	"	16 "	
Toney	" "	20	"	5 "	"	15 "	
Prince	" "	20	"	4 "	"	28 "	
Willington	" "	20	"	5 "	"		
Will	" "	15	"	4 "	"	27 "	
Jeffry	" "	20	"	6 "	"	29 "	
Allick	" "	15	"	6 "	"	28 "	
Daniel	" "	20	"	7 "			
Peter	" "	20	"	7 "	"	8 "	
Allick	" "	20	"	7 "	"	11 "	
Chambers	" "	5	"	13 "			
Joe	" "	10	"	10 "	"	"	
Toney	" "	10	"				

AGREEMENT TO PURCHASE CERTAIN SLAVES, 1851

March 14, 1851

Honble R. F. W. Allston

To Alonzo J White, Dr.

For purchase of 51 Negroes from Hugh Fraser, viz., Jack, Molly, Charlotte, Mary, L Jack, = Jim, Charity, Jacob, Pauline, Nancy, = George, Minda, Washington, Liddy, Anna, L George, = Sammy, Nancy, Molly, = London, Maggy, = Boston, Venus, Peter, Matilda, Jacie, = Linus, Brister, = Harriott, Bass, Ben, Ella, Julia, Amy, Fourpence, L Venus, Lucky, = Susannah, Flora, Mentor, Wellington, Desdimona, = Sancho, Abby, Harry, = Dianna, Betsey, Rose, = driver Harry, Harry, and Maroza @ $410 each $20,910.

conditions of payment

1/4 cash balance payable in 5 equal annual instalments with interest from date hereof payable annually, secured by a motgage of the above named negroes.

A DOCTOR'S BILL, 1853

Estate of J. W. Allston, Waverly
To Dr. A. Hasell   Dr

1853							$ cts
Jany.	1st	Mileage and pres[ence] for Prince					2.95
	2	"	"	"	"		2.95
	3	"	"	"	"	and dressing wound	3.95
	5	"	"	"	"	" "	3.95
	6	"	" a child and "	and dressings for			3.65
	8	"	"	"	" mede[cine] and "		3.75
	10	"	"	"	" and Peter, and operating on 3 carbuncles		6.95
	11	"	" Peter, and operating				3.95
	12	"	"	"	" and extr[acting] tooth of Johnny		4.95
	13	"	"	"	" and for Beck, and liniment		5.95
	14	"	"	"	"		5.95
	15	"	"	"	"		5.95
	16	"	"	"	" also Prince, Ben, and Venesection		5.95
	17	"	"	"	" " also Ben, and Porter for Peter		4.45
	18	"	"	" Prince and Ben			3.95
	19	"	"	"	" "		3.95
	20	"	"	"	" " and dressings		4.
	21	"	"	4			4.45
	22	"	"	3 Ben Philander and Rose			3.95
	23	"	"	Peter, Rose, Philander and 2 bottles of Porter			4.50
	24	"	"	2 and Mixture			4.45
	26	"	"	Peter, Rose, Philander and Ben			2.50
	28	"	"	3			3.95
	28	Mileage at night and pres[ence] for Violet					5.90
	29	" and pres[ence] for Violet, and Prince. Medi[cine] for Violet and Salve for Prince also for Philander, and powders for Peter and Porter for Chloe and liniment					6
	30	"	"	" for Violet and Philander			3.45
	31	"	"	" 2			3.45

								$ cts

Feby 1 Mileage and pres[ence] for Violet   2.95

4 and 6 "   "   "   "   Medi[cine] for Philander and Peter, lini[ment] and 2 bottles Porter   5.45

7   "   and 1 hours detention at night and pres[ence] for Jim who had 16 convulsions before my arrival   4.95

8   "   and pres[ence] for Jim   2.95

9   "   "   "   "   2.95

11   "   "   "   " Philander, and Peter   3.95

12   Medicines for Philander   1

24   "   "   "   Philander and Medi[cine]   3.45

26   Extr. tooth of Billy   1.

March 9   "   "   "   3 men, operating on finger of one and on thumb of another, and injection mixt[ure] for Philander   8.20

16   "   "   " 2 men   3.45

23   "   "   "   "   "   3.45

5   "   "   " Bob and extr[acting] teeth of Jack, and Betty   4.95

26   "   "   "   "   2.95

27   "   "   "   "   and other men   3.95

30   "   "   " York, and opening thumb   3.95

April 8   "   "   "   "   2.95

17   "   "   " a woman   2.95

20   Extr[acting] tooth of Philander 1.

21   "   2 teeth of Beck   2.

26th Mileage and pres. for Nanny   2.95

27   "   "   "   " Scotland, and a child   3.95

Vaccinating 3.   3.

28   "   "   " Nanny, Scotland, and a child   3.95

29   "   "   "   "   "   "   3.95

30   "   "   "   "   3.45

May 1   "   "   "   "   "   3.45

2   "   "   "   "   "   and medi[cines]   3.65

3   "   "   "   "   [child]   3.45

4   "   "   "   "   "   "   3.65

5   "   "   "   "   "   3.45

6   "   "   "   "   2.95

"   at night and pres. for Celia and a child   5.90

			$ cts
May	7	Mileage and pres. for Celia and a child	3.45
	8	" " " 2	3.45
	9	" " " "	3.45
	10	" " " "	3.45
	13	" " " "	3.45
	14	" " Celias child	1.
	16	" " " " "	1.
	26	" " Ben	1.
	28	" " "	1.
	29	" " " Isaac	2.95
	30	" " " " and Ben	3.45
	31	" " " " " and liniment	3.95
June	1	" " " " "	3.45
	2	" " " " "	3.45
	4	" " " " " and cupping	6.45
	6th	Mileage, and pres. for Isaac, and Ben	3.45
	6	" " " " and 6 powders for Anny	3.31
		extr[acting] tooth of Venus	1.
	12	" " " " and opening carbuncle, also for Ben	5.95
	13	" " " " and operating	4.
	14	" " " "	2.95
	15	" " " "	2.95
	18	" " " "	2.95
	23	" " " " and extr[acting] tooth of Peggy	3.95
	26	" " " "	2.95
	30	" " " "	2.95
Novr.	17th	" " " " and a woman	3.45
	19	" " " " and extr[acting] 2 teeth	4.95
	21	" " " of Isaac	2.
	22	" at night, and obstetrical attendance on Mollys daughter	33.90
	23	" and pres. for Doll	2.95
Decr.	4th	Attendance per Dr. Post	
		Mileage (after dark, and pres. for Servts child Sally	5.90
	5	" and pres[ence] for Servt. child Sally	2.95
	"	Extr[acting] tooth of Paul	1.
	6	" and pres[ence] for Servt. child Sally	12.80

$390.21

SLAVE CANDIDATES FOR CONFIRMATION AT
NIGHTINGALE HALL PLANTATION, 1857

Tom	January	Hannah	Fibbe
Marcus	Wallace	Rose	Eve
Robert	Trim	Delia	Jenny
Sam	Monday	Cicely	Decia
Richard	Jose	Mary Ann	Martha
Sammy	Scipio G	Nancy	Judy
Hard Times	Daniel	Stella	

DESCRIPTION OF LIFE AMONG THE SLAVES, 1858

James R. Sparkman to Benjamin Allston

Birdfield Mch 10th 1858

DEAR BEN,   Enclosed and accompanying this I have sent you a budget for what it is worth. I have no doubt all the answers received to the request made by the Executive for the benefit of Mr. Cobb[1] will if studiously waded through, not add much to his *digestion*. I have given many statements which to yourself and His Excellency may appear *small* and *unworthy*, but I have fancied myself catechised by an unbeliever and have purposely given in detail what would constitute answers to the many and varied questions of one *entirely ignorant* of our every day life on a Rice plantation. Such questions have repeatedly been propounded to me at the North by persons whose general acquirements and intelligence are noted but who really have fancied Slavery such a monster that no ordinary declaration of humanity and kindness and happiness etc. at the South, will be received with any credulity whatever. I myself have been asked if our slaves were not guarded by day with guns and secured at night with chains, and when in answer I stated that my negroes locked me and my family up every night and frequently went off with the Keys in their pockets, the smiles of incredulity and unbelief were too apparent. I dont know whether you intend to digest a report from S.C. of all the materials you receive, or to send the items as recd. on to Mr. Cobb. Please let me know. My notes could be very much condensed, but not knowing exactly what is wanted, I have extended them at the risk of their being too tedious and cumbrous for any other purpose than to light your candle of a frosty morning. Do what you like with them.

I am glad you are all getting surfeited with the City. We miss you too much in the country and shall be glad when Chicora Wood unfolds her doors to welcome you back. . . . .

[1] Probably Thomas R. R. Cobb (1823–62), of Georgia, whose *Inquiry into the Law of Negro Slavery* was published in this year.

[INCLOSURE:]

Statistics of a Rice plantation, with 100 Negroes, made in answer to a request from the Executive Department of the State of So Carolina.

1st Labor—The ordinary plantation task is easily accomplished, during the winter months in 8 to 9 hours and in summer my people seldom exceed 10 hours labor *per day*. Whenever the daily task is finished the balance of the day is appropriated to their own purposes. In severe freezing weather no task is exacted, and such work is selected as can be done with least exposure. During heavy rains and in Thunder showers, my people are always dismissed and allowed to go home. The task is allotted to each slave in proportion to his age and physical ability. Thus they are considered 1/4, 1/2, 3/4, or full task hands. Allowance is invariably made for the women so soon as they report themselves *pregnant* they being appointed to such light work as will insure a proper consideration for the offspring. No woman is called out to work after her confinement, until the lapse of 30 days, and for the first fortnight thereafter her duties are selected on the upland, or in the cultivation of the provision crops, and she is not sent with the gang on the low damp tide lands. Men and women are all engaged together in the planting, cultivation and harvesting of the Crop, but in the preperation of the Rice Lands, as ditching, embanking etc. the *men* alone are engaged with the spade. It is customary (*and never objected to*) for the more active and industrious hands to assist those who are slower and more tardy in finishing their daily task.

Foods—My habit has been for years to vary the weekly allowance of my people. As bread stuff, their diet consists of Rice Corn, Peas and Potatoes, with rations of Molasses, Salted fish Pork or Bacon and fresh beef. Corn is ground for them and given out in *Meal*. The allowance for one week is of Meal 10 quarts, of Rice or Peas 8 quarts, and of Sweet Potatoes one Bushel. This is the full allowance of every adult, and the younger negroes the same, no matter what their age, as soon as they are put to task work. Molasses is given throughout the year at proper intervals, Salt Fish only in winter, Pork or Bacon and Beef during summer. The allowance of Molasses is 1 pint (for one week), of Salted Fish (Mullet or Mackerel) 2 or 3 according to size, of Pork or Bacon 2 lbs. In giving fresh beef it is always made into soup, which is thickened with Rice and garden vegetables, and each hand receives of this *2 quarts daily*. Whenever I have been able to contract for the furnishing of Beef, it is supplied me twice a week from the 1st June to 1st Novr. and by care and attention, it is ordinarialy preserved so as to give my people this ration of soup every day in the week, and if from excessive hot weather the beef cant be preserved, it is usually made up by furnishing *mutton* from my flock. The children have their pot of soup independent of the adults 3 times a week during the summer months. A hand is detailed throughout the year to cook for the field laborers, and when the mid-day meal is ready, they are assembled together at a given hour, and from one hour to one hour and a half is allowed for eating and refreshing themselves.

Clothing—Is given out twice a year in May and November. For summer each adult male and female receives 6 Yds of widest cotton Osnaburgs and 6 Yds of unbleached cotton shirting. For Winter, Each man receives one Kersey or Pilot Cloth Sack, ready made, and one pr. Kersey Pants, or if they cant be had, 6 Yds best white welsh plains, also 6 Yds Cotton Shirting. The women receive 6 Yds each of best Welsh Plains and Cotton Shirting. The children receive Osnaburgs and shirting in Summer and Woolen and Shirting also in winter, in proportion to their size. Buttons, Needles and Thread are supplied as necessary. Flannel is given to those who are infirm by age, or from sickness, according to circumstances, whenever *health* requires it.

Blankets—Each infant at its birth is supplied with two entire suits ready made of flannel etc., and a blanket of small size. In distributing to my people generally, my habit has been for years to give in rotation, viz to the men, 1 year, to the women the 2d year, and to each child the 3d. year no matter what its age or how many in the family. This insures one new blanket 2 years out of three to each family and to those with several children the supply is abundant every 3d. year to make the average large. For my grown people I invariably purchase the heaviest and best 80 lb. Blankets (80 lbs to a bale of 16 Blankets) for my little Negroes a medium quality, at $45 the Bale. Shoes— Each working negro receives one pair of stout Bootees or Brogans. Mechanics, Stock Minders, Drivers etc. 2 pr each.

Our domestics or House Servants are clothed and furnished according to the fancy of individual owners. My own are supplied *without limit* to insure a genteel and comfortable appearance. Many of my servants take no regular allowance but are dieted from my own table.

Three days in each year are set apart for cleansing their houses. One in May, after the crop is planted, when all woolen clothing, Blankets etc. are to be washed and put in good condition for the ensuing cold season. One in October or Novr. after the Crops are harvested. And one of the *three* usually allotted for the Christmas holidays. On these occasions soap is furnished, and the women are expected to scour their houses, wash up every thing etc. while the men are (according to season) either planting, working, or harvesting their own little Crops, or laying in a supply of fuel.

On Christmas day, all plantation tools are inspected and a memorandum taken of each, as a check and guide for the overseer and master in the event of a change of overseers at the end of the year. This has been done regularly with me for 14 years past. I require it of every overseer, and find that it is a wholesome check upon my people in the preservation of their tools. To all who are not defaulters in showing their working utensils and who have not been guilty of any *greivous* offence during the year, an extra Ration of Rice, Peas, Molasses, and Meat, and Tobacco is given sufficient for a weeks consumption, independent of their regular allowance. This is their peculiar season for feasting and enjoyment, and for dress. Each woman after taking out her Rations receives a neat handkerchief, and each man a woolen cap.

Houses—Mine are all well framed buildings 18 by 22 feet, of best material. Hewn or sawed frames, milled weatherboarding, cover'd with best Cypress shingles, raised 2 feet from the ground, flooring closely jointed, glased lights to each room, and large fireplaces or chimneys made of a composition of Clay, Sand and Tar, as a substitute for brick, to which it is quite equal if properly done. Each house contains a hall and 2 sleeping apartments and is intended to accommodate an average of *five* people, or one family.

Medical Attendance—My Experience as a Physician covers 22 years, in this immediate neighborhood. During a large portion of this time have been the regular medical attendant and adviser on 25 to 30 Rice plantations, with a slave population of about 3000, and have had a field of observation covering 20 miles around. The advice of a Physician is generally sought in all serious illness. *It is the habit of the neighborhood to employ the Physician.* Each plantation has its Medical attendant, and when he is not employed, it is ordinairly the result of *ignorance* as to the danger of the malady or a blind confidence on the part of the owner or his agent as to his own skill. It is not more common among negroes than among the whites to find the hand of empyricism dealing heavily in drugs. Quackery does not arise oftener from *parsimony* than from other causes. Whenever their is *faith* in medicine as a science or art, the M.D. is not undervalued. Valuable Slaves, cherished family servants, like prominent and valuable citizens and heads of families, receive alike *extra* consideration and attention without reference or regard to *cost*. Professional consultations over negroes are quite common. In Surgical cases the advice of the most distinguished and experienced of the Profession is frequently had at a pecuniary cost from which the humanity of the Rice planter never shrinks, although I have known it in a few instances to exceed the value of the slave. The aged and infirm are not neglected when pain demands the kindly services of the Physician. I have personally received full compensation for continued attendance upon chronic cases hopelessly ill, and for years utterly useless, as an example and mark of fidelity of the master, in consideration for the fidelity and loyalty of his servant to a deceased ancestor. Native proprietors as a general rule are more kind, considerate and indulgent as slave holders, than foreigners who have settled among us. *Northerners* are generally *impatient* and *exacting*, without intending any unkindness. *They are ignorant of the negro character* and fail to secure the *attachment* of the slave on account of or by reason of their *mismanagement*. I have had experience with the three classes named, Foreigners, Northerners, and Native proprieters. The link between master and slave is *strongest with the native*. I feel warranted in asserting that the slave population *of this region* are *satisfactorily* cared for and provided for in sickness, and that *interest and humanity* go hand in hand together, leaving the M. D. a *carte blanche* to order and direct, with an abiding confidence and willingness to follow out his wishes and injunctions *faithfully and without stint*. There are difficulties incident, which are chargeable to the black race as *a people*, and which prevents the perfecting of any system of discipline by hospital or Infirmary institutions. The Medical police of any given plantation must therefore be only an approximation to what the Physician and Master both may religiously and studiously attempt. I bare willing testimony, however, to the kind, humane, considerate care for the sick whereever I have had charge, and can certify to the prompt resentment of the Master whenever his agent or overseer has shown a want of becoming consideration during his absence. On every well regulated Rice plantation, the *sick* receive the *first* and if necessary the undivided attention of the overseer. The Physician is the mutual friend of master and servant, and if he fails to gain their confidence and regard, the fault is his own.

Religious Instruction—My people are unbias'd in their selection of a church. They attach themselves to the Methodist, Baptist or Episcopal denomination without restraint or hindrance. A large portion of my adult negroes are in communion with the Methodists. Their place of worship (the Methodist Church) is situated immediately without my enclosure the land having been given by my ancestor for the location of their building. Religious services are held here once a day, on nearly every Sabbath in the year. An Episcopal Church (which I attend) is within one mile of settlement, and my people have the opportunity of attending here every Sunday from October to June. The Rector of this church visits my plantation once a fortnight from October to June for the catechetical instruction of all the smaller negroes who are arranged in a class and taught orally. The attendance is cheerful, and their instruction in no way compulsory, seems always pleasant and interesting. The fruit here is probably not more slow in ripening than among the whites. The harvest must depend much upon the tact, zeal and perseverance of the Missionary.

General Remarks—The moral and social condition of the Slave population in this district has vastly improved within 20 years. The control, management and entire discipline has materially changed, crime and rebellion are much less frequent. They have learnt in many instances to govern themselves and to govern each other and throughout this section, "*Runaways*" are fewer and "*less lawless*." The improvements in Machinery has relieved them of a large portion of the heaviest work. Agriculture has improved too, labor is more judiciously and economically bestowed. Comforts have multiplied, and although [*sic*] the routine of duty on a Rice plantation *to day* is incomparably less arduous to the slave than at any period heretofore. As an illustration of the "indulgencies" which my own people enjoy, I have during the past year kept an item of their perquisites from the sale (to me) of Eggs, poultry, Provisions saved from their allowance, and the raising of hogs, and it amounts in Money to upwards of $130, and in Sugar, Molasses, Flour, Coffee, Hand-kerchiefs, Aprons, Homespun and Calico, Pavilion Gause (Musquito Nets), Tin Buckets, hats, pocket knives, seives etc. to the am't of $110 more. One man received $25, and another $27, for hogs of their own raising and I had the satisfaction of seeing most of these am'ts spent in comforts and presents to their families.

The question has frequently presented itself whether or not this habit of buying for my people articles which are ordinarily only to be obtained through shop keepers, and retailing to them in exchange for their poultry etc. etc. might not lead to some *abuse* and cause them to pilfer or speculate upon each other. Limiting this rule strictly to my own people I have found it to work well. They frequently ask me to become *Treasurer* of their little funds. I have become satisfied that they get better bargains than can be made by themselves with the shop keepers. I hold now in this way upwards of $70, which will be called for in dimes and quarters, through the current year. As a *system* this can not be carried out in detail *generally*, for only those who are *permanent residents*, can very well undertake it. But the custom prevails with most of my neighbors of supplying all reasonable demands by exchange as indicated, whilst some prefer paying in *Money* and allowing them to trade for themselves. The point established is that by reasonable industry and ordinary providence, our people all have it in their power to add materially to their comforts and indulgencies, and that their owners very wisely and humanely offer every encouragement to this effort.

AGREEMENT BY ROBERT F. W. ALLSTON TO PURCHASE HOGS FROM THE SLAVES, 1859

In as much as during my absence of two years, my negroes have taken possession of my stock of Hogs, the best breed in the country, and I have few to kill, I will try the experiment of letting them raise for me. Therefore, Every negroe who is the head of a family will be allow'd the privelege to keep one hog. A Sow is universally prefer'd. So long as it does not trouble the fields, provided that in every October, on the Holiday after harvest (or at such time after as the overseer shall appoint before the 1st. Novr) they each shall bring to the overseer for the plantation-pen two yearling or young hogs, such as will be fit for killing during the ensuing winter. The overseer will weigh them both, and insert the weights against the name of the negroe presenting them in his journal and in his Report next succeeding. He will also give to each negroe a ticket for the smaller hog of the two he fetches, mentioning its weight. For this he shall be paid at the rate of Five dollars pr 100 lbs. Whatever else, the head of a family, by his diligence may raise, he may consume. But none must be sold off the plantation, except with the written consent of the [owner] or overseer. If any one offend against this regulation, he will thereby forfeit the privelege, now granted, of keeping a hog, and be liable besides to chastisement for disobedience.

AGREEMENT TO PURCHASE SLAVES, JANUARY 25, 1859

Agreed to purchase from Dr. Forster Forty one Negroes of Mrs. Withers of the "remainder" from the Estate of the late Francis Withers, to be deliver'd in all this week at $500. Titles to Ben Allston his Bond and mine payable in 8, 10, 12 yrs. secured by mortgage of the property, viz

$1000[1]	1	Andrew	38	yrs.	had	Blanket	in	1858	
800	2	Serena	36	"	"	"	"	56	
400	3	Jos.	10	"	"	"	"	57	
300	4	Judy	8	"	"	"	"	57	
200	5	Henry	5	"	"	"	"	54	
				[2]					
1000	6	Jack	30	"	"	"	"	1858	
800	7	Patience	27	"	"	"	"	56	pregnant
400	8	Daniel	11	"	"	"	"	49	
300	9	Prince	9	"	"	"	"	1850	
250	10	Phyllis	5	"	"	"	"	54	
200	11	Bess	3 1/2	"	"	"	"	55	
800	12	James*	28	"	"	"	"	56	carpenter, Drinks, delicate
800	13	Hagar	24	"	"	"	"	56	pregnant, near time of delivery
1200	14	Joe	39	"	"	"	"	56	carpenter and cooper
800	15	Levi	50	"	"	"	"	1858	
500	16	Betsey†	40	"	"	"	"	57	delicate
400	17	Murria‡	18	"	"	"	"	58	
400	18	Toby	14	"	"	"	"	57	

*Has Epileptic attacks produced by drink, would be valuable if kept from drink.
†With this family there is the incumbrance of an old man of 80 years, father of Betsy.
‡Murria is half witted.

1000	19	Paris	35	"	"	"	"	58
800	20	Hannah	33	"	"	"	"	56
800	21	Frank	16 1/2	"	"	"	"	58
500	22	William	14	"	"	"	"	56
350	23	Caty	9	"	"	"	"	50
300	24	Michael	6	"	"	"	"	53
150	25	Eleanor	3 1/2	"	"	"	"	55
50	26	Dandy	1	"	"	"	"	57

[1] The prices have been taken from a second list, also some of the remarks concerning individuals.

[2] The heavy lines probably indicate family groups.

800	27	Strephon	50 yrs.	had	Blanket	in		56	
700	28	Lucy	18	"	"	"	"	56	
500	29	Judy	14	"	"	"	"	57	
1000	30	Toney	38	"	"	"	"	56	an indifferent carpenter
800	31	Betty	35	"	"	"	"	58	
800	32	Daniel	16 1/2	"	"	"	"	56	3 years with Bricklayers to mix mortar
200	33	Francis	4 1/2	"	"	"	"	52	
100	34	Caesar	1 1/2	"	"	"	"	56	
500	35	O Sary	50	"	"	"	"	56	cook and washer
1000	36	Israel	31	"	"	"	"	57	
800	37	Esther	28	"	"	"	"	57	
100	38	William	1 1/2	"	"	"	"	57	
800	39	Dinah	18 1/2	"	"	"	"	58	
500	40	Quash	14 1/2	"	"	"	"	56	
300	41	William	9	"	"	"	"	56	

SLAVE BILL OF SALE, FEBRUARY 1, 1859[1]

The State of South Carolina.

To all to whom these Presents may come—I Mary Ann Petigru of Charleston Widow *Send Greeting.*

Whereas I the Said Mary Ann Petigru am lawfully possessed of and entitled to the negroe Slaves following that is to say: Nancy, Haramon, Francis, Dunkin, Esau, Clarinda, Maryan, Robert, Shaw, Molly, Lucy, Ned, Sukey, Amos, Prince, Maria, Beky, London, Rincky, Ned, Cupid, Amelia, Jim, Big Jacob, Dianna, Peggy, John, Patty, Jack, Patty, Rincky, London, Lizzy, William, Jim, Norrage, Jane, Tom, Frank, Lucy, Jim, Clarissa, Cotta, Nancy, Joe, Mary, Alice, Luna, Peggy, Stella, Abram, Conki, Hannay, Scipio, Jack, Edward, Betty, Rosan, Harklas, Friday, Affy, Hambleton, Snow, Nelly, Amy, July, Hannah, Minda, Liddy, Wallace, Hager, Eve, July, Phillis, Stepny, Elijiah, Judy, Sam, Jacob, Cloe, Daniel, Bina, Abram, Katy, Moses, Rose, Virgil, Scipio, Maria, Alice, Violet, Mary, James, Hannah, Carolina, Cupid, Louisa, Mary, Toney, Flora, Leah, Peter, Hager, Primus, Satira, Pompey, Liddy, Matilda, Sam, Harriet, John, Susannah, Rebecca, Catherine, Eliza and Stella and have contracted to Sell the Same to the Honorable Robert Francis Withers Allston at and for the price of Five hundred Dollars per head. *Now these Presents witness* that I the Said Mary Ann Petigru for and in consideration of the Sum of Fifty eight thousand Dollars to me duly Secured to be paid by the Said R. F. W. Allston *Have* bargained, sold and

[1] See above, p. 148.

delivered and by these Presents *Do* bargain Sell and deliver to the said R. F. W. Allston all those negroe Slaves above set forth by name one hundred and sixteen in number *To Have* and *To Hold* the same with their future issue and increase to the said R. F. W. Allston and his executors, Administrators and assigns forever: *And* I the Said Mary Ann Petigru all and singular the said slaves to him the said R. F. W. Allston against me and my heirs and against all other persons lawfully claiming or, to claim the same shall and will forever warrant and defend.

In witness whereof I have hereunto set my hand and Seal this first day of February in the year of our Lord one thousand eight hundred and fifty nine

Signed Sealed, and Delivered

in the presence of   M. A. PETIGRU

    JOS. BLYTH ALLSTON

State of South Carolina ⎱
Georgetown District ⎰

Personally appeared before me, Jos Blyth Allston and made Oath that he saw the above named M. A. Petigru sign seal and as her act and Deed deliver the within written Deed and that the Deponent witnessed the Execution thereof.—

Sworn before me, this   JOS. BLYTH ALLSTON
2d day of May 1859.

    HENRY F. DETJENS
    CCP & Ex offo Mgt

SLAVE BILL OF SALE, 1859[1]

The State of South Carolina
Georgetown District

TO ALL WHOM IT MAY CONCERN—

The following instrument of writing witnesseth. That in January 1859— R. F. W. Allston purchased of Mrs. M. A. Petigru her plantation and negroes on Sandy Island, for which he gave bonds to the amount of Seventy eight thousand dollars (78,000) and a mortgage of the property, to secure the payment thereof.

That having given to his Son Benjamin Allston the settled plantation, *Guendalos* with 215 acres of Rice land or thereabout; the undersigned desired to aid him in purchasing negroes to work it, and with this view chiefly, he agreed to the arrangement with Mrs Petigru.

Mrs. Petigru however prefering to hold the bonds of R. F. W. Allston, they were so given and dated 1st of February 1859. Now, in consideration of the said Benjamin Allston assuming to pay as his own debt a certain bond for

---

[1] An unsigned copy.

fourteen thousand five hundred dollars ($14,500) dated 1st of January 1859, and executed in favor of P. C. J. Weston by Ben Allston, R. F. W. Allston, and Jo. B. Allston, and in further consideration of the simple Bond of the said Ben Allston in favor of R. F. W. Allston, for the payment when demanded, of Six thousand ($6,000) dollars, with interest annually, on the 1st day of January, the undersigned has put him in possession of and hereby conveys to him, his heirs and assigns, Thirty four negroes, subject only to the mortgage to Mrs. Petigru, namely—

Jacob, Diana, Friday, Toney, Flora, Clarinda, Mary Ann (Billy, Molly, Lucy), Wallace, Hagar (Phillis, Stephney, Foxwood) Prince, Maria (Becky, London) Edward, Betty (Rosanna, Hercules) Luna (Peggy, Stella, Abram, Phebe) Robert, Affee (Hamilton) Kongue, Pompey, Eve and also the following negroes subject to no lien whatever namely Driver Sammy, Lydia, Chubby (Diana) Annette (Celia)

In witness whereof we do set our hands and seals hereto, ———.

A FREEDMEN'S CONTRACT, 1865[1]

STATE OF SOUTH CAROLINA.
Darlington District.

ARTICLES OF AGREEMENT.

This Agreement entered into between Mrs. Adele Allston Exect of the one part, and the Freedmen and Women of The Upper Quarters plantation of the other part *Witnesseth:*

That the latter agree, for the remainder of the present year, to reside upon and devote their labor to the cultivation of the Plantation of the former. And they further agree, that they will in all respects, conform to such reasonable and necessary plantation rules and regulations as Mrs. Allston's Agent may prescribe; that they will not keep any gun, pistol, or other offensive weapon, or leave the plantation without permission from their employer; that in all things connected with their duties as laborers on said plantation, they will yield prompt obedience to all orders from Mrs. Allston or his [*sic*] agent; that they will be orderly and quiet in their conduct, avoiding drunkenness and other gross vices; that they will not misuse any of the Plantation Tools, or Agricultural Implements, or any Animals entrusted to their care, or any Boats, Flats, Carts or Wagons; that they will give up at the expiration of this Contract, all Tools &c., belonging to the Plantation, and in case any property, of any description belonging to the Plantation shall be willfully or through negligence destroyed or injured, the value of the Articles so destroyed, shall be deducted from the portion of the Crops which the person or persons, so offending, shall be entitled to receive under this Contract.

[1] Indorsed: "Head Qts 2d Sub Dist, S.C., Darlington, S.C., July 31st, '65 Approved [signature illegible] Col. 29th Maine I. Vols Comdg 2d Sub Dist."

Any deviations from the condition of the foregoing Contract may, upon sufficient proof, be punished with dismissal from the Plantation, or in such other manner as may be determined by the Provost Court; and the person or persons so dismissed, shall forfeit the whole, or a part of his, her or their portion of the crop, as the Court may decide.

In consideration of the foregoing Services duly performed, Mrs. Allston agrees, after deducting Seventy five bushels of Corn for each work Animal, exclusively used in cultivating the Crops for the present year; to turn over to the said Freedmen and Women, one half of the remaining Corn, Peas, Potatoes, made this season. He [sic] further agrees to furnish the usual rations until the Contract is performed.

All Cotton Seed Produced on the Plantation is to be reserved for the use of the Plantation. The Freedmen, Women and Children are to be treated in a manner consistent with their freedom. Necessary medical attention will be furnished as heretofore.

Any deviation from the conditions of this Contract upon the part of the said Mrs. Allston or her Agent or Agents shall be punished in such manner as may be determined by a Provost Court, or a Military Commission. This agreement to continue till the first day of January 1866.

Witness our hand at The Upper Quarters this 28th day of July 1865.

Signed and delivered in the presence of
    W H EVANS
    A VANDER HORST

ADELE ALLSTON   *Executrix*
by her Agent
BEN ALLSTON

          His
1   GEORGE X GUNN
          mark

          His
2   BILLY X GRICE
          mark

          his
3   WILLIAM X [illegible]
          mark

          her
4   SYBANNA X KEITH
          mark

          her
5   SALLY X BROWN
          mark

          his
6   MURPHY X KEITH
          mark

INSCRIPTIONS FROM THE SLAVE BURIAL GROUND
AT CHICORA WOOD PLANTATION

Headstone:

In
Memory of
Joe of Warhees[1]
Who with fidelity served
My Grandfather
Wm Allston, Senr
My Father
Benj Allston and Me
Grateful,
Whose confidence and
Respect he had

Footstone:

J.
1840

Headstone:

In
Memory of
My Servant Thomas
Carpenter,
Honest and true
He died as for 40 years
He had lived
My faithful friend

Footstone:

1858

---

[1] Otherwise known as Mulatto Joe. "Warhees" is a name still applied to the section of Marion District where Joe lived and attended to the Allston farm.

FACTORS' CORRESPONDENCE

Charles Kershaw to Charlotte Ann Alston

Charleston May 8th, 1810

MADAM   Agreeably to your desire I paid to Mrs Vaux twenty Dollars to purchase the articles for your children and have since received a Letter from Miss Stone desiring me to send you Sixty dollars out of her money which I now inclose to you.

The Sale of Rice has become very dull and the price down to 2 1/4.[1] I very fortunately sold the last 118 Barrels that came down in Capt Toby at 2 1/2 dollars on a credit of Sixty days, which I will thank you to mention to Mr Tucker.

There is every probability that the Trade between this Country and Europe will be completely free in the course of a few days, but the scarcity of Shipping in our Port will prevent any advance in the price. I sold a very fine parcel of Rice two days ago at 2 3/8 D[ollars] which is the best sale I had made for a fortnight previous. . . . .

P.S.   I have settled with Mrs Jones and paid her twelve dollars in Cash the Barrel of small Rice came to 8 Dollars which made up the 20 Dollars, and for which Sum I have taken a recipt in full. . . . .

10th May—Since writing the above advices have been received that the Non Intercourse has been removed, it has not as yet had any influence on our market, the highest price now to be obtained is 2 3/8 D[ollars].

Charles Kershaw to Charlotte Ann Allston

Charleston 14 Decr, 1811

MADAM   By this days mail you will receive a Letter from Miss Mary[2] who I have the pleasure to inform you arrived in good health, the day before yesterday by the Ship Georgia Packet under the care of Mrs. Bunce wife of Captain Bunce. Mrs Bowman and Family being in the Country Miss Mary resides with my Family and will do so until I can find a good opportunity to convey her safe to you.

I have paid Mrs. Rivardi's account in full $160.11 which is correct, as she deducted the advance of $67 that was made to her formerly. You may rest assured of every attention being paid to Miss Mary during her stay with us and of my furnishing money to purchase such articles as may be wanted.

[1] Per hundredweight.

[2] Mrs. Allston's daughter, Mary Pyatt.

Charles Kershaw to Charlotte Ann Allston

Charleston July 30, 1812

MADAM   I have put on board of Capt Tarbox's Schooner
        1 Barrel Salt 10 1/2 Bushs at 7/- a Bushel
        1 Keg Glauber Salts
        1 paper parcel contg 1 lb Jalap
                        1/4 lb Rhubarb
                        1/4 lb Hyppo

Capt Davis did not deliver me any Box for Salts or demi Johns he sent two Empty Barrels only but did not know who put them on board his Vessel.

I have written on to New York to send me on the money for the Rice which I shipped to that place on account of the Estate when it arrives I will make the remittance you require and write you particularly on the subject of the debt due by Miss Newman's Estate. The Piano has been received, I will have it put in good order and sent to your House in George Town.

P.S.   Salt being so very dear, I have sent only one Barrel for the present.

Charles Kershaw to Charlotte Ann Allston

Charleston 25 Feb, 1815

MADAM   I have put on board Mr. Solomons Boat a Box containing the Medicines and a small packet with the Needles which I hope will arrive safe. As the Joyful News of Peace is come at last every one is anxious to reap some benefit from it and I have continual enquiries what Rice will sell for before the Buyers come into the Market. In consequence of the conversation we had about the disposal of Rice in Georgetown I would still recommend you to send for a flatt Load and sell it for the best price you can obtain in order to relieve the demands which you may have for money. If you can sell at two dollars it will be better than sending it down to this place for although I am offering the Estates Rice, which last came down, at 2 1/2 dollars I have not yet been able to dispose of it. Whenever you make a sale be good enough to inform me and I will advise you whether it will be best to go on to sell in Georgetown or send it on to this place. My first object is that you should be made as easy as possible, considering the heavy Debts we have to contend with. If you can sell at 2 1/4 dollars send for another flatt Load immediately or if the purchasers are willing, agree for one or two Loads more at that rate or as far as 100 Barrels if you are sure of the Money. I will write you from time to time and inform you how our Markets go. Please present my best respects to Mrs. Shackleford and to all your good Family.

P.S.   A Letter in which I put the Needles is on board Solomons Boat, in the Letter is a list of the Medicines.

Mrs. K[ershaw] cannot yet please herself with the Long Lawn. It is scarce and high.

Charles Kershaw to Charlotte Ann Allston

Charleston 12 May 1815

MADAM   I received your esteemed favor and beg leave to recommend you not to sell any more of the Estates Rice in Georgetown for as the price has advanced in this place in consequence of the late news from Europe, it is probable we can do better with it in Charleston. Yet at the same time should [you] have any very pressing occasion for money you must sell in Georgetown to answer these demands. I have not yet received one dollar from any Sale of the Estates Rice. I deemed it best to ship the old Rice to Europe and I am now pleased it is shipped away, for it is probable it may do well, indeed it must sell better than it would do in Charleston.

Your Brothers Affidavit is very clear. I am only sorry that his Letter was written in a moment of Irritation and that I cannot with prudence lay it before the Court.

My little Friend William[1] is with us, he seems very well pleased to stay with us, you will be good enough to permit [him] to remain for a Week or two, and we will send him home by some Friend.

P.S.   If Mr Saml Allston has any Rice ready pounded be good enough to request him to send it down to Charleston as it may sell to good advantage.

Charles Kershaw to Charlotte Ann Allston

Charleston 29 November 1815

MADAM   I had the pleasure to hear by Mr Saml Allston that the Negro Cloth was arrived, and as the remaining Articles are ready I have put them on board Capt Ca[rv]illes Schooner, Vizt

1 Cask containing 90 pair Shoes for Waccamaw and Peedee and 6 pair Shoes for your own people also a Bundle containing the following Articles

1 piece Bombarzet about 30 Yards cost................		13. –
3 London Duffil Blankets....................	a $5	15. –
6 quire paper.......................................		1.69
6 handkerchiefs.....................................		2.50
6 Yards Apron Check......................	a 2/8...	3.43
2 phials Calcined Magnesia........................		2. –

Agreeably to your desire I have had a Suit of Cloaths made for your Son William which I hope he will be pleased with. They are made of good Cloth and cost including the making $37.75. I have unfortunately lost the measure for his Shoes, one of the Children having thrown it by accident into the fire. Be good enough to inclose me the Length of his Shoe, on paper, in a Letter, and I will have two pair made for him. I send also two Demi Johns of Whiskey for the Negroes at Christmas and a small Bundle for Mr Saml Allston which you will be good enough to forward to him.

[1] Mrs. Allston's son, William Washington.

The Rice last shipped in the three Sisters has been sifted about three Barrels will be lost and as the appearance of the rest is hurt we shall not be able to get so good a price for it. 34 Barrels, however, are sold at $3 1/2.

Mr King has not yet arrived from Liverpool, but will be here by the middle of next Month, as the Court of Equity will meet in January next, if Mr Blanding attends, the Cause will go on.[1] And as it will be requisite that the Charge should be made for building the Mill I beg leave to suggest (if it meet with your approbation) that the two Carpenters that were employed should be ready to attend that every information may be obtained, or in Case the Court should appoint An Arbitration that they may be ready to point out what Work was done.

Charles Kershaw to Charlotte Ann Allston

Charleston 16th March 1816

MADAM   Agreeably to your desire I have made out a statement of the demands of the Estate Benjamin Allston against the Estate Dr Edwd H. Tucker which you will be good enough to look over and if you find it correct I beg leave to recommend your getting some Friend to deliver it personally to Mr Washington Heriot; the Friend who delivers the Statement should first read the Memorandum of the Notes, so as to remember the contents of the Letter.

I have put on board Capt Toby's Schooner two large Iron Pots for the purpose of boiling Salt, they contain from 30 to 40 Gallons Each. the articles you wrote for on your own account we have not yet been able to procure, the Dutch Oven and Chafing Dish are not to be had at the Stores in our Neighbourhood, but as they may probably be had in King Street, the first time I go that way will look out for them the Clothes Keetle you mention will cost thirty dollars, if you approve of the price I will send it to you.

I now inclose you $87.18 being the amount of the account for Weaving the Home Spun etc also One hundred dollars for the use of Miss Charlotte and Miss Mary. You will be good enough to sign the receipt and forward it by any opportunity at your leisure.

Be good enough to mention to Mrs Blyth that I have not yet been able to obtain the Table Sett of China at the limits she mentioned to me. These articles have been scarce in Town and do not sell at Vendue for less than 65 dollars.

Your two Servants Amy and Mary came under the care of Capt Toby who took them to the Persons they were to go to, should they have occasion for assistance in case of sickness I will take care they shall have attention paid to them.

Should you make the purchase of the plough Horses for the Estate be good

---

[1] The case involving a division of the Allston estate, which, however, was subsequently postponed until 1819. See above, p. 51.

enough to have a Bill made out in the name of the Estate and write an order upon it and it shall be paid. . . . .

Charles Kershaw to Charlotte Ann Allston

Charleston November 14, 1816

MADAM   I did not receive your esteemed favor of the 5th Instant until this morning. I have no objection to Major Savage Smith furnishing the Negro Shoes, if you wish to give him a preference provided he will supply them at one dollar a pair, to be paid for on the first of March next without Interest, on which terms I can obtain the Shoes in this place of the very best quality. But if the Shoes are not good, and it is a matter of indifference to you who supplys them, please send the measures down and I will have them fitted. I will also have two pair made for Masters Robert and William and if you think proper that your Son Robert should have Boots, be pleased to forward me the measure for them, he must get some Shoe Maker to take a measure of his Leg, instep etc.

You will please give me some explanation respecting the Blankets. If I understand your Letter right, it is that 120 Blankets *in all* are wanted, 30 of which are to be small Blankets. Be good enough to inform me if I am correct.

With respect to the Cloaths for your two Sons, I am very glad that you intend to have them made in Georgetown, as the Workmen in this place are very extravagant in their prices, perhaps it will be better to buy such Cloth as they may fancy at the Stores in Georgetown, but if you deem it best to have the Articles purchased here be good enough to let me know what quantities may be wanted. Your Servants shall be supplied with their Winter Cloaths and Shoes as you desire. I am on the look out for the Negro Cloth which will be ready to go by the return of Captain Davis. The Silk for Mrs Shackelford shall be purchased and forwarded.

Charles Kershaw to Charlotte Ann Allston

Charleston November 25th, 1816

MADAM   By this opportunity I forward to you—

3 Bales marked Est B. Allston No 1, 2 and 3
1 Cask Shoes etc. 4
1 Box Medicines. 5
1 Barrel Sugar. 6

which I hope will arrive safe and meet with your approbation. I purchased the Cloth for the People at Public Sale and obtained it at a cheaper rate than any of the same quality has been sold this Year. The Blue Cloth you will find of three different qualities, marked on the pieces of Lead No 1, 2 and 3, the number 3 is the best and from which you will please cut the 10 Yards for yourself as the pieces run together 124 1/2 Yards, 10 of which I charge to you and 114 1/2 to the Estate. The Shoes for your two Sons are making by the Boy James at Mr Blacks and if they are ready will go by this opportunity.

I am very glad to hear that the Estate will make a tolerable Crop of Rice as the price is likely to be high this Winter. Whenever the Mill can be set to Work, it will be best to have some of the Estates Rice sent down to obtain the favorable prices and enable me to pay off the demands that are pressing. The account for Master Robert and William Cloaths shall be paid whenever you think proper to give an order, please have the Account drawn out in the name of the Estate and let the Person specify how much for your Son Robert and how much for William.

I expect to set off for Columbia on Saturday and have much writing to prepare. I hope Mr Tucker will make it convenient to attend as Dr Blyth will be prevented by the indisposition of Mrs Blyth.

Please present my best respects to your good Family.

Charles Kershaw to Charlotte Ann Allston

Charleston Feby. 7. 1817

MADAM   Immediately on receipt of your favor I went up to Mr Kerrs respecting the Carpeting. He had one whole piece of 36 Yards which he would not cut. I therefore took the piece. On my wishing him to cut 5 Yards from another piece of the same kind he objected to do so, saying he had so many remnants that he would not make any more. I therefore took a remnant of nearly 3 3/4 Yds which he charges only 3 5/8 and it is probable as there is 3 Yds over in Mrs Blyths piece that you will be able to obtain what you want. If this plan will answer pray send me word how much you take from Mrs Blyths piece that I may charge accordingly. If the piece sent will not answer please return it and I will endeavour to prevail on Mr Kerr to cut off as much as you want, but it will be necessary for you to mark on the piece you return from what part of the Figure you begin the 5 Yard piece, otherwise the pattern will not match together on the floor. I send 15 Yards of bordering, 13 for Mrs Blyth and 2 for yourself. I am sorry to say that all the piece of Silk, like Miss Marys, is sold. Mr Mulligan says that in a day or two after your purchased the Silk he could have sold a dozen pieces and now there is not any in Town like it.

The other Articles will be procured as soon as the Weather will permit Mrs K[ershaw] to go out she has a bad cold which has confined her to the House during the bad Weather. She desires her best respects and requests me to say that she will be happy at all times to assist you in any purchases you may wish to make in this place. With respect to the Chairs, I am quite at a loss what to do, there is such a variety both in Pattern and Color that I wish you had mentioned the circumstance when you were in Charleston that you might have chosen the Pattern yourself. If you will be good enough to mention any Pattern or where you saw the sort that would suit you I will purchase them for you with pleasure.

Mr King has arrived safe and says he has a Letter from you which I must call for this Evening.

Charles Kershaw to Charlotte Ann Allston

Charleston March 13, 1817

MADAM Your Servant Amy goes by this opportunity, I suppose it is by your instructions, she takes with her the two Bottles of Castor Oil which I have charged to the Estate. In a former Letter I mentioned that the Silk could not be purchased and I therefore return you the balance of the 70 dollars with a Memorandum how the other part was expended. Capt Toby I make no doubt delivered you the Bundle containing the Stockings, Linen and Dowlass. The Stockings and Dowlass I paid out of the 70 Ds. but the Linen I have charged to the Estate, for Miss Charlotte, it cost One dollar a Yard. There will not be any difficulty in returning the Carpeting to Mr Ker, and when we settle with him, shall charge your Account with the 2 Yds of Bordering. With respect to the Chairs I really do not like to buy them, they appear to me so weak that they would not last you long. If you could possibly do without them for another Year I beg you to do so as I shall have so much money to raise this Year that it will be requisite to husband every Cent. I have enquired the price of those painted Green and Gilded next door to Mr Highams they ask 75 dollars for 12 Chairs that is 10 Common and 2 Arm, there are some in Setts of 10 without Arm Chairs that come about 56 dollars, if you want them I will purchase them for you. I return Mr Wm. Capers Bill, the Sum it is true is but small, but as the 1 April is near at hand it will be better to pay as the quarter comes round, it is not proper for an Estate to pay any account in advance.

Mrs Higham and Mrs King are both confined, they are as well as we could expect them to be and also the Children. Mrs King has met with a severe affliction in the loss of her Brother,[1] who was buried this Morning, he died after a short Illness at Columbia, and the Corpse was on its way down before they heard the account of his Death. Mr Higham will not forget to write for your Knives and forks, they will be out in the Fall.

Mrs K[ershaw] joins me in good wishes to yourself and Family.

Charles Kershaw to Charlotte Ann Allston

Charleston September 18, 1817

DEAR MADAM I received your esteemed favor of the 16th. and hope you will excuse my not writing to you before. I sent you by Capt Carville a Barrel of new Flour cost $12.50, and at the same time a small paper parcel, both of

---

[1] Alexander Shirras Campbell.

which I requested to be left for you at Mr Cheeseborough. I did not write as I had to be continualy going backward and forward to the Island to attend to Miss Mary Hasford who has been very Ill but is now I trust out of danger. We have had a most severe trial for these five Weeks past attending our own Families and those of our Friends, my Children have recovered, Mr Higham has three left out of five, Mr Kings eldest Son has recovered almost by a miracel, his daughter is now very ill, one of his Servants dying and another taken down, in short every Family less or more have suffered, and those who have been so fortunate as to escape are worn down with care and anxiety.

I was truly sorry to learn that my Friend Robert had been prevented by sickness, from coming round to take his passage for New York. Vessels are going continually to that place. I would therefore recommend that he come round by one of the Coasters, but you must contrive not to let him go back to Georgetown but have him taken from North Island, and a *positive agreement* must be made *that he is not to be taken up to Charleston but landed at Sullivans Island* you must excuse me being so particular but I cannot consent to receive Robert on any other terms. I would not have him visit Charleston on any consideration for he would as certain take the Strangers Fever as he now exists. My best respects and every good wish attend you and your family and I beg you will remember me kindly to Mrs. Shackelford and Mrs Cheeseborough.

Charles Kershaw to Charlotte Ann Allston

Charleston October 7, 1817

MADAM   I did myself the pleasure of writing to you about three Weeks ago and forwarded to you a Barrel of New Flour which I hope you have received safe. I have been on the look out for my Young friend Robert, but he has not yet appeared, in my last I mentioned to you to make an agreement with the Captain of the Vessel, that he has taken his Passage in for this place, to land him on Sullivans Island, and I must beg again to repeat this Caution for our City still remains sickly and although he has been taking medicine for his last Illness, he may not escape the malignant discorder that now prevails. Vessels are continually going to New York and I could get any of them to call at the Island and take Robert on board, this will be the most cautious plan, and if any accident was to happen we could console ourselves with having done every thing that was prudent, but if he was to land in Charleston, he might be taken away from us and we might continually reflect what little care we took, when there is so much danger.

I have had nobody in Town to look after the Silk for you agreeably to the pattern you sent, but hope to have it ready by the last of this month as you requested.

I have not been able to settle with Mr Saml Allston for his Shares of the Crop 1815, I will thank you to inform me if the Shares that Year was the same as for 1814 say 60 1/2 hands for the Estate and 7 for Mr Saml Allston making together 67 1/2. As I expect to receive some money soon and I will then advance the amount that is due to him.

There is another matter which I will thank you to inform me and that is if Mr Benjamin Allston returned the 270 Bushels of rough Rice he borrowed from the Estate the 15th March 1816. Mr Pyatt settled for the 200 Bushels he had at the same time, but I have never been informed whether Mr B. Allston returned the Rice in kind or sent clean Rice in place of it.

I am happy to inform you that my Family are now recovering from the effects of this malignant disorder. The Doctor has scarcely been away from my House these Six Weeks, my Son Tom is now Ill but is considered out of danger.

You will be good enough to let me know the Quantity of Negro Cloth that will be wanted this Year that I may be on the look out for it in time, also what Quantity of Thread and Needles.

If the Crop is forward, it will be as well to prepare some for market as soon as it will bear pounding as the first Sales will probably be the best.

P.S.   please to send the Shoe measures.

Charles Kershaw to Charlotte Ann Allston

Charleston December 19, 1817

MADAM   Mrs Kershaw requests me to say that the Gown you sent to be dyed has at last been obtained, but that the Woman has dyed it Black in place of lead Colour as she was directed, indeed at one time it appeared probable that you would have lost the Gown for it was missing and was not found until yesterday.

I have not heard anything from my Friends in New York respecting your Son Robert, but I am certain they will take care that he shall not want for any thing while he is there, but I will write to him and endeavour to obtain some information respecting him, at present I cannot form any Plan to assist him without knowing his particular situation.

Your Servants were too late for the Custom House, they must be regularly cleared out in the Manifest so that if Davis goes early in the Morning they cannot go with him, but if Capt Tobey arrives they will go by his Vessel.

Charles Kershaw to Charlotte Ann Alston

Charleston 24th Dec 1817

MADAM   Your Servants James and Pierce go by Capt Toby, but Madame Langlois cannot spare Mary. Pierce never came near me to get his Winter Cloaths until it was too late. I send you by Capt Toby a paper parcel containing, 1 pair Shoes for Master William, which will serve him for the present, I have requested James to take his measure and will then have three pair made for him, I send also one pair Shoes for your Servant.

Mr Hoff has received some Copies of Nelsons Devotions I therefore send you one and if it is approved of can forward what other Copies of it, that you may want, the price is $1.25

Capt Tobey delivered to us 60 Barrels of the Estates Rice which we have sold at 5 dollars.

I have not time to set down and answer the Letter you were good enough to write to me, but will do it very soon.

Charles Kershaw to Charlotte Ann Allston

Charleston December 30, 1817

MADAM   I have had the pleasure of receiving a Letter from my young Friend Robert dated the 17th Instant at West point, he gives me the agreeable information that he has been regularly admitted and seems to be much gratified in being enrolled a member of the Military Academy my Friend Mr Cary has advanced Robert one hundred and fifty dollars to purchase what was necessary for himself and the Furniture of his Room Bed etc as he says his pay will not commence until he receives his Warrant.

Your Servants have been on board Capt Tobeys Schooner several days. Mr Black complains much of James being very Idle, this is the last Year and the time when he should exert himself to be a good Workman, but he will not do what is proper, Mr Black says that he is capable of finishing Six pair of Shoes a Week and he seldom does more than three.

I have seriously reflected on your Letter respecting your staying on the Plantation and taking the management and find that I cannot advise you, it is a matter I am totally ignorant of and I would recommend your consulting with Mr B. Allston and Mr Tucker,[1] it is a duty they have undertaken and if I was to interfere I should give offence and do no good.

Charles Kershaw to Charlotte Ann Allston

Charleston 12 March 1818

MADAM   Capt Toby delivered the 42 Barrels Rice which was in time to obtain the highest price, 35 of them being sold at 6 1/4, this was so far fortunate as the price will certainly be down, as we have little or no demand at present.

I now inclose you $500 on your account and when I have the pleasure of seeing you will arrange all the several Sums which you have laid out on account of the Estate, if it will be agreeable to you we will settle accounts for all the small articles which you have paid for at different times from the

[1] Benjamin Allston and John H. Tucker, who had qualified as executors of the Allston estate.

Year 1809, the Charges you have been at in attending the Courts must be reimbursed to you, and it would give me great pleasure if you was relieved from the care and anxiety which you continually experience in the affairs of the Estate. I observe what you mention respecting Mr Joseph [Waties] Allston, and it gives me much pleasure to hear that he has taken an active part in the management of the Plantation, he will be of age this Year and it will meet with my concurence, if you thought it best that a division of the Estate should be made the next Year. The heavy Debts are closing by degrees I have lately paid the balance due on Savage Smith and Co's Bond, also the *Interest* in full of the Bonds for the Peedee Lands the Principal Debts are $6428.57 for the Peedee Plantation,[1] a balance due to the Estate Allard Belin, when the accounts are settled, about $3000 to Dr Blyth, a Debt to Mr B. Allston and a balance due to me. I shall strain every nerve to reduce the Debt for the Peedee Land and then there will be no Debt that is particularly pressing, so that if a division should be made the Debts could be divided into the several proportions the Younger Children are of sufficient Age to appoint Guardians and they might, after the division, unite their Interest and plant together, but there is a consideration, if the Estate is divided, how you are to receive your Annuity.

I throw out these Hints for your consideration and should be very happy if some Plan could be adopted that might be agreeable to all Parties. I must come to George town, some time next Month, to pass my Accounts with the Ordinary and I will then take the opportunity of seeing you and will pursue any measures that may be thought most advisable. It will be a source of great pleasure to me, if after struggling so long to keep the Estate together, we may be enabled to deliver over the property of the Children agreeably to the Will of my much respected Friend. Respecting your Son William I am quite at a loss what to advise, I feel the same difficulty with my own Children, William is certainly too Young to be sent to Charleston to put to Business, besides it could not be done without a heavy Expence. Merchants will not take Lads into their Stores or Counting Houses, without their Parents find them in everything, my Son William is now with Mr McCauley and I find him in Board, Clothing etc, it is considered that what they learn in the Stores is a full compensation for their Services. As far as I can Judge your Son William should be at School one or even two Years longer, and if that could be done under your own Eye it would be better, besides his delicate state of health requires the care of a Parent. I am willing to agree to any Plan that may be thought best for the Child, but after all it must rest with yourself, you are the Person who will feel the most for him and your feelings must be consulted I therefore beg of you to consider what ought to be done and I will assist you as far as lies in my power.

Mrs K[ershaw] thought that you had given up the purchase of the Plad

---

[1] Matanzas, later known as Chicora Wood.

Silk and has destroyed the Memorandum please mention the Quantity and it shall be purchased.

I have not been able to obtain the Sour Oranges, in a former Letter I mentioned that owing to the continual Rain in the fall of the Year that the Crop of Oranges had failed, now and then Six or Eight were brought to market, but although the Trees appeared full of Fruit, the Oranges either dropped before they were Ripe or withered upon the Tree. The Potatoes and ground Nuts will go by the Corsair for New York. Please to present my best respects to your Family.

P.S.   I have mentioned to Mr B. Allston that it will be best to purchase what Corn, that is wanting for the Plantation, in George town, the price here for good Corn is 125 Cents, please to draw on me when you purchase Corn and I will pay the order at sight.

Charles Kershaw to Charlotte Ann Allston

Charleston 16 May 1818

MADAM   Mr H. Gibbes was good enough to hand me your favor and since then Capt Harwicke arrived, but he had so much Cotton on board his Schooner that he mentioned he was not able to bring your Carriage down. When it arrives I will attend to your instructions in delivering it and receive the Money agreeably to the arrangement made by Mr Wilson. We hope the Carriage is on board Capt Gibbes or some of the Coasters now in George town as it may be wanted.

I am very sorry that I shall not be able to visit George Town this Spring, but I must come up in November or directly after the first Frost. I should have been glad to have seen you to talk over the affairs of the Estate, but there are so many of my Friends who are going away to the Northward, and who all want some little Business arranged previous to their departure, that it would be in vain for me to attempt to leave this place at this time.

I am glad you have determined on placing your Son William at Woodville Academy, I know Mr Wood Furman very well and shall write to him to pay some attention to him so as to bring him forward, he is too young to send to Charleston. With my best respects to yourself and your Family.

Charles Kershaw to Charlotte Ann Allston

Charleston 8th February 1819

MADAM   I wrote you by Mail to day to which beg leave to refer and now inclose you by Captn Tobey two hundred dollars being the amount which I received from Mr Joel Poinsett for the Carriage. I have seen Mr Black, he will give only ten dollars per month for James to find him, but you must find him in Cloaths and Shoes, pay Doctors accounts and allow for the time he is absent whenever you send for him to Georgetown either at Christmas or any other time. Mr Black says he is a good Workman and capable of turning out work equal to any of his Colour, but he is so very indolent that he requires a very tight hand kept over him, if therefore you consent to hire James to Mr Black you must give him a complete command over him and let him know no other person to apply to, but I assure [you] after all it will be more to your Son Roberts Interest to put him in the Field, he will earn more than double what he will do in this place. James may perhaps go on very well with Mr Black for a few Months, but after that he will have bad notions put into his head, he will want to work out and pay Wages which is much the same as giving him his freedom, I have had several young Lads whom I put apprentice but the moment they got out of their time they began upon the plan I mentioned of wanting to work out and pay Wages, which I found was one dollar or two dollars a Month and sometimes nothing, I therefore was compelled to send them in the Country and put them in the Field. All that I can do is to receive the Wages from Mr Black, if you think proper to hire him on the terms mentioned, but if you was to hint to him that I have any thing to say in the Business, you may be assured, James will not be obedient or attentive to his Work.

P.S.   James and his Sister go up by Capt Tobey.

Charles Kershaw to Charlotte Ann Allston

Charleston 27th February 1819

MADAM   I have written Mr Joseph W. Allston by Capt Tobey acknowledging receipt of 55 Barrels of the Estates Rice, and informing him that it was sold at $4 3/4, this makes 209 Barrels that have come to Market, the Average weight of which is full 600 lb Nett. It will be prudent to continue sending down such of the Estates Rice as it is pounded out, as the price will not probably be higher for some time to come and it is no doubt desireable to bring the Estates affairs to a close as soon as possible.

Dr R Nesbit was in Town and I proposed settling with him, after charging him with the purchases he made at the Sale and deducting some due Bills, which I hold, due to the Estate, there appears a balance due to him of $375, but he informs me that he owes for the Wages of a Negro Carpenter (I believe he said Thomas) please inform me how much the Wages amount to, that I may pay the balance and close that transaction.

I write Mrs Blyth by this opportunity to inform her that in the course of next Month I should be ready to pay her the $3000 which she was good enough to lend the Estate last Year, it will be better for me to pay this Debt to her as I am personally liable for it and then Mrs Blyth may, if she thinks proper, loan it to the Heirs and take their obligation for it, such a loan would help Mr Joseph W. Allston to purchase Negroes and with his own patrimony will be a handsome beginning for him. On the 9th of next month I shall pay the Exors of Rose the Interest due on the 5 Bonds and I have every reason to believe they will not require the Principal this Year, but remain satisfied with the Interest.

Charles Kershaw to Charlotte Ann Allston

Charleston March 19, 1819

MADAM   I have been unwell for some days or I would have written you sooner in answer to your two Letters, the first of which came by Major Bull inclosing the Bond and Mortgage, which is perfectly satisfactory, and I sincerely hope that the division will turn out equal to the most sanguine wishes of all the Heirs. I have lately paid the Interest on the Bonds in the hands of Mr Rose's Children, they are perfectly satisfied to receive the Interest and do not wish any part of the Principal of the Bonds this Year, therefore, there is no particularly pressing Debt upon the Estate and of course the Heirs will not be called upon for any payment until the Crop comes round.

Respecting the Wages for Charlotte I would advise you to make out an account of it and get it signed by the Heirs that they are satisfied with the Charge, and when I have any Funds in hand will discharge it.

Whatever necessaries you may want for the Plantations under your care had better be taken up in George town, the difference of the Cost will be a little more but then you can get what is wanted by degrees and at once, it will be better also to take the Corn from General Williams so as to have it landed at the Plantation until the Affairs of the Estate are quite settled you will be put to some inconvenience and trouble and you will also have to keep a particular account of all your transactions as Guardian of your Children, you must therefore be very cautious not to pay money away without a receipt, for you will have to settle every Year with the Masters in Equity. No Accounts can now be opened in the name of the Estate. I would beg leave to advise you to get Mr Shackelford, Mr Cheeseborough or some Friend you may deem best to open accounts for you in a Book expressly for the purpose. I am sorry to observe that there will be some difficulty in settling the Affairs of the Negro hire of Billey and Thomas, it is impossible for me to make any settlement of it and as I never interfered in the Business the settlement will not come through my hands, but as Mr Joseph Allston is so much interested it will be best for him to exert himself and where any Money is due to collect it for the right lays with himself to make the demand and receive from any one the one half of what may be due, for example if I knew exactly what was due by Dr Nesbit I would deduct it from his amount and pay the Money. Mr R F Withers you mentioned, had Billey the three first Years, that Money should be collected with Interest. I have never received a Cent of their Wages, your Idea that Mr B. Allston should have the Money collected is correct, but unless Mr Joseph Allston interferes it will not be done. I cannot interfere for if I do I shall be making myself a party in a Business that I know nothing about Mr F. Deliesseline wants much to settle and pay what Money he has to the Executors, but that Business remains with Mr Tucker and Mr B. Allston to settle. I cannot venture to interfere in that settlement. With a young and active mind like Mr Joseph Allston, with your assistance, much may be done to put matters in a train of settlement, but if it is left alone, many circumstances will be forgotten and the sufferers will be your Sons Joseph and Robert, I therefore recommend you to collect all the information you can in this Business and get the Assistance of some Friend in George Town to arrange this matter without delay, it is impossible for me to do it, but surely Mr R F Withers can be called upon and the Money collected from him, and when he is informed that it is to assist the Son of his Old Friend there is no doubt but he will make provision to discharge the amount due.

I wish I could say how much is due by the Estate. The principal Debt is due to Mr Roses Estate which is 5 Bonds of £300 Each, now if any of the Heirs want to pay they might take up any of the Bonds and have them transfered over to them, the next heavy Debt is Mrs Blyth which I shall discharge as soon as I have sold some more Rice.

P.S.   If you can ascertain how much is due by Mr B. Allston for the hire of Billey or Thomas, it can be deducted from the Debt due to Mr B. Allston by the Estate and the amount credited Mr Joseph Allston as so much in part of his proportion of the Estates Debt.

Charles Kershaw to Charlotte Ann Allston

Charleston 1 October 1819

MADAM   I came up from Sullivans Island yesterday when I received your esteemed favor Mr Lewis had opened the Letter and Mrs Lewis was good enough to procure and forward by the Stage the several Articles which you wrote for, as noted at foot, which I hope have arrived safe and are such as you approve of.

I am truly concerned for the distress of your Family and the loss you have sustained but I hope the Almighty will sanctify the Affliction and support you under the severe trials, please present my respects to your Son with my fervent wishes for his recovery.[1]

The Negro Shoes, the Negro Clothing and the Blankets I think may be obtained best in this place, if therefore you will be pleased to send the Shoe Measures down and mention the number of Yards of Cloth what are wanted for the different plantations I will take care to procure them and forward them by an early opportunity.

As soon as any of the Rice is threshed out I beg leave to recommend you to send it by the first good opportunity to this place and when it arrives I

---

[1] The reference is to the death of Joseph Waties Allston's wife.

will send it to a good Mill that will pound it well and find Barrels for it. As Capt Tobey may be detained in coming from the Northward, it will be best to take the first good Vessil that offers when the rough Rice is ready for Shipping, as there is no doubt the Rice that is early at Market will sell the best.

Mrs K[ershaw] and the Children are on the Island but they will not come up to Town until the Yellow Fever subsides in the City it is now very fatal to Strangers but the Subjects have most removed away. I will see Mr Rose respecting the Titles for the Land and write you when I obtain the intelligence you require, it will be best not to pay any more of the Bonds until this matter is determined as Mr Rose must make the Titles for the Land good. With my best respects to Miss Charlotte and Miss Mary. . . . .

Charles Kershaw to Charlotte Ann Allston

Charleston 25th February 1820

MADAM   I received the inclosed Note[1] from Mr King by which you will observe that he expresses a hope of having the Business of your Dower arranged by the Court in April next.

I send you by the Schooner Elizabeth and Jane Capt Smith a Box contg. the Cushions for the Altar and Reading Desk of All Saints Church, the Cushion for the latter wants two Silk Tassels which are not to be purchased in this City I shall have to send to New York for them. The Money has not held out to procure the Cloth and Cushions for the Communion Table, Mr Delorme has managed the Business very badly but after the Materials were put into his hands he would act without controul and I have been obliged to wait his leisure.

As I have much Business to attend to next Month, I shall not be able to see you before April, but in the mean time I will send you what Money may be needful to pay off the Accounts you mention to be due whenever you think proper.

The Sale of Rice continues very dull and the price down to $2 1/2 this depression in price has been a severe blow to many who have made heavy purchases under an expectation of Produce selling well.

Mr. Wilson Glover is in the Country, when he returns I will endeavour to obtain the Survey you mention. Please send the inclosed to Mr J. W. Allston.

Charles Kershaw to Charlotte Ann Allston

Charleston June 9th 1820

MADAM   I have been extremely sorry and much disappointed in not being able to wait on you in George Town, but so many of our Friends have this last month been making their arrangements to leave Carolina, that I have been constantly employed and not able to leave the Counting House. In-

[1] Missing.

closed you will receive the Account Sales[1] of the Rice from Peedee, it turned out 138 Barrels and Netted $2063.03, your share of which for 5 Hands is $448.49 which is carried to the credit of your private account. Inclosed you will also receive the account Current[1] of Robert and William by which you will observe that there still remains a balance in hand of $356.40 on that account. The Estate of Mr B. A[llston] is indebted to me about $270 as when Dr Nesbit was in Town a few Weeks ago he pressed the settlement of his Account in so particular a manner that I was obliged to advance the Money, there is also another Account due to Dr. Nesbit, since the death of Mr Allston, which has not been rendered but which I have engaged to pay when made out. As there was Money in hand and Robert and William are indebted to you I send you inclosed a Check on the Bank for $200 and should you want a further supply during the Summer we will assist you. The proportion of your Crop has, you will observe, not been equal to your Annuity, but we hope that another Year it will be better. There was a demand of $150 made against the Estate by Mr Bishop, which Mr Tucker mentioned was correct and it was threatened to be put in Suit, I was therefore obliged to take part of Robert and Wm Money to pay it as I had no Funds of the Estate, it will however be a sett off for so much against their Share of the Estates Debts. Mrs K[ershaw] had a very violent attack of the Spasms in her Stomach which had nearly proved fatal, she is now, I thank God, on the recovery. My daughter Ann is well and thanks you exceedingly for your kind remembrance of her, they join with me in their best respects to you and your Family.

Mr. McDowell has requested me to inform you that he cannot make you any payment this Year as his means are nearly exhausted owing to his Crop falling short and selling for so low a price. I will have imported for you One of the Cob Mills for yourself and one for Robert and William. I suppose you mean those that come from the Northward cost about 60 Dollars each.

[P.S.] I inclose Miss Charlotte and Miss Marys Account for Negro Cloth and return Mr McDowells bond for fear of being mislaid, when he can make you any payment be good enough to get an order on us and then indorse it on the Bond.[2]

Charles Kershaw to Charlotte Ann Allston

Charleston 11th May 1823

MY DEAR MADAM I received your esteemed favor and regret exceedingly that I had not the pleasure of seeing you, I had fully determined to wait another Week for you, but your Letter gave me no encouragement that if I had waited so long for you that you would be able to return to Town. Mr

---

[1] Omitted.

[2] The factors' documents of the years 1821–22 are few in number and of little significance.

Lewis informs me that he has remitted to you the proceeds of the Rice sold which I am very glad he has done, for I felt very much for your situation in seeing you so much embarrassed without having it in my power to assist you. We have advanced to one friend or another all our disposable Funds and in place of receiving what we have advanced, our Friends were in so much distress, occasioned by the low price of produce, that in place of being able to return to us what they borrowed they were in want of further help. It is in these times that our Business becomes very painful, we are compelled to refuse the assistance which we would willingly give, for want of the means of doing so, and as in these times Produce is very dull in the Sale and prices low we are often blamed for circumstances that are above our control.

When I was in George Town I passed my Accounts with the Estate before the Ordinary, there was still one Voucher wanting which I requested your Son, Mr Robert Allston, to present to you to sign, and to shew it to Mr Waterman[1] who would then be able [to] grant me a complete Certificate for passing my Account. I will thank you to obtain my Book in which are the Copies of the Accounts and retain it in your keeping until I have the pleasure of seeing you and I send at foot of this Letter a few lines to Mr Waterman for that purpose.

I am sorry to say to you that I have had another severe Attack of my complaint since my return to this place. I am now confined to the House and find much difficulty in writing. I shall not be able to see you this Year, for if you were to put yourself to the trouble of coming to this place, my head is now so confused that I should not be able to converse with you to any advantage.

Mr King will be in George Town to attend the Court of Equity on Monday the 19th Instant. It will be of much consequence that you see him personally upon two points, One respecting what is to be done in Bufords Bond and the other about the Debt due to Mr Rose in which Mr Vereens claim on your Land is involved. In the present State of my health it is impossible for me to attend to do what is necessary in this Business, all your Sons are now at that time of Life capable of assisting themselves, they are all interested in the Issue, for the Judgment of Mr Rose binds the whole of the Estate, and the Debt due by Buford is equally the property of them all. The Bonds due to Mr Rose, owing to my being an Executor and residing in Charleston were put into suit in this place and Judgment obtained, a writ to revive the Judgment was issued last Court, and in November the Judgment will be renewed and a levy of your property made, unless some plea can be set up to avert the proceedings, it is on this point that you must come to a complete understanding with Mr King what is to be done. As far as I can recollect, Mr Vereen did not make any claim to the Land until after the Judgment was obtained, and you must therefore claim from Mr Rose to be put into pos-

---

[1] Eleazer Waterman, ordinary of Georgetown District.

session of the Lands he sold before he can demand payment, but if Mr Rose obtains Judgment and you are compelled to arrange the Affair with Mr Vereen then we can manage to gain time by paying up the Interest that is due now there will be another difficulty Mr Tucker and Mr Joseph Allston have paid up their full proportion of the Debt by the kind assistance of Mrs Blyth, therefore the Interest will have to come from Miss Charlotte Miss Mary and Mr Rob and Mr William, Mrs. Blyth has given up to the Estate Mr R F Withers Bond, if payment can be obtained from that source, all will be well, but if not the heirs I have mentioned must provide for it.

Bufords Debt is involved in a mistery that I cannot unravel and on this point let me beg you will urge Mr King to give you the necessary information.

When I was in George Town Mr Flagg and myself had a meeting on the accounts of the Estate A Belin, he seemed satisfied with the Vouchers produced and after rectifying some Items that were evidently erroneous, there appeared a balance against the Estate of $548, this balance will draw Interest from 1809 and may amount to about $1000, but there is a Sum paid to Levy Futheroy of $200 which does not express what it was for, it is therefore deducted for the present, but subject to any information that you may be able to give, if therefore you can recollect what were the transactions that Mr Allston had with Mr Futheroy, Mr Flagg may be induced to pass the Voucher.

In order to settle the Estates Business with that of Mr Belins Estate, if money cannot be collected the Heirs will have to give each of them their Notes to Mr Flagg or pay their proportion of the Debt in Money.

Previous to Dr Nesbits Death we had a partial settlement of his demand which you will find charged in my last account, he had another demand of $150 which is not paid a copy of the account you have.

Dr Allstons account is still unpaid and remains to be arranged. I beg you will not trouble yourself to answer this Letter, I must be away at once the Warm Weather so affects me and I therefore will go by the first Vessel that sails to the Northward any where for it is immaterial where I go. I hope to have the pleasure of seeing you again in the Winter until then I pray that you may enjoy that invaluable blessing that I am in search of and with every good wish towards you and your Family I remain with the greatest respect. . . . .

P.S. In a former Letter to me you mentioned your anxiety to make your return of accounts to the Ordinary, there is no necessity for you to do this, Mr Robt Allston is now of age to sanction all your proceedings and I could arrange your accounts in a few Hours when needful, the great object is to get out of Debt the rest is easily done. The Ordinary has nothing to do with your accounts if you must return them for your own satisfaction it must be to the Master in Equity (Mr Heriot) as Guardian, but this is only throwing away money for no good purpose

N B   Dr. Allston claims a Sum of £72.5.3 as paid to Mr B. Allston during the time they were Trustees to Miss Butler, this amount I thought until lately, was justly due to him but upon looking over some of Miss Butlers papers I find that Dr. Allston had charged that Sum in his account. I can readily convince him that it is so and I am sure that he will be satisfied, the fact is that we have been both under a wrong impression in this affair, he did not know it was charged by the person he employed to make out his Accnts. nor did I know it was made until I saw it by accident in looking over some old papers.

Kershaw and Lewis to Charlotte Ann Allston

Charleston 12 Decr. 1823

MADAM   Your much esteemed favor came to hand this morning: when your rough rice arrives we shall pay the greatest attention to your interest in having it sent to a mill which will pound it out immediately in order that you may have the benefit of the present prices, altho low, may still be less. Below, you have a Statement of articles recd. on your account, which we are in hopes will answer the purpose required. Viz.—

Goods pr. Georgia Packet, Capt Bunce and reshipped pr. Schooner Rice Bird, 25 Octr.

passage and clearing out two women............		$32.00
3 Boxes 43 feet.........................	a 15¢	6.45
3 " 26 "	a 12 1/2	3.29
10 Small Boxes.........................	50	5. "
8 small trunks.........................	50	4. "
5 Jars..................................		1.25
6 packages.............................	50	3. "
2 Kegs.................................	25	.50
1 Barrel 50¢ 1 flag staff 25¢		.75
Wharfage landing $2.00, drayage 1.75..............		3.75
		————
		$59.99

2 Bbls flour pr. Wade Hampton and shipd. pr.
Rice Bird 11 Nov. freight wharfage and drayage...... 1.26
10 Bbls pr. Brig Rachel and Sally and shipd. pr.
Capt J. Davis 20 Nov. freight wharfage and drayage 5.85

$67.10

recd. of you per letter.......... 40.

Balance due K and L $27.10

There were 12 Barrels left at Nortons mill, which you are Cr. with at 50¢ which was the most he would allow. We received 73 Barrels per Capt Toby which we sold at 87 1/2¢ last June and passed to your Cr. $63.87

less freight paid Capt Toby. 4.56

to your Cr $59.31

The tomb stone is still here. Capt Davis says he will take it up, the first time he goes to the Oatland plantation of B. Allston Esqr., or shall we send it to Geo Town. The articles ordered shall be forwarded pr. Capt Howland.

Kershaw and Lewis to Charlotte Ann Allston

Cha[rle]ston 18 Decr. 1823

MADAM   Your much estd. favor, of the 15th Inst, is now before us. We regret that Capt Howland has been detained by head winds, but, as it has now shifted, we are in hopes he has arrived and commenced loading. Respecting the price of 50¢ we obtained for 12 Barrels that were left at Nortons mill last season, were the utmost that could be got, and you must be aware, from our willingness to serve you, that your interest should never suffer in our hands. Mr. Norton left it at our option to take that price or take them away, stating at the same time they wanted a good deal of repair. The empty rice Barrels, pr. Captain Toby, we should never have procured more than 62 1/2¢ for them, if we had not, at the time, wanted some at the mill for a parcel of rough rice that was pounding. It has always been the charge here of $1, for clearing servants out at the Custom house altho we agree with you that it ought to be the same every where. If you will have the goodness to look over the Statement we sent you you will find the drayage and wharfage only $4.86 instead of $9.50, the wharfage is established by law and the rates of wharfage may be found in some of the almanacks wherein you will find the charge a correct one. Whenever Capt Toby arrives we will send the tomb stone by him, if Capt Davis does not go up to the Oatland place the next trip.

As soon as Mr W. W. Jones presents your d[ra]ft it shall be duly honored. Mr. Charles Kershaw has arrived and is in much better health then he has been for some time, he desires particularly to be remembered to you.[1]

Kershaw, Lewis, and Robertson to Elizabeth Frances Blyth

Charleston 11 July 1833

MADAM   We did ourselves this pleasure on   Inst informing you of the Sale of your 2030 bushels Rough Rice at Chisolms Mill; and now beg to hand

---

[1] The factors' documents of the next ten years consist of accounts current and accounts sale (too detailed for printing) and brief notes of no significance.

you annexed account Sales[1] thereof, say 102 1/2 barrels. Nett pros. . $1387.48
and 5 1/2 barrels Small Rice   Nett pros. . . .   57.76
                                                  _____
making together. $1445.24

at your credit. We have allowed the Mill 7 1/2 pr cent Toll and taken the Small Rice which at the price it sold, is considerably to your interest.

When this sale was made $3 was higher than had been obtained for some time, and we thought it an excellent price, but the Market suddenly rose 2 days after, and it turned out an unfortunate one, which we assure you is as much regretted by us as it can possibly be, it was done for the best and could no more have been foreseen than the sudden decline which has since followed; for the market to day is as dull as we ever saw it, when only 2 days ago $3 1/4 was paid for a much inferior parcel to one for which not more than $3 can be obtained to day. It is many years since we have seen such fluctuations, and however we may regret missing the best price, we feel that we acted under the full impression that it was for your interest, at the time, and sincerely hope it will meet your approbation.

As soon as we receive your dividends on your 30 U S Bank Shares, and other Stock, we will send you a statement of the same.

Kershaw, Lewis, and Robertson to Elizabeth Frances Blyth

Charleston 15 August 1833

MADAM   Your favor of 12 inst came to hand this morning and we beg to hand you above, copy of our respects of 19th of last month,[1] acknowledgeing the receipt of your favor of 16th, and inclosing your account current, shewing a small balance of $167.47 at your debit, a copy of which we also beg to hand you, and trust it will be found correct. We are sorry that our letter has miscarried, and put you to the trouble of writing again, and we hope this will come to hand, and do away with any appearance of want of attention on our part, as you will perceive your favor of 16 July was answered the same day it was received.

We have not yet had any arrivals of Negro Cloth and Blankets, the season being rather too early for them, and as the prices here are so entirely regulated by the cost in England, it is almost impossible to say with any accuracy what they will be. We will however bear it in mind and inform you as soon as we can with certainty, when we shall be happy to receive your orders, which shall meet our best exertions, to be executed most to your interest.

We trust that you will not allow yourself to be at all troubled at this small balance of your account, as we assure you it will be perfectly agreeable to us to be refunded from the Sales of the coming crop; as well as for any advances, that you may wish before then, for which we beg you to draw on us without ceremony, as you may want.

[1] Omitted.

Lewis and Robertson to Elizabeth Frances Blyth

Charleston 19th June 1835

DEAR MADAM   We beg most respectfully to acknowledge the receipt of your esteemed favor of 16th inst

The writer has just returned from a visit to Mrs Jones who we are sorry to say is still very feeble. She begged us to say to you she was not better and thought Dr Simons had flattered her with the hope of getting her up again, yet she could not agree with him, though she was certainly no worse than when she left home.

We are sorry to advise you of the ill success in getting your Shares in the new Bank.[1] Your subscription has proved (like many persons) a mere nothing having procured you only 3 Shares, say 135 Shares, $13.500, Subscribed for and we got only 3 Shares and $3300 returned, say $75 only actually paid. We had however guarded against a heavy subscription to the greatest extent we could, as in your case we had in hand only $3291.75 from the Sale of your U S B[ank] Stock and we paid for you $3375.

We are much at a loss how to invest for you now, all Bank Stocks are too high, and we beg a little time to look about. If we can get a Bond, such a one as will pay you the interest regularly we will let you know. The Mill Stones shall be sent by Capt Christian now here.

Lewis and Robertson to Elizabeth Frances Blyth

Charleston 30 July 1835

DEAR MADAM   Your favor of 27 inst came to hand to day; and we hasten to acknowledge its receipt, and at the same time to advise you of our having invested your funds in Union Bank Stock on 6 inst which we omitted to mention to you when we last had this pleasure,

Say Nett proceeds of 30 United States Bk Shares $3291.75

disposed of as follows

vizt paid the 1st instalment on 3 Shares in the Charleston Bank .   75.

this Sum held to meet the 3 instalments due on the above 3 Shares   225

paid for 45 U B Shares at $66 $\frac{50}{100}$ $2992.50

$3292.50

We hope this Stock will prove lucrative in Jany next when the next dividend will be paid, the institution is in a very flourishing State, and we doubt not, but that it will declare as good a dividend as any other.

We will look out for the investment of your $459.40 in such a Bond or note as you have requested, and hope we will succeed very soon in putting it in such a shape as to yield its regular interest.

Our Rice market has not advanced as much as it was thought, but prices

[1] The Bank of Charleston, incorporated December 17, 1834.

are very good, say from \$3 3/4 to \$4, could these only continue through the winter, the planters would get a great lift, and all of us be benefitted.

We would beg to suggest the propriety of having your Rice shipped as soon as it is pounded, fresh beat sells readily at \$4, while all other kind is dull and difficult to be disposed of

We are happy to confirm the accounts of Mrs Jones improved health. She is really so much better as to be talking of going on to Philadelphia week after next, where she thinks she will be more at ease.

Hoping that your own health is better. . . . .

Lewis and Robertson to Elizabeth Frances Blyth

Charleston 6 Augt 1835

DEAR MADAM   We received last evening by Capt Christian, your favor of 3 inst, and the Rice therein mentioned was landed to day

We now have the pleasure of advising of the Sale as follows

 say 67 Barrels at \$4 1/8

  1 . . .do. . . cracked at \$3 1/2

and trust will meet your approbation, having done the best for you that our market would possibly admit of. The half barrel Small Rice with your letter for Mrs Dr. Allston have been sent to her.

We have been in much affliction at the loss of our amiable and best of friends Mr Kershaw, he died on the 31st Ulto from hemorrhage from the Stomach, with but a few hours illness, as easily as he had lived, and in perfect peace and charity with all men.

[P.S.]   We will send the Sales in a day or so the Rice is not yet weighed.

Lewis and Robertson to Elizabeth Frances Blyth

Charleston 12 Octor 1835

DEAR MADAM   Your esteemed favors of 12th and 30 Ulto were duly received, the latter by Capt Christian on Saturday last with your 27 Barrels Rice, which we sold on the wharf say 21 barrels good at \$4 and 6 barrels inferior at \$3 5/8, but so late in the day that we could not advise you of the same by mail. We held out all the morning for these prices, and in the afternoon when the purchasers saw that we would starve rather than abate them, they came forward and bought. We therefore feel fully satisfied that the very best has been done for you that our market would admit of. Annexed are the Sales,[1] shewing Nett proceeds at your credit \$498.26, which we trust will prove satisfactory.

We shall as usual, be happy for your instructions as to the disposal or remittance of the same.

Your Negro Cloth etc shall be sent up by Capt Christian to sail in a day or two, they come lower than last year say 65 cts for the white, and 78 for the Blue.

[1] Omitted.

The half Barrel Rice for Mrs Ann Guild was shipped properly marked with ink, by the Langdon Cheves.

We are very sorry that we have not been successful in getting you a Bond for the money received from Virginia, no one who is "good enough" will give so small a one, and as there is every prospect of all Bank Stocks being lower, in the course of the remainder of the year, in consequence of the larger amount which will be required to be paid in on Rail Road Stock and Charleston Bank, we deem it most to your interest to wait a little longer, in this way you can loose nothing, as no Bank will give a dividend til January. The subject shall meet our strict attention and best endeavours to make the most for you.

We are happy to say that all our friends here are quite well. Winter has set in early with us this season which allays all anxiety for fevers, and backened by abundant Crops gives us great cause to be thankful for the many mercies we have received.

Lewis and Robertson to Elizabeth Frances Blyth

Charleston 29 Decer 1835

DEAR MADAM   We duly received your favors of 18th inst, one by mail and the other by Capt Brown, with the 61 Barrels Rice therein mentioned, which were landed on the 24 inst, and we are afraid the price they sold at will fall short of your expectations. We however did the best for you that could possibly have been done.

Say .... 7 barrels E F B sold at $3 1/4

		H		Nett proceeds........	$884.47
50	do	E F B sold at 3 1/8			
4	do	Mid —sold at 2 5/8....do..............			51.90

as pr annexed Sales,[1] shewing nett proceeds at your credit........ $936.37 which we trust will prove satisfactory.

Without any intention, or view to injure the Proprietors of this Mill, and only with the view of your interest, we beg to suggest to you not to send any more to it to pound. Your Rice was badly milled by it, otherwise it would have been prime, but it was broken up, and no 3 barrels alike. Our wish not to speak against any one has detered us from writing sooner.

Enclosed we beg to hand you C M Furmans check on R D Smith Esq for... $895.77 .

Amount received from Virginia.......	$459.40	
do from Sale of Rice............	40.60	
Reserved in hand to be invested.......	$500.00	

which shall meet our earliest attention.

[1] Omitted.

Lewis and Robertson to Elizabeth Frances Blyth

Charleston 26 Jany 1836

DEAR MADAM We have duly received your two favors of 20 and 21 inst, and this day the Rice therein mentioned, say 85 who[le] and 17 half Barrels as reported by Capt Thomas, which we sold at $3 1/8 their utmost value in the present state of our declining market, which we are sorry to have to say, but such is the fact. The highest Sale made to day was $3 3/16 for prime, the market having fallen to this price from $3 1/2 and $3.56 1/4. We regret it much but there's no help for it.

Mr Cheesborough is to give us the man York tomorrow, when his time with the man he is hired to will be out. We wished much to get him today that he might be sent up by Capt Thomas' return. We will however send him up as soon as possible.[1]

The Wind is now fair for Capt T. Thomas and we will send your Sales by him.

P S. We have just been informed that Mrs Jones' Girl Catharine, is sold for $600, this is a great price for her.

Lewis and Robertson to Elizabeth Frances Blyth

Charleston 27 Jany 1836

DEAR MADAM We did ourselves this pleasure by yesterdays mail, and now beg to hand you annexed the Sales[2] of your 85 Who[le] and 17 hlf barrels received by Capt Thomas shewing Nett proceeds at you credit $1534.51, which we trust will be found correct and prove satisfactory.

We also beg to advise you that we purchased for you on 20th inst 4 Charleston Bank Shares at $28 advance. Three instalments have been paid on them, and the 4th and last is still due, this however will not be called in very soon, which when paid will make the 4 Shares Cost you $512, and we trust will prove a good investment.

Mr Cheesborough is [to] deliver York to us this evening, when we will pay him $1000 for him. This will leave you a balance of $519.43, exclusive of $175 which we reserve to meet the last instalment on the 7 Charleston Bank Shares you now own, say 3 subscribed for, and 4 now bought.

Pray instruct us how you wish your balance of $519.43 disposed of.

Enclosed we beg to hand you C M Farman's Check on Mr Smith for $94.50, the dividend due you on your 63 Union Bank Shares, and which should have been sent you in the beginning of the month.

---

[1] On the circumstances which led to the purchase of York see above, p. 66.

[2] Omitted.

Lewis and Robertson to Elizabeth Frances Blyth

Charleston 8 Sept 1836

DEAR MADAM   The receipt of your favor of 8th inst to day, acknowledging your having received from Mr Waterman, our remittance of $1591.25, made you on 1st inst we were glad to get. Mr Kirton who took it to Georgetown we knew but little of. Mr Waterman having made us a remittance by him, we consequently thought him safe to commit a return parcel by, but as he went by a private conveyance, we wrote you by mail the next day enclosing your account current, and advising you of the same. This we hope you have received ere this time Your Order for Negro Cloth is duly noted, and shall meet our early attention.

We beg to refer you to our respects of 2 inst, for a statement of your Bank Stock etc.

The dreadful Cholera still continues with us, tho it is altogether confined to the intemperate Whites and imprudent Blacks. We hope and trust it will keep confined to the City, for at this time its appearance in the Country, would be almost ruinous to the Crops, which about Harvest time what with Gales and wet weather, are causes generally enough of danger, to create anxiety and care with Planters, independent of this dreadful Scourge. But its progress rests with Power beyond that of man, and as is his Will, so it becomes us to submit.

Alexander Robertson to Elizabeth Frances Blyth

Charleston 7 Nover 1836

MY DEAR MRS. BLYTH   Your kind favor of 5 inst, came to hand to day, and I hasten to reply to it, and say that your Neice is with us, and that she is quite well. She arrived when we were in great affliction, and Mr Cheesborough was good enough to take her to his house for a few days.

The death of my dear good Sister has come upon us all, as a dreadful shock, and my poor Mother in particular, who was so ill, that we could not tell her more than that she was very ill. But Gods will be done and so we submit as cheerfully as we can. Only 3 days ill, in the prime of health and usefulness, and to be cut off so suddenly, without notice, teaches us the importance of being always prepared to die. Mrs R[obertson] and myself have joined my Mothers family. we are all together and I hope and trust to be able to help them, without toiling and labouring as they have done. If my life is spared to them we can all live together if not they will be in the care of Him who ordains all things. The Martha Pyatt will return in the morning and the articles you wrote for shall be sent in her.

Alexander W. Campbell to Robert F. W. Allston

Charleston 7 January 1837

DEAR ROBERT   I am pleased that I have it in my power to say, I have succeeded in disposing of Henry and his family.[1] I used my best efforts to accomplish this Sale myself, but I did not succeed, and concluded 'twas best to
put them in the hands of a Broker, after consulting with your Sister, they
were sold to Joshua W. Toomer for $4100, Cash, so they will nett precisely
$4000, that is $800 round which I think their full value, and hope you will
concur in opinion with me, if circumstances would have permitted I would
have consulted with you previous to closing the Sale, but I was afraid of
losing the offer. About the Sale of the rest, I am yet unable to say any thing
definite, I have off'd them to several without success, and have given a list
of them to Elliott and Condy, thinking it better to pay a commission, than
incur longer delay in accomplishing the Sale, will write you as soon as we
have an offer.

Robert F. W. Allston to Alexander W. Campbell[2]

Matanza 2d Feb 1837

DEAR CAMPBELL,   I have this instant return'd and seen the negroes embark'd on board the Industry. Immediately on the receipt of your favor of
the 28th informing that you had closed the Sale, I despatch'd a messenger to
Capt. Brown and agreed with him to take the negroes down, as he had only
1000 Bushels of Ro Rice and 80 or 100 Bbls of clean. I went over myself and
divided them and gave them a day to get ready. Last night, I received yours
of the 31st. But on going over early this morning and finding that they were
all down at the wharf, many of their things on board the vessel, there being
plenty of room in the hold and the wind fair withal I thought it would be
best not to wait a moment longer, for fear of having not so favorable a time.
I hope they will arrive safe. I hand you herewith the Bill of Lading. Sary
goes down for my sister to decide about, she is worse than useless on the
plantation and if her mistress determines not to sell her, I think she had
best leave her in the hospital of some Physician in town till she gets well.
Sandy, Mr Gotea tells me she wrote for herself. Letty belongs to the Estate
of my sister Mrs. Jones. I will trouble you to put her in the hands of Jervey,
Waring and White to be sold under the Will, proceeds to Lewis and Robertson for certain Legacies. Scotland the Driver I send to jolly the negroes and
gàve them confidence, they are accustom'd to him and will give you less
trouble.

[1] These and the Negroes mentioned below belonged to the estate of Joseph Waties
Allston, of which Campbell, Allston, and the widow Mary Allan Allston were acting as
executors.

[2] Copy.

I am sorry if the negroes shall reach you too soon, but as they were on the move I decid'd it best not to unsettle and harrass them any more.[1]

Robert F. W. Allston to Alexander W. Campbell[2]

Matanza 3d Feb. 1837

DEAR CAMPBELL, I am just in receipt of yours of the 1st Inst. the negroes being already embarked and clear'd, it is of course too late to stop either old Libba or Scotlands daughter, which I would have done otherwise, the wind today is fair but light, they may get down tonight.

On reflection, it seems to me not altogether proper that the Estate should be at the expense of a lawyer in this business (the purchaser will of course pay for the necessary papers) and therefore I have written to Petigru & Lesesne as my attorneys to render you such aid, in the various settlements incident to this transaction, as may be in their power, call upon them fully as in my place, and be so kind to furnish them with a copy of my first and longest letter to you on the subject, twill save me further writing at this hurried moment.

Lewis and Robertson to Robert F. W. Allston

Charleston 7 Feby 1837

DEAR SIR Your favors of 23 Ulto and 3rd inst have been received the latter only to day.

We have paid Mrs Allan $640 the amount of her annual interest on your Bond due 1st inst, and are to receive from Mr Campbell the $4000 and interest from 24 Nover last when the Bank Cashes your said Bond, which we hope will be next monday. It was to have been done yesterday but Mrs Allan did not bring us the Bond in time to submit it to the Board. This however will no doubt be all arranged. Watsons draft shall be duly paid.

We received 1250 Bushels Ro[ugh] Rice on your account by Chadwick, and put it into Chisolms Mill to be pounded having entered into a new arrangement with him to give up the offal at 10 p cent Toll.

We have sold 700 bus of your Seed Rice at $1 clear of all expences, and will hold the remaining 600 at $1.12 1/2

Our A[lexander] R[obertson] received the 2 doz Sercial Wine, and will send you the 5 doz Sherry by C's next trip, he could not get it for this, Mr De Saussure who hired the house in Meeting St. where the wine is, being sick; and could not get it out to day. It shall however be fixed next trip.

The woman Letty has been received, and is under offer to Mr Allan, who is to give his answer in the morning.[3]

Your draft for the Bank Stock shall be duly paid But we fear you will not get many Shares.

---

[1] See above, p. 68.   [2] Copy.   [3] See above, p. 68.

Alexander W. Campbell to Robert F. W. Allston

Charleston 11 Feby 1837

DEAR ROBERT   By the return of the Schr. Industry I have shipped the following articles for the Estate: 7 Pieces and one Box Castings, these are all the castings now ready. Kidd[1] sent down some patterns for Castings, and I sent them to the Foundary immediately, but they could not be got ready for the trip, should the vessel be detained by unfavorable winds I shall be able to send them.

I am afraid Kidd gets along very slow with the mill, I suppose it will be Summer before she will be in operation, as far as the price of Rice is concerned I do not think the Estate will lose any thing. I still think it decidedly to our interest to pound the whole of the crop now on hand.

I have returned by the Schr. the following negroes: Scotland, Sarah, Bob, Sibbah, this old woman Mr. A[llan] pays for, but wishes us to let her return. I have not seen your Sister since the arrival of the negroes, she has been and is now in the country, these that are returned, is done by the direction of Mrs. A[llston].

On next Monday I will submit your proposition to the Board, and have no doubt 'twill be granted.

I have consulted with Mr. Petigru, and told him in what manner Mr. Allan was to pay me, and he thought we had done well and made a very safe sale.

Will probably settle with Mr. A[llan] in the course of a week and will again have this pleasure.

Lewis and Robertson to Robert F. W. Allston

Charleston 25th March 1837

DEAR SIR   Your favors of 19th and 23rd inst and your Check on the Bank So Ca, have been duly received. Capt Chadwick got in yesterday with your 1400 Bus Seed Rice, which has been nearly all sold at $1.25. Mr Simons who had bought 750 bus having given up his purchase in conseqeunce of the detention, for which we are much obliged to him, as no doubt it will be sold for the $1 1/4, only between 3 and 400 being now unsold.

We hope to get the Altar Work for your Church done in time for Chadwick to take up. Mr Davidson who is doing it promised it the 1st of April. It corresponds to your dimensions exactly, and we doubt not will turn out all right. Your Note to the Jockey Club[2] must lie over until next Races, when it can be cancelled, but not before. Corn keeps up at 120¢ having paid this price to day for some very superior. Your order for 200 bus is therefore cancelled. Your Small Rice cannot be had until the parcels are beat out. We

---

[1] David Kidd, the machinist engaged in rebuilding the mill at Waverly.

[2] The South Carolina Jockey Club, which promoted horse-racing in Charleston.

sent you by Chadwicks last trip 3 barrels from your 1250 bus last beat by Chisolm. The flour shall be sold, as you direct.

We sent yesterday by Mr Jos Thurston your two Mortgages and Bond to H. M. Haig, under cover to our mutual friend Mr J W Coachman, with the request that he would enter satisfaction on the Records in Georgetown (all three having been recorded there) as well as here. We hope he will have no difficulty about it, having as seemed to us put it all straight for him. When you next see him pray bear in mind to [ask] him for them.

What arrangements our friend above will make to pay up the $4000 due, we wait to see, this however rests between you unless you say "call on him."

Your order for $12,000 to P[etigru] and L[esesne] was not used, the Bank having passed to our joint credit this amount, and the writer signed your Checks, say for $12,000 and paid to Mr Campbell $119 in addition being the month and 21 days interest due from 1 Feby. Your Bond to the Bank being dated 21 March, which is just the same thing to you.

Lewis and Robertson to Robert F. W. Allston

Charleston 28th March 1837

DEAR SIR We wrote you on 26th by mail to which we beg to refer you, and now hand you herewith Fifty dollars. Please credit this from Lewis and Robertson. Our J L[ewis] having joined the writer in subscribing to your Pee Dee Church.

We will have to send the Wood work of the Altar to Georgetown. Mr Davidson having not yet done it, nor do we see any prospect of getting it before the middle of the next week. We hope it will be up in time having exerted ourselves in pushing the work forward

Mr Weston is to pay this Expence, say $100. Otis and Roulain are daily expecting the Carriage for your Aunt. We have sent you by Chadwick 2 Bbls Salt 20 bus at 50¢ and 50 Bags Contg 150 bus Oats at 70. Your Seed Rice has turned out 1424 1/2 bus. We have sold 1150 bus, and have barreled the balance 274 1/2 to wait further Sales.

Our friend Dr Weston still continues very poorly. We look upon him in short as a very ill man, and begin to dread the worst.

Lewis and Robertson to Robert F. W. Allston

Charleston 24 April 1837

DEAR SIR Your favor of 21st is at hand this morning. Mr Mikell the purchaser of Letty has not yet returned her, nor do we think he will, should he, however, your limit of $600 for Mr Gotea, shall be carried out.[1] We rather think he will not make any further movement in the Business. Your orders to T. P. Alston, $50 each, shall be paid when presented. We received Stephen the other evening, he was sent to the writers yard, to wait your further in-

---

[1] See above, pp. 68, 69, 385.

structions which we now clearly understand, and will endeavor to get him fixed with Saunders. The other Boy we are not certain can be placed here for the Summer, during the winter their Services are valuable, as far as their food and clothing, but in the Summer after all the Strangers leave us, they are pretty much an expence, so 2 of the Coloured Barbers have told us, therefore we suggest to get him a place before you send him.[1]

On looking over your account we find you have now in Mill here 5130 Bushels Rough Rice, which we valued at 80¢ Nett when you was here in

Feby—say...................................	$4100
Deduct your Balance Dr this day about.........	2512
	$1588
Order to Moffett and Calder about 350	
T. P. Alston................... 100	450
Carried over.............	$1130
Brought forward.............	$1130
Taxes and sundry estimated drafts.............	330
	$ 800
Add 1000 bus Ro Rice not yet received.........	800
	$1600

Hence you will see that your item "of $2000 over and above outstanding demands," is not covered, even under this what we candidly think favorable estimation of the remainder of your Crop, for we cannot say what produce will fall to under the alarming prospects ahead. Two months ago we were all sanguine of fine prices for the remainder of the Crop, but now every one is gloomy and desponding, and anxious to realize whenever they can. Clean Rice has fallen from $3 3/4 to $2 3/4 and Rough from 103 to 85¢, Cotton from 17 to 12, and all within 60 days. The result is that our largest Capitalists are almost leveled, and in several instances, if our Banks had not, in self defence come forward and relieved them, they must have gone by the board, and their Real Estate sacrificed to their insolvency and ruin. Men who a month ago were considered as fully possessed of hundreds of thousands, and if now pushed would not pay their responsibilities and debts.

You ask us to tell you candidly as to your balance which will decide your going away. We have done so and add moveover, that there is considerable uncertainty in raising money in advance of your Rough Rice now in Mill, the Banks are all dreadfully hampered, and in very few instances do any new Business. Though for us, we do not doubt or question at all, any difficulty in

[1] The reference is to slaves whom Allston was seeking to place in Charleston for training.

getting what money we may want, being most fortunatley very free and clear of them. Yet as others find great difficulty to get accommodation it might possibly so happen with us if we were to apply, and only say so to you ahead, for these are times without paralel.

Should you however find it so that you are to go tell us candidly and we will do all, and what, we can to raise the "wherewithall," and refund by Sales during the Summer, which may be very low and fall short of the estimation annexed.

Bank Scrip which heretofore was like so much money is now no more than Common paper. No Bank in the City will loan on its Stock, in any new business. In this we are cut off most sadly, having always in the Summer raised money on our Stocks, now we would have to furnish a good Endorser.

We have given you our views freely in good feeling and trust it will be so viewed.

Lewis and Robertson to Robert F. W. Allston

Charleston 9th May 1837

DEAR SIR   Your favors of   inst have been duly received, and also your account Book, which shall be written up and returned to you.

In the meantime we enclose you herewith W A Mikell's Bill of Sale of the Woman Letty, sold yesterday the 8th for $300 which was a bona fide price without puffing. Mr Gotea will therefore, be no doubt well satisfied, with the price. We shewed all your letters to Mr Lesesne, and he arranged that the Sale be conducted, without any puffing, therefore the price, we look upon as a very fair one, for independent of the late fall in price of negroes, we cannot think that she would have fetched much more in the best of times. under the same circumstances.

We have charged your account for her $300
And for the Bill of Sale   1
                                                                    ———
Amount paid by us $301

And the Este Mrs Jones with $25 Dr Jervey's Certificate as to her unsoundness, The writer is on the Jury and must be off.

Alexander Robertson to Robert F. W. Allston

Charleston 13th May 1837

DEAR ALLSTON   . . . . What a dreadful Revolution we have had in the money World! I almost go beside myself when I think of the accounts to be received from Europe, after the failures and troubles have been received there, from this side the Water. Ruin, Ruin, Ruin, stares many a man in the face. I cannot but congratulate myself most heartily that "Wards scheme" did not go into opperation for without the consolation of feeling that we have no engagements to meet, which cannot be met tenfold, I believe I'd go mad. This however makes me settle down from all alarm for ourselves, for we cannot fail, unless the Banks go, for they will take all we have, with them and then go every one with Capital must. They cannot help themselves. But there's no fear yet of the Banks in this place though they must loose considerably and their Dividends will be small.

I have sent your articles by the Jas Hamilton as pr List accompanying.

Alexander W. Campbell to Robert F. W. Allston

Charleston 18 May [1837]

DEAR ROBERT   Your letter of the 8th ultimo respecting the Taxes shall receive proper attention, the Estate's Taxes will be paid as usual. For several weeks there has been very little business doing, and our commercial community kept in a state of continued anxiety. You will no doubt perceive by the newspapers, that as a measure of self defence our Banks have been compelled to suspend for a short time Specie payments, this measure we adopted with extreme reluctance, however 'twas forced upon us by the Northern Banks. I have just paid your order to Dr. Allston for $62.24/100 while things continue to be so extremely stagnant, and no sale for produce, I must beg you not to draw upon me on account of the Estate, as I am now in advance, and will be more so because the Taxes as a matter of course cannot be postponed. Rice I trust will in some measure recover before the Estate's comes to market.

Lewis and Robertson to Robert F. W. Allston

Charleston 26 May 1837

DEAR SIR   Your favor covering Receipt for 550 Bushels Seed Rice furnished Mrs Davis, came duly to hand. We applied to Mr Campbell her Factor, and then to her, and she said she would direct Mr C to pay it, but it is not yet done, but it will be, no doubt, very soon.

Your determination to remain at home this Summer we look upon as very judicious. Troubles are yet ahead which are not dreampt of by all, and we consequently feel much anxiety at all new responsibilities, in your case however we never hesitated a moment, but sent you our acceptance, on receipt of your desiring it.

Our J. Lewis left us this morning on a visit with his Son to Yale. And as the acts and deeds of the Concern now devolve on the writer he will be glad to accept your kind offer in part of Refunding us our advance by a draft on us, to be negotiated through the Bank of G[eorge] T[own] say to the amount of $1,000 which we will require from time to time through the Summer, to be paid in Georgetown though the larger part may be wanted at an early day for our mutual friend Dr Wm Allston. We therefore beg to annex you a dft for $1000. The date is blank, should you see the Doctor, and he has not yet drawn, tell him, we have funds now to check against, in this event pray fill up the blank and get the proceeds passed to our Cr. But should he have drawn on us or have made any other arrangement, pray leave the Date blank, and dont offer it for a month or so, and in this way save a little interest.

Your Wine in conjunction with the Govr has been ordered. We sent your Osnaburgs by the Waccamaw say 650 yds a 12¢ 4 lbs thread a 62 1/2 and 200 needles a 25. The quality was considerably better than Moffett and Calders at same price, and we therefore did the best for you by buying it.

The Pork shall be sent next time.

P S. Since writing the foregoing we find the date of the order is of no consequence, as it is payable on a given day and therefore filled it up. Bear in mind to endorse it over our's and let us know when it is discounted that we may give you credit for the Nett proceeds, which please state at same time.

Alexander Robertson to Robert F. W. Allston

Charleston 20 June 1837

DEAR ALLSTON Your favors of 17 and 18th are at hand today. I immediately turned out in search of a vehicle for you. Wm Heriot was with me, but after going the rounds with all the venders we came to the conclusion that nothing could be got, to suit you. All the Waggons at any thing like $150 are so common, and particularly inconvenient for Ladies to get in that of course they would not suit you. I however met in with an old (Revolutionary) Carriage which I bought for $50, and concluded to send you your old friend that I got from you, as an opportunity the Jas Hamilton will sail in the morning for Mr Westons Mill, and another may not offer for a month. Now I have only to say in regard to this, that if Mrs A[llston] or yourself either should not like it, send it back, and I can easily get rid of it in the fall, or use it for the Summers, and return it in the winter. My good old Mother found it difficult to get in and out, and when the coachman drove, it carried only 2 Ladies. The old carriage will carry 4 Ladies inside and suit me very well. We are all on the Island, for the Summer, and my three sisters and Mrs R[obertson] can ride together. It is either a great bargin or a humbug, anyhow I w[ill] not loose by it much, (and in these times this is more than most men can say.)

Your Aunts carriage is not yet in. The men from whom it was ordered failed, and Otis and Roulain ordered another. I told them it must be optional with her to take it on arrival.

I write you now very hurriedly, having consumed nearly all the morning in walking about for something for you. "Mr Wm" says he'll never go on such another expedition. Pray use no ceremony about the old friend I now send you, but use it on my account, for I could not sell it now, and it is of no use to me. I must mention tho. that I calculate on sending it up to night from the Island, and may possibly fail, if it can be got up, it shall be put on board the Hamilton. . . . . I am in treaty for the Sale of your parcel of 2000 and odd bus Ro[ugh] Rice in Napier's Mill at 3 1/4, if the quality suits it is a Sale, if not I must then do the best I can, $3 is the highest sale yet, but it must go to 3 1/4. The Books shall be sent if they can be got.

I have given you credit for the proceeds of your draft disc'td in G[eorge] T[own] Bank, but bear in mind the 1/2 per [cent] discount makes the odds against you, and we can raise the wind here at par.

The sample of your Rice will be out on Thursday, til then it is in suspense. I am happy to hear you are all well. My dear little girl has been very ill, but is on the mend again, she promises well, and is a source of much pleasure to us all, to hear her commence speaking, which she is getting in the way of right cleverly.

Thank God we have so far run the guantlet free, both in regard to loss of money and of friends a letter from Mr L[ewis] reports himself much better.

With my best wishes for you and yours, and all friends about you.

Alexander W. Campbell to Robert F. W. Allston

Charleston 1 July 1837

DEAR ROBERT Before you receive this you will no doubt have heard of the failure of Mr. Cheesb[orou]gh[1] produced by the failure of his partner in Phil[adelph]ia, as I am largely on their paper this will embarass me very much. I am about making an application to the Banks to endeavour to be relieved from my responsibilities on their a/c, whether I shall succeed or not I think is doubtful.

I have since I last wrote to you received some payments on account of the Estate and have disbursed a portion of the amt recd, say the years Int. on the Bond in the BSSC [Bank of the State of South Carolina] for $9000, and $950 on account of the principal. I will in a few days make up my a/c and write how it is, Mr. C's failure I fear will be fatal to my credit, but I will make a great effort to sustain myself.

Alexander Robertson to Robert F. W. Allston

Charleston 14 July 1837

DEAR ALLSTON I am in receipt of your two favors of 29 Ulto and that of 7 inst. You are quite welcome to the use of my Waggon, for I took my carriage to the island which suits there extremely well.

I have paid your man Thomas $20 agreeably to your desire, and furnished him with the articles he required as pr memorandum sent you, with the

[1] J. W. Cheesborough had been a short time before this, and probably still was, Campbell's partner.

claret from Paul and B. In a conversation with Mr Lance about his 39 acres of plowd Land, I could not bring him to any point, he seemed to dread the idea of parting with it. The truth is he is in no amiable mood, in consequence of his friend Campbell humbugging him as he says out of $3000, which is true as far as C[ampbell] owes him this sum, and cannot pay it. However I got him to say that if $10,000 was offered he would give an answer yea or nay, his mind seems altogether engrossed with his friend C[ampbell], who he has now cut, and I think if in the course of a week or say two weeks the offer is renewed, it might be considered by him more cooly than it was, when it first came to hand.

You will have seen the increase of capital in the Bank of Charleston has been postponed to a future day.

We have not yet done any thing with the collection of Mrs Davis' order for Seed Rice, but I shall call on her in a day or so, and have it arranged, one way or another.

And now that I have disposed of all the business matters, I can only say that I am sorry you did not know of C[ampbell]'s troubles sooner than you did. I was doubly anxious to give you a timely hint in consequence of learning that "one of the Allstons had sent him 4 Blanks," and I immediately thought of you, hearing that he was going to Waccamaw, and not knowing what applications he may make to you on propositions.

The Bubble long looked for, has at length burst and he is where he ought to have been 5 years ago. I am loth to express any opinion of him, he never treated me well, and always acted and spoke in direct contradiction to each other. But I look upon him as a dead man, and whatever his faults are let them remain with him. I only say to you keep a bright look out on him with your Brothers Este, for he owes every body money and his failure is hardly talked of by every one, for he is deficient to a large amount.

I have been tis true much gratified to find that Ward has not over looked us, tho more pleasant it would have been had it come without the "Cause," however we cannot always have things as we want them, and if I have said any thing uncharitable against my neighbour, it was not intended. I have spoken only with a view to guard you against what I honestly think is my duty to do by you.

I spent the last evening on the Island with my family, and left Pen and the little one quite well. My good old mother has been quite unwell, and is in Town for a few days.

Business set in heavily on me this month and I have applied myself to it very closely during all the excessive heat of the last week. But thank God that I have gotten thro with the payment of all our Bills, we owe nothing, have no endorsements, and cannot therefore fail, so long as the Banks keep up. The accounts to day from England are still worse, and more must go. I mean merchants. Factors have no right to fail. I cannot but feel grateful that we have stood the Blows, and on the contrary of loosing money, it will be as good an average business year with us as any other. I do not brag, I only express my feelings of gratitude.

Mr Lewis is at the Grey Sulphur. I had a letter from him lately in which he says he was considerably better.

Our Rice market has mended so cleverly that I have told Nowell to pound out your parcels there, I suppose it will be all of 3 weeks before we get it, by when I hope it will do still better. The turn out however I dread much.

Napiers[1] was infamous. I am at a loss about your Aunts Carriage. No one will allow more than $20 for her old one. I think she had best get it done up, for she will require a close one in winter, and it will be as good as new when repaired. I have written to her about it.

P.S. The accounts from England by to days mail, brought the news of the Roscoes arrival at Liverpool in 23 days. Mr Glennie and our other friends went in her.

Alexander W. Campbell to Robert F. W. Allston

Charleston 15 July 1837

DEAR ROBERT   I am devoting every moment of my time to bringing my affairs to an entire close that I may be enabled to resume my business in the fall perfectly freed from all my present liabilities. It is indeed a painful task, but it must be performed and shall be promptly and honorably as far as my judgement goes, assisted by the best counsel our city affords.

I send you the Estates a/c current,[2] there are some charges that will require explanation, and must be altered.

In making up my account for the last season I charged the Estate full commissions, whereas I was only entitled to 1/3, it was understood at the time to be done for regularity sake, at the time I had no intention of taking the commissions my object being to invest the amt. in some stock for the benefit of the children, little did I dream of what was in futurity, the only way it can be remedied now, is for me to pay Mrs. A[llston] and yourself your 1/3, another item you will see charged, paid Jail fees for the negroes, this I will arrange with Mr. Allan, and have it taken out. You will perceive my dear friend, the Estate is Cr. $3174.17/100 this I need not say I regret extremely, notwithstanding I know it must prove a perfectly good debt, be assured Robt. I will pay it. It is due to myself to bring to your view that since I have been acting as Exor. I have benefited the Estate considerably by making advances, for instance when I closed my last years a/c, the Estate owed me $4,663.98 on which I have made no charge for Int. I only ask a little indulgence, misfortune has overtaken me, but this will not deprive me of my industry or integrity, I may lose friends, at which I am not disposed to complain, what distresses me beyond all expression, is the breaking in upon the early and affectionate associations of my youth, but if my life is spared

[1] A rice mill in Charleston.   [2] Omitted.

in a few years I can pay every cent, of course much will depend upon the course pursued by my friends, sustained by a consciousness that I have not brought this calamity on myself either by extravagance or speculation, I feel that adversity will increase my energy, all that I ask is a trial, I have made arrangements with the Bank that I can deposit as usual without my money being subject to any charge growing out of my present difficulties. My dear Robert I am aware of your kind and manly feeling, and I am sure you can benefit me in an important manner, this is a great trial to me, my children just coming into Life, and my younger ones yet to be educated, with such incentives who could hesitate as to his course. Pray say to your Aunt Blyth I would write to her, but my letter to Mrs. A[llston] is full, and through that and yourself she will be made fully acquainted with my views.

I shall feel anxious to hear from you pray make my best respects to Mrs. A.

I have sent for the Estate 2 Lamps 1 Blank Book, 1 Bushel Tub, 2 Jugs Oil. Your man has got 2 small wheels for the Mill and some Iron.

The amt. I owe the Estate I think I can manage next winter, by paying it on the Bond in the B H C which will be equivalent to money.

Alexander Robertson to Robert F. W. Allston

Charleston 8 Augt 1837

Dear Allston I have to day sent your Aunt the proceeds of her Rice by Sea, in a check on your Bank. If you think it will be any accommodation to her, you can get the letter and send it up to her, it is true I have not been instructed by her to make this Remittance, but in these squally times, I would rather be punctual.

Mr Wm Carter offered me check on the G[eorge] T[own] Bank, the other day, but he seemed to hesitate at the time and when I went to him yesterday, he declined. Do pray see if he has any funds, and when we meet again you can say, it is not worth writing about.

I have paid Campbell the Expences on your Aunts and Dr Weston's Rice $325.50, and took his Receipt as Exor. The Carriage for your Aunt has come and shall be sent by Sea, as I have written to her.

Campbell made a statement of his concern on Saturday, as follows

Bank Debt	85,000
Individual debt	20,000
Liability	105,000
Assets	119,000
deduct Bad debts from Cheesborough and Campbell	69,000
	50,000
deduct his own bad debts	18,000
Leaving	$32,000

to pay 105,000 with; what a beautiful business? But I w[ill] say nothing more of him; for his creditors are calling on him for particulars, which they will no doubt get.

Alexander W. Campbell to Robert F. W. Allston

Charleston 8 August 1837

DEAR ROBERT   Your favor of the 21st ultimo came duly to hand, you are certainly correct in saying distress of mind must necessarily for a long time be my companion, my situation is as distressing as it well can be. I find my motives much misrepresented, and as I think much injustice done me, however time alone will prove to my friends that it is my wish to do what is right to all. If my friends prove friends in this time of affliction and sorrow to me, I can pay what I owe in a few years. I did not mention to you when I was up the payment made on Haig and Maxwells Bonds, I thought saying to you the Estate was Cr. on my Books was sufficient, * in regard to the debt I consider it the most Sacred on my Books, when I was with you I thought from all I could judge, I should retain a considerable portion of my business, and by lessening my expences, I could very soon surmount my troubles. I intended and intend now, as soon as I begin again to give the Estate my Bond with † security for the amount of the debt, in my present situation I will not ask a friend to involve himself in my troubles there cannot be a doubt of my capacity to reinstate myself if I am only sustained by most prominent friends, if they desert me because I am unfortunate, of course they will deprive me of a chance to pay. I have written to Dr. Magill fully on the subject of the cause of my embarassment, and will ask him to shew you the letter. . . . .

I have enquired about the Flour, they tell me they allow 2 1/2 Bushels to the Bbl. and they consider middling Rice as offal. I have made the inquiry about the rules of a Mill, but they say the question is so general, they dont know how to answer it. If you will specify I can get the information for you. In regard to charging the $200, paid Mr. Glennie to the Estate, I am of opinion it is a correct charge against the Estate, the minister in the parish is for the general good, and I really dont think Mrs. A[llston] ought to pay this from her private funds, when the children grow up they will receive the benefit.‡ In regard to the Taxes, you are right, it occured in this way, my clerk in making returns for my customers, returned the Estates property here, and with others was paid and some time after this, Mr. Vaught came down and it escaped us that the return had been made here, enclosed I hand you duplicate rects. for each payment.

You are correct about the payment to P J Allston and I will correct it. There was some misunderstanding about the Seed Rice, at first you remember the Estate was to have taken 300 Bushels, and I actually took Colo. Wards rect. and the entry passed through my Books, which I had to strike out afterwards, suppose then instead of my paying this small balance in the Bank, you give Colo. Ward an order on me for the Rice, and draw for the balance in any way you may wish. I only call your attention to this as I know you to be friendly to me, and feel assured that you cannot for a moment think I ever thought of any thing but what was right to the Estate.

Your letter about the Band was only received this morning consequently I have had no chance to have it made. Kidd I understand is in the city but I could not find him this morning, I will have the Band made as quick as possible and will send it up. I have sent the four sides of Band Leather as they will always be useful. I am sorry the Sheep Skins cannot be had in the city, but will send them by the first vessel.

*as I had advised you by Letter, under date of 15 June, and also beg leave to say I wrote you 18 May to say I was not in funds, which upon reference to my a/c will be found to be so.

†I have friends that will assist me and give me a chance to recover my former credit.

‡On this point however I am under the direction of yourself and Mrs A[llston].

Alexander Robertson to Robert F. W. Allston

Charleston 10 Augt 1837

DEAR ALLSTON . . . . About Toll. I have applied to Mr Lucas Mr Chisolm and Mr Nowell.[1] They have no regular Rates. They average all the parcels they beat, for the flour, Middling and small Rice, which they ascertain in this way and is all counted as offal, but not head Rice. You must however bear in mind their Mills are not on the same principle that yours are. Chisolm is the only one who makes middling Rice, and this is done by screening the small Rice.

I sold Dr Weston's Rice at $4 1/4 for the good, and $4 for the inferior, it arrived in good time, for since then the market has been very heavy and dull. The buyers seeming to think that $4 is high enough, but it must go to $4 1/2. I charged Hasell with the barrel he got of Dr W[eston] it amounted to $23.70, the average weight of the lot. We sent Mrs North her half barrel of whole and half barrel of small Rice on 25 May to the care of Collier and Hill in Augusta, and wrote to her at the time, but she has never acknowledged the receipt of either Rice or letter. I therefore fear she has not got them, pray let me know, that I may write to C and H about it.

I have of late come in for my share of a sick family. My Mother, sister Susan and my little pet have been all on their beam ends, but are better again.

Susan and Mary left us yesterday by Rail Road for Greenville. I want Mother and Helen to do the same. Change will do them all good no doubt, and I hope they will go. Penelope is quite well, the Island having brought her up to her old standard. I am as sick as death of it, and shall move up the first chance I can.

[1] Proprietors of rice mills in Charleston.

Mr Lewis writes me he is improved in his health and by no means surprized to hear that C[ampbell] had failed, the surprize to him has been his holding on so long. I always knew he was hampered and involved, but I must confess I had no idea he was to the extent he now shews. I gave you a statement of his statement in my last to you, which shews him to have been always insolvent.

Should you hear any thing of L and R [Lewis and Robertson] supporting him do pray contradict it. I refer you to Dr Heriot to whom I have written on the subject, perhaps more fully than I ought to have done. I heard it before, but took it for granted no one would believe it, til it occurred to me in reading Heriots letter, that my friends would have good reason to suspect my own solvency, for C[ampbell] is irretreivably lost in this community.

[P.S.]   We have sent you by the Schr Waccamaw A Barrel Ice 367 lbs a 1 1/2 cts and Bbl 87 1/2 which we hope may prove acceptable. We also send you, your Account Book written up to date, which we hope you may find correct.

Lewis and Robertson to Robert F. W. Allston

Received Charleston 17 Augt 1837 of Col R F W Allston by his agents Lewis and Robertson One thousand dollars in part of the principal and Three hundred and forty dollars eighty cents, in full of the interest on his and A Robertson's joint Bond to the Bank State South Carolina, leaving Eleven thousand dollars of principal due this day.

$1340.80   CHARLES M. FURMAN   CASHIER

Charleston 17th Augt 1837

DEAR SIR   Your favor of 8th inst came duly to hand. Above is Receipt for $1340 on your Bond in Bank So Ca leaving $11,000 of principal now due, which we hope will be cut down next winter. The acceptance in Bank Geotown is not provided for by this arrangement, but by the time, 1st Nover, that it will be payable, we can get a note discounted here, and take it up in full, please bear this in mind, in case you attend the meeting of Stockholders of the C C and L R Rail Road at Flat Rock.

We have given your message to Mr Belin, he will get you the pompoons. He has written to Mr King about his Rice, and you have no doubt heard from King about it. But he said nothing about "appropriating an occasional half hour to his rusticated neighbours," he however seemed to understand you. What has he been doing?

We have not been able to ascertain what has been done or what time has been appointed for the meeting at Flat Rock of Stockholders in the Rail Roads, it seems to have died a natural death, but will no doubt be revived.

The weather with us looks very stormy, our Barometer and Glasses indicate bad weather. But we can only hope for the best. . . . .

Alexander W. Campbell to Robert F. W. Allston

Charleston 22nd Augt. 1837

DEAR ROBERT I am just in receipt of your esteemed favor of the 15th and 19th inst, and feel much relieved to find that you are all safe on the beach, the crops I've no doubt have suffered materially, however we must be thankful that it is no worse. It seems to me I shall never get my assignment completed. I have had a lawyer engaged for a week, he says however that tomorrow it will be ready for my Signature. I wrote to Mrs. Allston some days since that I had made up my mind to prefer the Estates claim, this debt, and what I owe the Estate LaBruce, shall be paid first, the Balance of my assets shall be divided among my creditors proportionally.

I hope you will coincide with me in opinion as to the correctness of my course in giving the Estates claim a preference. I intend as soon as I complete my assignment to pass the Estates a/c with the ordinary and send the a/c Book up. I forget whether I mentioned to you that I had sent up to Mrs. Allston all the Estates papers that were in my hands.

I have employed Toney Weston to make the Band for the Mill, and I hope in a few days it will be ready.

I thank you for the justice you do me in explaining to others what may be misunderstood I wish I could be present in person, to remove any injurious and erroneous impressions that a misconstruction of my circumstances may lead to. I am very thankful to say I continue to receive the most friendly and sympathising letters from my Southern customers.

If I can be discharged from my present liabilities before the new Crop, I hope to retain a very good portion of my business.

I will have a petition drawn up for the Legislature, there is no difficulty in getting Back our money. The order to Ward shall be paid and the remaining paid on a/c of the Bond in the Bank, if they refuse so small a payment, I will deposit it to my credit as Exor. indeed this is the course I shall always pursue with all Estates that I have to manage, let my circumstances be ever so prosperous.

Lewis and Robertson to Robert F. W. Allston

Charleston 21 Sept 1837

DEAR SIR Your favor of 5th inst came duly to hand. The Waccamaw will return in a day or two, she is only waiting on one of her hands who has been ill. Your articles are all on board of her and judging from the present appearance of the weather, there is no doubt but that she will be up as soon as any. All storm seems to have blown over which God grant will prove so, for we have had a trying year, to contend with, in every way.

Our Rice market is a little higher this week, but not much, tho a few Sales were made at $4 7/16, and 15 barrels at $4 1/2. The purchasers buy only from hand to mouth, and nothing but dire necessity will drive them up to $4 1/2.

We did hope to see $5 before the season was out, but it is now so advanced, and the New Crop of Grain throughout the States generally is so very abundant, that it will be hard work to reach even $4 3/4, or even $4 1/2.

Our charge of $75 against you on 15 April last, was bottomed on your instruction dated 10th April, as follows "I have this day made sale of 5 Shares in the Bank of Georgetown held for The Este W. T. Jones at $5 advance; be good enough to put to the credit of the Estates account from mine $75 which is the sum received for them."

It was accordingly done by charging you, and crediting the Estate though our entry ought to have been differently and more ship shape like expressed.

We hope to see you next month, if you go to Greenville. And should there be any epedemic in our City, the writers family will hold out on the Island, until all such is gone, and he will be glad to have you with him there at nights, and through the day we can be in Town, and look after our Business.

[P.S.]   Your altered order for Lead has been attended to.

Alexander W. Campbell to Robert F. W. Allston

Charleston 16th October 1837

DEAR ROBERT   I am in receipt of your esteemed favor of the 8th inst. and assure you, I am quite aware of the Kindness of your feelings towards me, and therefore would not wish such feelings to lead you into any, the slightest indiscretion.

On the subject of the Estates business I will give you my views very frankly.

I have made up my mind for the present to continue my business, finding myself so situated with a large family that I am compelled to do it, not being accustomed to adversity, I had no idea I should be thus situated, and I really left myself perfectly destitute, and although there is a small pittance settled upon my children, for the present, that is perfectly unavailable. Even under the imperious circumstances of my situation I would not say, for the *present* I think the Estates Rice may be consigned to me without the slightest risk, if I did not know this to be the fact.

I am indebted to the Banks and to individuals, but this property could not be made liable to my debts, there is but one possible way that a loss could occur and that is my selling the Rice to any individual that I am indebted to, which of course I would avoid.

Do not understand me as insisting on this matter, I only say, there is no power that can reach the Estates property or prevent me from appropriating it as we may wish, I would like however on the Sale of each parcel of Rice to pay the proceeds to the Bank debt forthwith, this plan stops interest, and keeps my a/c balanced.

There are now a few small amts. due viz, the Band I sent up, and some other little things, shall I pay for them out of this Toll, I think twould be best. In consequence of heavy arrivals this morning Rice is not so brisk, and I believe that by the W[accamaw] has not been sold.

In regard to the future with me so much will depend upon circumstances that at present tis impossible to say any thing definite. I intend to pursue the same course towards the Estate LaBruce as I have suggested to you for your brothers Estate, intend writing to friend Josh on this subject and will consult with Mrs. LaB. It will shortly be time to purchase negroe clothing etc, I can buy them and have them charged to the Estate, if it meets your views.

Mr. Gotea has written to me for a Barn Lock and Oil for the mill, which articles I will send by the return of the Waccamaw.

[P.S.] The intelligence of the loss of the Steam Boat Home[1] has just been recd here, 'tis said there are about 90 passengers drowned.

Lewis and Robertson to Robert F. W. Allston

Charleston 17 Octor 1837

DEAR SIR   We are in receipt of your favors of 9th and 15th inst. The former by Capt Lea with 34 who[le] and 8 half Barrels Rice marked R F W A prime, which we sold on the wharf at $4 3/4 yesterday, also one half barrel *R F W A* sold to day at $4, Barrels 50/100. And we beg to annex your account Sales[2] of the same shewing Nett proceeds at your Credit $929.86, which we have just debited you with, as pr Receipt (also annexed) of the Bank of S[tate] So Ca. in further payment of your Bond, all which we trust will prove satisfactory. Our market got a considerable shock yesterday, by the large supply thrown on it in one day, say near 900 Barrels. All the prime parcels (except yours) consequently were stored, $3 5/8 being the highest offer made for them, and as we had the principal part, we held on, in hopes of doing a little better.

Your instructions in regard to the Toll etc due the Waverly Mill have been noted, and shall be complied with. We would however suggest that the Charges on every respective parcel, be kept distinct and that your claim against the Este[3] be made out clear, so that the one may go against the other, without confusion, and thus save Explanations at a future day. The act relative to Duty on Woolens has been acted on by the Senate, and agreed to, we shall therefore have all out the custom in a day or so, when prices will be fixed, as yet nothing at all has been done, in consequence of the duty being payable cash in Specie, and the Specie was not to be had. This however is now done away with. Toney Weston has bought the Rivets for your Band himself and will select the Band Leather, that sent you was from Cruickshanks. Lea's Cargo turned out all right, agreeably to Mr Gotea's letter.

[1] The steam packet "Home," leaving New York for Charleston on October 7, was wrecked in a storm off the coast of North Carolina, and the majority of her passengers and crew were lost.

[2] Omitted.   [3] The estate of Joseph Waties Allston.

The Resolution of the Cooper River planters to charge $1 for their Barrels, has been much talked of, of late. We have come to the more firm conviction that it is bad Policy. This however is between ourselves, for tho we express our opinion, we are bound to comply with all instructions from the planters, and to keep up an appearance to the purchasers who contend against the move.

In your Sale yesterday, we charged only 50¢, had the supply been light, and the demand active, we would have held out for $1, as we had to do so on Wards and Heriots, but the supply being heavy and full, and the demand very slack, we made the best terms for your interest, that we could, particularly as the proceeds were to kill interest, and as Luck would have it Wards Rice was mostly inferior, and bought by the retailers, one parcel and the only one good, we had to deduct 8¢ p 100 on, as broad as it was long to him. Heriots was prime, and we cannot get more than $4 5/8 for it, barrels 50/100. The man (M and L. Pezant) who offered this price assuring us that he will buy no Rice in which $1 is charged. We have therefore no alternative, but to hold on until some one else will buy at $1, deducting the 8¢. Leland Brothers and Co is the only house willing to come into the measure, so much for Boston, where they hail from.

Your Wine has arrived £120 pr pipe, or £60 a half Pipe this must be something extra. We will send it up by Lea with the Bill etc., and Gover[nor] Butlers we will also send as you direct.

Your account will be a cr when all the Toll is passed to it, we therefore made the payment to the Bank an even thousand, as p Receipt, and advanced it, Mr Cheesborough Jr having promised payment tomorrow. And to day being just 2 mos interest, and as you will be in Georgetown tomorrow, we have closed it, one day being of no consequence to us.

Robert Thurston[1] to Robert F. W. Allston

Charleston Octr 27, 1837

MY DEAR SIR   This morning I recd your kind favour of the 25th inst.

I will with pleasure accept the Business of your Brothers estate and hope by strict attention to deserve your and Mrs Allstons confidence.

As soon as the Saul gets in and the Rice by her can be sold, I will see the creditors you named and distribute the proceeds as you directed, in the mean time do let me advise the forwarding the balance of the old Rice as fast as possible, I fear that our market is already on the wane. . . . .

[P.S.] Plains are higher than usual 78 a 85c. Blankets are cheaper, very good can be purchased a 50 or 60 dolls pr piece, 8 pair. Will be happy to purchase and forward any supplies the Est may require.

---

[1] Thurston appears to have been an independent factor at this time, but in 1838 (see below, p. 407) he joined the firm of Lewis and Robertson.

Alexander W. Campbell to Robert F. W. Allston

Charleston 30th October 1837

DEAR ROBERT   I wrote you on yesterday that I would decline the Factorage, I was induced to come to this decision from the fact of the Estates business being withdrawn from me.[1] I have shewn Mr. Thurston your letter, and he without any hesitation acceded to your wish, that the consignment should be turned over to me. I will, be assured, disburse the proceeds of the Rice immediately as it is received. I confess I felt extremely mortified and hurt when I saw your letter to Mr. T[hurston] because I had conversed with Mr. Duncan, and he stated to me what he had written to you. Surely I would not allow the Estate to suffer by me now, when I considered my obligation so sacred as to secure it in my assignment. I applied to Messrs L[ewis] and R[obertson] for the Toll on your Rice, but Mr. R[obertson] declined paying me saying he had written to you on the subject.

Mr. Thurston has handed me your letter, I will make the payments as you desire.

The Saul I think will probably get in this evening.

Lewis and Robertson to Robert F. W. Allston

Charleston 7 Nover 1837

DEAR SIR   Without any of your favors to reply to We beg to introduce to you Capt Chadwick of the Schr Perseverance, who, will hand you this. He has come out to fill the place of his Brother Gayer Chadwick, who had the carrying of Mr Weston's Crop last winter, and is unfortunately too ill to undertake it this. We have told him that we did not think you were liable to the agreement you made with the writer, "to employ Gayer Chadwick provided he came out in a new vessel," in as much as he had neither come himself nor had sent out a new vessel. We however feel well satisfied that you will do by him, all that is right and proper, and if you employ him well and good, if not, the fault is with himself. We have known Capt Chadwick some time, his vessel the Perseverance though an old one, has been thoroughly overhauld, and put in complete repair and as we really think you will not be served better by any other Coaster, we recommend him to your patronage cheerfully, believing him to be worthy of it. The business of Mr Westons Mill and Waverly Mill, will give him full employment and if you have not taken up a vessel for the latter, Capt Chadwick is your man.

J. W. Cheesborough to Elizabeth Frances Blyth

Charleston 10th Nov 1837

DEAR AUNT   Knowing the intrest you feel in what concerns me and mine, I write to inform you of the result of the Sale of my Furniture and Negroes.

---

[1] Campbell was reported on November 10 to have left Charleston secretly. His last communication to Allston (March 23, 1838) was written in Savannah, Ga.

On the 8th the Furniture was sold. Through a friend, I bought *all* that we wanted at such price as my agent choose to bid for at much less than half its value. No one would bid for an article when it was understood it was wanted by my family, and we have now an ample supply of every thing of the sort necessary, at a Cost of less than $600, which John pays for out of the Salary that was due him.

The Negroes were sold on the 9th. It got out some how or other, that I wanted *but one* family, Viz a man his wife and 4 children, these people would probably sell for $3000 to any one wanting such and there were several at the sale who would have given that price, but they were bought for my family for $2100, no one would bid against them. My Cook was bought for us for $350 and a Female house Servant for $600, making $3050. The Bill of Sale is made to Mr Charles Graves, who pays for them. He is to allow John and myself to pay him as we may have it in our power, and he is then to turn them over for the benifit of my family. We can get *nearly* as much Wages for the man as will pay the Interst on the cost of himself and family. I expect to get from $1000 to $1200 in lieu of Dower on the House, which will be applied towards the payment of the negroes, and within two years I hope to be able to say that they belong to my wife and children, being then paid for. Persons at the Sales acted with great consideration and kindness towards me, no citizen of Charleston bid on any thing that Mr Graves said was wanted for my family. My worst trials are now over, and I feel in better spirits than for 4 or 5 months. We expect to move in about a fortnight, as soon as we are fixt I intend to pay a visit to Georgetown. Eliza has sustained herself nobly through our trials, and I believe if she had not seen me suffer so much and my spirits so depress'd, she would not have felt a pang at the privations which we have encounter'd and have still to encounter. As I commence life anew, it must be a year at least before I can get under way, by this time twelve months, I think I shall begin to go ahead, and I feel quite satisfied that integrity of purpose, capability in business, and untiring industry will within 6 or 8 years place me in a comfortable situation again. At all events I will do all that man can to deserve success, if I fail to attain it, why, I must submit.

Eliza and the Girls are busy in rearranging the household matters. All are well and desire their love, and I am with sincere affection and respect. . . . .

Lewis and Robertson to Robert F. W. Allston

Charleston 9 Decr 1837

Colo Robert F W Allston   Your favor of 25 Nover came duly to hand by the Waccamaw, with your 31 barrels Rice say 30 barrels of good, sold at 3 5/8 on the wharf 1 do inferior sold at 3 3/8 on 8th as pr account Sales annexed,[1] shewing Nett proceeds at your Credit $550.28, which we trust will prove

[1] Omitted.

satisfactory. We also annex you a Receipt from the Bank So Ca for $1100.09 in further part of the principal $1000 and in full of interest to date $101.09, leaving the balance due on said Bond $9000.

We have not sent for your 1000 bushels Ro[ugh] Rice you spoke of shipping, because the specimens we have seen of the Pee Dee Crop have in no instance warranted a Sale in the Rough, and it can be much better pounded at Waverly Mill, than here. We will therefore meet your payments cheerfully in the meantime and wait on you until you can pound. We are much perplexed how to decide as to Sales being postponed, that the Crop is the shortest since 1822 we are pretty certain of, but this will not be believed by the purchasers, until they feel it, and they cannot feel it until the Spring is well spent. In the meantime it is all conjecture how prices will range. There has not been a single Cargo yet made up of clean Rice for Europe; and unless shipments begin very soon, all the Coastwise and West India Markets must become stocked, and all active demand cease. They cannot take all the Crop. Foreign Orders must be brought into the market, or it must go down. The short Crop however must bring up prices in the Summer, and it will at all events be well to hold on with some til then.

We have been much gratified to learn Mrs Allston's improvement in health, for several days we experienced the heighth of anxiety to learn how she was.

Alexander Robertson to Robert F. W. Allston

Charleston 16 Jany 1838

DEAR ALLSTON I received yesterday your favor of 12 inst.

Miss Blamyer is out of Town. I have not therefore been able to see her. But it seems to me that we should keep in view the importance of putting your Neice[1] in such a place, that she will not be driven out in Summer by any epedemic. Now I can only say that Mad[ame] Talvande[2] hired a house on the Island last summer directly in my front, and had her Boarders all with her there, with a set of idle Catholic Priests. It may not have been wrong. I do not mean to scan the propriety or impropriety of it, or to judge others, but as my mind was impressed with the impropriety of the thing, I only mention it to you, "evil communications corrupt good manners." On the other hand to board her in the neighbourhood of Mad T's she will be subject to fevers etc being unacclimated, nor do I know that Mad T will take her as a scholar, while boarding with another. I think I have understood not, such is my impression, and I must have heard it somewhere.

It therefore seems to me that your course is to remain quiet, and let your

[1] Charlotte, daughter of Allston's deceased sister, Mary Pyatt Jones.

[2] Anne Marsan Talvande, whose school for girls was a favorite among Charlestonians for a number of years. For information concerning Mme Talvande the editor is indebted to Mrs. John Bennett.

Neice return to Miss Blamyer. In all probability others will turn up, and induce Miss B to continue. It is worth waiting for, for she is an excellent good lady, if any thing rather too straight laced but this is erring on the safe side.

I beleive Mad T's is the best school, where children live with their parents, but to be left to her care is quite another thing, she has too many Catholic priests about her (or rather she had) performing Mass rather too often for me. And as I have seen, so I tell you, frankly and openly. But at same time as it is no business of mine what she chooses to do, let this be for your own guidance and information.

I got home to my family all well. I hope Mrs Allston continues to mend. I have paid H and F for your 1/2 pipe of Wine, attend to Ward's share and got him to instruct us to charge accordingly. But the Govr's is unpaid. H and F say they sent him no draft, nor account either. It must have been some other wine he paid for thro the Bank. I told them to send him his Bill, which they will do. . . . .

Lewis and Robertson to Robert F. W. Allston

Charleston 8th March 1838

DEAR SIR   We are in receipt of your favors of 25th and 28th Ulto, and 5 inst.

Mr Thurston had not credited Mr Jno H Allston with the barrel of Middling Rice got by Capt Lea. We will therefore bring it into Dr Allston's Sales, when we close up his parcels now on hand, which we have not yet been able to do.

We are just closing up the Sales of Colo Wards and Colo Belins Seed Rice, which we had on hand. We did not therefore see our way clear to advise your shipping so soon, having understood you to say that you would hold back for late in the Season, and we had got down those, we were apprehensive so much at one time would interfere with one another. But as we have now got through with Wards and Belin's we can now go on with yours. Any of the Coasters in Georgetown will be glad of the job. They are all there, and beg to leave the engagement of one to you, not understanding precisely that you are ready for one, in case we should send him up.

Mrs Shackelfords five buckets have been made, and would have been painted for the Waccamaws present trip, but the late weather caused the leather to swell, and they are not yet finished, they shall however be sent up very soon.

Mr John H Allstons order for $700 has been passed to your credit, and $17.50 to our own.

Enclosed is Paul and Brown's account receipted in full, which came to hand this morning.

We have noted your price for Seed at the Barn, and will bear in mind any orders, in your neighbourhood, which we will have to execute.

We have handed Mr Thurston an account of the Seed Rice furnished

Mrs Davis last Spring, he will write to her for instructions to pay it, we have added "interest until paid agreeably to our understanding with her."

The payment of the instalments on your 60 Shares, in the C[harleston] C[incinnati] and L[ouisville] Rail Road, shall meet due attention.

Messrs Lazarus and Levy had only 1 doz and 2 hoes of the kind you wanted, we have therefore sent them to you, and charged them to your account, say $4.67.

Lewis and Robertson to Robert F. W. Allston

Charleston 20th March 1838

DEAR SIR We duly received your favor of 12th inst. Capt Eddy has not yet come in with your Seed Rice, which we have sold to arrive, to Mr Withers, at $1.37 1/2, say 900 Bushels, and hope it will turn out all right.

You were just in time to stop the insurance on your Threshing Mill, which has been accordingly done. We received your account Book, and the memorandum on it, which shall be executed, when Lea returns, and your instructions about the 1/2 pipe Wine, also.

It seems that we missed it, when we stored Rice for $4. Our market now is so void of purchasors, that to force Sales would bring it down to $31/4 a $31/2. We are therefore compelled to hold on, for it would be ruinous, with so short a crop to give way now, for what could be realized. We are sorry for it. The brunt falls heavily on us, but we must hold out a little longer at all events. In the meantime it is just as well to forego pounding on your own account. The worst feature in the business, is the large Stock which is accumulating, and must be worked off, before there can be any reaction.

Lewis and Robertson to Robert F. W. Allston[1]

Charleston Sep. 1st 1838

DEAR SIR We beg to inform you that we have made arrangements with our friend, Mr. Robert Thurston to join us in Business on the first of next month, under the firm of Lewis Robertson and Thurston, and we respectfully solicit the continuation of your Patronage.

DEAR SIR We wrote you under date of 17 Ulto care of Mr Laffan. Since then we are without any of your favors. Above we now beg to hand you our circular of 1st inst and trust it will meet your kind consideration.

We are sorry to confirm the sickliness of our City. The fever has been very fatal to all Strangers and those not acclimated. To the Natives, however, it is perfectly exempt.

We are extremely grieved to tell you of the death of Francis Westons little Son George, he died on the 31 of last month of Scarlet fever. We begin to fear that Dr Allston's Rice has lost a good market. None has been received since

---

[1] Addressed, New York, N.Y.

you left and the advanced Harvest on Cooper River, will interfere materially with prices. The weather however for several days has been unfavorable,
but no Gale we hope.

Lewis and Robertson to Robert F. W. Allston[1]

Charleston 20 Octr 1838

DEAR SIR   We have at last the pleasure of hearing from you. Your favor of
12 is at hand to day. It must be a surprize to you to find we have not received
any Rice lately from the Waverly Mill. It has been to us, and on the 15th we
wrote to Mr Ellis to know what Rice Dr Allston had on hand, and if he could
not beat it out at once, to ship it here in the Rough with the least possible loss
of time. We also asked him to say, how much of yours was remaining. The
Season is well advanced and Waverly Mill has done very little unless the
Waccamaw and the Julius Pringle both bring in large parcels from it. We
have lately sent the latter vessel there, for there is more Rice at Wards and
Waverly Mill than the Waccamaw could bring, and time is a matter of the
greatest importance to the owners now. We have in to day 2000 Bus of the
new Crop from Cooper River, W. A. Carson's, he has his Steam threshing
Mill at work, and contemplates supplying the little demand that the wretched
yellow fever has left us. We have not however been able to do anything with
it in the Rough, we shall be compelld to put it in Mill, and try the Experiment, for it is one, whether the Pestle will answer so early in the Season, or
not. The Harvest has been very forward and hence it will not do to wait and
hold back for an October market, as we did last year. We are therefore very
desirous to get to market all of the old Crop as early and as speedily as
possible.

We have only to day been able to get off your 5 1/2 Bar[rel]s of inferior
Rice, we almost can say we had to give it away, having sold at 2 1/2 and 2 3/4
(as pr Sales annexed).[2] But so it is, and even at this low rate, we had to consume more time, than selling very large parcels.

This afflicting fever has acted like a cramp to all Business. Without it,
and we would have worked off the old crop at famous prices, but as it now is,
we can scarcely sell, and every thing seems out of joint. We must however use
every exertion to meet the times. Thank God our families have so far kept
well. Your Niece is out of the reach of it. I thought of her, and made enquiry
a month ago, and found she was in as safe a situation, as she could be.

Your drafts shall meet due honor, none have yet come in pray let us know
what discount you pay. Exchange in New York here is at 1 1/2 prem. You
can judge whether you are best served by drawing, or our remitting, for
either way is the same to us, as long as you are satisfied.

If nothing turns up to interfere with the harvest it will be very abundant.

---

[1] Addressed, New York, N.Y.   [2] Omitted.

The late winds did no damage of any moment, and our friends seem satisfied with their prospects. There are however so many Risks to run, in all the next month, and the remainder of this, that there is no telling what the result will be, we can therefore only hope for the best.

We beg you to settle with J Stevens and Co and not leave them the trouble to remit the little matter of the value of Mr Rutledges Rice and grist, and when we meet we can arrange it.

We have now another favor to ask of you, provided you can do it without the least inconvenience to yourself. Our good and amiable friend Mrs Geo W Morris requested us to buy her a pair of horses. Now it seems to us that as you are to get Ward a pair, you will be on the look out, and it may so happen that you can select her "a pair of good well broke northern horses to cost not more than $500." These are her words, and if you can do so and travel them in, it may save you, and serve you, if not, ship them, and let us know that we may insure.[1] And as regards the needful, there is yet time for us to hear from you, whether you would prefer that we remit you for these, as for Wards also, and for any more funds you may want or whether you prefer to draw thro Laffan, drawing is most convenient to us, and we would not say a word about it, if it did not occur to us that Remitting would be the most saving. This however as we before said, rests with yourself.

We sent you the other day Our Circular of 1st inst. We hope you got it. The family at Hampstead have been well with the Exception of Miss Mildred who had an attack of Scarlet fever, she has however mended and is out again. The death of the little Boy has afflicted them very severely.

Your message to Colo Belin shall be delivered. The approaching Election for Congress seems to make no noise. I. E. Holmes has been nominated against Legare.[2]

Alexander Robertson to Elizabeth Frances Blyth

Charleston Friday 26, Octor 1838

MY DEAR MADAM I am very much grieved in having to write you now, but as I am certain you would blame me, if I did not; for I well know your great anxiety at all times, and particularly when sickness is in the way. I now write notwithstanding my great regret.

Miss Blamyer sent to let me know yesterday afternoon, that your Niece was sick. I immediately went up to her and found it was too true. She was taken on Tuesday night, and the fever still continued on her. She was however very collected, and spoke cheerfully and seemed very glad to see me. I sat sometime with her, and have been with her again to day, she appears much the same as last evening. Dr. Thos Y Simons attends her, he told me he was not much concerned about her case, that it was a plain one, and

[1] See above, p. 84.

[2] Hugh Swinton Legaré (1797–1843), the incumbent, who was defeated by Holmes.

whether it is my anxiety or not, I cannot tell, but I think she is very ill. She has not been out the house since the early part of August; and the situation was so completely considered safe from this wretched fever, that Mr Rawlins Lowndes moved his family (all perfect strangers) to Mr Aiken's immediately opposite. They have all kept well and poor Charlotte to be taken ill at this 11th hour when we were indulging the fond hope, that all danger was over, shews us the inscrutable ways of Providence, to whom we must at all times trust and confide.

I will write to you again tomorrow, when I trust and hope I will be able to tell you she is better. In the meantime she has my most earnest wishes.

Mrs Pyatt is well and her Daughter is getting well. Your Niece Mrs Weston looks poorly since her sad affliction her little daughter is much better.

We have had a dreadful Summer. God spare us from the like again. Mrs Robertson was quite ill, but she got over it cleverly, and the children too

2 o clock. I have just returned from seeing her and cannot say she is any better.

Alexander Robertson to Elizabeth Frances Blyth

Charleston 30th Octor 1838

MY DEAR MRS BLYTH Since yesterday midday Charlotte has continued much the same. The only change is in her symptoms which are not quite so good. This wretched fever is however so very insidious that while there is life there's hope, and she still holds out to the surprize of every one.

The Doctor recommended Old wine to day and I have got her the oldest and best I had. In this way we hope to keep up life. Mrs Withers laid in the same way, for a whole week, and was finally brought up by Wine. After her recovery, I shall never despond. I mean in protracted cases.

When she was first taken, I was very desponding for generally speaking, cases like hers were soon over, but now that we can keep her up, to her 7th day and 8th I truly hope her constitution will bear her through. This is now her only hope, for she is as low as she can possibly be.

P.S. We have to day closed the Sale of your Rice, at 3 3/4 and $3.68 3/4 and will send you the Sales tomorrow.

Alexander Robertson to Robert F. W. Allston

Charleston 14 Nover 1838

DEAR ALLSTON Yours of 7th and 8th with Mrs Morris' horses were received on Sunday. I like them much, and will, I am satisfied meet her full liking.

What I did for our late Orphan Child, was no more than I felt bound to do, could anxiety and care have kept her, she would now be with us. But it pleased God to call her. I look upon it that she would have been called from us, had she been any where, for taking all the circumstances attending her case, we cannot come to any other conclusion. I sat with her a good deal on Sunday the 28th Octo, she seemed as I thought then for the first time somewhat apprehensive of her situation and begged me to tell her, what sort of fever she had, but I did not wish to alarm her and finally soothed her into a sweet sleep, which was all important to her. Mr Trapier saw her on Tuesday, when she was very low, he was with her some time, and I am well satisfied that he was every way pleased with her. This was a consolation to me, and I am sure will be so to you all. I had every thing done as though she was my own, and discharged my last sad duty towards her by putting her in our private cemetary in St Pauls church Yard. I was desirous to take her up to Georgetown, and spoke with Mrs Pyatt about doing so, but it was so early in the season that there was too much risk attending it, and I was advised against it. I then did what I would have done by my own.

When we meet I will tell you all I know and in the meantime I will fall in with Thos Simons, and tell him you will be glad to hear from him.

Mr Lewis is mending, but very slowly, poor old gentleman, he has had a cruel and a severe bout of it, he is so dreadfully salivated that he cannot speak but with the most excruciating pain; it will be, must be, some time before he gets over it; he will no doubt be better when he recovers than he has been for years. But in the meantime, it is just as well that I have help in Thurston; for I dont know how I could have got along without an active and a responsible man of judgement for out door business, for it has so happened that we are without a clever man in doors, and I have to be in all day long.

Yesterday I had 19 Orders thro the Bank G[eorge] Town presented for acceptance. I had pretty nearly paid out all we had, and I must confess that the packet alarmed me so that I said rather promp[t]ly I could not accept. I offered to pay them if the discount deducted at the time would be refunded, but this was declined; and rather than accept (a most dangerous habit to get into) I paid the greater part of them. Amongst them was one of yours to Chapman $757.88 for your Rail R[oad] B[ank] Shares, which I had arranged here (but got refunded yesterday I hope). Now my good friend I have given you every evidence of the greatest confidence in you, and I tell you candidly, I am not sorry that yours was amongst the number, and I hope you will see how I was situated. I would not dishonor your paper and I could not get over it, but by paying it, for between ourselves there were some I could not accept for, and to do for one and not another was laying ourselves open to be cavailed at. Whereas no one can complain of making any preferences now. Therefore I have been particular in writing and just keep quiet about it. "We dont accept" is the old rule and one that we must adhere to, or we will soon become involved. You however know, that we dont hold always to it, with old and well tried friends, only to guard against— we must hold out the principle, and trust our old friends will support us in the stand, for it is pretty clear their true interest to do so.

Lewis, Robertson, and Thurston to Robert F. W. Allston

Charleston 26 Nover 1838

DEAR SIR   We are in receipt of your 2 favors of 16th and of 21st inst. We now hand you annexed a statement of The Estates account to 24 inst,[1] shewing a balance in hand $300.67, which it has occurred to us you may wish to be conversant with. The Bills against the late Proprietor are we believe all in, and paid and you have it all in a narrow compass. The next matter is the suggested Sale of the 19 Shares Bank Charleston Stock, the proceeds to be invested during the present winter.

To this it seems to us that the best interest to be realized will be from its own investment. There is now in hand $300, and on 1 Jany will be the annual interest on your Bond and Dividends, to enable the payment of 25 p cent on the increase of the Capital to be punctually met, for there is no question but that this Stock will always be worth $120, and the January Dividend will be secured. Whereas by selling now, only 142 can be got, and the $5 dividend (which is near at hand) would be lost. Therefore by selling now at $142 will make the purchaser stand at $121 when the increase is made, and the Seller will loose 5 months interest. But by holding on and getting the dividend of $5 and then selling at $120, will be a gain of $3 pr Share, to the Estate. We give you this minutiae to regulate you in deciding whether or not it is worth while to hold on for the funds can always be invested. We should not think it worth trying, though we give you the above facts of the case. With our own, we calculate to sell at $145, or to hold on and double.

Your Box of Clothes has not yet come to hand. J Chapman's Check for $300 has been placed to your credit, and your certificate of the 1st payment on your R[ail] R[oad] B[ank] Stock has been put away. We have charged you with $11 for Mrs Rutledges Rice sold by Mr Stevens in New Port.

Rice was brisk to day, clean 4 1/4 & 4 3/4, Rough 98 & 101¢.

Lewis, Robertson, and Thurston to Robert F. W. Allston

Charleston 4 Decer 1838

DEAR SIR   We received to day your favor of 30 Ulto. The late progress by the So[uth] W[estern] R[ail] R[oad] Bank has not caused its Stock to advance in value here, but between ourselves has had a contrary tendency; a good deal however, has yet to be done. In the meanwhile our views as to the Stock of the Bank of Charleston, have been strengthened, and we shall be regulated for the Estate's interest by our own movements in regard to Sales for our own account.

We received on 28th Ulto 86 who[le] and 11 hlf Bbls Rice on your account. The quality was very poor, being much broken and running uneven;

---

[1] Omitted.

at first we were unwilling to sell them at any thing like the value of similar parcels, and stored, but as the whole So[uthern] fleet is now in with about 1500 barrels of same description to land when the weather clears off, we closed your parcel to day at $4, which is all we could get offered on the wharf for it. We hope the next will be better, or you will require a very full crop to bring up a fair average. This result is unsatisfactory, but the quality did not warrant any thing more, though at first we were not inclined to think so. Prime Rice is still anxiously enquired after at $4 3/4 for Europe, but common is almost altogether neglected, and we apprehend some further decline.

The writer is much grieved to say that our J Lewis has had another severe attack in the head, he was taken last night, and though he has in a great measure recovered from the very alarming and dangerous symptoms he is still very ill, he had gotten so much better, as to be able to ride out, and intended to pay us a visit when the weather cleared off. But he is now scarcely able to sit up, and it must be some time longer before he can possibly be about again.

We will write to Mr Ellis about the Carriages and send up the old one by next trip of the U.S.

Lewis, Robertson, and Thurston to Robert F. W. Allston

Charleston 21 Decer 1838

DEAR SIR This will be handed to you by Bob belonging to Miss Sarah M Waring, who she has sent up to you. We do not know the circumstances, and only understand that you are welcome to the use of him until April next. Miss Waring has however no doubt written to you about him, and we only comply with her desire in forwarding him to you.

Your Boy left here last Summer with Dr Jervey is doing well. The Doctor called the other day to know whether you wished him to be returned, but we did not exactly know, and now beg your instructions in regard to his disposal. It is a good place that he is in, and if you do not wish him particularly he will learn and be well taken care of under the Doctors care.

Capt Bridges left here this morning. Our Rice Market is crippled. Every description but choice is dull and unsaleable, good 3 5/8 to 4, prime 4 1/4 to 4 1/2. Sales principally at $3 3/4 to 3 7/8.[1]

Robertson, Blacklock and Company to Robert F. W. Allston

Charleston Jany 13 1859

DEAR SIR We duly received your favors of 7 and 10 inst. We wrote to Dr Forster to know his prices terms etc. of the 50 negroes he offered to sell you,

---

[1] A third gap in the factors' documents occurs at this point. Such material as there is for the next twenty years does not lend itself to publication.

mentioning you were willing to give five hundred dollars round.[1] But we have not as yet had any reply to our letters.

We bought to day at Coln Thos Pinckney Alston's Sale the Bricklayer Wilchire and his wife Jenney agreably to your directions; we paid for them $750 ea, and have sent them to you by this trip of the Nina and will settle with Mr A J White for them in accordance with the terms of Sale, i e 1/3 cash Balance in 1, 2 and 3 years with interest from day of Sale payable annually: "Secured by Bond and Mortgage of the Property sold, and approved personal security Purchaser to pay A. J. White for requisite papers," unless we hear from you to the contrary! and in that event we beg your instructions in the premises.

The total average of the 177 Negroes is $635 i.e. 135 at auction at $630 and 42 at private Sale at $650.

We broke down on the Sale of Mrs Rutledge's Plantations on Santee to day, no bid or offer for those on the North River. Harrietta on the South River was sold to S. D. Doar for $25,000. There are some 60 negroes on same to be sold, can we do anything with you? at anything at or over $600 for them.[2] They will be sold to pay debt is the worst of it and money is the strong component part! Still as they have to be sold, we must do the best we can for the Heirs, not losing sight of the future welfare of the people, and our desire to get them a good owner. But a large portion of cash is indispensable.

Robertson, Blacklock and Company to Robert F. W. Allston

Charleston Jany 18, 1859

DEAR SIR   We received your favor of 17th. J B Allston has bought the Rutledge Negroes at $575 round. He will use the $10,000 paid in by Doar on his purchase of Harrietta. Please send us the amount of cash for T P Alston's negroes $1500, if perfectly convenient and agreeable, if not however we will pay here only as you said you could send us a check, pray do whichever is most convenient. We can settle the difference on cost of Papers, etc at any time.

Horses are dull of Sale just now, and we dont know but what Porcher and Bayn had better sell your Blacks for what they will fetch! Hockaway would no doubt be glad to have them on livery and give his own the preference all the time. Such has been our experience.

When Read comes to Town next month we will learn his views more fully, in regard to Pipedown.

[1] See above, p. 351.

[2] See above, p. 152.

Alexander Robertson to Robert F. W. Allston

Charleston March 22, 1859

DEAR ALLSTON   Spalatro has been bid in by "The family" at $3011. I went to $3010, and would have gone further for you, but there was no use; they seemed determined to give a dollar more than any one else.[1]

It was started by James Rose at $1000, E. N. Ball ran me to 2600, when he bid $3000, I 3010 and he $3011. There was no bona fide bid over $1600 (the Revd Mr Boyce's) by any outsider.

I could not well do otherwise than I have done; in the meanwhile no one has bought it over your head; and we have given every evidence of your value of the artist in your Relative.

If there had been only fair opposition but to bid against a family who were making every sacrifice to indulge their good Taste was painful to me in the extreme and I fear would be distasteful to you.

Robertson, Blacklock and Company to Robert F. W. Allston

Charleston 13th April 1859

DEAR SIR   Your favor of 9th Inst has just been handed to us by Mr Latrobe, who tells us that he has written to you advising the purchase of the Ashley Flouring Mills with Rail Road and Wharf appertaining thereto for $15,600.

We talked the matter over with him and afterwards saw Mr Petigru who tells us that you cannot be a Special Partner, without paying a Specific Sum into the Concern, which must also be published in the Daily Papers, as your Endorsement will not be sufficient of itself to define your position as a limited partner, and even then if you interfere in the management of the business, you will make yourself liable for all the engagements of the Concern, as a General Partner.

A still more serious difficulty is, that if you endorse for the Concern (being a Special Partner) you cannot be secured as a preferred Creditor, in case of the affairs becoming involved, but on the contrary you could not rank upon the Estate until every other debt due by it was liquidated, so that you would even stand in a worse position than a common creditor.

We must also mention in confidence, that from what we learn in other quarters, Mr L., has had some money difficulties to encounter, and in case of any check to the prosperity of the Mills, we fear you would have to meet it, if you once embarked in this project. Both Mr Latrobe and Mr T S Gourdin have seen us in reference to this matter, and wished us to write to

---

[1] "Spalatro," or "The Vision of the Bloody Hand," was painted in 1832 by Washington Allston for H. S. Ball, of Charleston. It later passed into the possession of H. R. Bishop and sometime after 1876 was burned at his home on the Hudson River.

you, as they are anxious to know whether you are still disposed to embark on this enterprize or not, as in the latter case, they must make other arrangements.

We have not yet been able to advise a Sale of your Monburnt [?] Rice, as we are holding it at $3 1/2, which price however we cannot yet realize.

The Books which you expect from Cambridge shall be taken care of on receipt. . . . .

Benjamin Allston to Robertson, Blacklock and Company[1]

Paris July 24, 1859

GENTLEMEN   About the end of May I had a negro man, named Levi sent down to your care to go to Dr. Peter Porcher to be cured of a hernia. Will you be pleased to inquire what has been done for him and how he is getting along. It seems to me quite time that he should have been cured if he be curable, if no good has been done him and no immediate good is probable from his longer stay in town have him sent home, as I would not have him remain there longer than necessary.[2]

I hope you will have a healthy summer in Charleston this season. Here we have had very warm weather, which no doubt you are also suffering at home

Alexander Robertson to Robert F. W. Allston

Charleston April 6, 1861

DEAR GOVERNOR   I have not written you in consequence of all sorts of idle reports, none reliable enough to report on. Our community has however been in considerable excitement for the 2 last days as you will see by the Various Telegrams from New York, and the ordering off of all the young men from the City to the different stations along the Harbor, the moving the Floating Battery to the Island (Back Beach for shelling) and Cutting off all further communication with fort Sumter: Provisions etc.

The latter 2 however are incorrect. Hatch told me confidentially to day that Genl Bouregard was not quite ready for either; the late high winds having prevented certain Sand moving or lifting to cover the Magasines (a couple of them) as soon as completed however, both will be done (i e the Battery etc). They are looking out for the Harriet Lane, and the Powhattan.

He also told me that something positive would turn up in the next 2 or 3 days. Gov Pickens is down at Morris Island to day, what with Saluting him, and idle curiosety most Business has ceased. We may as well be at Sea as on Shore for any good that we are doing with the Shop. Belin and Parker are talking heavy.

You had as well keep in place and learn what is going on which I will keep you posted up in, save and except idle reports. I rather think Mondays mail will take something definite.

[1] Copy.   [2] See above, p. 156.

I have to thank you for the favor you did me in sending over Dr Hasells letter to him. He came yesterday morning "pr Rail" and happily found Mr Lance mending. He is now considered convalescent but very ill in strength and Spirits, poor fellow he was in the jaws of death and will feel it for some-time to come. He is not altogether out of danger yet his throat is still very ugly.

You did me a great service when I see you I will explain.

The excitement in the community is greater than it has yet been; by the fact more idling and politics than ever.

One P M. Nothing positive transpired; no fight to day, unless Reinforcement is attempted. But on Monday, Anderson must either come out or be brought out Sumter, provided Beauregard is all ready of which there is now no question.

I will write you on Monday.

Alexander Robertson to Robert F. W. Allston

[Charleston] 1/2 past 2 April 9, 1861

DEAR GOVENOR   I wrote you yesterday.[1] Last night we were all in real great excitement about 11 o clock at the firing of 7 Guns to summon out the Militia to protect the coast from Invasion, or reinforcement of Fort Sumter. You will see the account of Capt Talbots mission by the mornings Papers. That part however referring to 7 men of War outside needs confirma-tion. In the meanwhile all the effective force is out the City, and the Home Guard is looked to with great respect. I cant beleive yet that there will be any fighting our way very soon, tho it squints very ugly that way.

Every thing is very quiet here to day. I was up all night, and feel damaged, men women and children were all mighty uneasy all night; but when morn-ing came and no fight or even the sound of a Gun, we began to feel easier. I never saw such a crowd in the Streets late at night, Old and Young. All turned out to see their friends off. My Boys are on the Island. Bouregard has summoned a large number of Men from the interior, Kershaws Regi-ment and some others. He wishes to place a large force on the Islands to guard against a large force landing on them; in the meanwhile Anderson is quiet in "Sumter" having made no reply to the Communication made him on Sunday. You will see Talbot took the back track. He has his election between that and "Lodgings in the West end of the City." There are all sorts of Reports about what he said and did, but no one beyond Pickens and Bouregard seems to know any thing as to his Mission, "nothing transpired." I dont begin to like it no how. I am uneasy but cant think there is immediate danger of any fight, hope not. . . . .

[1] Missing.

Alexander Robertson to Robert F. W. Allston

Charleston April 11, 1861

DEAR GOVENOR   I have written you daily since Saturday. I now write again with a heavy anxious heart. We are all bustle and confusion, and no doubt before the day is over, many many of us will be no more.

Fort Sumter is to be demanded to day and Anderson will give fight; I have this from head quarters. Now that a fight is to be dreaded, is of course true because the Pride of our State, the very pick of its best men, of all grades and dates, must be brought to bear against hierlings and the refuse of Gods Creation. It seems that Talbots Dispatches were taken from him, and the Governments plans to Anderson are all known to Bouregard. This is very important to us all.

Dr F J Parker has a commission in the Army. He and Gus Trapier have gone to Fort Moultrie to be in the thickest of the fight. All Business is at a stand, Our Shop may as well be closed. I hope and trust that the Nina will be in by 12 O clock to day. She will not return just now. The Charleston has been pressed into the Service of the State. Fort Sumpter will be under heavy fire by one o clock to day. The Tug Yankee from New York with Supplies and men will be along by evening. We think it likely that she will be protected by Men of War, who are to throw out heavy rienforcements all along the coast, and who will make their way to the scene of action the best way they can. There are however so many various stories this morning that one scarce knows where to take up the commencement of this Story, and I write accordingly, just off hand. The floating Battery has been lodged back of the (Cove) Back Beach of Sullivans Island. If Davis has ordered Bouregard to shell out Anderson at once and that Serious work and that preperations are going on this morning is unmistakable this last is a fixed fact, even if nothing else is true. We have a Telegram from Washington. Talbot had returned, great excitement. The Militia ordered out, and some 100 refused to take the oath to protect the Union. The U S. Mail has failed No[rth] of Richmond, in consequence of the old Post Master being replaced by a Black Republican, again, Virginia will join us right off, on the 1st Gun being fired.

This is the short hand of the Telegrams.

1/2 past 12—I have written the foregoing by snatches from time to time, just in from Head Quarters, the order has been sent to Anderson to surrender; supposed he wont be attacked before evening, when he cant see the different Sand Batteries, and he can be seen, and the Guns brought to bear on his range. He can be seen busily at work preparing for the action. I am truly anxious.

One o clock   The Nina not in sight. Keep cool and trust in God. Hot work is ahead.

Alexander Robertson to Robert F. W. Allston

Charleston April 12, 1861

DEAR GOVR 11 o clock The Ball opened this morning at day light. Since then a steady slow fire has been kept up from all quarters and from all the Batteries. Anderson commenced about 7 and has been steady in return; at 9 a boat came up from Cummins point, reported the iron battery as behaving handsomely and no one wounded, a special dispatch to Genl B[eauregard], nothing from Sullivan's Island, but great fears as to Fort Moultrie from the heavy and steady fire poured on and in it.

1/2 past 12. The iron battery continues to do good work, also the floating battery, no communication from fort Moultrie, too dangerous to approach. Anderson is doing all he can shooting and shelling. God grant we may never see such another day. The Battery is crowded with women looking on in anxiety and fear for their Relatives and Connexions exposed to the dreadful slow steady discharges that have been incessant since 1/2 past 4 this morning. You can form no idea of the death like sound, and feeling.

I saw Ben for a minute last evening. He went down to Morris' Island last night. I have paid Adger, and got your letter. No mail again to day, all communication no less mail and Telegraph stopped.

Anderson may hold out 3 days, Stevens has knocked in 3 of his Barbette Guns. It is confidently believed that a considerable breach is made in the back wall, this from the eye with the Glass, no one of course can go near it. 10 Shot penetrated the iron of the floating Battery, but did not go thro the Palmetto Logs, no[ne] badly hurt there. Hamilton in command. None thro the iron Battery; it is now hours since the firing has been going on steadily, no intermission, slow and steady, Anderson doing his best.

I must close—One o clock.

Alexander Robertson to Robert F. W. Allston

[Charleston] April 13th one o clock P M 1861

DEAR GOVR I have learnt that yesterdays mail was returned to the P. O. No Train went out, no telegram no nothing, except from Head quarters. The Bombardment continues without stoppage, further than the firing of Sumter. All the quarters have been burnt to day, a dense smoak, and several Explosions.

No Gun fired from it for 2 hours, and an awful fire poured into it from all sides and quarters. 3 War Steamers are at anchor off the Bar, Visable to the naked eye; they have not ventured up.

Anderson is said to be in a crippled condition; he cant hold out 48 hours longer, if as long. We have not a wounded man. All working and doing well at all the Batteries.

Robertson, Blacklock and Company to Robert F. W. Allston

Charleston June 10, 1861

DEAR SIR   We received your favor of 6th. Your order $1399.73 for Taxes was paid on presentment, the others have not yet come in, but shall meet due honor.

We will pay Mr Glennie $50 as desired. Our Port is still under strict Blockade. God only knows how long it will last. We are cut off all resources, and have to borrow to carry on all who have not got funds to draw against.

The writer will remain at home this Summer, and stand by the old Ship. [Illegible.] He will go to the Convention with Mr Petigru, from St Michaels, to leave on 17th night train, for a few days only. Hopes to see you along.

[P.S.]   Please send us The Este Sarah Warings a/c Book for the ordinary.

Alexander Robertson to Robert F. W. Allston

Charleston Augt 22, 1861

DEAR GOVERNOR   I received yours of 15th in due course, and should have acknowledged it last mail, but was left with only a couple of clerks, and was much occupied all the forenoon.

C A Thurston got back yesterday from Richmond, he seems satisfied with the result of his trip, having been "promised" that his Brother be promoted.

I have had your Trunk locked but the Brush could not be found.

I hope and trust that there will be no mischief amongst our people. It would be very dreadful, for our Enemies to get hold of such a story just at this time.

The Molasses and seeds were sent you by the Santee. We hope they reach all safe.

Our friend Memminger is in trouble at Richmond; no Treasury Notes can be got, no paper, nor no Engraver to get them up.

Our Banks are now in Session on the subject. The Board of the Bank of Charleston agreed to lend the Goverment 1,500,000 Dollars in its Notes at 6 per. It is thought about 6,000,000 (six millions) will be promptly made up here to enable the Army to move. Our whole existance depends on prompt and active measures. . . . .

Alva Smith to Robert F. W. Allston

Fair Bluff, S. C. June 28th 1862

DEAR SIR,   Your man Peter with flat loaded with rice, has arrived with (35) Thirty five tierces rice and one 3/4 tierce. I written Messrs Robe[rt]son Black-lock and Co. Columbia S. C. I am awaiting their instructions about the money will forward you a/c of sales next week of Last lot. Please send me statement of all the lots but the first by return mail and the marks of each lot. My young man has misplaced one of your letters, when I was from home.

I send you by your man Peter (15) fifteen bunches yarn. It is the quality we use here for negro clothing, it being heavy, and of course more durable.

I will endeavour to procure you some South Carolina Bank bills and send them enclosed in a letter to you at Kingstree S.C. by mail as bal[ance], that is after paying Robe[rt]son Blaclock and Co ($3,500) Thirty five Hundred Dollars.

P.S.   Will write you tonight at Kingstree S. C.

Alexander McKenzie to Robert F. W. Allston

Florence Augt 9th 1862

DEAR SIR   Enclosed you have Acct Current[1] balance due you Twelve Hundred and Seven 16/100 Dollars which amt I have placed to your cr. with Robinson Blacklock and Co Charleston, hoping the Sale will prove satisfactory.

You will see by the acct I have Cr you with 51 Casks instead of 52 during the time I was waiting to get possession of Mr Norris Ware House one of the Cars was broken open and part of one Cask stolen the balance of Cask was put in the casks that was overhauled and the damaged Rice taken out as soon as I found the cask broken open I immediately unloaded the cars in the Depot to prevent a similar depredation there was several casks very badly damaged

I have not heard from your Flat or Hands they are not at the Bridge unless they have come up today If I can make sale of the Rough or Clean Rice here I will do so on arrival or if the prospect is gloomy I will ship to Charleston as soon as I can get a sample I will send it to Wilmington and give that Market a trial a few days ago that Market was good prices fare and some demand for the article.

P S   I have calculated the Rice for Maddam Tugno at 4 1/4¢ to get at the commission the five casks amount to $135.11 at the above figures.

Robertson, Blacklock and Company to Robert F. W. Allston

Charleston Augt 14, 1862

DEAR SIR   We received yesterday your favor of 9 inst, too late to be answered by return mail

There seems to be some difficulty about the Captain of the Steamer Ripley, who is sick, and the crew too, "is out of line." Mr McCormick has promised to let us know when he can do any thing, and his rate of freights, etc. And the President of the No[rth] E[astern] Rail Road says he can do nothing with Rough Rice at the Pee Dee Bridge; at Kingstree he might be able to furnish Box Cars but does not speak to a point. He seems willing to buy Ro[ugh] Rice at Kingstree. It seems to us advisable to sell to him or any

[1] Omitted.

one else there, provided we get our price, as may be agreed upon, which will be the trouble; for there is no rule, no data nor precedents to govern us, therefore do please say what your views are, and instruct us accordingly; we should think about $1 to 1.10.

Mr Weston wrote us that you and he propose to purchase the Genl Ripley with 2 Lighters, and would be glad that we should take 1/3 interest etc. We have not been able to do any thing yet in the matter. As regards ourselves we are only sorry we cant own in Carriers or Mills; and particularly as we know nothing of the order or condition of the Boat or machinery now in question.

The writer got back on the 11th mended and feeling well, but this hot weather has pretty much put him back where he was.

We will write you again in a day or so.

[P.S.] The Engineer and one hand are all that are on board the Ripley. The Capt is very ill.

Duncan Malloy[1] and Son to Robert F. W. Allston

Cheraw S. C. Aug 18, 1862

DEAR SIR   Your favor of 9 inst came duly to hand. We note the contents We will invest the amts due you in Cotton we think it will pay better than the Bonds we can buy good Cotton 15 to 15 1/2 cts. there is not much offering for sale. as soon as we can make the purchase will write you.

Your Rough Rice had better remain at Florence. We are too high up to sell that article. There is none planted in this section and purchasers always buy the clean. When your casks arrive we will do the best we can with it.

P.S.   There is now no yarn to be had, it is worth at the Factory 3 1/2 to 4 pr [illegible] Tobacco is also scarce a common article is worth 1 to 1.25 p lb.

Alexander McKenzie to Robert F. W. Allston

Florence Sept 1st 1862

DEAR SIR   Your two favours of 27th and 28 Ultmo I recd Yesterday I regret I cannot get either Empty Bags or Barrels for the Rough Rice they are not to be had here I have wrote Messrs Robertson Blacklock and Co to send the bags back that went down some days since as soon as recd I will send them down to the Flat there is no chance to store Rice here the Ware House is full of Government Stores if you wish it stored out of the City of Charleston Cheraw will be the best place to send it the flat that is on the way up I will send directions to go on up unless you conclude to ship to the City if the Rice was pounded it will be in a worse condition than in the Rough there is no chance to get Bbls to put it in

---

[1] Malloy (1803–77), a native of North Carolina, had been a merchant and cotton buyer in Cheraw since 1835.

All the Rice delivered from Flats have been forwarded to Charleston 37 casks of the last lot was shipped on the 23th Augt 3 casks damaged will be sent to Kingstree by next train I closed your acct and sent Mess R[obertson] B[lacklock] and Co Charleston the balance due you You will please make arrangements to meet it in a short time I will pay the amt drawn for $200 when presented.

There is a Mill pounding at Wilmington I will write down there and assertain if I can sell the rough rice to them and at what price and let you know their offer.

Duncan Malloy and Son to Robert F. W. Allston

Cheraw So C. September 1, 1862

DEAR SIR Your Flat arrived last Tuesday evening, delivered to us 34 Casks Rice and about 360 w in a Cask after upsetting it. It appears to be a prime article we are asking 5 1/2 cts for it. Our advices from Charleston say it is worth 4 3/4 to 5 there, we will make Sale as soon as we can. We told the Skipper of your Flat to send the Rough Rice to Florence, as we think that the best place for it. We have also written to Capt. McKensie on the subject. Your Flat left Thursday afternoon.

Robertson, Blacklock and Company to Robert F. W. Allston

Charleston Sept 9th 1862

DEAR SIR Your favour of 3 inst came duly to hand. The Ro[ugh] Rice (407 Bags) has been sent to Mill and Sam on Saturday finished separating the damaged from the sound and we have sent 370 empty Bags to Mr McKensie Florence, the remainder Sam said were much damaged and he would take them to Salters and mend them.

We have sold on your account

16 1/2 Barrels Rice	JWI. a B	@	$4 5/8
17	Do	JBA	@ $4 1/2
1	Do	" ⊕	@ $4 1/2
1	Do	" SG	@ $4 1/4
4	Do	RHN w	@ $4 1/2
7	Do	BED	@ $4 1/2
2	Do	JBA ^	@ $4 1/2
1/2	Do	JBA damaged	@ $1
2	Do	JRS	@ $4 1/2

50 2/2 Barrels. As soon as we can get the Sales made we will forward them.

We have received a letter from J. Blyth Allston requesting us to send Frank to the Plantation. He will leave by to days train for Kingstree. Capt Allston had received a Telegram from your Son Col Benj Allston by whose order Frank is to be sent home instead of the West. Our Mr. Robertson has not yet returned to the City.

Alexander Robertson to Robert F. W. Allston

Charleston Oct. 14, 1862

DEAR GOVENOR.   I wrote you the other day by Jo Blyth hurriedly who was just going your way, I now beg to do so again. I have been trying to get such information as well [as] I could touching the welfare of our dear old City. I am truly sorry I have no good to report but on the contrary those high in authority seem to think our City is destined to be attacked, and seriously injured. They advise the removal of all negroes on navigable streams, clear beyond the reach of Gun Boats and their crews, and I have written to my friends advising them to make arrangements for the early removal of theirs and of their families also. Charleston and Georgetown Districts will no doubt be robbed of all their negroes that are not sent away beyond the reach of the enemy. The whole coast from Port Royal will likely be in their possession this fall and winter.

I hope therefore you have made your arrangements to purchase a place to take your negroes to. I will pilot you along for a year and a day, by when we can look about and see what is to be done. I hope to be your way by the end of the month to counsel and advise with my friends, and should you fall in with any of them who may be wanting to know what to do, please say to them I advise one and all to get out the way as soon as they can with their families and negroes.

Enclosed I hand you a/c Sales of 35 who[le] and 2 hlf Barrels Rice.[1] (all received to date for you) Showing net pro[ceeds] $802.93 at your credit, and hope will prove satisfactory. The market is very dull again no demand except for the retail trade. . . . .

Duncan Malloy to Robert F. W. Allston

Cheraw So C Nov. 6 1862

DEAR SIR.   Your people 24 in number arrived last night on the Cars. There are no wagons to day to take them up. We have sent [illegible] to Steer pen after the Ox Cart, and will forward them by that means if a wagon cannot be obtained.

Mr J. C. Yates was here yesterday we advanced him $1200 to purchase Mules etc for you. If you have any gear for ploughs, and also [illegible] Iron for repairing, you had better send up as Yates says he will need them. Yates

[1] Omitted.

has bot for you 100 bus [illegible] Oats. We have paid the negros R R fare from Florence $15.00.

Duncan Malloy and Son to Robert F. W. Allston

Cheraw So Ca Jany 1, 1863

DEAR SIR Mr J. C. Yates was here on Saturday last. We advanced him ($600) Six Hundred Dollars to pay for provisions etc purchased by him. Mr Yates has hired Duncan Barrentine to attend to your plantation he requested us to write you, he gives him $400 and furnishes him with a Cow. Barrentine is a sober prudent man and will take good care of your people, he passed up with his family yesterday on his way to your place. he is the man we recommended to you, we hope he will do well. You had better write him occasionally.

Duncan Malloy and Son to Robert F. W. Allston

Cheraw, So Ca Jany 6th 1863

DEAR SIR Your favor of 1st inst with Richard, your Blacksmith, and nine others (Eleven in all) arrived this morning. We will send all up to day on foot except one to take charge of their things, the wagon will be down tomorrow for their Baggage. We wrote you that Mr Yates had hired Duncan Barrentine as overseer. Your Blacksmith has only a few hand tools with him We think a [illegible] can be rented here for a short time until yours can be got up so as to have your Ploughs gotten ready. There is not such an article here as a grindstone. We have been told there are some in George Town. You can get there and send up. We will extend your instructions in regard to the wheat.

We will write Barrentine to come down tomorrow and see about the Ship, perhaps he may engage one.

A. O. DeRosset to Robertson and Blacklock[1]

Charleston 13th. March 1863.

GENTLEMEN,   Referring to the conversation with your Mr. Robertson to day I propose on behalf of my House at Wilmington N C (DeRosset Brown and Co) to purchase 300 Casks of Govr. Allston's Rice to be of good merchantable quality at $11.50 pr 100 lb. net deliver'd in prime shipping order at the Warehouse of the Wilmington and Manchester Rail Road at Pee Dee Bridge, each Cask to be plainly marked "Capt T D Hogg, Charlotte N C" and a Rail Rd. receipt sent to us at Wilmington. On receipt of which with a bill, the money will be remitted to you.

It is understood that the delivery is to be made with as much dispatch as possible, but should it be prevented by the interference of the enemy or by any unavoidable accident, the Seller is not to be bound and should the de-

1 Copy.

livery of the whole or any portion be delayed later than the end of April[1] proxo. it shall be at our option whether to receive it or not.

It is further understood that the Rice may be weighed at the Mill, or at the Warehouse at Pee Dee Bridge; if the latter it will be done by a public weigher to be sent from Wilmington at the joint expense of buyer and Seller and in any case notice is to be given us at Wilmington of the arrival of each parcel at the Bridge that we may attend to its delivery.

Robertson, Blacklock and Company to Robert F. W. Allston

Charleston 9th. May 1863.

DEAR SIR   Your favor of 5th inst is just received. We have notified DeRosset Brown and Co and Geo Hooper that their Rice had been sent forward. The latter had paid the Express Co the freight on the $5600 which they have refunded. We will notify Mr Hooper that the price of the Rice delivered at Fair Bluff will be $75 pr Bbl. We bought for the Estate of R S Izard in Jany. 1862 3 large Pots @ $25 each. No Pans have been furnished that we can find on our Books.

The Negro Brass was sold for $1700 pr a/c Sales enclosed,[1] Nett Proceeds $1648 at your credit

Mr Porcher has a list of Capt J Blyth Allstons Negroes (65) to be sold and has written him to send them down. We have ordered 2000 yds Osnaburgs to be purchased for you in Augusta and will forward same to Kingstree as soon as received. 400 Bags of your son's Ro[ugh] Rice has come to hand and we will return the Bags to Sam at Salters T[urn] O[ut].

Our A[lexander] R[obertson] has gone to Buncombe to bring home his daughters.

Robertson, Blacklock and Company to Robert F. W. Allston

Charleston 31st. August 1863.

DEAR SIR   Your favour of 21st. inst Came duly to hand. We sent for Mr Hicks and left messages for him to call on us, but he has not done so, and we must send again. Every thing is in great Confusion. Your carriage was sent to Cheraw some time since and last Saturday Nelson and Sam have taken a Car load of your Furniture to Society Hill by direction of Mrs Allston. We have sent 3 gls Castor Oil to Salters T[urn] O[ut] for yourself and son. We delivered your letter to Mr. Tunno[2] and he promised to write. On Saturday he informed us he had not written but would take your Rice delivered at Pee Dee Bridge at $72.50 pr Barrel to be of 600 lbs. Nett at the Cart. He also said you could arrange with Capt. Wigg at Georgetown for delivery of Rice at any Depot. He promised to send an Agent to Pee Dee Bridge and

---

[1] Omitted. On the circumstances leading to the sale of Brass see above, p. 194.

[2] Captain William M. Tunno, Confederate purchasing agent.

says Government has a Store house there. We have received a letter from Mr. Gilchrist dated 24th inst. He writes he had delivered to the Express Agent $2,400 in your account, but we have not yet received it. We have sent to the Express office to enquire about it.

Robertson, Blacklock and Company to Robert F. W. Allston

Charleston Octor 19, 1863.

DEAR SIR We beg to hand you annexed a/c Sales of 25 Barrels Rice received Pr N[orth] E[astern] Rail Way,[1] which we closed up to day, after giving it every trial to do better. Nett proceeds at your credit $1585.85, and trust will prove all right and satisfactory the quality was poor, and had been beat out some time.

We have made arrangements for Mr. Moody to go to Columbia and post up the books, which has not been done for nearly 4 months. The writer will remain here to answer all and any calls that may be made on us.

The city is sadly neglected and deserted. Most business men are away, and most of the Goods have been sent away. Living is very hard. Common wood is worth $40 a Cord, and every thing in proportion.

We understand that the Government is buying Rice at the Mills in your neighborhood at $15 cash, ie the ready money down, or checks on Charleston. The latter are very much preferable. In the present confusion, we think it advisable to sell on the Spot, to sending here. We wrote to Mr. DeRossett on 17th. and hope soon to advise a settlement with him.

We live in daily expectation of the "Swamp Angel."[2]

Robertson, Blacklock and Company to Robert F. W. Allston

Charleston Nover 6, 1863.

DEAR SIR We have reced your favor of 2nd. Contents noted; no one receives payment for good Bonds in these days, as investments cannot well be had. We hope the sale of 500 Barrels Rice to Government was agreed upon to be delivered at Mill; if on the River any where, there will be deductions and squabblings. This is our experience. But Sales at Mill for cash on delivery lead to plain dealing and pleasantness. Therefore we advise you not to deviate from the good old usage of Cash on delivery. Cotton Bonds sell at 150 and cannot be got for less.

We beg to enclose you a.c Sales[3] of 3 Barrels Rice reced on 26th. ulto, and the 85 sold Mr. Tunno. This is all to date. We will take your instructions to Mr. Moody, but it will be some time yet before he can get the Books up. He will be here to night, to relieve the writer for a week or 10 days, who

[1] Omitted.

[2] A Federal gun used in the bombardment of Charleston.

[3] Omitted.

is on his way to Buncombe to move his family to Columbia for the winter. He had intended remaining here and leaving them there, but the times seem to have made them so unhappy that he will place them nearer to him. God grant us some peace in this unhappy war. The writer will be absent as short a time as possible

Everything is quiet to day, nothing new.

Robertson, Blacklock and Company to Robert F. W. Allston

Charleston Jany 21 1864

DEAR SIR   We received your favor of 18th. We return you Risleys Mortgage. Please have your signature to the satisfaction proved, and send us back same, [that] it may be entered on the Record.

We enclose you statement showing the settlement of his Bonds,[1] say $2344.80 on your Sons A/c and $2245.80 on your nephews, and hope will prove satisfactory, as the parties used the money on their debts.

The Bombardment of the City is continued with unabated violence. All day yesterday and last night the Enemy shelled the lower portion i.e. East Bay and the Battery and from S[outh] Bay to Tradd St.

We have not been informed of any damage done your House lately. There is however great risk in leaving your Negroes there. They may be seriously hurt at any moment. We would therefore advise you to send for them and leave the House to take its chance along with others.

Hiring out Negroes (and particularly to Government) is a Business we have been obliged to give up and write our customers we could not attend to for want of time and means. We have no Clerks, and the writer has his hands full all the time and cannot well attend to negroes when abused, which is always happening, or he would take pleasure in hiring out yours.

Nothing special to day; all sorts of rumors and rumors upon rumors, adding to the cares and anxieties of the times; verily we are in a bad fix in this place, which must be pretty much destroyed if this violent and furious Bombardment is kept up, and no question but what it will.

P.S.   D[ea]r. Govr. I have directed your handsome Gas Chandeliers to be taken down. I will have them cared for somewhere the best I can.

Alexander Robertson to Adele Petigru Allston

Charleston April 13, 1864

DEAR MRS. ALLSTON   Major Vander Horst handed me your note to day. I had been truly grieved to learn your sad affliction, and I sympathise most deeply with you, and your family.[2] Truly we are surrounded with sorrow and trouble. Turn which way we will, we meet it, and it seems as if our fair

---

[1] Missing.

[2] The reference is to the death of Robert F. W. Allston on April 7.

Land is doomed to grievous sufferings. We have the consolation of knowing, however, that the hand of God is over us, and his Will not ours be done.

The sad accounts of the loss of the Juno and all her officers will afflict your poor Sister and Uncle Phil, beyond bearing up with the latter. Phil was a brave and generous fellow, admired and beloved by all his Brother officers.[1] Commo. Tucker seems more disturbed at his loss if possible than his own Sons. Poor fellow I thought his heart would break when he exclaimed "how sad" and then poor Mrs Odenheimer; he was the Son of Bishop Odenheimer, and married Miss Ball. They have one infant, I am told. You will no doubt see the particulars in the morning papers of this sad shipwreck.

And then our friend Dan Huger lost his 3rd Son to day in Sumpter, G Proctor Huger, about 18, he was killed by a shell. This is the 3rd in 1 year. But let us turn from scenes of such sorrowful and distressing cares.

It may be well for you to leave matters in charge of Mr Belflowers till we can learn what our duties are, which can only be thro the Will, if anything is done before that is proved we may do wrong; therefore if you should desire to return to your place of residence, dont hesitate to do so, and in the meantime to let me know what money you will require for the family etc, and I will anticipate promptly. When I can hear from Mr Lesesne, we will determine what can be done and let you know.

Robertson, Blacklock and Company to Adele Petigru Allston

Charleston Decer 7, 1864

DEAR MADAM   We beg to acknowledge the receipt of your favor of 3 inst.

As regards Captn Tunnos circular to Rice Planters, as we understand it: The application is made, merely in a formal manner, and it is therefore well that you replied in the way you did. We will deliver to him your instructions to send for the Governments Share at once, as you cannot be responsible for it. But we fear he will not bide our bidding, and will take his own time according to the convenience of the Government.[2]

Do pray dont give yourself any uneasiness about the interest on the Debts. The bulk of which will not be wanted while the War lasts, therefore the 4000 bus of Ro[ugh] Rice at $4; with money at Credit, and interest to be received, will certainly cover all the ground, and leave the family a surplus for Expences.

The loss of a pair of Carriage horses is truly a great misfortune at any time and particularly in times like these. There is no such thing on Sale in this place, the Government having pressed all they could, for its own uses. Verily we have fallen on hard times, and God only knows what the result will be.

[1] The Confederate armed steamer "Juno" foundered while running the blockade to Nassau. Lieutenant Philip Porcher was in command.

[2] See above, p. 203.

We will have the Cards and Candles purchased for you, and shipped, but the risk of your getting them safely, is very great. We have for a long time given up the execution of Orders in consequence of the frequent losses and constant quarelling with Express men and Rail Road Conductors and agents, independent of not having the means of purchasing and shipping, having only Mr Moody with the writer to carry on our indoor matters. We are here, we hope for the winter, at all events, if not for ever and a day, tho we apprehend Genl Sherman may not consult us as to our whereabouts, and are anxiously biding his movements.

The writer left his family last week all well, but anxious about Deserters, who are very naughty in the mountains, and had committed several depredations about Flat Rock, and threatened to shoot good old Doctor Hanckel and his wife, without provocation. It makes us anxious. But we must trust in an all good and all wise Providence, and hope for better times. The Seaboard is much neglected and exposed, and our dear old City presents a sad picture of ruin and desolation; we are sorry to say your house seems to have been badly damaged, tho we did not go into it. Please bear in mind your Chandeliers are at Mr John Rutledges house in Calhoun Street, where we had them sent, as we thought to be safe against the Shells, but there is no saying how soon the four mile house may be shelled out when the 7 mile gun is erected, which it is said the Enemy is about putting in place on Morris Island, we do not however beleive much in it.

Robertson, Blacklock and Company to Adele Petigru Allston

Charleston Jany 19 1865

DEAR MADAM We received yesterday your favor of 16th. The annual interest due on the Bonds held for Mrs Fraser and Mrs Roose cannot be paid. We have no authority to receive it ie $2435.37. The parties being in Scotland cannot use it, and we have in hand already for them more than we are willing to be responsible for, when the war is over.

The total annual interest on the Bond Debt is $13,815.03 falling due between this time and August next, as per annexed list. They will all receive their interest money no doubt, and be glad to get it, except those in Scotland, and we have no doubt that even they would be most happy to get theirs if they could. We have written to Mrs S E Alston Exex of T P Alston informing her we were ready to pay her $2030 due 1 inst. We have paid Miss Ann J Gadsden, Mrs Lowndes and The Este Col Ward, but we cant do any thing with the others till they fall due. We have credited the Este with 2 years interest due 1st by Jos B Allston $3500 on his Debt. We will pay your order to W Bull Pringle $2700 when presented. Then as regards the $5000 for School Expences of your Daughter Jane; we presume it will be payable quarterly in advance ie $1250, and you can draw on us accordingly. Mr Mouzon remitted us $3280.88 on account of The Este on 7 Novr last, which we acknowledged same day. Mr Tunno cannot do any thing with the Rice just now. We have not yet seen any thing of Blacksmith Sam.

We are making arrangements to leave the City in a few days, in search of some place to open our Business; we will go along with the Banks and Treasury Office. Every thing is topsy turvy. Little or no Business doing. The idea seems to be to defend the City to the last, and if we have to give it up, to hand it over in Ruins; we are truly in Sad times, not knowing which way to turn.[1]

Edward N. Thurston[2] to Benjamin Allston

Charleston March 6th 1866

DEAR BEN   I wrote you a few days ago, since when little of interest has occured here. The enquiry for Rice has improved somewhat, but I have not yet succeeded in selling the remaining 19 Barrels R F W A at the price which the 39 Barrels of the same parcel brought, the quantity of Rough in it is the objection. Nor have I been able to sell the Seed Rice yet, the quality is good, but not what would have been called extra prior to the War, and unfortunately there is another parcel here, the remnant of 9000 Bushels, which is superior to it, all of which, with the exception of a few hundred Bushels still on hand, brought $5. I have been offered $4 for yours but of course as you named $5 as the price at which you are willing to have it sold, I declined taking any less. As the Season is getting advanced, the fact of its being in the Country operates against its Sale, and it would be advantageous to have it here. The Party who offered for it this morning made that an objection.

I am much pleased to hear that the Negroes in your Section of Country show a better disposition. Some of them I hear are working very well now. No late news from Washington of consequence, I think Gen Howard seems to be somewhat innoculated with the everlasting Nigger. I dont remember if or not I asked in my last what you wanted done with 2 Bags of Wool received by the Boat from Georgetown. I have no instructions about them.

[1] The firm of Robertson, Blacklock and Company does not appear to have survived the war. In making his will in 1866, Robertson wrote: "Whereas the late war having left my estate in a complicated and, I fear, ruinous condition, and I cannot provide for my dear and dutiful daughters in that manner it would be my desire to do . . . . I therefore . . . . give, will, and bequeath to my said daughters . . . . all and whatever may remain after the payment of my said debts." The will was probated in 1889. The death of John Freer Blacklock was announced in the *News and Courier*, July 4, 1885.

[2] Edward N. Thurston was employed in some capacity by Robertson, Blacklock and Company as early as 1858. He may have been the son of the Robert Thurston who entered the firm in 1838 when it was known as Lewis and Robertson.

Edward N. Thurston to Benjamin Allston

Charleston March 10th 1866

DEAR SIR   I beg leave to acknowledge the receipt of your favor of 3d inst, and to advise that the Steamer Pilot Boy delivered this morning 46 Barrels Rice on account of the Estate R F W Allston from Waverly Mill. I have sold the 2 Barrels S G @ 8 1/2¢ but the quality of the 44 Barrels Chicora being very handsome I have stored same in hopes of doing better next week. Even in this parcel there are some grains of Rough remaining, could these have been removed the appearance of the Sample would have been much improved. I have succeeded in closing up the 58 Barrels R F W A previously received @ 11 1/2¢ which will I hope be satisfactory. The A/C Sales cannot be made out until Monday, when I will hand you a Copy of them as desired.

By the return of the Pilot Boy I have sent you to be landed at Waverly Mill 1 Barrel Prime Pork @ $30 (No Mess Pork here at present) and 1 Package to be landed in Georgetown which was received by Express and which is directed to "E S Allston Esq" to your care at Georgetown, and by direction of Hon H D Lesesne for the Est R F W Allston also to be landed at Waverly 280 Bags (in 2 Bundles) for the Seed Rice each bag is expected to hold 2 1/2 Bus, please have them well sewed up, as the season is getting advanced, it will be better to have this Rice here, in fact its being in the Country caused in two instances the purchasers to give a preference to other Rice.

I enclose the Receipt from Messrs J E Adger and Co for the Articles shipped by them on the 6th ulto which I hope you have received ere now.

Edward N. Thurston to Benjamin Allston

Charleston March 20th 1866

DEAR BEN   I have your letters of 12th and 17th insts, they reached me this morning together.

I'll do what I can in the matter of the $116, and expect that I can arrange it for you, so that need not trouble you any more. I can send your Friend a check on N York, or any other way that suits you.

I have not been able to close up the parcel Chicora yet quality handsome, but at present there is no demand, I have not an offer for it yet, the tumble in Gold has affected all produce, I hope this wont last long though.

The wool Mr Lesesne told me he would see your Mother and give me instructions about (after I wrote you) he thinks she wants it sent to New York.

I'll look into the "Stone" matter for you, but dont believe that Trescott is here, I have not seen him for a month, but will think over the matter and write you more particularly.

I am unusually busy to day and will write you a fuller letter next time.

Dr Forster has requested me to get a new Bond from you in place of the $10,000 one to Mrs Withers, which was burnt. Of course there can be no objection to it, tell me when you write how the Bond was secured, was it by a Mortgage of Guendalos or how.

[P.S.] Adger has exhanged the Hoes and sent them back by this Boat Say 2 Doz. difference in cost $10.

I shall look for the Seed Rice, by next trip, the remainder would have been sold if it had been here yesterday.

Benjamin Allston to Edward N. Thurston[1]

March 24 [18]66

Guendalos was not mortgaged for negroes, they were themselves mortgaged. I will not renew the bond at present. The State has passed an Act to meet such cases entitled "an act to provide a mode to perpetuate testimoney in relation to deeds, wills, and other papers lost or destroyed during the war." To renew the Bond I would consider a virtual concession of the point that these debts (negro) are to be paid in full, which I do not entend to concede. I will pay any interest that may be due up to the actual manumission of the negroes here, but not one cent of interest beyond this, until the matter is sifted by the courts and they decide whether such debts can be lawfully and equitably collected. I hold that the Bond and mortgage held by the vender is a sub or secondary title, so to speak, and must fall like the primary title to ownership falls, by the action of the Government. Now to execute a new Bond, would be simply to acknowledge that tho' my right of title and property in these negroes had fallen to the ground that the titles and proprietorship of those from whom I bought (and which from being the first became the secondary ones) are still good and that I am still bound in equity to pay as if I still owned the negroes or as if they had been lost by death or running away. None of the contingencies to which all looked and estimated for and against deprived me of the negroes, but the Government, under whose auspices they were held and sold etc has itself done away with all right in them. I would have no objection to renewing the bond except for the above reasons which seem to me sound and just. If the bond could be made so as to avoid the objections I urge then all right, that is to say, if it could be made so that I should by the renewal not commit myself to a violation of what I believe to be right, the non-payment of any further debt for negroes, I would renew it, but then of what value would it be?[2]

Thurston and Holmes to Benjamin Allston

Charleston April 23d 1866

DEAR SIR We beg leave to acknowledge the receipt of your favor of 16th inst. The Books of Robertson Blacklock and Co were burnt in Columbia last

---

[1] Copy.

[2] In a decree filed by Chancellor William D. Johnson, on December 18, 1866, in the case of *Calhoun* v. *Calhoun* mortgages of Negroes were held to be valid despite emancipation.

Spring by Gen Sherman, thus the Writer has no data from which to procure the information you desire as to the income and expenditures of the Est R F W. Allston and your plantation. The Balance Sheet, which was saved, of October 20th 1864 hows a balance of $4,939.19 at Cr of Est R. F. W. Allston, and of $7,153.84 at your own Debit.

As you desired we have written Col Jos Blyth Allston with a copy of the Entry, in R[obertson] and B[lacklock]'s Bond Book, of your Bond to the late Mrs S P Withers.

Your instructions, to hold your own and Mr Belflowers Rice for an improvement in the Market, are duly noted, we are very sorry to hear of his severe indisposition, and hope he will soon be out again. The Bill which Paul and Co have against you shall be paid when presented. The demand for Rice having improved somewhat we have sold R F W A 78 Barrels from Waverly Mill @ 12¢. The Storage and Insurance having nearly run out, we thought it best to take advantage of this offer and thus save those expenses the prices obtained being a 1/2¢ advance, over those which could have been obtained, when the Rice was landed, as soon as the question about the Toll can be arranged we will make up the A/c Sales.

P.S.   The Balance at Cr of Est R F W Allston on Oct 20th 1864 was reduced by Feb 13th 1865 to $1,388.91 at Cr. and that at your Debit was increased by then to $8,682.68, at Debit.

Edward N. Thurston to Benjamin Allston

Charleston April 23d 1866

DEAR BEN   I received your note of blank date by last trip of the Boat, there seems to be no use in writing, other than by the Boat, as Letters by the regular Mail tarry indefinitely on the route. I have seen Trescot, who seems to know more about the matter of Taxes than any one else, he says that he would not pay the U S Direct Tax, for the reason that there has been already collected from South Carolina more than her quota, that the only danger incurred is that you may be charged interest at the rate of 10 per Cent, as Mr McCullough the Secretary of the Treasury has issued an order prohibiting the Sale of any more property in this State for Taxes, and he, Trescot, believes that the money in excess will be refunded to the State, he seems very positive in the expression of the opinion that the Tax referred to should not be paid, and if I had property now subject to this Tax I would abide by it, but he may be wrong and it may be the best thing to pay up, only it seems to me that I would risk paying 10% additional in an effort to save the whole. I am very sorry that I cannot give you better information in the matter of the Income etc but you know all of our Books and Papers which could throw light upon the subject have been burnt, and like yourself I was many miles from here during 1864. I doubt very much if the Property paid expenses during that year, the Currency was almost valueless, and articles to be purchased enormously high. Nothing new here. Rice brisked up on Friday on account of a speculative demand, but is now quiet again.

[P.S.] I am really sorry and disappointed at not being able to leave here, but it would be wrong for me to go at present and so stay I must.

Edward N. Thurston to Benjamin Allston

Charleston April 30th 1866

My DEAR BEN Yours of 25th inst only reached me on Friday. I am extremely sorry to hear of the death of Mr Belflowers, and quite concerned about the little parcel of Rice sent down from Waverly Mill in his name. In accordance with your request I have stored same, but how I can make out the A/c Sales in your name puzzles me, unless you get Mr Tilton to write us a letter stating that the Rice was yours, and should have been shipped in your name, if there was an error at the Mill it can be corrected in that way, but if not, you will have to get an order from the Executor or Administrator to us to turn the Rice over, then we will be glad to make out A/c Sales in your name, this is the only way in which it can be done legally, I am sorry to put you to this inconvenience but in no other way can T[hurston] and H[olmes] get clear of their responsibilities in the matter and keep their Books straight. Of course it is needless for me to assure you that we believe implicitly the Statement of your part in the matter, the bare suspicion of there ever being a misunderstanding on your part has never crossed my mind, but we are obliged to do what is legal, and though you are inconvenienced, I am sure that you will on reflection, see that this is right.

It is nearly 10 P.M. and I am fairly tired out to day. Holmes is absent which gives me a good deal to do extra.

I shall be glad to see you, though Sincerely sorry for the cause which brings you. Mrs Allston's health will I trust be benefited by the change.

John Izard Middleton[1] to Benjamin Allston

Baltimore October 20th 1866

DEAR BEN Yrs 16th Inst has just been read, and I hasten to reply. You have been frank with me, and I will be equally so with you. In N. Y. you cannot get corn [MS torn] facility of getting freight, and regularity of communication, this is the best market for you, not excepting Norfolk or N. C.

Present prices are too high for you, viz, $1.12 for Prime Yellow and $1.25 Prime White, but next month the new Crop comes in, and prices will be ab't the same as last year, unless the demand is greater than we expect, owing to the scarcity in Europe and the South. Last year, 67¢ per *56 lbs* for White

---

[1] Son of John Izard Middleton, of Crowfield plantation. After service in the Confederate Army he resided in Baltimore, Md.

(it is always sold here by weight) was the lowest price paid, and that was late in Feby, while rates varied from that to 95¢ on 1st June. On 21 Dec 65. White corn was at 88¢ and oats a 55¢. Oats have been as low as 40¢ (15 August [18]66) and are now @ 56¢ per 32 lbs (sold by weight). My prices are only for *Prime* articles, dry and in best shipping order.

We buy here on Change daily and buy samples corn etc are weighed by sworn weighers on delivery and the charges are

In *bulk*—Tallying 20c pr 100 Bus. Commissions 2 1/2 %

   Insurance 1 to 1 1/2 %

   [MS torn]

   Holding and sewing 1¢ per Bus. Wharfage 1/4 to 1/2¢ per Bus.

Freight to Charleston by Steamer 12 to 16¢

     " Sail 10¢ to 12¢

  Georgetown "   "   14¢

    Smallest vessel to be had for G'town *3600 Bus*

Of course, you would have advantage of the best terms on the day of purchase. But I must have funds in hand, or be authorized to draw on a first class house in Charleston for amt of Invoice, which w'ld be maild on day of completion of Cargo. Here Provisions are Cash, strictly. Sh'ld you desire monthly shipments via Charleston yr best plan w'ld be to allow me to draw within 30 days of Invoice. Freight, of course, w'ld be paid at end of voyage, and w'ld form no part of my Invoice.

Bags, if only needed as a convenience for unloading, storage, and as securing a better rate of Insurance, can be had cheaper at second hand, and good for one voyage [MS torn]. Sh'ld 60 days be required yr Factor must accept yr Drafts against shipments and interest w'ld be charged, as I have to pay from 1/2 to 3/4 % per month.

I trust this has been made sufficiently clear to you, and beg you to bear in mind that I have choice of this market, of Norfolk, and of the No Ca ports and keep myself fully advised as to all these points.

Bacon is cheaper here than any where on the coast and can always be had at Western prices with freight thence added. Its quality can always be relied on, so also with Flour etc. and I sh'ld suppose you w'ld need an assorted cargo for yr Negroes, soap, Lard, Salt etc.

So much for business. I thank you sincerely for yr kind wishes [MS torn]. Mrs Middleton and Mrs Simons (now here on a visit to Mr Gittings, who arrived yesterday from Europe) both desire me to present them most kindly to you. Tom has not yet made his appearance and my sister is now near Phila. I hope you will not allow Mrs Allston to regard me as a stranger and that you will remember me most kindly to Joe Blyth and other friends.

P.S. Yellow Corn is generally worth from 5¢ to 20¢ per Bus less than White. It is suitable for Stock and for Negroes, if the latter can be induced to eat it.

Thurston and Holmes to Benjamin Allston

Charleston December 22d 1866

DEAR SIR   Your favor of 18th inst was duly received. We regret to hear such unhappy accounts from the Crops of your section, but can assure you that the bad and unexpected result is general. The Market is at a stand from $8 @ $8 1/4, a few barrels have been sold @ $8 1/2, but the demand is very limited, we hope that the New Year will bring an improvement in prices, when the fact that the Crop is very short will be appreciated at the North, if Congress repeals the present duty of 2 1/2¢ in gold on East India Rice, the effect will be unfortunate on Carolina, at present it costs about 9 1/2¢ p lb to import East India, but we hope that this will not be done directly if at all. We have heard of no Sales under 8¢, except a few barrels sold to the retailers by an outsider, this price is equal to a Sale in the Rough @ about $2 p bushel, if the Rice makes a fair turn out.

Your order in favor of Dr Hemingway for $20 has been paid.

[P.S.]   Thanks for your letter, and the kind feeling it evinces. Hope I shall see you early next month.

About 50 Barrels of *Choice* Rice is in demand and would bring a high figure.

Thurston and Holmes to Benjamin Allston

Charleston April 29th 1867

DEAR SIR   Referring to ours of 27th inst p Steamer Emilie we now beg leave to enclose you a copy of the Estimate made by you for the funds required for the Est Hon R. F. W. Allston during the year, which we obtained this morning from Mr C Richardson Miles.

Since the letter of the 5th ulto from the Executors, we have had no instructions to pay to your orders more than the $6,200, which was to include all the sums previously paid for plantation expenses. Since Dec 13th 1866 (the date at which the funds remaining from last year were exhausted) we have paid on account of Plantation Expenses $3,585.38, and if this amount is deducted from the $6,200 which we were ordered to pay on your Drafts, there would be left but $2614.62, but we are informed that the question, which you made last March, as to whether the expenditures paid this year, but incurred during 1866, are to come out or not of this $6,200, still is unsettled, and until the residue of the crop comes to market and the Accounts are made up, we cannot answer your question as to how much of this fund remains subject to your order. Under our present instructions we are authorized to pay the balance of the $6200—viz $2614.62.

We have been called upon several times to make up the Accounts and pay over to the Master in Equity the sum to be divided among the creditors, this we cannot do until the remainder of the Crop comes to Market, and this morning we were directed to request you to ship whatever may be left of this years crop as soon as convenient, that these payments may be made without unnecessary delay.

Messrs Adger and Co's Bill has been paid as you directed. Messrs Stoll and Webb presented your Draft this morning, we told them that we believed it would be paid on maturity, and they say they will hold it, it would have given us pleasure to have accepted it, but those very "calamitous" circumstances which might occur are precisely what we fear, we know full well, that if nothing happens you will place us in funds as you promise, but we are afraid that something entirely beyond your control may occur to put it out of your power to do so, we dont think though that you will have any further trouble in this matter, only hurry down your Rice etc and put us in funds.

Messrs B P and P W Fraser's Draft in your favor for Seventy five Dollars has also been received, we regret that we are not in funds for them, but we hope to be so shortly and will therefore hold the Draft and credit you with the amount of it as soon as we are unless you direct us to return it to you.

John Izard Middleton to Benjamin Allston

Baltimore, 30 May 1867

DEAR BEN—I thank you for your very friendly and kind letter 21st May recd yesterday. It is very pleasant to know that you have not forgotten your old friends and it's a sure way of making them preserve and keep alive their interest in you. You have my best wishes, as regards yourself, your family and your planting operations. I see too that you have been trying your hand at the political bellows and addressing the African Citizens of Prince George, but I hope my friend that you will succeed better in your agricultural labours than you are likely to do with your negro audiences at Public Meetings! I am not making fun of you, for I know full well the responsibilities that have devolvd upon all gentlemen in your position and while I can't say that I envy you, I sh'ld be the last to blame you, for doing your duty. As to Whiskey, my dear fellow, you said nothing ab't quality and so I sent the cheapest; I assure you we *pride* ourselves on our *liquors*, and I advise you not to order another Bbl, unless you are prepared to pay handsomely for it!! With regard to Corn, I bear in mind your wants, and if I can send it to you, at a reasonable price, shall do so. I have to send some *probably* to other parties direct, and shall certainly do the best I can for all of you. I shall write again in a fortnight, unless I see a good opportunity, before that, being governed by your letter, and my knowledge of your wants.

Thurston and Holmes to Benjamin Allston

Charleston June 6th 1867

DEAR SIR In compliance with the request of your Mother, the writer called on her last evening on the subject of the loss which the Est Hon.

R. F. W. Allston has sustained by the sinking of the Lighter of Keithfield Mill with 2020 Bushels of Rough Rice belonging to the Estate on board.

At this interview Mrs Allston informed us that the Lessees of the Mill had promised that the Estate should suffer no loss by the unfortunate accident. The preferable plan of settlement, to avoid all question as to the amount of loss, would have been to have turned over the whole Cargo of damaged Rice to the Mill, and then for the Lessees of the Mill to have paid for the number of Bushels, just as if they had purchased it, at the market value, but this not having been done, it remains to show the actual loss suffered by the Estate, and for this purpose as the quality of this damaged parcel is stated to have been precisely similar to that of the parcel pounded at the same Mill in November last, it is safe to assume that the following statement shows correctly the loss sustained, and which should be made good to the Estate by the Lessees of the Mill. Mrs Allston directs us to say to you that she desires you to present a claim for this amount to the Lessees of the Mill, which she hopes they will at once see the propriety of. She has instructed us to be extremely particular and not claim a single cent that is not fairly the due of the Estate. She regrets the whole unfortunate occurrence much, but must protect the interests of the Estate as she is bound to do.

The point settled by Mr James R Pringle and ourselves was only as to the difference in value between the damaged Rice received here, and the same Rice if not damaged, and does not in anyway affect the claim of the Estate to be indemnified for losses actually sustained over and above that amount. Rice once thoroughly wet must pound to great disadvantage, and it may even be that some portion of the Cargo was so thoroughly injured as to be unfit for use, and these losses should not fall upon the Estate.

MISCELLANY

CONTENTS OF THE WINE ROOM AT
CHICORA WOOD PLANTATION

Number mark'd	Description	When Imported	When bottled	When finished
No 1.	1/4 Pipe = 11 4/12 Dozen Newton, Gordon, Murdock and Co's Madeira 10 yrs. old	In 1830 with Ward, Magill and Heriot— $86	May 1831	4 Bottles on floor
No 2.	1/4 Pipe Madeira—same brand and character—in closet over the Piazza	in 1831, with Ward and Magill $90	May 1832	done
No 3.	1/2 Pipe *Sercial* Madeira, same brand—*22 Dozen*	In 1833 by myself, cost and charges $200 in the wood	July 1834	74 Btl 11 Shelf B
No 4.	8 *Dozen* Madeira of various quality—all good— some superior.	In and previous to 1830 a present from *Mrs. B. Huger*		18 Bottle Shelf B
No 5.	1/8 Pipe = dozen Madeira rich N. G. M. and Co's *Reserve* 1817?	Bo't by Ward and me of A. W. Campbell the 1/4 Pipe @ *$150*	Summer 1836	31 Btles Shelf G
No 6.	1/4 Pipe = *11 dozen Tinta* Madeira N. G. M. and Co. 2 Doz in box /62	In 1835 by me $112.50	1836	68 Bottles Shelf F
No 7.	1/4 Pipe = *10 4/12 dozen Burgundy*—Madeira N. G. M and Co.	In 1835 by me $70	"	
No 8.	1/4 Pipe = *11 dozen* fine nutty Madeira N. G. M. and Scott—*Govr's Wine*	In 1837 for Govr. Butler, W. Hampton, Ward and me the Pipe $*580*	May 1838	Shelf G

No 9.   1/4 Pipe Sercial Madeira ⎫ In 1838 in the   Summer   12 Bottles
        old as reputed but I   ⎪   name of Govr.   1839   on floor
        think 'fined = 7 dozen ⎬   Butler for
        and 7   N. G. M. and   ⎪   Ward, A Robert-
        Scott   ⎭   son J H Allston
                                   and me $120

No 10. 1/8 Pipe *Golden Sherry* in ⎫ In 1838, Gourdin   29 Bottles
        Demijohns   ⎬   and Math. or-   Shelf R
                                    ⎪   der'd by A.
                                    ⎭   J. White

No 11. 1 Demijohn *old Madeira* ⎫ bottled into Hock 1840   1 Bottle
        from my good Aunt Mrs.   ⎪   bottles and   on floor
        E. F. Blyth (Brown pa-   ⎬   placed on Shelf
        per tied over the cork)   ⎭   in Wine room

No 12. 15 Gall. Demijohn Amontillardo Sherry Wine   1844
        1840 bot at J. Vaughn's sale exposed to the
        Sun in its box till bottled—the box and
        straw about the Demi-john entirely decay'd
        at bottom.

No 13. 1 Do. Do. pale Sherry ex- ⎫ 1842 McNeil and   1844   Shelf S
        posed to the Sun and   ⎪   and Blair
        weather till bottled—In   ⎬
        attic N. E. side   ⎭

No 14. 1/2 Pipe O. P. Madeira *Leacock*—1842 in   May 14th
        name of Govr. *Butler* (1/4 pipe same for Hon
        A. P. Butler) This Cask was exposed to the   1844
        weather and turn'd over every day or two
        until bottled. Cost $210.04 = 22 8/12 Doz
        Bottles (School House up in Attic)

L. 1832 Leacock Wine from Dr ⎫ 1832 3 Doz. =   In boxes
        North's Est.   ⎬ $44.50
                             ⎭
        Brown Sherry Do . . . . .   3 Doz.—$44.50   "   "

No 15. 1/2 Pipe—20 4/12 Dozen ⎫ Imported for   July 28th
        bottles of all sorts & sizes ⎪ me in 1845   1846
        V.P. Leacock's Madeira. ⎪
        In School House Attic   ⎪
        north of No 14. In Cask ⎬
        it has been 6 months ex- ⎪
        posed to Sun and weath- ⎪
        er agitated ocasionally ⎪
        and [illegible]   ⎭

1/4 Cask Golden Sherry Cork leak'd and I got from it but a few Dozen placed in Wine room on Sherry shelf	imported same time		Shelf P
Brandy Larronde 1 Qr. Cask—8 Demijohns	Decr. 1846		Basement
Claret " 10 Cases	" "		"

No. 16. "Mansanilla" 1/4 Pipe— 12 Doz } March 1847. East attic.   Apl. 1847   Shelf R

2 Doz of this wine sent to Mr. J. H. Tucker

Brandy 2 Doz. in the Basement } Selected by J. H. Tucker in 1849   Mark'd 1805——

No 17. Madeira 1/2 of a 1/2 Pipe 2 Dozen sent as present to J. D. E. } Imported from J. D. Edwards taken with J. J. Ward. East Attic S. side   1849   Shelf D

No 18. Tinta 1 Qr Cask   Do. Do. Do.   1849   "   C

No 19. Sherry 1/4 Cask "Pale Curious"—14 2/12 Dozen —$250 } 1851 G and M. E Attic N. side   1851 Septr.   Shelf Q L & M

1856
Oct 31st Wine from the sale of R M Allan's Estate
Lot   Bottles
No 2. Leacock Madeira   20 on Shelf I
No 3.   "   "   52 on Shelf H
No 4.   "   "   65 on   "   A   2 Doz box'd /62
No 6. Pale Sherry   42 "   "   O 20 bot in box /62
No 7. Borodino Sherry   48 "   "   V 27 bot in boxes "
1 Demijohn and 8 bottles of Pale Sherry Imported in 1845, on floor.

REMARKS ON THE FREE SCHOOL SYSTEM OF SOUTH CAROLINA[1]

By ROBERT F. W. ALLSTON

GENTLEMEN Permit me a word of remark on the proposed changes in the Free School System. The numerous interesting papers communicated to the Legislature in 1838 thro' Govr. Noble the frequent Annual Reports on the subject since, and the more elaborate one made in 1847 to the State Agl. Society have had the good effect to awaken public attention and to attract to the work of reform several able young men now in public life, whose zeal in a good cause may possibly induce too much change, beyond the desired reform. I would venture a caution therefore.

In the commencement of his legislative ca[reer] the writer set about acquainting himself with the system then providing for Pauperism in the State, he thought it needed reform, and with a view to framing a better, he obtain'd, at no little cost of time and labor information as to the working of other systems, North, South and East. The excitement of the public mind occasion'd soon after by the Protective Tariffs of the Federal Congress and the consequent contest with the Federal Government so absorb'd all the interest of Statesmen as to put a stop to any further attempt to effect any State reform. Before it could again be taken up, he became convinced, that, in view of the habits of living and thinking among our people in the several sections of the State differing so materially from those of the people whose laws he had consulted it was entirely out of his power to frame a better system of poor laws.

Afterwards, he applied himself to understand the operation of the Free School System, with this view, he became a commissioner of Free Schools serving as such 9 years and applied to gentlemen of other states as before to know what they were doing in this line of education. Much consideration of the best systems elsewhere under good administration, satisfied him that the basis of their success is that all the children in the State were included in them, and that if we adopt the material features of those systems, we must begin with this pervading principle, which, after several partial discussions and some experience he was induced to believe is a principle not likely to be favor'd by the spirit of the people at large. A feature common to almost all of them invests the Commissioners or Controllers of the Schools with power to collect from the tax-payers within their several precincts a certain annual contribution equal or in proportion to the sum received from the State fund. This would apply to the existing system or to any other that might be [adopted].

No one system will be applicable alike and be effective in all parts of the

[1] Undated. See above, p. 97.

State. That which will work well among the urban population of St Philips and St Michaels[1] may be strange and fruitless in Winyah. Again that which does much good among the numerous rural population of Pickens, Anderson and Fairfield, may be very meagre in its results in the more sparce districts Williamsburgh, Marlborough, Horry. The Comrs and the people are becoming familiar with the present system such as it is, and the better plan for reforming it in my judgement is, instead of substituting for it another, to graft upon it such new features year by year as shall be clearly suggested by experience. Rather than supersede the old System, let it be efficiently administer'd, and from time to time amended in such manner as to have in it nothing superfluous, nothing if possible inoperative, but everything gradually tending to usefulness in proportion as it is better understood and discreetly practised.

It will be enquired, where will you begin to amend? It would be long before the members of the Legislature would agree on this point; each one, who has thought on the subject, having his own peculiar views, and those who have not given thought to it, being for the most part indisposed to any change. Much as I have dwelt upon the proposition, and decided as is the indication of my mind, I distrust too much the lights by which I have been guided, and am too sensible of the inadequacy of the practical information before us to allow myself to urge any material amendment at this moment, beyond provision for the accountability of its administration. Previous scrutiny into the actual working of the system in its several parts is necessary to a sound decision as to its judicious amendment. Fuller enquiry is necessary to form a sound determination. Here it may be ask'd, Hasn't frequent enquiry been made? Have not you for the space of half a score of years been making enquiry? Yes, but very unsatisfactorily, because without sufficient opportunity, and without the authority of law, so indispensable for the examination of details, and to personal observations. The only enquiry, whose results will be available, reliable, efficacious, will be that of an accountable, impartial, judicious, executive officer.

Let us take the important step to provide for and empower such a functionary, and leaving to him the scrutiny, which one will perform better than many, we may confidently turn our attention to other objects of public improvement, until the period comes round when he is to account for his division of labor, by laying before the Legislature his annual report. Furnishing as it will, the intelligible results of personal observation, practical information, together with the suggestions of a mind devoted to the subject and enlarged by the experience, and judgements of other minds, in all parts of the State. This report will supply the proper answer to the question just ask'd, when shall amendment begin? and it will constitute the legitimate and certain basis of amendment.

[1] The city of Charleston.

REMARKS BY ROBERT F. W. ALLSTON
CONCERNING THE NASHVILLE CONVENTION OF 1850[1]

The Nashville Convention I regarded with some hope as a means of saving the Union under the Constitution & reforming the Federal Government. I enter'd with alacrity, and earnestness, into its organization because also it was the obvious & most efficient way in which a conference could be held amongst the Southern States; and that unity & harmony in their several councils obtain'd without which the labors and the perils and the sacrifices of any *one* would be in vain.

I believed that the result of the deliberations of that Convention composed as I fondly trusted it would be, of delegates, wise men & true, from all the States having a common interest to protect & a common grievance to redress, and as it was in fact, of delegates from nine of those States, would have open'd the eyes of the majorities in Congress as to the extent & force of the injury which we had realized & now anticipated from their prepared Legislation, of the imminent dangers & peril into which they were madly urging their prosperous & beautiful country.

I yielded not to the self-deception of supposing that the Masses in the Northern States would be enlighten'd by its (congress') certified [?] conclusion or its deliberations. I was too sensibly aware of the selfish and interested views of the Northern press, a gigantic and all pervading Power, which is wielded with a few honorable exceptions, too exclusively for the personal advancement and the interest, political and pecuniary, of its proprietors, Editors & Agents. No sound of alarm & caution was given to its readers of the universal agitation of the Southern Mind, or of the waking indignation of your generous & confiding public.

No reprimand nor even gentle rebuke was adventured towards the designing and wicked policy of perverse or ambitious & reckless politicians of their own parties. No patriotic warning was offer'd and reiterated as to the tendency of such policy. But a plodding or a refined lust of gain was bow'd to, and subserved—a taste for the marvellous, the licentious, the excitement of inventive fiction was cater'd for by the managers of a venal press, faithless to the other, higher purposes which should actuate them. If the Southern Convention was mention'd at all, it was only to be condemn'd in advance, and prejudiced in the estimation of their public and every man who had the courage to appear at Nashville in June went there under a public protest founded on the bitter denunciations, the unmanly misrepresentations & ridicule of that press. No. I had no expectation of the Northern Masses being enlighten'd as to our true sentiments & growing alienation, except thro' the independent & just influence of their representatives in Congress.

[1] The manuscript furnishes no clue as to the occasion on which these remarks were made. See above, p. 102.

I confess I did expect to witness some effect produced upon the minds and the official action of members of Congress by the reasonable suggestions and firm conclusions of so grave and respectful a body as the Nashville Convention. And I cannot now persuade myself otherwise than to believe that this expectation fail'd of being realized only, in consequence of the opposition of Southern representatives, and chiefly that of a citizen of Kentucky, a native of Virginia, a Senator from a State lying South of the Ohio. I have reason to think that but for this opposition, a portion of the Pennsylvania Delegation would have sustain'd the line *36 30* besides some few other delegates. But with one Senator from Missouri bitterly hostile to the Convention, with 6 Southern Members urging upon the Senate a compromise (falsely so call'd) from which they profess'd to expect every satisfaction, how could the most liberal-minded & yielding Senator from Pennsylvania (Sturgeon) or New York (Dickinson), or Michigan (Cass) or Illinois (Douglas) take ground in favor of the line we proposed.

In the lower House the members for the same and other reasons dared not show it any favor. The masses upon whom they are dependent for political preferment, had been excited in times past on the subject of Southern Slavery by designing politicians for their own selfish purposes. Fanaticism had avail'd itself of this excitement, together with the ignorance which prevail'd as to the true condition of the South, and had fan'd it into a flame of consuming fire. They dared not meet the blaze of indignation which would have been kindled at home, had they exhibited any favor towards the "impudent exactions of the Slave holder!"

PROCLAMATION BY GOVERNOR ROBERT F. W. ALLSTON INVITING TEACHERS AND SCHOOL COMMISSIONERS OF SOUTH CAROLINA TO VISIT THE NORMAL SCHOOL IN CHARLESTON, APRIL 2, 1858

State of South Carolina   Executive Department

Whereas the last General Assembly of So. Ca., with a wise forecast, and a liberal regard to the public welfare, based as it is so essentially on the good sense and virtue of her citizens, enacted a law by which the Commissioners of Free Schools are authorized to establish a Normal School in the City of Charleston to which the Country districts will be entitled to send a certain number of pupils.

And whereas the enterprising Board of St Phillips and St Michaels, have now in operation at their excellent public school in the City, weekly exercises, which will serve to exemplify the benefits of such an establishment.

Now therefore I recommend to the several Boards of Commissioners of Free Schools in the State to appoint at their next quarterly meeting on the 4th Monday in April, and depute one or more of their number to visit the said public school (St Phillip's Street) in Charleston, at their convenience, so as to be able to report the result of their observations to the quarterly meeting on the 4th Monday of October next.

Also I do hereby invite all the Teachers of Free Schools, scholars throughout the State to come and see for themselves how the said public school is conducted, and what are the uses of a Normal School.

As the expenses of such a visit might put it out of the power of many to come, however much they may desire it, I will venture to say for the good citizens of Charleston that the houses of many residents will be opened to any Teacher who shall be provided with a letter of introduction, or with the certificate of the President and Secretary of the Board of Commissioners at home.

Failing this, it affords me pleasure to announce that Mrs. Kennedy of the American Hotel on King Street will, on account of this Department, take care of any Teacher of a Free School who will deposit with her, his or her certificate from the President and Secretary of the District Board of Commissioners for which he or she may be employed, from the 1st of June to the 5th inclusive.

Furthermore upon exhibiting the said certificates to the Agents of the Rail Road or other public conveyance by means of which they reach the city, I appeal to the proper authorities to instruct their agents to pass all such Teachers of Free Schools and one Commissioner from each Board, going down for the purpose herein set forth, one fare going and returning.

I am assured that the Commissioners of Free Schools of St Phillips and St Michaels will take pleasure in affording every facility to the Teachers and others to observe and profit by their improved methods. Visitors will only have to apply to C. G. Memminger Esqr. Chairman, or to any member of the Board, at the Public school house in St Phillip's Street, to be admitted at the proper hours.

A fixed time has been mentioned, viz, from 1st to the 5th of June. Better for all parties, if it be at all convenient, to adopt this appointment. But if there be any impediment to prevent any Teachers from coming at that time, the commissioners will receive them at any other time in May or June, including Saturday as one of the days.

Given under my hand and the seal of the State at Chicora near Georgetown, this second day of April in the year of our Lord one thousand eight hundred and fifty eight, and in the eighty second year of American Independence.

DESCRIPTION OF GUENDALOS PLANTATION, 1858[1]

Guendalos Island is Bounded on the *East* by Waccamaw River, *North* by Wando Passo, Long Creek and Lands of Governor Allston, *South* by Squirrell

[1] Copy of a newspaper advertisement. See above, p. 151.

Creek, Bullens Lake, and Lands of Mrs Nathaniel Barnwell, *West* by Pedee River.

Boundary of Main Land

East by Pedee River, *North* by lands of Gov Allston and Chapel Creek, *South* by public Road to landing and Lands of Mrs Nathaniel Barnwell, *West* by lands of Gov Allston and Glebe of Prince F[r]ederick.

The plantation consists of Six hundred and Fifty five 3/4 acres (655 3/4) of Rice Land, Surveyors measure, or 517 acres Planters measure, of which about 14 acres is very inferior, and Five hundred and Ninety Seven (597) acres Highland, Surveyors measures, of which about 100 acres, are fenced and under cultivation.

Buildings on Plantation

A Dwelling House built in 1854. Containing on ground floor, 1 large Hall, 1 Drawing Room, 1 Dining Room, 2 Bed Rooms, 1 pantry. In attics, 4 bed Rooms. Every Room Except Hall and pantry with Fireplaces, and the four downstair Rooms with Marble chimney pieces, the whole House plastered with two coats. 1 detached Kitchen, 1 Small Servants Hall. 1 Steam Thrasher, capable of doing 1000 bushels daily with corn mill attached capable of grinding 100 bush. daily. Two Barns. 1 corn and Blade House more than 100 feet long. 1 Plantation Store Room, 1 Cart House and Mule Stable, 1 Overseers house built in 1855 Contg. 5 Rooms, some of them lathed and plastered, 1 Stable, 1 Smoke House, 1 Servants House, 1 Hospital Contg 6 bed Rooms, 2 with fire places and piazza. 1 Childrens House in bad repair. Houses for 200 Negroes, some with brick chimneys, but rather old. 1 Large Potato Cellar. 1 Plantation Kitchen.

Furniture to go with the House

Drawing Room,	8 Chairs, 1 Marble top table, nest of Walnut tables, 1 Carpet, Fender and dog brass.
Dining Room	1 oval Table, 1 Walnut side Board, 8 Chairs, 1 Carpet, Fender, dogs brass
Hall	1 Carpet, 1 large Table, 1 small do. and Settee.
Pantry	2 presses, Dinner and Breakfast of white ware and glasses, Decanters, tumblers etc.
Bed Rooms	2 Mahog. Bedsteads, 2 drawers and glasses, 1 Looking glass, 3 Wash stands, 4 Tables, 2 Carpets, 10 Chairs, 2 fender and dogs
Kitchen	1 pair of Dogs

The Plantation has for many years made more than sufficient Provisions for the negroes.

The corn land has produced 40 Bush to the acre all round.

The rice [land] is generally of the first quality, and is in fine though not first
rate condition.

The Buildings except where otherwise stated are in thorough repair.

An Excellent Well of Water.

A DIARY KEPT BY ROBERT F. W. ALLSTON, 1859–60[1]

The river PeeDee has been full all the winter, so as to impede the work of
preparation in the Swamp whenever the wind blew hard from the East but
early in April the rains which had deluged the low country (about 11 inches)
having extended to the upper water courses of the PeeDee and Yadkin produced a freshet which at Cheraw (the bridge there is our standard) rose
within four feet of the high fresh in 1841. It reach'd us 12 to 17th April and
either cover'd the land or render'd it too boggy to plant.

Ten days of strong west wind have enabled us to dry the older rice at
Chicora before it was materially injured and the 20th found us again planting at Breakwater, 22nd at Exchange etc. Water cold. The Sun hot.

It was cold enough for frost on the 17th–18th April again 23d. March
has been wet & cold after being wet & warm, but not as blustering as April.
West winds prevail'd so long and so strong that the fresh ran off rapidly,
and on the 23d April the rise of the tide from low to high water was not
20 inches, the fields could not be flow'd.

On 24th April the channel of the Pee Dee was all that was cover'd with
water.

Pipe-Down

		Births
	Aug. 19th	Mary—boy
	Sept 22nd	Lucy—girl
		Deaths
	Aug 14th	Violet 71 Cholera Morbus
	Sept 28th	Lucy's child (girl) 6 days Lock Jaw

Guendalos

		Births
	Feb. 8th	Sampit Hagar girl
	May 26th	Margaret	boy
	June 4th	Patience	girl
	July 4th	Luna	"
	Oct 1	Susy	boy

Guendalos

One of Ben's boys, 13 yrs old, Kill'd by Lightening, and three stun'd

Francis Betty's child died   3 yrs. old in July

[1] These memoranda are entered on interleaves bound into a copy of *Miller's Planters
and Merchants' Almanac for the Year 1859*. With the exception of three or four medical pre-
scriptions and a few inconsequential notations they are printed without omission.

S. Esther's child died 2 yrs. old   William in Aug. of Dysentary
(P[ee] D[ee]) Hagar's 4th Sept   3 yrs. old worm fever   Elijah
Oct 1—Levi (65) died of Internal disease

27th Plant Slips at all the places.
July 4th Plant again "   "   "   as vines have been supplied by growth.
Turn'd out well notwithstanding the early frost 17th Oct. at N[ightingale]
H[all]. Plant few vines from the above for seed in Aug.

Chicora Wood　　　　　*Births*

April 2nd	L. Harriette	boy	
April 15	Jane	girl	
July 14th	B. Harriet	boy	
Aug. 28	Tobie's Maria		
Septr. 3d	Rachael	girl	
Ocbr 11	Linda Twins	Boy and Girl	allow her milk etc and 1/2 work for a year
Novr. 15	Katy	girl	
Decr 8	Lucy	boy	
Decr 15	Mary (York's)	"	

[Deaths]

Aug. 24th	Nancy	10 yrs. old	cholic	
Decr 1st	Abram	60	"	T. Pneumonia
Decr 7th	Edward	19	"	" "

N[ightingale]
Hall　　　　　　*Births*

Jan. 21st	Judy	boy	
Feb 6	Andrew's Nancy	girl	
" 20	Selina	"	
March 6	Fanny	"	
April 18th	Beck	"	
May 22nd	Charity	"	
June 11th	Iris	boy	
" 24th	R Maria	"	
Sept 16th	Rebecca	"	
Sept 24th	Hester	girl	(Had Twins boy and girl
Oct 6	L. Eve		The boy Still born)
	Phillis	Dead	
" 14th	Lydia	"	
Decr 17th	Sam's Peggy.		

Deaths

Minus 70 Indigestion

Aug 30th	Charity's child girl 2 months Consumption
	Phillis's " 1 month "
	Lydia's " 1/2 "
Oct 10th	Beck's "

6th July   Moved from Charleston to the Beach on the Waccamaw. Brought Ben's man Levi up with me for whom Dr. Porcher said he could do nothing. He has been ill ever since with some internal disease which every now and then induces hemorrhage from the bowels and intestines.

Took up 7 cows at Waterford 4 only with young calves. In driving home Mr. Foxworth Bob and Frank managed to Kill 1 calf, thus, it would not drive so it was run down and caught with the dogs mark'd and alter'd and then they undertook to drive it home. The weather was too hot and it died, or would have died and they kill'd it. Turn'd out cattle at the Farm. Milly came to the Beach.

Requested Dr Williams to order for me 50 copies of "Psalms and Testaments" plain for distribution. And to mention the opportunity afforded by the Normal School in Charleston, to those young persons in Georgetown who might be supposed desirous to profit by it.

Sent 2 Methst Catechisms and some other books to Catherine Moore to help teach the Smith's Children in Sunday School out on the Mill Pond.[1]

Sent to J M Stokes of "the Farmers and Planters" Five dollars to be credited as follows

to R F W A	$2.
" Jesse Belflowers	2.
" Ben Allston	1.

have not received the paper 3 months

Some of J Ward's servants pushing a boat beyond (S of) La Bruce's Stable have cut down for fire-wood between 20 and 30, young Live oaks at a point of woods projecting to the Marsh. Wrote to him on discovering the same and requested him to interpose. He does not seem to receive the notice kindly.

Mr Middleton's negroes on the river side seem disposed to cut right and left of the cart path without regarding ownership. Their object is bushes (pine tops). They have leveled since my absence in 1859, 30 or 40 pine trees and taken the tops away directly in front of Waterford pasture-bank! A good neighbor will instruct his people. No one else has a right to do it.

Aug. 29th Remit by mail $5 under cover to Milton and Grist to pay their bill of $4 for the Yorkville Enquirer to Jany 1860. They have credited the whole, and sent a receipt to 1st July 1860.

---

[1] See above, p. 161.

Crop of 1858 at—

Chicora Wood Exchange etc.

Rice 27,078 Bushels. Much of it [illegible] burn'd in consequence of Mr. B[elflowers] absence at the Springs for health   Corn shot 300 bushels   Potatoes and Peas fine.

Nightingale Hall and Waterford

Rice	370 Acres		18270	Bushels
Corn	50 "		990	"
Potatoes	30 "	(640 sold)	6600	"
Peas	100 "	(812 ")	1006	"
Turnips	5 "		1000	"

3d Sept   Cut Rice at Waterford and Guendalos

6th "   "   " " Chicora No 14, 11 in a hard rain. A great deal of water has fallen. N. winds and continued falling weather

5th 6th and 7th—7th Dined with Mr Gaillard in B. R

8th   clear, cool and fine.

15th and 16th   tides high wind N. E. and a swell in both Pee Dee and Waccamaw. 60 acres down at Chicora Wood (15th) 20 at Guendalos and   at N. Hall. Rain from E. N. E. with fresh breeze, at night wind S. E. with a storm of rain till 12 O'clock, the S. W.   Fortunate, as the tide was not inordinate. On thursday went round Ben's crop at Guendalos. The tide high, and weather threatening. It was a gratification to find that the work which I had done there last winter was well done and in the right places. But the rice cut on thursday should not have been brought in friday, as it was. That cut on Wednesday 1/2 it was very well to tie and stack in the field Thursday and fetch in on friday because there was a good sun out Wednesday, but on Thursday very little a sprinkle of rain too at 1 O'clock and a good shower friday morning at 9. The Sun was out bright and beautiful on Saturday, but even then the rice at Chicora which was cut on Thursday was not brought into the Yard (which is the worst place for wet rice) but tied up and the sheaves laid across the stubble. Found 3 acres of my best rice at N[ightingale] Hall in the yard wet in the same way. Stacks pull'd to pieces and covering a great deal of ground. If rain comes within 24 hours much of it will rot and be lost.

Oct 17th   Brot in the last of Chicora Wood, Chapel Field. The weather continuing fine the crop is reported well cured and put up in 335 Stacks which will probably average 100 bushels, 33500 besides straw and dirty rice, say 500 B.

At Nightingale Hall they finish'd a few days earlier 225 Stacks, 20,000 Bushels probably, besides straw etc. God be praised for his blessing on the labors of the year. The Frost in October has abridged the high land Pea crop, and Potatoes some what.

Novr 3   Gave out clothes for winter at all the places. Shoes were shared out on the first frost, from R. A. Pringle   Blankets to the Women. The children take *next year*. Great Coats and glazed hat to House Watch D. Sam Frank N[ightingale] H[all]   B. Sam Waverly Pea Jackets D. Richard, Jack, Phillip, D. Daniel, Sam N[ightignale] H[all].

Crop of Nightingale Hall Sent to Mill up to

		Rice	
Novr. 10th		5800	
Decr. 5th E[ast] W[aterford] prime	2170	$2136.42
" " W[aterford] main	700	1846.97
" 12th	1920	650.69
1860		
Jany	2224	2188.25

Harvested of Corn 2520 bushels of Cob corn, 1260 bushels. 370 bushels oats 1,585 Blankets Peas   6000 Bush Potatoes and Turnips

Chicora Wood up to—

			Rice		
22nd Novr.		c.	4890	bushels	$4990
	P[ipe] Down		3810	"	3307.10
	1, 2 and 3 D.		1644	"	1319.54
Decr 3d	1, 2, 3 C.		1950	"	1660.07
" 7th	4, 5, and 6 D		1950	"	1428.90
" 14th	4, 5, and 6 C		1770	"	1478.60
	Chapel F		800	"	798.51
1860					
Jany 6th	5, 6, 7, B W.		2350	"	2229.61
" 10th	Ex[change] Main		705	"	810.94
" "	Straw etc		305	"	206
" 17th	1, 2, 3 and 4 B W		1720		1646.50

Came home 9th Decr. for the remainder of the month, being the first time in 35 years excepting the year 1827, and a part of 1837, when my wife was ill after the birth of   and during this whole time 4 years as Surveyor Genl and 28 years as Representative (4) and Senator (24), I have not lost a day from my seat, with the exception of one week, when dispatch'd on duty to inspect the workshops of the So Ca Rail Road at Charleston, Hamburgh and Aiken and the proposed inclined plane at Aiken. This was the year when Mr Boyce (St. Philips & St. Michaels) was unseated and re-elected. Also one day in 184– when I had suffer'd an attack of Cholera.

Xmas—Marriages
Joe and Margaret   Guendalos

Guend[alos] Carp[enter] Joe and Betty
Bister and Emma
Salome and Tyra
Doctor and Alice P. D.
P[ee] D[ee] Pompey and Eve Guend.
P[ee] D[ee] Sam and Patty P[ee] D[ee]

Jany 14th   Thomas and Cupid P[ee] D[ee] were made to run the guantlet for taking a hog out of the pen. The whole plantation being shared out of Xmas until they found out the crimnal

Gave out 1/4 proportion of Small Rice to those who lost not a day of work last year, according to the list herewith—
Pipe Down Negroes bought of Mrs. Petigru   Allowance
Philip   Francis Duncan   1.   6.
Nancy   Esaw
Hammond
Clarinda   Shaw, Molly
Mary Ann   Lucy——   1.   4.
Ned
Suckey
Snow
Nelly
The women had Blankets in 1857.
The men   "   "   " 1858.
also the children mark'd X

Chicora Wood   1859

No of days lost by sickness
Names not lost a day to get a bushel of small Rice.

Tommy 57–8–9–1 1/4		Ladrus	1
Stephen	1 1/4	Salome	1
Hammerdy	1 1/4	Tim	1
B. Peter	1 1/4	Ancrum	1
Bowie	1 1/4	Jackey	1
Richard	1 1/4	Anthony	1
Jack	1 1/4	Alfred	1
Paul	1 1/4	Milly	1
Phebe	1 1/4	Bob	1
James	1 1/4	Carp[enter] Tom	1
B. Solomon	1 1/4	York	1
Auba	1 1/4	J. Charles	1
	15	Tenah	1
Charity	1/2	Harry	1
Wilson	1/2	H. Mary	1

Gabriel	1/2	Jacob	1
Doctor	1/2	Nancy	1
Page	1/2	Will	1
Emma	1/2	D. Venus	1
Maggy	1/2	Joe	1
			20
Sue	1/2	Betty C	1/2
Lavinia	1/2	Roger	1/2
January	1/2	Sancho	1/2
D Charles	1/2	June	1/2
March	1/2	Sandy	1/2
Matilda	1/2 6 1/2	Henry	1/2
	6 1/2	Jacob	1/2
	21 1/2	Anson	1/2
			4

21 1/2 + 20 + 4 = 45 1/2 Bushels

Nightingale Hall 1859

No of days lost by sickness in the year 706

Names to get 1 Bushel of Small Rice or a fraction

Acquiesence	1 B.	Chance	1/2 B
Dr Daniel	1	Carolina	1/2
C Daniel	1	Eleanor	1/2
Elsy	1	Allech	1/2
Y. Hannah	1	Fanny	1/2
W. Hannah	1	Gabe	1/2
Josey	1	B. Joe	1/2
N. Lydia	1	P. Joe	1/2
Mack	1	Jack	1/2
Monday	1	Martha	1/2
Q. Nancy	1	Primus	1/2
E. Prince	1	Snow	1/2
			6

Peter	1
Stepney	1
W Tom	1
Wd Tom Young	1
Trim	1
	17
	6
	23

Mr. Daniel's Beef bill for the summer = $267.82

Dr. Heriot's bill for N[ight-ingale] H[all] and Chicora = $46

1st Decr. 1859   Wiltshire and his apprentice Abram were taken by Mr. Gunn at $2 pr diem   Wiltshire lost 1 week by sickness

1st Jany 1860   Hammerday and his boy, Randall were taken by Mr. Gunn at   Hammerdy lost 3 days by sickness

Received from Mr Gunn for the foregoing by order of building com. $207.50 up to March 1860.

Early in Jany 1860 I paid Boston for a fat hog besides what he put in the plantation pen. Weigh'd by J. Belflowers 220 lbs @ 5¢—$11.00

17th Decr 1859—

Paid him 1st Jany 1 Hog and 10 cash—11.00

Jacky too brought a [*hog*] soon after weighing less—7.00 paid in cash.

1860 Jany gave out to Abram and Jim (Pipe Down) carpenters tools viz—

Square and Compass	Hand saw
Fire plane	1 Set of chisels each
Jack plane	

1st Feb   Mr Joshua LaBruce came to say that he had the money for the time of Jim and Abram deducting Doctors Bills etc. I told him I paid no bills except perhaps for Sam whom I sent to nurse Carolina her son. He also proposed to me from Mrs. Petigru to pay $100 for Phillip and $50 for Sary's hire. I told him to keep the money and pay for the other of the negroes as far as it would go. But that I had counted on making those negroes comfortable as long as they lived and not paying hire for them. If they are hired, they must be stirring, and when no longer so, their hire would cease and they must be cared for otherwise. I deem'd it therefore bad policy in Mrs. Petigru to insist upon hire for them. I have agreed to pay her interest money 1/2 yearly ($5,400) which is inconvenient and desire to gratify her in every way. But I think this disposition of servants whom she intends to benefit is not judicious. Both Phillip and Sary get here a supply of meat, sugar and coffee the first of every month to use as they please, and they each receive some gratification in money at Xmas.

Old July (blind) has his wife and a big boy waiting on him. Old Ned Do. Phillip has his wife Nancy working for him while minding the children and his crippled son doing little else (Hammond). When he and Sary come to be older, they will require help in larger proportion and God knows what the working gang will be by and by.

2 Jany   Cattle—13 head unaccounted for by E Foxworths own account, except 1 black ox shot at Enfield and died at the Farm not skin'd. 1 yearling stray'd off to [illegible] place and was kill'd. 1 Do of Ben's got from Mr Hunter 1 cow given him for me   Sandy Island [illegible] 1 yearling driven off with Dr Tucker's Stock. Including Columbias first Calf a Heifer heavy with her first calf, turn'd out fat. I paid $200 for the Dam ([illegible]) brought from Kentucky by Dove's at a year old and left her in Columbia to be impregnated by Dr Parker's Bull   I must mulcht Mr. Foxworth for such neglect of my interest or it will never be better. I regret to do it.

SALT PRODUCTION DURING THE
CONFEDERATE WAR, 1864

Sales of 34 Tierces Salt Received and Sold by order of Mrs Adele Allston
Executrix for Est R F W. Allston._____

1864

Augt 10	Cash	1	Tcs	Salt	642.95.547	lb.	10	By	47	lbs.	@	25.00	273.50
" 12	"	1	"	"	515.95.420	"	8	"	20	"	@	25.00	210.00
" 13	"	1	"	"	562.106.456	"	9	"	6	"	@	25.00	228.00
" 16	"	1	"	"	615.112.503 560.1155	"	10	"	3	"	@	25.00	251.50
" 18	"	2	"	"	595.195.960 590.1239	"	19	"	10	"	@	25.00	480.00
" 28	"	2	"	"	649.214.1025 561.1191	"	20	"	25	"	@	25.00	512.50
Sept 14	"	2	"	"	633.214.979	"	19	"	29	"	@	25.00	489.50
" 17	"	1	"	"	600.90.510 614.1209	"	10	"	10	"	@	25.00	255.00
" 22	"	2	"	"	595.180.1029 545.1770 630	"	20	"	29	"	@	25.00	514.50
" 23	"	3	"	"	595.2851.485	"	29	"	35	"	@	25.00	742.50
" 24	"	1	"	"	557.90.467 627.1754 532	"	9	"	17	"	@	25.00	233.50
" 27	"	3	"	"	595.310.1444 633.650.660	"	28	"	44	"	@	25.00	722.00
" 29	"	7	"	"	650.594.533.645								
" "	"	"			4365.725.3640 480.1074	72		"	40	"	@	26.00	1892.80
" "	"	"	2	"	"	594.100.794	"	17	"	44	"	@	26.00	464.88
Oct 12	"	1	"	"	564.110.454	"	9	"	4	"	@	26.00	236.08
" 18	"	1	"	"	531.100.431	"	8	"	31	"	@	27.00	232.74
" "	"	1	"	"	613.94.519	"	10	"	19	"	@	27.00	280.26
" 24	"	1	"	"	562.105.457	"	9	"	7	"	@	27.00	246.78
" 25	"	1	"	"	540.104.436	"	8	"	36	"	@	27.00	235.44

34 Tierces .... Charges........		8501.48
To Drayage and Storage	102.00	
" Commission on 8501.48 a 5%	445.07	547.07

$7954.41

E E CHERAW   Oct 31st 1864   D. MALLOY

TENANT LETTERS

Vincent Parsons to Adele Petigru Allston

Mill Creek, No Ca Jany 17th 1866

MADAM   As a tenant of yours I intrude this upon your notice.[1] I find your house on the Pearson place in need of many repairs, the house leaks in several places the chimneys all need work on them that is actually necessary to their preservation, and the Piaza flour is in bad order and their should be a gutter to the eves of the house to protect the flour. The frame at the [MS torn] of the upper pond should have a house or shelter over them or the frame will soon decay I consider this requisite. I will put a house suitable for a gin over the frame and put the running gear in it and build a screw and put all necessary repairs on the house and kitchen necessary for the rent of the place another year also build a plank garden and pale in the yard, the garden I intend building anyhow. The plantation is sadly out of repair Several gates are needed. The work I propose to do would be worth more than the rent of the place but the use of the gin would be a convenience to me and at any time could be changed to a flour mill. Should my proposition be accepted I would like to know it as early as possible that I could get the necessary timbers on the cleard land before planting time. I can get them there without troubling the wood land. The flour of the House has a quantity of grease on it put on I suppose by the Yanks while reveling here Mrs Parsons is endeavouring to get it up. I am an entire stranger to you I refer you to Capt R. Manard Marshall, and Capt G J Crafts of your city I served with Capt Marshall over two years in the Quarter Master Department and nearly a year with Majr [illegible] and had daily transaction with Capt Craft.

Your Servant at the Liles place is a good man I shall use every exertion to prevent depreciations on your Land in my charge, the Shanties on the Rail Road will I fear cause some homeless freedman to locate there for awhile should any one do so I will move them immediately.

Vincent Parsons to Adele Petigru Allston

Cheraw S. C. Augt 15th, [18]66

MADAM   I write enquiring if you purpose renting your plantations in Anson for the year 67, Mr Braswell who occupies the Liles place requested me to ascertain in regard to that place and I am anxious to know in reference to the Pearson place. It is getting time for persons to know what they will do for another season. There is always work to be done at this season of the year to put a plantation in order for the next crop, cleaning up and making

[1] Parsons was renting a portion of Morven or adjoining land acquired by the Allstons in 1863.

manure. I spoke to Mr Malloy to day, and he said that I had better write
to you, as he was not vested with power to Rent the Lands. My attention
to the preservation of your Lands has piqued some of my neighbors but duty
always points to the proper course. I would like to Rent, or lease the Pearson
place for the next year or a term of years. My crop on the Place was at one
time progressing but the severe drougth has materially cut off my expectations my corn was nearly made, but my cotton will fall short one half or
two thirds, my neighbors are in the same situation.

Will you please let me hear from you direct or through Mr Malloy at the
earliest moment in reference to the land. I wish to know so I can make my
arraingements accordingly.

Adele Petigru Allston to Vincent Parsons

Charleston 23d August 1866

Mr Parsons Your letter on the subject of renting the Pearson place is
receivd. I think the places will both be for rent the next year and I am willing
you should continue to rent the Pearson place, but I wish to be assured that
it is being taken care of in every respect. The land duly cultivated and the
timber not cut except what is necessary for farming purposes. All the new
land was fenced, and the buildings had been repaired. There cannot be a
great deal needed for the farm. The rent for 1867 should be five hundred
dollars ($500) with engagement to take care of the place and see that it
does not deteriorate in value, but improve.

I am also willing to rent the Pratt farm to those persons who have [it]
this year, for the year 1867 for one hundred and seventy five dollars, on the
same conditions, viz, that they take care of the place and buildings, and
suffer no trespass on the lumber or belongings.

I hope your wheat and small grain crops have done well. I hope you take
care of the fruit trees. I may possibly make my home on one of these farms
in the future. I wish them both preserved with care, the trees and even the
flowers.

Write and let me know if these terms suit you and Mr Braswell.

Is Mr J C Yates still living?

C. E. Braswell to Adele Petigru Allston

Morven Anson cty N. C. August the 15th 1867

Mrs. Adele P. Allston As the time is Drawing nigh for Farmers to Sow
their grain, I will drop you a few lines to find out what you are going to do
with your plantation, that I am Liveing on. If it is for rent, again, I would
like to rent it, if I can get it for more than one year. The Fences on the
Plantation is getting So rotten that it will take a good deal of work to repair
them. It will not Pay me to repair them unless I was going to Stay on the

plantation two or three years. It is worth the rent one year to repair the fences So that I can keep the Stock out of my Crop.

You will also have to have a Portion of the Dwelling house reshingled, as it is getting Very Leekey and is rotting the rafters and seiling, by keeping it wet. If you will rent me this Plantation for three years I will repair the Fences and Dwelling House and put the Plantation in good Farming order. I have made considerable Improvement on the Plantation Since I have bin here, and in the corse of two or three years could make a good deal more. I cannot afford to Do So Much repairing on the Plantation unless I have the Insureance for More than one year. I want you to write to me as Soon as you can and let me know what you are going to Do with your Plantation, So that I can Make arrangements for Sewing My wheat and oats. I have Sewed So late in the Season for the last two years that I have made but little grain you will Please let me know as Soon as you can So that I can Make my arrangements for another Crop.

INDEX